ALGORITHMS AND

DATA STRUCTURES:

THE SCIENCE

OF COMPUTING

ALGORITHMS AND DATA STRUCTURES: THE SCIENCE OF COMPUTING

DOUGLAS BALDWIN
GREG W. SCRAGG

CHARLES RIVER MEDIA, INC.
Hingham, Massachusetts

Publisher: David Pallai
Production: Eric Lengyel
Cover Design: The Printed Image

CHARLES RIVER MEDIA, INC.
10 Downer Avenue
Hingham, Massachusetts 02043
781-740-0400
781-740-8816 (FAX)
info@charlesriver.com
www.charlesriver.com

This book is printed on acid-free paper.

Douglas Baldwin and Greg Scragg. *Algorithms and Data Structures: The Science of Computing.*
ISBN: 1-58450-250-9

Library of Congress Cataloging-in-Publication Data
Baldwin, Douglas (Douglas L.), 1958–
    Algorithms and data structures : the science of computing / Douglas Baldwin and Greg Scragg.—1st ed.
        p. cm.
    Includes bibliographical references and index.
    ISBN 1-58450-250-9
    1. Computer algorithms. 2. Data structures (Computer science) I. Scragg, Greg W. II. Title.
    QA76.9.A43B35 2004
    005.1—dc22
                              2004008100

Printed in the United States of America
04 7 6 5 4 3 2 First Edition

CHARLES RIVER MEDIA titles are available for site license or bulk purchase by institutions, user groups, corporations, etc. For additional information, please contact the Special Sales Department at 781-740-0400.

Contents

Preface

*A*lgorithms and Data Structures: The Science of Computing* (which we usually refer to simply as *The Science of Computing)* is about *understanding* computation. We see it as a distinct departure from previous second-course computer science texts, which emphasize *building* computations. The *Science of Computing* develops understanding by coupling algorithm design to mathematical and experimental techniques for modeling and observing algorithms' behavior. Its attention to rigorous scientific experimentation particularly distinguishes it from other computing texts. *The Science of Computing* introduces students to computer science's three core methods of inquiry: design, mathematical theory, and the scientific method. It introduces these methods early in the curriculum, so that students can use them throughout their studies. The book uses a strongly hands-on approach to demonstrate the importance of, and interactions between, all three methods.

THE TARGET AUDIENCE

The target course for *The Science of Computing* is the second course in a computer science curriculum (CS 2). For better or worse, that course has become more varied in recent years. *The Science of Computing* is appropriate for many—but not all—implementations of CS 2.

The Target Student

The Science of Computing is aimed at students who are majoring in, or independently studying, computer science. It is also suitable for students who want to combine a firm background in computer science with another major.

The programming language for examples and exercises in this book is Java. We assume that students have had an introductory programming course using an object-oriented language, although not necessarily Java. The book should also be accessible with just a little extra work to those who started with a procedural language. An appendix helps students whose previous experience is with a language other than Java make the transition to Java.

There is quite a bit of math in *The Science of Computing*. We teach all of the essential mathematics within the text, assuming only that readers have a good pre-college math background. However, readers who have completed one or more college-level math courses, particularly in discrete math, will inevitably have an easier time with the math in this book than readers without such a background.

The Target School and Department

Every computer science department has a CS 2 course, and most could use *The Science of Computing*. However, this book is most suited to those departments that:

- Want to give students an early and firm foundation in all the methods of inquiry that they will need in later studies, or
- Want to increase their emphasis on the nonprogramming aspects of computer science, or
- Want to closely align their programs with other math and/or science programs.

WHY *THE SCIENCE OF COMPUTING*?

We believe that an introduction to computer science should be an in-depth study of the basic foundations of the field. The appropriate foundations lie not in *what* computer science studies, but in *how* it studies.

Three Methods of Inquiry

The Science of Computing is based on three methods of inquiry central to computer science (essentially, the three "paradigms" of computer science described by Denning et al. in "Computing as a Discipline," *Communications of the ACM*, January 1989). In particular, the book's mission is to teach:

Design—the creation of algorithms, programs, architectures, etc.

The Science of Computing emphasizes:

- Abstraction as a way of treating complex operations as "primitives," so that one can write algorithms in terms appropriate to the problem they solve.
- Recursion as a tool for controlling algorithms and defining problems.

Theory—the mathematical modeling and analysis of algorithms, programs, problems, etc.

The Science of Computing emphasizes:

- The use of mathematics to predict the execution time of algorithms.
- The use of mathematics to verify the correctness of algorithms.

Empirical Analysis—the use of the scientific method to study algorithms, programs, etc.

The Science of Computing emphasizes:

- The rigorous notion of "experiment" used in the sciences
- Techniques for collecting and analyzing data on the execution time of programs or parts of programs.

Advances in computer science depend on all three of these methods of inquiry; therefore, a well-educated computer scientist must become familiar with each—starting early in his education.

DISTINCTIVE FEATURES OF THIS BOOK

This book has a number of other features that the student and instructor should consider.

Abstract vs. Concrete

Abstraction as a problem-solving and design technique is an important concept in *The Science of Computing*. Object-oriented programming is a nearly ideal form in which to discuss such abstraction. Early in the book, students use object-oriented abstraction by designing and analyzing algorithms whose primitives are really messages to objects. This abstraction enables short algorithms that embody one important idea apiece to nonetheless solve interesting problems. Class libraries let students code the algorithms in working programs, demonstrating that the objects are "real" even if students don't know how they are implemented. For instance, many of the early examples of algorithms use messages to a hypothetical robot to perform certain tasks; students can code and run these algorithms "for real" using a software library that provides an animated simulation of the robot. Later, students learn to create their own object-oriented abstractions as they design new classes whose methods encapsulate various algorithms.

Algorithms and Programs

The methods of inquiry, and the algorithms and data structures to which we apply them, are fundamental to computing, regardless of one's programming language. However, students must ultimately apply fundamental ideas in the form of concrete programs. *The Science of Computing* balances these competing requirements by devoting most of the text to algorithms as things that are more than just programs. For example, we don't just present an algorithm as a piece of code; we explain the thinking that leads to that code and illustrate how mathematical analyses focus attention on properties that can be observed no matter how one codes an algorithm, abstracting away language-specific details. On the other hand, the concrete examples in *The Science of Computing* are written in a real programming language (Java). Exercises and projects require that students follow the algorithm through to the coded language. The presentation helps separate fundamental methods from language details, helping students understand that the fundamentals are always relevant, and independent of language. Students realize that there is much to learn about the fundamentals themselves, apart from simply how to write something in a particular language.

Early Competence

Design, theory, and empirical analysis all require long practice to master. We feel that students should begin using each early in their studies, and should continue using each throughout those studies. *The Science of Computing* gives students rudimentary but real ability to use all three methods of inquiry early in the curriculum. This contrasts sharply with some traditional curricula, in which theoretical analysis is deferred until intermediate or even advanced courses, and experimentation may never be explicitly addressed at all.

Integration

Design, theory, and empirical analysis are not independent methods, but rather mutually supporting ideas. Students should therefore learn about them in an integrated manner, seeing explicitly how the methods interact. This approach helps students understand how all three methods are relevant to their particular interests in computer science. Unfortunately, the traditional introductory sequence artificially compartmentalizes methods by placing them in separate courses (e.g., program design in CS 1 and 2, but correctness and performance analysis in an analysis of algorithms course).

Active Learning

We believe that students should actively engage computers as they learn. Reading is only a prelude to personally solving problems, writing programs, deriving and solving equations, conducting experiments, etc. Active engagement is particularly valuable in making a course such as *The Science of Computing* accessible to students. This book's Web site (see the URL at the end of this preface) includes sample laboratory exercises that can provide some of this engagement.

Problem Based

The problem-based pedagogy of *The Science of Computing* introduces new material by need, rather than by any rigid fixed order. It first poses a problem, and then introduces elements of computer science that help solve the problem. Problems have many aspects—what exactly is the problem, how does one find a solution, is a proposed solution correct, does it meet real-world performance requirements, etc. Each problem thus motivates each method of inquiry—formalisms that help specify the problem (theory and design), techniques for discovering and implementing a solution (design), theoretical proofs and empirical tests of correctness (theory and empirical analysis), theoretical derivations and experimental measurements of performance (theory and empirical analysis), etc.

THE SCIENCE OF COMPUTING AND COMPUTING CURRICULA 2001

Our central philosophy is that the foundations of computer science extend beyond programs to algorithms as abstractions that can and should be thoughtfully designed, mathematically modeled, and experimentally analyzed. While programming is essential to putting algorithms into concrete form for applied use, algorithm design is essential if there is to be anything to program in the first place, mathematical analysis is essential to understanding which algorithms lead to correct and efficient programs, and experiments are essential for confirming the practical relevance of theoretical analyses. Although this philosophy appears to differ from traditional approaches to introductory computer science, it is consistent with the directions in which computer science curricula are evolving. *The Science of Computing* matches national and international trends well, and is appropriate for most CS 2 courses.

Our central themes align closely with many of the goals in the ACM/IEEE Computing Curricula 2001 report, for instance:[1]

---

[1] Quotations in this list are from Chapters 7 and 9 of the Computing Curricula 2001 Computer Science volume.

- An introductory sequence that exposes students to the "conceptual foundations" of computer science, including the "modes of thought and mental disciplines" computer scientists use to solve problems.
- Introducing discrete math early, and applying it throughout the curriculum.
- An introductory sequence that includes reasoning about and experimentally measuring algorithms' use of time and other resources.
- A curriculum in which students "have direct hands-on experience with hypothesis formulation, experimental design, hypothesis testing, and data analysis."
- An early introduction to recursion.
- An introductory sequence that includes abstraction and encapsulation as tools for designing and understanding programs.

Computing Curricula 2001 strongly recommends a three-semester introductory sequence, and outlines several possible implementations. *The Science of Computing* provides an appropriate approach to the second or third courses in most of these implementations.

Effective Thinking

Most computer science departments see their primary mission as developing students' ability to think effectively about computation. Because *The Science of Computing* is first and foremost about effective thinking in computer science, it is an ideal CS 2 book for such schools, whether within a CC2001-compatible curriculum or not.

WHAT *THE SCIENCE OF COMPUTING* IS NOT

The Science of Computing is not right for every CS 2 course. In particular, *The Science of Computing* is not…

Pure Traditional

The Science of Computing is not a "standard" CS 2 with extra material. To fit a sound introduction to methods of inquiry into a single course, we necessarily reduce some material that is traditional in CS 2. For instance, we study binary trees as examples of recursive definition, the construction of recursive algorithms (e.g., search, insertion, deletion, and traversal), mathematical analysis of data structures and their algorithms, and experiments that drive home the meaning of mathematical results (e.g., how nearly indistinguishable "logarithmic" time is from "instantaneous"); however, we do not try to cover multiway trees, AVL trees, B trees, red-black trees, and other variations on trees that appear in many CS 2 texts.

The Science of Computing's emphasis on methods of inquiry rather than programming does have implications for subsequent courses. Students may enter those courses with a slightly narrower exposure to data structures than is traditional, and programs that want CS 2 to provide a foundation in software engineering for later courses will find that there is less room to do so in *The Science of Computing* than in a more traditional CS 2. However, these effects will be offset by students leaving *The Science of Computing* with stronger than usual abilities in mathematical and experimental analysis of algorithms. This means that intermediate courses can quickly fill in material not covered by *The Science of Computing*. For example, intermediate analysis of algorithms courses should be able to move much faster after *The Science of Computing* than they can after a traditional CS 2. Bottom line: if rigid adherence to a traditional model is essential, then this may not be the right text for you.

Software Engineering

Some new versions of CS 2 move the focus from data structures to software engineering. This also is distinct from the approach here. We lay a solid foundation for later study of software engineering, but software engineering per se is not a major factor in this book.

Data Structures

In spite of the coverage in Part III, *The Science of Computing* is not a data structures book. A traditional data structures course could easily use *The Science of Computing*, but you would probably want to add a more traditional data structures text or reference book as a supplemental text.

Instead of any of these other approaches to CS 2, the aim of *The Science of Computing* is to present a more balanced treatment of design, mathematical analysis, and experimentation, thus making it clear to students that all three truly are fundamental methods for computer scientists.

ORGANIZATION OF THIS BOOK

The Science of Computing has four Parts. The titles of those parts, while descriptive, can be misleading if considered out of context. All three methods of inquiry are addressed in every part, but the emphasis shifts as students mature.

For example, *Part I: The Science of Computing's Three Methods of Inquiry* has four chapters, the first of which is an introduction to the text in the usual form. It is in that chapter that we introduce the first surprise of the course: that the obvious algorithm may not be the best. The other three chapters serve to highlight the three methods of inquiry used throughout this text. These chapters are the only place where the topics are segregated—all subsequent chapters integrate topics from each of the methods of inquiry.

The central theme of *Part II: Program Design* is indeed the design of programs. It reviews standard control structures, but treats each as a design tool for solving certain kinds of problems, with mathematical techniques for reasoning about its correctness and performance, and experimental techniques for confirming the mathematical results. Recursion and related mathematics (induction and recurrence relations) are the heart of this part of the book.

Armed with these tools, students are ready for *Part III: Data Structures* (the central topic of many CS 2 texts). The tools related to algorithm analysis and to recursion, specifically, can be applied directly to the development of recursively defined data structures, including trees, lists, stacks, queues, hash tables, and priority queues. We present these structures in a manner that continues the themes of Parts I and II: lists as an example of how ideas of repetition and recursion (and related analytic techniques) can be applied to structuring data just as they structured control; stacks and queues as adaptations of the list structure to special applications; trees as structures that improve theoretical and empirical performance; and hash tables and priority queues as case studies in generalizing the previous ideas and applying them to new problems.

Finally, *Part IV: The Limits of Computer Science* takes students through material that might normally be reserved for later theory courses, using the insights that students have developed for both algorithms and data structures to understand just how big some problems are and the recognition that faster computers will not solve all problems.

Course Structures for this Book

Depending on the focus of your curriculum, there are several ways to use this text in a course.

This book has evolved hand-in-hand with the introductory computer science sequence at SUNY Geneseo. There, the book is used for the middle course in a three-course sequence, with the primary goal being for students to make the transition from narrow programming proficiency (the topic of the first course) to broader ability in all of computer science's methods of inquiry. In doing this, we concentrate heavily on:

- Chapters 1–7, for the basic methods of inquiry
- Chapters 11–13, as case studies in applying the methods and an introduction to data structures

- Chapters 16 and 17, for a preview of what the methods can accomplish in more advanced computer science

This course leaves material on iteration (Chapters 8 and 9) and sorting (Chapter 10) for later courses to cover, and splits coverage of data structures between the second and third courses in the introductory sequence.

An alternative course structure that accomplishes the same goal, but with a perhaps more coherent focus on methods of inquiry in one course and data structures in another could focus on:

- Chapters 1–9, for the basic methods of inquiry
- Chapter 10, for case studies in applying the methods and coverage of sorting
- Chapters 16 and 17, for a preview of what the methods can accomplish in more advanced computer science

This book can also be used in a more traditional data structures course, by concentrating on:

- Chapter 4, for the essential empirical methods used later
- Chapters 6 and 7, for recursion and the essential mathematics used with it
- Chapters 11–14, for basic data structures

Be aware, however, that the traditional data structures course outline short-changes much of what we feel makes *The Science of Computing* special. Within the outline, students should at least be introduced to the ideas in Chapters 1–3 in order to understand the context within which the later chapters work, and as noted earlier, instructors may want to add material on data structures beyond what this text covers.

SUPPLEMENTAL MATERIAL

The Science of Computing Web site,

http://www.charlesriver.com/algorithms

includes much material useful to both instructors and students, including Java code libraries to support the text examples, material to support experiments, sample lab exercises and other projects, expository material for central ideas and alternative examples.

ACKNOWLEDGMENTS

The Science of Computing represents the culmination of a project that has been in development for a very long time. In the course of the project, a great many people and organizations have contributed in many ways. While it is impossible to list them all, we do wish to mention some whose contributions have been especially important. The research into the methodology was supported by both the National Science Foundation and the U.S. Department of Education, and we are grateful for their support. During the first several years of the project, Hans Koomen was a co-investigator who played a central role in the developmental work. We received valuable feedback in the form of reviews from many including John Hamer, Peter Henderson, Lew Hitchner, Kris Powers, Orit Hazzan, Mark LeBlanc, Allen Tucker, Tony Ralston, Daniel Hyde, Stuart Hirshfield, Tim Gegg-Harrison, Nicholas Howe, Catherine McGeoch, and Ken Slonneger. G. Michael Schneider and Jim Leisy were also particularly encouraging of our efforts. Homma Farian, Indu Talwar, and Nancy Jones all used drafts of the text in their courses, helping with that crucial first exposure. We held a series of workshops at SUNY Geneseo at which some of the ideas were fleshed out. Faculty from other institutions who attended and contributed their ideas include Elizabeth Adams, Hans-Peter Appelt, Lois Brady, Marcus Brown, John Cross, Nira Herrmann, Margaret Iwobi, Margaret Reek, Ethel Schuster, James Slack, and Fengman Zhang. Almost 1500 students served as the front line soldiers—the ones who contributed as the guinea pigs of our efforts—but we especially wish to thank Suzanne Selib, Jim Durbin, Bruce Cowley, Ernie Johnson, Coralie Ashworth, Kevin Kosieracki, Greg Arnold, Steve Batovsky, Wendy Abbott, Lisa Ciferri, Nandini Mehta, Steve Bender, Mary Johansen, Peter Denecke, Jason Kapusta, Michael Stringer, Jesse Smith, Garrett Briggs, Elena Kornienko, and Genevieve Herres, all of whom worked directly with us on stages of the project. Finally, we could not have completed this project without the staff of Charles River Media, especially Stephen Mossberg, David Pallai, and Bryan Davidson.

Part

I

The Science of Computing's Three Methods of Inquiry

Does it strike you that there's a certain self-contradiction in the term "computer science"? "Computer" refers to a kind of man-made machine; "science" suggests discovering rules that describe how some part of the universe works. "Computer science" should therefore be the discovery of rules that describe how computers work. But if computers are machines, surely the rules that determine how they work are already understood by the people who make them. What's left for computer science to discover?

The problem with the phrase "computer science" is its use of the word "computer." "Comput*er*" science isn't the study of comput*ers*; it's the study of comput*ing*, in other words, the study of processes for mechanically solving problems. The phrase "science of computing" emphasizes this concern with general computing processes instead of with machines.[1]

The first four chapters of this book explain the idea of "processes" that solve problems and introduce the methods of inquiry with which computer scientists study those processes. These methods of inquiry include designing the processes, mathematically modeling how the processes should behave, and experimentally verifying that the processes behave in practice as they should in theory.

---

[1] In fact, many parts of the world outside the United States call the field "informatics," because it is more concerned with information and information processing than with machines.

1 What is the Science of Computing?

Computer science is the study of processes for mechanically solving problems. It may surprise you to learn that there truly is a science of computing—that there are fundamental rules that describe all computing, regardless of the machine or person doing it, and that these rules can be discovered and tested through scientific theories and experiments. But there is such a science, and this book introduces you to some of its rules and the methods by which they are discovered and studied.

This chapter describes more thoroughly the idea of *processes* that solve problems, and surveys methods for scientifically studying such processes.

1.1 ALGORITHMS AND THE SCIENCE OF COMPUTING

Loosely speaking, processes for solving problems are called *algorithms*. Algorithms, in a myriad of forms, are therefore the primary subject of study in computer science. Before we can say very much about algorithms, however, we need to say something about the problems they solve.

1.1.1 Problems

Some people (including one of the authors) chill bottles or cans of soft drinks or fruit juice by putting them in a freezer for a short while before drinking them. This is a nice way to get an extra-cold drink, but it risks disaster: a drink left too long in the freezer begins to freeze, at which point it starts to expand, ultimately bursting its container and spilling whatever liquid isn't already frozen all over the freezer. People who chill drinks in freezers may thus be interested in knowing the longest time that they can safely leave a drink in the freezer, in other words, the time that gives them the coldest drink with no mess to clean up afterwards. But since neither drinks nor freezers come with the longest safe chilling times stamped on them by the manufacturer, people face the problem of finding those times for themselves. This problem makes an excellent example of the kinds of problems and problem-solving that exist in computer science. In particular, it shares two key features with all other problems of interest to computer science.

First, the problem is general enough to appear over and over in slightly different forms, or *instances*. In particular, different freezers may chill drinks at different speeds, and larger drinks will generally have longer safe chilling times than smaller drinks. Furthermore, there will be some margin of error on chilling times, within which more or less chilling really doesn't matter—for example, chilling a drink for a second more or a second less than planned is unlikely to change it from unacceptably warm to messily frozen. But the exact margin of error varies from one instance of the problem to the next (depending, for example, on how fast the freezer freezes things and how willing the person chilling the drink is to risk freezing it). Different instances of the longest safe chilling time problem are therefore distinguished by how powerful the freezer is, the size of the drink, and what margin of error the drinker will accept. Things that distinguish one problem instance from another are called *parameters* or *inputs* to the problem. Also note that different instances of a problem generally have different answers. For example, the longest safe chilling time for a two-liter bottle in a kitchenette freezer is different from the longest safe chilling time for a half-liter in an commercial deep freeze. It is therefore important to distinguish between an answer to a single instance of a problem and a process that can solve any instance of the problem. It is far more useful to know a process with which to solve a problem whenever it arises than to know the answer to only one instance—as an old proverb puts it, "Give a man a fish and you feed him dinner, but teach him to fish and you feed him for life."

The second important feature of any computer science problem is that you can tell whether a potential answer is right or not. For example, if someone tells you that a particular drink can be chilled in a particular freezer for up to 17 minutes, you can easily find out if this is right. Chill the drink for 17 minutes and see if it comes out not quite frozen; then chill a similar container of the same drink for 17 minutes plus the margin of error and see if it starts to freeze. Put another way, a time must meet certain requirements in order to solve a given instance of the problem, and it is possible to say exactly what those requirements are: the drink in question, chilled for that time in the freezer in question, shouldn't quite freeze, whereas the drink in question, chilled for that time plus the margin of error in the freezer in question, would start to freeze. That you need to know what constitutes a correct answer seems like a trivial point, but it bears an important moral nonetheless: before trying to find a process to solve a problem, make sure you understand exactly what answers you will accept.

Not every problem has these two features. Problems that lack one or the other are generally outside the scope of computer science. For example, consider the problem, "In what year did people first walk on the moon?" This problem lacks the first feature of being likely to appear in many different instances. It is so specific that it only has one instance, and so it's easier to just remember that the answer is "1969" than to find a process for finding that answer. As another example, consider the problem, "Should I pay parking fines that I think are unfair?" This problem lacks the second feature of being able to say exactly what makes an answer right. Different people will have different "right" answers to any instance of this problem, depending on their individual notions of fairness, the relative values they place on obeying the law versus challenging unfair actions, etc.

1.1.2 Algorithms

Roughly speaking, an *algorithm* is a process for solving a problem. For example, solving the longest safe chilling time problem means finding the longest time that a given drink can be chilled in a given freezer without starting to freeze. An algorithm for solving this problem is therefore a process that starts with a drink, a freezer, and a margin of error, and finds the length of time. Can you think of such a process?

Here is one very simple algorithm for solving the problem based on gradually increasing the chilling time until the drink starts to freeze: Start with the chilling time very short (in the extreme case, equal to the margin of error, as close to 0 as it makes sense to get). Put the drink into the freezer for the chilling time, and then take it out. If it hasn't started to freeze, increase the chilling time by the margin of error, and put a similar drink into the freezer for this new chilling time. Continue in this manner, chilling a drink and increasing the chilling time, until the drink just starts to freeze. The last chilling time at which the drink did not freeze will be the longest safe chilling time for that drink, that freezer, and that margin of error.

Most problems can be solved by any of several algorithms, and the easiest algorithm to think of isn't necessarily the best one to use. (Can you think of reasons why the algorithm just described might not be the best way to solve the longest safe chilling time problem?) Here is another algorithm for finding the longest safe chilling time: Start by picking one time that you know is too short (such as 0 minutes) and another that you know is too long (perhaps a day). Try chilling a drink for a time halfway between these two limits. If the drink ends up frozen, the trial chilling time was too long, so pick a new trial chilling time halfway between it and the time known to be too short. On the other hand, if the drink ends up unfrozen, then the trial chilling time was too short, so pick a new trial chilling time halfway between it and the time known to be too long. Continue splitting the difference between a time known to be too short and one known to be too long in this manner until the "too short" and "too long" times are within the margin of error of each other. Use the final "too short" time as the longest safe chilling time.

Both of these processes for finding the longest safe chilling time are algorithms. Not all processes are algorithms, however.

To be an algorithm, a process must have the following properties:

- It must be unambiguous. In other words, it must be possible to describe every step of the process in enough detail that anyone (even a machine) can carry out the algorithm in the way intended by its designer. This requires not only knowing exactly how to perform each step, but also the exact order in which the steps should be performed.[1]
- It must always solve the problem. In other words, a person (or machine) who starts carrying out the algorithm in order to solve an instance of the problem must be able to stop with the correct answer after performing a finite number of steps. Users must eventually reach a correct answer no matter what instance of the problem they start with.

These two properties lead to the following concise definition: an algorithm is a finite, ordered sequence of unambiguous steps that leads to a solution to a problem.

If you think carefully about the processes for finding the longest safe chilling time, you can see that both really do meet the requirements for being algorithms:

- No ambiguity. Both processes are precise plans for solving the problem. One can describe these plans in whatever degree of detail a listener needs (right down to where the freezer is, how to open it, where to put the drink, or even more detail, if necessary).
- Solving the Problem. Both processes produce correct answers to any instance of the problem. The first one tries every possible (according to the margin of error) time until the drink starts to freeze. The second keeps track of two bounds on chilling time, one that produces drinks that are too warm and another that produces drinks that are frozen. The algorithm closes the bounds in on each other until the "too warm" bound is within the margin of error of the "frozen" one, at which point the "too warm" time is the longest safe chilling time. As long as the margin of error isn't 0, both of these processes will eventually stop.[2]

---

[1] For some problems, the order in which you perform steps doesn't matter. For example, if setting a table involves putting plates and glasses on it, the table will get set regardless of whether you put the plates on first, or the glasses. If several people are helping, one person can even put on the plates while another puts on the glasses. This last possibility is particularly interesting, because it suggests that "simultaneously" can sometimes be a valid order in which to do things—the subfield of computer science known as *parallel computing* studies algorithms that take advantage of this. Nonetheless, we consider that every algorithm specifies some order (which may be "simultaneously") for executing steps, and that problems in which order doesn't matter can simply be solved by several (minimally) different algorithms that use different orders.

[2] You may not be completely convinced by these arguments, particularly the one about the second algorithm, and the somewhat bold assertion that both processes stop. Computer scientists often use rigorous mathematical proofs to explain their reasoning about algorithms. Such rigor isn't appropriate yet, but it will appear later in this book.

Computer science is the science that studies algorithms. The study of algorithms also involves the study of the data that algorithms process, because the nature of an algorithm often follows closely from the nature of the data on which the algorithm works. Notice that this definition of computer science says nothing about computers or computer programs. This is quite deliberate. Computers and programs allow machines to carry out algorithms, and so their invention gave computer science the economic and social importance it now enjoys, but algorithms can be (and have been) studied quite independently of computers and programs. Some algorithms have even been known since antiquity. For example, Euclid's Algorithm for finding the greatest common divisor of two numbers, still used today, was known as early as 300 B.C. The basic theoretical foundations of computer science were established in the 1930s, approximately 10 years before the first working computers.

1.1.3 Describing Algorithms

An algorithm is very intangible, an idea rather than a concrete artifact. When people want to tell each other about algorithms they have invented, they need to put these intangible ideas into tangible words, diagrams, or similar descriptions. For example, to explain the longest safe chilling time algorithms described earlier, we wrote them in English. We could just as well have described the algorithms in many other forms, but the ideas about how to solve the problem wouldn't change just because we explained them differently.

Here are some other ways of describing the longest safe chilling time algorithms. For instance, the form of algorithm you are most familiar with is probably the computer program, and the first chilling-time algorithm could be written in that form using the Java language as follows (with many details secondary to the main algorithm left out for the sake of brevity):

```java
// In class FreezerClass...
public double chillingTime(Drink d, double margin) {
    Drink testDrink;
    double time = 0.0;
    do {
        time = time + margin;
        testDrink = d.clone();
        this.chill(testDrink, time);
    } while (!testDrink.frozen());
    return time - margin;
}
```

The second algorithm can also be written in Java:

```
// In class FreezerClass...
public double chillingTime(Drink d, double margin) {
    double tooWarm = 0.0;
    double tooCold = …    // A time that ensures freezing
    double time;
    while (tooWarm + margin < tooCold) {
        time = (tooWarm + tooCold) / 2.0;
        Drink testDrink = d.clone();
        this.chill(testDrink, time);
        if (testDrink.frozen()) {
            tooCold = time;
        }
        else {
            tooWarm = time;
        }
    }
    return tooWarm;
}
```

Both programs may well be less intelligible to you than the English descriptions of the algorithms. This is generally the case with programs—they must be written in minute detail, according to rigid syntax rules, in order to be understood by computers, but this very detail and rigidity makes them hard for people to understand.

Something called *pseudocode* is a popular alternative to actual programs when describing algorithms to people. Pseudocode is any notation intended to describe algorithms clearly and unambiguously to humans. Pseudocodes typically combine programming languages' precision about steps and their ordering with natural language's flexibility of syntax and wording. There is no standard pseudocode that you must learn—in fact, like users of natural language, pseudocode users adopt different vocabularies and notations as the algorithms they are describing and the audiences they are describing them to change. What's important in pseudocode is its clarity to people, not its specific form. For example, the first longest safe chilling time algorithm might look like this in pseudocode:

Set chilling time to 0 minutes.
Repeat until drink starts to freeze:
     Add margin of error to chilling time.
     Chill a drink for the chilling time.
(End of repeated section)
Previous chilling time is the answer.

The second algorithm could be written like this in pseudocode:

Set "too warm" time to 0 minutes.
Set "too cold" time to a very long time.
Repeat until "too cold" time is within margin of error of "too warm" time:
    Set "middle time" to be halfway between "too warm" and "too cold" times.
    Chill a drink for "middle time."
    If the drink started to freeze,
        Set "too cold" time to "middle time."
    Otherwise
        Set "too warm" time to "middle time."
(End of repeated section)
"Too warm" time is the answer.

Finally, algorithms can take another form—computer hardware. The electronic circuits inside a computer implement algorithms for such operations as adding or multiplying numbers, sending information to or receiving it from external devices, and so forth. Algorithms thus pervade all of computing, not just software and programming, and they appear in many forms.

We use a combination of pseudocode and Java to describe algorithms in this book. We use pseudocode to describe algorithms' general outlines, particularly when we begin to present an algorithm whose details are not fully developed. We use Java when we want to describe an algorithm with enough detail for a computer to understand and execute it. It is important to realize, however, that there is nothing special about Java here—any programming language suffices to describe algorithms in executable detail. Furthermore, that much detail can hinder as much as help you in understanding an algorithm. The really important aspects of the science of computing can be expressed as well in pseudocode as in a programming language.

Exercises

1.1. We suggested, "In what year did people first walk on the moon?" as an example of a problem that isn't general enough to be interesting to computer science. What about the similar problem, "Given any event, *e*, in what year did *e* happen?" Does it only have one instance, or are there more? If more, what is the parameter? Is the problem so specific that there is no need for a process to solve it?

1.2. Consider the problem, "Given two numbers, *x* and *y*, compute their sum." What are the parameters to this problem? Do you know a process for solving it?

1.3. For most of your life, you have known algorithms for adding, subtracting, multiplying, and dividing numbers. Where did you learn these algorithms? Describe each algorithm in a few sentences, as was done for the longest safe chilling time algorithms. Explain why each has both of the properties needed for a process to be an algorithm.

1.4. Devise your own algorithm for solving the longest safe chilling time problem.

1.5. Explain why each of the following is or is not an algorithm:

1. The following directions for becoming rich: "Invent something that everyone wants. Then sell it for lots of money."
2. The following procedure for baking a fish: "Preheat the oven to 450 degrees. Place the fish in a baking dish. Place the dish (with fish) in the oven, and bake for 10 to 12 minutes per inch of thickness. If the fish is not flaky when removed, return it to the oven for a few more minutes and test again."
3. The following way to find the square root of a number, *n*: "Pick a number at random, and multiply it by itself. If the product equals *n*, stop, you have found the square root. Otherwise, repeat the process until you do find the square root."
4. How to check a lost-and-found for a missing belonging: "Go through the items in the lost-and-found one by one. Look carefully at each, to see if you recognize it as yours. If you do, stop, you have found your lost possession."

1.6. Describe, in pseudocode, algorithms for solving each of the following problems (you can devise your own pseudocode syntax).

1. Counting the number of lines in a text file.
2. Raising a number to an integer power.
3. Finding the largest number in an array of numbers.
4. Given two words, finding the one that would come first in alphabetical order.

1.7. Write each of the algorithms you described in Exercise 1.6 in Java.

1.2 COMPUTER SCIENCE'S METHODS OF INQUIRY

Computer science is the study of algorithms, but in order to study algorithms, one has to know what questions are worth asking about an algorithm and how to answer those questions. Three *methods of inquiry* (approaches to posing and answering questions) have proven useful in computer science.

1.2.1 Design

When we invented algorithms for solving the longest safe chilling time problem, we were practicing one of computer science's methods of inquiry—*design*. Design is the process of planning how to build something. The things that computer scientists design range from the very abstract, such as algorithms, to the very concrete, such as computers themselves. Computer scientists also design programs, but programming is just one of many forms of design in computer science. No matter what you are designing, remember that design is planning for building. Building a product from a good set of plans is straightforward, and the product usually performs as expected; building from poor plans usually leads to unexpected problems, and the product usually doesn't work as expected. The most common mistake computer science students make is to try to write a program (i.e., build something) without first taking the time to plan how to do it.

1.2.2 Theory

Having designed algorithms to solve the longest safe chilling time problem, one faces a number of new questions: Do the algorithms work (in other words, do they meet the requirement that an algorithm always solves its problem)? Which algorithm tests the fewest drinks before finding the right chilling time?

These are the sorts of questions that can be answered by computer science's second method of inquiry—*theory*. Theory is the process of predicting, from first principles, how an algorithm will behave if executed. For example, in the previous section, you saw arguments for why both algorithms solve the chilling time problem. These arguments illustrated one form of theoretical reasoning in computer science.

For another example of theory, consider the number of drinks each algorithm chills. Because the first algorithm works methodically from minimal chilling up to just beyond the longest safe chilling time, in increments of the margin of error, it requires chilling a number of drinks proportional to the longest safe chilling time. The second algorithm, on the other hand, eliminates half the possible chilling times with each drink. At the beginning of the algorithm, the possible chilling times range from 0 to the time known to be too long. But testing the first drink reduces the set of possible times to either the low half or the high half of this range; testing a second drink cuts this half in half again, that is, leaves only one quarter of the original possibilities. The range of possible times keeps halving with every additional drink tested. To see concretely what this means, suppose you start this algorithm knowing that two hours is too long, and with a margin of error of one minute. After chilling one drink, you know the longest safe chilling time to within one hour, and after two drinks to within 30 minutes. After a total of only seven drinks, you will know exactly what the longest safe chilling time is![3] By comparison, after seven drinks, the first algorithm would have just tried chilling for seven minutes, a time that is probably far too short. As this example illustrates, theoretical analysis suggests that the second algorithm will generally use fewer drinks than the first. However, the theoretical analysis also indicates that if the longest safe chilling time is very short, then the first algorithm will use fewer drinks than the second. Theory thus produced both a general comparison between the algorithms, and insight into when the general rule does not hold.

Theory allows you to learn a lot about an algorithm without ever executing it. At first glance, it is surprising that it is possible at all to learn things about an algorithm without executing it. However, things one learns this way are among the most important things to know. Precisely because they are independent of how it is executed, these are the properties that affect every implementation of the algorithm. For example, in showing theoretically that the longest safe chilling time algorithms are correct, we showed that anyone who carries them out faithfully will find a correct chilling time, regardless of what freezer, drink, and margin of error they use, regardless of whether they carry out the algorithms by hand or program some robotic freezer to do it for them, etc. In contrast, properties that do depend on how an algorithm is executed are likely to apply only to one implementation or user.

1.2.3 Empirical Analysis

The longest safe chilling time problem also raises questions that can't be answered by theory. For example, is the longest safe chilling time for a given freezer, drink, and margin of error always the same? Or might the freezer chill more or less efficiently on some days than on others? This type of question, which deals with how algorithms interact with the physical world, can be answered by computer science's third method of inquiry—*empirical analysis*. Empirical analysis is the process of learning through observation and experiment. For example, consider how you could answer the new question through an experiment.

Even before doing the experiment, you probably have some belief, or *hypothesis*, about the answer. For example, the authors' experience with freezers leads us to expect that longest safe chilling times won't change from day to day (but we haven't actually tried the experiment). The experiment itself tests the hypothesis. For the authors' hypothesis, it might proceed as follows: On the first day of the experiment, determine the longest safe chilling time for your freezer, drink, and margin of error. On the second day, check that this time is still the longest safe chilling time (for example, by chilling one drink for that time, and another for that time plus the margin of error, to see if the second drink starts to freeze but the first

---

[3] Mathematically, this algorithm chills a number of drinks proportional to the logarithm of the longest safe chilling time.

doesn't). If the first day's longest safe chilling time is not the longest safe chilling time on the second day, then you have proven the hypothesis false and the safe chilling time does change from day to day. On the other hand, if the first day's longest safe chilling time is still the longest safe chilling time on the second day, it reinforces the hypothesis. But note that it does not prove the hypothesis true—you might have just gotten lucky and had two days in a row with the same longest safe chilling time. You should therefore test the chilling time again on a third day. Similarly, you might want to continue the experiment for a fourth day, a fifth day, and maybe even longer. The more days on which the longest safe chilling time remains the same, the more confident you can be that the hypothesis is true. Eventually you will become so confident that you won't feel any more need to experiment (assuming the longest safe chilling time always stays the same). However, you will never be able to say with absolute certainty that you have proven the hypothesis—there is always a chance that the longest safe chilling time can change, but just by luck it didn't during your experiment.

This example illustrates an important contrast between theory and empirical analysis: theory can prove with absolute certainty that a statement is true, but only by making simplifying assumptions that leave some (small) doubt about whether the statement is relevant in the physical world. Empirical analysis can show that in many instances a statement is true in the physical world, but only by leaving some (small) doubt about whether the statement is always true. Just as in other sciences, the more carefully one conducts an experiment, the less chance there is of reaching a conclusion that is not always true. Computer scientists, therefore, design and carry out experiments according to the same scientific method that other scientists use.

Exercises

1.8.   In general, an algorithm that tests fewer drinks to solve the safe chilling problem is better than one that tests more drinks. But on the other hand, you might want to minimize the number of drinks that freeze while solving the problem (since frozen drinks get messy). What is the greatest number of drinks that each of our algorithms could cause to freeze? Is the algorithm that is better by this measure the same as the algorithm that is better in terms of the number of drinks it tests?

1.9.   A piece of folk wisdom says, "Dropped toast always lands butter-side down." Try to do an experiment to test this hypothesis.

1.10.   Throughout this chapter, we have made a number of assertions about chilling drinks in freezers (e.g., that frozen drinks burst, etc.). Pick one or more of these assertions, and try to do experiments to test them. But take responsibility for cleaning up any mess afterwards!

1.3 CONCLUDING REMARKS

Computer science is the science that studies algorithms. An algorithm is a process for solving a problem. To be an algorithm, a process must:

- Be unambiguous.
- Solve the problem in a finite number of steps.

In order to be solved by an algorithm, a problem must be defined precisely enough for a person to be able to tell whether a proposed answer is right or wrong. In order for it to be worthwhile solving a problem with an algorithm, the problem usually has to be general enough to have a number of different instances.

Computer scientists use three methods of inquiry to study algorithms: design, theory, and empirical analysis.

Figure 1.1 illustrates the relationships between algorithms, design, theory, and empirical analysis. Algorithms are the field's central concern—they are the reason computer scientists engage in any of the methods of inquiry. Design creates algorithms. Theory predicts how algorithms will behave under ideal circumstances. Empirical analysis measures how algorithms behave in particular real settings.

Each method of inquiry also interacts with the others. After designing a program, computer, or algorithm, the designer needs to test it to see if it behaves as expected; this testing is an example of empirical analysis. Empirical analysis involves experiments, which must be performed on concrete programs or computers; creating these things is an example of design. Designers of programs, computers, or algorithms must choose the design that best meets their needs; theory guides them in making this choice. Theoretical proofs and derivations often have structures almost identical to those of the algorithm they analyze—in other words, a product of design also guides theoretical analysis. Empirical analysis tests hypotheses about how a program or computer will behave; these hypotheses come from theoretical predictions. Theory inevitably requires simplifying assumptions about algorithms in order to make mathematical analysis tractable, yet it must avoid simplifications that make results unrealistic; empirical analysis shows which simplifications are realistic and which aren't.

The rest of this text explores more fully the interactions between algorithms, design, theory, and empirical analysis. The goal is to leave you with a basic but nonetheless real ability to engage in all three methods of inquiry in computing. In the next chapter, we introduce some fundamental concepts in algorithm design. The two chapters after that provide similar introductions to theory and empirical analysis.

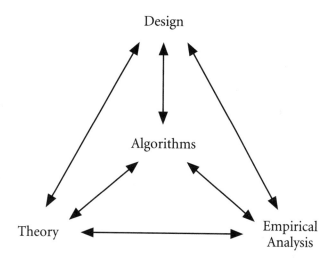

FIGURE 1.1 Algorithms and methods of inquiry in computer science.

1.4 FURTHER READING

For more on the meaning and history of the word "algorithm," see Section 1.1 of:

> Donald Knuth, *Fundamental Algorithms* (*The Art of Computer Programming*, Vol. 1), Addison-Wesley, 1973.

For more on how the field (or, as some would have it, fields) of computer science defines itself, see:

> Peter Denning et al., "Computing as a Discipline," *Communications of the ACM*, Jan. 1989.

The three methods of inquiry that we described in this chapter are essentially the three "paradigms" of computer science from this report.

2 Abstraction: An Introduction to Design

We begin our presentation of computer science's methods of inquiry by considering some fundamental ideas in algorithm design. The most important of these ideas is *abstraction*. We illustrate these ideas by using a running example involving a simulated robot that can move about and spray paint onto the floor, and we design an algorithm that makes this robot paint squares. Although this problem is simple, the concepts introduced while solving it are used throughout computer science and are powerful enough to apply to even the most complex problems.

2.1 ABSTRACTION WITH OBJECTS

Abstraction means deliberately ignoring some details of something in order to concentrate on features that are essential to the job at hand. For example, abstract art is "abstract" because it ignores many details that make an image physically realistic and emphasizes just those details that are important to the message the artist wants to convey. Abstraction is important in designing algorithms because algorithms are often very complicated. Ignoring some of the complicating details while working on others helps you turn an overwhelmingly large single problem into a series of individually manageable subproblems.

One popular form of abstraction in modern computer science is object-oriented programming. *Object-oriented programming* is a philosophy of algorithm (and program) design that views the elements of a problem as active objects. This view encourages algorithm designers to think separately about the details of how individual objects behave and the details of how to coordinate a collection of objects to solve some problem. In other words, objects help designers ignore some details while working on others—abstraction!

The remainder of this chapter explores this idea and other aspects of object-oriented abstraction in depth. While reading this material, consult Appendix A for an overview of how to express object-oriented programming ideas in the Java programming language.

2.1.1 Objects

An *object* in a program or algorithm is a software agent that helps you solve a problem. The defining characteristic that makes something an object is that it performs actions, or contains information, or both. Every object is defined by the actions it performs and the information it contains.

Some objects correspond very literally to real-world entities. For example, a university's student-records program might have objects that represent each student at the university. These objects help solve the record-keeping problem by storing the corresponding student's grades, address, identification number, and so forth. Objects can also represent less tangible things. For example, a chess-playing program might include objects that represent strategies for winning a game of chess. These objects help the program play chess by suggesting moves for the program to make. The robot in this chapter is an object that doesn't correspond to any real robot, but does correspond to a graphical software simulation of one.[1]

Programming with objects involves defining the objects you want to use, and then putting them to work to solve the problem at hand. Something, usually either another object or the program's main routine, coordinates the objects' actions so that they collectively produce the required result.

2.1.2 Messages

A *message* is a signal that tells an object to do something. For instance, here are some messages one can send to the simulated robot and the actions the robot takes in response to each:

move: This message tells the robot to move forward one (simulated) meter.[2] The robot does not turn or spray paint while moving. However, if there is some obstacle (e.g., a wall of the room) less than one meter in front of the robot, then the robot will collide with the obstacle and not move.

turnLeft: This message tells the robot to turn 90 degrees to the left without changing its location. Robots are always able to turn left.

turnRight: This message tells the robot to turn 90 degrees to the right without changing location. Robots are always able to turn right.

---

[1] Java classes that implement this simulation are available at this book's Web site.
[2] For the sake of concreteness when describing robot algorithms, we assume that the robot moves and paints in units of meters. But the actual graphical robot in our software simulation moves and paints in largely arbitrary units on a computer monitor.

paint(*Color*): This message tells the robot to spray paint onto the floor. The message has a *parameter*, (*Color*), that specifies what color paint to spray. The robot does not move or turn while painting. The paint sprayer paints a square exactly one meter long and one meter wide beneath the robot. Therefore, when the robot paints, moves forward, and then paints again, the two squares of paint just touch each other.

Here is an algorithm using these messages. This algorithm sends move and turnLeft messages to a robot named Robbie, causing it to move two meters forward and then turn to face back towards where it came from:

```
robbie.move();
robbie.move();
robbie.turnLeft();
robbie.turnLeft();
```

Here is a more elaborate example, this time using two robots, Robbie and Robin. Assuming that the robots start out side by side and facing in the same direction, this algorithm draws parallel red and green lines:

```
robbie.paint(java.awt.Color.red);
robbie.move();
robin.paint(java.awt.Color.green);
robin.move();
robbie.paint(java.awt.Color.red);
robbie.move();
robin.paint(java.awt.Color.green);
robin.move();
```

2.1.3 Classes

One often wants to talk about features that groups of objects share. For example, it is far easier to say that all robots respond to move messages by moving one meter forward than to say that Robbie responds to move messages in this manner, and by the way, so does Robin, and if a third robot ever appears, it does too, and so on. A group of objects that all share the same features is called a *class*, and individual members of the group are called *instances* of that class. For example, Robbie and Robin are both instances of the robot class.

The most important features that all instances of a class share are the messages that they respond to and the ways in which they respond to those messages. For example, the robots discussed here all share these features: they respond to a move message by moving one meter forward, to a turnLeft message by turning 90 degrees to the left, to a `turnRight` message by turning 90 degrees to the right, and to a `paint` message by spraying a square meter of paint onto the floor.

The mathematical concept of set is helpful when thinking about classes. A *set* is simply a group of things with some common property. For example, the set of even integers is a group whose members all share the property of being integers divisible by two. Similarly, the class (equivalent to a set) of robots is a group whose members share the property of being objects that respond to `move`, `turnLeft`, `turnRight`, and `paint` messages in certain ways. As with all sets, when we define a class by stating the property that its members have in common, we implicitly mean the set of *all possible* objects with that property. For example, the class of robots is not just the set of robots referred to in this book, or used in a particular program, but rather it is the set of all possible robot objects.

2.1.4 Objects as Abstractions

Objects are very abstract things that are used to build algorithms. For example, our description of the robot was abstract because we concentrated on what it can do to draw (move, turn, spray paint), but ignored things not relevant to that task, such as what shape or color the robot is.

More significantly for algorithm design, our description of the robot concentrated on what a user needs to know about it in order to draw with it, but ignored details of what happens inside the robot—how it moves from one place to another, how it detects obstacles, and so forth. Imagine what it would take to move the robot forward without this abstraction: you would have to know what programming commands draw an image of the robot, what variables record where the robot is and where obstacles are, and so forth. Instead of a simple but abstract instruction such as "move" you might end up with something like, "If the robot is facing up, and if no element of the obstacles list has a y coordinate between the robot's y coordinate and the robot's y coordinate plus one, then erase the robot's image from the monitor, add one to the robot's y coordinate, and redraw the robot at its new position; but if the robot is facing to the right … ." This description would go on to deal with all the other directions the robot might face, what to do when there were obstacles in the robot's way, etc. Having to think at such a level of detail increases opportunities for all kinds of oversights and errors. Using abstraction to separate what a user needs to know about an object from its internal implementation makes algorithms far easier to design and understand.

Exercises

2.1. Design algorithms that make Robbie the Robot:

1. Move forward three meters.
2. Move one meter forward and one meter left, then face in its original direction (so the net effect is to move diagonally).
3. Turn 360 degrees without moving.
4. Test its paint sprayer by painting once in each of red, green, blue, and white.

2.2. Robots Robbie and Robin are standing side by side, facing in the same direction. Robbie is standing to Robin's left. Design algorithms to:

1. Make Robbie and Robin turn to face each other.
2. Make each robot move forward two meters.
3. Make Robbie and Robin move away from each other so that they are separated by a distance of two meters.
4. Make Robin paint a blue square around Robbie.

2.3. Which of the following could be a class? For each that could, what features do the instances share that define them as being the same kind of thing?

1. Bank accounts.
2. Numbers.
3. The number 3.
4. The people who are members of some organization.
5. Beauty.
6. Things that are beautiful.

2.4. Each of the following is something that you probably understand rather abstractly, in that you use it without knowing the internal details of how it works. What abstract operations do you use to make each do what you want?

1. A television.
2. A car.
3. A telephone.
4. An elevator.
5. The post office.
6. An e-mail message.

2.5. For each of the following problems, describe the objects that appear in it, any additional objects that would help you solve it, the behaviors each object should have, and the ways abstraction helps you identify or describe the objects and behaviors.

1. Two busy roads cross and form an intersection. You are to control traffic through the intersection so that cars coming from all directions have opportunities to pass through the intersection or turn onto the other road without colliding.
2. A chicken breeder asks you to design an automatic temperature control for an incubator that will prevent the chicks in it from getting either too hot or too cold.

2.2 PRECONDITIONS AND POSTCONDITIONS

Now that you know what the robot can do, you could probably design an algorithm to make it draw squares—but would it draw the right squares? Of course, you have no way to answer this question yet, because we haven't told you what we mean by "right": whether we require the squares to have a particular size or color, where they should be relative to the robot's initial position, whether it matters where the robot ends up relative to a square it has just drawn, etc. These are all examples of what computer scientists call the *preconditions* and *postconditions* of the problem. As these examples suggest, you can't know exactly what constitutes a correct solution to a problem until you know exactly what the problem is. Preconditions and postconditions help describe problems precisely.

A *precondition* is a requirement that must be met before you start solving a problem. For example, "I know the traffic laws" is a precondition for receiving a driver's license.

A *postcondition* is a statement about conditions that exist after solving the problem. For example, "I can legally drive a car" is a postcondition of receiving a driver's license.

To apply these ideas to the square-drawing problem, suppose the squares are to be red, and take "drawing" a square to mean drawing its outline (as opposed to filling the interior as well). Furthermore, let's allow users of the algorithm to say how long they want the square's sides to be (as opposed to the algorithm always drawing a square of some predetermined size). Since the robot draws lines one meter thick, it will outline squares with a wide border. Define the length of the square's side to be the length of this border's outer edge. All of these details can be concisely described by the following postcondition for the square-drawing problem: "There is a red square outline on the floor, whose outer edges are of the length requested by the user." Figure 2.1 diagrams this postcondition.

Note that a postcondition only needs to hold after a problem has been solved—so the postcondition for drawing a square does not mean that there is a red outline on the floor now; it only means that after any square-drawing algorithm finishes,

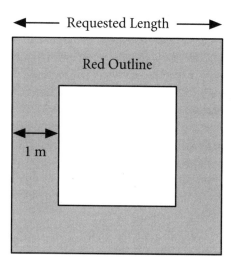

FIGURE 2.1 A square drawn as a red outline.

you will be able to truthfully say that "there is a red square outline on the floor, whose outer edges are of the length requested by the user."

Every algorithm has an *implementor,* the person who designs it, and *clients,* people who use it. Sometimes the implementor and a client are the same person; in other cases, the implementor and the clients are different people. In all cases, however, postconditions can be considered part of a contract between the implementor and the clients. Specifically, postconditions are what the implementor promises that the algorithm will deliver to the clients. For instance, if you write an algorithm for solving the square-drawing problem, you can write any algorithm you like—as long as it produces "a red square outline on the floor, whose outer edges are of the length requested by the user." No matter how nice your algorithm is, it is wrong (in other words, fails to meet its contract) if it doesn't draw such a square. Conversely, as long as it does draw this square, the algorithm meets its contract and so is correct. Postconditions specify the *least* that an algorithm must do in order to solve a problem. For example, a perfectly correct square-drawing algorithm could both draw the square and return the robot to its starting position, even though the postconditions don't require the return to the starting position.

As in any fair contract, an algorithm's clients make promises in return for the postconditions that the implementor promises. In particular, clients promise to establish the problem's preconditions before they use the algorithm. For example, clients of the square-drawing algorithm must respect certain restrictions on the length of a square's sides: the length must be an integer number of meters (because the robot only moves in steps of a meter), and it has to be at least one meter (because the robot can't draw anything smaller than that). Clients also need to know where to place the robot in order to get a square in the desired location—for concreteness's sake, let's say at a corner of what will be the border—with the future square to the right and forward of the robot (Figure 2.2). Finally, clients will need to make sure there is nothing in the border region that the robot might run into. These requirements can be concisely described by a list of preconditions for the square-drawing problem.

1. The requested length of each side of the square is an integer number of meters and is at least one meter.
2. The future square is to the right and forward of the robot (as in Figure 2.2).
3. There are no obstacles in the area that will be the border of the square.

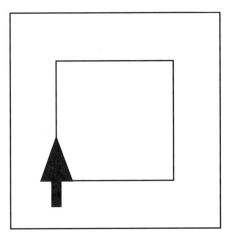

FIGURE 2.2 The robot starts in the lower left corner of the square it is to draw.

An algorithm needn't take advantage of all of its problem's preconditions. For example, you might be able to design a square-drawing algorithm that let the robot navigate around obstacles in the border region. This algorithm is also a good solution to the problem, even though it doesn't need the precondition that there are no obstacles in the border. Preconditions describe the *most* that an algorithm's implementor can assume about the setting in which his or her algorithm will execute.

Never make an algorithm establish its own preconditions. For instance, don't begin a square-drawing algorithm with messages that try to move the robot to the place you think the square's left rear corner should be. Sooner or later your idea of where the corner should be will differ from what some client wants. Establishing preconditions is solely the clients' job. As an implementor, concentrate on your job—establishing the postconditions.

Preconditions and postconditions are forms of abstraction. In particular, they tell clients what an algorithm produces (the postconditions) and what it needs to be given (the preconditions) while hiding the steps that transform the given inputs into the desired results.

Exercises

2.6. Can you think of other postconditions that you might want for a square-drawing algorithm? What about other preconditions?

2.7. Think of preconditions and postconditions for the following activities:

1. Brushing your teeth.
2. Borrowing a book from a library.
3. Moving Robbie the Robot forward three meters.
4. Turning Robbie the Robot 90 degrees to the left.

2.8. Find the preconditions necessary for each of the following algorithms to really establish its postconditions.

1. Make Robbie the Robot draw a green line two meters long:

```
robbie.paint(java.awt.Color.green);
robbie.move();
robbie.paint(java.awt.Color.green);
```

Postconditions: The one-meter square under Robbie is green; the one-meter square behind Robbie is green.

2. Make Robin the Robot paint a red dot and then move out of the way so people can see it:

```
robin.paint(java.awt.Color.red);
robin.move();
```

Postconditions: Robin is one meter forward of where it started; the one-meter square behind Robin is red.

3. Make Robin the Robot paint the center of a floor blue:

```
robin.paint(java.awt.Color.blue);
```

Postcondition: The center square meter of the floor is blue.

2.9. Suppose you want to divide one number by another and get a real number as the result. What precondition needs to hold?

2.10. Consider the following problem: Given an integer, x, find another integer, r, that is the integer closest to the square root of x. Give preconditions and postconditions for this problem that more exactly say when the problem is solvable and what characteristics r must have to be a solution.

2.3 ALGORITHMS THAT PRODUCE EFFECTS

Many algorithms produce their results by changing something—changing the contents of a file or the image displayed on a monitor, changing a robot's position, etc. The things that are changed are external to the algorithms (that is, not defined within the algorithms themselves), and the changes persist after the algorithms finish. Such changes are called *side effects*. Note that this use of the term "side effect" differs somewhat from its use in everyday speech—computer scientists use the term to mean any change that an algorithm causes to its environment, without the colloquial connotations of the change being accidental or even undesirable. Indeed, many algorithms deliver useful results through side effects. In this section, we examine how to use object-oriented programming, preconditions, and postconditions to design side-effect-producing algorithms.

2.3.1 Design from Preconditions and Postconditions

A problem's preconditions and postconditions provide a *specification*, or precise description, of the problem. Such a specification can help you discover an algorithm to solve the problem. For instance, the precise specification for the square-drawing problem is as follows:

Preconditions:

1. The requested length of each side of the square is an integer number of meters and is at least one meter.
2. The future square is to the right and forward of the robot (as in Figure 2.2).
3. There are no obstacles in the area that will be the border of the square.

Postcondition:

1. There is a red square outline on the floor, whose outer edges are of the length requested by the user. The square is to the right and forward of the robot's original position.

With this specification, we finally know what an algorithm to draw squares must do.

Drawing Squares

The basic algorithm is simple: start by drawing a line as long as one side of the square (the precondition that the robot starts in a corner of the square, facing along a side, means that the algorithm can start drawing right away). Then turn right (the precondition that the square is to be to the robot's right means that this is the correct direction to turn), draw a similar line, turn right again, draw a third line, and finally turn right a last time and draw a fourth line.

This square-drawing algorithm demonstrates two important points: First, we checked the correctness of some of the algorithm's details (when to start drawing, which direction to turn) against the problem's preconditions even as we described the algorithm. Preconditions can steer you toward correct algorithms even at the very beginning of a design!

Second, we used abstraction (again) to make the algorithm easy to think about. Specifically, we described the algorithm in terms of drawing lines for the sides of the square rather than worrying directly about painting individual one-meter spots. We used this abstraction for two reasons. First, it makes the algorithm correspond more naturally to the way we think of squares, namely as figures with four *sides*, not figures with certain spots colored. This correspondence helped us invent the algorithm faster, and increased our chances of getting it right. Second, the abstract idea of drawing a side can be reused four times in drawing a square. So for a "price" of recognizing and eventually implementing one abstraction, we "buy" four substantial pieces of the ultimate goal.

Here is the square-drawing algorithm, drawSquare, using a robot named Robbie to do the drawing. The algorithm has a parameter, size, that indicates the desired length of each side of the square. Also note that for now the abstract "draw a line" steps are represented by invocations of another algorithm, drawLine, that will draw the lines. We will design this algorithm in the next section.

```
static void drawSquare(int size) {
    drawLine(size);
    robbie.turnRight();
    drawLine(size);
    robbie.turnRight();
    drawLine(size);
    robbie.turnRight();
    drawLine(size);
}
```

Drawing Lines

Algorithm drawSquare looks like it should draw squares, at least if drawLine draws lines. So to finish solving the square-drawing problem, we need to design a line-drawing algorithm. It may seem backwards that we used an algorithm that doesn't exist yet in designing drawSquare, but doing so causes no problems at all—we just have to remember to write the missing algorithm before trying to execute the one that uses it. In fact, it was a helpful abstraction to think of drawing a square as drawing four lines, and writing that abstraction into the drawSquare algorithm is equally helpful (for example, it helps readers understand the algorithm, and it avoids rewriting the line-drawing steps more often than necessary).

The way we used drawLine in drawSquare implicitly assumes a number of pre-conditions and postconditions for drawLine. We need to understand these conditions explicitly if we are to design a drawLine algorithm that works correctly in drawSquare. For example, note that every time drawSquare invokes drawLine, Robbie is standing over the first spot to be painted on the line, and is already facing in the direction in which it will move in order to trace the line (i.e., facing along the line). In other words, we designed drawSquare assuming that drawLine has the precondition "Robbie is standing over the first spot to paint, facing along the line."

Now consider what we have assumed about postconditions for drawing a line. The obvious one is that a red line exists that is size meters long and in the position specified by the preconditions. More interesting, however, are several less obvious postconditions that are essential to the way drawSquare uses drawLine. Since the only thing drawSquare does in between drawing two lines is turn Robbie right, drawing one line must leave Robbie standing in the correct spot to start the next line, but not facing in the proper direction. If you think carefully about the corners of the square, you will discover that if each line is size meters long, then they must over-lap at the corners in order for the square to have sides size meters long (see Figure 2.3). This overlap means that "the correct spot to start the next line" is also the end of the previous line. So the first assumed postcondition for drawing lines can be phrased as "Robbie is standing over the last spot painted in the line." Now think about the right turn. In order for it to point Robbie in the correct direction for starting the next line, Robbie must have finished drawing the previous line still fac-ing in the direction it moved to draw that line. So another assumed postcondition for drawing a line is that Robbie ends up facing in the same direction it was facing when it started drawing the line. Notice that much of the thinking leading to these postconditions is based on how Robbie will start to draw the next line, and so relies on the preconditions for drawing lines—for example, in recognizing that the "cor-rect spot" and "correct direction" to start a new line are the first spot to be painted in the line and the direction in which it runs.

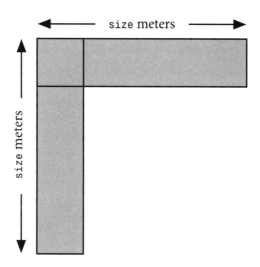

FIGURE 2.3 Lines overlap at the corners of the square.

Knowing the preconditions and postconditions for drawing lines, we can now design algorithm drawLine. drawLine's basic job will be to spray red paint and move until a line size meters long is painted. One subtle point, however, which the preconditions and postconditions help us recognize, is that because Robbie both starts and finishes over ends of the line, Robbie only needs to move a total of size−1 steps while painting a total of size times. Further, Robbie must both start and end by painting rather than by moving. These observations lead to the following drawLine algorithm:

```
static void drawLine(int size) {
    robbie.paint(java.awt.Color.red);
    for (int i = 0; i < size-1; i++) {
        robbie.move();
        robbie.paint(java.awt.Color.red);
    }
}
```

Algorithms drawSquare and drawLine together form a complete solution to the square-drawing problem. Algorithm drawSquare coordinates the overall drawing, and drawLine draws the individual sides of the square. The design processes for both algorithms illustrated how preconditions and postconditions guide design. Careful attention to these conditions clarified exactly what each algorithm had to do and called attention to details that led to correct algorithms.[3]

2.3.2 Subclasses

You now have an algorithm that you can use to make Robbie draw red squares. However, you have to remember the algorithm and recite it every time you want a square. Furthermore, if you ever want to draw a square with another robot, you have to change your algorithm to send messages to that other robot instead of to Robbie.

You could avoid these problems if there were a way for you to program the drawSquare and drawLine algorithms into robots, associating each algorithm with a message that caused the robot to execute that algorithm. This, in effect, would allow you to create a new kind of robot that could draw squares and lines in addition to being able to move, turn, and paint. Call such robots "drawing robots." Once you created as many drawing robots as you wanted, you could order any of them to draw squares or lines for you, and you would only need to remember the names of the drawSquare and drawLine messages, not the details of the algorithms.

Subclass Concepts

Object-oriented programming supports the idea just outlined. Programmers can define a new class that is similar to a previously existing one, except that instances of the new class can respond to certain messages that instances of the original class couldn't respond to. For each new message, the new class defines an algorithm that instances will execute when they receive that message. This algorithm is called the *method* with which the new class responds to, or *handles*, the new message. This is the fundamental way of adapting object-oriented systems to new uses.

A class defined by extending the features of some other class is called a *subclass*. Where a class is a set of possible objects of some kind, a subclass is a subset, corresponding to some variation on the basic kind of object. For example, drawing robots are a subclass of robots—they are a variation on basic robots because they handle drawSquare and drawLine messages that other robots don't handle. Nonetheless, drawing robots are still robots. So every drawing robot is a robot, but not all robots are necessarily drawing robots—exactly the relationship between a subset and its superset, illustrated in Figure 2.4. Turning the relationship around, we can also say that the original class is a *superclass* of the new one (for example, robots form a superclass of drawing robots).

---

[3] At least, both algorithms seem to be correct. Chapter 3 will examine the question of whether they really are, and will introduce methods for rigorously proving correctness or lack thereof.

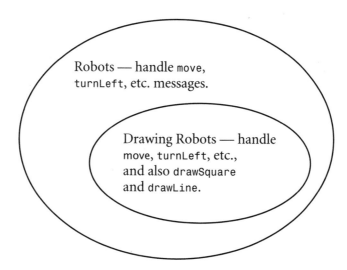

FIGURE 2.4 Drawing robots are a subclass (subset) of robots.

Since instances of a subclass are also instances of the superclass, they have all of the properties that other instances of the superclass do. This feature is called *inheritance*—instances of subclasses automatically acquire, or *inherit,* the features of their superclass. For example, drawing robots inherit from robots the abilities to move, turn, and paint.

Objects Sending Messages to Themselves

One problem remains before you can turn the drawSquare and drawLine algorithms into methods that any drawing robot can execute. The original algorithms send messages to Robbie, but that is surely not what every drawing robot should do. Poor Robbie would be constantly moving and turning and painting to draw squares that other robots had been asked to draw! Each drawing robot should really send these messages to itself. In other words, a drawing robot should draw a square by telling itself to paint certain tiles, move, and turn in certain ways, etc. So far, all our examples of messages have been directed to a specific individual, such as Robbie. But you can also direct messages to a special name, such as Java's this, to indicate that the object executing a method sends itself a message—for example, this.move(). This idea may seem odd at first, but there is nothing wrong with it. It's certainly familiar enough in real life—for example, people write themselves reminders to do things. From the point of view of the algorithm, a message is simply being directed to an object, like messages always are.

Example

Here is a Java description of drawing robots, illustrating all of the foregoing ideas:

```
class DrawingRobot extends Robot {

    public void drawSquare(int size) {
        this.drawLine(size);
        this.turnRight();
        this.drawLine(size);
        this.turnRight();
        this.drawLine(size);
        this.turnRight();
        this.drawLine(size);
    }

    public void drawLine(int size) {
        this.paint(java.awt.Color.red);
        for (int i = 0; i < size-1; i++) {
            this.move();
            this.paint(java.awt.Color.red);
        }
    }
}
```

The methods in this example are the algorithms from Section 2.3.1, except that all messages inside the algorithms are sent to this. Moreover, since drawLine is now a message to drawing robots, the drawSquare method sends a drawLine message to this instead of just saying drawLine(size). Finally, note that the description of drawingRobot does not define move, turnLeft, turnRight, or paint methods. These methods do not need to be mentioned explicitly here, because they are inherited from DrawingRobot's superclass.

2.3.3 Method Abstraction

Messages and methods are actually very general concepts. Objects don't use methods only to handle messages defined by subclasses—they handle all messages that way. A message is thus a signal from outside an object that causes the object to do something. A method is an algorithm that the object executes internally in order to do that thing. Figure 2.5 illustrates this relationship.

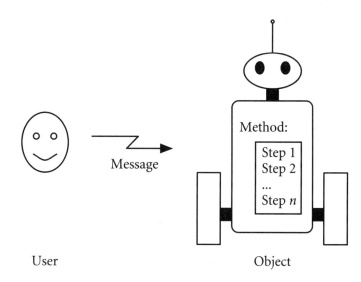

FIGURE 2.5 An external message causes an object to execute the corresponding internal method.

The relationship between methods and messages corresponds very neatly to the relationship between algorithms' implementors and clients. Indeed, just as an algorithm has an implementor and clients, so too do classes. A class's implementor is the person who creates the class's methods; clients are the people who send messages to instances of the class. Because methods are algorithms invoked by messages, class implementors are algorithm implementors and class clients are algorithm clients. Focusing the client's role on sending messages and the implementor's role on writing methods is the key to objects as abstractions. Clients can send messages that cause objects to do useful things without knowing the algorithms the objects will execute in response, and implementors can write methods without knowing which clients will send the corresponding messages or why. Each party can think abstractly about the other's contribution while making their own, thus freeing their mind to concentrate on the tasks most important to themselves.

In studying the class DrawingRobot earlier, you became a class implementor. You learned how to create a new abstraction (in this case, a new kind of robot) via a class definition. Every class provides certain operations whose detailed realizations are spelled out in methods inside the class definition. However, once the methods are defined, they remain hidden inside the class definition. The class *encapsulates* the methods, in other words, isolates them from clients. Encapsulation allows clients to use the operations without having to know how they are implemented. Clients only need to know which messages elicit which behaviors from instances of the class.

Encapsulating an algorithm in a method hides many details of its design from clients, and many details of its use from implementors. However, two things remain shared by clients and implementors: the algorithm's preconditions and postconditions. Good preconditions and postconditions describe all, and only, the properties of the algorithm that abstraction should not hide. Preconditions and postconditions are thus a particularly important part of a method's specification—they are the interface between implementor and client that sets forth their agreement about what a method is to do.

Exercises

2.11. Design a subclass of Robot that provides the following new messages:

1. turnAround, which causes its recipient to turn 180° without changing position.
2. stepAndPaint(*Color*), which causes its recipient to paint the floor under itself and then move one meter forward. The color in which to paint is a parameter to this message.
3. quickStep, which causes its recipient to move two meters forward.
4. uTurn, which causes its recipient to turn 180° and move one meter to the right of its original position, as illustrated in Figure 2.6.

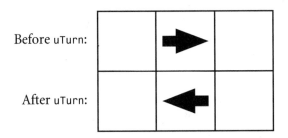

Before uTurn:

After uTurn:

FIGURE 2.6 A robot's position and orientation before and after handling a uTurn message.

2.12. Suppose you are writing a program that acts like a telephone book—users enter a person's name into the program, and the program responds with that person's telephone number. Internally, such a program might be built around a telephone book object, which handles messages such as:

■ find(*Person*), which searches the telephone database for an entry for *Person*, and returns that person's telephone number if they are listed in the database. Assume this message returns telephone numbers as strings and returns an empty string if *Person* isn't listed in the database.

- ▪ add(*Person*, *Number*), which adds *Person* to the database, with telephone number *Number*. Assume both *Person* and *Number* are strings.
- ▪ remove(*Person*), which removes the entry (if any) for *Person* from the database.

1. Using these messages, design an algorithm for updating a telephone book, in other words, an algorithm that takes a telephone book object and a person's name and telephone number as inputs, removes any existing entry for that person from the telephone book, and then creates a new entry for that person, with the given telephone number.
2. Using pseudocode or English, outline methods that telephone book objects could use to handle these messages. Assume that the telephone database is stored in a file using an organization of your own devising (a very simple organization is fine). (Note that since you aren't using a specific programming language's file and string handling commands, you will necessarily have to treat files and strings as abstractions in these algorithms. How does this abstraction appear in your algorithms? How does it correspond to what you know of particular languages' mechanisms for working with strings and files?)
3. Code a telephone book class in Java based on your abstract algorithms from the preceding step.

2.13. Robots can "print" certain block letters. Figure 2.7 presents some examples, each of which occupies a 5-meter-high by 3-meter-wide section of floor, and each of which is produced by painting appropriate one-meter squares within the 5-by-3 section.

Design a subclass of Robot that provides messages for printing each of the letters in Figure 2.7. Design an algorithm that uses an instance of this subclass to write a simple message. Try to abstract reusable subalgorithms out of this problem as you design your class—in other words, try to describe drawing each letter in terms of steps intermediate between drawing the whole letter and painting a single square, so that the steps can be reused in drawing other letters. A number of different preconditions and postconditions are possible for drawing letters—pick some that seem appropriate to you and design your methods around them.

2.14. Suppose the postconditions for the square-drawing problem were that there be a *filled* square (rather than just an outline) on the floor. Define a subclass of DrawingRobot that draws such squares. Your subclass may handle a new message distinct from drawSquare to draw filled squares, or it may define a new method for the drawSquare message. (The latter option is called *overrid-*

ing a superclass's method. Overriding is a feature in object-oriented programming that allows a subclass to handle a message with its own method rather than with the one that it would normally inherit from its superclass.)

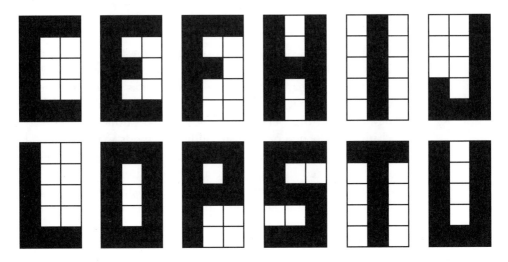

FIGURE 2.7 Letters that robots can draw.

2.4 ALGORITHMS THAT PRODUCE VALUES

So far, all of our example algorithms have produced their results in the form of side effects. However, there is another way for algorithms to produce results: they can calculate some sort of value, or answer. Such algorithms are called *value-producing algorithms*, and you have probably seen examples before (for instance, an algorithm that calculates the average of a set of numbers). All of the forms of abstraction that we introduced in connection with side effects (encapsulating algorithms in methods, preconditions and postconditions, etc.) remain important when designing value-producing algorithms.

2.4.1 Expressions

Consider an algorithm that calculates the area of a square that is *n* meters on a side. In English, this algorithm might be stated as:

Take the value n, and multiply it by itself.

In Java, this algorithm corresponds to the *expression*:

```
n*n
```

Although this expression looks different from the algorithms seen so far, it none-theless describes the algorithm just given in English. Of course, expressions can also describe more complicated algorithms. For example, here is one that uses the Pythagorean Theorem to calculate the length of a square's diagonal (*n* again being the length of the side, and Math.sqrt being a Java function that computes square roots):

```
Math.sqrt(n*n + n*n)
```

The corresponding algorithm might be described in English as:

Multiply the value of n by itself.
Multiply n by itself a second time.
Add the two products together.
Calculate the square root of the sum.

The concept of "expression" is surprisingly broad. In particular, expressions are not always numeric. For example, here is a Java expression that carries out a calculation on strings—it first joins together (*concatenates*) the strings "bird" and "dog", and then extracts a part (or *substring*) of the result, extending from the third through sixth characters (Java counts positions in strings from 0, so the third character is the one in position 2):

```
"bird".concat("dog").substring(2, 6)
```

This expression consists of a series of messages to objects—each message, from left to right, produces a new object, to which the next message is sent. The concat message produces a string ("birddog"), to which the substring message is then sent, producing the final result: "rddo". Although this *syntax*, or grammatical form, is quite different from that of the earlier arithmetic expressions, it is still an expression. Expressions that consist of such a series of messages are useful anytime you need to do a calculation that operates on objects.

Similarly, one can construct expressions from operations on other types of data—finding the day before or after a particular date, the operations of logic ("and", "or", "not", etc.) on truth values, and so forth. Regardless of the type of data on which they operate, or the kinds of operations they involve, however, all expressions share one important feature: they correspond to algorithms that take one or more values as input and produce a value (rather than a side effect) as a result.

Like all algorithms, expressions have preconditions and postconditions. For example, the expression:

```
x / y
```

has a precondition that y is not 0. Similarly, the expression:

```
Math.sqrt(x)
```

has a precondition that x is greater than or equal to 0. In Java, this expression also has a postcondition that its result is non-negative. This postcondition is important, because mathematically any nonzero number has both a positive and a negative square root, and knowing which is produced can be important to understanding why and how this expression is being used. As these examples illustrate, preconditions for an expression often make explicit the inputs for which the expression is valid, while postconditions often clarify exactly what results it produces.

When considering an expression as an algorithm, the *operators* (symbols such as "*" or concat that denote a computation) are the steps of the algorithm, and the *operands* (values on which computations are done) are the data manipulated by those steps. But here an interesting difference between expressions and our earlier algorithms appears: expressions are less precise about the order in which their steps are to be carried out. Sometimes this imprecision doesn't matter. For example, the expression:

```
x + y + z
```

contains no indication whether x and y should be added first, and then their sum added to z, or whether y and z should be added first, and then x added to their sum. But since the final sum will be the same in either case, this ambiguity is inconsequential.

Unfortunately, there are also situations in which imprecision about the order of operations makes it impossible to determine exactly what algorithm an expression represents. For example, the expression:

```
3 * 4 + 5
```

could correspond to the algorithm, "Multiply 3 by 4, and then add that product to 5" (an algorithm that produces the value 17), or to, "Add 4 to 5, and multiply that sum by 3" (an algorithm that produces 27).

Luckily, there are a number of ways to resolve such ambiguity. For one, note that the ambiguity is due to the syntax used in the expression (specifically, the fact that operators appear in between their operands, so that the example expression can be interpreted either as a "*" whose operands are "3" and "4 + 5", or as a "+" whose operands are "3 * 4" and "5"). There are other syntaxes, in both mathematics and programming, that eliminate such ambiguity (Exercise 2.15 explores this topic further).

Alternatively, conventional mathematical notation and most programming languages (including Java) allow parts of an expression to be parenthesized to indicate that those parts should be evaluated first. Using this convention, the ambiguity we saw could be resolved by writing either:

```
(3 * 4) + 5
```

or:

```
3 * (4 + 5)
```

Another common approach is to adopt implicit rules that resolve ambiguity. For example, Java (and most other programming languages, as well as much of mathematics) evaluate multiplications before additions, and so would interpret the ambiguous example as meaning "(3 * 4) + 5". However, because such rules are implicit, you shouldn't rely heavily on them when writing algorithms that people are supposed to understand—the reader might not use the same implicit rules you do.

While expressions describe algorithms in their own right, they often also appear as parts of larger algorithms. For example, the expression:

```
m * 60
```

describes an algorithm that calculates the number of seconds in m minutes. It might sometimes be interesting to talk about this algorithm by itself, but it is also likely to appear embedded in other algorithms. For instance, here it is inside an algorithm that calculates the total number of seconds in m minutes and s seconds:

```
m * 60 + s
```

Here it is providing a parameter for a wait message to object x:

```
x.wait(m * 60);
```

Do not be surprised if you find yourself using expressions as parts of other algorithms more often than you use them as complete algorithms by themselves.

2.4.2 Abstractions of Expressions

In Section 2.3 you saw how messages cause objects to execute algorithms. The algorithms in Section 2.3 were all side-effect-producing ones, but messages can also cause objects to execute value-producing algorithms. We call messages that do this *value-producing messages* to distinguish them from messages that invoke side-effect-producing algorithms (*side-effect-producing messages*).

Basic Concepts

A value-producing message is a two-way exchange: first a client sends the message to an object, and then the object :r*returns* the resulting value, that is, sends it back to the client. Value-producing messages thus act as questions asked of an object (which answers), while side-effect-producing messages are commands given to an object. For example, our robots have a value-producing message heading, to which they reply with the direction in which they are facing (north, south, east, or west). Figure 2.8 shows how a client could exchange such a message and its reply with a robot.

Because a value-producing message returns a value, the message must be sent from a point in an algorithm where that value can be used—basically, anyplace

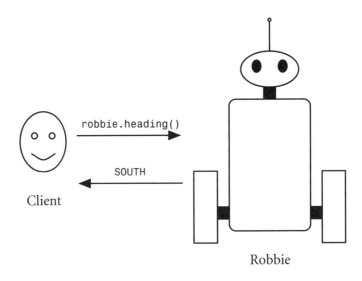

FIGURE 2.8 A value-producing message and its resulting value.

where an expression could appear. In fact, sending a value-producing message really is a kind of expression. For example, if you want a program to tell its user the direction in which Robbie is facing, you could include the following statement in the program:

```
System.out.println("Robbie is facing " + robbie.heading());
```

Value-producing messages are also frequently sent as parts of larger expressions. For example, the following comparison expression is true if and only if Robbie and Robin are facing in different directions:

```
robin.heading() != robbie.heading()
```

Other places where value-producing messages often appear include the right-hand sides of assignment operations or as parameters to other messages. Apart from being used in different contexts, however, value-producing messages are just like side-effect-producing messages—they are named and directed to objects in the same way, their parameters are specified in the same way, etc. This text normally uses the word "message" by itself, qualifying it with "value-producing" or "side-effect-producing" only in discussions that pertain to one kind of message but not the other.

Value-producing messages are handled by value-producing methods. The crucial difference between a value-producing method and a side-effect-producing one is that the value-producing method returns a value, and ideally produces no side effects, whereas the side-effect-producing method produces one or more side effects but returns no value. Just as side-effect-producing methods allow you to abstract side-effect-producing algorithms into messages, value-producing methods allow you to abstract value-producing algorithms into messages. For example, here are the algorithms for a square's area and diagonal encapsulated in a "square calculations" class:

```
class SquareCalculations {

    public static double area(double size) {
        return size * size;
    }

    public static double diagonal(double size) {
        return Math.sqrt(size*size + size*size);
    }
}
```

An Extended Example

Suppose you want to calculate your probability of winning a lottery. Specifically, consider lotteries in which the lottery managers pick a set of numbers from a large pool of possibilities and players win if they guess in advance all the numbers that will be picked. For example, to play the lottery in the home state of one of the authors, a player guesses six numbers between 1 and 59, and hopes that these are the same six numbers the lottery managers will pick in the next drawing.

Your probability of winning the lottery depends on how many different sets of numbers the lottery managers could pick. Mathematically, if the managers pick n numbers (for example, 6 in the previous paragraph's example) from a pool of p (e.g., 59 in the example), the number of sets is:

$$\frac{p!}{n!(p-n)!} \tag{2.1}$$

The probability of guessing the one winning set is simply the reciprocal of the number of sets, or:

$$\frac{n!(p-n)!}{p!} \tag{2.2}$$

(The "!s" in these equations—and in mathematical expressions generally—represent factorials. $x!$ is the product of all the integers between 1 and x; for example, $4! = 1 \times 2 \times 3 \times 4 = 24$.)

Equation 2.2 by itself is a rough description of a "probability of winning the lottery" algorithm. To phrase this algorithm in Java, you will need a method for calculating factorials, but that is a good thing to abstract out of the main algorithm. The details of how you calculate factorials would distract from how you use factorials in the "probability of winning" algorithm, and a "factorial" method defined once can be used three times while evaluating Equation 2.2. Notice how similar these reasons for abstracting "factorial" out of "probability of winning" are to those for abstracting drawing a line out of drawSquare in Section 2.3. This is no accident—the reasons for and benefits of abstraction are the same in all algorithms.

Here is Equation 2.2 as a chanceOfWinning method of a Java "lottery calculator" class:

```
// In class LotteryCalculator...
public static double chanceOfWinning(int n, int p) {
    return factorial(n) * factorial(p-n) / factorial(p);
}
```

Now consider the `factorial` method. Its parameter will be *x*, the number whose factorial is needed. The idea that *x*! is the product of all the integers between 1 and *x* provides the central plan for the algorithm: multiply together all the integers between 1 and *x*, and return the final product. This product can be very large, so we declare it as `double`, a Java numeric type that can represent very large values. The lottery calculator class with `factorial` looks like this:

```
class LotteryCalculator {

    public static double chanceOfWinning(int n, int p) {
        return factorial(n) * factorial(p-n) / factorial(p);
    }

    public static double factorial(int x) {
        double product = 1.0;
        while (x > 0) {
            product = product * x;
            x = x - 1;
        }
        return product;
    }
}
```

The `factorial` method illustrates how a value-producing method isn't limited to containing a single expression; it can contain any algorithm that eventually returns a value. This is a very useful feature, since many calculations aren't easily written as single expressions. Encapsulating such calculations in value-producing methods allows them to be invoked via the corresponding message anywhere an expression could appear, even though the algorithm that eventually gets carried out is not itself an expression.

2.4.3 Values and Side Effects

So far, we have presented value-producing algorithms and side-effect-producing ones as completely separate things. This separation ensures that every algorithm produces only one kind of result, either a set of side effects or a value; such algorithms are easier to think about than ones that produce multiple results in multiple forms. Unfortunately, value-producing and side-effect-producing algorithms are not always separated so strictly. In some situations, it may make sense to define a message that produces both side effects and a value (for instance, if the value is a status code that indicates whether the intended side effects were successfully produced), and almost all programming languages allow programmers to do so. There are even languages in which some of the built-in operators produce side effects.[4]

Regardless of what programming languages permit, however, side-effect-free algorithms are easier to reason about than side-effect-producing ones. Every condition that holds before executing a side-effect-free algorithm will also hold afterward, and the only postconditions one needs for such an algorithm are the postconditions that specify the value it returns. For example, consider the two fragments of Java in Listing 2.1. Both use an add method to add 1 and 2, placing the sum in variable result. It is probably much easier for you to understand how the top fragment does this, and what value it leaves in the other variable, x, than it is to understand the bottom fragment.

LISTING 2.1 Two Code Fragments That Place a Value in Variable Result

```
// In class ValueExample...
private static int x;
public static void normal() {
    x = 1;
    int result = add(1, 2);
}


// In class SideEffectExample...
private static int x;
public static void weird() {
    x = 1;
    add(1, 2);
    int result = x;
}
```

The reason for the difference between the code fragments in Listing 2.1 is that the top one was written for a value-producing add method, whereas the bottom one was written for a side-effect-producing method. The top of Listing 2.2 shows a possible value-producing add, while the bottom shows a side-effect-producing one.

LISTING 2.2 Value- and Side-Effect-Producing Implementations of an add Method

```
// In class ValueExample...
public static int add(int a, int b) {
    return a + b;
}
```

---

[4] For instance, the "++" and "--" operators in Java and C++.

```
// In class SideEffectExample...
public static void add(int a, int b) {
    x = a + b;
}
```

Side effects are certainly necessary for solving some problems. For instance, we could not have solved the square-drawing problem at the beginning of this chapter without the side effect of painting a square on the floor. However, do not use side effects unnecessarily, and if you have a choice between a side-effect-producing algorithm and a value-producing one (e.g., as in the add examples), prefer the value-producing algorithm.

Exercises

2.15. Using your library and similar resources, find out what other syntaxes for expressions exist and which have been adapted for use in programming languages.

2.16. Write, as expressions, algorithms for calculating the following:

1. The area of a circle whose radius is r.
2. The perimeter of a square whose side is n units long.
3. The amount of paint needed to paint a wall h feet high by w feet wide. Assume that 1 gallon of paint paints 400 square feet of wall.
4. The cost of driving d miles, assuming that your car can drive m miles per gallon of gasoline and that gasoline costs p dollars per gallon.
5. The value of x at which a function of the form $f(x) = mx + b$ is equal to 0.
6. A value of x at which a function of the form $f(x) = ax^2 + bx + c$ is equal to 0.
7. The average of three numbers, x, y, and z. (Think carefully! Simple as it appears, many students get this wrong on their first attempt!)

2.17. Write an expression that calculates the area of the red border that Section 2.3.2's drawSquare algorithm draws, assuming that the square is size meters on a side.

2.18. List the items that you have for a hypothetical restaurant meal, along with the price of each item. Write an expression for calculating the total cost of the meal (including tax and tip).

2.19. You worked 38 hours last week at $5.57 per hour. Your employer withheld 15% for federal taxes and 4% for state tax. You also paid $3.50 for union dues. Write an expression to calculate your take-home pay.

2.20. Write, as a series of English sentences, the algorithms described by each of the following mathematical expressions:

1. $3^3/(4+5)$
2. $(4+7)\times((8-3)\times6)$
3. $((9-7)-5)-(5-(7-9))$
4. $(x+y)/2$
5. $4!/2!+7$

2.21. Find preconditions for the following expressions:

1. $1/y$
2. $\sqrt{(x+y)/(x-y)}$
3. The 17th character of string w
4. $\tan\alpha$
5. The uppercase version of a given character (for instance, the uppercase version of "a" is "A", the upper-case version of "A" is "A" itself.)
6. The letter that is alphabetically after a given letter (for instance, the letter alphabetically after "B" is "C").
7. $\log_2 x$
8. $y!$

2.22. Many programming languages' built-in trigonometric operators include one that computes the inverse tangent of its operand, but nothing to compute an inverse sine. Programmers who need inverse sines must thus write expressions to compute them. Devise an expression that computes $\sin^{-1} x$, assuming you have a $\tan^{-1}$ operator. What preconditions must hold in order for this expression to have a value? Recall that $\sin\alpha$ is not strictly invertible, that is, for any α such that $\sin\alpha = x$, an infinite number of other angles also have sines equal to x. Provide a postcondition for your $\sin^{-1} x$ expression to clarify exactly which angle it yields. (Assume that your $\tan^{-1}$ operator produces a result strictly greater than $-\pi/2$ and strictly less than $\pi/2$.)

2.23. Define a calculator class that has methods for handling the following messages:

1. cube(n), which returns n^3, given the precondition that n is a real number.
2. sum(n), which returns the sum of all integers i such that $1 \le i \le n$, given the precondition that n is an integer greater than or equal to 1.
3. average(x, y), which returns the average of x and y, given the precondition that x and y are both real numbers.

2.24. Use Equation 2.2 to calculate the probability of winning a lottery in which the lottery managers:

1. Choose 2 numbers out of a pool of 6.
2. Choose 3 numbers out of a pool of 5.
3. Choose 4 numbers out of a pool of 6 (compare this probability to that for item 1—can you explain why you see the result you do?)

2.5 ENCAPSULATING VALUES

Most of the preceding examples of value-producing methods calculate their results from parameters supplied with a message. Often, however, this is not a very convenient way to provide inputs to a method. For instance, the `heading` method within robots must determine a robot's orientation for itself rather than being told it via a parameter.

This problem can be solved by allowing objects to contain pieces of data that methods can use. For example, a robot could contain data about its orientation, which the `heading` method could retrieve, and which the `turnLeft` and `turnRight` methods would presumably alter. The mechanism for doing such things is *member variables*. Like other variables, member variables are named containers in which to store data. Unlike other variables, however, member variables are contained within objects. Think of a member variable as a pocket inside an object. The object can place a piece of data into this pocket, and examine the data in it. The only restriction is that the pocket always contains exactly one piece of data. For example, a "time-of-day" object could represent a time as the number of hours since midnight, the number of minutes since the start of the hour, and the number of seconds since the start of the minute. Each of these values would be stored in a separate member variable as Figure 2.9 illustrates for an object that represents 10:15:25 a.m.

An object's class determines what member variables that object will contain. Thus, all instances of a class contain member variables with the same names. However, each instance has its own copy of these member variables, so different instances can have different values stored in their member variables. For example, the time-of-day class might be declared, in part, like this:

```
class Time {
    private int hour;
    private int minute;
    private int second;
    ...
}
```

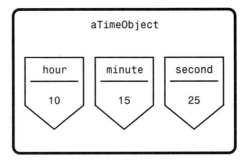

FIGURE 2.9 A "time-of-day" object with member variables.

Two Time objects could then describe different times by storing different values in their member variables, as shown in Figure 2.10.

Any method executed by an object can access any of that object's member variables by simply referring to the variable by name. For example, you could give the Time class methods for setting the time and for calculating the number of seconds since midnight as follows:

```
class Time {

    private int hour;
    private int minute;
    private int second;

    public void setTime(int h, int m, int s) {
        hour = h;
        minute = m;
        second = s;
    }

    public int secondsSinceMidnight() {
        return  hour * 60 * 60 + minute * 60 + second;
    }
}
```

The setTime method uses assignment statements to copy its parameters' values into the member variables; secondsSinceMidnight reads values from those same member variables. Thus, the values used by secondsSinceMidnight will often have been stored by setTime. Such cooperative use of member variables between an object's methods is common. However, this cooperation requires that methods be

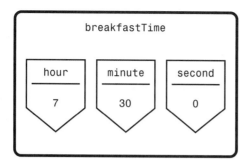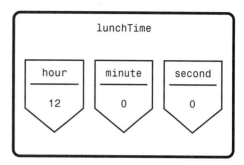

FIGURE 2.10 Two Time objects with different values in their member variables.

able to use member variables without interference from outside the object, so nothing other than an object's own methods should ever try to access its member variables. This is why we declared the member variables in the Time example private. As a general rule, member variables should be private unless there is a specific reason why they must be accessed by clients.

Just as was the case with messages and methods, subclasses inherit their superclass's member variables. Also as with messages and methods, you can define additional member variables for a subclass as part of its definition.

Objects can encapsulate data in member variables and encapsulate algorithms that operate on that data in methods. Such combinations are particularly powerful abstractions. They represent things that internally may use very complicated representations of information, possibly with subtle algorithms, but that clients can nonetheless work with as if they were simple, even primitive, data types. This happens because clients see the data simply as objects, not as their internal representations, and the operations on that data as messages, not as complex algorithms.

Exercises

2.25. Define a class that represents dates. Use member variables to represent the day, month, and year parts of a date. Provide methods to handle the following messages:

1. set(d, m, y), a side-effect-producing message that makes a date represent day d of month m of year y. Preconditions are that m is between 1 and 12, d is between 1 and the number of days in month m, and y is greater than or equal to 2000.

2. day, month, and year, value-producing messages that return the day, month, and year parts of a date respectively.

3. julianForm,[5] a value-producing message that returns the number of days between a date and January 1, 2000. For example, if d is a date object that represents January 2, 2000, then d.julianForm() should return 1. The precondition is that the date object represents a day on or after January 1, 2000.

4. precedes(d), a value-producing message that returns a Boolean value. d is a second "date" object, and precedes should return true if its recipient represents a date before d, and should return false otherwise.

5. getLaterDate(n), a value-producing message that returns a new "date" object that represents the date n days after the date represented by the message's recipient. For example, if d represents January 1, 2000, then d.getLaterDate(3) would return a "date" object that represents January 4, 2000.

2.26. Devise another solution to Exercise 2.25 in which the "date" class does not explicitly store the day, month, and year, but instead uses an integer member variable to record the number of days between the date being represented and January 1, 2000. The message interface to this version of the date class should be exactly as defined in Exercise 2.25, despite the different internal representation of dates.

2.27. Add a "tick" message to the text's Time class. This message increments a time by 1 second, "carrying" if necessary into the minute or hour member variables in order to keep second and minute between 0 and 59 and hour between 0 and 23. (For example, time 23:59:59 would increment to 0:0:0.)

2.28. Design classes that represent each of the following. For each, decide what member variables will represent an object's value, and design methods for a few typical operations.

1. Fractions.
2. Complex numbers.
3. Circles.
4. Playing cards.
5. Vectors in 3-dimensional space.
6. Polynomials.
7. Entries in a dictionary.

---

[5] The "Julian" representation of a date gives that date as a number of days since some agreed-upon starting date.

2.6 CONCLUDING REMARKS

Abstraction, selectively concentrating on some aspects of a thing while ignoring others, is a powerful theme throughout computer science. This chapter introduced you to abstraction in algorithm design, in particular, to the way in which designers focus on different aspects of a problem or solution at different times. Object-oriented design helps designers do this by letting them think of the overall solution to a problem in terms of the actions of one or more objects that each solve a subproblem. The details of how each object solves its subproblem can be dealt with at a different time or even by a different person. Preconditions and postconditions, both those of the overall problem and those of the various subproblems, connect the different pieces of the large design: they provide a "contract" through which implementors and clients agree on exactly what the interface to an algorithm should be, without concern for how that algorithm will be implemented or used.

Algorithms can be divided into two groups: those that produce results in the form of side effects and those that produce results in the form of values. Both kinds of algorithm, however, rely on the same abstraction mechanisms: preconditions and postconditions, objects and messages, etc.

After you design an algorithm, the same abstractions that helped you design it help you reason about it. For example, preconditions and postconditions are the keys to determining whether the algorithm is correct—it is correct if and only if it produces the specified postconditions every time it is run with the specified preconditions. Similarly, encapsulating an algorithm in a method also encapsulates knowledge of its correctness—to know that a use of the algorithm is correct you only need to show that the algorithm's postconditions are what its client wants and that the client establishes the algorithm's preconditions. You do not need to repeatedly show that the algorithm's internals are correct every time it is used. The next chapter explores these issues in more detail.

2.7 FURTHER READING

Object-oriented programming is a long-standing interest among computer scientists. The idea was first implemented in the late 1960s in a programming language named Simula, which inspired the development of SmallTalk in the 1970s. For more information on these languages, see:

Graham Birtwistle et al., *Simula Begin*, Auerbach, 1973.

Adele Goldberg and David Robson, *SmallTalk-80: The Language*, Addison-Wesley, 1989.

Currently popular object-oriented languages include C++, and of course, Java. The primary references for these languages are:

Bjarne Stroustrup, *The C++ Programming Language: Special Edition*, Addison-Wesley, 2000.

Ken Arnold, James Gosling, and David Holmes, *The Java Programming Language* (3rd ed.), Addison-Wesley Longman, 2000.

Research on the theory and practice of object-oriented design and programming is a lively and growing area of computer science supported by a number of conferences and journals (for example, the annual ACM OOPSLA—"Object-Oriented Systems, Languages, and Applications"—conference). Innumerable textbooks provide introductions to the area for students, for example:

Angela Shiflet, *Problem Solving in C++*, PWS Publishing Co, 1998.

Paul Tymann and G. Michael Schneider, *Modern Software Development Using Java*, Thomson/Brooks-Cole, 2004.

The idea of treating preconditions and postconditions as contracts has been widely promoted by Bertrand Meyer. It is well-supported by his Eiffel programming language, and is a central element of his approach to object-oriented design, as described in:

Bertrand Meyer, *Object-oriented Software Construction* (2nd edition), Prentice-Hall, 1997.

3 Proof: An Introduction to Theory

This chapter introduces theoretical techniques for reasoning about correctness and other aspects of algorithm behavior. You have surely written at least one program that looked right but didn't deliver correct results, so you realize that an algorithm may seem correct without actually being so. In fact, the correctness of any algorithm should be suspect until proven.

For example, consider the following algorithm for making any amount of change between 1 and 99 cents in U.S. currency, using as few coins as possible:

Algorithm MakeChange
    *Give as many quarters as you can without exceeding
       the amount owed.*
    *Give as many dimes as you can without exceeding the
       amount still owed after the quarters.*
    *Give as many nickels as you can without exceeding
       the amount still owed after the dimes.*
    Give whatever is left in pennies.

Most people accept that this algorithm uses as few coins as possible. But suppose the currency were slightly different—suppose there were no nickels. Then a similar algorithm would not always use the fewest coins! For example, the similar algorithm would make 30 cents change as 1 quarter and 5 pennies, a total of 6 coins, but doing it with 3 dimes would use only 3 coins. With this example in mind, how can you be sure there isn't some obscure case in which the original algorithm fails too? (We'll show you the answer later, but in the meantime, see if you can work it out for yourself.)

3.1 BASIC IDEAS

We begin with correctness. Chapter 2 developed a number of algorithms, but used only careful design and intuition to convince you that they worked correctly. Now we will look at how you can determine more rigorously whether an algorithm works.

3.1.1 Correctness

Computer science uses a specific definition of what it means for an algorithm to "work." An algorithm for solving some problem works, or is correct, if and only if the algorithm ends with all of the problem's postconditions true whenever it is started with all of the problem's preconditions true. Note that an algorithm is not correct if it only produces the right postconditions most of the time—it must do so every time the preconditions hold. On the other hand, if any of the preconditions don't hold, then all bets are off. If started with even one precondition false, an algorithm can do anything, however inappropriate to the problem, and still be considered correct.

When deciding whether an algorithm is correct, most people's first thought is to execute the algorithm and see what happens. This is called *testing*, and is an empirical analysis of correctness. Unfortunately, testing cannot completely prove correctness. When you test an algorithm, you pick certain input values to test it on, but you cannot test it on all values. This means that, at best, testing only shows that the algorithm produces correct results some of the time, not that it always does so. Furthermore, an algorithm is an abstract idea about how to solve a problem, but testing necessarily tests a concrete implementation of that idea. This means that testing can confuse flaws in the implementation with flaws in the idea. For example, a programmer might use a programming language incorrectly in implementing an algorithm, causing the program to produce incorrect results even though the underlying algorithm was correct.

The alternative to testing is to prove, using logic, that an algorithm is correct. These proofs have strengths and weaknesses complementary to those of testing. Proofs can show that an algorithm works correctly for all possible inputs, and do deal directly with the abstract algorithm. But because they treat the algorithm as an abstraction, proofs cannot tell you whether any specific implementation is correct.[1]

We will present many proofs in this book about algorithms written in Java, but remember that our theoretical reasoning is always about the abstract algorithm, not about the details of Java. We use Java as a convenient way to describe a sequence of

---

[1] It is, in principle, possible to prove concrete implementations correct, but such proofs are hard to create in practice.

operations, and we prove that performing that sequence of operations has certain consequences. However, we rely on your and our shared, informal understanding of what the Java operations mean, and do not claim to "prove" those meanings, to prove things about the limitations or lack thereof of individual machines that execute Java, etc.

3.1.2 Proof

Proof simply means an argument that convinces its audience, beyond any possible doubt, that some claim, or *theorem*, is true. This is not to say that proofs needn't be rigorous and logical—quite the contrary, in fact, because rigorously identifying all of the possibilities that have to be discussed, and then being sure to discuss them all, is essential to a convincing argument. Logic is one of the best tools for achieving this rigor. But the first task in any proof is to decide informally whether you believe the theorem, and why. Then rigor and logic can make your intuition precise and convincing.

A Theorem

Let's look at a simple example from mathematics. Suppose you wanted to convince someone that the sum of two odd numbers is always even. This statement, "The sum of two odd numbers is always even," is your theorem.

Testing the Theorem

The first thing you might do is try a couple of examples: $3+5=8$, $7+7=14$, $1+9=10$, etc. These examples are the mathematical equivalent of testing an algorithm. They show that the idea is right in a number of cases, but they can't rule out the possibility that there might somewhere be a case in which it is not. (For instance, what if the two numbers differ greatly in size? Could it matter whether one of them is a multiple—or some other function—of the other? What about cases where one or both numbers are negative?) Thus, the examples help the theorem seem believable, but they aren't completely convincing. Something stronger is called for.

Intuition

You can start making a stronger argument by thinking about why you intuitively believe the claim. One intuition is that every odd number is one greater than some even number, so adding two odd numbers is like adding two even numbers plus two "extra" 1's, which should all add up to something even. For example, $3+5$ can be rephrased as $(2+1)+(4+1)$, which is the same as $2+4+(1+1)$, which in turn is the same as $2+4+2$. This intuition sounds good, but it is not very rigorous—it assumes that adding even numbers produces an even sum, and it is based on addition of odd numbers being "like" something else, reasoning that may overlook subtle differences.

Rigorous Argument

To dispel the above worries, examine the intuition carefully. To do this, consider exactly what it means to say that every odd number is one greater than some even number. An even number is one that is an exact multiple of 2, in other words, a number of the form $2i$ where i is some integer. So an odd number, being greater by one than an even number, must be of the form $2i+1$, for some integer i. If you have two odd numbers, you can think of one as $2i+1$, and the other as $2j+1$ (i and j are still integers). The sum of these odd numbers is $2i+1+2j+1$. This sum can be re-written as $2i+2j+2$, which can in turn be written as $2(i+j+1)$. Anything that is twice an integer is even, and since i and j are integers, so is $i+j+1$. Therefore, $2(i+j+1)$ is an even number! This shows that any sum of two odd numbers is necessarily even, and so the argument is finished. The original intuition was indeed sound, but you had to go through it carefully to make certain.

3.1.3 Proving an Algorithm Correct

An algorithm is correct if it establishes its problem's postconditions whenever it starts with its problem's preconditions established. Proving an algorithm correct therefore amounts to showing rigorously that the problem's postconditions follow from its preconditions and the actions that the algorithm takes. Such proofs are often just a series of deductions, corresponding one-for-one to steps in the algorithm. Each deduction convincingly demonstrates that the corresponding step in the algorithm transforms the conditions holding before that step into others that hold after it (and so before the next step). The algorithm is proven correct if this process ends by showing that all of the problem's postconditions hold after the last step. This is the same proof structure—a series of deductions, each building on the previous ones—as in the mathematical proof above.

As a simple example, consider an algorithm that makes a robot named Robbie draw a two-tile-long blue line. To say precisely what Robbie has to do, let the preconditions and the postconditions for the problem be as follows:

Preconditions:

1.   There are no obstacles within two tiles in front of Robbie.

Postconditions:

1. Robbie is two tiles (in the direction it was originally facing) from the place where it started.
2. There is a two-tile blue line behind Robbie.

The following algorithm should solve this problem:

```
robbie.paint(java.awt.Color.blue);
robbie.move();
robbie.paint(java.awt.Color.blue);
robbie.move();
```

We can prove that this algorithm is indeed correct:

PRECONDITION: There are no obstructions within two tiles in front of Robbie.

THEOREM: After the above algorithm finishes, Robbie is two tiles from the place where it started (in the direction it was originally facing) and there is a two-tile blue line behind Robbie. □

PROOF: The algorithm's first step is a paint(java.awt.Color.blue) message to Robbie. Robbie responds to this message by painting the tile beneath itself blue (thereby making a one-tile-long blue line). The algorithm's second step is a move message to Robbie. Since there are no obstructions, Robbie moves one tile (in the direction it was originally facing, since it hasn't turned) from its original position. The one-tile blue line is now behind Robbie. The third step is another paint(java.awt.Color.blue) message, which causes Robbie to paint the tile now beneath it blue. This tile just touches the previous one, so there is now a two-tile blue line starting one tile behind Robbie and extending under it. The last message, another move, moves Robbie one more tile forward—since Robbie is still facing in its original direction, this leaves Robbie two tiles in its original direction from its original position. The blue line is now behind Robbie. The algorithm ends here, and both parts of the postcondition have been shown to hold. ■

Notice the format of this proof. It is one that all proofs in this book will follow—even though the theorems will be less obvious, and the proofs will become more complex. First, there is a statement of assumptions, or preconditions, that will be used in the proof. In this case (and most other correctness proofs for algorithms), the assumptions are just the problem's preconditions. Second, there is a statement of the theorem that is to be proven. For correctness proofs, this is just a statement that the problem's postconditions hold at the end of the algorithm. Finally, there is the proof proper, in other words the argument for why the theorem is true, given the assumptions.

3.1.4 Proof Methods

The above proofs, although simple, demonstrate several features common to all proofs. In particular, they demonstrate one of the most common forms of logic in proofs and illustrate a clear and logically sound way of presenting proofs.

Modus Ponens

Both of the proofs in this section used the same strategy, or *proof technique*, for proving their claims: start with the known facts or preconditions and make a series of deductions until you obtain the desired goal. Each deduction involved reasoning of the form:

> "I know that...
> *P* is true, and
> *P* implies *Q*
>
> So, therefore, *Q* must be true."

For example:

> "I know that...
> Robbie receives a move message and is unobstructed, and
> Robbie receiving a move message when unobstructed implies that Robbie moves
> one tile forward
>
> So, therefore, Robbie must move one tile forward."

Despite its simplicity, this form of deduction is so useful that logicians have a name for it: *modus ponens*.

Equation 3.1 summarizes modus ponens symbolically:

$$P \Rightarrow Q$$

$$\frac{P}{Q} \tag{3.1}$$

Read this equation as saying that whenever you know all the things above the line (in other words, that *P* implies *Q*, and that *P* is true), you can conclude the things below the line (in this case, that Q is true). This notation is a common way to describe rules of logical deduction.

Statements of the form "P implies Q", or, equivalently, "if P then Q" are themselves very common, and are called *implications*. The "if" part of an implication (P) is called its *antecedent*; the "then" part (Q) is its *consequent*.

Implications and modus ponens are simple, but they are easily distorted into invalid forms. For example, consider the following: "If something is an alligator, then it eats meat. My dog eats meat. Therefore, my dog is an alligator." This argument's conclusion is clearly false, and the problem is that the argument's "logic" is "modus ponens backwards"—deducing an implication's antecedent (that something is an alligator) from its consequent (that the "something" eats meat). The problem is clear if you try to plug the pieces of the claim into Equation 3.1:

$$\frac{\text{Something is an alligator} \Rightarrow \text{Something eats meat} \qquad \text{My dog eats meat}}{\text{My dog is an alligator}} \qquad (3.2)$$

Equation 3.1 says that when you know an implication and the statement on its *left* (P), you can conclude the statement on its right (Q). But in Equation 3.2 you know an implication and the statement on its *right*—a mismatch to the rule of modus ponens. Modus ponens only allows you to deduce the consequent from the antecedent; it never permits you to go the other way around.

Rigor and Formality

Rigor and *formality* are two important properties of any proof. Rigor means that the proof is logically sound and that there are no oversights or loopholes in it. Formality refers to the extent to which the proof uses accepted logical forms and techniques. Mathematicians and computer scientists have a small set of well-accepted proof techniques that they use over and over again, each of which is usually clearest when presented in one of a few standard forms. Rigor and formality go hand in hand, since formal proof techniques are well-accepted precisely because they embody rigorous logic and help people use it. But the two are not completely inseparable. Logic can be rigorous even if it isn't presented formally, and there are mathematical pranks that use subtly flawed logic in a formal manner to "prove" obvious falsehoods (for instance, that 0 equals 1).

Both proofs in this section are rigorous and moderately formal. Formally, using a series of deductions to prove desired conclusions from initial assumptions is a well-accepted proof technique. Each proof's rigor depends on each deduction being justified by the previous ones and standard definitions (for example, definitions of "even number", of the move message, etc.) Both proofs could be written more formally as lists of steps, with each step consisting of exactly one deduction and all of the things that justify it. We chose a less formal but more readable presentation, however, using English prose rather than lists of steps and spelling out the most important or least obvious justifications but leaving others implicit. For example, in proving that the sum of two odd numbers is even, we explained carefully why every odd number is of the form $2i+1$, but assumed you would recognize by yourself why such steps as rewriting $2i+1+2j+1$ as $2i+2j+2$ are justified. This practice of leaving the reader to fill in "obvious" justifications is common in proofs. By not belaboring the obvious, it makes a proof shorter and easier to follow. However, it also involves an important risk: what is superficially "obvious" may turn out not to be true at all in some situations, and by not carefully listing and checking each justification, one risks overlooking those situations. In short, one jeopardizes the proof's rigor. So always think through the justifications for every deduction in a proof, even if you then choose not to write them all down.

Exercises

3.1. Prove that the sum of two even numbers is always even. Prove that the sum of an even number and an odd number is always odd.

3.2. Prove that the sum of any number of even numbers is even. Is it also true that the sum of any number of odd numbers is even?

3.3. Prove that the product of two even numbers is even. Prove that the product of two odd numbers is odd.

3.4. Consider the problem of making Robin the robot back up one tile. The precise preconditions and postconditions for this problem are as follows:

Preconditions:

■ There are no obstructions within two tiles of Robin, in any direction.

Postconditions:

■ Robin is one tile behind (relative to its original direction) its original position.
■ Robin is facing in its original direction.

Prove that each of the following algorithms correctly solves this problem:

```
Algorithm 1
    robin.turnLeft();
    robin.turnLeft();
    robin.move();
    robin.turnLeft();
    robin.turnLeft();
```

```
Algorithm 2
    robin.turnLeft();
    robin.move();
    robin.turnLeft();
    robin.move();
    robin.turnLeft();
    robin.move();
    robin.turnLeft();

Algorithm 3
    robin.turnRight();
    robin.turnRight();
    robin.move();
    robin.turnLeft();
    robin.turnLeft();
```

3.5. Explain why each of the following is or is not a valid use of modus ponens:

1. Birds have wings. Having wings implies being able to fly. Therefore, birds are able to fly.
2. Sue always wears sunglasses when driving. Sue is driving now. Therefore, Sue is wearing sunglasses now.
3. Dogs do not have wings. Having wings implies being able to fly. Therefore, dogs can't fly.
4. Birds fly. Having wings implies being able to fly. Therefore, birds have wings.
5. If A and B are both positive, and $A < B$, then $1/A > 1/B$. $2 < 2.5$, and $2.5 < 3$. Therefore, $1/2.5$ lies between $1/2$ and $1/3$.
6. Any composite number is the product of two or more prime numbers. 18 is composite. Therefore, 18 is the product of two or more prime numbers.
7. Any composite number is the product of two or more prime numbers. 18 is composite. Therefore, $18 = 3 \times 3 \times 2$.
8. If a baseball player drops the ball, then he or she is a bad baseball player. I once saw a college baseball player drop the ball. Therefore, all college baseball players are bad baseball players.
9. Any person who hand-feeds piranhas is crazy. Therefore, this book's first author is crazy.

3.2 CORRECTNESS OF METHODS

Most algorithms are more complicated than the two-tile blue line algorithm. As you saw in Chapter 2, designers use abstraction to cope with that complexity. In object-oriented design, one of the important forms of abstraction is encapsulating algorithms inside methods. These methods and their underlying algorithms can be proven correct by building on the basic proof techniques just introduced.

3.2.1 An Example

Recall the Time class from Section 2.5, whose instances represent times of day. Instances of this class handle a secondsSinceMidnight message by returning the number of seconds from midnight until the time they represent. Section 2.5 presented one method for this message; another one appears here. When reading this method, remember that hour, minute, and second are member variables of Time objects. hour contains the number of whole hours from midnight until the time in question, minute the number of whole minutes since the start of the hour, and second the number of whole seconds since the start of the minute.

```
// In class Time...
public int secondsSinceMidnight() {
    return (hour * 60 + minute) * 60 + second;
}
```

Here is a proof that this secondsSinceMidnight algorithm is correct. It is convenient in this proof to write times using the standard "H:M:S" notation, where H is an hour, M a minute, and S a second; this notation assumes a 24-hour format for H. For example, one-thirty a.m. would be written 1:30:0, while twelve-thirty a.m. would be 0:30:0, and one-thirty p.m. would be 13:30:0.

To begin proving that secondsSinceMidnight is correct, we need to know its intended postcondition: its return value should be the number of seconds from midnight until time hour:minute:second. Knowing this postcondition, we can then turn to the proof.

> **PRECONDITION:** hour, minute, and second are integers; $0 \le \text{hour} \le 23$; $0 \le \text{minute} \le 59$; $0 \le \text{second} \le 59$.

> **THEOREM:** The above secondsSinceMidnight algorithm returns the number of seconds from midnight until time hour:minute:second. □

These statements tell us exactly what our goal is (the "Theorem"), and what we can assume in getting to it (the "Precondition"). The proof proper is now a step-by-step analysis of `secondsSinceMidnight` to see why (and if) it establishes the goal:

> **PROOF:** Since $0 \leq$ hour ≤ 23, and hour contains no fractional part, the expression hour * 60 computes the number of minutes between midnight and time hour:0:0. Since minute also contains no fractional part and $0 \leq$ minute ≤ 59, hour * 60 + minute is then the number of minutes between midnight and time hour:minute:0. Since there are 60 seconds in a minute, multiplying that number by 60 yields the number of seconds between midnight and time hour:minute:0. Finally, since $0 \leq$ second ≤ 59, adding second gives the number of seconds between midnight and time hour:minute:second. The algorithm returns this final value. ∎

3.2.2 Proof Structure

Like the proof for the two-tile blue line algorithm, the proof about `secondsSinceMidnight` is a series of deductions, each showing why some step in the algorithm produces a certain result. The steps in this algorithm are arithmetic operations, not messages to a robot, but both algorithms are nonetheless sequences of steps, and all proofs about sequences of steps have the same structure. For instance, the algorithm's first step is to multiply hour by 60, and the proof's first sentence explains why doing that computes the number of minutes between midnight and time hour:0:0. The proof continues, one sentence for each step in the algorithm, until the final sentence explains why the return in the algorithm returns the correct number. Also notice that `secondsSinceMidnight`'s postcondition is that the number the algorithm returns has a certain property (namely, being equal to the number of seconds between midnight and time hour:minute:second), rather than visible effects on the world around a robot, but this difference does not change the basic nature of the proof either.

Although the proof doesn't say so explicitly, each of its steps uses modus ponens. The implications are items of common knowledge, which is why we didn't state them explicitly. For example, we don't need to tell you that if h is a number of hours, then $h \times 60$ is the corresponding number of minutes. But it is that implication, and the fact that hour is a number of hours, that formally allows us to conclude by modus ponens that hour * 60 is the number of minutes between midnight and hour:0:0.[2] Many proofs use modus ponens in this implicit way, so you will use the technique frequently even if you don't see the phrase very often.

---

[2] In fact, this conclusion relies on another use of modus ponens, too. The second implication is that if h is an integer between 0 and 23, then h:0:0 is a valid time of day.

Exercises

3.6. Which steps in the correctness proof for the secondsSinceMidnight method would be invalid if hour or minute included a fractional part? What if hour were greater than 23, or minute or second greater than 59?

3.7. Identify some uses of modus ponens in the correctness proof for secondsSinceMidnight other than the ones mentioned in the main text.

3.8. Consider a class that represents cubic polynomials, in other words, polynomials of the form:

$$ax^3 + bx^2 + cx + d \qquad (3.3)$$

Suppose this class represents polynomials by storing their coefficients (a, b, c, and d) in member variables, and that it handles a value message by evaluating the polynomial at x, where x is a parameter to the message. The relevant parts of the class definition might look like this:

```
class CubicPolynomial {
    private double a, b, c, d;
    public double value(double x) {
        return ((a*x + b) * x) + c) * x + d;
    }
}
```

Prove that this value method really does evaluate Equation 3.3 at x, given the preconditions that a, b, c, d, and x are real numbers.

3.9. The Kingdom of Dystopia computes every citizen's income tax as 10% of their wages plus 90% of their other income. Dystopians can take a deduction from their income prior to computing the percentages, but the deduction must be divided between wage and other income proportionally to the amounts of those incomes. For example, if two-thirds of a Dystopian's income is from wages, and one-third is from other sources, then two-thirds of that person's deductions must be used to reduce their wage income, and one-third to reduce other income.

Prove that the following method computes the correct tax for a Dystopian, given that wages is the Dystopian's wage income, misc his income from other sources, and ded his deduction:

```
// In class DystopianCitizen...
public double tax(double wages, double misc, double ded) {
    double wageFraction = wages / (wages + misc);
    double miscFraction = misc / (wages + misc);
    double adjustedWages = wages - deduction * wageFraction;
    double adjustedMisc = misc - deduction * miscFraction;
    return adjustedWages * 0.1 + adjustedMisc * 0.9;
}
```

3.10. Prove that the following algorithm computes the number that is halfway between real numbers a and b:

```
public static double halfWay(double a, double b) {
    return (a + b) / 2.0;
}
```

3.3 CORRECTNESS OF SIDE EFFECTS

Correctness proofs for side-effect-producing algorithms are almost exactly like proofs for value-producing algorithms. The only difference is that the postconditions to prove for a side-effect-producing algorithm describe the changes the algorithm makes to its environment rather than the value it returns.

3.3.1 The Square-drawing Problem Revisited

Recall Chapter 2's square-drawing problem. It requires a robot to draw a red square of a client-specified size. The heart of the solution is a drawSquare method, which receives the size of the square as a parameter. This method coordinates the overall drawing of squares but uses a secondary algorithm, drawLine, to draw the individual sides of the square. The preconditions and postconditions for drawing a square are as follows:

Preconditions:

1. The requested length of each side of the square is an integer number of tiles, and is at least one tile.
2. The future square is to the right and forward of the robot.
3. There are no obstacles in the area that will be the border of the square.

Postcondition:

1. There is a red square outline on the floor, whose outer edges are of the length requested by the user. The square is to the right and forward of the robot's original position.

Let's try to prove that Chapter 2's solution to this problem is correct.

3.3.2 drawLine

Since drawSquare uses drawLine, we will begin by proving that drawLine is correct. Here is the drawLine method:

```
// In class DrawingRobot...
private void drawLine(int size) {
    this.paint(java.awt.Color.red);
    for (int i = 1; i <= size-1; i++) {
        this.move();
        this.paint(java.awt.Color.red);
    }
}
```

Chapter 2 developed the preconditions and postconditions for drawing a line. Those preconditions and postconditions were spread over a page and a half, and some of them were rather vague (for example, part of the postcondition was simply that the line is "in the position specified by the preconditions"). Furthermore, two preconditions for drawSquare, that the requested size is an integer greater than or equal to one, and that there are no obstructions along the sides of the square, are implicitly preconditions for drawLine. While it wasn't important to state these as explicit preconditions of drawLine when designing it, it is helpful to acknowledge all preconditions explicitly for a proof. A simple but important beginning for the correctness proof is thus to collect all preconditions and postconditions relating to drawLine into "Precondition" and "Theorem" statements, making the vague parts more precise as we do so.

PRECONDITION: A drawing robot is standing where some t-tile-long line should begin, and facing along that line. t is an integer greater than or equal to one. There are no obstructions on the $t-1$ tiles in front of the robot.

THEOREM: After the robot handles a drawLine message with parameter t, there is a t-tile-long red line on the floor, starting at the robot's original position and running in the direction the robot was originally facing; the robot is standing over the end of that line; the robot is facing in its original direction. □

PROOF: In the first step of drawLine, the robot sends itself a paint(java.awt.Color.red) message. Since the robot is standing over the beginning of the line, and the line will be at least one tile long, this paints the first tile of the line red.

The remainder of drawLine is a loop, and reasoning rigorously about the correctness of loops requires proof techniques that you won't encounter until Chapter 8. However, we can describe the general ideas now. On each iteration, the robot sends itself a move message followed by a paint(java.awt.Color.red) message. Since there are no obstacles, the move makes the robot move one tile. The paint message then makes the robot paint that new tile red. The loop repeats size-1 times. In this invocation of drawLine, parameter size stands for the number t, so the loop repeats $t-1$ times. Thus, the robot moves a total of $t-1$ tiles, painting a $(t-1)$-tile red line that starts one tile after the robot's initial position and that ends at its final position. Note that the robot remains facing in its original direction throughout the loop, meaning that the line runs in the direction the robot was originally facing.

When the loop starts, the robot is standing over the one-tile red spot it painted in the first step; the $(t-1)$-tile line drawn during the loop therefore starts just after this tile, to make a total line of t tiles, starting at the robot's original position. As noted above, the line runs in the direction the robot was originally facing. Since the loop is the last thing drawLine does, drawLine ends with this t-tile red line on the floor, the robot standing over the end of that line, and the robot facing in its original direction. ■

Structure and Complications

drawLine contains several complicating features not present in the two-tile blue line algorithm. For one, the two-tile blue line algorithm is a single sequence of messages, and its proof is, correspondingly, a single sequence of deductions. drawLine, on the other hand, contains a loop, and its proof contains a paragraph that deals with the effects of that loop, surrounded by additional arguments to show how the loop and the first paint message act together to produce the whole line. Both proofs' structures reflect the control structures in their algorithms. This is typical of proofs about algorithms and can often help you plan such proofs.

Furthermore, the two-tile blue line algorithm draws a line of a specific length (two tiles), whereas drawLine draws a line of any length, depending on the value of its parameter. The proof for drawLine must therefore deal with the line's length in general terms, without knowing exactly what that length is. It therefore uses a generic value, *t*, in place of a specific numeric length, and makes no assumptions about *t* other than those given as preconditions.

3.3.3 drawSquare

Now we can turn to drawSquare, whose method is as follows:

```
// In class DrawingRobot...
public void drawSquare(int size) {
    this.drawLine(size);
    this.turnRight();
    this.drawLine(size);
    this.turnRight();
    this.drawLine(size);
    this.turnRight();
    this.drawLine(size);
}
```

The idea behind this algorithm is, roughly, to make the robot draw lines between the corners of the desired square. drawSquare's correctness proof will be easier to read and write if we have short, standard ways to refer to those corners. Call the corner in which the robot starts corner 1, the next corner 2, then 3, and finally 4, as shown in Figure 3.1.

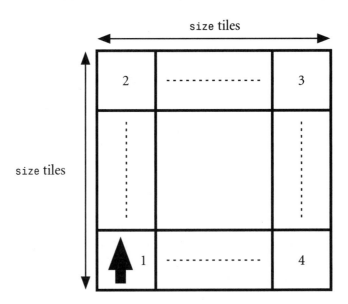

FIGURE 3.1 Labels for the corners of the square.

With these labels for corners, the proof can talk concretely about how drawSquare makes a robot draw lines from corner to corner. Begin by rephrasing the square-drawing problem's preconditions and postconditions in terms of the labels. Also, replace the awkward phrase "the requested length of the square's sides" with a generic value.

PRECONDITION: A drawing robot is standing at corner 1 and facing corner 2 of a future t-tile square. t is an integer greater than or equal to one. There are no obstacles in the area that will be the border of the square.

THEOREM: After the robot handles a drawSquare message with parameter t, there is a red square outline on the floor whose outer edges are t tiles long. The square's sides meet at corners 1, 2, 3, and 4, as shown in Figure 3.1. □

PROOF: The algorithm starts by sending the robot a drawLine message with parameter size. In this invocation of drawSquare, size $= t$. Furthermore, t is an integer greater than or equal to one, and there are no obstacles anywhere in the border area, and thus particularly none between corners 1 and 2. Therefore, the preconditions hold for drawLine to draw a t-tile red line from corner 1 to corner 2. After the robot handles the drawLine message, such a line exists and the robot is in corner 2 facing in its original direction. This position and orientation mean that corner 3 is to the robot's right. Thus, the next step, sending the robot a turnRight message, makes the robot face corner 3, while still standing at corner 2. The third step, another drawLine message with parameter size, draws a red line from corner 2 to corner 3, and leaves the robot in corner 3, facing in the corner-2-to-corner-3 direction, and so with corner 4 to its right. The fourth step, a turnRight message, makes the robot face corner 4; then a drawLine message moves it to that corner, drawing a red line as it does so. The algorithm's sixth step turns the robot to face corner 1, and the last step draws a red line from corner 4 to corner 1. At the end of the algorithm, there are thus red lines from corner 1 to corner 2, corner 2 to corner 3, corner 3 to corner 4, and corner 4 to corner 1, in other words, a red square outline whose sides are t tiles long, and meet at corners 1, 2, 3, and 4. ∎

Abstraction in Proofs

Notice that the correctness proof for drawSquare doesn't repeat the proof for drawLine every time drawSquare sends a drawLine message. Instead, all that the proof for drawSquare has to do is show that the preconditions for drawLine hold right before each drawLine message; if they do, then the postconditions for drawLine will necessarily hold afterwards. The original correctness proof for drawLine essentially proved the implication, "If drawLine is given its preconditions, then it will produce its postconditions." With this implication, any time you know that the preconditions hold before a drawLine message, you can use modus ponens to conclude that the postconditions hold after it. This one implication summarizes all the relevant behavior of a drawLine message. Since the reasons why the preconditions hold are straightforward, we explained them carefully only for the first drawLine. You should, however, convince yourself that they really do hold prior to every drawLine in the algorithm. This treatment of drawLine demonstrates a new benefit of method abstraction: prove a method correct *once*, and you know that *all* invocations of it that start with its preconditions will establish its postconditions. Method abstraction encapsulates an algorithm's correctness, just as it encapsulates the algorithm's design.

Not having to repeat the correctness proof for drawLine in the correctness proof for drawSquare made the latter easier to write and read than it otherwise would have been. Simplifying one proof by relying on a previous one is very common, and not just in proofs about algorithms. In fact, people will sometimes deliberately break a large proof into separate proofs of smaller "subtheorems," in order to reduce the large proof to a few sentences that cite the subtheorems and provide some logic to connect their results (very much analogous to breaking a large program into subprograms). The technical term for such a "subtheorem" is *lemma*. For example, we could say that the correctness of drawLine was a lemma for the correctness proof for drawSquare.

Exercises

3.11. Figure 3.1 seems to imply that robots start drawing a square in the square's lower left corner. In fact, no matter where the robot starts, there is a way of labeling the corners of the square 1, 2, 3, and 4 that is consistent with the text's definition of the labels and the problem's preconditions. Show that this claim is true.

3.12. A "corner" is a figure that robots can draw, defined by the following preconditions and postconditions and Figure 3.2 (the figure defines labels for key tiles relative to which the robot moves and paints).

Preconditions:

■ The robot is standing over tile 1.
■ The robot is facing tile 2.
■ There are no obstructions on tiles 1, 2, 3, or 4.

Postconditions:

■ The robot is standing over tile 4.

- The robot is facing away from tile 3.
- Tiles 1, 2, and 3 are green.

Prove that the following algorithm correctly draws a corner:

```
// In class DrawingRobot...
public void corner() {
    this.paint(java.awt.Color.green);
    this.move();
    this.paint(java.awt.Color.green);
    this.turnRight();
    this.move();
    this.paint(java.awt.Color.green);
    this.move();
}
```

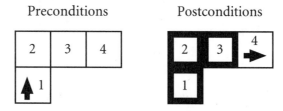

FIGURE 3.2 Preconditions and postconditions for drawing a corner.

3.13. Design an algorithm for drawing corners (see Exercise 3.12) that is different from the algorithm shown in Exercise 3.12. Prove your algorithm correct.

3.14. A "table" is a figure that robots can draw, defined by the following preconditions and postconditions and Figure 3.3 (the figure defines labels for key tiles relative to which the robot moves and paints):

Preconditions:

- The robot is standing over tile 1.
- The robot is facing tile 2.
- There are no obstructions on tiles 1, 2, 3, 4, 5, 6, or 7.

Postconditions:

- The robot is standing over tile 7.
- The robot is facing away from tile 6.

■ Tiles 1, 2, 3, 4, 5, and 6 are green.

The following algorithm draws a table, using the `corner` message introduced in Exercise 3.12. Prove that this algorithm is correct. You may assume that `corner` works correctly.

```
// In class DrawingRobot...
public void table() {
    this.corner();
    this.corner();
}
```

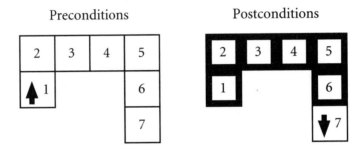

Preconditions   Postconditions

FIGURE 3.3 Preconditions and postconditions for drawing a table.

3.15. Here's a solution to the square-drawing problem that uses multiple robots instead of just one. Specifically, suppose four drawing robots are positioned as described by the following preconditions and Figure 3.4.

Preconditions:

■ Drawing robot `robbie` is at position 1a, facing towards position 1.
■ Drawing robot `robin` is at position 2a, facing towards position 2.
■ Drawing robot `roberta` is at position 3a, facing towards position 3.
■ Drawing robot `rob` is at position 4a, facing towards position 4.
■ There are no obstacles in the area that will be the border of the square, nor within one tile of the edges of that area.
■ It is t tiles from the bottom of position 1 to the top of position 2, from the left edge of position 2 to the right edge of position 3, from the top of position 3 to the bottom of position 4, and from the right edge of position 4 to the left edge of position 1.
■ t is an integer greater than or equal to one.

Prove that the following algorithm solves the square-drawing problem:

```
robbie.move();
robbie.drawLine(t);
robbie.move();
robin.move();
robin.drawLine(t);
robin.move();
roberta.move();
roberta.drawLine(t);
roberta.move();
rob.move();
rob.drawLine(t);
rob.move();
```

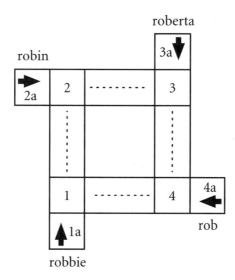

FIGURE 3.4 Preconditions for a multi-robot square drawing algorithm.

3.16. Consider the following "simpler" form of the four-robot square-drawing algorithm from Exercise 3.15. Start the robots on corners 1, 2, 3, and 4, rather than positions 1a, 2a, 3a, and 4a. Face the robots in the same initial directions as in Exercise 3.15, with the same definition of t. Then use the following algorithm to draw the square:

```
robbie.drawLine(t);
robin.drawLine(t);
roberta.drawLine(t);
rob.drawLine(t);
```

Why can this algorithm not be proven correct?

3.4 CORRECTNESS OF CLASSES

Imagine that you have defined a new class, and you want to show that it is correct. What does this entail? Partly, it requires proving that the individual methods within the class are correct. But correctness of a class requires more than just that the methods are correct in isolation. The methods must also interact with each other in the proper ways.

3.4.1 Class Invariants

Whether interactions between methods are "proper" is often determined by conditions called *class invariants*. Informally, a class invariant is a condition that is true whenever an object is "at rest," that is, not in the midst of executing a method. Formally, a class invariant is a postcondition of every method in a class, and a precondition of every method in the class except ones that initialize new objects. Because they are universal postconditions, and nearly universal preconditions, class invariants govern all of a class's behaviors, regardless of when those behaviors are invoked, how often, or in what relation to each other. This universal need to obey invariants constrains how the class's methods can interact with each other.

For example, imagine a credit card company keeping track of its cardholders' balances (the amount a cardholder owes the credit card company). Two things change credit card balances: making a purchase with a credit card increases the balance, and paying a credit card bill decreases the balance. You can therefore think of credit card accounts as objects, with three messages: purchase, pay, and getBalance. purchase records a purchase made with the card, pay records a payment to it, and getBalance returns the current balance. If you think about it, you can see that a balance is simply the difference between the total amount charged to a credit card, and the total payments made to the company. getBalance should therefore always return a value equal to the difference between the total purchases and the total payments. That defines a class invariant for credit card accounts—a getBalance message to an account will always return the sum of all purchases made on that account minus the sum of all payments made to it. Even though you don't know any details of the purchase, pay, and getBalance methods, this invariant tells you a lot about how they interact. In particular, it tells you that purchase and pay somehow communicate purchase and payment amounts to getBalance.

3.4.2 Object Initialization and Constructors

Class invariants impose special significance on methods that initialize new objects. No object can be assumed to respect its class invariant until it has been initialized. This is why initialization methods do not have the invariants as preconditions, and why they must initialize objects in ways that make the invariants hold. In Java (and many other object-oriented programming languages), an initialization method is executed automatically in the course of creating an object. Automatically executed initialization methods are called *constructors*. Because they execute automatically whenever an object is created, constructors eliminate any danger of using objects that violate their class invariants due to lack of initialization.

3.4.3 Proving Class Invariants

To illustrate how you can prove that something is a class invariant, consider the following implementation of credit card accounts:

```
class CreditCardAccount {

    private double balance;

    public CreditCardAccount() {
        balance = 0;
    }

    public void purchase(double amount) {
        balance = balance + amount;
    }

    public void pay(double amount) {
        balance = balance - amount;
    }

    public double getBalance() {
        return balance;
    }
}
```

Proving that the class invariant for credit card accounts holds in this implementation simply requires proving that the invariant is a postcondition of every method, including the constructor. Since by definition a class invariant is a precondition of every method except constructors, you can assume that the invariant holds before every method except the constructor.

PRECONDITION: Prior to sending any purchase, pay, or getBalance message to a CreditCardAccount object, a getBalance message to that object will return the sum of all purchases so far made on that account minus the sum of all payments so far made to it.

THEOREM: After a CreditCardAccount object executes its constructor, or purchase, pay, or getBalance methods, a getBalance message to that object will return the sum of all purchases so far made on that account minus the sum of all payments so far made to it. □

PROOF: getBalance simply returns member variable balance, so it suffices to prove that the claim "balance equals the sum of all purchases so far made on an account minus the sum of all payments so far made to it" is a class invariant. As a class invariant, you can use this statement about balance as a precondition for each method except the constructor during your proof.

The constructor executes only when a new credit card account is created. At that time, there have been no purchases on the account, and no payments to it, so the sum of all purchases minus the sum of all payments is 0. This is what the constructor initializes balance to.

Suppose that prior to receiving a purchase message, the sum of all purchases on a credit card is p and the sum of all payments is q. By assumption, balance is then equal to $p-q$. After the purchase message, the sum of all purchases has increased by *amount*, to $p+amount$, while the sum of all payments has not changed. The difference between the sum of all purchases and the sum of all payments has thus become $(p+amount)-q$, which can be rewritten as $p-q+amount$. Since balance was originally $p-q$, this is the original value of balance plus *amount*. This is what the assignment statement in purchase sets balance equal to.

Using the same notation, after a pay message, the sum of all purchases has not changed, but the sum of all payments has increased to $q+amount$. The difference between the sum of all purchases and the sum of all payments has thus become $p-(q+amount)$, or $p-q-amount$. This is the original value of balance minus *amount*, which is what the assignment statement in pay sets balance equal to.

Finally, neither purchases nor payments have changed when a credit card account receives a getBalance message. getBalance correspondingly leaves balance unchanged, that is, still equal to the sum of all purchases minus the sum of all payments. ■

By proving the class invariant, we have proven that the methods in the credit card account class really do interact in the desired ways. For instance, we are now certain that purchase and pay communicate effectively with getBalance, that the constructor initializes accounts in a manner consistent with this communication, etc.

As this example illustrates, class invariants often hinge on the values of member variables. This means that a class invariant cannot be counted upon to hold if an object's clients can arbitrarily change its member variables. This is a further compelling reason to protect member variables from direct access by clients, as recommended in Section 2.5.

Exercises

3.17. Ohm's Law describes how the electrical current (amount of electricity) flowing through a conductor depends on voltage (the force pushing electricity along) and the conductor's resistance (opposition to electrical flow). Specifically, Ohm's Law says $E = IR$, where E is voltage, I is current, and R is resistance. A conductor designed to have a relatively high resistance is called a *resistor* and is (perhaps surprisingly) very useful in electrical circuits.

Computer programs for analyzing electrical circuits might use the following class to represent resistors. Clients define a resistor's resistance when they create it, but they can later set either voltage or current and have the resistor calculate the other:

```
class Resistor {

    private double resistance;
    private double current;
    private double voltage;

    public Resistor(double initialResistance) {
        resistance = initialResistance;
        current = 0;
        voltage = 0;
    }
```

```
public void setCurrent(double newCurrent) {
    current = newCurrent;
    voltage = current * resistance;
}

public void setVoltage(double newVoltage) {
    voltage = newVoltage;
    current = voltage / resistance;
}

public double getCurrent() {
    return current;
}

public double getVoltage() {
    return voltage;
}
}
```

Prove that the relation voltage = resistance × current (Ohm's Law, expressed in terms of the class's member variables) is a class invariant for this class.

3.18. Design your own implementation of the credit card account class, but track purchases and payments in some other way than keeping a running total in a balance member variable. Prove that your implementation respects the class invariant for credit card accounts.

3.19. Design a class whose instances generate sequences of perfect squares. In other words, the first time an instance is asked for a perfect square it should return 0, the next time it should return 1, then 4, then 9, and so forth. Your class should handle (at least) the messages reset and getNext, respond to reset by preparing to start its sequence over at 0, and responding to getNext by returning the perfect square after the one most recently returned. State a class invariant for your class, and prove that your design respects that invariant.

3.5 APPLYING THE PROOF TECHNIQUES

This chapter opened with the algorithm MakeChange, which supposedly makes change between 1 and 99 cents using the fewest coins. We deliberately raised doubts about whether this algorithm is correct. It turns out that it is, and you now know enough about correctness proofs to follow one for MakeChange. Furthermore, you also know that a variant on MakeChange is *not* correct for a different currency. This will offer an opportunity to see what proofs can tell you about incorrect algorithms.

3.5.1 The Correctness of MakeChange

Our correctness proof for MakeChange is subtler than the other proofs in this chapter. However, it is an important proof, since it isn't obvious that MakeChange is correct, and you should be able to follow it even if you might not be able to invent it by yourself yet.

Formally, this proof uses a technique called *proof by contradiction*, which amounts to showing that it is impossible for a theorem *not* to be true. In particular, we will show that MakeChange must use the fewest coins because any scenario in which a smaller number of coins might suffice actually entails some paradox or contradiction, and so is impossible.

PRECONDITION: C cents change is to be given, where C is an integer, $1 \leq C \leq 99$.

THEOREM: Algorithm MakeChange delivers C cents using the fewest possible coins. □

PROOF: There are really two parts to the proof: first, that MakeChange delivers exactly C cents, and second, that it does so with the fewest possible coins. The first part is easy: the steps in MakeChange that give quarters, dimes, and nickels explicitly do so without exceeding C cents. Thus, after these steps finish, C cents or less has been given. The last step then adds pennies until exactly C cents has been given.

For the second part, we know that there is *some* smallest collection of coins worth C cents, whether MakeChange finds it or not. Let's think about how this smallest collection compares to the one produced by MakeChange:

Conceivably, the smallest collection could contain a different number of quarters. Since MakeChange gives the greatest number of quarters that doesn't exceed C cents, the smallest collection would have to contain fewer quarters than MakeChange uses. Therefore, the smallest collection would contain at least one quarter's worth of dimes, nickels, and pennies. But think carefully about those dimes, nickels, and pennies:

1. There could be two or fewer dimes. Then there would have to be at least enough nickels and pennies to get the rest of the way to 25 cents. This in turn would mean that some subset of the dimes, nickels, and pennies had a value of exactly 25 cents, and so could be replaced by one quarter. But doing that would produce a smaller collection of coins worth C cents, which is

impossible because we are already thinking about the smallest such collection.

2. Evidently, therefore, there would have to be three (or more) dimes in the smallest collection. But then three of those dimes could be replaced by one quarter and one nickel, again producing a smaller collection, which is again impossible.

This analysis rules out every way in which the smallest collection of coins worth C cents could differ from MakeChange's collection in number of quarters. Therefore, MakeChange must produce a collection of coins with the same number of quarters as the smallest collection (and so both collections have the greatest number of quarters that doesn't exceed C cents).

Another possibility is that the smallest collection could have a different number of dimes than MakeChange's. We just showed that both collections contain the greatest possible number of quarters, and MakeChange's contains the greatest number of dimes subject to that constraint, so the smallest collection could only have fewer dimes than MakeChange's. This means the smallest collection would have to contain at least ten cents in pennies and nickels. But then two or more of those coins could be replaced by one dime, reducing the total number of coins. As above, this is impossible, because it would produce a collection smaller than the smallest one. Thus, the smallest collection must have the same number of dimes as MakeChange's.

A similar argument shows that the smallest collection must have the same number of nickels as MakeChange's. The smallest collection can't have more nickels, since both collections have the greatest possible number of dimes and quarters, and MakeChange's collection has the greatest number of nickels subject to that constraint. If the smallest collection had fewer nickels, then it would have to have at least five cents in pennies, which could be replaced by one nickel.

Now we know that the smallest collection of coins worth C cents contains the same number of quarters, dimes, and nickels as MakeChange's. The only coins left are pennies, which in both collections must make up the difference between C and the value of the quarters, dimes, and nickels. Both collections therefore contain the same number of pennies.

We have now shown that the collection of coins produced by MakeChange contains exactly the same number of each kind of coin as the smallest collection. MakeChange's collection is therefore identical to the smallest. ∎

3.5.2 Proofs and Incorrect Algorithms

So far, you have only studied correctness proofs for algorithms that really are correct. It is also instructive to see what happens if you attempt a correctness proof for an incorrect algorithm. For example, the introduction to this chapter described a currency consisting of quarters, dimes, and pennies, and pointed out how the corresponding variant of MakeChange does not always give the fewest possible coins (for example, it gives 30 cents as a quarter and five pennies rather than as three dimes). Consider what happens if we try to adapt our correctness proof for the original MakeChange to this variant.

The proof applies perfectly to the variant until considering how the number of coins produced by the variant compares to the smallest possible number. Then, when considering whether the smallest collection of coins could contain fewer quarters than the variant's collection, but three or more dimes, the argument that three dimes could be replaced by a quarter and a nickel no longer applies, because there are no nickels in this currency. Indeed, this currency provides no way to replace three dimes with fewer than three coins. This tells you that the variant may fail to give a minimal number of coins in situations involving trading quarters for three or more dimes—and indeed, that is exactly the situation in our example of the variant's incorrectness.

Notice how the proof in this example failed in a way that told you a lot about where the algorithm was wrong. A "correctness" proof for an incorrect algorithm typically will lead you to a specific flaw in the algorithm. Indeed, correctness proofs can be more useful for the help they give you in fixing incorrect algorithms than for the confirmation they offer that correct algorithms are correct.

Exercises

3.20. The preconditions for MakeChange's correctness proof include the statement that C is an integer. Does the proof really require this condition? If so, why?

3.21. The new pan-European currency, the Euro, has 1- and 2-Euro coins plus fractional Euro coins in denominations of 0.50, 0.20, 0.10, 0.05, 0.02, and 0.01 Euro. Prove that the variant of MakeChange for making change of up to 4.99 Euros (the smallest bill is worth 5 Euros) is correct. You may assume that change is never made in units smaller than 0.01 Euro.

3.22. Imagine a currency just like U.S. currency, except that it includes an additional coin worth four cents. Is the variant of MakeChange for this currency correct? Prove your answer.

3.23. Robbie the Robot is supposed to draw a 3-tile by 3-tile checkerboard. Preconditions and postconditions for this problem follow, using the labeling for tiles in the checkerboard shown in Figure 3.5.

Preconditions:

- Robbie is standing on tile 1.
- Robbie is facing tile 2.

■ There are no obstructions on tiles 1 through 9.

Postconditions:

■ Tiles 1, 3, 5, 7, and 9 are red.
■ Tiles 2, 4, 6, and 8 are white.

Try to prove that each of the following algorithms correctly solves this problem. Fix any that your proofs show to be incorrect.

```
Algorithm 1
    robbie.paint(java.awt.Color.red);
    robbie.move();
    robbie.paint(java.awt.Color.white);
    robbie.move();
    robbie.paint(java.awt.Color.red);
    robbie.turnLeft();
    robbie.move();
    robbie.paint(java.awt.Color.white);
    robbie.turnLeft();
    robbie.move();
    robbie.paint(java.awt.Color.red);
    robbie.move();
    robbie.paint(java.awt.Color.white);
    robbie.turnRight();
    robbie.move();
    robbie.paint(java.awt.Color.red);
    robbie.turnRight();
    robbie.move();
    robbie.paint(java.awt.Color.white);
    robbie.move();
    robbie.paint(java.awt.Color.red);

Algorithm 2:
    robbie.paint(java.awt.Color.red);
    robbie.move();
    robbie.paint(java.awt.Color.white);
    robbie.move();
    robbie.paint(java.awt.Color.red);
    robbie.turnLeft();
    robbie.move();
    robbie.paint(java.awt.Color.white);
```

```
        robbie.turnLeft();
        robbie.move();
        robbie.paint(java.awt.Color.red);
        robbie.move();
        robbie.paint(java.awt.Color.white);
        robbie.turnRight();
        robbie.move();
        robbie.paint(java.awt.Color.red);
        robbie.move();
        robbie.paint(java.awt.Color.white);
        robbie.move();
        robbie.paint(java.awt.Color.red);
```

Algorithm 3

```
        robbie.paint(java.awt.Color.red);
        robbie.move();
        robbie.paint(java.awt.Color.white);
        robbie.move();
        robbie.paint(java.awt.Color.red);
        robbie.turnLeft();
        robbie.move();
        robbie.paint(java.awt.Color.white);
        robbie.move();
        robbie.paint(java.awt.Color.red);
        robbie.turnLeft();
        robbie.move();
        robbie.paint(java.awt.Color.white);
        robbie.move();
        robbie.paint(java.awt.Color.red);
        robbie.turnLeft();
        robbie.move();
        robbie.paint(java.awt.Color.white);
        robbie.turnLeft();
        robbie.move();
        robbie.paint(java.awt.Color.red);
```

Algorithm 4

```
        robbie.paint(java.awt.Color.white);
        robbie.move();
        robbie.paint(java.awt.Color.red);
        robbie.move();
```

```
robbie.paint(java.awt.Color.white);
robbie.turnLeft();
robbie.move();
robbie.paint(java.awt.Color.red);
robbie.turnLeft();
robbie.move();
robbie.paint(java.awt.Color.white);
robbie.move();
robbie.paint(java.awt.Color.red);
robbie.turnRight();
robbie.move();
robbie.paint(java.awt.Color.white);
robbie.turnRight();
robbie.move();
robbie.paint(java.awt.Color.red);
robbie.move();
robbie.paint(java.awt.Color.white);
```

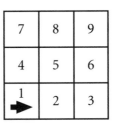

FIGURE 3.5 Preconditions for drawing a checkerboard.

3.24. Robin the Robot has to get from tile 4 to tile 6 as shown in Figure 3.6, but the way is blocked. Exact preconditions and postconditions for this problem are as follows:

Preconditions:

- Robin is on tile 4.
- Robin is facing tile 5.
- There is an obstacle on tile 5.
- There are no obstacles on tiles 1, 2, 3, 4, 6, 7, 8, and 9.

Postconditions:

- Robin is on tile 6.
- Robin is facing away from tile 5.

Try to prove that each of the following algorithms correctly solves this problem. Fix any that your proof shows to be incorrect.

```
Algorithm 1:
    robin.turnLeft();
    robin.move();
    robin.turnRight();
    robin.move();
    robin.move();
    robin.turnRight();
    robin.move();

Algorithm 2:
    robin.move();
    robin.move();

Algorithm 3:
    robin.turnLeft();
    robin.move();
    robin.turnRight();
    robin.move();
    robin.move();
    robin.turnRight();
    robin.move();
    robin.turnLeft();

Algorithm 4:
    robin.turnLeft();
    robin.move();
    robin.turnRight();
    robin.move();
    robin.turnRight();
    robin.move();
    robin.turnLeft();
```

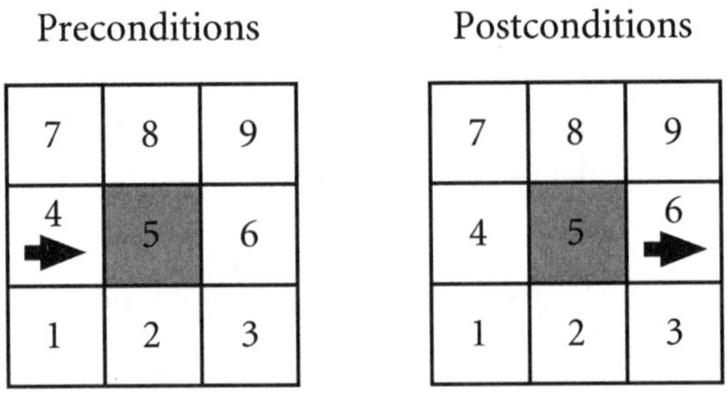

Preconditions   Postconditions

FIGURE 3.6 Preconditions and postconditions for moving Robin the Robot.

3.6 ANALYZING EFFICIENCY

In addition to correctness, algorithms' efficiency can also be analyzed theoretically. For example, which of the following algorithms for moving Robbie the Robot two tiles forward looks most efficient to you?

```
Algorithm 1
    robbie.move();
    robbie.move();

Algorithm 2
    robbie.move();
    robbie.turnLeft();
    robbie.turnLeft();
    robbie.turnLeft();
    robbie.turnLeft();
    robbie.move();
```

You probably chose algorithm 1, because it executes fewer steps. If you did, you're right. And more importantly, you have discovered a key idea behind theoretical efficiency analysis—counting the number of steps an algorithm executes.

3.6.1 An Example

As you might suspect, counting takes more cleverness in algorithms more complicated than the ones above. Later chapters will teach you some mathematical techniques that can help. In the meantime, less formal methods can accomplish a lot.

For instance, there is an interesting inefficiency lurking in the algorithms we have
developed for drawing squares:

```
public void drawSquare(int size) {
    this.drawLine(size);
    this.turnRight();
    this.drawLine(size);
    this.turnRight();
    this.drawLine(size);
    this.turnRight();
    this.drawLine(size);
}


private void drawLine(int size) {
    this.paint(java.awt.Color.red);
    for (int i = 1; i <= size-1; i++) {
        this.move();
        this.paint(java.awt.Color.red);
    }
}
```

Think about how many `paint` messages `drawSquare` sends while drawing a
square `size` tiles on a side: `drawSquare` doesn't send `paint` messages directly, but it
does send `drawLine` messages, and the `drawLine` method sends `paint` messages. Specifically, `drawLine`'s loop repeats $size-1$ times, and sends one `paint` message on
each repetition. The loop thus sends $size-1$ paint messages all together. `drawLine`
sends one more paint message outside the loop, for a total of *size*. `drawSquare` sends
four `drawLine` messages, each with parameter size; since each `drawLine` sends `size`
paint messages, the total number of `paint` messages is $4 \times size$.

Now compare this expression to the number of tiles in the border of a `size`-tile
square. Figure 3.7 shows how such a square consists of four $(size-2)$-tile side regions, and four one-tile corners. The total area of the border is thus
$4(size-2)+4 = 4 \times size - 4$ tiles. So `drawSquare` paints four tiles more than it needs
to (more precisely, it paints four tiles twice)! This is not a huge inefficiency, and
you will see in later chapters that overwhelmingly bigger differences in algorithms'
efficiencies are common. But this inefficiency is nonetheless interesting to discover,
and it can be corrected if you wish (see Exercise 3.26).

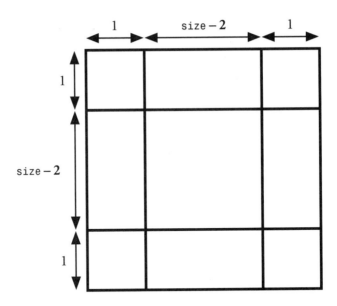

FIGURE 3.7 The structure of a size-by-size-tile square's border.

3.6.2 Efficiency and Problem Size

The above analysis of drawSquare demonstrates a common feature of efficiency analyses: the amount of work an algorithm does (in this case, the number of tiles it paints) usually depends on the size of the problem it solves (in this case, the size of the square). The goal of most efficiency analyses is to find a formula that relates the amount of work an algorithm does to some measure of the size of the problem it solves (as, for example, the formula $4 \times$ size relates the number of paint messages drawSquare sends to the size of the square).

3.6.3 Execution Time

The number of steps that an algorithm executes is an abstraction of its actual execution time, in that each step takes some amount of time to execute, but you don't know exactly how much. For example, counting the paint messages that drawSquare sends suggests that drawSquare takes more time than absolutely necessary to paint a square, but does not indicate how many extra seconds it takes. This abstraction reflects the abstract nature of algorithms themselves. An algorithm is a description of a problem-solving process that ignores many implementation details. But without those details (for example, how fast the computer is) you cannot determine concrete execution costs. Analyses of algorithms (as opposed to analyses of implementations) are therefore forced to analyze abstractions of the real-world costs of executing an algorithm. Nonetheless, abstract efficiency analysis is very useful. An abstract algorithm can have many different concrete implementations, and the information provided by an abstract efficiency analysis pertains to all of them. For example, abstract analysis could tell you that one algorithm will always be faster than another, regardless of their implementations.

Counting steps as an abstract measure of execution time is further justified by the idea's deep roots in theoretical computer science. Computer scientists have developed many abstract mathematical "machines" as models of computing. While these machines are never implemented physically, they provide extraordinarily good predictions about the limits of real algorithms and real computers (see Chapter 16 and Chapter 17 for some examples). Each of the mathematical models provides a different definition of a "step" in an algorithm, but comparisons of the models indicate that these differences don't matter very much—an algorithm will have comparable efficiencies on most models, regardless of what their definitions of a step are. Thus, although counting the pseudocode (or even Java) steps in an algorithm ignores many details of how a particular computer will execute that algorithm, you can expect all computers to execute it in comparable ways. In particular, the broad patterns in the algorithm's execution time will not change with the computer that executes it or the language that describes it.

3.6.4 Resources

The number of steps an algorithm executes is the most important theoretical measure of efficiency. It is therefore the measure that this text concentrates on. However, efficiency analysis needn't always count steps. In general, you can count the number of units an algorithm uses of any kind of resource. A *resource*, in efficiency analysis, is anything that represents a cost of executing an algorithm. For example, algorithms consume time executing, so time (or its abstraction, steps) is an important resource. Similarly, it requires memory space to store the data on which an algorithm works, so space is another commonly counted resource.

Exercises

3.25. Exercise 3.23 and Exercise 3.24 each presented a problem along with several algorithms for solving it. For each problem, decide which of the associated algorithms you expect to be the fastest, and which the slowest. (Since the algorithms may not all be correct, you only need to compare the ones that are.)

3.26. Design a drawing robot that uses $4 \times \text{size} - 4$ paint messages to draw a size-tile square. Derive the number of paint messages your methods send, to confirm that you have the right number. Prove that your algorithm is correct.

3.27. Prove that each of this section's algorithms for moving Robbie two tiles is correct.

3.7 CONCLUDING REMARKS

Two important questions that can be asked about any algorithm are whether or not it correctly solves its problem, and, if so, how efficiently it does so.

An algorithm correctly solves a problem if, whenever the algorithm starts with all of the problem's preconditions satisfied, it stops with all of the problem's postconditions satisfied. Rigorous proofs can help you show that an algorithm does this. Indeed, proofs can help you study almost any aspect of an algorithm's behavior (for example, what does the algorithm do if its preconditions don't hold? Does it ever produce undesirable side effects?)

Efficiency, in general, means how much or how little of some resource an algorithm uses. Time is one of the most important resources, and the number of steps that an algorithm executes is a good abstraction of the time it will take to run.

An algorithm's behavior can be studied both theoretically and empirically. This chapter introduced some of the central questions computer scientists ask about behavior and the theoretical tools for answering those questions. These tools can tell you a lot about an algorithm, and they have the advantage of being independent of any particular implementation of the algorithm. But theoretical results are abstract, and you will often want to know how they manifest themselves in concrete implementations. For this, you need to combine the theoretical results with empirical results. The best empirical results in any science come from sound, convincing experiments. The next chapter discusses what makes a *sound, convincing* computer science experiment.

3.8 FURTHER READING

Theoretical analysis of algorithms' correctness and efficiency are the prime concerns of the subfield of computer science known as *analysis of algorithms*. Several classic textbooks cover this subfield. For example:

T. Cormen, C. Leiserson, and R. Rivest and C. Stein, *Introduction to Algorithms*, (2nd ed.) MIT Press, 2001.

Techniques for proving algorithms correct date to the 1960s. The most influential publications in this area were:

C. A. R. Hoare, "An Axiomatic Basis for Computer Programming," *Communications of the ACM*, Oct. 1969.

R. Floyd, "Assigning Meanings to Programs," Proceedings of the American Mathematical Society Symposia in Applied Mathematics, 1967.

Hoare's paper extended the ideas in Floyd's. Both developed the idea of deducing postconditions from preconditions and the meanings of individual steps. Floyd and Hoare were mainly concerned with proving programs, rather than algorithms, correct. For this reason, their papers described formal ways of defining programming language constructs, and so were also seminal to research on programming languages.

Over the years, the correctness of algorithms and the correctness of programs have become separate concerns. Correctness of algorithms remains an important issue in analysis of algorithms. Correctness of programs, on the other hand, has become a problem that some people probably wish would go away, but that is too important to do so. Practicing programmers generally resist proving their work correct, yet as anyone who uses software can see, current informal approaches to correctness frequently fail. Formal methods for producing correct programs are thus an active interest in software engineering. For example:

E. Clarke et al., "Formal Methods: State of the Art and Future Directions," *ACM Computing Surveys*, Dec. 1996.

Constructing correct object-oriented programs from preconditions, postconditions, and class invariants is discussed in:

B. Meyer, *Object-Oriented Software Construction* (2nd edition), Prentice-Hall, 1997.

One of the first textbooks in which mathematical efficiency analysis figured significantly was:

D. Knuth, *The Art of Computer Programming* (Vol. 1: *Fundamental Algorithms*, 1968; Vol. 2: *Seminumerical Algorithms*, 1969; Vol. 3: *Sorting and Searching*, 1973), Addison-Wesley.

For more on the currency change-making problem, see:

G. Brassard and P. Bratley, *Fundamentals of Algorithmics*, Prentice-Hall, 1996.

This book presents several solutions to the problem, and a number of exercises that address variations on it.

For a survey of proof techniques from a mathematician's perspective, see:

D. Velleman, *How to Prove It*, Cambridge University Press, 1994.

4 Experimentation: An Introduction to the Scientific Method

Section 3.6 introduced the idea that you can abstractly estimate an algorithm's execution time from the number of steps it executes. How do you know whether this idea is valid? On the one hand, each step takes time to execute, and the overall time an algorithm takes depends on the total time of all its steps, so the number of executed steps could be a good surrogate for time. On the other hand, algorithms are abstract processes that don't execute directly—only programs (or other implementations of algorithms) execute. Program steps are far from uniform: different operations take different amounts of time, different computers run at different speeds, and even two instances of the same operation on the same computer can take different times depending on what part of the computer's memory they fetch their data from. Thus, just the number of steps an algorithm executes may not accurately reflect the time its concrete implementations require, after all. So perhaps theoretical step counts provide good estimates of execution time, and perhaps they don't. Theoretical considerations alone cannot tell us how much faith to place in step counts. In order to be confident that we understand program behavior, both in general (for example, whether counting steps ever really tells us anything) and in particular (for example, how fast a specific program runs), theoretical predictions must be compared to the actual behavior of programs. The need to compare theory to reality arises in all sciences and is the reason that science depends so critically on experiments. This chapter describes the role of experiments in science in general, and in computer science in particular.

4.1 THEORIES AND HYPOTHESES

The idea that an algorithm's execution time depends on the number of steps it executes is an example of a scientific *theory*. A theory, in science, is an explanation for certain phenomena that summarizes science's understanding of them. In the case of algorithms and time, the theory summarizes certain aspects of algorithm execution (each step takes time to execute, steps execute one at a time, etc.) by stating one of their main consequences.

Calling something a scientific theory usually implies that it is a profound explanation, one on which whole bodies of scientific thought rest.[1] In order to attain theory status, an explanation thus has to be widely respected by scientists, which in turn requires it to have survived extensive scientific scrutiny. Scientists generally don't call scientific theories "facts," because any theory may change over time. However, to gain widespread acceptance by scientists, a theory has to be tested and refined until current knowledge and technology can find no flaws in it. "Theory" as a scientific term thus connotes much more authority than "theory" does in common usage.

In computer science, some theories deal solely with mathematical entities, in which case "extensive scientific scrutiny" entails mathematical proof. However, as the example of steps and time indicates, computer science also has theories that describe connections between mathematical entities and their real-world implementations. These theories must be empirically tested, just as theories in the natural sciences must.

4.1.1 The Role of Experiments

One of the most important forms of empirical testing is the experiment, which, in its ideal form, proceeds as follows:

1. The need for an experiment arises when a scientist forms a *hypothesis*, a belief about how something works. This belief may be an attempt to explain prior, informal observations of that thing, in which case the hypothesis could, after enough scrutiny, become accepted as a new theory. Alternatively, the hypothesis may be a new implication of an existing theory.
2. Next, the scientist uses the hypothesis to predict the consequences of some action.
3. Then the scientist designs an *experimental procedure* for causing that action and observing its consequences. The things in which the scientist causes the action and observes the consequences are *experimental subjects* (for example, laboratory rats in biology or psychology, programs in computer science).

---

[1] Which is indeed the case with the theory that an algorithm's execution time depends on the number of steps it executes. While perhaps not as ingenious as some other scientific theories, this one is fundamental to computer science. It is a foundation upon which whole subfields of computer science rest, and it provides a crucial connection between the theoretical analysis of algorithms and the practical design of programs.

4. The scientist performs the action on or with the subjects and observes the results by measuring the subjects' reactions. These measurements provide *data* against which to test the prediction.

5. The prediction cannot always be tested with just the directly measurable data (called *raw data*). Thus, the raw data are often input to further calculations, or *data analysis*, whose outputs the scientist can compare to predicted values.

6. The scientist reaches a *conclusion* about whether or not the original hypothesis is correct based on whether the results of the data analysis are consistent with the prediction. The scientist shares this conclusion with other scientists.

7. Often, particularly if the hypothesis is an important one or the conclusion surprising, other scientists (or the original one) redo the experiment in order to verify that the results are repeatable.

The word "hypothesis" usually means an explanation for which the supporting evidence is not overwhelming enough to qualify it as a theory. Most experiments do test hypotheses in this sense of the word. Some experiments, however, test established theories (for instance, when a scientist discovers a new implication of the theory to test, or when new technology makes tests possible that were previously impossible). Don't be confused if you see a well-accepted theory called the "hypothesis" of such an experiment—the word "hypothesis" has a slightly broader meaning when used as the idea an experiment tests than it does in other contexts.

Exercises

4.1. By reading other books and/or talking with scientists, find out some of the criteria besides experiments by which scientists judge hypotheses.

4.2 PREDICTIONS

An experiment starts with a prediction, which in turn is based on a hypothesis. Many hypotheses involve cause-and-effect relationships from which you can develop predictions. For example, the belief that an algorithm's execution time depends on the number of steps it executes follows from the idea that executing steps causes the algorithm to consume time.

Causes, or conditions established by the experimenter (for example, the number of steps in an algorithm), are called *independent variables*. Effects, or results measured by the experimenter (for example, the amount of time an algorithm takes to execute), are called *dependent variables*. Note that "variable" in these phrases does not mean quite the same thing it means in programming or mathematics. A *variable* in an experiment is literally something that varies, either because the experimenter directly causes it to (an independent variable) or because changes in the independent variables indirectly cause it to (a dependent variable).

One way to devise predictions is to ask how you can vary your hypothesis's independent variables and what effects that should have on its dependent variables. For instance, you could vary the number of steps an algorithm executes (the example independent variable above) by including in the algorithm a loop that can repeat different numbers of times. The expected effect on execution time (the example dependent variable) is that if you execute the algorithm several times, each time changing the number of repetitions of the loop, then the runs with more repetitions will take more time.

It is surprisingly easy to trick yourself into making predictions you shouldn't. In particular, if you wait until after you see an experiment's results to make predictions, human nature will lead you to decide that the results you saw are the ones you should have expected, even if they aren't really implied by your hypothesis. Therefore, predictions must be made *before* doing experiments.

Exercises

4.2. Identify the independent and dependent variables in each of the following hypotheses:

1. The amount of disk space required to store a word processing document depends on the number of words in the document.
2. The size of a file determines the amount of time required to print it.
3. The length of a lecture is inversely proportional to how interesting it is.
4. The time required to display a picture on a computer monitor depends on the height, width, and color resolution of the picture.
5. The number of entries in a dictionary determines both the time required to look up a word in it and the number of pages in it.

4.3. For each of the hypotheses in Exercise 4.2, state a prediction that you could test in order to test the hypothesis.

4.4. State a prediction other than the one in the text that you could make from the hypothesis that an algorithm's execution time depends on the number of steps it executes.

4.3 EXPERIMENTAL PROCEDURE

Think about how you would test our prediction about the execution time of an iterative algorithm. The prediction itself provides a crude outline of the experiment: find a suitable algorithm, code it, execute it with a varying number of repetitions of the loop, measure running times, and see if the runs with more repetitions really take more time. This outline, however, is only a starting point—many details remain to be filled in before you have a good experiment. (For instance, which algorithm should you use? Should you use more than one? In what language should you code it or them? How should you measure times?) The following guidelines, applicable to any experiment, can help you work out these details.

4.3.1 Define Variables

A hypothesis tells you roughly what the independent and dependent variables are in an experiment, but you need very precise definitions in order to know exactly what to measure during the experiment. These precise definitions aren't always easy to find. For example, we have been talking about the number of steps an algorithm executes, but "step" is an ambiguous notion (if something takes one statement to describe in pseudocode, but two in a concrete programming language, is it one step or two?) In any experiment, look carefully for ambiguities in the definitions of variables and resolve any that you find.

4.3.2 Use Appropriate Instruments

Once you know what to measure, you have to decide how to measure it. You need to consider three things when choosing tools, or *instruments*, with which to make measurements: the instruments' accuracy, precision, and range.

Accuracy and precision are related, but not identical, concepts. *Accuracy* refers to how close a measurement is to the correct value; *precision* refers to how fine a distinction the instrument can make between one measurement and another. For example, the distance between New York City and Los Angeles is more accurately given as 3000 miles than as 2000 miles (the *1998 Rand-McNally Road Atlas* gives the driving distance between the two as 2824 miles). It is more precisely given as being between 2500 miles and 3000 miles than as being between 1000 and 5000 miles. Note that both "between 2500 and 3000 miles" and "between 1000 and 5000 miles" are correct descriptions of the distance, but the first distinguishes it more finely (to within a 500-mile range) than the second does (to within a 4000-mile range).

An instrument can, in principle, be accurate, precise, both, or neither. For instance, look at the four-centimeter scales in Figure 4.1. Scale A is as accurate as this text allows, but has a precision of only 1 cm. Scale B is visibly inaccurate, but still

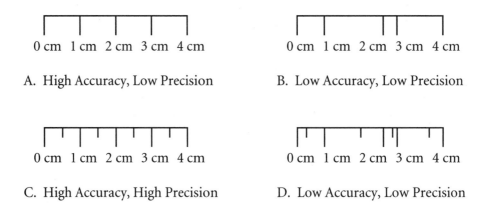

FIGURE 4.1 Accuracy and precision.

has a nominal 1 cm precision. Scale C is accurate and has a better, 0.5 cm, precision. Scale D also has this better precision, but is inaccurate. The inaccuracy of scales B and D is so great that whatever precision they claim is irrelevant; scale A is accurate, but its low precision makes it hard to use that accuracy to measure anything except an integral number of centimeters. As these observations suggest, the levels of accuracy and precision in an instrument should be about the same.

Range refers to the size of the values an instrument can measure. An instrument that cannot measure values as large as you expect to encounter in an experiment is clearly not suitable for that experiment. But on the other hand, if you try to measure values much smaller than your instrument is designed for, it may not have the precision to distinguish those values from 0, and even if it does, it may not measure them very accurately. As a general rule, pick an instrument whose range is sufficient to measure values somewhat larger than you expect to encounter and whose accuracy and precision are sufficient to distinguish values substantially smaller than you expect to encounter. For example, if you want to measure how long a lecture lasts and you expect it to last about an hour, a watch with an accuracy and precision of one minute and a range of one day would be a good instrument.

Instrumentation Code

Many of the instruments used in computer science experiments are actually software instructions embedded in programs. Such software is called *instrumentation code.* For example, an experimenter who wants to know how many times some event happens in a program could create a counting "instrument" by putting into the program a statement that increments a counter whenever the event happens and putting in another statement that prints the counter at the end of the program.

It would be easy, in Java, to give this instrument a range of roughly two billion counts,[2] with an accuracy and precision of one count.

Be careful when writing instrumentation code that it doesn't measure itself along with the parts of the program that are the real experimental subject. For example, if you are trying to count certain events and time how long they take, be sure that you don't accidentally time the counting code, or count events associated with the timing code.

4.3.3 Thoroughly Explore the Independent Variable

Most predictions describe a relationship between independent and dependent variables. For example, the relationship in our prediction about an iterative algorithm is that the dependent variable (running time) increases as the independent variable (number of steps executed) increases. For an experiment to thoroughly test whether a predicted relationship exists, it must look for that relationship in as many different subjects, representing as wide a range of values of the independent variable, as possible.

In some sense, this idea is just "more is better"—more subjects, a larger range of values for the independent variable, etc. This suggests that you should keep doing every experiment forever, on an ever-increasing number of subjects, which is clearly impossible. The practical compromise is to start with some small value of the independent variable, and then systematically work up to larger and larger values. You would proceed until you believe that you have enough data to lead you to a conclusion and to convince others of that conclusion's validity.

In some experiments, the hypothesis being tested will suggest a suitable starting value for the independent variable. If it doesn't, start with the smallest value for which you can accurately measure both the independent variable and the corresponding value of the dependent variable.

In many computer science experiments, a good way to "systematically work up" through values of the independent variable is to repeatedly double it. In other words, if x is the smallest value of the independent variable that you study, the next smallest value should be $2x$, then $4x$, and so on. Using this strategy, the values grow quickly, so you can test a large range without needing too many subjects. At the same time, the gaps between values aren't too big compared to the values themselves. Together, these features give you a reasonably good chance of discovering any range of values where the prediction fails to hold, if such a range exists.

For example, suppose you were testing the prediction about an iterative algorithm and could measure how long one repetition of the loop takes. A good set of experimental subjects would start with a run of the program in which the loop repeated once, then a run in which the loop repeated twice, then one with four repeti-

---

[2] 0 to 2,000,000,000 is roughly the range of positive values that Java's int data type can represent.

tions, and so on. Table 4.1 shows the numbers of repetitions in the first ten subjects in this experiment.

TABLE 4.1 Example Subjects for Testing the Iterative Algorithm Prediction

Subject	Repetitions of Loop
1st	1
2nd	2
3rd	4
4th	8
5th	16
6th	32
7th	64
8th	128
9th	256
10th	512

4.3.4 Control Differences between Subjects

Every experiment's goal is to produce evidence for or against some hypothesis. An experiment in which the dependent variable shows the predicted relationship to the independent variable should be strong evidence for the hypothesis, and an experiment in which the predicted relationship is not apparent should be strong evidence against the hypothesis. But both of these interpretations are undermined if anything other than the independent variable (and its dependent variables) differs from subject to subject. In that case, the apparent relationship (or lack thereof) between dependent and independent variables could be due to the incidental differences between subjects, not to the independent variable. Experimenters must therefore be careful that their experimental subjects differ only in the value of the independent variable.

Environmental Influences

Start controlling differences between subjects by eliminating, as far as possible, ways in which the environment outside the experiment can affect subjects inside the experiment. This ensures that changes in the environment can't translate into changes in the subjects. For programs, *environment* generally means the computer hardware and operating system on which the program runs. There are many ways in which these things can affect a program. Some examples, and ways experimenters can control them, include:

- If your operating system provides multitasking (the ability to run multiple programs simultaneously—most modern operating systems have this ability), then other programs running at the same time as an experiment will effectively slow down the experimental subject. Don't run other programs on a computer that is running an experiment, and measure execution time as the time the experimental subject actually spends running, not total elapsed time, whenever possible. See Section 4.7 for more on the subtleties of measuring time.
- If network traffic, or other input, arrives while a program is running, then the operating system will pause that program in order to deal with the incoming data. If possible, disconnect a computer running an experiment from networks and other sources of input, and be careful not to provide input through the remaining sources (even idly moving a mouse while waiting for a program to finish can measurably delay that program).
- Input and output statements (for example, writing text to a monitor, reading or writing a file) take a relatively long and variable time to execute. Avoid such statements in experimental subjects whenever possible.

Unfortunately, there will always be elements of an experiment's environment that you either can't control, or don't realize you need to control. Avoiding changes in subjects due to these elements is the reason you should keep all subjects as similar as possible, even in ways that seem not to matter. For example, if the subjects are programs, they should all be written in the same language, they should all be run on the same computer, they should all be run at about the same time, etc.

Garbage Collection

Garbage collection is a technique that Java and some other languages use to reclaim memory occupied by objects that a program no longer needs. Programs in garbage-collected languages automatically (in other words, without explicit commands from programmers) include code that notices when objects can no longer be accessed by programmer-written instructions and makes the memory occupied by those objects available for reuse. Garbage collection helps prevent programs from running out of memory. However, garbage collection is also very time-consuming, and programmers have very limited control over when it happens. Thus, programs can easily differ in the amount of garbage collection they do, leading to dramatic differences in execution time.

If you do an experiment whose subjects are Java programs (or programs in other garbage-collected languages), it is very important that you minimize garbage collection. The best ways to do this are to avoid creating any more objects than you absolutely need and to make sure that any objects you do create remain in use throughout your experiment. See the sample experiment in Section 4.8 for a demonstration of these strategies.

Controls

Even with the best efforts, it is usually impossible to eliminate all chance differences between subjects. Scientists therefore use special subjects, called *controls*, to help them distinguish intended experimental effects from the effects of unintentional influences. A classic example of controls comes from biology. To determine if a certain drug inhibits the growth of certain organisms, biologists will grow some organisms in the presence of the drug and will grow others (the controls) under identical conditions except without the drug.

Controls serve two important purposes:

1. As checks against unexpected influences. In the biology example, if some of the control organisms grow differently than others, then something other than the drug influences growth, and that same "something" probably also influences the treated organisms. The "something" may be nothing more than inevitable random variation between subjects ("random error"—see Section 4.4.2), in which case the amount of variation between controls provides a guide to how much variation between treated subjects is also due to randomness rather than to the treatment.
2. As references. If our example biologist predicts that the drug will inhibit growth, then treated organisms should grow less than untreated ones. The biologist can measure the extent to which this is true by comparing the growth of the treated organisms to the growth of the controls.

Computer science experiments usually use less obvious controls than the classic example, but they nonetheless have controls:

1. Subjects can serve as their own controls for unexpected influences. A computer scientist should test the same subject under the same conditions multiple times. All of these tests should produce the same results. If they don't, then something unexpected is influencing the experiment. As in the biology example, this "something" might be unavoidable random error, but the computer scientist should make every effort to rule out correctable influences before attributing variations to random error.
2. Subjects can serve as reference controls for each other. The prediction in many computer science experiments is that some calculation done during data analysis will produce the same value for all subjects. The subjects then

become references for each other, to the extent to which the calculations for each do or do not agree with the calculations for the others.

Replication

The very nature of unexpected influences on an experiment is such that experimenters don't know what those influences are, and even the best scientist can't rule out every one of the nearly infinite number of things that might influence an experiment. Thus, confidence that the results of an experiment aren't due to accidental differences between subjects increases if a different experimenter, working at a different time and place, repeats the experiment and gets the same results. An independent replication of the experiment reproduces the parts of the experiment believed to affect its outcome (for example, the changes to independent variables and measurements of dependent variables), but doesn't reproduce incidental factors. If the replication obtains the same results as the original experiment, then confidence increases that those results are due to the deliberate features the experiments had in common, and not to incidental ones in which they differed.

4.3.5 Make Multiple Measurements

As Section 4.3.4 discussed, repeating measurements multiple times is an important control in computer science experiments. A good rule of thumb is to repeat each measurement three to five times at first. For example, if you want to know how long it takes a program to process a certain input, run the same program on the same input five times and measure how long each of those runs takes.

Interpreting the Measurements

Ideally, all three to five initial measurements will be within your instrument's accuracy and precision of each other. If so, then they are as close to identical as it is physically possible for measurements taken with that instrument to be. Making more measurements is unlikely to change your results. You can use the average of the measurements as the typical value. For example, suppose you are measuring the execution time of a program, using a timer whose accuracy is ±1 millisecond (mSec). Further suppose you run the program five times, collecting the following measurements: 50 mSec, 51 mSec, 50 mSec, 50 mSec, 51 mSec. Even though these times are not exactly identical, the differences between them can be entirely explained by the timer's limitations, and so you cannot interpret the measurements as meaning that the program's running time varied. You should report the running time of that program on that input as 50.4 mSec (the average of 50, 51, 50, 50, and 51).

Unfortunately, the differences between measurements will usually be greater than your instrument's accuracy and precision. This may mean that something unexpected is affecting the experiment. You should try to identify the unexpected influence and correct it. Ultimately, however, nature has a great deal of inherent randomness, and this will unavoidably cause some variation between measurements. If this randomness is the only explanation for the differences between your measurements, you can use averaging and other statistical methods to compensate for it. Doing so will probably require additional measurements beyond the original three to five, however. Section 4.5 explores this subject in greater detail.

Outliers

Sometimes when you make multiple measurements, a few will be wildly different from the rest. Such wildly different measurements are called *outliers*. Outliers cast doubt on the measurements and any conclusions you reach from them, but there is no universally good way to deal with outliers. Some people discard outliers from their data sets, but this risks discarding valid but unusual measurements based on an ultimately subjective judgement as to what constitutes an outlier. Other people always discard the largest and smallest values from a data set, but this may discard perfectly good data while overlooking some outliers (if, for example, the two highest measurements are outliers, while the lowest is valid). Still other people keep all the data they measure, relying on later statistical analysis to minimize the effect of outliers, but this requires having enough valid data to make the outliers statistically insignificant. The best approach is probably not to have obvious outliers in the first place, something that is often possible in computer science with careful design and control of an experiment.

Exercises

4.5. We quoted the distance between New York City and Los Angeles as 2824 miles. This figure apparently has a precision of ±1 mile, that is, it is distinguishable from 2825 miles and from 2823 miles. Do you believe this measurement warrants such precision?

4.6. In which of the following scenarios do the instruments have appropriate accuracy, precision, and range for the measurements being made?

1. Using a stopwatch and a 50-meter track to measure how fast a person runs.
2. Using a stopwatch and a 50-meter track to measure how fast a snail crawls.
3. Using a micrometer to measure how tall a person is.
4. Using a wristwatch to measure how long a computer program takes to run.
5. Using a bathroom scale to measure how heavy a dog is.

6. Using a meter stick to measure how thick a sheet of paper is.
7. Calculating the thickness of a page in a book by counting the number of pages, then using a meter stick to measure the thickness of the book and dividing the measurement by the number of pages.

4.7. Section 4.3.3 suggested selecting values for an independent variable by doubling each value to generate the next. It claimed that the gaps between values "aren't too big compared to the values themselves." If the largest value is n, what is the size of the largest gap?

4.8. Using sources outside of this text, discover ways other than those already mentioned in which a computer's operating system or hardware can affect programs (and thus the results of experiments).

4.9. Phineas Phoole tests his programs by running them on one or two inputs. If a program works in these tests, Phineas concludes that it is totally correct. What element of the scientific method is Phineas overlooking, and what problems are likely to occur as a result?

4.10. Study the history of cold fusion in the 1980s. How does it illustrate the importance of replicating experiments?

4.11. In which of the following sets of measurements do you suspect that the variations between individual measurements are due to something other than the measuring instrument's accuracy and precision?

1. The following program execution times, measured to an accuracy of ± 1 mSec: 150 mSec, 150 mSec, 149 mSec, 150 mSec, 149 mSec.
2. The following times for a computer's user to respond to a prompt, measured to an accuracy of ± 1 second: 2 Sec, 3 Sec, 2 Sec, 2 Sec, 17 Sec.
3. The following measurements of the width of an image on a computer monitor, measured to an accuracy of ± 0.25 cm: 31.5 cm, 32.3 cm, 32.0 cm, 31.9 cm, 32.2 cm.

4.12. For each set of measurements in Exercise 4.11, give a number that you would use as "the" value of the variable being measured. Explain your choices.

4.4 EXPERIMENTAL ERROR

Experimental error is anything that makes a variable's apparent value, as measured in an experiment, different from the variable's "true" value. Some amount of error is inevitable in any experiment, since measurements cannot be infinitely accurate or precise. You therefore cannot eliminate experimental error completely from an experiment, but you must keep the amount of it small enough that it doesn't affect the experiment's conclusions.

There are two types of experimental error:

- *Systematic* errors distort all measurements in the same way. An excellent example comes from a physics experiment the first author did as a student (and still remembers with horror), in which an improperly connected meter consistently produced readings 100 times higher than they should have been. As this example suggests, systematic errors often result from flaws in experimental procedure. Many systematic errors can therefore be eliminated from an experiment by planning and executing it properly.

- *Random* errors distort measurements literally at random, sometimes making them higher than they should be, and sometimes lower. For example, flip a coin several times and compare the number of "heads" to the number of "tails." Theoretically, you should get equal numbers of "heads" and "tails," and on average, over many flips, you will come very close to that. But in any single, short series of flips you will sometimes get more "heads" than "tails," and sometimes fewer, due to the randomness of coin flipping. As this example suggests, you can never eliminate all random error.

There is a frustrating duality between systematic and random error. Random error is readily detectable, because it makes measurements that should be similar differ, but there is little you can do to eliminate it once you detect it. Systematic error, on the other hand, can often be eliminated if you detect it, but because it affects all measurements in the same way, it is not easily detectable.

4.4.1 Systematic Error

Often the only indication of systematic error in an experiment is a difference between the data you measure and the data you expect. But this is not a sure sign of error, since your expectations could be wrong—the whole point of an experiment, after all, is to *test* expectations. The best way to cope with systematic error is therefore to avoid it from the start. The guidelines for experimental procedure in Section 4.3 will help you do this to some extent. Unfortunately, these guidelines are only a beginning. Every experiment has its own sources of systematic error, and you must thoroughly understand each experiment in order to do a really good job of avoiding systematic error in it. The more practice you get doing your own experiments and evaluating other people's experiments, the better you will become at recognizing and avoiding systematic errors.

4.4.2 Random Error

In contrast to systematic error, random error cannot be eliminated before it happens, but it can be controlled afterwards. In particular, certain statistical calculations can estimate, and even reduce, the severity of random errors.

To understand random error, you have to understand that a variable does not have a single "true" value. This is partly because no instrument measures with perfect accuracy, and partly because nature is filled with random processes (for example, electrical noise, Brownian motion, etc.) that cause a variable's value to change slightly from one observation to the next. Different measurements of a variable will therefore produce slightly different values, and it is impossible to say that one of these values is "right" and the others are "wrong." Fortunately, however, the changing measurements of the variable almost always center around some unchanging average, and scientists consider this average to be the variable's "true" value. Figure 4.2 illustrates this situation, using dots to show a variable's value at different instants in time, and a line to show the average of these values. If you could measure the variable infinitely often, you could simply average your measurements to discover the variable's "true" value. But of course an experiment can only measure a variable a finite number of times. Figure 4.3 shows the result: the measurements catch only a sample of the variable's values. Each measurement in the sample will generally differ from the variable's average value, and these differences will be random—some will be higher than the average, some lower, some will be far from it, some near, etc. This is random error.

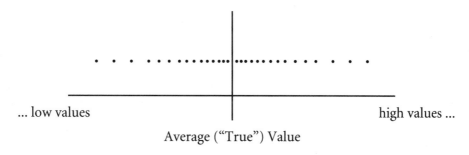

FIGURE 4.2 Instantaneous and average values of a variable.

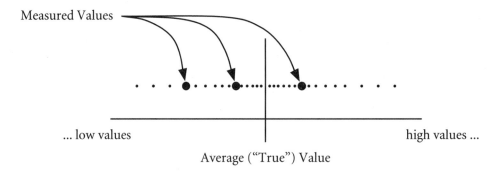

FIGURE 4.3 Measured values are a sample of instantaneous values.

Exercises

4.13. Try the coin-flipping experiment outlined above. Specifically, flip a coin 10 times. Theoretically, it should land heads up 5 times. Does it? Now do four sets of 10 coin flips, and count how many times the coin lands heads up in each set. Calculate the average of your four counts. How close is the average to 5? How many sets of 10 flips yielded counts further from 5 than your average is?

4.5 DATA ANALYSIS

After collecting data, you need to analyze it to see if it confirms the experiment's prediction. Section 4.2 pointed out that you should form the prediction before doing the experiment, since after you have done the experiment it is easy to convince yourself that whatever results you get are what you should have expected. For the same reason, you should decide how you will analyze data, and which results you will consider to confirm the prediction, before collecting the data.

No single way of analyzing data is appropriate for all experiments—what is appropriate depends on the prediction and the data itself. In some experiments, a simple data analysis is sufficient; in others, much more complex analyses are necessary. You will learn data analysis techniques appropriate for various kinds of experiments throughout the rest of this book.

Error analysis, the analysis of data to estimate and reduce the amount of random error in it, plays a role in most experiments. The following subsections therefore introduce some statistical techniques for error analysis.

4.5.1 Estimating True Values

Section 4.4.2 described how the average of a variable's various instantaneous values is considered to be the variable's "true" value. While no finite set of measurements can measure all of the instantaneous values, you can capture a sample of them. The average of this sample is a good estimate of the variable's "true" value. The more measurements there are in the sample, the more accurate this estimate is.

For example, suppose you make the following five measurements of some program's running time: 2 seconds, 1 second, 2 seconds, 3 seconds, and 3 seconds. Your best estimate of the program's "true" running time is the average of these measurements:

$$\frac{2+1+2+3+3}{5} = \frac{11}{5} = 2.2 \tag{4.1}$$

4.5.2 The Error in an Average

Once you know the average of a set of measurements, the next question is how accurately does that average estimate the variable's "true" value? Put another way, it is important to know how much random error remains in the average itself. Two factors are important in determining this: the variation among the measurements (whether the individual measurements are widely spread out, as opposed to being tightly clustered around the same value) and the number of measurements you make. More spread suggests greater random influence on each individual measurement and so less likelihood that their average is close to the "true" value. On the other hand, more measurements provide a more comprehensive sample of the variable's instantaneous values, meaning that the sample's average is more likely to be close to the variable's "true" value.

Standard Deviation

The degree to which measurements are spread out is summarized by a statistic called the *standard deviation* of the measurements. Suppose you have measured the value of variable x a total of n times. Call the measured values x_1, x_2, and so on up to x_n. Let x_{avg} stand for the average of these measurements. The standard deviation of the measurements, denoted s, is then given by Equation 4.2 (if you aren't familiar with the "Σ" notation in this formula, see the "Summation Notation" sidebar):

$$s = \sqrt{\frac{\sum_{i=1}^{n}(x_i - x_{avg})^2}{n-1}} \tag{4.2}$$

Summation Notation

The "Σ" (an uppercase Sigma) in the standard deviation formula indicates adding up a series of values. The values to add are given by the expression immediately to the right of the "Σ": "$(x_i - x_{avg})^2$" in this instance. The "i" in this expression is defined by the expressions "$i=1$" and "n" appearing below and above the "Σ". The expression below the "Σ" tells you the starting value for i, the expression above the ending value for i; i takes on all integer values between and including these bounds. Thus, the expression:

$$\sum_{i=1}^{n}(x_i - x_{avg})^2$$

means:

$$(x_1 - x_{avg})^2 + (x_2 - x_{avg})^2 + \cdots + (x_n - x_{avg})^2$$

Intuitively, the standard deviation is like an average difference between the measured values and the sample's overall average. Each measurement's difference from the average is given by an $(x_i - x_{avg})$ term. If you averaged these terms directly, you would get 0, because the measurements above the average (with positive differences) would cancel out the ones below the average (with negative differences); squaring the differences eliminates this cancellation, since all the squares are positive. The sum of the squares, divided by $n-1$, is (nearly) the average squared difference (the reasons for dividing by $n-1$ in this "average" instead of by n are beyond the scope of this text). Finally, the square root produces a value that better corresponds to the notion of "average difference" as opposed to "average squared difference."

Let's continue the example in Section 4.5.1 by calculating its standard deviation. The original example provided five measurements of a program's running time: 2 seconds, 1 second, 2 seconds, 3 seconds, and 3 seconds. The average of these measurements (x_{avg}) was 2.2 seconds. To calculate the standard deviation, work from the inside of Equation 4.2 outwards, in other words, start with the summation. It tells you to subtract the average from each individual measurement, square the result, and add up the squares. Subtracting the average and squaring produces:

$$(x_1 - x_{avg})^2 = (2-2.2)^2 = (-0.2)^2 = 0.04$$
$$(x_2 - x_{avg})^2 = (1-2.2)^2 = (-1.2)^2 = 1.44$$

$$\left(x_3 - x_{avg}\right)^2 = \left(2 - 2.2\right)^2 = 0.04$$

$$\left(x_4 - x_{avg}\right)^2 = 0.64$$

$$\left(x_5 - x_{avg}\right)^2 = 0.64 \tag{4.3}$$

Add these values up to complete the summation:

$$0.04 + 1.44 + 0.04 + 0.64 + 0.64 = 2.8 \tag{4.4}$$

Now you have finished evaluating the summation. The next step is to divide by $n-1$. Note that in this example, n, the number of measurements, is 5.

$$\frac{2.8}{5-1} = \frac{2.8}{4} = 0.7 \tag{4.5}$$

Finally, take the square root of the quotient to get the standard deviation:

$$s = \sqrt{0.7} \approx 0.84 \tag{4.6}$$

This standard deviation tells you that the measurements typically differ from their average by about 0.84 seconds. Unfortunately, that is not a fact you can do much with. It would be more helpful to know how accurate the average itself is, in other words, how close it is likely to be to the "true" running time. The standard deviation is a starting point for estimating this statistic, as we will shortly see.

Standard Error

When a set of measurements is averaged, those measurements that are higher than the "true" value tend to cancel out those that are lower than the "true" value, making the average closer to the "true" value than any single measurement is. This improved accuracy of the average is captured in a statistic called the *standard error* of the set of measurements:

$$E = \frac{s}{\sqrt{n}} \tag{4.7}$$

where s is the standard deviation of the measurements and n is the number of measurements. The standard error of a set of measurements is normally used as the estimated random error when the set's average is used as a variable's estimated "true" value.

For example, you can now estimate how accurate our example of an average running time is. You just saw that the standard deviation of the measurements is

0.84, and there are five measurements. Plugging these numbers into Equation 4.7 yields Equation 4.8:

$$E = \frac{s}{\sqrt{n}} = \frac{0.84}{\sqrt{5}} \approx 0.36 \tag{4.8}$$

This result tells you that the calculated average (2.2 seconds) is probably within 0.36 seconds of the program's "true" running time. Equivalently, the "true" running time is probably somewhere between 1.84 seconds (2.2−0.36) and 2.56 seconds (2.2+0.36). (One caution about this example is necessary though: standard errors are not always accurate when the number of measurements is small, and five is in fact a very small number of measurements to calculate a standard error on. We used such a small set of measurements to make the examples easy to follow, but in reality you should use 20 or 30 or more measurements if you plan to calculate their standard error.)

The formula for standard error provides an interesting insight into how the error in an average decreases with the number of measurements: it decreases in proportion to the square root of n (standard deviations stay roughly constant as n increases). This means that in order to decrease the random error in a set of measurements by some factor, you have to increase the number of measurements by about the square of that factor. For example, if you want to reduce random error to half its initial value, you need to make about four times as many measurements, if you want to reduce random error by a factor of three you need about nine times as many measurements, etc.

4.5.3 Relative Error

You now know how to estimate a variable's "true" value from a set of measurements and how to gauge the error in that estimate. There are two ways to express this error: as an absolute number and as a fraction, or percentage, of the estimate. For example, saying that a variable's value is 10±1 expresses the error in absolute terms; saying that the value is 10±10% expresses the same error as a percentage. Error expressed as a fraction or percentage of the estimate is called *relative error*. Error's significance depends on its size relative to the estimate, so relative error is often more useful to know than absolute error. For instance, an error of ±1 unit is minor if the estimate it goes with is 100 units, but overwhelming if the estimate is 1 unit. In the former case, the error is ±1%, in the latter it is ±100%.

Exercises

4.14. Calculate the average, standard deviation, and standard error of each of the following sets of numbers:

1. 2, 1, 3, 3, 2
2. 1, 1, 2, 3, 3
3. 1.5, 2.2, 1.6, 0.9, 1.3
4. 3, 5, 2, 6, 1, 3, 7, 0, 2, 1
5. −10, 25, 60, 0, 100, −50, 70, −90, −100, 50
6. −100, 100, 10, 12, 9, 10, 8, 15, 10, 11

4.15. Below are measurements of some variables' values. What would you estimate as the "true" value of each variable, and what amount of error would you associate with each estimate?

1. 0.9 seconds, 1.1 seconds, 1.2 seconds, 1.0 seconds.
2. 123 centimeters, 120 centimeters, 125 centimeters, 122 centimeters.
3. 17 seconds, 20 seconds, 18 seconds, 21 seconds, 22 seconds, 18 seconds.
4. 1214 bytes, 985 bytes, 1538 bytes, 1184 bytes.

4.16. Rephrase the standard error from the running time example as a relative error.

4.17. Suppose that in doing some experiment you make a number of measurements from which you calculate an average. Your friend, doing a similar experiment, makes only one tenth as many measurements as you do. About how much more accurate would you expect your average to be than your friend's?

4.18. Each of the following measurements represents a variable's estimated value with an absolute error. Restate each using relative error.

1. 5 ± 1 seconds
2. 10 ± 0.5 centimeters
3. 2 feet $\pm$ 1 inch
4. 12 ± 3 units
5. 17.5 ± 0.3 inches

4.19. Each of the following measurements includes a relative error. Restate each using absolute error.

1. 60 centimeters $\pm$ 10%
2. 13 seconds $\pm$ 2%
3. 37 degrees centigrade $\pm$ 4%

4.6 FORMING CONCLUSIONS

Experimental "proof" is very different from logical "proof." Every time a prediction is borne out in an experiment, scientists' confidence in the underlying hypothesis increases. However, the hypothesis may lead to other predictions that are wrong, or there may even be rare subjects, which the experiment simply didn't find, for which the original prediction is wrong. Therefore, experiments cannot prove a hypothesis with complete certainty, no matter how many one does. The proper positive conclusion to draw from an experiment is always that it *supports* the hypothesis—not that it *proves* the hypothesis.

On the other hand, a negative conclusion is definitive—a well-constructed experiment whose prediction is wrong proves the hypothesis wrong. But before drawing such a conclusion, you have to be very careful that the experiment's result reflects a real flaw in the hypothesis, not an error in the experiment. Furthermore, there are degrees of wrongness, ranging from predictions that are wildly inaccurate in all cases, to those that are off by only a small amount in a single case. You should temper your conclusions correspondingly. A wildly wrong prediction justifies rejecting a hypothesis, but a prediction that is only slightly wrong often calls for modifying, rather than completely rejecting, the hypothesis.

4.7 MEASURING TIME IN COMPUTER SCIENCE EXPERIMENTS

Time is one of the most frequently measured variables in computer science experiments. Most programming languages (including Java) provide some way to measure time. Unfortunately, it is surprisingly hard to measure time accurately on a computer, and the mechanisms for measuring it introduce an inherent error source into experiments.

4.7.1 Defining Time as a Variable

Time is one of the hardest variables to define for a computer science experiment. Even while a program is running, most operating systems will occasionally take control away from it in order to do other things. Thus, the time a program spends doing work for its user (*user time*) is less than the elapsed time between the moment the program starts and the moment it finishes. The difference between elapsed time and user time reaches extremes in so-called *multitasking* systems, where the operating system may take control away from one program for a while in order to let other programs run. For example, if you listen to music on your computer while doing other work, you have seen multitasking—your computer alternates between doing small pieces of your other work and playing small pieces of music (the alternation is so fast that you usually don't notice it). With multitasking, a considerable fraction of an experiment's elapsed time may actually be consumed by programs completely unrelated to the experimental subject. Even if there were no multitasking (and unfortunately, most operating systems do multitask), and the distinction between elapsed time and user time were insignificant, most experimental programs don't spend 100% of their time executing experimental code—they also spend time initializing the experiment, printing results, etc. Thus, an experimenter interested in "the time" that a program takes to do something must decide whether this means user time or elapsed time, whether multitasking is a factor in the computer, what part of the time consumed by the program is really the part of interest, etc.

4.7.2 Measuring Time

One of the most common forms of instrumentation code measures the time part of a program takes to execute. Such code typically uses a so-called *clock function*. This is a method that returns the amount of time that has passed since some start time or *time zero* Depending on the particular clock function, "time zero" could be an actual time, or it could be something like the moment at which your program started running or your computer was turned on.

Java's clock function is the built-in method System.currentTimeMillis. It returns a long integer representing the current time as a number of milliseconds since midnight of January 1, 1970. Beware that measuring time in milliseconds does *not* necessarily mean that System.currentTimeMillis has a precision of one millisecond. While it often does, a Java implementation is free to increment its millisecond counter less than once per millisecond, as long as it increments by the proper amount. For example, a Java implementation could increment its counter by 10 every 10 milliseconds, giving System.currentTimeMillis a precision of 10 milliseconds rather than one. Also notice that System.currentTimeMillis is an elapsed time clock, not a user time clock. However, it is the only standard Java tool available for measuring time in experiments.

To time something with a clock function, you record the time at which the event starts (startTime in the outline below) and the time at which it finishes (endTime). The difference between these times is how long the event took (executionTime in the outline). For example, Java timing code looks like this:

```
long startTime = System.currentTimeMillis();
// The code you want to time goes here
long endTime = System.currentTimeMillis();
long executionTime = endTime − startTime;
```

4.7.3 Error Sources in Time Measurements

Clock functions are an important source of random error. Clock functions are based on a counter, which the computer periodically increments. A clock function returns an integral value: 0 for any time between "time zero" and the counter's first increment, 1 for any time between the first and second increments, and so forth. Figure 4.4 illustrates this behavior—tick marks indicate instants at which the counter increments; the numbers between tick marks represent time as reported by the clock function.

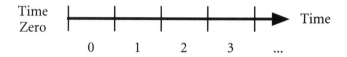

FIGURE 4.4 Time as seen through a clock function.

The time between increments of the counter is the clock function's precision. You cannot accurately measure times shorter than this. Figure 4.5 illustrates the problems: Event 1 starts just after the counter increments and ends just before the next increment. It thus takes almost one unit of real time, but no time as seen by the clock function. Event 2, on the other hand, starts just before an increment and ends just after it. This event takes almost no real time, but appears to take one unit according to the clock function. As these examples illustrate, times measured by a clock function have a random error of plus or minus the clock's precision.

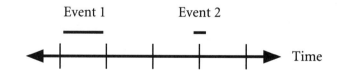

FIGURE 4.5 Possible errors in measuring time with a clock function.

Exercises

4.20. Why do you not need to know when "time zero" is in order to use a clock function to time part of a program?

4.21. Assume each of the following sets of data was measured using a clock function. Calculate how long each event took:

1. Start time = 109 milliseconds, end time = 200 milliseconds.
2. Start time = 32 seconds, end time = 40 seconds.
3. Start time = 150 milliseconds, end time = 350 milliseconds.
4. Start time = 982 sixtieths of a second, end time = 1165 sixtieths of a second.

4.22. Suppose each of the following sets of measurements was made using a clock function with the precision indicated. Calculate the elapsed time and absolute random error for each set.

1. Measured with a precision of 1 millisecond: start time = 10 milliseconds, end time = 20 milliseconds
2. Measured with a precision of 0.5 millisecond: start time = 4 milliseconds, end time = 6 milliseconds.
3. Measured with a precision of 0.1 second: start time = 0.6 seconds, end time = 1.4 seconds.
4. Measured with a precision of 1 millisecond: start time = 5 milliseconds, end time = 5 milliseconds.

4.23. The following outline illustrates a way to change the inherent error in an elapsed time calculation from plus or minus one unit of the clock's precision to plus one unit, minus zero (in other words, the measurement may be as much as one unit lower than the true value, but will never be higher). Explain why this is so, assuming that the computer executes many statements in between clock increments.

```
long synchronizer = System.currentTimeMillis();
while (System.currentTimeMillis() == synchronizer) { }
long startTime = System.currentTimeMillis();
// The code you want to time goes here
long endTime = System.currentTimeMillis();
long executionTime = endTime - startTime;
```

4.24. The robots introduced in Chapter 2 respond to heading messages by returning the direction in which they are facing. Phineas Phoole wants to know how long it takes a robot to handle such a message. He uses the following code to find out:

```
// Assuming that theRobot is a robot object...
long start = System.currentTimeMillis();
System.out.println(theRobot.heading());
long end = System.currentTimeMillis();
System.out.println("Elapsed time = " + (end - start));
```

What systematic error does this code contain? (It's a very common one in computer science experiments.)

4.8 AN EXAMPLE EXPERIMENT

Some of the most popular algorithm analysis and experimentation examples involve sorting, in other words, rearranging a sequence of data into ascending or descending order. For instance, a typical sorting algorithm might take an array as input and output the same array with its contents rearranged into ascending order. In this section, we use a simple sorting algorithm, Selection Sort, to develop and demonstrate a complete experiment. See the "Selection Sort" sidebar for details of Selection Sort.

In *Chapter 9: Iteration and Efficiency*, you will learn mathematical techniques for determining how many steps an algorithm such as this executes. But even without those techniques, one can form hypotheses about the algorithm's execution time. In particular, notice that the number of times Selection Sort's loops repeat depends on the length of the array. This means that Selection Sort executes more steps while sorting a long array than while sorting a short one, which in turn suggests the hypothesis "Selection Sort's execution time increases as the size of the array increases." The remainder of this section describes an experiment in which the authors tested this hypothesis.

We began designing the experiment by formulating a prediction and determining what the independent and dependent variables would be. We also decided how we would analyze the data. The hypothesis suggests array size as the independent variable and running time as the dependent variable. Further, the hypothesis led us to predict that if we wrote a Selection Sort program and ran it on arrays of increasing size, we could measure running time increasing as size did. Since this was a qualitative prediction (it only said that times should increase with array size, not what the mathematical relation between array size and time should be), a qualitative way of testing the prediction was appropriate: we decided to graph the measured running times against array size and see if the plotted line was always rising (i.e., increasing). Note that we made all of these decisions about the prediction and data analysis before gathering any data.

We wrote a SortableArray class in Java. Objects of this class represent integer arrays that use Selection Sort to put themselves into ascending order in response to a sort message. A SortableArray's size is the number of integers it contains. SortableArray objects have a constructor that takes the maximum size the SortableArray will ever have as a parameter. A reset message, whose parameter is a size less than or equal to the maximum, causes a SortableArray to adopt that size and fill itself with integers in decreasing order. The combination of constructor and reset allowed us to send all the sort messages we timed to a single SortableArray object, which we reset to the appropriate size before each sort. We thus ran the entire experiment in only one object, eliminating any risk of garbage collection (see Section 4.3.4). We timed many sorts, in arrays of different sizes (thus both exploring the prediction over many array sizes—Section 4.3.3—and getting multiple measurements for each size—Section 4.3.5), while keeping those arrays similar to each other in as many ways as possible (to control differences between subjects, as discussed in Section 4.3.4).

Selection Sort

Selection Sort sorts an n-item array as follows: First, search the entire array for the smallest item and swap it with the item in position one. This leaves the smallest item in its final, sorted position. Then, to put the second smallest item in its final position, find the smallest item in positions two through n and swap it with the item in position two (since the smallest item is already in position one, the smallest item in positions two through n is the second smallest overall). Then find the smallest item in positions three through n to swap into position three, then the smallest in positions four through n to swap into position four, and so forth.

Here is Selection Sort in Java. theArray is the array to sort, and size is the number of items in it; both are member variables of the class that contains sort. This class also provides a swap method that swaps two elements of the array, given their indices. The cur loop selects the position into which to swap, and the seek loop finds the item to swap into that position:

```java
public void sort() {
    for (int cur = 0; cur < size-1; cur++) {
        int min = cur;
        for (int seek = cur+1; seek < size; seek++) {
            if (theArray[seek] < theArray[min]) {
                min = seek;
            }
        }
        this.swap(min, cur);
    }
}
```

We also wrote a main program that creates the `SortableArray` object, and then measures how long it takes to process many `sort` messages at each of many sizes (resetting the object before each `sort`, so that all `sort`s operate on initially reverse-ordered arrays). We defined sorting time to be the time from sending the `sort` message until control returns to the main program. We used the timing technique from Section 4.7.2 to time each sort, namely:

```
long startTime = System.currentTimeMillis();
subjectArray.sort();
long endTime = System.currentTimeMillis();
long time = endTime - startTime;
```

Our complete program is available at this book's Web site, in file SortableArray.java.

We ran our program on an Apple PowerBook® G4 running at 550 MHz with a 100 MHz bus; the computer had 768 MB of main memory and 256 KB of level two cache. The computer was disconnected from its network while running this experiment, and we turned off all screen effects and energy saving options (since the programs that provide these features multitask with others—see Section 4.3.4). The operating system was Mac OS® X 10.2.6. The only other programs running during the experiment were the experimental subject itself and its development environment (Apple's ProjectBuilder 2.1).

We did some exploratory runs of the experiment in order to identify and correct additional error sources and to determine how big an array had to be in order for us to measure its sorting time. We found that times were easily measurable when the arrays contained about 1000 numbers. We therefore ran the main experiment on sizes that started at 1000 numbers, and that doubled (as recommended in Section 4.3.3) until 64000, at which point we felt we could reach a clear conclusion. We found that the first sort after the program started was often an outlier (slower than later sorts—we have also seen similar behavior in other Java programs), so we modified the program to do one untimed sort before beginning the sorts it would time. We also noticed that our time measurements were more variable during the first few hours after the computer was turned on than later, so we waited to do the actual data collection run until the computer had been on for several hours. Even then, the times for each array size differed by more than our `System.currentTimeMillis`' 1 millisecond precision, so we decided to average 20 sorts for each size (Section 4.5.1 discusses averaging to control random error), using the relative standard error to gauge how accurate the averages were (see Section 4.5.2 on standard error and Section 4.5.3 on relative error). We chose 20 sorts because 20 is the smallest number of measurements we felt comfortable applying standard error to.

After the above adjustments to our experimental procedures, we were ready to gather the data we would actually analyze. Table 4.2 shows the data we collected and the error analysis we performed. All times are in milliseconds. The estimated relative errors (the last row of the table) are very low, with the largest being only 1.16% and most being substantially less than 1%. We therefore believe that the average times are within 1% or less of the "true" time for this particular program to perform these sorts.

TABLE 4.2 Sorting Times and Error Analysis for Java Selection Sort

Size	1000	2000	4000	8000	16000	32000	64000
Times	16	55	225	894	3635	14783	63591
	14	56	223	895	3630	14776	63619
	14	56	225	895	3633	14785	63576
	14	56	224	895	3640	14774	63585
	14	57	225	893	3631	14780	63608
	14	56	224	893	3634	14784	63624
	16	56	224	896	3636	14773	63636
	14	56	223	895	3631	14776	63615
	14	57	225	895	3635	14785	63622
	15	57	223	897	3634	14774	63616
	13	56	224	895	3632	14784	63585
	15	56	223	895	3636	14776	63598
	15	55	225	892	3635	14788	63614
	14	56	222	895	3632	14777	63871
	14	56	223	893	3634	14788	63511
	15	56	224	894	3634	14779	63545
	14	57	225	897	3633	14781	63590
	14	56	223	893	3633	14775	63584
	14	56	223	895	3634	14782	64084
	14	56	223	895	3632	14776	63675
Average	14.35	56.1	223.8	894.6	3633.7	14779.8	63637.5
Std. Err.	0.17	0.12	0.21	0.29	0.5	1.08	28.15
Rel. Err.	0.0116	0.0022	0.001	0.0003	0.0001	0.0001	0.0004

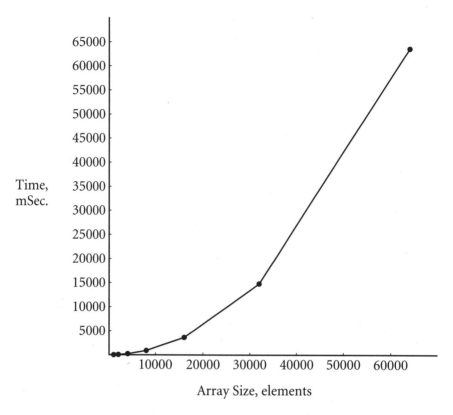

FIGURE 4.6 Sorting time versus array size for java selection sort.

The graph that tests our prediction appears in Figure 4.6. The graph does indeed show sorting time always increasing with array size,[3] supporting our prediction. We therefore concluded that this experiment supports the hypothesis that Selection Sort's execution time increases with array size.

The foregoing experiment is really a replication (see Section 4.3.4) of an experiment we first did several years earlier. The earlier experiment tested the same prediction about Selection Sort, using a similar class and the same array sizes. However, we wrote the original class in C++ and ran the experiment on an Apple PowerBook G3 running at 333 MHz. The computer had 256 MB of main memory, 512 KB of level two cache, and was running with virtual memory turned off. The

---

[3] Actually, the graph's resolution is too low to show how time changed with array size for the smallest arrays. Graphs are powerful tools for displaying broad patterns in data, but are not good for showing detailed behavior. However, inspecting Table 4.2 confirms that even at small sizes, time did always increase with size.

computer was disconnected from its network while running the experiment. The operating system was Mac OS 9.1. The program we used for this experiment is at this book's Web site, in file sortablearray.cc.

Table 4.3 shows the times we measured in the original experiment, while Figure 4.7 graphs them against array size. All times are in 60ths of a second, because that is the unit in which our C++ program measured time. All times for each array size were within the clock's precision of each other, so we needed no error analysis and took fewer measurements than in the Java experiment.

TABLE 4.3 Sorting Times for C++ Selection Sort

Size	1000	2000	4000	8000	16000	32000	64000
Times	0	4	15	58	256	1047	4224
	1	3	15	58	255	1047	4224
	1	3	14	58	255	1048	4224
	1	4	15	59	255	1048	4224
	1	4	14	59	256	1048	4224
	1	3	15	59	256	1048	4225
	1	3	15	58	255	1047	4224
Average	0.9	3.4	14.7	58.4	255.4	1047.6	4224.1

Note that the original experiment differed from the Java one in the computer and operating system on which we ran it, and in the language in which we wrote it. The times it measured were slightly longer than those in the Java experiment. Nonetheless, the results from the original experiment also supported our prediction. Since its results agree with those of the Java experiment in this respect, it is quite likely that those results reflect something fundamental to Selection Sort (or to the exactly out-of-order arrays both experiments sorted), not something peculiar to one computing environment or programming language.

Exercises

4.25. Replicate the experiment described in this section. How similar are your results to the authors'?

4.26. It is possible that the experiment described in this section really reveals something about sorting exactly out-of-order arrays, not something about Selection Sort. Design and conduct an experiment that tests the hypothesis that Selection Sort takes increasing time to sort increasingly large arrays regardless of their initial order.

4.27. Look at the shape of the graphs in Figure 4.6 and Figure 4.7. Is anything about it surprising to you? Does it suggest a more specific relationship between array size and Selection Sort's execution time than the relationship in the original hypothesis?

4.28. Phineas Phoole believes that the world is run by a secret society of "Hidden Masters." The Hidden Masters have mysterious powers by which they can make any event happen exactly as they wish. Is this belief scientifically testable? Why or why not?

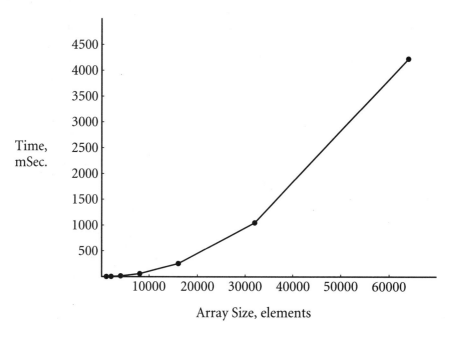

FIGURE 4.7 Sorting time versus array size for C++ Selection Sort.

4.9 OTHER USES OF EXPERIMENTS IN COMPUTER SCIENCE

Section 4.8's experiment concerned the execution time of an algorithm. Execution time is an important subject of experimental study, and almost all of the experiments discussed in this book deal with it. However, there are also many other important applications of experiments in computer science.

4.9.1 Programming

Programming and experimentation interact in a number of ways. Perhaps the most obvious is program testing. Every time someone tests a program, the tester is, in effect, testing a hypothesis of the form, "This program is correct". The more one approaches this hypothesis in the same frame of mind as one would approach any experiment, the more thorough and reliable the tests are likely to be. For instance, testers should identify the relevant inputs to provide (independent variables), identify the relevant outputs to observe (dependent variables), determine before testing what results are consistent with a working program, think about errors that might confuse the results, etc.

Similarly, debugging (locating and fixing the source of a problem once testing has revealed one) can be approached as an experimental process: gather exploratory data about the problem, eventually form a hypothesis about where the problem originates, make a prediction that certain changes to the program will correct the problem, and then systematically test that prediction.

Sometimes the very act of creating a program can be seen as an experiment, whose hypothesis is, "I can write a program that does such-and-such". If one is only interested in demonstrating that a specific algorithm can be written, then writing the algorithm in pseudocode and giving a theoretical correctness proof can be sufficient. But complete programs are more than just a few algorithms expressed in a programming language: they also have to present a comfortable user interface, interact with external system components such as databases, networks, hardware, etc., and meet users' requirements for such things as usability, speed, cost, etc. Faced with such complex interactions and requirements, it is essential to write the program (or at least a prototype of it) and see if users really accept it.

4.9.2 Hardware/Software Systems

The box that users think of as "the computer" is in fact a complicated system of interacting hardware and software. The electronic components in the box ultimately store and manipulate data, and execute program instructions, but it is software that provides users an interface through which they can enter data and commands, that translates high-level language programs into a form the electronics can execute, that makes decisions about what the hardware should do at what times, etc. Each part of such a system interacts with the other parts in ways that purely theoretical models of the systems cannot fully capture. Computer scientists who study computer systems must thus experimentally test their beliefs about whether a new piece of software or hardware will be more reliable, faster, easier to integrate with other components, or in some other way better, than previous versions. Typically, a computer scientist constructs a prototype system incorporating his ideas, and then measures its performance. Areas of computer science in which such experiments are important include networking, computer architecture (the design of computer hardware and hardware organizations), operating systems (the software that manages the raw hardware), and more.

4.9.3 Human Considerations

Human beings are tremendously unpredictable. Computer systems that either interact with humans or simulate humans are thus likely to need to behave in ways different than those computer systems' designers expected the computer systems to behave. Experimentally testing such systems is an important way of confirming that they perform acceptably even in unforeseen situations.

For example, designers of user interfaces develop ideas about ways to make computers easier for people to use, less error-prone, etc. But how a person really uses a user interface is unique to that person and the task they are performing, so interface designers must test their ideas experimentally. Typically, the designers have people use a new interface, while the designers measure such things as error rates, learning times, task completion times, and similar variables. The data thus collected lets the designers test their belief that the new interface is better in some respect than previous ones.

Simulating human behavior, particularly mental behavior, is increasingly important in computing. Such simulations appear, for example, in programs that play games, that communicate with people using human rather than machine-oriented languages, that complement human decision-making, that serve as models for studying human intelligence, etc. Mathematical descriptions of human behavior that are complete enough to prove the underlying simulation algorithms correct do not exist, so experiments are needed to gauge how close to human such an algorithm's behavior is. These experiments may measure the fraction of offered problems that the algorithm solves, or solves in the same way a human does, the quality of the algorithm's solution as judged by human experts, etc.

4.10 CONCLUDING REMARKS

The search to understand how and why the universe works the way it does is among the oldest of human endeavors. This effort has led down many paths—religions, sciences, philosophies, etc. Of the resulting disciplines, those that are now called sciences share a common concern: verifying that theoretical models are in fact consistent with observable reality. This coupling of theoretical reasoning with empirical verification is the heart of the scientific method. Experiments are the current state of the art for empirical verification within the scientific method.

An overarching goal in every experiment is to test a hypothesis as objectively as possible. Many elements of good experimental practice follow from this goal:

- A concrete prediction about measurable results, made *before* collecting data, ensures that the outcome of an experiment can't be retroactively interpreted as "what should have happened" regardless of its real consistency with the hypothesis.
- Isolating the experimental system from outside influences ensures that the experiment tests the hypothesis in question rather than the idiosyncrasies of a particular experimenter or laboratory. In particular, this helps to ensure that the experimenter's expectations don't influence the results, even unconsciously.
- Carefully identifying and eliminating error sources further ensures that the experiment tests only the hypothesis.
- Assessing the importance of any remaining errors, especially random ones, indicates how much confidence one can have in the results.
- Replicating an experiment minimizes the chances that its outcome is due simply to mistakes on the part of the experimenter.

This chapter has provided an introduction to the scientific method and experimentation. You will find further experimental techniques and data analyses throughout the remainder of this book. It is essential that you practice these techniques and analyses, whether in assigned laboratory exercises or in some other way. Proficiency in experimentation (as in most other things) comes only through practice!

This completes your introduction to design, theory, and empirical analysis. This part of the book has concentrated on what these methods of inquiry are, keeping the algorithms used to demonstrate them simple. In the next part of the book, you will learn to apply all three methods to more complex algorithms. In the next chapter, we look at algorithms that can make decisions.

4.11 FURTHER READING

Through most of the history of computer science, the care and rigor that computer scientists devote to experimentation has lagged behind that devoted to theory and design. However, some branches of computer science (for example, parallel computing) have relatively strong experimental traditions—see, for instance:

L. Crowl, "How to Measure, Present, and Compare Parallel Performance," *IEEE Distributed and Parallel Technology*, Spring 1994.

Other branches have weak experimental traditions—articles that critique, comment on, or exemplify experimentation in general computer science appear in:

Computer, May 1998.

There are movements to make experimentation more prominent in computer science, for instance:

The ACM Journal of Experimental Algorithmics, http://www.jea.acm.org/.

A great deal has been published on the philosophy and history of the scientific method, both for specialists and for the general public. One example that we find helpful and accessible is:

J. Losee, *A Historical Introduction to the Philosophy of Science* (2nd edition), Oxford University Press, 1980.

You can delve deeper into the mathematical analysis of error with any statistics text. For example, we find the following to be very thorough and accessible:

D. Moore and G. McCabe, *Introduction to the Practice of Statistics* (2nd Edition), W. H. Freeman and Company, 1993.

Program Design

Much of the introductory section side-stepped issues created by control structures, treating computing as if algorithms were mostly sequential in nature. Sequential algorithms offer little of interest for either theoretical or empirical analysis. We now begin the exploration of algorithms containing non-sequential control structures, starting with the conditional or if statement and then considering recursion and iteration. These control structures enable more powerful and interesting algorithms, ones that can respond to a variety of situations, including those not known precisely at the time of program writing. Unfortunately, their inclusion often complicates the analysis of the algorithm. For example, the use of conditionals creates multiple paths through an algorithm. When constructing a proof of correctness or estimating execution time, the programmer must account for such multiple paths. We will also see that in spite of the complexities introduced, the tools we develop for the formal analysis can actually help the program-design process. After exploring the major control structures, we will tie it all together with some extended examples.

5 Conditionals

On the surface, the simplest control structure is probably the *conditional*, or "if" statement. But simple as it may be, the conditional introduces the need for new evaluation tools. We will begin the study of the conditional with a brief review of the terminology. Then we'll introduce the needed tools for evaluation and explore the implications for programming.

5.1 REVIEW OF TERMINOLOGY

Every conditional has the same standard structure. Although the appearance of and terminology for the parts of that structure vary widely across programming languages, every conditional has the following three parts:

- A *test*, which is a Boolean expression
- An *action* that is executed when the test is true
- An *alternative action* that is executed when the test is false (may be empty)

Test

The test can be any question that has a true/false (yes/no) answer—and is describable within the computing language. Although the most familiar tests involve arithmetic comparisons, any true-false question is legal, including true/false value-producing methods, non-numeric comparisons, and more complicated combinations of questions.

Action and Alternative Action

Each conditional has two (possibly empty) sets of actions to be executed depending on the result of the test. The action is executed if the test is true, and the alternative is executed when the test is false. Because some languages (although, not Java) explicitly introduce the action with the word then, the action is often referred to as the "then clause." Similarly, the alternative action is often called the "else clause." Each clause can contain zero or more steps, possibly including other control structures. When the clause is empty, we say it is *null*. (This use of the word "null" is closely related to—but slightly different from—the Java term `null`. Empty collections turn out to be a powerful concept in computer science—and not surprisingly, will reappear often in this text). Null action (or alternate) clauses usually have no visual representation. For example, we could represent an empty else clause explicitly as:

```
if (foo > 1)
    { foo = 0 }     // then clause
else { };           // empty else clause
```

but usually simplify it and write just:

```
if (foo > 1)
    { foo = 0 }     // then clause
```

We will see, when we attempt to analyze conditional statements, that it is often useful to treat the else clause as if it is always there—even when empty.

Exercises

5.1.   Rewrite the following pseudocode segments using an explicitly stated null series of actions:

(a) `if (value > 3)`
        `print value;`

(b) `if (not integer (value))`
        `value = Math.round(value);`

5.2 THE TEST: BOOLEAN EXPRESSIONS

Although many programmers usually think of the test portion of a conditional statement as if it were restricted to questions with a simple yes/no answer, we often want to ask more complicated questions. For example, suppose you are purchasing a computer. Suppose you feel that anything under $100 would almost certainly be of poor quality. On the other hand, you know you can't afford more than $1000. In that case, selecting a computer price really requires two questions:

Is the price greater than $100?

and:

Is the price less than $1000?

Boolean logic (named for the English mathematician George Boole (1815–1864) who formalized and developed the system) is a system for representing and combining values in a world where there are only two values—normally the two logical values *true* and *false*. In the current example, we see an equivalent set: the possible answers to yes/no questions. Boolean logic is exactly the tool needed. Although a very simple system—it allows just two values and has only three basic operators—it just may be the most fundamental tool of all computer science. Boolean logic and Boolean algebra enable us to build very complicated descriptions by combining just the two logical values. Note that Boolean logic is also called *propositional logic*, since it combines propositions.

5.2.1 Conjunction (And)

The two questions above can be restated as a single true/false question:

Is the answer to both of the following questions true?:
    Is the price above $100?
and
    Is the price below $1000?

The logical operator *and*, does exactly that: it combines two questions into one question. Historically, we refer not to the question form ("Is the price above $100?") but to the *proposition*, or proposed statement of fact (e.g., "the price is above $100"). The proposition is true or false if the answer to the corresponding question is "yes" or "no" respectively. A combination of the general form:

$$proposition_1 \text{ And } proposition_2 \tag{5.1}$$

is true if both propositions are true, taken individually. It is false in all other cases: if $proposition_1$ is false; if $proposition_2$ is false; or if they are both false. The behavior of the "And" operation can be summarized as a table of results, called a *truth table*:

proposition₁	*proposition₂*	*proposition₁* **And** *proposition₂*
false	false	false
false	true	false
true	false	false
true	true	true

Notice that the first two columns contain every possible combination of two true/false values. The third column shows the result of combining two propositions using the "And" operator. If the two propositions:

The price is above $100.

and:

The price is below $1000.

are individually true (as in the fourth row of the table) then the last column of the table shows that

(*The price is above $100*) And (*The price is below $1000*)

is also true. But if either proposition is false (e.g., if the price is too low or if it is too high) then the conjunction is false. It may appear to some that the second and third rows are redundant since both show that the combination of one true and one false value is false. We will see later cases in which it is important to be specific about which proposition—the first or the second—is true and which is false.

For discussions, the formal name *conjunction* is often less confusing than the equivalent logical operator "And." For example: "Conjunction is a Boolean operator." is likely to cause less confusion than "And is a Boolean operator." For that reason, the formal terms are used throughout the remainder of this text. For similar reasons, mathematicians use formal symbols to indicate conjunction. For better or worse, there is more than one standard mathematical symbol or notation.

Symbol	Example
and	*proposition₁* and *proposition₂*
$\wedge$	$proposition_1 \wedge proposition_2$
$\cdot$	$proposition_1 \cdot proposition_2$

The $\wedge$ is probably more common in mathematics (and will be used here), but $\cdot$ is more common in computer engineering.

Conjunction in Programming Languages

Every language provides a built-in operator exactly equivalent to logical conjunction. Most languages use an infix notation analogous to the basic arithmetic operators. The symbol used varies from language to language, but in Java, it is the infix:

&&, and an expression involving && can appear anywhere a true/false value can appear such as:

```
if (p && q) {...
```

On the other hand, few (if any) languages provide a direct representation of mathematical ranges such as $1 > n \geq K$. But conjunction allows us to represent the combination in a program as:

```
if ((1 > n) && (n >= K)) {...
```

In general, it is best to explicitly delimit all logical expressions with parentheses, as in this example. This both avoids issues of precedence between the operators (which in some languages produces very surprising results) and makes your intentions clearer and easier to read.

5.2.2 Disjunction (Or)

Logical values can be combined in other fundamental ways, such as:

$proposition_1$

or

$proposition_2$

For example, the criteria for admission to a campus event might be:

Is the person a student?

or

Does the person have a university activity card?

This is equivalent to:

Are either of the following propositions true?:
   The person is a student.
   The person has a university activity card.

Propositions of the form:

$$proposition_1 \text{ Or } proposition_2 \qquad (5.2)$$

are called *disjunctions*. Notice that the disjunction is an *inclusive disjunction*: the result is true if the first alternative is true, or if the second alternative is true—and also if both are true. This contrasts slightly with common English usage. For example, to most students, the question, "Do you want to study or go to the party?" implies that you expect them to do one or the other, but not both. The Inclusive Or, as used in computer science, however, allows for the possibility that a student would do both,[1] as summarized in the truth table:

proposition₁	*proposition₂*	*proposition₁* Or *proposition₂*
false	false	false
false	true	true
true	false	true
true	true	true

Our original question can be restated again as:

Is at least one of the following true?
    The person is a student.
or
    The person has a university activity card.

Disjunction, like conjunction, is usually represented using infix notation, and again there are many different mathematical symbols with identical meanings:

Symbol	Example
or	*proposition₁* or *proposition₂*
$\vee$	*proposition₁* $\vee$ *proposition₂*
+	*proposition₁* + *proposition₂*

We will use the most common symbol, $\vee$, when speaking mathematically. In Java, the operator, || represents disjunction, as in:

---

[1] This treatment of "or" as a yes/no question is a frequent source of obnoxious jokes and responses from computer scientists, who when asked, "Would you like chicken or roast beef for dinner?" might be all too likely to answer "yes," rather than a more informative "chicken."

```
if (p || q) { ...
```

Disjunction and Numeric Expressions

Notice that you have already encountered an implicit use of disjunction: the numeric expressions "$a \geq b$" (math) or "a >= b" (programming languages) really represent the disjunction: $(a > b)$ Or $(a = b)$.

Exclusive Or

Another form of "or" used in computer science, the *exclusive or*, is roughly equivalent to the common English usage: one or the other but not both. The *exclusive or* has its own important uses in computer science, and its own symbols. It is summarized by the truth table:

*proposition*₁	*proposition*₂	*proposition*₁ Exclusive-Or *proposition*₂
false	false	false
false	true	true
true	false	true
true	true	false

Although the inclusive or is much more common, exclusive or has its own uses and important characteristics. We will see later (Exercise 5.11) that you can construct an exclusive or from other basic operators.

5.2.3 Negation (Not)

One more logical operator, *negation* or *not*, completes the basic set. Negation is just the logical inverse, or *complement*, of a proposition. It provides a way of asking:

> *Is the following proposition false?*
>   *any proposition*

For example:

> *Are you a nonstudent?*

is roughly

> *Is it false that*
>   *You are a student?*

If a proposition is true, its negation is false; if the proposition is false, its negation is true, as shown by the truth table:

proposition	**Not** *proposition*
false	true
true	false

Infix notation is not really an option for negation: it is always a *unary* (only one operand), never a binary, operation. Conventionally, we use *prefix* notations meaning simply that the operator (not) goes before the operand (proposition). As with conjunction and disjunction, negation also has several standard and concise mathematical representations:

Symbol	Example
not	not *proposition*
$\neg$	$\neg proposition$
$-$	$-proposition$
$\sim$	$\sim proposition$
(overbar)	$\overline{proposition}$

We will use "$\neg$" in the remainder of this text. Java uses the operator "!" to negate a proposition, as in:

```
if (!(a = b)) { ...
```

Negation, like the other operators, can be applied to any logical expression

```
!(a > b) or !(p && q).
```

Arithmetic Operations and Negation

Negating common arithmetic expression often generates alternative but equivalent ways of representing the same relationship. The familiar "not equals," (a != b) means the same thing as !(a == b). It is not the case that: a == b. Negation could be combined with arithmetic operands such as "greater than or equal to." The expression "greater than or equal to" includes all cases except "less than." Thus, A >= B has the same meaning as !(A < B). If *A* is less than *B*, then it is not greater than or equal to *B*, and vice versa.

5.2.4 Implication

Although it is not usually considered a primitive operation, *implication* is an important Boolean operator because it corresponds directly to the logical proof technique modus ponens (and incidentally to the conditional statement). We say that $p \Rightarrow q$ (pronounced: p implies q) if whenever p is true, q is also true. From that definition, it is easy to build (most of) the truth table:

p	q	$p \Rightarrow q$
false	false	true
false	true	true
true	false	false
true	true	true

The only part that seems strange to some students is the first line. The definition seems to specify the value of q only if the *antecedent*, p, is true; it says nothing about q (the *consequent*) when p is false. Since the definition of implication doesn't restrict the consequent when the antecedent is false, we say it is true no matter what the value of the consequent. Java does not provide a symbol for the implication operator, but you will see in the next section that you can easily construct it whenever you need it.

5.2.5 Boolean Expressions and Java

Boolean expressions in Java are not restricted to the test of a conditional. They can be used any place a `boolean` value may be used. For example, suppose you wanted to write a method `inARow` to determine if three integers were in strictly increasing order. You might be tempted to write the code as:

```java
static boolean inARow(int first, int second, int third) {
    if ((first < second) && (second < third))
        return true;
    else return false;
}
```

But you could just as legally return the value of the Boolean expression as in:

```java
static boolean inARow(int first, int second, int third) {
    return (first < second) && (second < third);
}
```

The result of a Boolean operation could also be assigned to a boolean variable:

```
p = q || r;
```

Exercises

5.2. Write a segment of legal Java code containing expressions equivalent to $p \wedge q$, $p \vee q$, and $\neg p$.

5.3. Write a program to build the truth tables for conjunction, disjunction, and negation. The program should actually calculate the last column.

5.4. A truth table showing a combination of two arguments has $4 = 2^2$ rows. How many rows must a table representing a function of three arguments have? Four arguments?

5.5. How many distinct three-column, four-value truth tables are there involving two propositions? Create the ones you have not seen yet.

5.6. Write Java code to test if a given value is outside of a specific range of values.

5.7. Build a truth table for the imaginary Boolean operator: "the first, but not the second."

5.3 BOOLEAN ALGEBRA

Once you can combine two logical values with one Boolean operation, it is only a small extension to imagine the need for combining many propositions into a single complex expression. For example, suppose you wanted to move a robot to the northeast corner of its world. You might want to ask if it could currently take a productive step toward that goal. This would mean that it is OK to move and also that the robot is facing an appropriate direction. Since there are two appropriate directions, this involves both a conjunction (direction and mobility) and a disjunction (two directions). Fortunately, since the results of a Boolean operation are always Boolean values, one Boolean operator can be applied to the results of another. We call an expression in which one operation is applied to another a *complex Boolean expression*. Stated formally, the above query is:

OkToMove

and   (5.3)

(*heading* = NORTH or *heading* = EAST)

Notice the use of parentheses to distinguish this question from the similar, but entirely distinct:

$$(OkToMove \text{ and } heading = \text{NORTH})$$

$$\text{or} \tag{5.4}$$

$$heading = \text{EAST}$$

which seems to succeed if either it is OK to move north, or if the robot is facing east (without regard to mobility). The desired query is a conjunction of two propositions, the second of which is itself a disjunction. It is good programming practice to use parentheses to clarify complex Boolean expressions.

In general, Boolean expressions can be arbitrarily complex. In order to write correct code—and to reason about that code—we must be able to interpret these more complex expressions. One simple tool for understanding a given complex proposition is creating a visual representation as a structure[2] built up from simpler logical operations as in Figure 5.1. Unfortunately, such structures can get large quickly. More importantly, although they provide a good intuitive view of the expression, they provide no tools for interpretation. A formal set of rules for constructing complicated expressions from simpler ones (or breaking down complicated ones into simpler ones) is called *Boolean algebra*.

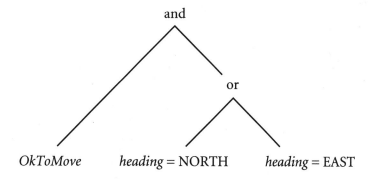

FIGURE 5.1 A visualization of a complex conditional.

---

[2] Similar structures will appear again in Chapter 13.

5.3.1 Complex Truth Tables

Like the basic Boolean operators, complex expressions can also be represented as truth tables, which can be built from the simpler truth tables:

OkToMove	heading = NORTH	heading = EAST	heading = NORTH ∨ heading = EAST	OkToMove ∧ (heading = NORTH) ∨ (heading = EAST)
false	false	false	false	false
false	false	true	true	false
false	true	false	true	false
false	true	true	true	false
true	false	false	false	false
true	false	true	true	true
true	true	false	true	true
true	true	true	true	true

The left-hand columns show all possible combinations of values for the three basic propositions. The right-hand columns were built by substituting those values into the truth table for the primary operator heading that column. The fourth column shows the result of looking for either direction. The last column is the conjunction of that result with the mobility test. Notice that the truth table now requires eight rows to account for all possible tests. Collectively, the values in the rightmost column show the exact situations under which the action would be executed.

5.3.2 Truth Tables as a Proof Technique

A truth table can actually be thought of as a compact form of proof. Since the left columns describe every possible set of circumstances, a complex proposition can be shown to be universally true if every line yields a value of true in the appropriate column. Thus, for example, we could "prove" that two expressions (p or q) and (q or p) are equivalent:

p	q	p or q	q or p	Same?
false	false	false	false	true
false	true	true	true	true
true	false	true	true	true
true	true	true	true	true

In this case the final column shows that the two expressions have the same value in every case. A logical expression that is necessarily true in all circumstances is called a *tautology*. A truth table containing all possibilities can be used to demonstrate tautologies—and serves as an informal proof of the equivalence of the expressions.

Suppose that we wanted to demonstrate that a given statement will always be executed. And suppose we have:

```
q = !p;
```

and later:

```
if (p || q)
    { /* some action */ };
```

Because q is currently related to p (as its negation), not all circumstances are possible. We might summarize possibilities for the test as:

p	q [not p]	p or q
false	false (can't happen)	(can't happen)
false	true	true
true	false	true
true	true (can't happen)	(can't happen)

showing that the conditional is always true in any possible circumstance. Thus, the test is always true and the action will always be executed.

Law of the Excluded Middle

Consider, for example, the law of the excluded middle, which states in effect that in Boolean logic there is no "maybe," that any proposition and its negation cover all possibilities. Put logically, this is:

THEOREM: For any proposition p, either p or its negation must be true. $\square$

p	$\neg p$	$p \vee \neg p$
false	true	true
true	false	true

Simple as this law is, it forms the basis for an important tool for mathematical proof, as we will see in Section 5.4.

5.3.3 Manipulating Boolean Expressions

Boolean algebra actually refers not only to the rules for combining simple comparisons into more complex comparisons, but to a set of rules for manipulating Boolean expressions to create new and equivalent expressions. For example, one of the simplest rules, the rule of double negation is:

$$\neg(\neg p) \approx p \qquad\qquad (5.5)$$

where "$\approx$" is read as "is equivalent to" and means that the two expressions must always have the same logical value. When two expressions are equivalent, one can be substituted for the other without changing the meaning. Thus, an expression containing a double negation can always be replaced by the expression with no negations (notice how this reflects the rule of English grammar that says "never use a double negative"). A simple truth table shows the *validity* of the double negation rule:

Double Negation

p	$\neg p$	$\neg(\neg p)$	$p \approx \neg(\neg p)$
true	false	true	true
false	true	false	true

The final column shows the equivalence of the first column and the third column (which was derived as the negation of the second). The two expressions are therefore equivalent. Since two equivalent expressions will always have the same value, one can be substituted freely for the other. This has several implications for the design process. Most obviously, it allows a programmer to substitute simpler expressions for equivalent—but more complex—expressions. Thus, the conditional:

```
if (!(a != b))
    { ...
```

can be replaced with the much more obvious:

```
if (a == b)
    { ...
```

Such substitutions result in code that is marginally faster, but much more importantly, they result in code that is easier to understand.

Familiarity with some other basic rules can help you simplify your logical expressions. Proof of most of these rules is left as exercises.

Simplification

Any repeated expression in a conjunction or disjunction can be reduced by removing the redundant operand:

$$(p \wedge p) \approx p \tag{5.6}$$

p	$p \wedge p$	$p \approx (p \wedge p)$
true	true	true
false	false	true

$$(p \vee p) \approx p \tag{5.7}$$

Proofs of this and most remaining rules are left to exercises.

Commutative Laws

Conjunction and disjunction are *commutative*: the two propositions can be written in either order:

$$(p \vee q) \approx (q \vee p)$$
$$(p \wedge q) \approx (q \wedge p) \tag{5.8}$$

We have already seen a truth table proof of the commutative rule for disjunction, here is the proof for conjunction:

p	q	$p \wedge q$	$q \wedge p$	$(p \wedge q) \approx (q \wedge p)$
false	false	false	false	true
false	true	false	false	true
true	false	false	false	true
true	true	true	true	true

Associative Laws:

When combining multiple disjunctions or multiple conjunctions, the parentheses make no difference; when the operations are the same, they can be evaluated in any order.

$$(p \wedge (q \wedge r)) \approx ((p \wedge q) \wedge r)$$
$$(p \vee (q \vee r)) \approx ((p \vee q) \vee r) \tag{5.9}$$

Vacuous Cases:

When one proposition has a constant Boolean value, the expression can always be reduced, by removing one operand:

$$(p \vee \text{true}) \approx \text{true}$$
$$(p \vee \text{false}) \approx p$$
$$(p \wedge \text{true}) \approx p$$
$$(p \wedge \text{false}) \approx \text{false} \tag{5.10}$$

de Morgan's Law:[3]

For evaluating the negation of a conjunction or disjunction:

$$\neg (p \vee q) \approx (\neg p) \wedge (\neg q)$$
$$\neg (p \wedge q) \approx (\neg p) \vee (\neg q) \tag{5.11}$$

Distributive Laws

For combining disjunctions with conjunctions:

$$(p \vee (q \wedge r)) \approx (p \vee q) \wedge (p \vee r)$$
$$(p \wedge (q \vee r)) \approx (p \wedge q) \vee (p \wedge r) \tag{5.12}$$

In each case, p, q, and r may be any Boolean expression. The last two of these rules (de Morgan's law and the distributive law) are both the hardest to see and the most important. Notice that for any complex Boolean expression, one or more of the above laws will apply. Thus, every complex expression has more than one representation. The programmer can use these rules to find the simplest, most readable, or most appropriate expression.

---

[3] After Augustus de Morgan (1806–1871), a British mathematician and logician who helped lay the foundations for modern logic. Notice that he was a contemporary of George Boole.

Applying the Rules

To see how these rules can help you write simpler code, suppose a programmer had generated the following code (it's a bit convoluted, but that sometimes happens after several rounds of debugging):

```
if (((robbie.colorOfTile() == java.awt.Color.red) &&
    (robbie.heading() == Robot.NORTH)) ||
   ((robbie.heading() == Robot.EAST) &&
    (robbie.colorOfTile() == java.awt.Color.red))) { ...
```

Notice that the test has the general form:

$$(p \wedge q) \vee (r \wedge p) \tag{5.13}$$

which, by applying the commutative rule, can be rewritten as:

$$(p \wedge q) \vee (p \wedge r) \tag{5.14}$$

and then applying the distributive law yields:

$$(p \wedge (q \vee r)) \tag{5.15}$$

which means the final code could be written more simply as:

```
if ((robbie.colorOfTile() == java.awt.Color.red) &&
   ((robbie.heading() == Robot.NORTH) ||
    robbie.heading() == Robot.EAST)){ ...
```

This is only one line shorter, but the intent is much clearer.

Exercises

5.8. Prove the associative law and vacuous case rules by creating the appropriate truth tables.

5.9. Prove de Morgan's law and the distributive laws rules by creating the appropriate truth tables.

5.10. Build a truth table to show that you can construct implication from negation and disjunction.

5.11. Build a truth table to show that you can construct exclusive or from disjunction and conjunction.

5.12. For the remaining two-variable truth tables in Exercise 5.5, create each from the basic Boolean operators.

5.13. Prove that $A \geq B$ is actually the negation of $(A < B)$.

5.14. Prove that $A \leq B$ is actually the negation of $(A > B)$.

5.15. The eight-line truth table in Section 5.3.1 seems to imply that there are three possible combinations of Boolean values for the question. How many are there really? Explain the difference.

5.4 CORRECTNESS: PROOF BY CASE

The downside of using conditionals is that they may make proofs of correctness more difficult. Since some actions may or may not be executed, assertions about the state of the world following a conditional are more difficult to prove. An addition tool—*proof by case*—will help.

5.4.1 Separation of Cases

One essential part of any proof is the statement of the assumptions. The body of the proof almost always makes use of these assumptions. Unfortunately, not all results can be proved from the assumptions in a straightforward manner—or perhaps the result is actually independent of the assumptions. In fact, many theorems need to be proved for two distinct cases: when some assumption or condition is true, and when that assumption is false. Conditional statements generate exactly such a situation. Figure 5.2 represents the classic proof by modus ponens. But any proof of correctness when conditionals are involved must be valid if the given conditional action is executed and also valid if it is not executed. Thus, proofs involving conditionals are essentially the same as in Figure 5.2 with one small added twist: essentially, we divide the possible situations into separate (usually two) groups or *cases*—typically those that satisfy some key assumption and those that do not. Then we separately prove the result for each case, as in Figure 5.3. Since the cases cover all possibilities, and the result has been shown for each case, the result must be true for any possible situation. It is not necessary to be able to describe all examples—only to be sure that the cases cover all possibilities. The law of the excluded middle assures that any assumption and its negation will indeed cover all possibilities. For example, suppose you wanted to show that all human children grew up to be adult humans. You could start by noting that children are either boys or girls. Then show that little boys grow up to be men (male adult humans) and that little girls grow up to be women (female adult humans). Since the two cases cover all possibilities and you proved the desired result for each case, you have shown the theorem to always be true.

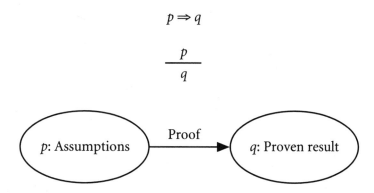

FIGURE 5.2   General proof technique.

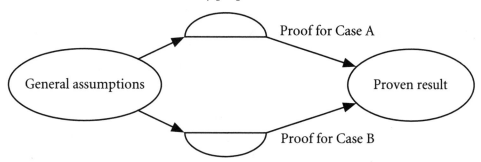

FIGURE 5.3   Proof by case.

For a slightly more practical example, consider a more formal proof of the rule of double negation:

THEOREM: $p \approx \neg(\neg p)$. $\square$

PROOF: Consider the two cases: p is true, and p is not true.

> **Case 1:** Assume p is true. Then $\neg p$ is false and $\neg(\neg p)$ must be ($\neg$false), that is, true. So when p is true, $\neg(\neg p)$ is also true.
>
> **Case 2:** Assume p is false. Then $\neg p$ is true and $\neg(\neg p)$ must be ($\neg$true), that is, false. So when p is false, $\neg(\neg p)$ is also false.

Since p and $\neg(\neg p)$ were the same in each possible case, they must always be the same. ∎

Proof by case may also entail more than two cases. Suppose that you wanted to show that the square of any number is positive:

THEOREM: The square of any number, N is greater than or equal to zero. ☐

PROOF: The sign of the product of two numbers depends on the signs of the two multiplicands. Since N may be any number, it may be positive, negative, or zero. Consider the three cases:

Case (a): Suppose that $N > 0$. Then $N^2 = N \times N$, the product of two positive numbers is positive. Therefore, N^2 is greater than zero.

Case (b): Now suppose that $N < 0$. Then N is negative. The product of two negative numbers is positive. So N^2 is again positive and greater than zero.

Case (c): Finally, suppose $N = 0$. In that case, $N^2 = 0 \times 0 = 0$.

Since the proposition holds for each of the three possible cases, the theorem is proved: the square of N is always greater than or equal to 0. ∎

You may already be thinking that proof by case will be a very useful tool for proving results about a computer program involving conditionals. For example, suppose you have a robot that paints the tile surface it walks on. At some point in the program, it may be necessary to prove the assertion:

The tile that the robot is currently standing on is painted red.

Consider the statement:

```
if (robbie.colorOfTile() != java.awt.Color.red)
    robbie.paint(java.awt.Color.red);
```

Now we can prove the above assertion as a postcondition of the conditional statement:

ASSERTION: A postcondition for this conditional statement is: "The tile that the robot is currently standing on is painted red." ☐

PROOF: Either the tile was initially red or it was not. So consider the two cases separately:

Case 1: The tile is already red. Then the conditional statement is not executed. No action occurred; so the tile must still be red.

Case 2: The tile is not red prior to the conditional. In this case, the test will be true, so the conditional action will be executed. The conditional action clearly makes the tile red. Thus, it is red after executing the conditional.

Since the tile is red in either of the two possible cases, it must indeed be red after the conditional statement. ∎

Finally, consider an example that might not be quite so obvious. Most computer languages recognize two forms of number: real (or floating) numbers and integers. In many languages, an attempt to assign a real value to an integer location results in a truncated number. For example, in Java:

```
integerLocation = (int) 3.2;
```

and

```
integerLocation = (int) 3.8;
```

would each result in `integerLocation` containing the value: 3. For many human endeavors however, the rounded result (e.g., 3.8 rounds to 4) is more useful. It would be nice to have a method that rounds any number to the nearest integer value. Java, in fact, provides such a method, but many languages do not.

CLAIM: The method:

```
static int myRound(float realValue) {
    return (int) (realValue + 0.5);
}
```

will successfully round a floating point number `realValue` to the nearest integer. □

PROOF: By design, the `myRound` method returns:

$$\lfloor realValue + 0.5 \rfloor \tag{5.16}$$

where the notation $\lfloor realValue \rfloor$ is read "floor of *realValue*" and is the result of truncating off the noninteger portion of the number. Divide the problem into two cases based on the fractional part of *realValue*. The fractional part can be defined as:

$$fractionalPart = realValue - \lfloor realValue \rfloor$$
$$realValue = fractionalPart + \lfloor realValue \rfloor \qquad (5.17)$$

Consider the cases where *fractionalPart* is less than 0.5, greater than 0.5, or equal to 0.5.

Case 1: Suppose the fractional part of *realValue* is less than 0.5. Then:

$$fractionalPart + 0.5 < 0.5 + 0.5 = 1 \qquad (5.18)$$

and:

$$realValue + 0.5 = fractionalPart + \lfloor realValue \rfloor + 0.5 < \lfloor realValue \rfloor + 1 \quad (5.19)$$

$$\lfloor realValue + 0.5 \rfloor < \lfloor realValue \rfloor + 1 \qquad (5.20)$$

So the resulting integer value is strictly less than $1 + \lfloor realValue \rfloor$ and therefore must be just $\lfloor realValue \rfloor$. That is, it rounded down, which was what was needed.

Case 2: If the fractional part of *realValue* is greater than 0.5. Then:

$$1 < fractionalPart + 0.5 < 2 \qquad (5.21)$$

So:

$$1 < realValue - \lfloor realValue \rfloor + 0.5 < 2 \qquad (5.22)$$

$$1 + \lfloor realValue \rfloor < realValue + 0.5 < 2 + \lfloor realValue \rfloor \qquad (5.23)$$

$$1 + \lfloor realValue \rfloor \leq \lfloor realValue + 0.5 \rfloor < 2 + \lfloor realValue \rfloor \qquad (5.24)$$

That is, the result is an integer greater than the truncated value, but no more than 1 greater: the method rounded up, which is again the desired case.

Case 3: If the fractional part is 0.5. In that case, the method should round up.

$$fractionalPart + 0.5 = 1 \qquad (5.25)$$

So:

$$\lfloor realValue + 0.5 \rfloor = \lfloor realValue + 1 \rfloor \qquad (5.26)$$

which is the needed value.

Thus, the formula yields the rounded value in all possible cases. ∎

Exercises

5.16. Prove the laws from Exercise 5.8, this time by means of a formal proof by case.

5.17. Prove the laws from Exercise 5.9 again, this time by means of a formal proof by case.

5.18. Prove by case that the method inARow returns the needed results.

5.5 PERFORMANCE ANALYSIS AND CONDITIONALS

Conditionals add a new level of complication to the execution-time analysis of algorithms. In earlier chapters, we suggested you could get a good estimate of running time by simply counting the number of steps you expect an algorithm to take. But a conditional action may or may not be executed—often depending on information that may not be available in advance. How, then, are we to analyze the execution time for an algorithm containing conditionals?

5.5.1 Expanding the Definition of Execution Time

Consider an algorithm of the form:

> *action*$_1$
> *if test*
>   *then action*$_2$
> *action*$_3$.

If, as we have assumed previously, each action requires approximately the same amount of time (one time unit), then this algorithm will run either 2 or 3 time units depending on the value of the *test*. The whole point of conditionals was to enable us to create algorithms that work under variable or unknown situations, so they are important structures, but in general they make it impossible to say exactly how long an algorithm will run.

Average Time

One obvious solution might be to find the average execution time. Unfortunately, any calculation of average execution time analysis is likely to require more information than we have available at this point. It might appear at first glance that the average execution time should be 2.5 units (just the simple average of the two possible cases). However, that assumes that the two cases are equally likely. True average time analysis requires some knowledge of the expected conditions existing at the time of the test. For an extreme example, consider the test:

> *If today is the first of the month*
> *   then display the calendar.*

Clearly, any empirically measured average execution time for this algorithm is likely to be less than the simple average of the two possibilities, possibly about 2 and 1/30 time units. Unfortunately, even knowing the relative likelihood of the two possibilities is often nontrivial. If the above example were part of a bill-paying program, the odds of it being executed on the first of the month might be much higher.

5.5.2 Bounding Execution Time

As an alternative to average time, we can *bound* the execution time:

- ■ Upper bound: The algorithm will require *no more* than 3 time units.
- ■ Lower bound: It will require *at least* 2 units of time.

We call these two bounds the *worst-case* and *best-case* times, respectively. Worst-case analysis behaves as if the slower of the two conditional actions is an unconditional action (and that for all practical purposes, the other alternative doesn't even exist). The best-case and worst-case times are easier to obtain, and together they actually tell us much about the expected execution time. One simple approach to calculating the worst-case time (or at least an upper bound) might be:

> *For each conditional*
> *   Ignore the faster alternative*
> *   Ignore the test itself*
> *   (leaving only the slower alternatives)*
> *Count the steps as in previous sections.*

In conditionals with a null action, since the null action must necessarily be as fast or faster than the other alternative, this reduces to:

Ignore the tests and always perform the conditional actions.

Best case analysis assumes exactly the opposite—that the test always leads the algorithm to the faster choice (or at least a lower bound).

> *For each conditional*
> *   Ignore the slower alternative*
> *   Ignore the test*
> *Count the steps as in previous sections.*

Why Worst-Case Analysis?

It may seem surprising that worst case analysis is perhaps the most common form of performance analysis in computer science. It is not so important to know that an algorithm may sometimes (or even usually) run very fast as it is to know that it will never run very slowly. Worst-case analysis can be paraphrased as:

> *What is the longest time that we will ever have to wait for this algorithm to complete — (even if this bad case doesn't happen very often)?*

If you were getting your computer repaired you might want to know:

> *What is the absolute maximum that this repair might cost me?*

This is worst-case analysis. Consider a system that controls a life and death situation, perhaps a program that controls part of an aircraft. The designer of the control needs to know:

> *How long from the time the pilot activates the button until the plane responds?*

If the time might *ever* be too long for safety, another mechanism will be needed. Notice that in this case, it doesn't matter if the system works fast enough on average or even "almost always" performs well enough. If it doesn't work fast enough every single time, it is not good enough. For reasons such as this, worst case has historically been the dominate form of theoretical performance analysis in computer science.

5.5.3   What the Best Case and Worst Case Can Tell Us

In reality, worst-case and best-case analysis taken together often tell us most of what we need to know. The worst case provides an upper bound on possible execution times, and the best case, a lower bound. The expected execution time must fall between these two bounds. If the two bounds are sufficiently close, computer scientists will often feel they have enough information. Taken together, they tell us that the program will run at least some minimum time, but will definitely be completed by some definite, but potentially long, time.

Problem Size

Execution time analysis describes execution time as a function of the size of the problem. Unfortunately, "size of the problem" is a slippery term at best: in most of the Robot class examples, size was measured as a function of the size of the floor or the distance the robot will traverse. The most common measure in computer science expresses execution time as a function of the size of the input. In other examples in this text (in programs without conditionals), the number of statements has served as a proxy for the size: the more statements, the longer the execution time. Incorporation of conditional statements creates a complication because some statements may or may not be executed. If we draw a graph of the relevant values above we get something like Figure 5.4.

In general, we have:

$$\textit{number of statements} \geq \textit{worst case} \geq \textit{expected time} \geq \textit{best case} \geq 0 \qquad (5.27)$$

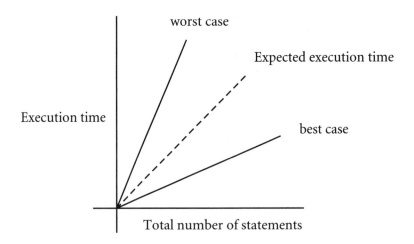

FIGURE 5.4 Bounded execution time.

Thus, if the number of conditionals is small, the worst case and best case will not be far apart, and the two values will bind the expected result fairly tightly. For example, if there are 1000 statements and 100 are conditionals, then we have:

$$1000 \geq \text{expected time} \geq 900 \text{ time units} \tag{5.28}$$

Even in more extreme cases, the time is bounded reasonably well. Suppose there are $2n$ statements, and half of them (n) were conditional actions. Then the expected run time would be proportional to n (which, conveniently, is proportional to $2n$). Thus, the expected run time is proportional to either n or $2n$. We will see later (Chapter 9) that both of these are not only appropriate, but equivalent, measures. In fact, the difference between n and $2n$, or any other difference attributable solely to conditional statements, is insignificant compared to the differences introduced by other control structures. Finally, remember that although this shows us the relationship between best, worst, and expected times, in computer science, expected execution time is seldom (if ever) actually measured in terms of the number of statements. In general, we will prefer to describe the expected execution time in terms of the problem rather than the lines of code.

Exercises

5.19. The calculations in this section were unusually simple. Use the following algorithm as an example to show where the suggested calculation can go wrong.

> *If this is the first day of the month*
> *   then action$_1$.*
> *If this is the second day of the month*
> *   then action$_2$.*
> ...
> *If this is the thirty-first day of the month*
> *   then action$_{31}$.*

5.20. Exercise 5.19 provides a counter-example to the above claim (that execution time is approximated by the number of statements). Give a better worst case execution time for that algorithm.

5.21. Suppose a program has 500 statements of which 200 are conditionals. Give a statement of best and worst time measures for each.

5.6 BOOLEAN ALGEBRA AS A PROGRAM DESIGN TOOL

The use of conditional statements helps create better or more flexible programs. The use of Boolean algebra in the design process can be a valuable tool for interpreting and evaluating those programs by helping to assure their accuracy.

5.6.1 Robust Algorithms: the Power of Conditionals

Every method has its set of preconditions. And as you've seen, it is the client program's responsibility to ensure that the preconditions are satisfied prior to invoking the method. We say that a method that accomplishes the same goal with fewer preconditions is more *robust*. Robust programs are often more desirable since they both result in fewer run-time errors and require less preventive action on the part of the client. Conditional statements can be used to create more robust algorithms. Consider the Robot method, move, which may be abstractly summarized as:

> *move()*
> *Precondition: There is an empty tile in front of the robot.*
> *Action: The robot moves to the tile directly in front of it.*
> *Postcondition: The robot is on that tile.*

An alternative action, safeMove, could be defined as:

```
// in class ExtendedRobot ...
public void safeMove() {
    if (this.okToMove())
        this.move();
    }
}
```

safeMove has no preconditions and is therefore more robust. Since the method move is invoked only if the test indicates it is OK to do so, the use of the conditional action actually reduces the need for explicitly stated preconditions. Rather than stating a precondition to a procedure, the procedure can perform a test equivalent to the precondition and either perform the action or not, as appropriate. On the other hand, the method's postconditions are less specific:

> *Either the robot is on the next tile or it is on the same tile facing a wall.*

and therefore it may be more difficult to prove statements about the status of the world after this method is invoked. In practice, robust methods will report back unexpected or problematic conditions.

This technique can be generalized and used throughout your programs. Suppose you had a method with a precondition that the robot face north. The following code could be included as a precondition-free method.

```
// in class ExtendedRobot ...
public void faceNorth() {
    if (this.heading() != NORTH)
        this.turnLeft();
    if (this.heading() != NORTH)
        this.turnLeft();
    if (this.heading() != NORTH)
        this.turnLeft();
}
```

Clearly, as long as the robot is not facing north, it keeps turning to the left—up to a maximum of three turns. Since there are only four possible directions, it will have to face north within three moves. And once it does, it will make no further moves. Notice that this example reduces the preconditions without reducing what can be said about the postconditions. A second method can thus become more robust by employing faceNorth to remove a precondition.

5.6.2 Construction of Boolean Methods

All languages provide some number of built-in Boolean operators. But most programmers will discover that they need to ask far more questions than are easily answered with this limited set. This is especially true in cases involving user-created classes.

Creating explicit functions to perform Boolean comparisons provides several advantages—the same advantages provided in general by other abstractions. Just as:

```
if (score <= 5) { ...
```

is easier to read than:

```
if ((score < 5) || (score = 5)) { ...
```

it is also easier to read:

```
// used with some class Clothing
if (shirt.warmColor()) { ...
```

than the equivalent:

```
if (shirt.color() = "red" ||
    shirt.color() = "orange" ||
    shirt.color() = "yellow") { ...
```

Boolean abstraction also guarantees that the proper format for a question need only be worked out once; thereafter, it can simply be reused. This saves time and reduces errors. So build and use Boolean methods liberally—but use some caution.

Avoid Side Effects

Boolean methods are intended to produce a value—a Boolean value. A side effect in a Boolean method can be dangerous indeed. And it can make debugging almost impossible. For example, suppose an ExtendedRobot class contained a Boolean method, okToWalk, which determined not just if the robot could move at all, but if it could traverse multiple tiles. Further suppose that it did so by asking the robot to take one step and then see if it was OK to move at least one more step:

```
// in class ExtendedRobot ...
public boolean okToWalk() {
    if (!this.okToMove()) {
        return false;
    }
    else {
        this.move();
        return this.okToMove();
    }
}
```

This test will find the correct result. Unfortunately, it sometimes moves the robot—even when the result is false. In debugging any code that uses this method, it is virtually impossible to tell by inspection where the robot will be after the test. In general, good programming practices say that you should avoid combining side effects and value-producing code in a single method. Boolean methods are designed to return a value, and they are often used in the test part of conditional statements. It is especially important to avoid side effects.

Conditionals, Java and Side Effects

In some languages (including Java), the importance of avoiding side effects is amplified by the language's own rules. In Java, the evaluation of conditionals takes shortcuts based on the simplification rules. If the test is a conjunction and the first proposition is false, the simplification rules say we can ignore the second proposition. In order to create slightly faster code, Java does exactly that: in a conjunction, if the first test is false, Java skips the second test. This means there are even more circumstances in which the status of the world is hard to predict after a conditional, That is, the status depends not just on the action steps and the side effects of the test methods, but also on the order of the test methods. Thus, in Java code containing Boolean methods with side effects, the commutative rule may not strictly apply. That is, if either of the methods foo or bar produce side effects:

```
if (foo() && bar()) { ...
```

may not be strictly equivalent to:

```
if (bar() && (foo()) { ...
```

The rules of Boolean algebra suggest that, by extension, more complex tests may also yield hard-to-interpret results when side effects are involved. And of course the same is true for disjunction. Avoiding side effects in your Boolean methods assures that such interaction will not cause problems.

5.6.3 Interpreting Nested Conditionals

In a conditional statement, the action part can be any action allowable within the system—including another conditional. How do we interpret a complex statement such as:

> If $test_1$
>> then if $test_2$
>>> then $action_1$
>>> otherwise $action_2$
>> otherwise if $test_3$
>>> then $action_3$
>>> otherwise $action_4$.

The third conditional is evaluated only if the first test is false. Therefore, $action_3$ is performed only if $test_1$ is false and $test_3$ is true. When the tests are themselves complex, that can become quite confusing. We can use Boolean algebra to make sure we understand those conditions and perhaps even improve on their form. For example, consider a more concrete code segment. We know that $action_3$ will be taken if and only if $test_1$ is false and $test_3$ is true. That is if

$$(\neg test_1) \wedge test_3 \tag{5.29}$$

is true. If $test_1$ is $(p \vee q)$ and $test_2$ is $(r \wedge s)$, this becomes:

$$\neg(p \vee q) \wedge (r \wedge s) \tag{5.30}$$

which by de Morgan's rule is:

$$(\neg p \wedge \neg q) \wedge (r \wedge s) \tag{5.31}$$

which is, by the associative rule, simply the conjunction of four distinct propositions:

$$(\neg p) \wedge (\neg q) \wedge r \wedge s \tag{5.32}$$

Since this is a simple list of discrete propositions, it is hopefully easier to visualize.

5.6.4 Finding Design Flaws

Boolean algebra can often help the designer find flaws in the logic of complex conditionals. By building a table of legal values for Boolean expressions, you can ensure there is a path through the code corresponding to each possible combination. Suppose you built a table and discovered that no path corresponded to $(p \vee \neg q \wedge r)$, yet there is no logical reason why that combination can't exist. That tells you that you need to provide for another explicit set of circumstances. Remember that if the combination might exist, someday it will. If the program doesn't account for that circumstance, it will eventually fail. Always make sure a program accounts for every combination of possible Boolean values. Building a truth table-like structure will help you keep track of those and recognize exactly when a given path will be taken.

Avoiding Redundant Comparisons to "True"

Boolean methods, such as okToMove, return Boolean values—exactly what is needed for conditional tests. It is not necessary to explicitly ask if the test returned a true value. The semantics of the conditional statement itself ask this question. Asking if okToMove is exactly the same as asking if it was a true value, which can be seen simply by building a simple truth table:

okToMove	okToMove = true	okToMove ≈ (okToMove = true)
false	false	true
true	true	true

Thus:

```
if (this.okToMove() == true) { ...
```

yields exactly the same result as:

```
if (this.okToMove()) { ...
```

but is more verbose. Most experienced programmers also find the latter version easier to understand.

Other Redundant Tests

Less dangerous, but still important, are code segments that are more complex than they need to be. Consider the following algorithm designed to calculate letter grades (familiar to many students from earlier courses):

> *If (score > 90)*
>   *then grade = "A"*
>   *otherwise if score ≤ 90 and score > 80*
>   *then grade = "B"*
>   *otherwise if score ≤ 80 and score > 70 ...*

Applying an analysis similar to the previous section indicates that a "B" grade will be assigned only if both:

$$(score > 90) \tag{5.33}$$

is false and:

$$(score \leq 90 \wedge score > 80) \tag{5.34}$$

is true. Formally, these expressions are equivalent to:

$$\neg(score > 90) \wedge (score \leq 90 \wedge score > 80) \tag{5.35}$$

$$(score \leq 90) \wedge (score \leq 90 \wedge score > 80) \tag{5.36}$$

$$(score \leq 90 \wedge score \leq 90) \wedge (score > 80) \tag{5.37}$$

But this repeats the condition $(score \leq 90)$ twice. Thus, by the vacuous case rules, this is really just:

$$(score \leq 90) \wedge (score > 80) \tag{5.38}$$

which, in turn, shows that was not necessary to reiterate the comparison to 90 in the second test. The simplified algorithm becomes:

> If $(score > 90)$
>   then grade = "A"
>   otherwise if score > 80
>   then grade = "B"
>   otherwise if score > 70 …

Make Redundant Questions Explicit

Another common stylistic problem for many programmers is the inclusion of redundant questions. Such redundant questions come in at least two forms, the repeated question:

> If $(total = 3)$
>   then $action_1$.
> If $(total = 3)$
>   then $action_2$.

rather than the simpler:

> If $(total = 3)$
>   then $action_1$,
> $action_2$.

and the unneeded alternative question:

> If $(total = 3)$
>   then $action_1$.
> If $(total \neq 3)$
>   then $action_2$.

rather than:

If (total = 3)
    then action₁,
    else action₂.

Redundant questions are not as clear as their simpler equivalents and are more likely to produce errors. This is particularly true when the two tests are written in different—but equivalent—forms, in which it might not even be obvious to the programmer that the tests are repetitious. A truth table sort of evaluation will help detect these circumstances. Consider the impact of making a minor correction in these examples such as changing the desired value of *total* from 3 to 4. The single-question form guarantees that when you make the change, the conditions for both *action₁* and *action₂* are changed at the same time. Finally, notice that repeated questions interact very poorly with methods containing side effects. If the test has side effects, then a repetition of the same test may yield different results.

5.6.5 Establishing Test Data

Once a program is designed, the task of course isn't over—you still need to test it. When testing a program containing conditionals, it is essential that you exercise every code segment within the program. Alternatively stated, you must be sure to test all possible conditional values for any Boolean test. By describing each nested conditional in terms of the basic conditions for which it is true, you can establish clear criteria for data that will force the program through that path.

Exercises

5.22. Build a method that tests whether a numeric value is greater than, less than, or equal to zero. Use the function in an algorithm that prints out the words "greater than", "less than", or "equal". Make sure there are no redundant tests.

5.23. Build a function to compute a letter grade for the traditional A, B, C, D, F system. Make sure there are no redundant tests.

5.24. Create a boolean method isRightTriangle, which accepts three numbers and returns true if the three values form a legal combination for the sides of a right triangle.

5.25. Create a method faceSouth that does not use turnLeft.

5.26. Assume SmallRoomRobot is a subclass of Robot, with a room limited to six tiles by six tiles in size. Create a method goToEdge that takes a SmallRoomRobot to the edge of the room. The procedure should have no preconditions with respect to the robot's location within the room or direction it is facing. (Do not use iteration or recursion—that's for another chapter).

5.27. Prove (by case) the needed postcondition for `goToEdge`.

5.28. Make a method `faceRoom` which assures that the robot faces into a room (hint: it must have its back to the wall).

5.29. Use proof by case to prove the needed postconditions for the previously discussed methods:

■ `faceNorth`
■ `faceRoom`
■ `goToEdge`

5.30. Evaluate the conditions under which `action3` will be executed:

```
if ((c <d) || (a!=b))
    { /* action1 */}
else if ((e < f) && (b==a))
        { /* action2 */}
        else { /* action3 */}
```

5.31. Suppose a program contains the following conditionals:

$If(a \lor b)$
    then $action_1$.
$If(a \land c)$
    then $action_2$
    else if $(a \land d)$
        then $action_3$
        else $action_4$.

List the logical combinations that must be accounted for in the test data.

5.7 EMPIRICAL MEASURE AND CONDITIONAL STATEMENTS

Although theoretical analysis of performance of programs containing conditional statements is usually conducted in terms of the worst case analysis, it may be difficult to find the worst case running time via experimental methods. Straightforward empirical studies to find an unknown time usually generate something more like an average execution time. In general, negative results are difficult (or even impossible) to demonstrate empirically. There is no empirical way to show that a program will *never* run slower (or faster) than a given time. At best, you can show that within the context of some large number of trials, the program was never *observed* to run slower (or faster) than the given time. This does not mean that it can't run faster the next time you try. But empirical results do generate a very good measure of average expected execution time. The more trials, the more reliable the estimate for the average will be. Recall that a scientific theory is accepted though an accumulation of evidence. But even this assumes proper selection of data.

It is also possible to confirm empirically a worst-case running time predicted through theoretical means. Thus, if you derive an expected run time and know the circumstances that should generate the worst results, that expectation can be compared to theoretical results to confirm the theory (we will see examples of this later in the text).

Empirical study of conditionals introduces an additional source of variation. You have already seen that empirical measure may be subject to errors in measurement—systematic or otherwise. In the case of conditionals, different trials with different data can result in legitimately different measures. That is, sometimes a program may use more time because it actually performs a different number of steps. It is also possible that no single instance of the program will ever yield execution time equal to the average execution time—or the best or worst case. Recall the example in the previous section in which a program might run either two or three steps, but the average was 2.5 units—a time which would never actually occur. This is not a problem, just a distinction between the average of several instances and any single instance. After a sufficiently large number of trials, the average observed time should become a useful predictor of future execution time. Unfortunately, no number of trials will ever show the exact upper and lower bounds.

Data Set Selection

Not only must we perform a significant number of trials, it is also essential that we have a representative sample within those trials. For example, suppose a program contained a step something like:

> *If N is odd*
> > *then perform some action foo.*

If we tested this algorithm using a random collection of integers, we should get a good measure, but if we used a collection of prime numbers as values of *N*, we would get a very skewed result since almost all prime numbers are odd. Thus, it is essential that in testing execution time, any sample data must be truly representative of the set of possible or likely values. The same applies to worst-case analysis.

For testing programs with conditionals for correctness, we must also ensure that we exercise the program under every possible set of conditions. Unfortunately, this may not be feasible in practice. A program with just 20 conditional statements could theoretically have some $2^{20} = 1$ million possible paths through the program. Since it is clearly impossible to create that many distinct tests, we need some guidelines for generating the appropriate set of empirical tests. In particular, data must be included to test every comparison—both the test and the possible actions. You can ignore a combination of conditionals only if you can demonstrate that one has no impact on the other—a task easier said than done. But the tools of this chapter can help with the selection:

- Try to create the extreme cases: those situations in which all (or most) conditionals yield true tests or false tests.
- For every conditional, include test data that yields both true and false values. It is impossible to generate every single combination of possibilities, but be sure to get every possibility in isolation.
- Use hierarchical diagrams to make sure that all possible paths are actually accounted for.
- Use Boolean logic to assure that your tests cover all possible cases.

Exercises

5.32. Consider the following algorithm:

> *For i between 1 and n, do:*
>   *If n is prime*
>   *perform some expensive action.*

Describe what happens if you test this algorithm for small n (say, less than 7). Large n (say, greater than 1000). What does this tell us about data set selection?

5.33. Describe appropriate data selection for the first of the month algorithm described in Section 5.5.1.

5.8 CONCLUDING REMARKS

The conditional or `if` statement is the first nonlinear control structure. On the one hand, it enables the creation of much more robust programs. But that power comes at a price: added complications in the theoretical or empirical analysis of the algorithms. Fortunately, the conditional statement itself provided insight into new tools for working with algorithms, notably Boolean algebra. Proof by case—which itself looks very much like a conditional statement—is an essential tool for proving things about any algorithm for which there may be multiple possible initial conditions. Most theoretical run-time analysis estimates worst case rather than average time, both because it is actually easier and because it is in many ways the more crucial measure. While conditionals forced the issue of worst-case analysis into view, it is with the remaining control structures that we will see truly significant differences.

5.9 FURTHER READING

For an original approach to logic and Boolean algebra that works heavily with the notion of equivalence and the idea that you can "do" logic by rewriting expressions to replace equivalents with equivalents, see:

David Gries and Fred Schneider, *A Logical Approach to Discrete Math*, Springer-Verlag, 1993.

6 Designing with Recursion

"A journey of a 1000 miles begins with a single step."

What does this familiar proverb have to do with computer science? There are two important messages in this proverb. The less exciting, but more commonly given, interpretation is:

"You gotta get started. If you don't take the first step, you'll never get there."

But there is a deeper and more fundamental message for our field:

"The first step is just one of many. The entire journey is made up of steps. After that first step, you will be closer to your goal. The remaining journey closely resembles the original—but it is shorter."

6.1 BASICS OF RECURSIVE THINKING

The proverb represents the basis for an important problem solving technique used throughout computer science: *recursion*. Recursion provides a tool for writing short solutions for large problems: reducing each problem to a similar—but smaller—one. In computer programming, recursion requires the use of a method as part of its own definition.

6.1.1 Stating the Problem Recursively

Let's examine the "1000 mile journey" problem. For the moment, assume that we know the route and that the problem is one of getting there at all. And let's reword the problem slightly. If the average step is 2.5 feet, then there are about 2000 steps to the mile, so:

"A journey of 2,000,000 steps begins with a single step."

That leaves a journey of 1,999,999 steps. We could amplify the proverb:

"A journey of 2,000,000 steps begins with a single step—leaving only 1,999,999 steps to go."

This may not sound like a major improvement, but the form of the improvement is essential, because it provides the clue for solving the remaining problem:

"A journey of 1,999,999 steps begins with a single step—leaving only 1,999,998 steps to go."

This problem is identical in *form* to the original—but just a bit smaller. If we kept the process up, we would create paraphrases with 1,999,997 steps, 1,999,996 steps, and so on. Eventually we must get to a final instruction:

"A journey of 1 step(s) begins with a single step—leaving only 0 steps to go."

If there are no steps to go we must be there! So the last step is actually:

"A journey of 0 step(s) is no journey at all."

In any finite problem, if we consistently reduce the size of the problem enough times we will eventually discover that there is nothing more to do to reach the goal.

At first glance, this description may appear to require 2,000,000 instructions—two million essentially identical instructions before reaching that last step. The set of instructions would be better if we can distill out and use the common part of those two million nearly identical instructions, perhaps something like:

"A journey of any number of steps begins with a single step—followed by a journey requiring one less step."

6.1.2 Restating in Computational Terms

Unfortunately, this last statement is not really an instruction—certainly not in the sense that we think of an instruction for computing. It is just a guide or template. But this guide can easily be translated into a pair of instructions:

Take one step.
Take all remaining steps.

This may not seem very satisfactory because it does not say how many steps are actually needed nor when to stop walking. In addition, it really doesn't explicitly say that the "remaining steps" should be taken in the same manner as the steps for the original problem. It is this essential assumption that provides a restatement of the algorithm as:

>*Take one step.*
>*Take all remaining steps—in the same manner.*

This can be formalized by naming that manner:

>*Algorithm takeJourney   [first attempt]*
>>*Take one step.*
>>*takeJourney—but one that is smaller.*

We must still formalize the idea of "smaller." Given the assumption that we are going in the right direction, we are guaranteed that the remaining distance will get smaller with each step—until we reach our destination. Finally, we need to specify how to recognize the destination. This is a second underlying—but essential—assumption. Even if we are traveling in the right direction, that direction will become the wrong direction if we pass the destination. We need to incorporate a way to recognize success into the algorithm description:

>*algorithm takeJourney   [second attempt]*
>>*If we are not yet at the destination*
>>>*then take one step,*
>>>>*takeJourney—but a smaller one.*
>>*(otherwise we must be at the destination, so stop).*

The algorithm specifies two possible situations—either we are at the destination or we are not—and describes what to do in either case. So far it does not specify how to take a step or how to recognize that we are there.

6.1.3 A Recursive Java Method

In programming terms, a recursive method asks the object to send itself a message to perform exactly the same method (but somehow smaller). To make the algorithm explicit, let's consider the analogous problem within the Robot class. In that case, one step is really moving one tile. And a robot's travel must stop when it reaches the wall. This discrete world makes things easier to specify: it can't go a thousand miles; only until it bumps into a wall. So let's design a method for moving a robot until it bumps into the wall.

Algorithm toTheWall
   If you can take a step
      Then take one step,
         keep moving
         otherwise (since you can't take a step, you must be at the destination).

Translating to Java from this point is straightforward:

```
// in class ExtendedRobot ...
public void toTheWall() {
   if (this.okToMove()) {
      this.move();
      this.toTheWall();
   }
   else {};
}¹
```

Equivalent syntaxes

Notice that the terminating step of toTheWall is simply a null else clause (called a *degenerate* step). It does make it clearer that this algorithm fits the general pattern for recursive methods. But since it doesn't actually do anything, most programmers just leave it out:

```
// in class ExtendedRobot ...
public void toTheWall() {
   if (this.okToMove()) {
      this.move();
      this.toTheWall();
   }
}
```

Suppose we wanted to make a robot face north. In Chapter 5 we saw that we could do that with a series of conditionals within a single method—turning the robot right until it faced the desired direction. Some may have felt that algorithm was a bit awkward because it asked three times if it was facing north—even if the robot

---

[1] Some, but not all, of the algorithms used as examples in this chapter may have a relatively simple straightforward iterative equivalent. Many students at this point may have considered those tried-and-true approaches first. We urge you to focus on the recursive versions: compare their visual and structural simplicity to the iterative versions. The recursive tool is very powerful and we will soon see many problems that do not have any obvious iterative approaches.

were initially facing that direction. A recursive algorithm for achieving the same
goal is:

If the robot is facing north
    then do nothing (because it has reached its goal).
    otherwise turn to the left and
        ask again.

Using the methods `turnLeft` and `heading` this translates to:

```
// in class ExtendedRobot ...
public void faceNorth() {
    if (this.heading() == NORTH)
        {}
    else {
        this.turnLeft();
        this.faceNorth();
    }
}
```

This algorithm actually has an identical structure as the first example—it only appears slightly different because the "then clause" rather then the "else clause" contains the null final step. It could easily be rewritten, with the clauses reversed as:

```
// in class ExtendedRobot ...
public void faceNorth() {
    if (this.heading() != NORTH) {
        this.turnLeft();
        this.faceNorth();
    }
}
```

And most programmers would probably write it this way. It just doesn't correspond
quite so obviously to the algorithm as originally written.

6.1.4 Recursion is Ubiquitous

Your English teacher probably told you never to define a word using itself in its
own definition. In spite of this, recursion and recursion-like definitions are actually
very common in the world. In fact, recursion can be used for almost any problem
or situation for which smaller versions of the problems can be found.

Songs

Many folk songs have an inherently recursive structure. Typically, each verse is defined in terms of the previous verse—sometimes getting longer (*There was an old lady who swallowed a fly*), sometimes shorter (*Row, Row, Row your Boat*), sometimes just different. But in each case, if we can do one verse, we can do later verses. One very familiar kid's camp song goes something like:

99 bottles of beer on the wall, 99 bottles of beer
If one of those bottles should happen to fall—98 bottles of beer on the wall.

Another 99 very similar verses follow (keeping young campers nicely busy). The final verse is sometimes sung:

No bottles of beer on the wall, no bottles of beer.
There's nothing left on top of the wall, no bottles of beer on the wall.

It would be easy (or at least straightforward) to write an algorithm for singing all of the verses. There are almost 100 verses, all but one of which look like:

Sing (someNumber) bottles of beer on the wall,
    (someNumber) bottles of beer.

A much better solution is a recursive method using the recursive principle: "Sing one verse and then sing the rest of the verses":

Algorithm singBottlesOnWall (someNumber)
    if someNumber is zero
        then   Sing: No bottles of beer on the wall,
                    no bottles of beer,
                Sing: There's nothing left on top of the wall,
                    no bottles of beer on the wall!
    otherwise
                Sing: (someNumber) bottles of beer on the wall,
                Sing: (someNumber) bottles of beer,
                Sing: if one of those bottles should happen to fall,
                Sing: (someNumber −1) bottles of beer on the wall,
                singBottlesOnWall (one fewer than someNumber).

We don't have quite all the tools we need to convert this example to Java, and the conversion of this example to Java is left to Exercise 6.7.

Games

Consider the childhood game of telegraph in which one child starts a message and each one passes it along to another. At the end, the final message is compared to the original. Usually there seems to be no connection between the two. It becomes apparent that big changes are accomplished a little bit at time. Instead of immediately comparing the big differences between the original and the final, we might try to describe the general connection between two tellings, perhaps:

>*New telling = small variation on previous.*

The overall process then might be:

>*Algorithm telegraph*
>>*If some child has not yet heard the story*
>>>*then make a small variation,*
>>>>*telegraph it to another.*

Looking ahead

Recursion appears in many other places—not surprisingly, you will meet several of those later in this text. In mathematics (where the equivalent term is called *induction*), both sets and functions are often defined recursively. We will see examples of those in the next section. In Chapter 11, we will see that classes can be defined recursively. We will see in several places (e.g., Chapter 10 and Chapter 13) that recursion can be used in astonishingly efficient algorithms. But we will also see in Chapter 15 that it can be used in equally astonishingly inefficient algorithms.

Exercises

6.1.   Rewrite the *toTheWall* algorithm (not a Java method)—with a non-degenerate trivial step (i.e., even the trivial step should have at least one instruction for the robot). Why won't this work in the `Robot` class?

6.2.   Write a Java method to make a robot face south.

6.3.   Write a method `circleNorth` that makes a robot walk "around" so that it takes three steps forward and turns left—until it is facing north. If it is facing west at the start, it will walk a full perimeter of a square. Otherwise it will walk less than the full square.

6.4.   Write a Java method that causes the robot to draw a diagonal line until it runs into a wall similar to Figure 6.1. You may assume that it will first find a wall on the north-south rather than east-west step.

FIGURE 6.1 A robot-painted diagonal line.

6.5.   The song "Row row row your boat" is often sung in a repeating manner—but each time through the song you sing one less word. Write an algorithm for singing the entire song through all 19 verses. There are only 18 words; why are there 19 verses?

6.6.   Sketch algorithms for "There Was an Old Lady Who Swallowed a Fly" and "The 12 Days of Christmas" (but sing from the twelfth day to the first).

6.2 CONTROLLING RECURSION: INDICES

Not every problem has an explicit built-in terminating test such as okToMove. In fact, most recursive algorithms differ from those discussed so far in a fundamental way. Instead of a simple test of final success, but no measure of how large a problem remains, most recursive algorithms are defined in terms requiring solving a similar *but smaller* problem. Often it is known precisely how much smaller the new problem is and how far away the goal is.

6.2.1 Simple Indices

In the original (proverb) version of the takeJourney problem, each step of the journey implicitly contained a measure of how many steps remained. At each stage, the algorithm had access to that remaining distance. The journey ended when that number fell to zero. The Java methods in the previous section instead rely on tests explicitly provided by the Robot class that could tell a robot when the goal was reached (e.g., okToMove). To generalize the concept for other situations, we need a way to state the recursive problem to ensure that the remaining problem does indeed get smaller at each recursive step—and to determine when it is sufficiently small so that we can declare success. Consider the original travel problem. If we know the distance of the current journey, then a smaller one is easy to describe explicitly. The smaller problem may always be stated in terms of the original problem: it is one step less. The measure of the smaller problem may be passed as a parameter to the method—just as a parameter can be passed to any other method. So we can define a new version of *takeJourney*:

> *Algorithm takeJourney (distance)*   *[third attempt]*
>   *If you can take a step*
>   *then take one step,*
>   *takeJourney (distance −1).*

At each stage, the algorithm takes a step and then takes a journey one step shorter. In a computer program, that distance is simply passed as a parameter within the message:

```
// in class ExtendedRobot ...
public void takeJourney(int distance) {
    if (distance > 0) {
        this.move();
        this.takeJourney(distance - 1);
    }
}
```

At each stage, if you read the algorithm using the current value of distance, it would read just like the original statements. This algorithm is not only explicit; it always assures a smaller problem because a parameter distance−1 is necessarily less than distance. We call this controlling factor the *index*. Usually (but not always) the index is the parameter. The terminating condition for a recursive method with an index is generally stated in terms of that index—typically, "Has the index been reduced to zero?" The index not only serves as part of the terminating condition, it provides a sort of measure of "how much remains to be solved?" When the robot is at the destination, the distance remaining to travel must be zero steps. If the journey's distance = 0, it should simply stop. And in fact, if the test fails (i.e., if the distance is zero), then the algorithm does nothing.

    Consider another example. Suppose you wanted a generic method to print out a series of repeating characters, perhaps to build one row in a histogram. The method *printStars*(5) might print out:

    *****

Printing 5—or any other positive number of—stars is just:

> *Print one star.*
> *Print n−1 stars.*

Thus, the algorithm can be:

Algorithm printStars(n):
   If n is positive
      Then   print (""),*
              printStars(n−1).

Or in Java, just:

```java
static void printStars(int n) {
    if (n > 0) {
        System.out.print("*");
        printStars(n-1);
    }
}
```

Now further suppose for some reason you wished to print out a series of lines of decreasing length:

```
*****
****
***
**
*
```

Notice that each line contains one less character than the previous line. Use that fact to create a general description:

Print a line of n characters
Do the same for n−1 characters (and fewer) characters

This leads to the algorithm:

Algorithm seriesOfStars(n)
   if n is positive
   then   printStars(n),
          seriesOfStars(n−1).

Yes, a recursive algorithm can use any legal command—including invoking another recursive algorithm. The complexity of the resulting overall process is totally hidden. Creating the Java method for this algorithm is left as an exercise (in fact, most future examples without code appear as exercises). That's all there is to it. You can now even create a Java method equivalent to the sing algorithm. The trivial steps are a little longer than previous examples (e.g., it requires two lines to write out the last verse). But the general structure is identical (see Exercise 6.7).

6.2.2 General Principles for Indices

When exploring other possible recursive algorithms, it is helpful to keep a few general guidelines concerning the index in mind.

Terminating at Zero

Many new programmers instinctively try to build an index that counts down to 1, rather than 0. The traveling robot example could indeed have been written that way:

```
// in class ExtendedRobot ...
public void takeJourney(int distance) {
    if (distance > 1) {
        this.move();
        this.takeJourney(distance - 1);
    }
    else this.move();
}
```

But this form is not quite as intuitive. Consider the equivalent pseudocode:

> *If there are more than one step to go*
> > *then   take one step,*
> > > *continue on the journey.*
> > *Otherwise   take one step and stop.*

In this case, the test wouldn't really be one of, "Is the goal satisfied?" but one of, "Will one more step satisfy the goal?" Generally, recursive problems are best stated in terms of, "Is it completely done?" When the index reaches zero, there is usually nothing left to be done, making for a deceptively simple algorithm. Interestingly, such a test will almost always make the algorithm's mathematical analysis simpler too.

Coordination of Index and Terminating Condition

Consider one variant of the earlier `faceNorth` method that starts with a turn:

```
// in class ExtendedRobot ...
public void faceNorth() {
    this.turnLeft();
    if (this.heading() != NORTH) {
        this.turnLeft();
        this.faceNorth();
    }
}
```

This attempt has a problem: when this method starts, the terminating condition may already be true, yet the robot turns anyway—making the terminating condition no longer true. Since the robot turns before making the test, it will not be facing north at the first test and will actually start turning. The test will not be true again until it has turned all the way around. A similar situation could occur in any recursive algorithm. For another example, consider an algorithm intended to take a sequence of characters and print out as many "*"s as there were characters:

```
static void replaceWithStars(String inString) {
    System.out.print("*");
    if (inString.length() >= 1) {
        System.out.print("*");
        replaceWithStars(inString.substring(1));
    }
}
```

Unfortunately, this prints out a star with every recursion—whether or not there is any input. In general, if it is at all possible that the goal state has already been reached at the time the method is used, the trivial step should always be null.

Always Smaller

It may seem like the index could be increasing, with the problem terminating when the index became sufficiently large. Thus, *printStars* might conceivably look like:

Algorithm printStars   *[not quite right]*
     If we have not yet reached the upper limit
         then   *print one star,*
              printStars (one larger).

This would work fine if we always wanted to print exactly five stars. But the algorithm was supposed to print any number of stars. As written, the recursive calls have no way of knowing when they have reached the target. For an upward progressing recursion to work, the parameters would have to include both the current position and the target:

> *Algorithm printStars(currentNumber, maxSize)*   *[not very practical]*
> *If currentNumber < maxSize*
> *then   print one star,*
> *printStars (currentNumber+1, maxSize).*

and its initial reference would look something like:

> *printStars(1, 5)*

The index virtually always counts down toward zero, or some equivalent measure such as the empty string.

6.2.3 Non-numeric Indices

The index need not be numeric; it can be any measurable quantity that can signal the end of recursion. For example, a method that processes the letters of the alphabet might work from *z* down to *a*. Recursion is very often used for string manipulation, in which case either the string itself or the length of the string can be used as the index: each recursion works on a shorter string. For example, one might make an algorithm to print a string omitting any blank spaces:

> *Algorithm removeSpaces(theString)*
> *if theString is not empty*
> *then   if the first character is not a space*
> *then print the first character*
> *remove spaces from the rest of the string.*

The string itself acts as the index indicating how much problem is left to be solved. Each invocation works with a smaller string until it finds the empty string. In Java:

```
static void removeSpaces(String theString) {
    if (theString.length() >= 1) {
        if (theString.charAt(0) != ' ')
            System.out.print(theString.charAt(0));
        removeSpaces(theString.substring(1));
    }
}
```

Notice that even though the index is a string, the algorithm terminates when there was nothing left to process.

Exercises

6.7. The algorithm *singBottlesOnWall* needed an index to work completely. Write a Java method to "sing" (that is, print out) all 100 verses of "99 Bottles of Beer."

6.8. Write a method that causes the robot to move twice as many squares as its parameter calls for.

6.9. Create and use together the Java methods `printStars` and `seriesOfStars`, based on the corresponding algorithms.

6.10. Write a method that prints the letters of the alphabet.

6.11. Write an algorithm that accepts a `StringBuffer` and replaces each occurrence of space with a star.

6.12. Write a method that prints the digits from 9 down to 1.

6.3 VALUE-PRODUCING RECURSION

The examples thus far all achieve their results through side-effects. Many problems require algorithms that produce values. Fortunately the concept of recursion is flexible enough to handle these situations just as it handles side effects. Recursive algorithms can be value-producing, just like any nonrecursive algorithm. Suppose that instead of printing n stars as in `printStars` you wanted to create a string of n stars. The solution is almost identical to `printStars`: the central notion is that n stars is just 1 star followed by $(n-1)$ stars. We could write the algorithm as:

> *Algorithm stringOfStars*
>   *if n is zero*
>   *then   return the empty string (that is: no stars)*
>   *otherwise   return one star followed by (n−1) stars.*

In Java that is simply:

```java
static String stringOfStars(int n) {
    if (n <= 0)
        return "";
    else
        return "*" + stringOfStars(n-1);
}
```

Notice that the logic is identical to the side-effect-producing algorithms we have looked at. However, because value-producing methods must always return a value, it is always necessary to take an action for both possible results of the test. But notice that returning the empty string is about as close to doing nothing as you can get.

6.3.1 Inductive Definitions in Mathematics

Many students will recognize recursion as a concept they have seen in mathematics. Actually, value-producing recursive algorithms bear a striking resemblance to a mathematical concept you may have already seen: the inductive definition. Consider the classic mathematical definition of factorial.

$$factorial(n) = \begin{cases} 1 & \text{if } n \leq 1 \\ n \times factorial(n-1) & \text{if } n > 1 \end{cases} \tag{6.1}$$

The definition defines factorial for one small base case, and then defines all larger cases in terms of smaller cases. Thus:

$$
\begin{aligned}
factorial(1) &= 1 \\
factorial(2) &= 2 \times factorial(1) = 2 \times 1 = 2 \\
factorial(3) &= 3 \times factorial(2) = 3 \times 2 = 6 \\
factorial(4) &= 4 \times factorial(3) = 24
\end{aligned}
\tag{6.2}
$$

and so on.

Similarly, Peano's axioms[2] are a set of definitions of arithmetic operators using a very small set of primitive operators. His primitive objects are just 0 and 1, and his primitive operations are *successor* $(n+1)$ and *predecessor* $(n-1)$. He defined the set of natural numbers[3] as:

0, 1 are natural numbers.
If n is a natural number
   then the successor of n is also a natural number.

So 0 and 1 are natural numbers by the first rule. Two is a natural number by applying the second rule to 1. Three is a natural number by applying it to 2 and so on. Peano also defined addition in terms of *successor* and *predecessor*:

---

[2] After their creator, Giuseppe Peano, (1858–1932), a pioneer in mathematical logic and the axiomatization of mathematics which helped make computing possible.
[3] A natural number is an integer greater than or equal to 0: 0, 1, 2, 3, etc.

$$a+b = \begin{cases} a & \text{if } b = 0 \\ successor(a + predecessor(b)) & \text{if } b > 0 \end{cases} \tag{6.3}$$

Thus:

$$0+0 = 0$$
$$1+0 = 1$$
$$2+0 = 2 \tag{6.4}$$

by the first rule and:

$$1+1 = (1+0)+1 = 2$$
$$2+1 = (2+0)+1 = 3$$
$$2+2 = (2+1)+1 = 4 \tag{6.5}$$

by the second rule.

6.3.2 Converting a Mathematical Definition to a Method

Actually, value-producing recursive algorithms are almost identical to inductive definitions. In fact, creating a value-producing recursive algorithm may require little more than the writing down of the inductive definition.

Consider factorial again. The definition from Equation 6.1 is repeated here:

$$factorial(n) = \begin{cases} 1 & \text{if } n \leq 1 \\ n \times factorial(n-1) & \text{if } n > 1 \end{cases} \tag{6.6}$$

We can first simply rearrange the parts into an algorithm statement:

Algorithm factorial(n)
   if n less than or equal to 1
      then the answer is 1
      otherwise the answer is: $n \times factorial(n-1)$.

It is easy to see that this algorithm is a straightforward piece-by-piece rewriting of the inductive definition: every piece of the algorithm comes directly from the mathematical definition. The Java method for factorial can be derived just as easily from the algorithm:

```
//method for class Calculator
static int factorial(int  n) {
    if (n <= 1)
        return 1;
    else return n * factorial(n - 1);
}
```

Each component of the definition—and essentially nothing else—appears in the method. It is not uncommon for value-producing recursive algorithms to flow just as directly from the original definition of the needed result. Any mathematical function that can be defined inductively can be similarly translated into a recursive method. This transforms the problem from one of writing methods to solve problems to one of just defining the problem or the mathematical function.

The same approach will work for any inductively defined mathematical functions such as summation:

$$\sum_{i=1}^{n} i = \begin{cases} 1 & \text{if } n = 1 \\ n + \sum_{i=1}^{n-1} i & \text{if } n > 1 \end{cases} \tag{6.7}$$

becomes:

```
//method for class Calculator
static int sum(int  n)  {
    if (n <= 1)
        return 1;
    else return n +  sum(n - 1);
}
```

And it gets better: this example extends directly—almost template-like—to any other summation equation. Thus, the sum of squares:

$$\sum_{i=1}^{n} i^2 = \begin{cases} 0 & \text{if } n = 0 \\ n^2 + \sum_{i=1}^{n-1} i^2 & \text{if } n > 0 \end{cases} \tag{6.8}$$

becomes:

```
//method for class Calculator
static int sumSquares(int  n)  {
   if (n <= 0)
      return 0;
   else return n*n + sumSquares(n - 1);
}
```

String Manipulation

Recursive value-producing methods are especially useful for processing strings, because they can build a new string from an old one. Recall that the basic string operations in Java are substring, length, charAt, and + (concatenation). The typical
string manipulation algorithm may be described as:

Take care of the first character.
Now take care of the rest of the string.

—exactly what we want. One could build a recursive method to double-up the individual characters of a string, e.g., transform "abc" into "aabbcc":

If the string is empty
   then do nothing (since twice an empty string is an empty string!)
   otherwise concatenate the first character with the first character and with
      double-up of all characters after the first.

That is, the string is the first character used twice followed by doubling up the remaining portion of the string:

double ("abc") = "a" + "a" + double ("bc")

Notice the simplicity created by avoiding temporary variables and loop counters.
The method could be written:

```
//method for class StringManipulator
static String doubleUp(String inString) {
   if (inString.length() < 1)
      return "";
   else return inString.substring(0,1)
      + inString.substring(0,1)
      + doubleUp(inString.substring(1));
}
```

Notice that we couldn't actually avoid writing the degenerate case altogether: even though there was no work to do when the string was empty, we still needed to return the empty string as a value.

Many basic string manipulation algorithms can be created in exactly the same way. For example, Java provides a method `replace` to replace all occurrences of a given character with another character (for example, `"abcabc".replace('b','x')` returns `axcaxc`). Not all languages provide such a method, and for that matter, someone had to write the Java method. You could build it yourself simply as:

> *Algorithm myReplace(oldCharacter newCharacter)*
> > *If the string is empty*
> > > *then return the empty string*
> > > *else if first character is oldCharacter*
> > > > *then return newCharacter + myReplace applied to rest of string*
> > > > *else return oldCharacter + myReplace applied to rest of string.*

6.3.3 The Index as Result

The previous examples start with a target, often one that is directly translatable into the number of recursive invocations that will be needed (e.g., the summation problems counted down taking the index from *n* to zero) and returned a result based on those recursions. Some problems do the opposite: they specify a goal state and ask how many times a given calculation needs to be performed in order to reach that state. These problems want to know the index. For example, suppose you needed a function to determine the length of a string. In general, it is one more than a shorter string:

> *Algorithm myLength(someString)*
> > *If the string is empty*
> > > *then return 0*
> > > *otherwise return 1 plus the length of the string without its first character.*

Consider the question: How many digits are required to print out a large number? The number 123,456,789 requires 9 digits.[4] Such a calculation might be needed by a

---

[4] The question of how many digits are required to represent a given value actually turns out to be of fundamental importance in computer science because it addresses the amount of information that any computer must store in order to represent a given value. You may recognize this question as essentially an integer–only equivalent of *logarithm*. The $\log_{10}$ of *n* is roughly the number of digits required to represent the number, or alternatively: if $y = \log_{10} n$ then $n = 10^y$. For the moment, think of "the numbers less than *n*." For example the numbers *less than* 1000 can be represented in 3 digits (and there are 1000 such numbers, if you include zero). Since computers are binary instruments, the log base 2 is particularly closely related to the computer representation of numbers.

program that needed to determine in advance how much space to allow for inserting a calculated value. One approach to this problem is to recurse, dividing the number by 10 until there is nothing to left to divide. The recursive algorithm becomes:

> *howManyDigits(n):*
>   *If n < 10*
>   *then return 1*
>   *otherwise return* $1 + howManyDigits(n/10)$.

Or in Java:

```
//in class Calculator ...
public static int howManyDigits(int someValue) {
    if (someValue < 10)
        return 1;
    else return 1 + howManyDigits(someValue / 10);
}
```

Notice that this effectively reverses the role of index and returned value: rather than being told how many times to repeat a calculation, the method performs a calculation and counts how many times it did so. More importantly, however, the recursive technique is structurally the same as always: the index clearly gets smaller with each recursive call and will eventually reach a base case: $n < 10$.

Envisioning Problems Recursively

Writing recursive code is very closely tied to finding ways to state the problem. For example, consider the following seemingly complex problem: many people would like to be millionaires. They could retire, travel, or do whatever they felt like. But what would it take for you to retire as a millionaire? It's surprising how easy it really is (well, at least how easy the computation is)! Let's start with a few assumptions:

- You will retire in about 40 years.
- You have the opportunity to buy bonds that pay 10% interest per year.[5]

---

[5] 10% is actually a rather high return for a bond—certainly higher than the historical average and considerably higher than the current rate. However, it is not high at all for a return on a stock investment—actually slightly under the historical average. This example uses bonds because they have consistent return, predictable from year to year. You could restate the problem in terms of "average return" without seriously affecting the validity of the argument.

And a question: How much must you invest (all at once) right now to eventually retire as a millionaire?

To see the solution, first remind yourself: "An investment of 40 years begins with a single year." The fact that you do not know yet how much to invest this year is not important—it is actually what we want to find. Imagine that you have solved the problem and have now moved 39 years through time. You now must become a millionaire in a single year. How much must you have this year, in order to have a million next year? This can easily be found from the equation:

$$nextYear = thisYear \times 1.1 \qquad (6.9)$$

Solving for *thisYear* gives:

$$thisYear = nextYear/1.1 \qquad (6.10)$$

In fact, this relationship is always true—even for the first year. It specifies the general situation. So we can write the general case:

If this is the last year
> *then you must now have $1,000,000*
> *otherwise you must now have* $nextYear/1.1$.

Writing this as a formal method gives:

```
static double mustHave(int yearsToGo, double goal)  {
    if (yearsToGo == 0)
        return goal;
    else return mustHave(yearsToGo-1,goal/1.1);
}
```

The example illustrates that you need not be able to envision all of the steps of the answer in order to start the process. In this case, we did not know how much we needed for the first year: that number was not calculated until all other years were calculated. (See Exercise 6.21).

Design Hint

Remember that a value-producing method must always produce a value. This means that both the base and the general case must produce and return values. Every recursive value-producing method must have at least *two separate* return points. A method of the form:

If n is 0

  then perform calculation (with no return statement)
  otherwise return (some value).

will fail because there is no value for the base case $n = 0$.

Exercises

6.13. Write Java code corresponding to the pseudocode for the algorithm *myReplace*. Compare your results to the Java method `replace`.

6.14. Write a method `myAdd` based on Peano's definition of addition. You may use the Java increment (++) and decrement (--) operators, but not the actual addition (+) and subtraction (-) operators.

6.15. Peano also defines multiplication as:

$$a \times b = \begin{cases} 0 & \text{if } b = 0 \\ a + (a \times (b-1)) & \text{if } b > 0 \end{cases} \tag{6.11}$$

Write this definition in the form of a recursive algorithm and then convert the algorithm to Java. First use the regular addition operator, and once that version is working, replace Java's addition operator with your own from Exercise 6.14.

6.16. The remaining definitions from Peano are:

Exponentiation:

$$a^b = \begin{cases} 1 & \text{if } b = 0 \\ a \times a^{b-1} & \text{if } b > 0 \end{cases} \tag{6.12}$$

Subtraction:

$$a - b = \begin{cases} a & \text{if } b = 0 \\ 0 - (b-a) & \text{if } b > a \\ pred(a - pred(b)) & \text{if } b < a \end{cases} \tag{6.13}$$

Division:

$$a/b = \begin{cases} 0 & \text{if } b > a \\ 1 + \dfrac{a-b}{b} & \text{if } b \le a \end{cases} \tag{6.14}$$

Write Java methods corresponding to each of these definitions.

6.17. Write Java methods that print the following mathematical series. Each method should accept one parameter indicating the starting or ending point.

- 1, 2, 3, 4, 5, 6, 7, 8, 9
- 9, 8, 7, 6, 5, 4, 3, 2, 1
- 0, 2, 4, 6, 8, 10
- 1, 2, 4, 8, 16, 32, 64, ...
- 64, 32, 16, 8, 4, 2, 1
- 1, 2, 4, 7, 11, 16, 22, 29 (the difference between any two numbers is one more than between the previous two)

6.18. Write a `boolean` method in Java that determines if there are any blank spaces in a string.

6.19. Write a `boolean` method in Java that determines if an integer is an exact power of two.

6.20. Write a Java method `Coder` that takes a string and codes it into a secret code. The secret code is simply: a becomes b, b becomes c, ... y becomes z and z becomes a. You may want to build a helper method to convert one single character.

6.21. Copy and run the method `mustHave` using the number of years from the time you expect to graduate until you turn 65.

6.22. Create a Java method corresponding to the algorithm *howManyDigits*.

6.4 ENSURING TERMINATION

When the index for recursion is an integer, it is usually easy to see that the terminating condition will indeed eventually hold: as long as the terminating condition is zero and the index is positive and counting downward, the terminating condition must eventually be reached, right? Well, *almost* right. In some cases, it is actually possible to step over or to pass the target termination point. For example, suppose you were creating an algorithm to print out the positive integers in decreasing order down from *n*:

> Algorithm printDown(n)
>   If n is 0
>   then   {do nothing we are done}
>   otherwise   print n
>   printDown(n−1)

Thus far, this works fine. Now suppose we wanted to print just the odd or just the even positive integers. We might try simply changing the algorithm to subtract 2 at each recursive call:

> *Algorithm printDown(n)*
> > *If n is 0*
> > *then*
> > *otherwise   print n,*
> > > *printDown(n − 2).*

That should work. Or does it? It looks fine and in fact works fine for even numbers. But what about odd numbers? Suppose the method were called with initial $n = 5$. The first call would print 5 and the next call 3, then 1 and then—oops— −1, followed by −3, −5 and so on forever. The algorithm stepped past its terminating condition of $n = 0$! The programmer must ensure that any algorithm that counts down by values greater than zero properly tests its terminating condition.

Failures to hit the terminating condition may not always be quite so obvious in advance. Consider the following attempt at a recursive algorithm that should stop when you run out of money:

> *Algorithm spendMoney:*
> > *If there is any money left*
> > > *then   purchase a new item,*
> > > > *spend some more money.*

So far so good, but suppose as you attempt to make this more concrete, the form might become:

> *spendMoney(totalFunds)*
> > *If totalFunds ≠ 0*
> > > *then   purchase a new item,*
> > > > *spendMoney(totalFunds minus purchase price (of the new item)).*

This is fine until the time comes that there are $3 left and the new item costs $4. The *spendMoney* algorithm hides the fact that the number to be subtracted from the total may vary. The problem with this algorithm occurs if it attempts to purchase an item that costs more than the remaining funds. But computationally there is a much larger problem: after purchasing that $4 object, the *totalFunds* remaining is −$1. Mathematically, that is just fine. Unfortunately, it is not *equal* to zero. And once the number becomes negative, no additional subtraction will ever result in the *totalFunds* becoming exactly zero. The algorithm will run forever (in reality it will run until there is an error).

There are two approaches to assuring that a recursive algorithm can't step over its terminating condition:

First, think about the logic of the problem to make sure that the decrement will hit the target exactly. For example, decrementing a positive value by one will necessarily hit zero eventually. Decrementing by two will hit zero if—and only if—the initial index is even. This approach is also a helpful technique for detecting logical errors. For example, in the *spendMoney* example, the observation that the algorithm could step over zero also reveals that the purchase price of the new item isn't taken into consideration in the decision of whether or not to make a purchase.

Second, you can almost always avoid the infinite recursion aspect of the problem by avoiding exact tests. Ask instead if you have exceeded the target. Don't ask simply:

Are the total funds exactly zero?

ask instead:

Are the funds exhausted?

or

Are the total funds less than or equal to zero?

In that case, even if you inadvertently step past the target, the method will still terminate.

The Step Must Make Progress

A similar problem can occur if somehow the increment becomes zero (for example, the purchase price above became zero; more likely, somehow a value just never got set). A string algorithm terminates when the string is empty. Each recursion should use a shorter string. The following incorrect method could result from a misunderstanding about how the length of strings is reported:

```
// won't work
static int badCounter(String inString) {
    System.out.println(inString);
    if (inString == "")
        return 0;
    else
```

```
        // intent: starting at zero, length
        // characters should get to position: length - 1
        return (1 + badCounter(inString.substring(0, inString.length())));
    }
```

In this case, inString never gets any smaller and the algorithm will never terminate.

Nonintegral Tests

If the step is not integral, it is possible to create a recursive algorithm with an index that does in fact get smaller with each invocation but that nonetheless never reaches the terminating target. The classic example for this situation is usually stated in terms of a man who is trying to cross a room. However, he does it by taking steps that are each $1/2$ of the remaining distance. Thus, to cross a 10-foot-wide room, he would take steps of 5 (half of 10), 2.5 (half of the remaining 5 ft.), 1.25 (half of 2.5), 0.6125, 0.30625, ... feet. Although the walker actually goes half way to the wall with every step, that still leaves the walker just as far from the target as the length of that step. The steps are indeed taking the walker closer to the goal but by ever decreasing amounts. The walker will never reach the goal since he always has as far still to travel as he came on the most recent step. Thus, no positive step can ever take him to his destination.

This problem can be fixed by rewriting the terminating test as, "Are we sufficiently close to a solution?" In the case of the walker, although he never gets to the wall, he does get arbitrarily close. So perhaps ask, "Is he close enough so that his clothing touches the wall?" Suppose that is 0.001 of a foot. The test would then be written as:

$$\textit{If distance} < 0.001 \ ...$$

rather than:

$$\textit{If distance} = 0 \ ...$$

Be Wary of Double Conditions

Sometimes it seems as if there are two conditions under which the algorithm should terminate: the index has reduced to zero or some problem has appeared. Be very careful to always ensure that the index actually runs to the needed target.

Exercises

6.23. Code the "walking halfway to the wall" example in Java.

6.24. Fix the badCounter string length method.

6.25. Write a method dance that makes a robot turn right, turn left, move forward, and then repeat that pattern until it has either repeated the pattern the requested number of times (specified by a parameter to the method), or it can't move forward.

6.26. Write a method that counts the blank spaces in a string.

6.5 RECURSIVE DESCRIPTIONS AS ALGORITHMS

The recursive algorithm may look quite different from algorithms you have written previously. But it is indeed an algorithm. It satisfies all of the requirements in the definition:

> A finite ordered sequence of unambiguous steps that leads to a solution to a problem.

Notice that the definition says "sequence of ... steps," not "list of individual instructions." The visual representation may not look like the sequence of steps that are taken, but a recursive algorithm does describe how to perform the full sequence of steps. The number of steps still must be finite. The executed steps are ordered— although that ordering is not always immediately clear to the beginner. The algorithm says what to do at each instant. That is, it specifies a series of steps—without listing them individually. It is this alternate specification that makes recursion so useful. In general, it is best to view a recursive algorithm as just that: directions for solving a problem in terms of a smaller problem, but not as a sequence of steps. Nonetheless, for learning purposes, it is sometimes useful to watch the "sequence of steps" unfold as an algorithm is executed.

6.5.1 Understanding the Execution of Recursive Algorithms

Consider a detailed instance of the execution of the algorithm *toTheWall* for moving a robot to the wall. Let's assume for this evaluation that we have a team of specialists (human or machine, it doesn't matter) to help the robot move. Most of these specialists are "management"—they don't really do much work; they just tell others how and when to do their tasks. In fact, we will assume that we have a large collection of these managers called *toTheWall$_n$* for $n = 1, 2, 3, \ldots$. Each manager is not really interested in doing much actual work, just in "getting the job done" and telling his superiors what a good job he has done. Each manager is capable of performing a single action, called move. But he also has a more important capability: he can ask others to do some work. When a manager is given a task, he does perhaps one simple step and decides who should really do the rest of the work, assigns the task to that other manager, and—when it is complete—reports that success to his own superior. Even though each manager does very little actual work, he still needs to make the decisions and be able to observe the world. In this case, the manager can simply ask if the robot can move. Described in this way, each manager's work may be paraphrased as:

> *Ask: Can the robot move?*
> *If the answer is no*
> > *then   the task must be complete, so report back on this great success*
> > *otherwise   move the robot one small step,*
> > > *ask the next manager to take over the rest of the task.*

Let's trace the individual actions, assuming that the robot is three tiles from the edge and that the task is initially given to *toTheWall*$_1$, as in Figure 6.2 (a):

1. *toTheWall*$_1$ asks "can the robot move?"   (a)
   Since the answer is "yes"
   it moves the robot a single step and
   asks toTheWall$_2$ *to finish the task*

2. *toTheWall*$_2$ asks "can the robot move?"   (b)
   Since the answer is again "yes"
   it moves the robot a single step and then
   asks toTheWall$_3$ *to finish the task*

3. *toTheWall*$_3$ asks "can the robot move?"   (c)
   Since the answer is still "yes"
   it moves the robot a single step and then
   asks toTheWall$_4$ *to finish the task*

4. *toTheWall*$_4$ asks "can the robot move?"   (d)
   This time the answer is "no"
   so toTheWall$_4$ *simply reports its success (to toTheWall*$_3$ *)*
   (this in spite of the fact that toTheWall$_4$ *has done no work at all!)*

(3.) *On hearing of toTheWall*$_4$*'s success, toTheWall*$_3$ *is also finished & reports its success (to toTheWall*$_2$ *)*

(2.) *Similarly toTheWall*$_2$ *is also finished & reports its success (to toTheWall*$_1$ *)*

(1.) *And finally, toTheWall*$_1$ *can report (to the original client) that it has succeeded.*

When one method, recursive or otherwise, sends a message, the sender must wait for the response to the message to be complete. After *toTheWall*$_1$ asks the robot to move, *toTheWall*$_1$ must wait until the move is complete before taking its next

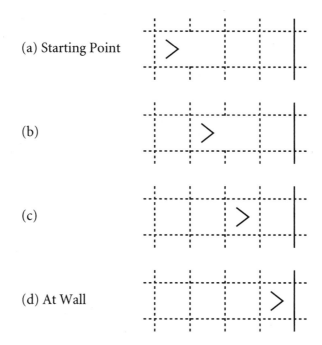

(a) Starting Point

(b)

(c)

(d) At Wall

FIGURE 6.2 Trace of robot moving to wall.

step: asking *toTheWall₂* to work; similarly *toTheWall₂* must wait until it's subordinates have completed their work before reporting success. Thus, *toTheWall₃* must be complete before *toTheWall₂* can report success, and *toTheWall₂* must be complete before *toTheWall₁* can report its own success. This causes a sort of inversion—the last one to start must be the first one done. This is always true in every recursive method! When an algorithm refers to itself recursively, it cannot continue until the recursion is complete. This inversion is an important characteristic of all recursive methods—a characteristic which will be used to advantage in the next section.

Design Hint

Although the robot moves only three steps, it requires four managers to do so. This is because the final manager does nothing (except report its own success). Never worry about the fact that your algorithm appears to send an "extra" or "unneeded" message. Any extra computation required for this message is insignificant when compared to the clarity created by a simpler algorithm.

6.5.2 Classifying Recursive Algorithms

Recursive algorithms have a surprisingly consistent—and simple—structure, a structure that follows directly from the design suggestions. In fact, every recursive solution has three parts:

1. General step: involving solving a smaller problem—in the same terms as the original problem—this step will always include a recursive call.
2. Final step: a trivial step—usually no more than one line.
3. A test: to determine which of the above two situations applies.

Almost all recursive algorithms fit into three basic structural groups, based on their behavior, or equivalently, the relative position of the recursive statement. It is easy to recognize the behavior of an algorithm by its structure—and vice versa. Consider the algorithm *countDown*, which prints the natural numbers less than (or equal to) *n*:

Algorithm countDown(n)
    If n is positive
        then   print n,
                countDown(n−1).

If invoked with *countDown*(3), the algorithm will print:

    3   2   1

The individual steps are:

Enter with n = 3.
Print n = 3.
Recurse:
    Enter with n = 2.
    Print n = 2.
    Recurse:
        Enter with n = 1.
        Print n = 1.
        Recurse:
            Enter with n = 0.
            Return immediately without doing anything.
        Return (from n = 1).
    Return (from n = 2).
Return (from n = 3)—all done!

This algorithm printed the numbers in decreasing order. Notice that this is exactly the same order as the various indices were passed to the successive invocations of countDown. Would it be possible to print values in the usual numerical order? At first glance, it may seem tricky: since we want to print numbers in increasing value, one might be tempted to try to have the index count upwards. But we have seen that that seldom works well. In the example as shown, the process prints a value and then recurses. Since it starts at 3 and the test looks for 0, it is not surprising that the printout appears in decreasing order.

We can reverse the output order in a surprising way. If the action is not taken until the recursion is complete, as in:

> *Algorithm countUp(n):*
> *If n is positive*
> *then   countUp(n − 1),*
> *print n.*

the order of output is reversed, as indicated in this trace of the individual steps taken:

> *Enter with n = 3 .*
> *Recurse:*
> *Enter with n = 2 .*
> *Recurse:*
> *Enter with n = 1 .*
> *Recurse:*
> *Enter with n = 0 .*
> *Return immediately without doing anything.*
> *Print n = 1 .*
> *Return.*
> *Print n = 2 .*
> *Return.*
> *Print n = 3 .*
> *Return (Exit).*

The only difference between these two algorithms is the relative order of the two subactivities of the recursive part. *countUp* calls the "helper" first, and then prints. But this means that the helper must complete its entire task—including any output within its additional recursive calls—before writing its own index. Thus, the side effects of printing the numbers occur on the way out of the recursion: 2 must be written before the 3; all numbers less than 2 before that.

If we can write this series in either order by proper positioning of the action and the recursion, could we do both at once? Yes, just include the action both before and after the recursion. The algorithm:

Algorithm downAndUp (n)
        If n is positive
                then
                        Print n.   */* prerecursion action */*
                        downAndUp(n − 1).
                        Print n.   */* postrecursion action */*

called with $n = 3$, will write:

```
3  2  1  1  2  3
```

You can exploit these behavior patterns in any recursive algorithm. For example, consider the following task: Ask a robot to go to the wall and return to the exact position where it started. We already know how to get a robot to the wall. So we are tempted to think that all that remains is to move it back:

Go to wall.
Turn around.
Return to starting point.

With this statement of the algorithm, the central remaining problem is, "How to get back to exactly the same tile?" Without adding a counter of some sort, there appears to be no nice test like okToMove for checking, "Is this where I started?" This is where thinking recursively comes to the rescue. The inversion characteristic of recursive algorithms is exactly what we need. The robot must take exactly as many steps back as it takes to the wall. So all it needs to do is take one step back for each step forward as the algorithm unwinds. So let's envision a recursive algorithm:

If we are not there yet:
        Take one step forward,
        Go the rest of the way to the wall and back to here,
        Take one step backwards.

With no further effort, the steps toward the wall and those coming back are exactly balanced. The Java method looks like:

```
//in class ExtendedRobot
public void thereAndBack() {
    if (!this.okToMove()) {          /* has it reached the wall */
        this.turnLeft();            /* two left turns gets */
        this.turnLeft();            /* half way around */
    }
    else  {
        this.move();                /* toward the wall */
        this.thereAndBack();
        this.move();                /* now away from the wall */
    }
}
```

The actual execution of the code results in a series of actions that looks like:

$move_1$ (from original tile)
$move_2$ (from tile next to original tile)
...
$move_n$ (to edge tile)
(turn around)
$move_n$ (from edge tile)
...
$move_2$ (to tile next to original tile)
$move_1$ (to original tile)

Perhaps an even more impressive example of the reversing effect is simply reversing a string. That is, given "abc", return "cba":

Algorithm reverse someString
    If someString is empty
        then return the empty string (since an empty string is its own inverse)
        else return reverse (all but the first character), followed by the first
            character.

The algorithm fits the reversing pattern since the recursive reference comes before the character is added. Similarly, you could create a palindrome by writing the string first and then its reverse (see Exercise 6.38). In general, any action specified before (above) the recursive step will reflect the decreasing order of the index. Any action after the recursive step will occur in the reverse or increasing order. Algorithms with both will have a mirror image effect.

6.5.3 Algorithms with Multiple Recursive References

Some recursive algorithms do not fit any of the above models. How can that be? We have seen algorithms with the action before or after the recursive step as well as both before and after. It is possible to have more than one recursive call within the algorithm. The behavior of such algorithms might be a little harder to understand at first—but their structural simplicity makes them very interesting. Such algorithms can be both powerful and problematic.

Consider an attempt to find the square root of a number greater than one. We could start by guessing and then asking if the guess was too high or too low. Then make another guess based on that answer. Not quite the rigorous method we may have learned in high school, but it will get us there.[6] To start, we know that the square root of any such number n must certainly be no greater than n (the upper bound) but no less than one (the lower bound). So we will guess halfway between these two:

Guess = average(lowerBound, upperBound)

At each step, we will assume that we have previously bounded the range of possible solutions. The algorithm looks like:

Algorithm guessSquareRoot(lowerBound, n, upperBound):
    Make a guess = average of lowerBound & upperBound
    If the guess is very close to n
        then return guess
            /* we have found the answer (or close enough) */
        else if guess^2 < n
            then return guessSquareRoot(guess,n,upperBound)
            else return guessSquareRoot(lowerBound,n,guess)[7]

Notice how the recursive parts of the algorithm work: they search in one portion of the allowable range and disregard the values that can't possibly be right. Each new recursive call makes a new guess, but limits the possible values for that guess: at each step, the possible range gets smaller, until the guess is constrained to be arbitrarily close to the needed result. Even though it is very hard to see in advance which of the two recursions will happen in any given invocation, it is easy to see

---

[6] And surprisingly quickly as you will see in later chapters.
[7] If you look closely, you will notice that this algorithm is structurally almost identical to the beverage cooling algorithm discussed in the very first chapter. This structure will come up yet again in Chapter 8. You should not be surprised that certain basic algorithms appear over and over.

that the algorithm produces closer and closer guesses. In fact, with each recursion, this algorithm moves substantially closer to its goal.

Design Note

Although the above algorithm contains two separate recursive calls, note that necessarily only one can be called (since they are in opposite clauses of a conditional). In general, beware of any recursive method containing more than one recursive call if such calls are not mutually exclusive. You will see in Chapter 15 that such methods are likely to run very slowly—so slowly that they may not even be usable. Thus:

> *Algorithm*
> > *If test*
> > > *then*
> > > *otherwise if situation1*
> > > > *then   recurse*
> > > > *otherwise   recurse.*

may be good, even very powerful, but an algorithm of the form:

> *Algorithm*
> > *If test*
> > > *then*
> > > *otherwise   recurse*
> > > > *recurse.*

is a candidate for problems.

6.5.4 Recursive Call is Never First

Notice that no recursive algorithm ever places the recursive call before the test. This is essential. If the algorithm recurses before it decides if it is done it will recurse forever.

6.5.5 Hiding Recursion

When a method such as *guessSquareRoot* has extra parameters that seem irrelevant to the client (or human programmer or user), many designers will hide the process in a dummy calling method:

> *squareRoot(n)*
> > *guessSquareRoot(0,n,n)*

The visible routine, *squareRoot*, then does not require the user to know about the two guesses required for *guessSquareRoot*. In such a case, *guessSquareRoot* might be a private method and *squareRoot* a public one.

Exercises

6.27. Create a Java method corresponding to *downAndUp*.

6.28. Create a Java method like *downAndUp*, but which prints down to zero—but prints the zero value only once—and back up.

6.29. Write a method that gets the robot to the same point on the wall as in Exercise 6.4 but does so by going straight to the wall, turning, and going an equal number of steps along the wall.

6.30. Write Java code corresponding to the pseudocode for the algorithm *reverse*.

6.31. Write a method that writes out a balanced series of parentheses (e.g., "((()))"). Your method should take the number of opening parentheses in the series as a parameter.

6.32. Write a method that causes the robot to paint a "V" with the tip at a wall, as in Figure 6.3 (a).

6.33. Make a method similar to that in Exercise 6.32, but making a "U" rather than a "V", as in Figure 6.3 (b).

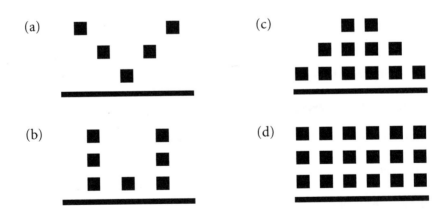

FIGURE 6.3 Robot painting.

6.34. Write a method to tell a robot to draw a pyramid. You may assume that the robot begins on an appropriate edge with enough space available. The pyramid should have an even number of cells on the bottom, corresponding to the initial parameter, as in Figure 6.3 (c).

6.35. Write a method that fills in all cells between the robot and the corner, as in Figure 6.3 (d).

6.36. Write another method to tell a robot to draw a pyramid. You may assume that the robot begins on an appropriate edge and has enough space available. The pyramid should have one cell on top and more cells on each level going toward the edge.

6.37. The thereAndBack method could actually be written without recursion—if you stood on your head a little. Write the iterative version. Comment on the extra difficulties.

6.38. A palindrome is a string that reads the same forward and backwards. Create a method that generates a palindrome from any input string by first repeating the string and following it with its inverse. Thus, "abc" produces "abccba".

6.39. Write a recursive algorithm that takes a string as its parameter and returns true if the string is a palindrome and false if it is not (see Exercise 6.38 for more information on palindromes).

6.40. Modify Exercise 6.36 to build a pyramid with an odd number of cells on the bottom.

6.41. Write a method, badBoy, to tell the robot to move to a corner.

6.42. Combine the pyramid and badBoy exercises to build a pyramid without assuming that the robot is at the edge before you start.

6.43. Write a method spiral that causes the robot to draw a spiral pattern.

6.44. Write a method enabling a robot to count how far it is from the wall (the one it is facing). It may move around, as long as it ends up where it started.

6.6 CONCLUDING REMARKS

Recursion is one of the most powerful techniques in all of computer science, so powerful that it often seems to the new programmer like it doesn't really solve the problem at all—just passes it off or assumes that it has already been solved. In fact, the power comes from that very appearance: every recursive algorithm is simply a test determining if it is done followed by two simple alternatives: one for what to do when done and the other reducing the problem to a smaller one. It is worth doing as many exercises as you need until you feel comfortable with it. It is also related to concepts outside of computer science ranging from mathematical definitions to songs and games. In the next chapter you will see a mathematical proof technique that looks strangely like recursion. In the data structures chapter, you will see that objects as well as programs can be defined recursively. Chapter 10 and Chapter 13 will show that recursion can create some of the fastest algorithms, but Chapter 15 will show that recursion can also create some of the slowest.

6.7 FURTHER READING

Although recursion is a very simple idea, it is incredibly pervasive in computer science. There have actually been entire books written about using this idea, for example:

Roberts, E.S. *Thinking Recursively.* John Wiley and Sons, 1986.

is a language-independent guide aimed at introductory students, while

Odifreddi, P. *Classical Recursion Theory, Volume II,* North Holland, 1999.

is a comprehensive reference manual aimed at mathematics and computer science professionals.

7 Analysis of Recursion

Now that you know something about recursion, you probably realize that even short recursive descriptions can produce complex, nonobvious behaviors. For example, suppose a calculator class uses the following method to compute 2^n for any natural number n:

```
public static long powerOf2(int n) {
    if (n > 0) {
        return powerOf2(n-1) + powerOf2(n-1);
    }
    else {
        return 1;
    }
}
```

This turns out to be a horribly inefficient way to compute 2^n, although that may not be evident from looking at the algorithm (in fact, it may not even be evident that the algorithm computes 2^n at all). Understanding recursive algorithms often requires more powerful mental tools than you need for other kinds of algorithm. This chapter thus introduces mathematical ways of analyzing correctness and efficiency in recursive algorithms. This math not only helps you understand how individual algorithms behave, but it also helps you understand recursion in general.

7.1 CORRECTNESS

Proving recursive algorithms correct is a good place to start studying the mathematics of recursion. The proof techniques of earlier chapters (case analyses and simple series of deductions) fail here because they do not deal well with the way recursion repeats actions. Elegantly, the key to dealing with such repetition is a proof technique that itself looks a lot like recursion—one called "induction."

7.1.1 Induction in Mathematics

In its broadest sense, *induction* is a kind of reasoning that generalizes individual observations to universal rules. For example, over the course of your life you have probably observed the sun set in the evening a few thousand times. If you conclude from these observations that the sun sets *every* evening, you are thinking inductively. Mathematical induction similarly generalizes from individuals to universals, but in a uniquely rigorous way suitable for proofs.

Mathematical induction works as follows: suppose you have some statement about the natural numbers that you want to prove. You start by finding an example (i.e., an individual observation) of a natural number for which the statement holds. This example is called the *base case* for the proof. Of course, one example does not make a complete proof, and so a base case by itself is not very useful. Every induction proof, therefore, has a second part, called the *induction step*, in which you show that if the statement holds for smaller natural numbers, then it must hold for larger ones. For example, many induction steps consider consecutive natural numbers, $k-1$ and k, and show that if the statement is true of the smaller $(k-1)$, then it must also be true of the larger (k). The combination of an example (the base case) *and* grounds for generalizing it to larger numbers (the induction step) does make a complete proof.

The Sum of the First *n* Natural Numbers

For a concrete example of induction, consider the following claim about the sum of the natural numbers from 1 to n (a sum that appears in the analyses of many algorithms' execution times, so this claim will be helpful to you in the future):

$$\sum_{i=1}^{n} i = \frac{n(n+1)}{2} \tag{7.1}$$

It is easy to find examples of particular n's for which this claim is true. For instance, the sum of the naturals between 1 and 4 $(1+2+3+4)$ is 10, which in turn is equal to $4(4+1)/2$. However, examples cannot prove that the claim is true of every n. To do that, we need more rigorous reasoning, rigor for which induction is ideal.

Before starting the proof, let's preview what it will do and why: first, the base case will show that Equation 7.1 holds when $n=1$. Second, the induction step will show that whenever Equation 7.1 holds for a natural number $k-1$, it also holds for k. That's all there is to the proof per se, but consider what its two parts together imply. From the base case, 1 is a value of $k-1$ for which Equation 7.1 holds. Therefore, by the result from the induction step, the equation also holds for the corresponding k, in other words, 2. If Equation 7.1 holds for 2, then the induction step similarly means that it holds for 3. And if it holds for 3, then it holds for 4, and then 5, and so on through all larger natural numbers. Mathematical induction sets up a chain of logic that shows that a statement holds from a base case on to infinity. Because this chain starts at the base case, induction proofs should use the smallest natural they can as their base case, to ensure that the proof applies to as many naturals as possible.

To start the induction proof, we need a base case. So let's try to prove the equation for the smallest plausible value of n, $n = 1$ (but also see Exercise 7.1):

$$\sum_{i=1}^{1} i = 1$$ The sum of the naturals between 1 and 1 is just 1 by itself.

$$= \frac{1(2)}{2}$$ Multiplying by 2/2 to introduce the desired denominator, 2, into the expression.

$$= \frac{1(1+1)}{2}$$ Rewriting 2 in the numerator as $1+1$.

$$= \frac{n(n+1)}{2}$$ Since $n = 1$ in this case.

Next, we need an induction step. The induction step's goal is to show that whenever Equation 7.1 holds for $n = k - 1$, it also holds for $n = k$. We have to do this in a way that applies to all k, in other words, we cannot assume that k stands for any specific value. So let's simply plug $k - 1$ into the original Equation 7.1 in place of n and assume for the moment that the purported equality holds (such assumptions are called *induction hypotheses*):

$$\sum_{i=1}^{k-1} i = \frac{(k-1)((k-1)+1)}{2} = \frac{(k-1)k}{2} \tag{7.2}$$

We will try to conclude from this that:

$$\sum_{i=1}^{k} i = \frac{k(k+1)}{2} \tag{7.3}$$

We do so by starting with the summation on the left side of Equation 7.3 and rewriting it into the quotient on the right:

$$\sum_{i=1}^{k} i = \left(\sum_{i=1}^{k-1} i \right) + k$$

Writing the last term in the sum separately from the first $k-1$ terms.

$$= \frac{(k-1)k}{2} + k$$

Using the induction hypothesis to replace the summation with its equivalent expression.

$$= \frac{(k-1)k}{2} + \frac{2k}{2}$$

Multiplying k by $2/2$ to give both terms a common denominator.

$$= \frac{(k-1+2)k}{2}$$

Factoring k out of each term.

$$= \frac{k(k+1)}{2}$$

Simplifying and rearranging terms.

This completes the proof. Notice the proof's structure:

1. Base Case. Find a small example for which the theorem is true.
2. Induction Step.
   a. Assume the theorem is true of $k-1$ (induction hypothesis).
   b. Use this assumption to show that the theorem must be true of k.

Every induction proof has such a structure. Deliberately follow it in your own induction proofs, particularly as you are gaining experience with induction. In particular, think consciously about every induction proof's base case and induction step; start induction steps by plugging $k-1$ into your theorem and assuming the resulting statement is true, and then plug k into the theorem and try to prove that that statement is true. Start proving this by looking for a way to use the induction hypothesis to simplify something complicated into a more tractable form (as the example used its induction hypothesis to remove a summation).

The Sum of the First *n* Powers of Two

To see how the above structure of induction proofs appears in another context, consider the following claim:

$$\sum_{i=0}^{n} 2^i = 2^{n+1} - 1 \tag{7.4}$$

This sum also appears in many algorithm analyses and will be useful to you in the future.

Once again, we use the smallest reasonable value of n for the base case. In this equation, the smallest reasonable value is $n = 0$, so we need to show that:

$$\sum_{i=0}^{0} 2^i = 2^{0+1} - 1 = 1 \qquad (7.5)$$

This equality is easy to show, because:

$$\sum_{i=0}^{0} 2^i = 2^0 = 1 \qquad (7.6)$$

For an induction hypothesis, replace n with $k-1$ in Equation 7.4:

$$\sum_{i=0}^{k-1} 2^i = 2^{(k-1)+1} - 1 = 2^k - 1 \qquad (7.7)$$

Then assume that the resulting statement is true and show that:

$$\sum_{i=0}^{k} 2^i = 2^{k+1} - 1 \qquad (7.8)$$

$$\sum_{i=0}^{k} 2^i = \left(\sum_{i=0}^{k-1} 2^i \right) + 2^k$$

Writing the last term in the sum separately from the first $k-1$ terms.

$$= \left(2^k - 1 \right) + 2^k$$

Using the induction hypothesis to replace the remaining summation with $2^k - 1$.

$$= 2 \cdot 2^k - 1$$

Adding the 2^k terms

$$= 2^{k+1} - 1$$

Because 2×2^k is 2^{k+1}.

7.1.2 Induction and the Correctness of Recursive Algorithms

Induction is exactly the tool we need to prove a recursive algorithm correct. As you will learn through the following examples, an induction proof's induction step provides a way to reason about recursive messages, while induction's base case provides a way to reason about a recursive algorithm's base case.

Introduction

Let's prove that Chapter 6's algorithm for moving a robot an arbitrary distance works correctly no matter what the distance is. The algorithm is as follows:

```
// In class ExtendedRobot...
public void takeJourney(int distance) {
    if (distance > 0) {
        this.move();
        this.takeJourney(distance-1);
    }
}
```

In mathematical analyses, computer scientists use the variable n to stand for the size of the problem an algorithm is solving. The size of a journey-taking problem is just the distance the robot has to move. Thus, let's suppose n is the value of `takeJourney`'s `distance` parameter and see if we can show that `takeJourney` works correctly no matter what n is. We will do this by using induction on n.

The claim we are proving is a statement about an algorithm, rather than a mathematical equation. This difference means that the proof will consist of prose instead of a series of mathematical equations, but the proof will nonetheless have exactly the same form as the proofs in Section 7.1.1: a base case and an induction step. Just as Section 7.1.1's induction hypotheses assumed that a mathematical statement was true about $k-1$ in order to show that it must be true about k, this proof's induction hypothesis will assume that an algorithm works correctly when its parameter is $k-1$ in order to show that it must also work correctly when the parameter is k.

PRECONDITIONS: An `ExtendedRobot` object receives a `takeJourney` message with parameter n, with n being a natural number. There are no obstructions within n tiles in front of the robot.

THEOREM: After handling the `takeJourney` message, the robot is n tiles forward of its initial position. □

PROOF: The proof is by induction on n.

Base Case: The smallest natural number for which this algorithm is supposed to work is 0, so the base case is $n = 0$. In this case, the test if (distance > 0) fails, and so the algorithm does nothing. This leaves the robot where it started, that is, 0 tiles forward of its initial position, as required.

Induction Step: For the induction step, show that whenever the method works with $n = k - 1$, where $k - 1 \geq 0$, it necessarily works with $n = k$. To do this, reason through what the method would do if given a parameter value of k (and, per the preconditions, no obstructions within k tiles in front of the robot). The first thing the algorithm does is evaluate the test if (distance > 0). Since $k - 1 \geq 0$, k must be strictly greater than 0, so this test succeeds. The robot therefore sends itself a move message followed by a takeJourney$(k-1)$ message. Since there are no obstructions within k tiles in front of the robot, and $k > 0$, the move message moves the robot one tile forward. From the induction hypothesis, takeJourney$(k-1)$ works correctly, in other words, moves the robot an additional $k - 1$ tiles if $k - 1 \geq 0$ and there are no obstructions within $k - 1$ tiles in front of the robot. We assumed that $k - 1 \geq 0$, and since there were initially no obstructions within k tiles in front of the robot and it has moved only one tile forward, the second requirement also holds. Thus, the takeJourney message moves the robot $k - 1$ tiles. This, and the one tile moved by the move message, add up to a total forward movement of $(k - 1) + 1 = k$ tiles. ∎

This proof illustrates the parallels between mathematical induction and recursion. Induction is a recursive proof technique: both induction and recursion use a result about a small instance (of a theorem and problem, respectively) to derive a result about a larger instance. Both use a base case to ensure that this regression to smaller and smaller instances eventually stops. These parallels lead to close parallels between a recursive algorithm's structure and that of its inductive correctness proof. The proof's base case analyzes what the algorithm does in its base case, and the proof's induction step analyzes what the algorithm does in its recursive case. The induction hypothesis is essentially that the recursive messages work correctly.

When using induction to prove an algorithm correct, the induction hypothesis can only be applied to a recursive message if you can show that all of the message's preconditions hold when the message is sent. This is simply because, by definition, all preconditions must hold in order for a message to produce its specified results. This is why the proof above claims that the recursive takeJourney message moves the robot $k - 1$ tiles only after showing that this message meets the explicit requirements for applying the induction hypothesis *and* that all of the preconditions for takeJourney$(k-1)$ hold.

We described the above proof as using induction *on* the value of n. The phrase "on the value of n" identifies n as the natural number that changes during the induction—the quantity that is equal to $k-1$ in the induction hypothesis and equal to k elsewhere in the induction step, the quantity that takes on its minimum value in the base case, etc. Every induction proof is by induction on something. For example, Section 7.1.1's proofs about various sums were by induction on the upper bound in the sums.

An Implicit Induction Variable

Many recursive algorithms have a parameter that changes during the recursion, and such a parameter is usually an ideal thing on which to do induction. However, the quantity on which to do induction is less obvious for some recursive algorithms. For example, consider the following algorithm for moving a robot forward until it reaches a wall:

```
// In class WalkingRobot...
public void moveToWall() {
    if (this.okToMove()) {
        this.move();
        this.moveToWall();
    }
}
```

This algorithm doesn't have an explicit parameter on which to do induction. Nonetheless, there is still a quantity that changes during the recursion: the distance between the robot and the wall. You can do induction on this distance just as you could on an explicit parameter. Here is a correctness proof that does so:

PRECONDITIONS: A `WalkingRobot` receives a `moveToWall` message. The robot is facing towards a wall, with $n \geq 0$ tiles between the robot and the wall. n is a natural number. There are no obstructions in the space between the robot and the wall.

THEOREM: After handling the `moveToWall` message, the robot is standing beside the wall. □

PROOF: The proof is by induction on n, the distance from the robot to the wall.

Base Case: Consider $n = 0$. In this case, the robot is already beside the wall. The `okToMove` message returns false, the algorithm does nothing, and so the robot is still beside the wall when the algorithm ends.

Induction Step: Assume that the algorithm leaves the robot standing beside the wall when $n = k - 1 \geq 0$, and show that the algorithm also leaves the robot standing beside the wall when $n = k$. If $k - 1 \geq 0$, then $k > 0$, in other words, the robot is not initially beside the wall. Thus, the `okToMove` message returns true. The robot therefore moves, which leaves it one tile closer to the wall, since the robot was initially facing towards the wall and there were no obstructions between the robot and the wall. In other words, the robot is $k - 1$ tiles from the wall after the move. The robot then sends itself a `moveToWall` message. Because the robot is $k - 1$ tiles from the wall, still facing the wall, and there are still no obstructions between the robot and the wall, the induction hypothesis applies to this message, meaning that the message leaves the robot standing beside the wall. ∎

Value-producing Recursion

Both of the algorithms studied above produce side effects. Induction is also useful for proving the correctness of recursive algorithms that return values. The classic example of value-producing recursion is recursive computation of factorials, which we show below. Note that mathematically, $0! = 1$, and the algorithm's base case relies on this fact. Our Java version of the algorithm is a static method of a hypothetical `MoreMath` class, which provides mathematical operations not provided by Java's standard `Math` class.

```
// In class MoreMath...
// Precondition: x is a natural number.
public static long factorial(int x) {
    if (x > 0) {
        return x * factorial(x-1);
    }
    else {
        return 1;
    }
}
```

We can use induction on x to prove this algorithm correct. The fact that we aren't reasoning about side effects makes the proof a little shorter than our previous induction proofs about algorithms, but the proof follows exactly the same induction outline that the earlier ones did.

THEOREM: Whenever x is a natural number, `factorial`(x) returns $x!$. □

PROOF: For a base case, consider $x = 0$. The test `if (x > 0)` fails, so the algorithm returns 1, which, as noted above, is $0!$.

Induction Step: Assume that if $k-1$ is a natural number, factorial$(k-1)$ returns $(k-1)!$. Show that factorial(k) returns $k!$. Consider what the factorial method will do when $x=k$. $k-1$ being a natural number means, in part, that $k-1 \geq 0$, so $k>0$. This means the test if $(x > 0)$ succeeds, so the algorithm returns $k \times$ factorial$(k-1)$. From the induction hypothesis and the fact that $k-1$ is a natural number, factorial$(k-1)$ is $(k-1)!$, so $k \times$ factorial$(k-1)=k \times (k-1)!=k!$. ∎

More Complicated Recursion

As recursion itself becomes more complicated, induction becomes an even more valuable tool for reasoning about algorithms. For example, the following algorithm from Chapter 6 moves a robot forward to a wall and then brings it back to where it started:

```
// in class ExtendedRobot
public void thereAndBack() {
    if (!this.okToMove()) {      /* has it reached the wall */
        this.turnLeft();         /* two left turns gets half */
        this.turnLeft();         /* way around */
    }
    else  {
        this.move();             /* toward the wall */
        this.thereAndBack();
        this.move();             /* now away from the wall */
    }
}
```

Many people have trouble understanding how this algorithm works. They find the move message after the recursive thereAndBack particularly puzzling. An induction proof that the algorithm really does move a robot to a wall and then back to its starting point clarifies what this move does. Specifically, the proof shows how the move after the recursion balances the one before the recursion in a manner that brings the robot back exactly the distance that it originally moved forward. This clarity comes from the induction hypothesis summarizing the effects of the recursive message, which in turn makes it easier to understand the actions that must be taken before and after the recursion. Using an induction hypothesis in this manner eliminates the need to trace execution through layers of recursion, greatly simplifying reasoning about recursion. Such an inductive view is also useful when designing recursive algorithms.

PRECONDITIONS: An ExtendedRobot facing towards a wall n tiles away receives a thereAndBack message. n is a natural number. There are no obstructions between the robot and the wall.

THEOREM: After handling the thereAndBack message, the robot has moved to the wall and has returned to its original position. The robot is facing away from the wall. □

PROOF: The proof is by induction on n.

Base Case: Consider $n = 0$. This means the robot is next to the wall, so the test if (!this.okToMove()) succeeds. The robot does not move, but does turn left twice. Therefore, the robot has trivially moved to the wall and returned to its original position; the two turns leave it facing away from the wall.

Induction Step: Assume that when $n = k-1$, and $k-1$ is a natural number, thereAndBack moves the robot forward to the wall, returns it to its original position, and leaves it facing away from the wall. Show that thereAndBack also does so when $n = k$. $k-1$ being a natural number means that $k-1 \geq 0$, so $k > 0$. The robot is therefore not at the wall, so the test if (!this.okToMove()) fails, and the robot sends itself a move message. From the preconditions, there are no obstructions between the robot and the wall, so this message moves the robot one tile forward. There are still no obstructions between the robot and the wall, so the induction hypothesis applies to the recursive thereAndBack message that the robot then sends itself. In other words, this message moves the robot forward to the wall and returns it to its present position, facing away from the wall. Combined with the one tile previously moved, the robot has thus moved forward from its original position to the wall, but has returned to a place one tile closer to the wall than it originally was. However, because the robot is facing away from the wall, the final move message brings it back to that last tile, that is, returns it to its original position. The robot is still facing away from the wall. ■

Strong Induction

All the induction proofs we have presented so far have made an induction hypothesis about $k-1$ and used it to prove an inductive claim about k. Such induction is called *weak induction*. Sometimes it is easier to do an induction proof if you assume as an induction hypothesis that the claim is true for *all* natural numbers less than k, not just for $k-1$. This form of induction is called *strong induction*. Strong induction sets up a chain of conclusions from the base case on to infinity, just as weak induction does. A proof by strong induction is much like one by weak induction, with two exceptions:

1. Where a weak induction hypothesis assumes that the theorem is true of one number less than k, a strong induction hypothesis assumes that the theorem is true of all numbers less than k.

2. Where the base case in a weak induction proof shows that the theorem is true of some natural number, b, the base case in a strong induction proof must show that the theorem is true of all natural numbers less than or equal to b. This is a good reason to use 0 as the base case in strong induction proofs, because there is only one natural number less than or equal to 0 (0 itself).

For an example of a situation in which one would use strong induction, consider the following class. This class extends Java's library class Random with the ability to print a random selection of objects from an array.[1] The selection method prints the selection. It randomly picks a position within the first n elements of array items, prints the object at that position, and then recursively prints a selection of the items before that position.

```
class RandomSelector extends Random {
    public void selection(Object[] items, int n) {
        if (n > 0) {
            int pos = this.nextInt(n);
            System.out.println(items[pos]);
            this.selection(items, pos);
        }
    }
}
```

Strong induction is better than weak induction for proving statements about the selection method, because while one knows that the recursive selection message's n will be less than the original n, one doesn't know how much less it will be. For example, consider the following claim:

THEOREM: The selection method prints elements of array items chosen without repetition from the first n elements. □

PROOF: The proof is by induction on n.

---

[1] While this class offers a good introduction to strong induction, it isn't a very fair selector. Objects near the beginning of the array have a higher probability of being selected than objects near the end, and in fact the first element is always selected.

Base Case: Suppose n is 0. There is nothing to print within the first 0 elements of an array. And indeed, the `if (n > 0)` test fails, so the algorithm returns without printing.

Induction Step: Assume that whenever n is less than or equal to $k-1$, where $k-1$ is a natural number, `selection` prints elements of `items` chosen without repetition from the first n elements. Show that when $n = k$, `selection` prints elements of `items` chosen without repetition from the first k. Since $k-1$ is a natural number, $k > 0$, so the `if (n > 0)` test succeeds. The `nextInt` message generates a random integer between 0 and $k-1$, which the algorithm stores in `pos`. The `println` message then prints the element at this position, in other words, an element chosen from the first k elements of `items`. Finally, the algorithm sends the `selection(items, pos)` message. Since $pos \leq k-1$, the induction hypothesis says that this message prints elements of `items` chosen without repetition from the first `pos` elements. All such elements are within the first k elements. Further, this range does not include `pos` itself, so none of these elements repeat the one already printed. ■

Weak and strong induction are interchangeable—anything you can prove using one you can prove using the other. Thus, computer scientists often talk about just "induction," without distinguishing between "strong induction" and "weak induction." In all inductions, the induction step proves something about k by using an induction hypothesis about one or more values less than k, but not all induction hypotheses have to be about $k-1$. We often follow this practice in this book, describing a proof as being "by induction," without saying explicitly whether the induction is strong or weak.

The "`powerOf2`" Algorithm

As a final example, let's use an inductive correctness proof to understand the `powerOf2` algorithm from this chapter's introduction. Here is the algorithm again, for reference:

```java
public static long powerOf2(int n) {
    if (n > 0) {
        return powerOf2(n-1) + powerOf2(n-1);
    }
    else {
        return 1;
    }
}
```

THEOREM: powerOf2(n) returns 2^n. $\square$

PROOF: The proof is by induction on n.

Base Case: Consider $n = 0$. The test if (n > 0) fails, and so the algorithm returns 1, which is indeed 2^0.

Induction Step: Assume that $k-1$ is a natural number such that powerOf2$(k-1)$ returns 2^{k-1}. Show that powerOf2 with parameter k returns 2^k. Since $k-1$ is a natural number, $k > 0$, so the test if (n > 0) succeeds, and the algorithm returns powerOf2$(k-1)$+powerOf2$(k-1)$. From the induction hypothesis, powerOf2$(k-1)$ returns 2^{k-1}, so this expression is equal to $2^{k-1} + 2^{k-1} = 2 \times 2^{k-1} = 2^k$. $\blacksquare$

Exercises

7.1. Could we also use 0 as a base case for proving Equation 7.1? Why or why not?

7.2. At the beginning of the proof of Equation 7.1, we said that we needed to find a base case. Actually, this wasn't strictly true. We had already seen a base case, albeit not a very satisfying one. Where?

7.3. Note that the conclusion from the proof of Equation 7.1 is that the equation holds for all natural numbers greater than or equal to 1. Could the conclusion be simply that the equation holds for all numbers greater than or equal to 1? Why or why not?

7.4. Use induction to prove each of the following:

1. $\sum_{i=1}^{n}(2i-1) = n^2$ (in words, the sum of the first n odd integers is equal to n^2).

2. A set with n members has 2^n distinct subsets.

3. $\sum_{i=0}^{n}a^i = \frac{a^{n+1}-1}{a-1}$, where a is a constant.

4. The sum of any n even numbers is even, where n is any natural number greater than or equal to 1.

7.5. Prove that the following algorithm returns the sum of the natural numbers between 0 and n, given the precondition that n is a natural number.

```
// In class Calculator...
public static int sum(int n) {
    if (n > 0) {
        return n + sum(n-1);
```

```
        }
        else {
            return 0;
        }
    }
```

7.6. Prove that the following algorithm causes a robot to draw a red line from its initial position to a wall, assuming that there is a wall somewhere in front of the robot and there are no obstructions between the robot and that wall:

```
// In class WalkingRobot...
public void drawToWall() {
    if (this.okToMove()) {
        this.paint(java.awt.Color.red);
        this.move();
        this.drawToWall();
    }
    else {
        this.paint(java.awt.Color.red);
    }
}
```

7.7. Prove that the following algorithm outputs a string of n letters "A", assuming that n is a natural number:

```
// In class Writer...
public void writeA(int n) {
    if (n > 0) {
        System.out.print("A");
        this.writeA(n-1);
    }
}
```

7.8. Prove that the following algorithm moves a robot n tiles forward and then back to where it started. More precisely, the preconditions for the algorithm are that n is a natural number, and there are no obstructions within n tiles in front of the robot. The postconditions are that the robot has moved forward n tiles, has returned to its original position and is facing in the opposite of its original direction:

```
// In class WalkingRobot...
public void forwardAndBack(int n) {
    if (n > 0) {
        this.move();
        this.forwardAndBack(n-1);
        this.move();
    }
    else {
        this.turnLeft();
        this.turnLeft();
    }
}
```

7.9. Prove that the output of the following algorithm consists of a string of "("
and ")" characters, in which all the "(" characters come before all of the ")"
characters, and in which there are exactly *n* "(" characters and *n* ")" characters. Assume that *n* is a natural number:

```
// In class Writer...
public void parens(int n) {
    if (n > 0) {
        System.out.print("(");
        this.parens(n-1);
        System.out.print(")");
    }
}
```

7.10. Prove that the following algorithm leaves a robot facing in the same direction
as it faced before it received the "getDizzy" message:

```
// In class SpinningRobot...
public void getDizzy(int n) {
    if (n > 0) {
        this.turnLeft();
        this.getDizzy(n-1);
        this.turnRight();
    }
}
```

7.11. Number theorists claim that every natural number greater than or equal to 2
can be written as a product of prime numbers. In other words, if *n* is a natu-

ral number and $n \geq 2$, then $n = p_1 \times p_2 \times \cdots \times p_k$, where the ps are prime numbers and $k \geq 1$. Prove this claim. Note that the "product" may be a single prime (that is, k may be 1) when n itself is prime. Also note that the ps needn't all be different—for example, 8 factors as $2 \times 2 \times 2$.

7.2 EFFICIENCY

You have seen how a recursive proof technique, induction, helps you prove recursive algorithms correct. Similarly, a recursive counting technique called a *recurrence relation*, or simply *recurrence*, helps you determine how many steps a recursive algorithm executes.

7.2.1 Recurrence Relations in Mathematics

A recurrence relation is a recursive definition of a mathematical function. We therefore examine the mathematical nature of recurrence relations before considering their applications to recursive algorithms.

Recursively Defined Mathematical Functions

As an example of how a recurrence relation might arise, suppose you have an opportunity to deposit $100 in a fund that pays one half of one percent interest per month. More technically, the fund pays simple monthly interest. Your deposit increases in value by 0.5% all at once at the end of the first month; at the end of the second month, it increases by 0.5% (of its value at that time) again. It continues growing in this manner for each full month you leave it in the fund. Every month, you earn interest on previously paid interest as well as on your initial principal, so it is not immediately obvious what your investment's value will be after a number of months.

To figure out how good this investment is, you want to know how your money will increase with time—in other words, you want to know the function that relates the value of your deposit to the number of months you leave it in the fund. Call this function V, for "Value." One step toward discovering V is to notice that 0.5% monthly interest means that after being in the fund for m months, your deposit is worth 1.005 times what it was worth after being in the fund for $m-1$ months. Mathematically, $V(m) = 1.005V(m-1)$. Notice that this is a recursive description of V. As with any recursion, this one needs a base case and some way to choose between the base case and the recursive case. A good base case comes from the observation that if you deposit your money and then immediately withdraw it, in other words, you leave it in the fund for 0 months, it earns no interest. In other words, $V(0) = 100$. Interest only accrues if you leave your money deposited for at least 1 month, so the recursive case only applies if $m > 0$. Putting all of these ideas together produces the following definition of V:

$$V(m) = \begin{cases} 100 & \text{if } m = 0 \\ 1.005\,V(m-1) & \text{if } m > 0 \end{cases} \tag{7.9}$$

Equation 7.9 is a recurrence relation. Recurrence relations are multipart function definitions, with each part associated with conditions under which it applies. In this example, there are two parts, one of which applies when the function's argument is 0 and one of which applies when the argument is greater than 0. One or more parts of every recurrence relation must involve recursion, as does the second line in Equation 7.9. This is the essential characteristic that makes a definition a recurrence relation. One or more parts must be nonrecursive, as is the first line of Equation 7.9. Finally, recurrence relations usually define functions whose arguments are restricted to the natural numbers. And indeed, if you think carefully about Equation 7.9, you will realize that it does not define V for fractional or negative values of m.

At first glance, Equation 7.9 seems to do no more than restate the original problem. But, in fact, it determines a unique value of $V(m)$ for every natural number m. For example, consider $V(1)$: Since 1 is greater than 0, the second line of Equation 7.9 applies, saying that $V(1) = 1.005\,V(1-1) = 1.005\,V(0)$. Now we have to (recursively) calculate $V(0)$. This time, the recurrence directs us to use the first line, $V(0) = 100$. Plugging this into the expression for $V(1)$, we find that

$$V(1) = 1.005\,V(0) = 1.005 \times 100 = 100.5.$$

Similarly, we can calculate

$$V(2) = 1.005\,V(1) = 1.005 \times 100.5 = 101.0025,$$

$$V(3) = 1.005\,V(2) = 1.005 \times 101.0025 = 101.5075,$$

and so forth. Notice how much like a recursive algorithm for calculating $V(m)$ Equation 7.9 is. This similarity between recurrence relations and recursive algorithms is one of the reasons recurrences are so useful for analyzing algorithms.

Closed Forms

Evaluating recurrence relations as we just did provides a sense for how they work, but it is painfully laborious. Fortunately, there is an easier way to evaluate functions defined by recurrence relations. Many recurrence relations have equivalent *closed forms*, nonrecursive expressions that produce the same values the recurrence relation does. Thus, one typically uses a recurrence relation as an initial but easily discovered definition of a function and then derives a closed form from the recurrence relation to use when the function actually needs to be evaluated.

To find a closed form for Equation 7.9, think about the equation as follows: it tells you directly that $V(0)$ is 100. $V(1)$ is 1.005 times $V(0)$, or 1.005×100. Leave this expression in this form, and turn to $V(2)$:

$$V(2) = 1.005 V(1) = 1.005 \times 1.005 \times 100 = 1.005^2 \times 100.$$

Similarly, $V(3) = 1.005 V(2) = 1.005^3 \times 100$, and $V(4) = 1.005 V(3) = 1.005^4 \times 100$. There seems to be a pattern emerging here, namely that $V(m) = 1.005^m \times 100$. This formula, if it is correct for *all* values of m and not just the ones tried here, is a closed form for the recurrence relation.

As always in mathematics, observing a pattern is intriguing but not conclusive. To be sure that $V(m) = 1.005^m \times 100$ really is a closed form for Equation 7.9, we need a rigorous proof. Given the recursion in the recurrence relation, it is no surprise that induction is a good way to do this proof:

THEOREM: $V(m)$, as defined by Equation 7.9, is equal to $1.005^m \times 100$, for all natural numbers m. □

PROOF: The proof is by induction on m.

Base Case: Consider $m = 0$. From the first line of Equation 7.9, $V(0) = 100$. But $100 = 1 \times 100 = 1.005^0 \times 100$, which is what the theorem requires when $m = 0$.

Induction Step: Assume that $k - 1$ is a natural number such that $V(k-1) = 1.005^{k-1} \times 100$ and show that $V(k) = 1.005^k \times 100$. Since $k - 1$ is a natural number, k is also a natural number, and $k > 0$. The second line of Equation 7.9 thus defines $V(k)$:

$V(k) = 1.005 V(k-1)$ From Equation 7.9.

$\qquad = 1.005 \left(1.005^{k-1} \times 100 \right)$ Using the induction hypothesis to rewrite $V(k-1)$ as $1.005^{k-1} \times 100$.

$\qquad = 1.005^k \times 100$ Multiplying the outer 1.005 and the 1.005^{k-1} together. ∎

We found this closed form for Equation 7.9 by evaluating the recurrence relation on some small parameter values and looking for a pattern. We then proved that the pattern we thought we saw was indeed the general closed form. Although it may seem ad hoc, this is an accepted and surprisingly effective way to find closed forms for recurrence relations. The patterns are usually easiest to recognize if one phrases the values calculated from the recurrence as simple expressions (for example, $1.005^2 \times 100$), rather than as single numbers.

7.2.2 Recurrence Relations and Recursive Algorithms

Recurrence relations provide a "bridge" between a recursive algorithm and a formula for the number of steps the algorithm executes. You start "crossing" this bridge by finding a recurrence relation for the number of steps the algorithm executes. There are usually strong parallels between the recursion in the algorithm and recursion in the recurrence relation, making the recurrence easy to discover. Once you have the recurrence relation, you finish "crossing the bridge" by deriving a closed form that concisely describes the algorithm's efficiency.

A First Example

Let's calculate how many move messages the takeJourney algorithm studied in Section 7.1.2 sends. Here is the method again:

```
// In class ExtendedRobot...
public void takeJourney(int distance) {
    if (distance > 0) {
        this.move();
        this.takeJourney(distance-1);
    }
}
```

As we did to prove this algorithm correct, we'll let the mathematical variable n stand for the value of takeJourney's distance parameter. The first thing to observe about this algorithm is that the number of move messages it sends depends on the value of n—if nothing else, a glance at the code reveals that if n is 0, the algorithm sends no move messages, whereas if n is greater than 0, the algorithm sends at least one. More generally, one might expect that moving farther (in other words, giving takeJourney a larger n) would require more move messages. Thus, figuring out how many move messages takeJourney sends really means deriving a function for the number of moves in terms of n. Let's call this function M, for "Moves."

The algorithm contains a surprising amount of information about M. For instance, we have already noted that when n is 0, the algorithm sends no move messages. In mathematical terms, this means:

$$M(n) = 0 \quad \text{if } n = 0 \tag{7.10}$$

We also noted that when n is greater than 0, the algorithm sends at least one move message. Specifically, it sends the one move in the this.move() statement, plus any that might be sent indirectly as a result of the this.takeJourney($n-1$) statement. We can't count these indirect moves explicitly, but there is an expression for their number: $M(n-1)$ (since M gives the number of move messages in terms of takeJourney's parameter, and $n-1$ is the parameter to this particular takeJourney). So takeJourney's recursive case sends one move directly, plus $M(n-1)$ more indirectly. Mathematically:

$$M(n) = 1 + M(n-1) \quad \text{if } n > 0 \qquad (7.11)$$

Together, Equation 7.10 and Equation 7.11 define $M(n)$ for all values of n that takeJourney could sensibly receive. In other words, they are the parts of a recurrence relation for M:

$$M(n) = \begin{cases} 0 & \text{if } n = 0 \\ 1 + M(n-1) & \text{if } n > 0 \end{cases} \qquad (7.12)$$

This completes the first step across the "bridge" from the takeJourney algorithm to a formula for the number of move messages it sends. Notice how many parallels there are between Equation 7.12 and the takeJourney algorithm. Both have the same condition ($n > 0$) for choosing between their base and recursive cases; both use recursion in the same manner (one recursive "message," with a parameter of $n-1$). These parallels are not coincidental; it is precisely because certain features of the algorithm are relevant to the number of move messages that parallel features are present in the recurrence relation. In many ways, the recurrence relation is thus a synopsis of the algorithm that abstracts away everything not relevant to counting move messages.

The second step across the "bridge" is to find a closed form for the recurrence relation. As in Section 7.2.1, a good guess confirmed by a proof can produce this closed form. In M's case, the recurrence relation says explicitly that when n is 0, $M(n)$ is also 0. When n is 1, $M(1) = 1 + M(1-1) = 1 + M(0) = 1 + 0 = 1$. Similarly, $M(2) = 1 + M(1) = 1 + 1 = 2$. Continuing in this manner, we find the values shown in Table 7.1.

TABLE 7.1 Some values of M, as defined by Equation 7.12

$M(0) = 0$
$M(1) = 1 + M(0) = 1$
$M(2) = 1 + M(1) = 2$
$M(3) = 1 + M(2) = 3$
$M(4) = 1 + M(3) = 4$

A pattern certainly seems to be emerging, namely that $M(n)=n$. The proof that this is always true is as follows:

THEOREM: $M(n)$, as defined by Equation 7.12, is equal to n, for all natural numbers n. $\square$

PROOF: The proof is by induction on n.

Base Case: Consider $n=0$. The proof for this case follows immediately from Equation 7.12: the first line says explicitly that $M(0)=0$.

Induction Step: Assume that $k-1$ is a natural number such that $M(k-1)= k-1$ and show that $M(k)=k$. Since $k-1$ is a natural number, so is k, and $k>0$. Therefore, $M(k)$ is defined by the second line of Equation 7.12:

$$M(k)=1+M(k-1) \qquad \text{From Equation 7.12.}$$

$$=1+(k-1) \qquad \text{Using the induction hypothesis to replace } M(k-1) \text{ with } k-1.$$

$$=k \qquad \text{Cancelling "1" and "–1".} \blacksquare$$

An Implicit Parameter

Just as the quantity on which to do induction when proving a recursive algorithm correct is not always a parameter to the algorithm, so too the quantity that determines how many steps an algorithm executes is not always a parameter. For example, we can count the move messages sent by the moveToWall algorithm, even though that algorithm has no parameters:

```
// In class WalkingRobot...
public void moveToWall() {
    if (this.okToMove()) {
        this.move();
        this.moveToWall();
    }
}
```

Even without parameters, there is still a quantity that distinguishes "larger" (requiring more steps to solve) instances of a problem from "smaller" ones. In this particular example, that quantity is whatever makes moving to a wall require more or fewer `move` messages. With a little thought, you can probably guess that this is the robot's distance from the wall. So let's call this distance n and see if we can derive $M(n)$, a function for the number of `move` messages in terms of n.

The first observation to make is that if the robot is already at the wall, in other words, if $n = 0$, then the algorithm sends no `move` messages. So $M(n) = 0$ if $n = 0$. On the other hand, if n is greater than 0, then it will be OK for the robot to move when `moveToWall` starts executing, and so the algorithm will send one `move`, plus perhaps others due to the recursive `this.moveToWall()`. However, since the robot is one tile closer to the wall when it sends the recursive message, there will only be as many other `move`s as it takes to move $n-1$ tiles—namely, $M(n-1)$. Thus, when $n > 0$, $M(n) = 1 + M(n-1)$. Since the robot moves in whole-tile steps and it doesn't make sense to talk about a negative distance from a wall, we can assume that n is a natural number and put the above observations together in a recurrence relation for M:

$$M(n) = \begin{cases} 0 & \text{if } n = 0 \\ 1 + M(n-1) & \text{if } n > 0 \end{cases} \tag{7.13}$$

Equation 7.13 is the same as Equation 7.12! Thus, the closed form for Equation 7.13 is $M(n) = n$, precisely the closed form for Equation 7.12. This demonstrates one of the benefits of recurrence relations as abstract synopses of algorithms: two algorithms that appear different may nonetheless lead to the same recurrence relation, in which case the closed form only has to be found and proved once.

Recurrences and Value-producing Recursion

In value-producing algorithms, the steps are often operators rather than distinct statements, but recurrence relations can still count those steps. For example, let's figure out how many steps the recursive factorial algorithm from Section 7.1.2 executes while computing $x!$:

```
// In class MoreMath...
public static long factorial(int x) {
    if (x > 0) {
        return x * factorial(x-1);
    }
    else {
        return 1;
    }
}
```

The basic steps in this algorithm are the operators that do the arithmetic calculations, namely the multiplication and subtraction operators. Since it takes time to execute, we can also consider the x > 0 comparison to be a step. Let $A(x)$ (for "arithmetic," since all the steps do some sort of arithmetic calculation or comparison) be the function for the number of these steps executed while calculating $x!$. We can assume that x is a natural number, since $x!$ is only defined for natural numbers. Thus, a recurrence relation can define $A(x)$ for all the relevant "x"s. To set up this recurrence, note that when $x = 0$, the algorithm executes one step, the comparison itself. Therefore, $A(x) = 1$ if $x = 0$. On the other hand, when $x > 0$, factorial directly executes the comparison, one multiplication, and one subtraction (3 steps), and indirectly executes however many additional steps the recursive factorial$(x-1)$ entails. Since the recursive message has a parameter of $x-1$, this number is $A(x-1)$. Therefore, $A(x) = 3 + A(x-1)$, if $x > 0$. Putting these observations together yields the recurrence relation:

$$A(x) = \begin{cases} 1 & \text{if } x = 0 \\ 3 + A(x-1) & \text{if } x > 0 \end{cases} \qquad (7.14)$$

Once again, the recurrence relation can be considered an abstract synopsis of the algorithm. As before, the recurrence and the algorithm use the same condition to select between their base and recursive cases and have the same pattern of recursion. Even the constants in the recurrence are abstractions of the algorithm, in that they reflect information about how many steps the algorithm executes while suppressing details of what kinds of step they are. The 1 in the recurrence's base case reflects the fact that the algorithm executes one step in its base case, while the 3 in the recurrence's recursive case reflects the fact that the algorithm executes three steps in its recursive case.

As with previous recurrences, we can guess the closed form for Equation 7.14 by looking for a pattern in its values. Table 7.2 shows the results.

TABLE 7.2 Some values of *A*, as defined by Equation 7.14

$A(0) = 1$
$A(1) = 3 + A(0) = 3 + 1$
$A(2) = 3 + A(1) = 3 + (3 + 1) = 3 \times 2 + 1$
$A(3) = 3 + A(2) = 3 + (3 \times 2 + 1) = 3 \times 3 + 1$
$A(4) = 3 + A(3) = 3 + (3 \times 3 + 1) = 3 \times 4 + 1$

The pattern seems to be that $A(x) = 3x + 1$.

THEOREM: $A(x)$, as defined by Equation 7.14, is equal to $3x+1$ for all natural numbers x. $\square$

PROOF: It probably comes as no surprise that the proof is by induction on x.

Base Case: Suppose $x = 0$. Equation 7.14 defines $A(0)$ to be 1, which can be written as $3 \times 0 + 1$.

Induction Step: Assume $k-1$ is a natural number such that $A(k-1) = 3(k-1)+1$ and show that $A(k) = 3k+1$. k is a natural number greater than 0, so $A(k)$ is defined by the second line of the recurrence:

$$A(k) = 3 + A(k-1) \qquad \text{From Equation 7.14.}$$

$$= 3 + [3(k-1)+1] \qquad \text{Using the induction hypothesis to replace } A(k-1) \text{ with } 3(k-1)+1.$$

$$= 3 + 3k - 3 + 1 \qquad \text{Multiplying 3 through } (k-1) \text{ and removing parentheses.}$$

$$= 3k + 1 \qquad \text{Cancelling "3" and "−3".} \blacksquare$$

More Complicated Recursion

As was the case with inductive correctness proofs, the usefulness of recurrence relations for analyzing recursive algorithms becomes greater as the algorithms become more complicated. For example, recall the algorithm for making a robot move forward to a wall, turn around, and return to its original place:

```
//in class ExtendedRobot
public void thereAndBack() {
    if (!this.okToMove()) {      /* has it reached the wall */
        this.turnLeft();         /* two left turns gets half */
        this.turnLeft();         /* way around */
    }
    else  {
        this.move();             /* toward the wall */
        this.thereAndBack();
        this.move();             /* now away from the wall */
    }
}
```

The presence of steps both before and after the recursive message, as well as in the base case, makes it hard to judge how many steps this algorithm executes. However, a recurrence relation, as a synopsis of the algorithm, is particularly helpful for overcoming these difficulties.

Let's define a step in thereAndBack to be any one of the basic robot messages (move, turnLeft, or okToMove) and count how many the algorithm executes. The distance between the robot and the wall, n, is the quantity that determines how many steps the algorithm executes. Assume that n is a natural number. Let $S(n)$ be the function that relates the number of steps to n. To find a recurrence relation for S, notice that when it is not OK for the robot to move, in other words, when $n = 0$, the algorithm sends one okToMove message and two turnLeft messages. This observation means mathematically that $S(n) = 3$ if $n = 0$. When it is OK for the robot to move, in other words, when $n > 0$, thereAndBack sends one okToMove message, a move, a recursive thereAndBack, and another move. Three of these messages (okToMove and the two moves) count directly as steps, and the recursive thereAndBack leads indirectly to other steps being executed. Since the robot is $n-1$ tiles from the wall when it sends the recursive message, the number of indirectly executed steps is $S(n-1)$. Thus, the total number of steps executed when $n > 0$ is $3 + S(n-1)$. The recurrence relation for $S(n)$ is therefore:

$$S(n) = \begin{cases} 3 & \text{if } n = 0 \\ 3 + S(n-1) & \text{if } n > 0 \end{cases} \tag{7.15}$$

Notice how concisely the recurrence relation summarizes this algorithm's behavior. First, the recurrence handles the presence of steps both before and after the recursive message by condensing all the steps directly executed in the algorithm's recursive case down to a number, 3, abstracting away concern for when those steps execute. This makes sense, because all that really matters in counting steps is how many steps are executed, not when they are executed. Second, although someone reading the algorithm might get distracted trying to understand how the steps in the algorithm's base case interact with those in the recursive case, the recurrence relation avoids this distraction by providing a familiar mathematical framework for counting both.

Our usual strategy of looking for a pattern works well for finding a closed form for $S(n)$ (see Table 7.3).

TABLE 7.3 Some values of S, as defined by Equation 7.15

$$S(0) = 3$$
$$S(1) = 3 + S(0) = 3 + 3 = 3 \times 2$$
$$S(2) = 3 + S(1) = 3 + (3 \times 2) = 3 \times 3$$
$$S(3) = 3 + S(2) = 3 + (3 \times 3) = 3 \times 4$$
$$S(4) = 3 + S(3) = 3 + (3 \times 4) = 3 \times 5$$

The pattern that appears is $S(n) = 3(n+1)$. Prove that this closed form is correct as follows:

THEOREM: $S(n)$, as defined by Equation 7.15, is equal to $3(n+1)$ for all natural numbers n. □

PROOF: By induction on n.

Base Case: Equation 7.15 defines $S(0)$ to be 3. 3 can be equivalently written as $3 \times 1 = 3(0+1)$.

Induction Step: Assume that $k-1$ is a natural number for which $S(k-1) = 3((k-1)+1) = 3k$. Show that $S(k) = 3(k+1)$. k is a natural number and $k > 0$, so $S(k)$ is defined by the second line of Equation 7.15:

$S(k) = 3 + S(k-1)$ From Equation 7.15.

$\quad = 3 + 3k$ Using the induction hypothesis to replace $S(k-1)$ by $3k$.

$\quad = 3(k+1)$ Factoring 3 out of both arguments to the addition. ∎

Recurrences and Execution Time

As Section 3.6 points out, the number of steps an algorithm executes is an abstraction of its execution time. The main reason for counting the steps that an algorithm executes is to produce a mathematical description of that algorithm's execution time. In the case of a recursive algorithm, we use a recurrence relation to count some or all of the steps that the algorithm executes and then conclude that the execution time is proportional to the closed form for the recurrence relation (we can't conclude that the execution time is equal to the closed form, because each step doesn't usually take exactly one unit of time).

As an example of this process, recall that we said that the powerOf2 algorithm at the beginning of this chapter is "horribly inefficient." Recurrence relations allow us to find out how inefficient the algorithm is. Here is the algorithm again:

```
public static long powerOf2(int n) {
    if (n > 0) {
        return powerOf2(n-1) + powerOf2(n-1);
    }
    else {
        return 1;
    }
}
```

To begin analyzing this algorithm's execution time, we need to pick some step or steps to count as representatives of execution time. For simplicity, let's count only the number of additions the algorithm executes. Because we ignore the subtractions and the n > 0 comparison, we may consider the result a lower bound on efficiency (in other words, an estimate that is probably less than the actual number of steps), but as you will see, even a lower bound for this algorithm is startling.

The number of additions that powerOf2 executes depends on n. Call the number of additions $A(n)$. We begin setting up a recurrence relation for A as we have before. When $n = 0$, powerOf2 does no additions, so $A(n) = 0$ if $n = 0$. However, when n is greater than 0, powerOf2 behaves a bit differently from the algorithms we have analyzed in the past: it executes one addition directly, but sends *two* recursive messages. The double recursion poses no problem in the recurrence relation, however. We simply add the number of additions entailed by each recursive message together. Since both recursive messages have parameter $n-1$, both cause $A(n-1)$ additions to be performed. Adding these to the one addition executed directly yields $A(n) = A(n-1)+1+A(n-1) = 2A(n-1)+1$. The recurrence relation is therefore:

$$A(n) = \begin{cases} 0 & \text{if } n = 0 \\ 2A(n-1)+1 & \text{if } n > 0 \end{cases} \tag{7.16}$$

Next, we need a closed form for Equation 7.16 with which to characterize execution time. We find this closed form in the usual way, by looking for patterns in the values of $A(n)$. Table 7.4 shows the specifics.

TABLE 7.4 Some values of A, as defined by Equation 7.16

$$A(0) = 0$$
$$A(1) = 2A(0) + 1 = 2 \times 0 + 1 = 1$$
$$A(2) = 2A(1) + 1 = 2 \times 1 + 1 = 2 + 1$$
$$A(3) = 2A(2) + 1 = 2(2+1) + 1 = 2^2 + 2 + 1$$
$$A(4) = 2A(3) + 1 = 2(2^2 + 2 + 1) + 1 = 2^3 + 2^2 + 2 + 1$$
$$A(5) = 2A(4) + 1 = 2(2^3 + 2^2 + 2 + 1) + 1 = 2^4 + 2^3 + 2^2 + 2 + 1$$

The pattern here is more complicated than we have seen before, but it appears that $A(n)$ is the sum of the powers of 2 from 1 (which is 2^0) up through 2^{n-1}. This sum can also be expressed as:

$$\sum_{i=0}^{n-1} 2^i \tag{7.17}$$

Lo and behold, this is an instance of one of the sums we discussed in Section 7.1.1! (Remember we said those sums appear in many algorithm analyses? Here's your first example.) From the proof in Section 7.1.1, we know that:

$$\sum_{i=0}^{n-1} 2^i = 2^n - 1 \tag{7.18}$$

Therefore, our guess at a closed form for Equation 7.16 is:

$$A(n) = 2^n - 1 \tag{7.19}$$

We still need to prove that this closed form is correct, which we do by induction as we have before.

THEOREM: $A(n)$, as defined in Equation 7.16, is equal to $2^n - 1$, for all natural numbers n. $\square$

PROOF: The proof is by induction on n.

Base Case: Equation 7.16 defines $A(0)$ to be 0. For the closed form to be correct, this should be equal to $2^0 - 1$, which it is: $2^0 - 1 = 1 - 1 = 0$.

Induction Step: Assume $k-1$ is a natural number such that $A(k-1) = 2^{k-1} - 1$ and show that $A(k) = 2^k - 1$. k is a natural number greater than 0, so:

$$A(k) = 2A(k-1) + 1 \qquad \text{From Equation 7.16, second line.}$$

$$= 2(2^{k-1} - 1) + 1 \qquad \text{Using the induction hypothesis to rewrite } A(k-1) \text{ as } 2^{k-1} - 1.$$

$$= 2^k - 2 + 1 \qquad \text{Multiplying the 2 through } 2^{k-1} - 1.$$

$$= 2^k - 1 \qquad \text{Combining "-2" and "1".} \blacksquare$$

Since execution time should be proportional to this closed form, we conclude that the execution time of powerOf2 grows approximately like 2^n does (actually, it might grow faster, since our analysis only estimated a lower bound on number of steps). 2^n grows extremely rapidly. For example, a computer that could execute a billion operations per second would spend about one second (a long time when you can do a billion of something in it) doing the additions to evaluate powerOf2(30), it would spend about 20 minutes doing the additions for powerOf2(40) and almost two weeks doing nothing but additions to evaluate powerOf2(50). That such a seemingly innocuous use of recursion can lead to such an appallingly slow algorithm is one of the pitfalls in recursion; detecting such problems is an important reason for analyzing algorithms' efficiency.

Exercises

7.12. What difficulty do you encounter if you try to use Equation 7.9 to calculate $V(2.5)$?

7.13. Calculate $f(1)$, $f(2)$, and $f(3)$ by directly evaluating the recurrence relations for the following functions f:

1. $f(n) = \begin{cases} 2 & \text{if } n = 0 \\ 4 + f(n-1) & \text{if } n > 0 \end{cases}$

2. $f(n) = \begin{cases} 1 & \text{if } n = 0 \\ 10f(n-1) & \text{if } n > 0 \end{cases}$

3. $f(n) = \begin{cases} 0 & \text{if } n = 0 \\ 3 + f(n-1) & \text{if } n > 0 \end{cases}$

4. $f(n) = \begin{cases} 2 & \text{if } n = 1 \\ 5 + f(n-1) & \text{if } n > 1 \end{cases}$ \qquad (Watch out! This one is different!)

7.14. Find closed forms for each of the recurrence relations in Exercise 7.13. Prove each of your closed forms correct.

7.15. Letting c and k be constants, prove the following:

1. Every recurrence relation of the form

$$f(n) = \begin{cases} c & \text{if } n = 0 \\ kf(n-1) & \text{if } n > 0 \end{cases}$$

has a closed form

$$f(n) = k^n c$$

2. Every recurrence relation of the form

$$f(n) = \begin{cases} c & \text{if } n = 0 \\ k + f(n-1) & \text{if } n > 0 \end{cases}$$

has a closed form

$$f(n) = kn + c$$

7.16. A biologist is growing a population of bacteria with the unusual property that the population doubles in size every hour on the hour. At the beginning of the first hour, the population consists of one bacterium. Construct a recurrence relation for the function that describes the number of bacteria in the population after h hours. Find (and prove correct) a closed form for this recurrence relation.

7.17. Our analyses of `takeJourney` and `moveToWall` might represent execution times more accurately if they counted the $n > 0$ and `okToMove` operations as well as the `move` messages in the algorithms. Redo the analyses counting these operations as well as the `move`s.

7.18. The following algorithm makes a robot draw a line n tiles long. Derive the number of `paint` messages this algorithm sends.

```
// In class DrawingRobot...
public void redLine(int n) {
    if (n > 0) {
        this.paint(java.awt.Color.red);
        this.move();
        this.redLine(n-1);
    }
}
```

7.19. The following algorithm writes the natural numbers between n and 0, in descending order. Derive the number of `println` messages it sends.

```
// In class NaturalNumbers...
public static void countDown(int n) {
    if (n > 0) {
        System.out.println(n);
        countDown(n-1);
    }
    else {
        System.out.println(0);
    }
}
```

7.20. The following algorithm multiplies natural numbers x and y by repeated addition. Derive the number of "+" operations this algorithm executes.

```
// In class Calculator...
public static int multiply(int x, int y) {
    if (y > 0) {
        return x + multiply(x, y-1);
    }
    else {
        return 0;
    }
}
```

7.21. The following algorithm makes a robot move forward n tiles and then back twice that far. Derive the number of `move` messages this algorithm sends.

```
// In class WalkingRobot...
public void bounceBack(int n) {
    if (n > 0) {
        this.move();
        this.bounceBack(n-1);
        this.move();
        this.move();
    }
    else {
        this.turnLeft();
        this.turnLeft();
    }
}
```

7.22. The following algorithm writes the natural numbers from n down to 0 and then back up again to n. Derive the number of println messages this algorithm sends.

```
// In class NaturalNumbers...
public static void countDownAndUp(int n) {
    if (n > 0) {
        System.out.println(n);
        countDownAndUp(n-1);
        System.out.println(n);
    }
    else {
        System.out.println(0);
    }
}
```

7.23. The following algorithm writes a long string of "x"s. Derive the length of this string, as a function of n:

```
// In class Writer...
public static void longString(int n) {
    if (n > 0) {
        longString(n-1);
        longString(n-1);
    }
    else {
        System.out.print("x");
    }
}
```

7.24. Estimate as much as you can about the execution times of the algorithms in Exercise 7.18 through Exercise 7.23.

7.25. Consider the following alternative to this chapter's powerOf2 algorithm:

```
public static long otherPowerOf2(int n) {
    if (n > 0) {
        long lowerPower = otherPowerOf2(n-1);
        return lowerPower + lowerPower;
    }
    else {
        return 1;
    }
}
```

Estimate the execution time of this algorithm.

7.26. Redo the analysis of `powerOf2`'s execution time, counting

1. The `n > 0` comparisons as well as the additions
2. The `n > 0` comparisons and the subtractions as well the additions

Do these more complete analyses still suggest execution times more or less proportional to 2^n, or do the times become even worse?

7.27. What function of x does the following algorithm compute (assume x is a natural number)?

```
public static int mystery(int x) {
    if (x > 0) {
        return mystery(x-1) + 2*x - 1;
    }
    else {
        return 0;
    }
}
```

(Hint: The algorithm practically *is* a recurrence relation for the function it computes. Write this recurrence explicitly, and then find a closed form for it.)

7.3 CONCLUDING REMARKS

Recursion takes many forms:

■ In algorithms, recursion solves a large problem in terms of solutions to smaller instances of the same problem. The algorithm's base case solves the smallest problems, and the recursive case builds from there to solutions to larger problems.

■ In proofs, recursion appears in induction, proving a theorem true of large numbers from its truth of smaller numbers. The proof's base case proves the theorem for the smallest numbers, and the induction step builds from there to larger numbers. By building in a way that does not depend on the exact values of the numbers, a single induction step proves the theorem from the base case out to infinity.

■ In mathematical function definitions, recursion appears in recurrence relations, defining a function's value at large numbers in terms of its values at smaller numbers. The recurrence's base case defines the function at the smallest numbers, and the recursive part builds from there to larger numbers. Despite their apparent dependence on recursion, many recurrence relations have equivalent nonrecursive closed forms.

In many ways, induction, recurrence relations, and recursive algorithms are all the same thing, albeit approached from different perspectives and used for different purposes.

The connections between a recursive algorithm and its associated induction proofs and recurrence relations are very strong. The quantity that changes during the algorithm's recursion is also the quantity represented by the proof's induction variable, and the quantity that changes during the algorithm's recursion is the parameter that changes during the recurrence's recursion. The base cases in the proofs and recurrence relations analyze the algorithm's base case; the proofs' induction steps and the recursive parts of the recurrence relations analyze the algorithm's recursive case. Similarly, induction proofs about closed forms for the recurrence relations will have base cases that deal with the recurrences' base cases and induction steps that deal with the recurrences' recursive parts. These connections can help you translate any form of recursion into the others and understand each form in terms of the others.

Recursion, induction, and recurrence relations will reappear throughout this book. Many of the algorithms that we will design will be recursive, and their analyses will be based on induction and recurrence relations. As the algorithms become more sophisticated, you will learn correspondingly more sophisticated forms of the mathematics. You will also see that this mathematics, particularly induction, has applications in computer science beyond recursive algorithms. The next chapter explores one of these applications, analyzing algorithms based on loops.

7.4 FURTHER READING

Induction and recurrence relations are important elements of what is sometimes called "discrete math" or "discrete structures." Despite ambiguity about exactly what "discrete math" is (the term lumps together parts of many subareas of mathematics), many texts on it have been written, both by mathematicians and by computer scientists. For example, the following are good introductions to discrete math, the first from a mathematician's perspective and the second from a computer scientist's. The second text also places particular emphasis on recurrence relations:

K. Rosen, *Discrete Mathematics and Its Applications* (4th edition), WCB/McGraw-Hill, 1999.

R. Graham, D. Knuth, and O. Patashnik, *Concrete Mathematics: A Foundation for Computer Science*, Addison-Wesley, 1994.

Most algorithms or data structures texts also contain brief introductions to induction and recurrence relations, for instance:

G. Brassard and P. Bratley, *Fundamentals of Algorithmics*, Prentice Hall, 1996.

Induction in mathematics dates to long before the use of recursion in computing. The first complete use of induction appears to be due to French mathematician Blaise Pascal, in his circa 1654 "Traité du Triangle Arithmétique" ("Treatise on the Arithmetic Triangle"). Portions of this text, including the proof, are available in English in:

D. Struik, ed., *A Source Book in Mathematics, 1200–1800*, Harvard University Press, 1969.

Glimmers of induction seem to have been understood by some Arabic and Jewish mathematicians as long ago as the Middle Ages. See:

I. Grattan-Guinness, *The Norton History of the Mathematical Sciences*, W. W. Norton & Co., 1997.

Our "find-a-pattern-and-prove" approach to deriving closed forms for recurrence relations is simple, but surprisingly effective. More sophisticated and powerful techniques also exist—for a survey, see:

G. Lueker "Some Techniques for Solving Recurrences", *ACM Computing Surveys*, Dec. 1980.

The previously mentioned discrete math books by Graham, Knuth, and Patashnik, and by Brassard and Bratley, also each cover other ways to solve recurrences.

8 Creating Correct Iterative Algorithms

In the previous two chapters, you learned how to design and analyze recursive algorithms. If you are like many newcomers to recursion, you found it a strange and foreign way to program, and you wished you could program with loops, or *iteration*. But beware of what you wish for—you might get it! Recursion has simpler mathematical foundations than iteration, so formal analysis of a recursive algorithm is more straightforward than analysis of an iterative one. Thus, while it may be easy to think of an iterative outline for an algorithm, it is hard to be sure that the idea really works and is efficient. Hard or not, though, you will eventually have to reason about iteration. This chapter and the next give you the theoretical foundations for doing so. This chapter discusses the theory and design of correct iterations, while the next discusses performance issues.

8.1 LOOP INVARIANTS

For many people, the natural way to think about a loop is to think about the changes that happen as the loop executes. However, the deepest understandings of loops often come from things that *don't* change as the loop iterates. Loosely speaking, conditions that remain unchanged even as a loop repeats are called *loop invariants*.

8.1.1 Formal Definition

Consider the following loop, which sets every element of array A to 100:

```
for (int i = 0; i < A.length; i++) {
    A[i] = 100;
}
```

One way to describe this loop is to say that it steps through the elements of A, changing each to 100. But a slightly different description simply notes that every time the loop's body finishes executing, elements 0 through i of A are (somehow) 100. After executing the body the first time, A[0] (that is, elements 0 through 0 of A) is 100; after executing the body for the second time, elements 0 through 1 of A are 100; and so forth. Although the value of i changes, this statement about the relationship between i and the elements of A always remains true. Therefore, this statement is a loop invariant.

Formally, a loop invariant is a condition, associated with a specific point in a loop's body, that holds every time control reaches that point in the body. In the example, the condition is "elements 0 through i of A are 100," and it is associated with the end of the body. In other words, every time the loop finishes an iteration, it is true that elements 0 through i of A are 100.

The invariant "elements 0 through i of A are 100" doesn't say how those elements become 100, but it does do many other things. It helps one understand the loop's correctness (the loop exits when i has reached the number of elements in A, at which point the invariant implies that all elements must be 100), it helps one understand why i has the bounds it does, etc. Loop invariants are valuable ways of exposing order in a loop.

A loop invariant that holds at the point where a loop makes the decision whether to exit or to start a new iteration serves two roles. As a loop invariant, it reveals order within the loop. But it is also a condition that is true when the loop exits, and so is a postcondition for the loop as a whole. In this latter role, the invariant helps ensure that the loop as a whole is correct. Thus, loop invariants that hold at such exit points (usually the beginning or end of the loop's body) are the most useful and widely used. However, loop invariants can also be stated for other points in a loop, and it is sometimes useful to do so.

8.1.2 Design with Loop Invariants

The key to designing an iterative algorithm, an algorithm that contains one or more loops, often lies in finding good loop invariants. Once you find the right loop invariants, the loops may practically design themselves. A good example occurs in a classic algorithm for searching arrays.

Binary Search

Suppose you have a sorted array, and you wish to search it for a particular value, x. You may already know an algorithm named Binary Search that solves this problem. If you don't know the algorithm, don't worry—we're about to explain it. The key idea is that since the array is sorted, you can narrow your focus to a section of the array that must contain x if x is in the array at all. In particular, x must come before every element greater than x, and after every element less than x. We call the section of the array that could contain x the *section of interest*. We can iteratively home in on *x* with a loop that shrinks the section of interest while maintaining the loop invariant that *x* is in that section, if it is in the array at all. The general algorithm is then:

> *Initially, the section of interest is the whole array.*
> *Repeat the following until either the section of interest*
>   *becomes empty, or you find x:*
> *If x is less than the middle item in the section of interest,*
>   *Then x must be in the first half of that section if*
>   *it's in the array at all;*
>   *so now the section of interest is just that first half.*
> *Otherwise, if x is greater than the middle item in the section of interest,*
>   *Then x must be in the second half of that section if*
>   *it's in the array at all;*
>   *so now the section of interest is just that*
>   *second half.*

Binary Search is easy to understand in the abstract, but if you tried to write it in a concrete programming language you would almost certainly get it wrong—even computer scientists took 16 years after the first publication about Binary Search to develop a version that worked in all cases! (See the "Further Reading" section of this chapter for more on this story and the history of Binary Search.) The details of keeping track of the section of interest are surprisingly hard to get right. However, designing code from the loop invariant can guide you through those details to a working program.

You already know that algorithm design is a process of refining broad initial ideas into more and more precise form until they can be expressed in code. When designing an algorithm from a loop invariant, you will frequently refine the loop invariant in order to refine the code ideas. In the case of Binary Search, we should refine the loop invariant to specify exactly what the section of interest is, since that section is the central concept of the whole algorithm. Programmers often use two indices, typically named `low` and `high`, to represent a section of an array. `low` is the index of the first element that is in the section, and `high` is the index of the last element in the section (because the elements at positions `low` and `high` are in the section, we say that `low` and `high` are *inclusive* bounds for the section). If we use this convention to represent the section of interest, our loop invariant can become:

If *x* is in the array, then it lies between positions `low` and `high`, inclusive.

Figure 8.1 illustrates this invariant. Using this invariant, we can outline the algorithm in greater detail. In particular, the invariant helps us make the following refinements:

- The invariant helps us refine the idea of "updating" the section of interest. When we find that x is less than the middle item in the section, we "update" by setting high equal to the position before the middle (since the invariant specifies that x could be at position high, but we just learned that x is too small to be at the middle position). Similarly, when x is greater than the middle item, we set low to the position after the middle.
- Since x must lie between positions low and high, inclusive, the section of interest becomes empty when there are *no* positions between low and high, including low and high themselves. In other words, when low > high.
- The middle of the section of interest is the position halfway between low and high.

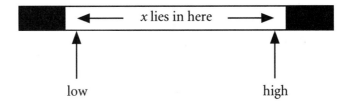

FIGURE 8.1 Bounding the section of an array in which a value may lie.

These considerations lead to the following outline of Binary Search:

Initialize low and high to include the whole array.
Repeat the following until either low > high, or you find x:
    If x is less than the item half way between positions low and high,
        Then set high equal to the position before the halfway point.
    Otherwise, if x is greater than the item half way
        between positions low and high,
    Then set low equal to the position after the halfway point.

The outline of Binary Search is now detailed enough to rewrite in Java. It is a good idea whenever you program to design in pseudocode until you are ready to express ideas that correspond to individual statements in a concrete programming language. This is why we have written Binary Search in pseudocode until now.

Now, however, we begin to want the precise, concrete meanings of programming language operations, so it is time to refine the algorithm into Java.

To provide a context for the Java version of Binary Search, let's make it a method of an ExtendedArray class. ExtendedArray objects will act like arrays do in most programming languages (in other words, as sequences of values whose elements can be individually accessed), but they will also provide additional operations beyond what most languages offer on arrays—in particular, a binarySearch message that searches a sorted ExtendedArray. ExtendedArray objects will store their contents in a member variable that is a standard array. A partial definition of ExtendedArray is thus as follows (for concreteness's sake, we made the member array an array of integers, but other types would also work):

```
class ExtendedArray {
    private int[] contents;
    public boolean binarySearch(int x) {
        ...
    }
    ...
}
```

The binarySearch method takes an integer as its parameter, returning true if that integer appears in the ExtendedArray and false if it does not.

Writing Binary Search in Java is now mostly just a matter of expressing the ideas in the pseudocode in Java. For example, the pseudocode says to "initialize low and high to include the whole array." The invariant reminds us that low and high are inclusive bounds, so this must mean initializing low to 0 and high to the array's largest index:

```
low = 0;
high = contents.length - 1;
```

The position halfway between low and high can be computed as:

```
(low + high) / 2
```

Remember that integer division in Java truncates away any fractional part of the quotient, so this expression really does produce an integer position.

The pseudocode loop repeats *until* low > high, or *until* x is found (that is, contents[(low+high)/2] == x). Java doesn't have an "until" loop, so in Java we will need to loop *while* the pseudocode's test is false. Equivalently, the Java test should be the logical negation (recall Chapter 5) of the pseudocode test. De Morgan's Law

(Chapter 5) tells us that this negation is the "and" of the negations of the two individual tests:

```
while (low <= high && contents[(low+high)/2] != x)
```

Our concrete `binarySearch` is supposed to return a Boolean value. The loop invariant helps us determine how to calculate this value from the values of `low` and `high`: if the loop exits with `low > high`, then there are no positions left between `low` and `high`, so *x* must not be in the array and `binarySearch` should return false. Otherwise, *x* must have been found, and `binarySearch` should return true:

```
if (low > high) {
    return false;
}
else {
    return true;
}
```

The complete Java version of Binary Search is thus as follows:

```
public boolean binarySearch(int x) {
    // Precondition: The array is in ascending order.
    int low = 0;
    int high = contents.length - 1;
    while (low <= high && contents[(low+high)/2] != x) {
        if (x < contents[(low+high)/2]) {
            high = (low+high)/2 - 1;
        }
        else {
            low = (low+high)/2 + 1;
        }
    }
    if (low > high) {
        return false;
    }
    else {
        return true;
    }
}
```

We mentioned earlier that Binary Search is a hard algorithm to code correctly. Common mistakes include not adding one to, or subtracting one from, `(low+high)/2` when updating `high` or `low`, and assuming that the search has failed when `low` still equals `high`, instead of waiting until `low > high`. Notice how the loop invariant explicitly helped us code these points correctly. This is an excellent example of the value of loop invariants in designing iterative algorithms. Such uses of loop invariants are typical of many algorithm designs, and are by no means unique to Binary Search.

Greatest Common Divisors

For another example of loop invariants in algorithm design, consider designing an algorithm that computes greatest common divisors. The *greatest common divisor* of natural numbers x and y, denoted $GCD(x,y)$, is the largest natural number that evenly divides both x and y. For example, $GCD(12,8) = 4$, because 4 divides evenly into both 12 and 8, and no larger natural number does. On the other hand, $GCD(12,7) = 1$, because nothing other than 1 divides both 12 and 7 evenly. One interesting corollary to this definition is that $GCD(x,0) = x$, no matter what x is. The reason is that any x divides into itself once, and into 0 zero times, so x divides into both itself and 0 evenly. Clearly, no larger number divides evenly into x, so x is the greatest number that divides both x and 0.

Mathematicians know a lot about greatest common divisors. One of the things they know is that:

$$GCD(x,y) = GCD(y, x \bmod y) \text{ if } x \geq y > 0 \tag{8.1}$$

($x \bmod y$ is basically the remainder from dividing x by y, for example, 11 mod 3 is 2, while 10 mod 5 is 0.) For example, Equation 8.1 means that:

$$GCD(12,9) = GCD(9, 12 \bmod 9) = GCD(9,3) \tag{8.2}$$

Algorithmically, Equation 8.1 means that code such as:

```
int oldX = x;
x = y;
y = oldX % y;
```

changes the values of variables x and y, *without* changing their greatest common divisor. Any time you can change values without changing some relationship between those values, you have a possible loop invariant. Indeed, you could put these three statements into a loop, which would have the condition:

x and y have the same greatest common divisor they had before entering the loop.

as a loop invariant that holds at the beginning of every iteration. Moreover, x mod y is smaller than y (since the remainder after dividing x by y can't be greater than or equal to y),[1] so this hypothetical loop will make y smaller on every iteration. If the loop iterates often enough, y will eventually become 0. When this happens, GCD(x,y) is trivial to compute, because GCD(x,0) is always just x. So this simple loop will reduce y until its greatest common divisor with x becomes trivial to compute, without changing the value of that greatest common divisor. What an elegant algorithm for computing greatest common divisors! (So elegant, in fact, that it was described by the Greek mathematician Euclid over 2000 years ago, and is known as Euclid's Algorithm in his honor.) In Java, this algorithm might be a static method of some mathematical utilities class, as follows:

```java
public static int greatestCommonDivisor(int x, int y) {
    // Preconditions: x >= y >= 0
    while (y > 0) {
        int oldX = x;
        x = y;
        y = oldX % y;
    }
    return x;
}
```

A reader who didn't understand the origins of this algorithm would have no idea what it does. Only by understanding its loop invariant can you understand what the algorithm does and why. Loop invariants often help you understand an algorithm in a much deeper way than simply reading its code can do.

Exercises

8.1. The grade-school algorithm for multiplying multidigit integers x and y is as follows:

---

[1] When we write algorithms in Java, we use the % operator to represent the mathematical "mod" operator. Java's % and math's "mod" are exactly the same as long as the left operand is positive or zero (which it always will be in this algorithm). However, mathematicians usually define "mod" so that it never produces a negative result, whereas Java's % produces a negative result if the left operand is negative.

Initialize a running product to 0.
For i = 1 to the number of digits in y, do the following:
    Multiply x by the i-th digit of y
      (counting from the right).
    Multiply that product by 10^{i-1}, and add the result to
      the running product.

When this algorithm's loop exits, the running product is the final, full product. State an invariant for the loop to justify this claim.

8.2. Another fact about greatest common divisors is that $GCD(x, y) = GCD(y, x - y)$ if $x \geq y > 0$. Use this fact to devise another loop invariant and iterative algorithm for computing greatest common divisors.

8.3. Design a loop that capitalizes the letters in a string, based on the invariant "all letters from the first through the i-th are capitals."

8.4. If $x \geq y > 0$, then $x \bmod y = (x - y) \bmod y$. Convince yourself that this is true, and then use it to find a loop invariant and loop for computing $x \bmod y$ without using division.

8.5. A hypothetical electronic puzzle features two counters, which can display arbitrary positive or negative integers. Two buttons change the values in the counters, as follows: Button A adds two to each counter; Button B subtracts four from the first counter but adds one to the second. The object of the puzzle is to make the sum of the counters become zero. Give an algorithm for doing so. (Hint: look for an invariant involving the sum mod three.)

8.6. Design an iterative search algorithm for `ExtendedArray` that does not require the array to be sorted. What loop invariant(s) does your algorithm use? (Even if you didn't think consciously about loop invariants while designing the algorithm, there are nonetheless certain to be some on which it relies.)

8.7. Design a search algorithm for sorted arrays that uses the same loop invariant as Binary Search, but that chooses a different element of the array to compare to x. Convince yourself that your algorithm works correctly.

8.2 CORRECTNESS OF ITERATIVE ALGORITHMS

Designing loops from their invariants improves your chances of designing them correctly, but can't by itself guarantee perfection. As with any algorithm, you should review an iterative algorithm while you design it to convince yourself that it is correct.

As in all correctness arguments, the goal when reasoning about the correctness of an iterative algorithm is to prove that certain postconditions hold when the algorithm finishes. This reasoning, however, is harder for loops than for other control structures. Proving a loop correct typically requires all of the following:

1. Prove that the loop actually *terminates*, that is, exits. Some loops don't stop looping. Any conclusions you reach about what happens after a loop finishes are moot if the loop never finishes.
2. Prove that any loop invariants on which the algorithm relies really do hold on every iteration, including the first.
3. Prove the postcondition(s) from conditions that you know hold when the loop exits. Generally, these will be the conditions that the loop tests in deciding to exit, plus any loop invariants that hold where the loop makes that test.

8.2.1 Proving Termination

The clearest termination proofs show that every iteration of a loop makes at least some minimum, nonzero, amount of progress toward satisfying the loop's exit condition. As a simple example, recall Section 8.1.1's loop for making all elements of an array of 100:

```
for (int i = 0; i < A.length; i++) {
    A[i] = 100;
}
```

This loop will exit whenever $i \geq$ A.length. Furthermore, every iteration of the loop increases i by one. Since A.length is constant, increasing i by one often enough will eventually make i exceed A.length. Therefore, the loop must eventually exit.

To see why there must be a "minimum, nonzero" amount of progress toward the exit condition, consider the following pseudocode:

Initialize x to 1
while x > 0, do the following:
    Set x to x/2

This loop exits when $x \leq 0$, and every iteration of this loop reduces x, so it seems that the loop should eventually exit. But the actual values of x are 1, 1/2, 1/4, 1/8, and so on. Even though these numbers always get smaller, they never actually get to zero. The problem is that every iteration of the loop makes less progress towards

$x \leq 0$ than the previous iterations, and there is no limit to how small the amount of progress can get.[2]

Termination of Binary Search

For a more realistic example of a termination proof, recall the loop in Binary Search:

```
while (low <= high && contents[(low+high)/2] != x) {
    if (x < contents[(low+high)/2]) {
        high = (low+high)/2 - 1;
    }
    else {
        low = (low+high)/2 + 1;
    }
}
```

THEOREM: The loop in Binary Search must exit. □

PROOF: This loop will certainly exit if low > high, even if x is not in the array. So we will concentrate on showing that every iteration makes progress toward low becoming greater than high. Every iteration either changes high or changes low. Those iterations that change high change it to (low+high)/2 - 1, and since low can be as large as high, but no larger, this quantity must be at most:

$$\frac{\text{high}+\text{high}}{2} - 1 = \text{high} - 1 \tag{8.3}$$

Similarly, since high can't be smaller than low, the iterations that change low replace it with a value that is at least:

$$\frac{\text{low}+\text{low}}{2} + 1 = \text{low} + 1 \tag{8.4}$$

Thus every iteration reduces high by at least one, or increases low by at least one, and so low must eventually exceed high. ■

---

[2] In programming languages this loop probably would exit. Programming languages can't represent real numbers infinitely precisely, so x would probably become indistinguishable from 0 eventually. But this conclusion assumes that the language's implementation behaves reasonably even when its representation of numbers breaks down, so we can't be sure what will really happen.

Note that this argument only determined that `high` and `low` change by *at least* one, it didn't say exactly how much progress each iteration makes towards termination. Indeed, different iterations will generally make different amounts of progress. However, proving termination only requires showing that every iteration makes at least some minimum amount of progress, which we did.

8.2.2 Proving Loop Invariants

The strategy for proving that a condition is a loop invariant is simple: prove that the condition holds on the first iteration of the loop, and then prove that if it holds on any iteration it continues to hold on the next. You can think of this proof strategy as directly verifying the definition of "loop invariant," namely a condition that is true on every iteration.

Formally, this strategy for proving that a condition is a loop invariant is induction on the number of times the loop has repeated. Proving that the condition holds on the first iteration is the induction's base case. Proving that if the condition holds during one iteration then it holds during the next is the induction step—in other words, this part of the proof shows that if something is true during the $(k-1)$-th iteration, then it must also be true during the k-th.

Binary Search's Invariant

To illustrate this strategy, let's prove that Binary Search really does have the invariant "if x is in the array, then it lies between positions `low` and `high`, inclusive," at the point where the loop evaluates its test. We state this claim formally as:

PRECONDITION: An `ExtendedArray` object's `contents` array is in ascending order.

THEOREM: Whenever that `ExtendedArray`'s `binarySearch` method evaluates the test in `while (low <= high && contents[(low+high)/2] != x)`, x lies between positions `low` and `high` of `contents`, inclusive, if x is in the array at all. □

PROOF: To prove the base case, consider the loop's first iteration. When the first iteration evaluates the test, `low` and `high` have just been initialized to 0 and `contents.length−1`, respectively. Since these are the first and last positions in the array, x must lie between them (inclusive) if it is anywhere in the array.

Induction Step: Suppose the invariant holds in the $(k-1)$-th iteration, and show that it also holds in the k-th. Consider what happens during the $(k-1)$-th iteration. The body of the loop consists of two cases, corresponding to `x < contents[(low+high)/2]` and `x > contents[(low+high)/2]`. Consider each case in turn:

1. x < contents[(low+high)/2]. The algorithm sets high equal to (low+high)/2 − 1, and leaves low unchanged. Since the array is in ascending order, and x < contents[(low+high)/2], x must appear at or before position (low+high)/2 − 1, the new value of high. From the induction hypothesis, x must appear at or after position low. In other words, at the end of this iteration, and so at the test in the next, x still lies at a position between low and high, if it is in the array at all.

2. x > contents[(low+high)/2]. The algorithm sets low to (low+high)/2 + 1, and leaves high unchanged. By reasoning similar to that for the first case, x must lie at or after position (low+high)/2 + 1 (the new value of low), and at or before position high. Once again, the loop invariant still holds at the beginning of the next iteration. ∎

Invariants in Euclid's Algorithm

The loop invariant for Euclid's Algorithm is "x and y have the same greatest common divisor they had before entering the loop." We want to show that this invariant holds every time the loop evaluates its test. Proving this, however, introduces some complexities of loop invariant proofs that did not appear in the proof for Binary Search. As we explore the proof and its complexities, it will be helpful to refer back to the algorithm, so here it is again:

```
public static int greatestCommonDivisor(int x, int y) {
    // Preconditions: x >= y >= 0
    while (y > 0) {
        int oldX = x;
        x = y;
        y = oldX % y;
    }
    return x;
}
```

The first complexity is that we will need to talk about the values of variables in specific iterations of the loop. For example, we need to say things like "the value of x in the k-th iteration is the same as the value of y in the $(k-1)$-th." To say such things concisely, we use a subscript notation that is often useful when talking about loop invariants: if v is some variable used in a loop, v_i denotes the value of v at the point associated with the loop invariant during the loop's i-th iteration (we define v_i relative to a specific point in the loop because a variable's value can change within an iteration). For example, we can use this notation to state the aforementioned relation between x in the k-th iteration and y in the $(k-1)$-th by saying "$x_k = y_{k-1}$." We use v_0 to denote the variable's value before the first iteration.

The subscript notation allows us to make a more precise statement of our loop invariant, namely:

$$\mathrm{GCD}(x_i, y_i) = \mathrm{GCD}(x_0, y_0) \text{ for all } i \geq 1 \qquad (8.5)$$

(In other words, the greatest common divisor of x and y in every iteration of the loop is the same as their greatest common divisor before entering the loop.)

The second complexity is that Euclid's Algorithm relies on Equation 8.1 to justify the idea that the loop's changes to x and y don't change x and y's greatest common divisor. However, Equation 8.1 only applies if $x \geq y$ and $y > 0$. The test while (y > 0) immediately guarantees that y will be greater than 0 in the body of the loop, but it is less clear that x is always greater than or equal to y. It is therefore helpful to prove $x \geq y$ as a lemma (recall Section 3.3.3) that the main proof can use later.

PRECONDITION: $x \geq y \geq 0$.

LEMMA: Every time greatestCommonDivisor(x, y) begins executing the body of its loop, $x \geq y$. $\square$

PROOF: The proof is by induction on the number of times the loop has repeated.

Base Case: The first iteration. $x \geq y$ is one of the preconditions, and nothing changes x or y before entering the loop. Thus x is still greater than or equal to y when the loop's body begins executing for the first time.

Induction Step: Assume that $x_{k-1} \geq y_{k-1}$, and show that $x_k \geq y_k$ for any $k > 1$. According to the assignment statements in the loop's body, $x_k = y_{k-1}$, and $y_k = x_{k-1} \bmod y_{k-1}$. Because $y_{k-1} > 0$, and $x_{k-1} \geq y_{k-1}$, x_{k-1} and y_{k-1} are both positive. Thus $x_{k-1} \bmod y_{k-1}$ must be less than y_{k-1} (because, when dividing two positive numbers, you can't have a remainder greater than or equal to the divisor). Putting these observations together we have:

$$x_k = y_{k-1} > x_{k-1} \bmod y_{k-1} = y_k \qquad (8.6)$$

Thus in fact $x_k > y_k$, but that implies $x_k \geq y_k$. ∎

The fact that x is greater than or equal to y whenever the greatestCommonDivisor method begins executing the body of its loop is a loop invariant. This is why we proved it using exactly the same proof technique (induction on number of iterations) we use for any loop invariant. Many iterative algorithms require such secondary loop invariants in order to prove their primary ones. The need to state and prove secondary loop invariants significantly lengthens many iterative algorithms' correctness proofs.

In the course of proving this lemma, we showed that the operands to the algorithm's "mod" operation are both positive. While this wasn't the main goal of the proof, it is a nice fringe benefit, because it ensures that the % operator in our Java version of the algorithm will behave exactly like the mathematical "mod" operator that we intend it to represent. (Java's % does not obey the usual mathematical definition of "mod" when the left operand is negative.)

We can now state and prove our main claim about the loop invariant in Euclid's Algorithm.

PRECONDITION: $x \geq y \geq 0$.

THEOREM: For all $i \geq 1$, $GCD(x_i, y_i) = GCD(x_0, y_0)$ when greatestCommonDivisor(x, y) evaluates the test in while (y > 0). □

PROOF: The proof is by induction on loop iterations.

Base Case: We show that the invariant holds in the loop's first iteration, in other words, that $GCD(x_1, y_1) = GCD(x_0, y_0)$. Since x and y don't change before the evaluating the test for the first time, x_1 is x_0 and y_1 is y_0. Therefore, $GCD(x_1, y_1)$ is the same as $GCD(x_0, y_0)$.

Induction Step: Assume that the invariant holds in iteration $k-1$ (in other words, that $GCD(x_{k-1}, y_{k-1}) = GCD(x_0, y_0)$), and then show that it holds in iteration k (in other words, that $GCD(x_k, y_k) = GCD(x_0, y_0)$):

$GCD(x_k, y_k)$

$= GCD(y_{k-1}, x_{k-1} \bmod y_{k-1})$

| x_k and y_k equal the values assigned to x and y during the preceding iteration of the loop, namely y_{k-1} and $x_{k-1} \bmod y_{k-1}$.

$= GCD(x_{k-1}, y_{k-1})$

$x_{k-1} \geq y_{k-1}$ by the lemma, and $y_{k-1} > 0$ because of the test in the while. Thus Equation 8.1 applies to x_{k-1} and y_{k-1}, that is, $GCD(y_{k-1}, x_{k-1} \bmod y_{k-1}) = GCD(x_{k-1}, y_{k-1})$.

$= GCD(x_0, y_0)$

By the induction hypothesis. ■

Vacuous Truth

Many loop invariants are statements about all members of some set. For example, recall the loop with which we introduced loop invariants:

```
for (int i = 0; i < A.length; i++) {
    A[i] = 100;
}
```

We proposed a loop invariant that elements 0 through i of A are 100 at the end of each iteration of this loop's body. This is a statement about all members of a set, specifically all members of the set of elements of A whose positions are between 0 and i.

A similar invariant holds at the *beginning* of every iteration of this loop (where it is probably more useful than the original, because it holds at the point where the loop evaluates its exit test). In particular, since at the beginning of each iteration the i-th element of the array is not necessarily equal to 100 yet, but all previous elements should be, the new invariant is simply:

At the beginning of each iteration, elements 0 through $i-1$ of A are 100.

The new invariant is still a statement about all members of a set, namely the set of elements of A whose positions are between 0 and $i-1$. But think about this invariant during the loop's first iteration: in that iteration, i is 0, so the invariant says that all elements of A that lie between positions 0 and -1 are 100. But there are no such elements! Can this statement really be true?

Surprisingly, it turns out that *any* statement about all elements of an empty set is true. This rule is called *vacuous truth*. To see why vacuous truth is logically sound, suppose that P is any proposition, and consider the statement:

$$P \text{ is true of all members of the empty set} \qquad (8.7)$$

Equation 8.7 is equivalent to the implication:

$$x \text{ is a member of the empty set} \Rightarrow P \text{ is true of } x \qquad (8.8)$$

The left hand side of this implication is always false, because nothing can be an element of the empty set. Recall from Chapter 5's truth table for implication that an implication is always true when its left side is false, regardless of whether its right side is true or false. Therefore, it doesn't matter whether P really is true for any given x or not; the implication in Equation 8.8 is true nonetheless, and thus so is the statement in Equation 8.7. Note that the rule of vacuous truth does *not* say that

P is ever true—vacuous truth says something about the *empty set*, not about the proposition P.

With the aid of vacuous truth, we can easily prove that the new invariant for the array-initializing loop holds on every iteration:

THEOREM: At the beginning of every iteration of the array-initializing loop, elements 0 through $i-1$ of A are 100. □

PROOF: The proof is by induction on loop iterations.

Base Case: Consider the loop's first iteration. The theorem is vacuously true in that iteration, because there are no elements 0 through -1 of A.

Induction Step: Assume that at the beginning of the iteration in which $i = k-1$, elements 0 through $k-2$ of A are equal to 100. Show that at the beginning of the iteration in which $i = k$, elements 0 through $k-1$ of A are equal to 100. They are, because during the iteration in which $i = k-1$, the body of the loop sets $A[k-1]$ equal to 100, and all previous elements were already 100 by the induction hypothesis. ∎

Vacuous truth is useful for showing that claims are true about all elements of anything that is empty, or null. You can use vacuous truth to justify claims about all members of the empty set, about all characters in the null string, etc. For this reason, vacuous truth figures in the base cases of many inductive proofs. It is useful not only in proving loop invariants, but also in proofs about recursive algorithms whose base cases operate on something empty.

8.2.3 Proving Postconditions

Once you know that the loop in an iterative algorithm terminates, you can think about whether the algorithm establishes its intended postconditions. Showing that an iterative algorithm establishes certain postconditions just requires showing that the conditions that hold when the loop exits are transformed into those postconditions by any statements that the algorithm executes after the loop. In general, two kinds of conditions hold when a loop exits: conditions that the loop tests in deciding whether to exit and loop invariants that hold where the loop makes that decision.

Correctness of Binary Search

For example, let's prove that Binary Search returns the correct result. For reference, recall that the algorithm is as follows:

```
public boolean binarySearch(int x) {
    // Precondition: The array is in ascending order.
    int low = 0;
    int high = contents.length - 1;
    while (low <= high && contents[(low+high)/2] != x) {
        if (x < contents[(low+high)/2]) {
            high = (low+high)/2 - 1;
        }
        else {
            low = (low+high)/2 + 1;
        }
    }
    if (low > high) {
        return false;
    }
    else {
        return true;
    }
}
```

We need to show that if some element of contents equals x, then the returned value is true, and if no element of contents equals x, then the returned value is false. This statement contains two implications, and we give each a separate proof.

PRECONDITION: An ExtendedArray object's contents array is in ascending order.

THEOREM: If that ExtendedArray executes binarySearch(x), and some element of contents equals x, then binarySearch returns true. □

PROOF: The loop invariant for binarySearch states that if x is anywhere in contents, then it lies between positions low and high, inclusive. This invariant holds every time binarySearch evaluates the test in the while statement. In particular, it must hold the last time the loop evaluates the test, in other words, when the loop finally exits (and we know from the termination proof—see Section 8.2.1—that the loop does eventually exit). By the assumption of this theorem, x *is* somewhere in contents, so when the loop exits low must still be less than or equal to high (so that there are positions between low and high for x to lie in). Therefore, the test low > high immediately after the loop fails, causing binarySearch to return true. ∎

PRECONDITION: An ExtendedArray object's contents array is in ascending order.

THEOREM: If that ExtendedArray executes binarySearch(x), and no element of contents equals x, then binarySearch returns false. □

PROOF: The loop in binarySearch exits when contents[(low+high)/2] = x, or when low > high. Because no element of contents equals x, there can never be a value of (low+high)/2 for which contents[(low+high)/2] = x. Therefore, since the loop does eventually exit, it must do so because low > high. This in turn means that the test low > high immediately after the loop must succeed, causing binarySearch to return false. ∎

Most of the effort in both of these proofs revolved around finding the right combination of information from loop invariants and exit conditions to deduce the results we wanted. There was little reasoning about statements after the loop, because this algorithm does little substantive computing after its loop. Many iterative algorithms have this feature—all the real computing happens inside the loop, after which the algorithm simply returns a result. The correctness of such algorithms hinges on when the loop exits and what invariants it maintains.

Correctness of Euclid's Algorithm

We can also prove that Euclid's Algorithm really does return GCD(x, y).

Euclid's Algorithm is harder to prove correct than you might expect. The problem is this: when we designed the algorithm, we expected the while loop to exit with $y = 0$, and x and y still having their original greatest common divisor, in which case x would have to be equal to that greatest common divisor. Unfortunately, the algorithm's actual loop statement is while (y > 0), which exits when $y \leq 0$, not necessarily when $y = 0$. Thus, to make the original logic rigorous, we need another lemma to show that y cannot be negative when this loop evaluates its test.

PRECONDITION: $x \geq y \geq 0$.

LEMMA: $y \geq 0$ immediately before each evaluation of the test in while (y > 0) in greatestCommonDivisor(x, y). □

PROOF: The proof is in two parts, one dealing with the loop's first iteration, and one dealing with subsequent iterations.

For the first iteration, notice that $y \geq 0$ is one of the preconditions and is still true the first time the algorithm evaluates the test.

Subsequently, consider the k-th iteration, for any $k > 1$. In this iteration, $y_k = x_{k-1} \bmod y_{k-1}$. "Mod" always produces a result greater than or equal to zero, so $y_k \geq 0$ (recall that Java's % operator behaves like "mod" when the left operand is positive, and we discovered in Section 8.2.2 that x_{k-1} would be positive). ■

We can now prove the main theorem, that Euclid's Algorithm establishes its intended postcondition:

PRECONDITION: $x_0 \geq y_0 \geq 0$.

THEOREM: `greatestCommonDivisor(`x_0`, `y_0`)` returns $GCD(x_0, y_0)$. □

PROOF: We can show (see Exercise 8.9) that `greatestCommonDivisor`'s loop eventually exits. When it does, $y = 0$. This is because the loop's exit condition is $y \leq 0$, and we also showed that y must be greater than or equal to 0; $y \leq 0$ and $y \geq 0$ implies $y = 0$. Since $y = 0$ upon loop exit, $GCD(x, y)$ is simply x. Furthermore, the loop invariant says that $GCD(x, y)$ at loop exit is still the greatest common divisor of x_0 and y_0. Therefore, by returning x immediately upon exiting the loop, the algorithm establishes the desired postcondition. ■

8.2.4 A Complete Correctness Proof

You have now encountered all three parts of correctness proofs for iterative algorithms—termination proofs, proofs of loop invariants, and proofs of postconditions. In explaining these parts, we proved Euclid's Algorithm and Binary Search correct, but in piecemeal fashion, not in well-organized proofs. Proofs should, of course, be well-organized, so we now demonstrate how the three parts work together.

A Multiplication Algorithm

The following algorithm multiplies natural numbers m and n. It is easily implemented in hardware, forming the basic multiplier in some computers. Broadly speaking, the algorithm decreases m while increasing n and another term in such a way that the desired product eventually emerges. The algorithm's design starts with the observation that halving m and doubling n shouldn't change their product, since:

$$\frac{m}{2} \cdot 2n = mn \tag{8.9}$$

Thus the product of m and n could equivalently be computed as the product of $m/2$ and $2n$, which might be an easier computation, since $m/2$ is smaller than m. Doubling and halving natural numbers are easy things to do in computer hardware, but there is one pitfall: to avoid fractions, computer hardware halves natural numbers by doing exactly the sort of truncating division that Java's integer division does. This produces the mathematically exact quotient when m is even, but for odd m it effectively computes:

$$\frac{m-1}{2} \tag{8.10}$$

Thus, when m is odd, "halving" m and doubling n does change their product, to:

$$\frac{m-1}{2} \cdot 2n = mn - n \tag{8.11}$$

When m is odd, an actual multiplier therefore halves m and doubles n, but also notes that it needs to add a correction term equal to n in order to get the right product:

$$\frac{m-1}{2} \cdot 2n + n = mn \tag{8.12}$$

The multiplier repeatedly halves m, doubles n, and accumulates corrections in a running product until m decreases all the way to zero. The loop invariant relating m, n, and the running product (p) at the beginning of every iteration of this loop is:

$$m_i n_i + p_i = m_0 n_0 \text{ for all } i \geq 1 \tag{8.13}$$

We use the usual subscript notation in this invariant, so m_i, n_i, and p_i are the values of m, n, and p at the beginning of the i-th iteration of the loop, while m_0 and n_0 are the initial values of m and n. From this invariant, the running product must contain the full product when m decreases all the way to zero.

Here is the algorithm (we present it in pseudocode because many of its operations are those of electronic circuits rather than of a high-level programming language):

> *Algorithm "multiply"—multiply natural numbers m and n:*
>   *Initialize the running product to 0.*
>   *Repeat while m > 0:*
>   *If m is odd*
>   *Increment the running product by n.*
>   *Halve m.*
>   *Double n.*
>   *(When the loop exits, the running product is the product*
>   *of the original m and n)*

Correctness Proof

To prove the multiplication algorithm correct, we need all the typical parts of an iterative algorithm's correctness proof: a proof that the loop terminates, proofs that loop invariants hold when they should, and a proof that the algorithm establishes the required postcondition. We will prove termination and loop invariants as lemmas, and then use those lemmas to prove a final theorem about the algorithm's postcondition.

We begin by proving that the loop terminates.

PRECONDITION: m and n are natural numbers.

LEMMA: When algorithm "multiply" runs with arguments m and n, the loop in the algorithm eventually exits. □

PROOF: The loop exits when $m \leq 0$. Every iteration of the loop halves m, truncating the quotient to an integer if necessary. Since:

$$\frac{m}{2} < m \tag{8.14}$$

and truncation cannot increase the quotient, the result of the halving operation is strictly less than m. Further, the result of the halving operation is a natural number, so it must be at least one less than m. Thus every iteration of the loop reduces m by at least one, meaning m must eventually drop to or below 0. ■

We will need two loop invariants to prove the final theorem. One of these is the primary loop invariant, given in Equation 8.13. The second is that $m \geq 0$ whenever the loop evaluates its "while m > 0" test. We need this invariant for the same reasons we needed a similar invariant to prove Euclid's Algorithm correct: the multiplication algorithm's design assumes the loop will reduce m exactly to 0, but the loop could apparently exit with $m < 0$.

We prove the primary loop invariant first. Throughout this proof, we use variable p to stand for the value of the running product, as we did in Equation 8.13.

PRECONDITION: m and n are natural numbers.

LEMMA: When algorithm "multiply" runs with arguments m and n, Equation 8.13 holds whenever the algorithm evaluates the test in "while $m > 0$." □

PROOF: The proof is by induction on loop iterations.

Base Case: The loop's first iteration, the iteration for which i from Equation 8.13 is 1. The algorithm initializes p to 0. Furthermore, $m_1 = m_0$ and $n_1 = n_0$, because neither m nor n change before the loop begins. Thus, when the test is evaluated in iteration 1:

$$m_1 n_1 + p_1 = m_0 n_0 + 0 = m_0 n_0 \tag{8.15}$$

Induction Step: Assume that for some $k > 1$:

$$m_{k-1} n_{k-1} + p_{k-1} = m_0 n_0 \tag{8.16}$$

and show that:

$$m_k n_k + p_k = m_0 n_0 \tag{8.17}$$

The proof has two cases, one for m_{k-1} even, and one for m_{k-1} odd.

Case 1, m_{k-1} is even: the "if m is odd" test fails, so the loop's body leaves $p_k = p_{k-1}$, and sets $m_k = m_{k-1}/2$ (since halving an even number is exact) and $n_k = 2n_{k-1}$. We can use these values to rewrite $m_k n_k + p_k$ as follows:

$$m_k n_k + p_k = \frac{m_{k-1}}{2} \cdot 2n_{k-1} + p_{k-1} \qquad \text{Rewriting values in the } k\text{-th iteration in terms of values from the } (k-1)\text{-th.}$$

$$= m_{k-1} n_{k-1} + p_{k-1} \qquad \text{Cancelling the 2s.}$$

$$= m_0 n_0 \qquad \text{By the induction hypothesis.}$$

Case 2, m_{k-1} is odd: the "if m is odd" test succeeds, so the algorithm sets $p_k = p_{k-1} + n_{k-1}$, $m_k = (m_{k-1} - 1)/2$ (since halving an odd number truncates), and $n_k = 2n_{k-1}$. Thus:

$$m_k n_k + p_k = \frac{m_{k-1} - 1}{2} \cdot 2n_{k-1} + p_{k-1} + n_{k-1} \qquad \text{Rewriting values in the } k\text{-th iteration in terms of values from the } (k-1)\text{-th.}$$

$$= m_{k-1} n_{k-1} - n_{k-1} + p_{k-1} + n_{k-1} \qquad \text{Cancelling the 2's and multiplying } n_{k-1} \text{ through } m_{k-1} - 1.$$

$$= m_{k-1} n_{k-1} + p_{k-1} \qquad \text{Cancelling the } -n_{k-1} \text{ and } n_{k-1} \text{ terms.}$$

$$= m_0 n_0 \qquad \text{By the induction hypothesis.} \blacksquare$$

We next prove the secondary loop invariant.

PRECONDITION: m and n are natural numbers.

LEMMA: When algorithm "multiply" runs with arguments m and n, $m \geq 0$ every time the algorithm evaluates the "while $m > 0$" test. □

PROOF: By induction on iterations of the loop.

Base Case: The base case follows from the fact that m is initially a natural number and therefore greater than or equal to 0, and does not change before the loop.

Induction Step: Assume that $m_{k-1} \geq 0$ for some $k > 1$, and show that $m_k \geq 0$. m_k is the result of halving m_{k-1}. Dividing a non-negative number by two produces a non-negative result, and truncating this result still leaves it non-negative. Thus $m_{k-1} \geq 0$ implies that m_k is also greater than or equal to 0. ■

We finally have all the intermediate conclusions in place and can prove that algorithm "multiply" really does multiply. Once again, we use variable p to denote the value of the running product.

PRECONDITION: m_0 and n_0 are natural numbers.

THEOREM: When algorithm "multiply" runs with arguments m_0 and n_0, it ends with $p = m_0 n_0$. □

PROOF: Since the loop terminates, "multiply" does in fact end. When the loop finds $m \leq 0$ and so exits, we know from the secondary loop invariant that $m \geq 0$ also. Thus m must be exactly equal to 0 when the loop exits. From the primary loop invariant, we know that:

$$mn + p = m_0 n_0 \tag{8.18}$$

at the time the loop exits. Since $m = 0$, this simplifies to:

$$p = m_0 n_0 \quad \blacksquare \tag{8.19}$$

Exercises

8.8. A common *incorrect* implementation of Binary Search looks something like this:

```
public boolean binarySearch(int x) {
    int low = 0;
    int high = contents.length - 1;
    while (low <= high && contents[(low+high)/2] != x) {
        if (x < contents[(low+high)/2]) {
            high = (low+high)/2;
        }
        else {
            low = (low+high)/2;
        }
    }
    if (low > high) {
        return false;
    }
    else {
        return true;
    }
}
```

Show that the loop in this algorithm will *not* always terminate. (Hint: Try to create a termination proof, and note where your attempt fails. Use the reason the proof fails to help you find a specific example of a search in which the loop repeats forever.)

8.9. Prove that the loop in Euclid's Algorithm terminates. Hint: recall from our discussion of the algorithm that x mod y is always less than y.

8.10. Prove that the following loop terminates. The division operator is Java's truncating integer division. You should assume as a precondition for this loop that n is an integer greater than or equal to one.

```
while (n % 2 == 0) {
    n = n / 2;
}
```

8.11. Prove $y \geq 0$ every time greatestCommonDivisor evaluates the test in its while loop (the lemma we needed in order to prove greatestCommonDivisor correct) by using the standard inductive approach to proving a loop invariant. (Hint: the proof will look a lot like the proof we already gave.)

8.12. The following algorithm returns true if n is an exact power of two, and returns false if n is not an exact power of two. The loop is based on the invariant that the original value of n is equal to the value of n at the beginning of each iteration of the loop times some exact power of two (in terms of the subscript notation: for all i such that $i \geq 1$, $n_0 = n_i 2^i$). Prove that this invariant holds every time the loop evaluates its test.

```
// In a mathematical utilities class...
public static boolean isPowerOf2(int n) {
    // Precondition: n >= 1
    while (n % 2 == 0) {
        n = n / 2;
    }
    if (n == 1) {
        return true;
    }
    else {
        return false;
    }
}
```

8.13. The following algorithm finds the largest value in an extended array:

```
// In class ExtendedArray...
public int findLargest() {
    // Precondition: the array contains at least 1 element
    int max = contents[0];
    for (int i = 1; i < contents.length; i++) {
        if (contents[i] > max) {
            max = contents[i];
        }
    }
    return max;
}
```

Prove that max is the largest value in positions 0 through $i-1$ of contents at the beginning of every iteration of this algorithm's loop.

8.14. Here is an iterative algorithm to compute $n!$:

```
// In a mathematical utilities class...
public long factorial(int n) {
    long product = 1;
    for (int i = 1; i <= n; i++) {
        product = product * i;
    }
    return product;
}
```

Prove that the loop invariant $product = (i-1)!$ holds at the beginning of every iteration of this algorithm's loop. (Remember that $0! = 1$.)

8.15. Prove that the loops in each of the algorithms in Exercise 8.12 through Exercise 8.14 terminate.

8.16. Prove that the algorithms in Exercise 8.12 through Exercise 8.14 are correct.

8.17. Prove any loops you designed in Exercise 8.2 through Exercise 8.7 correct.

8.18. The following algorithm computes x^n, for any real number x and any natural number n. The algorithm's loop invariant is analogous to the one for algorithm "multiply":

```
// In a mathematical utilities class...
public static double power(double x, int n) {
    // Precondition: n >= 0
    double runningPower = 1.0;
    while (n > 0) {
        if (n%2 == 1) {
            runningPower = runningPower * x;
        }
        n = n / 2;
        x = x * x;
    }
    return runningPower;
}
```

State the exact loop invariant for this algorithm, and then prove that the algorithm really does return x^n.

8.19. Which of the following statements are true, and which false? Of those that are true, which are vacuously true, and which true for some other reason?

1. All odd numbers evenly divisible by two are negative.
2. All negative numbers are odd and evenly divisible by two.
3. Some odd number evenly divisible by two is negative.
4. Some negative number is odd.

5. All 10-meter tall purple penguins in the Sahara desert are ex-presidents of the United States.
6. All right triangles have three sides.
7. None of my friends from the planet Pluto have three eyes.
8. All of my friends from the planet Pluto have three eyes.

8.3 CONCLUDING REMARKS

Loop invariants are the guideposts to correct iteration. They are conditions that are true every time control reaches a particular point in a loop. Loop invariants play central roles both in the design of iterative algorithms and in proofs of those algorithms' correctness.

When designing iterative algorithms, start by identifying invariants in the problem the algorithm solves. Those invariants often become loop invariants for the algorithm. From loop invariants you can in turn deduce the right initializations for loop variables and the right ways of updating variables within the loop; you may also be able to deduce exit conditions for the loop.

To prove an iterative algorithm correct, you need to do three things:

1. Prove that the loop terminates, by showing that the loop makes at least some minimum amount of progress towards its exit condition in every iteration.
2. Prove that loop invariants you need in the other two steps really are loop invariant. Use induction on the number of times the loop has repeated to prove this.
3. Prove that the algorithm establishes its postconditions. You will often use loop invariants that hold where the loop evaluates its exit test to prove this.

Once you know that the loops in an algorithm are correct, your next concern is likely to be for how fast they are. The next chapter therefore takes up theoretical and experimental analyses of loops' performance.

8.4 FURTHER READING

Theoreticians have studied loops since the first work on proving algorithms correct. One of the first papers to deal comprehensively with proving properties of algorithms was:

Robert Floyd, "Assigning Meanings to Programs," *Mathematical Aspects of Computer Science*, XIX American Mathematical Society, 1967.

One of this paper's contributions (although Floyd suggests that others deserve the credit for it) is proving that an algorithm terminates by showing that some value decreases towards a fixed limit with every step of the algorithm. C. A. R. Hoare, in:

C. A. R. Hoare, "An Axiomatic Basis for Computer Programming," *Communications of the ACM*, Oct. 1969.

built on Floyd's ideas, He introduced loop invariants, using "an assertion which is always true on completion of [a loop's body], provided that it is also true on initiation" to define what can be proven about the postconditions of a loop.

David Gries, The *Science of Programming*, Springer-Verlag, 1981.

discusses design from loop invariants, and methods by which invariants can be discovered, at length.

Binary Search has long been known to be a surprisingly subtle algorithm. Donald Knuth describes its history at the end of Section 6.2.1 of:

Donald Knuth, *Sorting and Searching* (*The Art of Computer Programming*, Vol. 3), Addison-Wesley, 1975.

He points out that 16 years elapsed between the first published description of Binary Search and the first published version that worked for all array sizes.

Jon Bentley, "Programming Pearls: Writing Correct Programs," *Communications of the ACM*, Dec. 1983.

describes a course in which Bentley asked practicing programmers to code Binary Search from an English description; almost none were able to implement the algorithm correctly.

Many other algorithms discussed in this chapter are also classics. The original description of Euclid's Algorithm is in Book VII of Euclid's Elements, Proposition 2. Translations are widely available and provide interesting comparisons between ancient and modern ways of describing mathematics and algorithms. The "mod" algorithm suggested in Exercise 8.4 is embedded in Euclid's greatest common divisor algorithm, which never explicitly uses division or remainders. The natural number multiplication algorithm can be found in most computer architecture books, for example:

John Hennessy and David Patterson, *Computer Architecture: A Quantitative Approach*, Morgan Kaufmann, 1990.

This algorithm has a fascinating history—it is sometimes known as the "Russian Peasants' Algorithm," in the belief that it was used by Russian peasants prior to the introduction of modern education, and it is closely related to the multiplication strategy used in ancient Egypt. For more on historical multiplication algorithms, see:

L. Bunt et al., *The Historical Roots of Elementary Mathematics*, Prentice-Hall, 1976.

9 Iteration and Efficiency

The previous chapter introduced some ways to increase your confidence that loops are correct. However, questions about loops don't end with correctness. Loops can have a big impact on an algorithm's efficiency, and a thorough understanding of this impact is important in many settings. This chapter therefore explores the theoretical and empirical relationships between iteration and efficiency.

9.1 COUNTING THE STEPS IN ITERATIVE ALGORITHMS

We begin by developing theoretical techniques for counting how many steps a loop executes. This is the same measure of efficiency we analyzed for other algorithms (e.g., recursive algorithms in Section 7.2), although the mathematical tools used to count loops' operations are different than the tools needed for other control structures.

9.1.1 Overview

As in other efficiency analyses, the basic goal is to derive formulas that relate the number of steps an algorithm executes to the size of its input. Recall that computer scientists use the variable n in these formulas to stand for input size, and we follow that convention in this book.

Each analysis generally selects a few operations or statements from the overall algorithm and counts how many times they execute. What makes a good choice of steps to count depends on the question you want to answer—do you want an estimate of the overall amount of work an algorithm does, do you want to know how many times it sends a particular message to a particular object, etc.

Iterative algorithms often have distinctly different best- and worst-case efficiencies. Chapter 5 introduced the idea that different inputs may lead an algorithm to execute different numbers of steps. Even for the same input size, some problems of that size may require fewer steps to solve than others. (For example, consider searching an array: the size of the array is a natural measure of input size, but even within the same size array, some searches will find what they are looking for sooner than others.) The problem that requires the fewest steps is the best case for that size; the problem that requires the most steps is the worst case. The corresponding numbers of steps are the algorithm's best-case and worst-case efficiencies for that input size. You can often find one formula that relates input size to the best-case number of steps for all input sizes and a different formula that relates input size to the worst-case number of steps. Computer scientists therefore often do two analyses of an algorithm's efficiency: one to derive the formula for the best case and the other to derive the formula for the worst case.[1]

In all analyses, counting the steps that a loop executes boils down to adding up, over all the loop's iterations, the number of steps each iteration executes. To do this, you have to know two things about the loop:

- The number of iterations
- How many steps each iteration executes

9.1.2 Simple Loops

As a first example, consider an algorithm in which both the number of times the loop repeats and the number of steps it executes are easy to determine. The algorithm is Sequential Search, an alternative to Binary Search for searching arrays. This algorithm simply looks at each element of an array in turn until it either finds the value it is seeking or comes to the end of the array. We present it as another method for Chapter 8's ExtendedArray class:

```
// In class ExtendedArray...
public boolean sequentialSearch(int x) {
    int cur = 0;
    while (cur < contents.length && contents[cur] != x) {
        cur = cur + 1;
    }
    if (cur >= contents.length) {
        return false;
    }
    else {
        return true;
    }
}
```

---

[1] Computer scientists may also derive a formula for the average number of steps an algorithm executes. Those analyses are beyond the scope of this book.

Multiple Iterations

Let's count the worst-case number of times `sequentialSearch` executes its `contents[current] != x` comparison, as a function of the size of the array. As described in the preceding overview (Section 9.1.1), we need to know how many times the loop iterates and how many times each iteration executes the comparison.

The loop in `sequentialSearch` can iterate as many times as there are elements in the array—after that many iterations, the `current < contents.length` test fails and causes the loop to exit. The worst-case number of iterations is therefore `contents.length`.

Every iteration of the loop executes the `contents[current] != x` comparison once.

Since the loop repeats `contents.length` times, and each repetition executes the step we are counting once, it is easy to see that the step must be executed `contents.length` times. Conveniently, `contents.length` is the parameter (array size) that we wanted to express the number of comparisons as a function of, so the analysis is finished. To put this result in computer scientists' usual notation, we would let n stand for array size (our measure of input size, the parameter we are expressing our result in terms of), and say that `sequentialSearch` executes its `contents[current] != x` comparison n times in the worst case.

In this loop, every iteration executes the step we are counting the same number of times. Therefore, summing the number of executions over all iterations simplifies to multiplying the number of iterations (`contents.length`, or n, in this example) by the number of times each iteration executes the step (1 in this example). Such multiplication is a helpful shortcut for analyzing loops in which every iteration executes the same number of steps. Be aware, however, that not all loops have this property. For loops without it, you must explicitly add up the number of steps in each iteration.

No Iterations

Next, let's look at the best-case number of times that `sequentialSearch` executes the `contents[current] != x` comparison. The loop in `sequentialSearch` may find x, and so exit, as early as the loop's first iteration. In this case, the algorithm executes the comparison only once.

Deriving this best case didn't require any summing of steps over iterations. This is because in its best case, `sequentialSearch` doesn't complete even one iteration of its loop. Many algorithms' best cases happen when loops never repeat. In these cases, summing steps over iterations degenerates into simple, direct counting.

9.1.3 Varying Number of Steps per Iteration

Most loops don't execute the same number of steps in every iteration. Rather, the number of steps varies from iteration to iteration, a situation that requires explicitly summing the number of steps executed over all iterations. To demonstrate, consider Selection Sort, which you may remember as the subject of an experiment in Section 4.8. Here it is again, this time as a sort method for class ExtendedArray:

```
// In class ExtendedArray...
public void sort() {
    for (int cur = 0; cur < contents.length-1; cur++) {
        int min = cur;
        for (int i = cur+1; i < contents.length; i++) {
            if (contents[i] < contents[min]) {
                min = i;
            }
        }
        this.swap(min, cur);
    }
}
```

Setting Up the Analysis

Before starting to analyze any algorithm's efficiency, we need to decide what steps we want to count, what measure of input size we want to express the result in terms of, and whether we want to analyze the best case or the worst case.

Taking these decisions in order, let's count the number of times Selection Sort executes the contents[i] < contents[min] comparison.

Second, the size of the array (i.e., the number of items being sorted) is a natural measure of input size for sorting. Thus, in this analysis, the variable n will stand for the number of items in the array, equivalent to contents.length in the Java code. (The algebra in the analysis will be easier to read if we don't use names like "contents.length" as math variables though.)

Finally, there are no best and worst cases for Selection Sort, so we only need to do one analysis. Both of the loops simply step a variable from an initial value to a fixed final value—there is no way either loop can exit early. Nor is there any way that some iterations can choose to execute the contents[i] < contents[min] comparison while others choose not to execute it. Thus, array size is the only thing that affects how many times the algorithm executes the comparison.

We will divide our analysis into two parts, one for each of the two loops in Selection Sort:

■ We will start the analysis by figuring out how many comparisons the inner loop executes. We will do this in the usual manner, figuring out how many times the loop repeats and how many comparisons each repetition executes.

■ Analyzing the inner loop will produce an expression that tells us how many comparisons one iteration of the outer loop executes. We will sum that expression over all iterations of the outer loop in order to get the final count.

One can analyze most nested loops using a similar strategy, feeding analysis results for inner loops into the analyses of outer ones.

Analyzing the Inner Loop

The inner loop iterates once for each integer between $cur+1$ and $n-1$, inclusive. The number of integers between $cur+1$ and $n-1$, inclusive, is:[2]

$$(n-1)-(cur+1)+1 = n-1-cur-1+1 = n-cur-1 \qquad (9.1)$$

Every iteration of the inner loop executes the comparison once. Thus, the number of comparisons executed by the inner loop is:

$$n-cur-1 \qquad (9.2)$$

Equation 9.2 depends on cur, the variable defined by the outer loop. In each iteration of the outer loop, the inner loop therefore repeats a different number of times. This is why we must add up the values of Equation 9.2 over the iterations of the outer loop rather than simply multiplying it by the number of times the outer loop repeats.

Analyzing the Outer Loop

Selection Sort's outer loop repeats once for each value of cur between 0 and $n-2$. Equation 9.2 therefore takes on the values $n-1$ (when $cur=0$), $n-2$ (when $cur=1$), and so forth. Adding together all of the values that Equation 9.2 takes on as cur ranges from 0 to $n-2$ yields the sum:

$$\sum_{i=0}^{n-2}(n-i-1) \qquad (9.3)$$

Equation 9.3 would be easier to understand and use if we found a closed form for it, that is, an equivalent expression that does not involve the summation operator. We can do this as follows:

---

[2] For any two integers, a and b, where $b \geq a$, the number of integers between a and b, inclusive, is $b-a+1$.

$$\sum_{i=0}^{n-2}(n-i-1) = \sum_{i=0}^{n-2}n - \sum_{i=0}^{n-2}i - \sum_{i=0}^{n-2}1$$

Using associativity (see the "Simplifying Summations" sidebar) to split the $(n-i-1)$-summation into separate summations of n, i, and 1.

$$= (n-1)n - \sum_{i=0}^{n-2}i - \sum_{i=0}^{n-2}1$$

The n-summation is simply $n-1$ n's added together, or $(n-1)n$.

$$= (n-1)n - \frac{(n-2)(n-1)}{2} - \sum_{i=0}^{n-2}1$$

The i-summation simplifies to $(n-2)(n-1)/2$ (see Section 7.1.1).

$$= (n-1)n - \frac{(n-2)(n-1)}{2} - (n-1)$$

The 1-summation is just $(n-1)$ 1's added together, or $n-1$.

$$= \frac{2n(n-1)-(n-2)(n-1)-2(n-1)}{2}$$

Putting all terms over a common denominator.

$$= \frac{(2n-(n-2)-2)(n-1)}{2}$$

Factoring $(n-1)$ out of each term in the numerator.

$$= \frac{n(n-1)}{2}$$

Simplifying $(2n-(n-2)-2)$.

$$= \frac{n^2-n}{2}$$

Multiplying n through $(n-1)$.

Discussion

By adding up the number of contents[i] < contents[min] comparisons that each iteration of Selection Sort's outermost loop performs, we have calculated the total number of those comparisons that the algorithm executes, as a function of the size of the array. Our final answer is that Selection Sort executes:

$$\frac{n^2-n}{2} \tag{9.4}$$

comparisons while sorting an n-element array.

Simplifying Summations

You can simplify many summations by exploiting some algebraic properties of addition.

First, consider a sum of the form:

$$\sum_i (a_i + b_i)$$

This summation is shorthand for:

$$(a_1 + b_1) + (a_2 + b_2) + (a_3 + b_3) + \ldots$$

Because addition is associative, you can group the a and b terms together, as

$$(a_1 + a_2 + a_3 + \ldots) + (b_1 + b_2 + b_3 + \ldots)$$

This in turn is equivalent to:

$$\sum_i a_i + \sum_i b_i$$

Therefore:

$$\sum_i (a_i + b_i) = \sum_i a_i + \sum_i b_i$$

Second, because multiplication distributes over addition, constant coefficients (coefficients that don't depend on the summation variable) can be factored out of summations:

$$\sum_i c a_i = c a_1 + c a_2 + \ldots = c(a_1 + a_2 + \ldots) = c \sum_i a_i$$

This analysis says a lot about Selection Sort. If the number of comparisons Selection Sort does (let alone other work) grows more or less proportionally to n^2, then its overall execution time must grow at least that fast, too. This suggests that as array size increases, Selection Sort's subjective performance will probably deteriorate quickly from "good" to "slow" to "totally unacceptable." You may have sensed this in the graph of execution time versus array size from Section 4.8's experiment, which curved upwards rather than following a straight line. This curve can be explained by the roughly n^2 comparisons you now know the algorithm was doing.

9.1.4 Deriving the Number of Iterations

It is not always as easy to determine how many times a loop will iterate as in the previous examples. Sometimes you need a mathematical analysis of the loop, or of the problem it solves, in order to derive the number of iterations. For example, consider deriving the worst-case number of times the loop in Binary Search (from Section 8.1) can repeat.

```java
// In class ExtendedArray...
public boolean binarySearch(int x) {
    // Precondition: The array is in ascending order.
    int low = 0;
    int high = contents.length - 1;
    while (low <= high && contents[(low+high)/2] != x) {
        if (x < contents[(low+high)/2]) {
            high = (low+high)/2 - 1;
        }
        else {
            low = (low+high)/2 + 1;
        }
    }
    if (low > high) {
        return false;
    }
    else {
        return true;
    }
}
```

The worst-case number of iterations isn't immediately obvious from the algorithm, but you can derive it by recalling how Binary Search works: it keeps track of which section of the array should contain x; with every iteration, it compares one of the elements in this "section of interest" to x and divides the rest of the section into two halves. The search continues in one of these halves during the next iteration.

From this idea of halving a section of interest, we can do a two-step derivation of the worst-case number of iterations of Binary Search's loop:

1. Derive the number of elements in the section of interest as a function of the number of iterations of the loop (in other words, derive a formula for the number of elements in the section during the *i*-th iteration, for any *i*).
2. Binary Search can only repeat its loop until the section of interest contains one item. So find out how many iterations that takes by solving the formula

from step 1 for the iteration number in which the section of interest contains one item.

As usual in efficiency analyses, we let n represent the input size, in this case, the number of elements in the array.

The Size of Binary Search's Section of Interest

During Binary Search's first iteration, all n elements are in the section of interest. From the "compare one and divide into halves" rule, the number of elements in the section of interest during the second iteration must be:

$$\frac{n-1}{2} \tag{9.5}$$

Binary Search further compares one of *these* elements to x and divides the others into two sections, each of size:

$$\frac{\frac{n-1}{2}-1}{2} = \frac{(n-1-2)/2}{2} = \frac{n-(2+1)}{4} \tag{9.6}$$

The pattern continues in subsequent iterations as shown in Table 9.1:

TABLE 9.1 Sizes of Binary Search's Section of Interest

Iteration Number	Elements in Section of Interest
1	n
2	$\dfrac{n-1}{2}$
3	$\dfrac{\frac{n-1}{2}-1}{2} = \dfrac{n-(2+1)}{4}$
4	$\dfrac{\frac{n-(2+1)}{4}-1}{2} = \dfrac{n-(4+2+1)}{8}$
5	$\dfrac{\frac{n-(4+2+1)}{8}-1}{2} = \dfrac{n-(8+4+2+1)}{16}$

Let s stand for the number of elements in the section of interest. The general pattern then seems to be that in the i-th iteration:

$$s = \frac{n - \sum_{j=0}^{i-2} 2^j}{2^{i-1}} \tag{9.7}$$

You can, in fact, prove that this formula is correct (see Exercise 9.13). The closed form for the sum of the first powers of 2 (see Section 7.1.1) is:

$$\sum_{k=0}^{m} 2^k = 2^{m+1} - 1 \tag{9.8}$$

Substituting this closed form into Equation 9.7 allows us to simplify that equation to:

$$s = \frac{n - \left(2^{i-1} - 1\right)}{2^{i-1}} \tag{9.9}$$

The Maximum Number of Iterations of Binary Search's Loop

Binary Search's loop can continue only as long as there is at least one element in the section of interest. Thus, we can find the maximum number of iterations by setting s equal to 1 in Equation 9.9 and solving for i:

$1 = \dfrac{n - \left(2^{i-1} - 1\right)}{2^{i-1}}$	Original equation with s set to 1.
$2^{i-1} = n - \left(2^{i-1} - 1\right)$	Multiplying both sides by 2^{i-1}.
$2^{i-1} + 2^{i-1} = n + 1$	Adding 2^{i-1} to both sides and simplifying the resulting $n - (-1)$ on the right.
$2 \times 2^{i-1} = n + 1$	Replacing $2^{i-1} + 2^{i-1}$ with $2 \times 2^{i-1}$.
$2^i = n + 1$	$2 \times 2^{i-1} = 2^1 \times 2^{i-1}$, which in turn is 2^i.
$i = \log_2 (n+1)$	Taking base 2 logarithms of both sides. (Recall that the base 2 logarithm of x, written $\log_2 x$, is the power to which 2 must be raised in order to get x. For example, $16 = 2^4$, so $\log_2 16 = 4$. More generally, whenever $k = 2^i$, $\log_2 k = i$.)

The maximum number of times Binary Search's loop can repeat is therefore:

$$\log_2 (n+1) \qquad (9.10)$$

where n is the array size. This result came from the mathematics of a particular aspect of Binary Search, namely the way it halves the array's section of interest. You can now use this formula to derive step counts for Binary Search. For example, since every iteration can perform two comparisons between x and `contents[(low+high)/2]`, the worst-case number of such comparisons Binary Search makes must be:

$$2\log_2 (n+1) \qquad (9.11)$$

Exercises

9.1. The following algorithm computes n! for a hypothetical mathematical utilities class:

```
public static long factorial(int n) {
    long product = 1;
    for (int i = 2; i <= n; i++) {
        product = product * i;
    }
    return product;
}
```

Derive the number of multiplications this algorithm executes, as a function of n. (Note that the best and worst cases are the same for this algorithm.)

9.2. The following algorithm computes the sum of the integers between 1 and n for a hypothetical mathematical utilities class:

```
public static int sum(int n) {
    int total = 0;
    int i = 1;
    while (i <= n) {
        total = total + i;
        i = i + 1;
    }
    return total;
}
```

Derive the number of "+" operations this algorithm executes, as a function of n. (Note that the best and worst cases are the same for this algorithm.)

9.3. The following algorithm determines whether or not n is a prime number. The algorithm returns true if n is prime, false if it is not. Derive the best and worst case number of % operations this algorithm executes, as functions of n.

```
public static boolean isPrime(int n) {
    // Precondition: n >= 2
    boolean mayBePrime = true;
    int limit = Math.round(Math.sqrt(n));
    for (int f = 2; f <= limit && mayBePrime; f++) {
        if (n % f == 0) {
            mayBePrime = false;
        }
    }
    return mayBePrime;
}
```

9.4. Design a method for the ExtendedArray class that determines whether an extended array is in ascending order. Your method should return true if the array is in order, false if not. Derive the best- and worst-case numbers of comparisons between array elements that your algorithm performs.

9.5. Here is an algorithm that initializes every element of a square two-dimensional array to 0. The algorithm appears as an initialize method for a hypothetical Extended2DArray class, in which member variable contents contains the values in the array, and member variable n is the number of rows and columns in it. Derive the number of assignments to elements of contents that this algorithm executes, in terms of n:

```
// In class Extended2DArray...
public void initialize() {
    for (int row = 0; row < n; row++) {
        for (int col = 0; col < n; col++) {
            contents[row][col] = 0;
        }
    }
}
```

9.6. Do the best- and worst-case number of times Selection Sort executes its min = i statement differ? If so, derive expressions for each in terms of array size.

9.7. Insertion Sort is another simple sorting algorithm, often preferred to Selection Sort. To see why, derive formulas for the best- and worst-case (they differ) number of comparisons between elements of the array that Insertion Sort makes, in terms of array size. Here is Insertion Sort, as an alternative sort method for ExtendedArray. The algorithm works by maintaining a loop invariant in the outer loop that elements 1 through cur−1 of contents are in sorted order; the algorithm extends this sorted region to include the cur-th element by moving that element to its proper place in the sorted region (using the inner loop to do the moving):

```
// In class ExtendedArray...
public void sort() {
    // Insertion Sort
    for (int cur = 1; cur < contents.length; cur++) {
        int j = cur - 1;
        while (j >= 0 && contents[j] > contents[j+1]) {
            this.swap(j, j+1);
            j = j - 1;
        }
    }
}
```

9.8. Bubble Sort is another sorting algorithm, that like Insertion Sort (Exercise 9.7) can take advantage of the extent to which parts of an array are already sorted to reduce the amount of work it does. Here is Bubble Sort, as an alternative sort method for ExtendedArray. The key idea is to swap adjacent elements that are out of order in a way that "bubbles" large values to the upper end of the array and to keep doing so as long as at least one element moves:

```
// In class ExtendedArray...
public void sort() {
    // Bubble Sort
    int limit = contents.length - 1;
    boolean moved;
    do {
        moved = false;
        for (int i = 0; i < limit; i++) {
            if (contents[i] > contents[i+1]) {
                this.swap(i, i+1);
                moved = true;
            }
```

```
        }
        limit = limit - 1;
    } while (moved);
}
```

Derive the best- and worst-case number of comparisons between elements of the array that Bubble Sort makes, in terms of array size.

9.9. Our analyses of sorting algorithms have concentrated on the number of comparisons an algorithm makes. Another popular measure of the work a sorting algorithm does is the number of times it swaps array elements. Derive the best- and worst-case numbers of swap messages that Selection Sort, Insertion Sort, and Bubble Sort send, in terms of array size (Insertion Sort is defined in Exercise 9.7, Bubble Sort in Exercise 9.8).

9.10. Find closed forms for the following summations:

1. $\displaystyle\sum_{i=0}^{n}(i+2)$

2. $\displaystyle\sum_{i=0}^{n}3i$

3. $\displaystyle\sum_{i=0}^{n}(2i+5)$

4. $\displaystyle\sum_{i=0}^{n}10(i-1)$

5. $\displaystyle\sum_{i=0}^{n}3\cdot2^{i}$

6. $\displaystyle\sum_{i=0}^{n}2^{i-2}$

7. $\displaystyle\sum_{i=0}^{n}(2^{i}+3i-1)$

9.11. Derive an expression for the worst-case number of division operations Binary Search can do.

9.12. Imagine a class `NaturalNumber` that represents natural numbers. The main member variable in `NaturalNumber` is an integer, `value`, that holds the value a `NaturalNumber` object represents; $value \geq 0$ is a class invariant for `NaturalNumber`. One of the messages `NaturalNumber` objects handle is `countDigits`, which returns the number of digits needed to print a natural number in decimal. Here is the method that handles this message:

```
// In class NaturalNumber...
public int countDigits() {
    int power = 10;
    int digits = 1;
    while (power <= value) {
        power = power * 10;
        digits = digits + 1;
    }
    return digits;
}
```

Derive the number of times the loop in this algorithm repeats, in terms of value.

9.13. Prove that Equation 9.7 gives the correct number of elements in Binary Search's section of interest. Assume that dividing sections into halves as Binary Search does always produces equal-sized subsections. (Hints: you might find it easier to work with the closed form in Equation 9.9 than with Equation 9.7; consider using an induction proof.)

9.2 RELATING STEP COUNTS TO EXECUTION TIME

By now, you have seen a lot of theoretically derived operation counts for algorithms. You have also learned how to measure the execution times of algorithms. You are thus prepared to study how theoretical operation counts relate (or don't) to empirically measured execution times.

9.2.1 Introductory Examples

This section examines relationships between operation counts and execution times in the ExtendedArray class. We study the Selection Sort and Sequential Search algorithms discussed earlier, and two new algorithms: one that initializes an array to be in descending order, and one that finds the "rank" of each element in an array. An element's *rank* is the position that element would have if the array were sorted into ascending order—the smallest element has rank 1, the second smallest rank 2, and so forth. Code and efficiency analyses for these new algorithms appear in the "Ranking and Initializing Arrays" sidebar.

The number of operations each algorithm executes depends on the array size, *n*. We count the number of comparisons to array elements executed by Sequential Search, Selection Sort, and Ranking, and the number of assignments to array elements executed by Initialization. You saw in Section 9.1.2 that Sequential Search

Ranking and Initializing Arrays

We use a simple, if inefficient, ranking algorithm: count, for each element of the array, the number of elements less than or equal to it. This count is the element's rank, which we store in a second array, `result`:

```
public int[] rank() {
    int[] result = new int[contents.length];
    for (int cur = 0; cur < contents.length; cur++) {
        int rank = 0;
        for (int j = 0; j < contents.length; j++) {
            if (contents[j] <= contents[cur]) {
                rank = rank + 1;
            }
        }
        result[cur] = rank;
    }
    return result;
}
```

The outer loop iterates n times, where n is the array size. Each iteration causes the inner loop to iterate n times, so the total number of iterations of the inner loop is n^2. Each of those iterations executes one comparison between array elements, so the total number of comparisons is also n^2.

Our algorithm to initialize an array executes one assignment to an array element in each iteration of its loop. The loop iterates n times, so the total number of assignments is n:

```
public void descendingOrder() {
    for (int cur = 0; cur < contents.length; cur++) {
        contents[cur] = contents.length - i;
    }
}
```

executes n comparisons to array elements (in the worst case), and Section 9.1.3 showed that Selection Sort executes $(n^2 - n)/2$ comparisons. Our ranking algorithm executes n^2 comparisons, and our initialization algorithm executes n assignments.

In addition to deriving theoretical operation counts for our algorithms, we also measured the algorithms' actual execution times. Table 9.2 shows the average execution times of each algorithm for several array sizes. We gathered these measurements from a Java implementation of `ExtendedArray`, running on a 550 MHz Apple PowerBook G4 under Mac OS X 10.2.6. The times for Sequential Search are worst-case times.

TABLE 9.2   Execution Times of Some Array Algorithms (in Microseconds)

Algorithm	Array Size						
	8	16	32	64	128	256	512
Selection Sort	2.8	6.9	23.6	87.6	318	1258	4836
Ranking	5.1	15.2	51.6	188	721	2840	11240
Sequential Search	0.4	0.6	1.1	2.2	4.4	8.4	16.7
Initialization	0.4	0.7	1.3	3.0	4.7	9.0	17.6

Figure 9.1 graphs the execution times against array size. The most striking thing about this graph is the gross difference between the times for Selection Sort and Ranking on one hand, and Sequential Search and Initialization on the other. Sequential Search and Initialization are so fast that their times are indistinguishable from zero when compared to Selection Sort and Ranking. In contrast, Selection Sort and Ranking both fit well on the graph.

Figure 9.2 presents another graph of the four algorithms' execution times, now with the vertical axis scaled to show the times for Sequential Search and Initialization. This graph has a problem complementary to that of Figure 9.1: the lines for Selection Sort and Ranking immediately climb off it, while Sequential Search and Initialization fit comfortably on it.

Figure 9.1 and Figure 9.2 suggest that some differences between algorithms matter much more than others. Two of the algorithms are overwhelmingly slower than the others; the slow algorithms are exactly those that have an n^2 term in their operation counts, while the fast ones are those with only an n term. The differences in performance between the two n^2-operation algorithms, or between the two n-operation algorithms, pale in comparison to the differences between an n^2- and an n-operation algorithm. For example, it is all but irrelevant that Selection Sort only executes about half as many comparisons as Ranking when one considers that Sequential Search and Initialization are both essentially instantaneous compared to either. In fact, differences such as those between Ranking and Selection Sort, or between Initialization and Sequential Search, may vanish if you just code one algorithm more efficiently than the other. However, differences such as those between

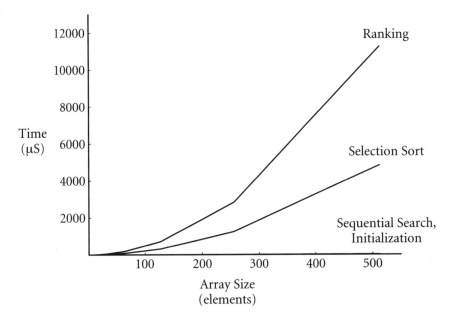

FIGURE 9.1 Execution times of four algorithms.

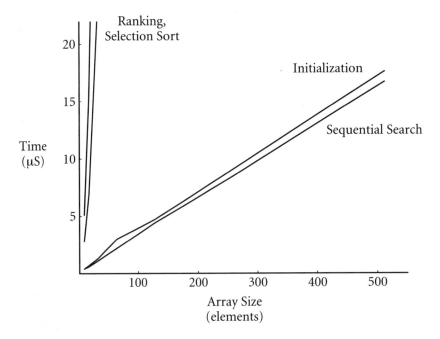

FIGURE 9.2 Execution times of four algorithms, emphasizing the smaller times.

Ranking or Selection Sort on one hand, and Sequential Search or Initialization on the other, are so huge that no amount of clever implementation can overcome them.

9.2.2 Asymptotic Notation

As illustrated by the comparison of Selection Sort, Ranking, Sequential Search, and array Initialization, the most important thing about a theoretical operation count is its fastest-growing term (n^2 in the cases of Ranking and Selection Sort, n in the cases of Sequential Search and Initialization). In light of this fact, computer scientists generally state theoretical operation counts using *asymptotic notation*, an abstraction of a formula based on its fastest-growing term.

Informal Meaning

If $f(n)$ and $b(n)$ are functions, a computer scientist will say that "$f(n)$ is order $b(n)$", written:

$$f(n) = \Theta(b(n)) \tag{9.12}$$

if (informally) the fastest-growing term in $f(n)$ is proportional to $b(n)$. For example:

$$4n^2 + 1 = \Theta(n^2) \tag{9.13}$$

because the fastest-growing term in $4n^2 + 1$ is $4n^2$, which is proportional to n^2.

Be aware that the "=" sign in asymptotic expressions such as Equation 9.12, is somewhat misleading. "$\Theta(b(n))$" does not represent a function that $f(n)$ is identical to; at best, $\Theta(b(n))$ is a whole set of functions, of which $f(n)$ is one member, that are all roughly proportional to $b(n)$. Nonetheless, the use of "=" in asymptotic notation is so deeply ingrained in tradition that it is universally understood and unlikely to change.

When you analyze an algorithm's efficiency, you are usually more interested in how it performs on large problems than on small ones. This is why asymptotic notation concentrates on the fastest-growing term in a function—it is the term that determines the function's behavior when n is large. The possible presence of other, slower-growing terms in a function means that asymptotic notation is not simply a way of saying that one function is perfectly proportional to another, though. Rather, asymptotic notation says that one function is *roughly* proportional to another, for large values of the parameter. For example, Figure 9.3 demonstrates an $\Theta(n)$ function. The function is $\Theta(n)$ because its graph is generally proportional to that of n, except when n is small.

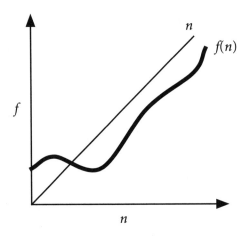

FIGURE 9.3 An $\Theta(n)$ function.

Formal Definition

You can usually read "$\Theta(\dots)$" as "roughly proportional to...," but sometimes you will need the precise, formal definition. The precise definition is that $f(n) = \Theta(b(n))$ if and only if f grows no faster than proportional to b for sufficiently large n, nor does f grow slower than proportional to b, for sufficiently large n. These conditions are usually stated formally as:

■ (f grows no faster than proportional to b) there exists a pair of constants, c_1 and n_1, with $c_1 > 0$, such that:

$$f(n) \le c_1 b(n) \text{ for all } n \ge n_1 \tag{9.14}$$

■ and (f grows no slower than proportional to b) there exists another pair of constants, c_2 and n_2, with $c_2 > 0$, such that:

$$f(n) \ge c_2 b(n) \text{ for all } n \ge n_2 \tag{9.15}$$

To illustrate how one might use this definition, let's prove the asymptotic equivalence we asserted informally in Equation 9.13, namely:

$$4n^2 + 1 = \Theta\left(n^2\right) \tag{9.16}$$

All that such a proof requires is to find values for c_1 and n_1 that make Equation 9.14 hold, and values for c_2 and n_2 that make Equation 9.15 hold. For example, notice that:

$$4n^2 + 1 \le 5n^2 \text{ for all } n \ge 1 \tag{9.17}$$

In other words, $c_1 = 5$ and $n_1 = 1$ make Equation 9.14 hold. Similarly:

$$4n^2 + 1 \ge 4n^2 \text{ for all } n \ge 0 \tag{9.18}$$

so that $c_2 = 4$ and $n_2 = 0$ make Equation 9.15 hold. That's all there is to the proof—we have shown that both Equation 9.14 and Equation 9.15 can be made to hold for $f(n) = 4n^2 + 1$ and $b(n) = n^2$, so therefore $4n^2 + 1$ must indeed be $\Theta(n^2)$. The values we found for n_1, c_1, n_2, and c_2 are not the only four values that prove this equivalence; many others will also work. This is generally the case when proving that one function is asymptotically equivalent to another—you aren't looking for *the* values that work, you are looking for *any* of many values that do.

Asymptotic Step Counts and Execution Time

The asymptotic forms of theoretical step counts provide an excellent approximation of an algorithm's real-world execution time. Suppose you heroically counted every single step the algorithm executes, and miraculously defined "step" in such a way that each of the things you counted takes the same amount of time to execute as every other. You could still only conclude that the actual running time of programs based on that algorithm is *proportional* to your step count, because different computers run at different speeds. A program's actual running time depends both on what executes it and how many steps it executes. Therefore, an asymptotic step count, which gives a simple expression that is roughly proportional to actual running time, provides all the information that one can reasonably expect from a theoretical execution time analysis.

For example, you know that Selection Sort performs:

$$\frac{n^2 - n}{2} \tag{9.19}$$

comparisons between array elements. If you want to turn this count into an estimate of Selection Sort's execution time, you can say that the time is:

$$\Theta(n^2) \tag{9.20}$$

If you measured the execution time of a Selection Sort program, you would indeed measure times proportional to n^2. Any effect of the division by two in Equation

9.19 would be indistinguishable from (and probably dwarfed by) effects of running the program on faster or slower computers. Similarly, any effect of the low-order "$-n$" term in Equation 9.19 would be so small relative to the n^2 term that it would be indistinguishable from random error in the measurements.

Because only the asymptotic form of a theoretical operation count matters in the end, you can be quite cavalier about what operations you count in theoretical analyses of execution time. As long as you count an operation whose number of executions grows as fast as any other operation's in the algorithm, you will get the correct asymptotic execution time.

9.2.3 Testing Asymptotic Hypotheses

Suppose you derive a theoretical execution time of $\Theta(f(n))$ for some algorithm, and then measure that algorithm's running time in a program. How can you analyze your data to see if the measured times are really $\Theta(f(n))$?

One good analysis follows from the definition of $\Theta(f(n))$:

If your measurements are $\Theta(f(n))$, it means that:

■ The measurements are less than or equal to $c_1 f(n)$, and
■ the measurements are greater than or equal to $c_2 f(n)$, for some positive constants c_1 and c_2, and sufficiently large values of n.

This in turn implies:

$$c_2 \leq \frac{measurements}{f(n)} \leq c_1 \tag{9.21}$$

Thus, to analyze your data, divide each measurement by $f(n)$, where n is the value of the independent variable for that measurement. If, as n increases, this ratio seems to settle between two nonzero bounds, then the data is consistent with your $\Theta(f(n))$ hypothesis.

Note that it makes no sense to ask if a single measurement is $\Theta(f(n))$. Asymptotic notation describes how a function grows as its parameter increases. Therefore, you can only ask if a sequence of measurements, each corresponding to a different input size (i.e., a different n), grows as $\Theta(f(n))$.

For example, suppose you want to verify that a certain program's running time is $\Theta(n^2)$. You measure the execution times in Table 9.3 for this program:

TABLE 9.3 Execution Times for a Hypothetical Program

Input Size (n)	Time (seconds)
1	2
2	3
5	26
10	99
20	405
50	2498
100	10004

Since $f(n)$ is n^2 in this case, you should divide each running time by the corresponding n^2, as shown in Table 9.4:

TABLE 9.4 Analysis of Table 9.3's Data for $\Theta(n^2)$ Growth

n	Time	n^2	Time / n^2
1	2	1	2.000
2	3	4	0.750
5	26	25	1.040
10	99	100	0.990
20	405	400	1.013
50	2498	2500	0.999
100	10004	10000	1.000

The ratios don't consistently increase or decrease as n increases; instead, they seem to settle around 1. You can therefore conclude that your measured times are consistent with your $\Theta(n^2)$ hypothesis.

Exercises

9.14. A certain sorting algorithm runs in $\Theta(n^2)$ time. A program that uses this algorithm takes two seconds to sort a list of 50 items. How long do you estimate this program will take to sort a list of 500 items?

9.15. Decide whether each of the following statements is true or false, and prove your answers.

1. $n+1 = \Theta(n)$
2. $1/n = \Theta(n)$
3. $n/1000 = \Theta(n)$
4. $3n^2 = \Theta(n^2)$
5. $2n^2 + n = \Theta(n^2)$

9.16. Each inequality in the definition of $\Theta(...)$ can also be used by itself, leading to two other asymptotic notations used in computer science:

■ $f(n) = O(b(n))$ if and only if there exist constants $c > 0$ and n_0 such that:

$$f(n) \leq cb(n) \text{ for all } n \geq n_0 \tag{9.22}$$

■ $f(n) = \Omega(b(n))$ if and only if there exist constants $c > 0$ and n_0 such that:

$$f(n) \geq cb(n) \text{ for all } n \geq n_0 \tag{9.23}$$

Using these definitions, prove or disprove each of the following:

1. $n^2 + 1 = O(n^2)$
2. $n^2 + 1 = \Omega(n^2)$
3. $n^2 = O(n)$
4. $n = O(n^2)$
5. $n^2 = \Omega(n)$
6. $n = \Omega(n^2)$

9.17. A very useful theorem about asymptotic notation says, informally, that any polynomial is of the same order as its highest-degree term. Stated precisely, the theorem is that if $a_n > 0$, then:

$$a_n x^n + a_{n-1} x^{n-1} + \ldots + a_1 x + a_0 = \Theta(x^n) \tag{9.24}$$

Prove this theorem.

9.18. Determine whether the times in each of the following tables are consistent with the associated asymptotic expressions.

1. $\Theta(n^2)$

n	Time (seconds)
1	1
5	26
10	101
50	2505
100	10010

2. $\Theta(n^2)$

n	Time (seconds)
1	10
5	510
10	1990
50	50050
100	199900

3. $\Theta(n^2)$

n	Time (seconds)
1	1
5	59
10	501
50	62005
100	499990

4. $\Theta(n)$

n	Time (seconds)
1	10
5	49
10	99
50	495
100	990

5. $\Theta(n)$

n	Time (seconds)
1	1
5	3
10	4
50	7
100	11
500	22
1000	30

6. $\Theta(2^n)$

n	Time (seconds)
1	0.5
2	1.5
5	8
10	250
15	8200
20	260000

9.3 ITERATION AND MEASURING SHORT EXECUTION TIMES

Section 9.1 dealt with consequences of loops for theoretical analyses of algorithms' performance, and Section 9.2 described how to relate theoretical analyses to empirical running times. With this information, plus what you learned earlier in this book, you can make theoretical predictions about any algorithm's execution time. But can you test those predictions against the actual behavior of the algorithm? Many algorithms' real-world execution times are so short that they are hard to measure using the technique presented earlier in this book (the difference between two calls on a clock function, see Section 4.7). For example, did you notice that the times for Sequential Search and Initialization in the previous section are only about 1/100th of the smallest time Java's System.currentTimeMillis clock function can supposedly measure? Fortunately, iteration can help you measure times less than the precision of your clock function.

9.3.1 The Basic Technique

The basic idea for measuring short times is simple: even if executing an algorithm once takes too little time to measure, executing it many times does take a measurable time. For example, if executing an algorithm once requires a thousandth of a second, doing it 1000 times should take a second. Therefore, to measure a fast algorithm's execution time, place it inside a loop that repeats many times, and measure the time that loop takes. The time for one execution of the algorithm can then be estimated as the total time for the loop divided by the number of times the loop repeated:

> *Call the clock function, and store the result in StartTime.*
> *Repeat many times:*
>> *Run the algorithm.*
> *Call the clock function, and store the result in EndTime.*
> *One execution of the algorithm took*
>> *(EndTime − StartTime) / (number of times loop repeated)*
>> *ticks of the clock.*

As a concrete example of this technique, here is the heart of the Java code we used to measure the execution times reported in Section 9.2. This code measures the descendingOrder (array initialization) method, but we simply replaced descendingOrder with other messages to measure the other methods. We chose to repeat the loop 50,000 times because preliminary tests showed us that 50,000 repetitions produced acceptably accurate measurements of descendingOrder's execution time. We don't show the calculation of one message's time here, because our actual calculation controlled for loop overhead, as described in the next subsection. Our complete code appears in that subsection. Note that theArray is an ExtendedArray object created elsewhere in the program:

```
final int repetitions = 50000;
...
long startTime = System.currentTimeMillis();
for (int i = 0; i < repetitions; i++) {
    theArray.descendingOrder();
}
long endTime = System.currentTimeMillis();
```

9.3.2 Controlling for Overhead

There is one danger in using a loop to time fast algorithms. Loop bookkeeping, such as the test that determines whether to exit the loop, may take a measurable amount of time. If so, the time you measure is really the time the algorithm takes plus the overhead time for bookkeeping. This introduces a systematic error into your experiment.

You can compensate for loop overhead by timing a second, empty loop. Any time measured for the empty loop is entirely loop bookkeeping, so subtracting that time from the time measured for the main loop subtracts the overhead from the main loop measurement.

We used such an empty loop in our example measurement. Thus, the code we used to time descendingOrder really looks like this:

```
final int repetitions = 50000;
...
long startTime = System.currentTimeMillis();
for (int i = 0; i < repetitions; i++) {
    theArray.descendingOrder();
}
long endTime = System.currentTimeMillis();

long controlStart = System.currentTimeMillis();
for (int i = 0; i < repetitions; i++) { }
long controlEnd = System.currentTimeMillis();

long mainTime = endTime - startTime;
long contTime = controlEnd - controlStart;
double time = ((double)(mainTime - contTime))/repetitions;
```

In calculating the time one message takes, endTime - startTime is the time it took the main loop to execute, while controlEnd - controlStart is the time the empty loop took (i.e., the loop overhead). Subtracting the latter value from the former yields the time for the initializations without overhead. Dividing this time by the total number of initializations yields the time for a single initialization. Casting the dividend to double ensures that Java will do the division as real-valued division, rather than integer division (which would truncate away the fractional part of the quotient).

9.3.3 Error

Like any measurements, times measured using this technique include some amount of random error. The most important source is the inherent plus-or-minus one tick error due to the clock function. You should include this error in your estimate of the time for one execution of the fast algorithm. To do so, notice that the timing technique involves two measurements based on the clock function, one of the main loop and one of the empty loop. Each of these measurements has an inherent random error of ±1 tick, so you can estimate the inherent random error in their difference (i.e., in the time required to execute the fast algorithm many times) as ±2 ticks. Since you estimate the time for one execution by dividing the time for many executions by the number of times you repeated the algorithm, you similarly estimate the random error in the time for one execution by dividing the ±2 tick random error in the time for many executions by the number of repetitions.

For example, our smallest estimate of the execution time of descendingOrder was 0.0004 milliseconds. Since this figure is based on 50,000 repetitions of the algorithm, and our clock has a precision of 1 millisecond, we estimate the random error in it as ±2/50000, or ±0.00004 milliseconds. Relative to the measurement, this is 10% relative error.

Estimating random error can help you select an appropriate number of times to repeat the fast algorithm. The more repetitions you do, the longer you will have to wait for them to finish, but the lower the random error in the time estimate will be. Thus, you would like to use the smallest number of repetitions that yields an acceptable level of error. Calculating the random error for a given number of repetitions allows you to do this. For example, we like to have relative errors of at most a few percent in an experiment, so the 50,000 repetitions used to get 10% relative error in the previous example was the smallest number we would tolerate—fewer repetitions would have compromised accuracy more than we wanted, while more would have made each run of the experiment take more time than necessary.

Exercises

9.19. Each of the following sets of data describes a different, hypothetical time measurement made using the technique described in this section. For each set of data, calculate the time required for one execution of the fast algorithm, and estimate the relative error in that time. Assume that the clock has a precision of 1 millisecond.

1. Main loop time = 10 milliseconds; empty loop time = 1 millisecond; 1000 repetitions.
2. Main loop time = 1 second; empty loop time = 0.005 second; 100,000 repetitions.
3. Main loop time = 500 milliseconds; empty loop time = 0 milliseconds; 100 repetitions.
4. Main loop time = 106 milliseconds; empty loop time = 2 milliseconds; 100,000 repetitions.
5. Main loop time = 57 milliseconds; empty loop time = 1 millisecond; 35,000 repetitions.

9.20. Suppose you are planning an experiment that will use the timing technique described in this section, and you want to know how many repetitions of the loops to use. You do some preliminary timings, using arbitrarily chosen numbers of repetitions. Below are some hypothetical data from these timings, along with desired levels of relative random error. For each data set, estimate the minimum number of repetitions of the loops that would give you the desired error level. Assume the clock's precision is 1 millisecond.

1. Main loop time = 10 milliseconds; empty loop time = 0 milliseconds; 10 repetitions. Relative error should be 2% or less.
2. Main loop time = 10 milliseconds; empty loop time = 0 milliseconds; 10 repetitions. Relative error should be 1% or less.
3. Main loop time = 100 milliseconds; empty loop time = 2 milliseconds; 1000 repetitions. Relative error should be 2% or less.
4. Main loop time = 102 milliseconds; empty loop time = 2 milliseconds; 5000 repetitions. Relative error should be 2% or less.
5. Main loop time = 103 milliseconds; empty loop time = 3 milliseconds; 100 repetitions. Relative error should be 10% or less.
6. Main loop time = 275 milliseconds; empty loop time = 3 milliseconds; 12,000 repetitions. Relative error should be 5% or less.
7. Main loop time = 97 milliseconds; empty loop time = 1 millisecond; 3500 repetitions. Relative error should be 1% or less.
8. Main loop time = 200 milliseconds; empty loop time = 0 milliseconds; 100 repetitions. Relative error should be 0.2% or less.

9.21. (For students with a good statistics background). In Chapter 4, we used standard error to argue that the random error in an average decreases with the square root of the number of samples. The iterative technique for measuring a fast algorithm's execution time basically computes an average execution time for the fast algorithm, yet we claim that the random error in this average decreases linearly with the number of samples. Why is this claim valid?

9.4 CONCLUDING REMARKS

Repetition is the origin of all significant time complexity in algorithms. Repetition can happen either through recursion or through loops (iteration). This chapter has examined the implications of iteration for time complexity.

The most obvious connection between iteration and time complexity is that loops in an algorithm generally raise its time complexity. To see what the algorithm's execution time depends on, and how, you can analyze the algorithm and its loops theoretically. All such analyses involve summing the operations the algorithm executes over the iterations of its loops. This simple idea is complicated by the need to figure out how many iterations the loops perform and how many operations each iteration executes—these complications mean that loops often require more cleverness than other control structures to analyze.

Given mathematical techniques for analyzing an algorithm's performance, one wants to describe theoretical complexity in a way that corresponds to observable behavior. Asymptotic notation provides such a description. Mathematically, $f(n) = \Theta(b(n))$ if the value of $f(n)$ lies between two nonzero multiples of the value of $b(n)$ as n grows large. This is exactly the kind of relationship that can be observed between the size of a program's input and its running time—the time can usually be seen to be proportional to some function of input size, with the proportionality often becoming clearer as the inputs get larger.

You can also use iteration to increase time complexity deliberately. This idea manifests itself in the technique for timing operations too fast to time individually: put one of those operations inside a loop, and time how long the loop as a whole takes. Divide this time by the number of times the operation was performed to estimate the time to perform the operation once.

In this chapter and the three preceding it, you learned to design recursive algorithms, analyze their correctness and performance, design iterative algorithms and prove them correct, and analyze iterative algorithms' performance. You studied each of these topics largely in isolation from the others, yet in real use they often work together. The next chapter studies two examples of how this happens, namely two widely used and very efficient sorting algorithms.

9.5 FURTHER READING

Analysis of loops' performance is one of the persistent themes in every book on the analysis of algorithms. There are many such books. A good current example aimed at about the same level as this text is:

Clifford Shaffer, *A Practical Introduction to Data Structures and Algorithm Analysis* (2nd ed.), Prentice Hall, 2001.

Two classics of the field, aimed at more advanced students, are:

Thomas Cormen, Charles Leiserson, Ronald Rivest, and Clifford Stein, *Introduction to Algorithms* (2nd ed.), MIT Press, 2001.

Alfred Aho, John Hopcroft, and Jeffrey Ullman, *The Design and Analysis of Computer Algorithms*, Addison-Wesley, 1974.

The searching and sorting algorithms appearing in examples and exercises in this chapter are favorites of analysis of algorithms authors, and you can learn more about them in the texts cited above.

For more on the mathematics of summations and asymptotic notation, see:

Donald Knuth, *Fundamental Algorithms* (*The Art of Computing Programming*, Vol. 1), 2nd ed., Addison-Wesley 1973.

Ronald Graham, Donald Knuth, and Oren Patashnik, *Concrete Mathematics*, Addison-Wesley 1994.

10 A Case Study in Design and Analysis: Efficient Sorting

Imagine computerizing the census information for a large city. Such a data set might contain about 5 million entries. It seems reasonable to keep the data sorted (for example, alphabetized according to people's names), so that you can search it using a fast algorithm such as Binary Search. You have seen several sorting algorithms in this text, most prominently Selection Sort. But recall, for a moment, some of Chapter 9's results on Selection Sort—in particular, the theoretical analysis that showed that its execution time is $\Theta(n^2)$, and the empirical analysis that measured a time of about 4800 microseconds for a particular implementation to sort an array of 512 values. From these facts, you can estimate how long a similar implementation would take to sort 5 million census entries: 5 million is roughly 10,000 times bigger than 512. Since Selection Sort's execution time grows as the square of problem size, a factor of 10,000 increase in problem size translates into a factor of $10,000^2$, or 100,000,000, increase in execution time. So you should expect to wait $100,000,000 \times 4800$ microseconds, which is 480,000 seconds, or about five and a half days, for Selection Sort to sort the census data. Evidently Selection Sort is not the tool to use for this application!

This chapter illustrates how design and analysis techniques from earlier chapters help one develop faster sorting algorithms. The processes we use to develop and analyze these algorithms are useful for many other algorithms, too. They illustrate how algorithm designers can methodically reason their way to fast and correct algorithms without those algorithms being obvious at the outset. Studying and analyzing these algorithms will therefore teach you much that generalizes beyond the specific sorting examples.

10.1 AN INITIAL INSIGHT

We will examine two sorting algorithms, known as Quicksort and Mergesort. Both are motivated by the same insight about execution time, but the two algorithms build on that insight in different ways. This section explains the basic insight, while subsequent sections develop actual sorting algorithms from it.

10.1.1 The Insight

Every sorting algorithm you have seen so far has an execution time of $\Theta(n^2)$. The insight is that when an algorithm's execution time is $\Theta(n^2)$ (or, for that matter, anything greater than $\Theta(n)$), solving two problems of size $n/2$ takes less time than solving one problem of size n. Mathematically, this is because:

$$2\left(\frac{n}{2}\right)^2 = 2\left(\frac{n^2}{4}\right) = \frac{n^2}{2} < n^2 \tag{10.1}$$

Thus, one possible way to speed up sorting would be to split an unsorted array[1] into two smaller subarrays, use some $\Theta(n^2)$ algorithm to sort those subarrays, and finally combine the results back into a single sorted array. Since the two subarrays need to be sorted too, we might do even better to split them into sub-subarrays before using the same $\Theta(n^2)$ algorithm. Continuing this line of thought, the sub-subarrays could also be split, and so on until each sub-sub-...-subarray had only one value in it. Carrying the splitting to its extreme in this manner conveniently eliminates the need for $\Theta(n^2)$ sorting at all, because any one-value fragment is already sorted.

10.1.2 Example

Suppose we want to sort an array containing the numbers

     7 2 4 1

The insight says we should split this array into two pieces, sort each piece, and then combine the sorted pieces back into a sorted whole. There are many ways to split the array and recombine the sorted pieces. Different choices of how to do these things lead to different sorting algorithms, as you will see in later sections. For now, let's split the array by simply dividing it into halves, so the pieces are:

---

[1] For discussion purposes, we assume that the data to be sorted are in an array. However, the algorithms adapt easily to other sequential structures, for instance files, vectors, etc.

7 2   and   4 1

Now we need to sort each of these pieces. We start by splitting them into parts, too:

7   and   2   and   4   and   1

Now each piece contains only one value, so we can't do any more splitting. Also, notice how each piece, considered by itself, is sorted—no piece contains values that are out of order relative to other values in that piece (simply because each piece contains just one value, with no "others"). It's time to combine the pieces back into a sorted whole. Without worrying about the details yet, suppose we somehow decide to combine the piece containing 7 with the piece containing 4, and the piece containing 2 with the piece containing 1. Further, suppose we combine in a way that leaves the results sorted. We end up with two pieces again, but they are:

4 7   and   1 2

Then we combine these two pieces, still doing it in some way that produces a sorted result, to yield:

1 2 4 7

We are now back to a single piece, which is the sorted form of the original array.

10.1.3 Strategy: Divide and Conquer

The broad strategy for sorting that we have discovered is to divide an array into parts and recursively sort each. So far, we have glossed over dividing the array into parts and combining the sorted parts back into a sorted whole, but as long as we can do these things quickly (and you will soon see that we can), this strategy should lead to sorting algorithms that execute in less than $\Theta(n^2)$ time. Both Quicksort and Mergesort use this "divide and conquer" approach.

10.2 QUICKSORT DESIGN

The overall strategy for sorting an n-element array with Quicksort is

*Rearrange the data so that the smallest n/2 values are
    in the low-indexed half of the array, and the largest
    n/2 values are in the high-indexed half. (This is the*

> *ideal, although in reality Quicksort won't always put*
> *exactly n/2 values in each half.)*
> *Recursively sort each half.*

While rearranging the data in the first step, the algorithm does not try to put the small values into sorted order relative to each other, nor the large values—the algorithm only separates the small values from the large ones. This step is called *partitioning* the array. After the array has been partitioned, the recursive sorting step takes care of putting the values in each half into the proper order relative to each other.

10.2.1 Refining Quicksort's Design

The preceding description of Quicksort is very abstract. Much more concrete descriptions exist, of course, and it is interesting to see how they follow from the abstract idea. Refining a rough idea into a working implementation is central to algorithm design, and studying the refinement process in the case of Quicksort, will help you carry out similar refinements when you invent algorithms of your own. In particular, Quicksort demonstrates the interplay of correctness proofs and algorithm design, and the roles of preconditions, postconditions, loop invariants, and abstraction.

As with other array algorithms in this book, we will present Quicksort as a method of our ExtendedArray class. The data to sort is in the ordinary array contents that is a member variable of ExtendedArray.

Sorting Subsections of Arrays

The first detail to refine is that Quicksort doesn't always sort an entire array—the recursive messages that Quicksort sends to itself only sort subsections of the array. Therefore, we need some way to tell Quicksort what section of the array it should sort. We solved a similar problem when we kept track of a section of an array for Binary Search to search (Section 8.1.2). We can apply the ideas we used then here. Specifically, the Quicksort message can have parameters indicating the upper and lower bounds of the segment to be sorted. As in Binary Search, we will use inclusive bounds, meaning that both the first position and the last will be in the section.

Goals for Partitioning

Much of the remaining refinement of Quicksort deals with partitioning. Ideally, partitioning places the smallest $n/2$ values from an array section in the first half of the section, and the largest $n/2$ values in the second half. Unfortunately, you can't identify exactly $n/2$ small values and $n/2$ large ones without almost sorting the section in the process. Thus, actual Quicksort departs from the ideal. It classifies values as "small" or "large," but doesn't guarantee a half-and-half split.

Partitioning separates the small values and the large ones into distinct subsections of the array, and tells the rest of Quicksort where the boundary between these subsections lies. Partitioning is likely to be fairly complicated, so it should be a separate method invoked by the main Quicksort method. The partitioning method needs to receive the bounds of the section being sorted as parameters, and to return the position of the boundary between small values and large ones. Its header therefore looks like this:

```
private int partition(int first, int last)
```

partition is a private method because it should be used only by the Quicksort method, not by clients of ExtendedArray.

What it means for an array section to be partitioned, and how the boundary between small and large values can be indicated, is illustrated in Figure 10.1, and is described formally by partition's postcondition:

Let p be the position returned by partition. Then first $\leq p \leq$ last, and for all positions i such that first $\leq i \leq p$, contents[i] $\leq$ contents[p]; for all positions j such that $p \leq j \leq$ last, contents[p] $\leq$ contents[j].

The precondition for partition defines precisely what first and last represent:

first $\leq$ last, and the section of contents to partition lies between positions first and last, inclusive.

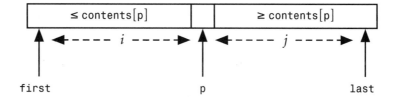

FIGURE 10.1 Partitioning places small values before position p and large values after.

The Main Quicksort Algorithm

With `partition`'s interface in place, the rest of Quicksort falls together easily. Quicksort's general case is partitioning a section and sorting the resulting subsections. Since any section with one value (or fewer) is necessarily in order, the algorithm only needs to execute this general case when there is more than one value in the section. The fact that one-value sections are already sorted means that Quicksort needn't do anything in its base case. The code for Quicksort (assuming that a `partition` method is available) is thus:

```
// Within class ExtendedArray...
public void quicksort(int first, int last) {
    if (first < last) {
        int mid = this.partition(first, last);
        // sort the small values:
        this.quicksort(first, mid-1);
        // sort the large values:
        this.quicksort(mid+1, last);
    }
}
```

The most subtly important statement in this method is:

```
int mid = this.partition(first, last);
```

This statement, executed over and over by `quicksort` and its recursive invocations, is what actually sorts the array. In particular, it is `partition` that puts small values before large ones within array sections. The position that `partition` returns is useful to the `quicksort` method, but is really a reflection of `partition`'s main effect of rearranging values.

Correctness

We can now verify that the `quicksort` method sorts correctly. We can, and should, do this even though we have not yet designed the `partition` method that `quicksort` uses. We *should* try to prove `quicksort` correct now, because the attempt may reveal errors in our design. The sooner any designer finds and corrects errors, the less impact those errors can have on other parts of a program. We *can* do this proof because we know `partition`'s preconditions and postconditions, and so we know exactly what `partition` will do. We can assume, for the sake of proving `quicksort` correct, that `partition` is correct, and then confirm that assumption with another proof after we design `partition` in detail. In other words, we can use the correctness of `partition` as a lemma for proving `quicksort` correct, but defer proving the lemma until later.

To start, we must say exactly what correct sorting entails. We have implicitly assumed that sorting means putting the elements of an array into ascending order. Thus, our main postcondition for sorting is:

For all i such that $0 \le i < n-1$, `contents`$[i] \le$ `contents`$[i+1]$ where n is the number of values in the array.[2]

We can now prove that `quicksort` sorts correctly.

PRECONDITION: $0 \le$ `first` $\le$ `last` $< n$, where n is the length of an `ExtendedArray`'s contents array.

THEOREM: After the `ExtendedArray` handles the message `quicksort(first, last)`, `contents`$[i] \le$ `contents`$[i+1]$ for all i in the range `first` $\le i \le$ `last` -1. □

PROOF: The proof is by induction on the length of the section being sorted. Note that this length is `last` $-$ `first` $+1$, since `first` and `last` are inclusive bounds.

Base Case: Suppose the length of the section is less than two, so that `last` $-$ `first` $+1 \le 1$. Then `last` $\le$ `first`, so there are no values of i such that `first` $\le i \le$ `last` -1, and the postcondition holds vacuously (corresponding to our observation that a section containing only one value—or fewer—cannot be unsorted).

Induction Step: Assume that `quicksort` correctly sorts all array sections whose length is less than or equal to $k-1$, where $k-1 \ge 1$. Show that `quicksort` correctly sorts array sections of size k. We know that $k \ge 2$, and when sorting a section that long, `quicksort`'s `first < last` test succeeds. Therefore, `quicksort` executes its recursive case. Assuming that `partition` works correctly, `mid` receives a value such that `first` $\le$ `mid` $\le$ `last`. `quicksort` then recursively sorts the subsection extending from position `first` through `mid` -1, and the subsection from position `mid` $+1$ through `last`. Because `mid` is between `first` and `last`, both of these subsections have sizes less than or equal to $k-1$. Therefore, by the induction hypothesis, both subsections get sorted. Figure 10.2 summarizes the state of `contents` after sorting the subsections. Formally, for all i such that `first` $\le i \le$ `mid` -2, `contents`$[i] \le$ `contents`$[i+1]$, and for all j such that

---

[2] For complete rigor, the postcondition should also state that all values present in `contents` before sorting are present in `contents` afterwards, and *vice versa*. See Exercise 10.3.

$mid+1 \le j \le last-1$, contents$[j] \le$ contents$[j+1]$. Furthermore, after partitioning, every value in positions first through $mid-1$ is less than or equal to contents[mid], so in particular contents$[mid-1] \le$ contents[mid]. Similarly, contents$[mid] \le$ contents$[mid+1]$. Taken together, these relations mean that for all i such that first $\le i \le last-1$, contents$[i] \le$ contents$[i+1]$. ∎

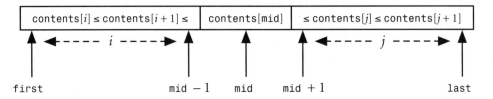

first   mid − 1   mid   mid + 1   last

FIGURE 10.2 The effect of quicksort's recursive messages.

10.2.2 Partitioning

We now need to design and prove correct a concrete partition method.

The Pivot Value

Recall that partition's postcondition requires small values to be separated from large values. The simplest way to classify values as small or large is to simply select one value to compare all the others to. This special value is called the *pivot* value. Any value smaller than the pivot will be considered small, and any value larger than the pivot large. The partition method will rearrange the contents of the array section so that all small values come first, then the pivot, and then all large values. After doing this, partition can return the pivot's final position as the boundary between the small and large subsections.

There are several ways to choose a pivot, the simplest being to use the value originally in the section's first position. Part A of Figure 10.3 shows an array section with this first value chosen as the pivot. Part B shows the section after partitioning, with the small values, pivot, and large values moved to new positions, thus creating "small value" and "large value" subsections.

Designing the Partition Algorithm

To devise an algorithm that partitions around a pivot, we will generalize partition's postcondition into a condition that holds when the array section is only partially partitioned. Our partition algorithm will then iteratively transform this general condition into the postcondition. The general condition will be a loop invariant for

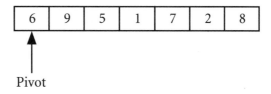

Pivot

A. The pivot before partitioning

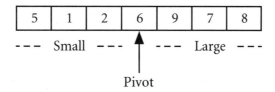

--- Small --- ↑ --- Large ---

Pivot

B. The pivot in the partitioned array

FIGURE 10.3 Values classified as small or large relative to a pivot.

the iteration, and the loop will exit when the postcondition holds. Generalizing a problem's postcondition into something that can iteratively evolve into the postcondition is a good way to discover loop invariants and iterative algorithms for many problems.

To generalize the postcondition, suppose that the small-value and large-value sections exist while partition is executing, but do not yet extend all the way to their eventual meeting point. In between the small-value and large-value sections lie values whose relation to the pivot is still unknown. As the algorithm executes, this unclassified-value section shrinks, until it finally vanishes. Figure 10.4 illustrates this idea, using a new variable, uFirst, to indicate the first position in the unclassified section, and uLast to indicate the last position in it.

To describe this idea formally, notice that every value whose position is strictly before uFirst is known to be a small value, and every value whose position is strictly after uLast is known to be large. In other words, if the pivot value is v then:

$$\text{for all } i \text{ such that first} \leq i < \text{uFirst, contents}[i] \leq v$$
$$\text{and for all } j \text{ such that uLast} < j \leq \text{last}, v \leq \text{contents}[j] \tag{10.2}$$

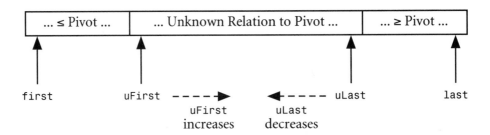

FIGURE 10.4 Partitioning shrinks the region of unclassified values until it vanishes.

Equation 10.2 is the generalization of the postcondition, in that it describes a fully partitioned array section if uFirst > uLast (indicating that there are no more unclassified values), but until uFirst becomes greater than uLast, the equation describes an array section that is partially partitioned. In particular, the equation says nothing about values at positions between uFirst and uLast, inclusive, because those are the values whose relation to the pivot is still not known.

Equation 10.2, the generalization of the postcondition, is the loop invariant around which we will design the partition algorithm. Using this loop invariant, partition's basic strategy will necessarily be to find initial values for uFirst and uLast that make Equation 10.2 hold, and then move uFirst and uLast toward each other until every value has been classified as small or large, making sure that Equation 10.2 continues to hold:

> *initialize uFirst and uLast*
> *while some values remain unclassified (that is, while uFirst ≤ uLast)*
>   *increment uFirst and/or decrement uLast in some way that*
>   *maintains Equation 10.2.*

To refine the algorithm, let's first figure out how to initialize uFirst and uLast. If we pick the first element in the array section as the pivot, then we can initialize uFirst to first+1. This choice satisfies the requirement that for all i such that first $\leq i <$ uFirst, contents[i] $\leq v$, because the only such i is first itself, and contents[first] is less than or equal to the pivot because it *is* the pivot. We can take advantage of vacuous truth to initialize uLast: if we initialize uLast to last, then there are no values j greater than uLast but less than or equal to last, so the requirement that for all j such that uLast $< j \leq$ last, $v \leq$ contents[j] is vacuously true.

Next, let's devise a way to increment uFirst or decrement uLast until they pass each other. We can't just increment uFirst, or decrement uLast, blindly, because uFirst can't increase past a position containing a value greater than the pivot, nor uLast decrease past a position containing a value less than the pivot, without violating Equation 10.2. Fortunately, there is a clever solution to this problem. Start by decrementing uLast until uLast indexes a value less than the pivot. Then swap that value with the pivot—since the pivot is greater than or equal to itself, the swap leaves position uLast containing a large value, and the pivot's old position containing a small value (which is legal there, since the pivot's old position is less than uFirst). Decrement uLast one more time, so that it once again indexes a not-yet-classified value. Then start incrementing uFirst until it encounters a value greater than the pivot, and swap that value with the one in the pivot's new position. Continuing in this fashion, the pivot is always either the last value in the small-value subsection, or the first value in the large-value subsection, while the unclassified region shrinks from the end opposite the pivot.

Here is concrete Java code for this partitioning algorithm. This code records the pivot's position in variable p, which eventually provides the return value.

```java
// In class "ExtendedArray"...
private int partition(int first, int last) {
    int uFirst = first + 1;
    int p = first;
    int uLast = last;
    while (uFirst <= uLast) {
        if (p == uFirst - 1) {
            // Check unclassifieds at uLast
            if (contents[uLast] < contents[p]) {
                this.swap(uLast, p);
                p = uLast;
            }
            uLast = uLast - 1;
        }
        else {
            // Check unclassifieds at uFirst
            if (contents[uFirst] > contents[p]) {
                this.swap(uFirst, p);
                p = uFirst;
            }
            uFirst = uFirst + 1;
        }
    }
    return p;
}
```

```
private void swap(int i, int j) {
    int temp = contents[i];
    contents[i] = contents[j];
    contents[j] = temp;
}
```

Correctness

We need a number of lemmas to show that partition works correctly. The first shows that partition's loop terminates.

LEMMA: The loop within partition always exits. □

PROOF: The body of the loop is a conditional, one arm of which decreases uLast by one, and the other arm of which increases uFirst by one. Every iteration of the loop executes one of these arms, so uFirst and uLast get closer in value by one in each iteration. Thus, uFirst must eventually become greater than uLast, which is the loop's exit condition. In fact, since uFirst and uLast get closer by exactly one in each iteration, the loop must exit with uFirst = uLast + 1, as long as the loop starts with uFirst ≤ uLast + 1. ■

Next, we need to show that partition really maintains the loop invariants around which we designed it. The obvious condition is Equation 10.2, our main invariant. However, in designing the algorithm we also wanted the pivot to always be either the last value in the small-value subsection or the first in the large-value subsection. Further, our Java implementation supposedly records the pivot's position in variable p. These design decisions correspond to two secondary loop invariants:

$$p = \text{uFirst} - 1 \text{ or } p = \text{uLast} + 1 \tag{10.3}$$

$$\text{pivot} = \text{contents}[p] \tag{10.4}$$

Proving Equation 10.4 to be a loop invariant is very similar to proving that Equation 10.2 is, because both proofs depend on how partition swaps array elements and updates uFirst, uLast, and p. Thus, we will prove Equation 10.4 and Equation 10.2 together as one lemma, and Equation 10.3 as another. We begin with Equation 10.3.

LEMMA: Whenever the loop in partition evaluates its uFirst <= uLast test, p = uFirst − 1 or p = uLast + 1. □

PROOF: The proof is by induction on the number of iterations of the loop.

Base Case: The first iteration. Before entering the loop, p is initialized to first, and uFirst to first+1, so in the first iteration p = uFirst−1.

Induction Step: Assume that p = uFirst−1 or p = uLast+1 at the beginning of iteration k, and show that p = uFirst−1 or p = uLast+1 at the beginning of iteration $k+1$. Consider each possible value of p during iteration k:

> **Case 1.** p = uFirst−1. The algorithm executes the first arm of its conditional. This arm may set p equal to uLast and then decrement uLast, in which case p = uLast+1 at the end of iteration k and the beginning of iteration $k+1$. If the arm doesn't change p, then p still equals uFirst−1 at the end of iteration k.

> **Case 2.** p ≠ uFirst−1. By the induction hypothesis that p = uFirst−1 or p = uLast+1, p must equal uLast+1. The algorithm executes the conditional's second arm. By reasoning similar to that for the first arm, either p is set equal to uFirst and then uFirst incremented, so that p = uFirst−1 at the end of iteration k, or p remains equal to uLast+1.

These two cases show that for all possible values of p at the beginning of iteration k, p = uFirst−1 or p = uLast+1 at the end of that iteration and so at the beginning of iteration $k+1$. ∎

We next prove the combination of Equation 10.2 and Equation 10.4. The combined condition is:

$$\text{for all } i \text{ such that first} \le i < \text{uFirst, contents}[i] \le v$$
$$\text{and for all } j \text{ such that uLast} < j \le \text{last, } v \le \text{contents}[j] \qquad (10.5)$$
$$\text{and } v = \text{contents}[\text{p}]$$

LEMMA: Whenever the loop in partition evaluates its uFirst <= uLast test, Equation 10.5 holds. □

PROOF: The proof is by induction on iterations of the loop.

Base Case: The first iteration. $v = $ contents[p] upon entering the loop because the algorithm uses contents[first] as the pivot, and initializes p to first. The other two clauses hold by the argument given while developing the algorithm, namely that initially the only i such that first $\le i <$ uFirst is first itself, and contents[first] *is* the pivot, while the statement that $v \leq$ contents[j] for all j such that uLast $< j \leq$ last is vacuously true.

Induction Step: Assume that Equation 10.5 holds at the beginning of iteration k, and show that it must hold at the beginning of iteration $k+1$. The body of the loop does one of two things, depending on the value of p:

> **Case 1.** p = uFirst − 1. The algorithm compares the value of contents[uLast] to contents[p], which is v. The comparison has one of two outcomes:
>
> > **Case 1a.** contents[uLast] < contents[p]. The algorithm swaps contents[uLast] and contents[p]. Then the algorithm sets p to uLast, restoring the condition that $v =$ contents[p]. Furthermore, Equation 10.5's "for all i..." clause now holds for all possible i values except uFirst−1 by the induction hypothesis, and of uFirst−1 because the swap placed a value less than v at that position. Finally, the algorithm decrements uLast by one. The rest of the loop invariant is now restored, because the "for all j..." clause holds of all possible j values except uLast+1 by the induction hypothesis, and of uLast+1 because the swap placed v at that position.
> >
> > **Case 1b.** contents[uLast] ≥ contents[p]. Iteration k just decrements uLast. The loop invariant holds at the beginning of iteration $k+1$ because uFirst hasn't changed and so the "for all i..." clause is still true. The "for all j..." clause is true because it was just discovered to be true of the value that now lies at position uLast+1, and is true of all other possible values of j by the induction hypothesis. $v =$ contents[p] because neither p nor any value in contents has changed.
>
> **Case 2.** p ≠ uFirst − 1. This case is similar to the one for p = uFirst − 1, except that uFirst rather than uLast changes. Also, p must equal uLast + 1 because p = uFirst − 1 or p = uLast + 1, and p ≠ uFirst − 1. ∎

Finally, recall that partition's postcondition requires the returned value to be between first and last. Our partition method returns the value of p. The easiest way to ensure that this value really is between first and last is to state and prove it as a final loop invariant:

PRECONDITION: first ≤ last.

LEMMA: Whenever the loop in partition evaluates its uFirst <= uLast test, first ≤ p ≤ last. □

We sketch the proof, but leave a fully formal version as an exercise.

PROOF: Notice that uFirst is initialized to first+1, and only increases thereafter. Thus, in every iteration of the loop, first ≤ uFirst−1. Similarly, uLast is initialized to last, decreases to last−1 in the first iteration, and only decreases more thereafter. Thus, in the second and later iterations, uLast+1 ≤ last. Moreover, first ≤ last implies that:

$$first+1 \le last+1 \qquad (10.6)$$

Since first+1 is the initial value of uFirst, and last the initial value of uLast, Equation 10.6 implies that uFirst ≤ uLast+1 initially. As noted in the termination proof, this means that the loop will exit when uFirst = uLast+1. Therefore, uFirst ≤ uLast+1 every time, including the last, that the loop evaluates its test. Combining all these inequalities, the following holds in all iterations of the loop except the first:

$$first \le uFirst-1 < uLast+1 \le last \qquad (10.7)$$

Since p = uFirst−1 or p = uLast+1, and Equation 10.7 shows that both of these possible values lie between first and last, first ≤ p ≤ last in the second and later iterations. Furthermore, first ≤ p ≤ last in the first iteration too, because p is initialized to first, and the precondition says that first ≤ last. ∎

We have finally assembled all the lemmas we need to prove that partition is correct.

PRECONDITION: $0 \le first \le last < n$, where n is the size of an ExtendedArray's contents array.

THEOREM: partition(first, last) returns a value p such that first ≤ p ≤ last, and for all positions i such that first ≤ i ≤ p, contents[i] ≤ contents[p], and for all positions j such that p ≤ j ≤ last, contents[p] ≤ contents[j]. □

PROOF: The main loop invariant is:

$$\begin{aligned} &\text{for all } i \text{ such that } first \le i < uFirst,\, contents[i] \le v\\ &\text{and for all } j \text{ such that } uLast < j \le last,\, v \le contents[j] \end{aligned} \qquad (10.8)$$

One of the other invariants is that $v = contents[p]$, so we can rewrite Equation 10.8 as:

$$\text{for all } i \text{ such that } \texttt{first} \leq i < \texttt{uFirst}, \texttt{contents}[i] \leq \texttt{contents}[p]$$
$$\text{and for all } j \text{ such that } \texttt{uLast} < j \leq \texttt{last}, \texttt{contents}[p] \leq \texttt{contents}[j] \tag{10.9}$$

As we reasoned when proving that $\texttt{first} \leq p \leq \texttt{last}$, the precondition that $\texttt{first} \leq \texttt{last}$ implies that $\texttt{partition}$'s loop will exit with $\texttt{uFirst} = \texttt{uLast}+1$, or equivalently, $\texttt{uLast} = \texttt{uFirst}-1$. But one of $\texttt{uLast}+1$ or $\texttt{uFirst}-1$ is equal to p, so we can also say that the loop exits with $p = \texttt{uLast}+1 = \texttt{uFirst}$ or $p = \texttt{uFirst}-1 = \texttt{uLast}$. Consider each possibility in turn:

Case 1. $p = \texttt{uFirst}$. From Equation 10.9:

$$\text{for all } i \text{ such that } \texttt{first} \leq i < \texttt{uFirst}, \texttt{contents}[i] \leq \texttt{contents}[p] \tag{10.10}$$

Since $p = \texttt{uFirst}$, we can rewrite Equation 10.10 as:

$$\text{for all } i \text{ such that } \texttt{first} \leq i < p, \texttt{contents}[i] \leq \texttt{contents}[p] \tag{10.11}$$

Then, since $\texttt{contents}[p]$ is less than or equal to itself, we can extend the range of i to include p:

$$\text{for all } i \text{ such that } \texttt{first} \leq i \leq p, \texttt{contents}[i] \leq \texttt{contents}[p] \tag{10.12}$$

Moreover, because $p = \texttt{uFirst} = \texttt{uLast}+1$, the second clause of Equation 10.9 becomes:

$$\text{for all } j \text{ such that } p \leq j \leq \texttt{last}, \texttt{contents}[p] \leq \texttt{contents}[j] \tag{10.13}$$

Equation 10.12 and Equation 10.13 and the invariant that $\texttt{first} \leq p \leq \texttt{last}$ are the desired theorem, since $\texttt{partition}$ returns p.

Case 2. $p = \texttt{uLast}$. From Equation 10.9:

$$\text{for all } j \text{ such that } \texttt{uLast} < j \leq \texttt{last}, \texttt{contents}[p] \leq \texttt{contents}[j] \tag{10.14}$$

Since $\texttt{uLast} = p$ and $\texttt{contents}[p]$ is less than or equal to itself, this becomes:

$$\text{for all } j \text{ such that } p \leq j \leq \texttt{last}, \texttt{contents}[p] \leq \texttt{contents}[j] \tag{10.15}$$

Meanwhile, because $p = \texttt{uLast} = \texttt{uFirst}-1$, the first clause of Equation 10.9 becomes:

$$\text{for all } i \text{ such that } \texttt{first} \leq i \leq p, \texttt{contents}[i] \leq \texttt{contents}[p] \tag{10.16}$$

As in Case 1, Equation 10.15 and Equation 10.16 and $first \leq p \leq last$ are the desired theorem. ■

Exercises

10.1. Consider the sequence of numbers 12, 10, 3, 22, 1, 19, 20, 8.

1. Partition this sequence by hand.
2. Quicksort this sequence by hand.

10.2. Design an algorithm that finds the i-th smallest value in an extended array (in other words, the value that $i-1$ other values are less than or equal to), where i is a parameter to the algorithm. Your algorithm may use a partition message as defined in this section.

10.3. Prove that after being sorted by quicksort, an array section contains the same values it did before quicksort ran. You may assume that partition leaves a section containing the same values it contained before partitioning.

10.4. Prove that after partition partitions an array section, that section contains the same values it contained before partitioning.

10.5. The "median of three" strategy is another popular way of selecting a pivot. In this strategy, the pivot is the median of the first, middle, and last values in the section being partitioned. Design a partitioning algorithm that uses this strategy. (The *median* of a set is the value that half of the other values are smaller than, and half larger than. For example, the median of 1, 3, 7, 9, and 10 is 7, because two of the other four values are less than 7 and two are greater.)

10.6. Design an algorithm that partitions an n-value array by moving the exactly $n/2$ smallest values to the first half of the array, and the exactly $n/2$ largest values to the last half. Your algorithm may have slightly different postconditions than those of our partitioning algorithm. Does your algorithm sort the array in order to partition it? If not, characterize how close to sorted the array is.

10.7. Give the details of the $p \neq uFirst - 1$ case in the proof that Equation 10.5 is a loop invariant.

10.8. Give a formal proof by induction on iterations that $first \leq p \leq last$ is a loop invariant at the beginning of partition's loop.

10.3 QUICKSORT PERFORMANCE

Now we can see if Quicksort's divide-and-conquer strategy yields the good performance we hoped it would. As we did with other sorting algorithms (see Chapter 9), we will count comparisons between array elements to estimate execution time. All such comparisons happen in `partition`, so we will need to know how many comparisons `partition` performs. Further, since each recursive invocation of `quicksort` invokes `partition`, we must total the comparisons in `partition` over all its invocations.

10.3.1 The Number of Comparisons in Partition

It is easy to calculate how many comparisons between array elements a *single* invocation of `partition` performs. Every iteration of `partition`'s loop does exactly one such comparison. Let n be the number of values in the section being partitioned. Initially, $n-1$ of these values are in the unclassified region (since `uFirst` is one greater `first`), and each iteration of the loop reduces the size of this region by 1. Therefore, the loop must iterate $n-1$ times, doing a total of $n-1$ comparisons.

10.3.2 Accounting for Quicksort's Recursion

The easiest way to add up `partition`'s comparisons over *all* its invocations is to use a recurrence relation to count the comparisons, based on the recursion in `quick-sort`. Specifically, let $C(n)$ be the number of comparisons `quicksort` causes while sorting an n-value section. Further, suppose the section partitions into subsections containing n_1 and n_2 values. $C(n)$ must then equal $n-1$ for partitioning the section, plus $C(n_1)+C(n_2)$ for the recursive sorting. In the nonrecursive case, `quicksort` does no comparisons, so $C(n) = 0$. Since the nonrecursive case happens when $n \le 1$, and the recursive case when $n > 1$, the recurrence relation for $C(n)$ is:

$$C(n) = \begin{cases} 0 & \text{if } n \le 1 \\ (n-1)+C(n_1)+C(n_2) & \text{if } n > 1 \end{cases} \qquad (10.17)$$

Equation 10.17 has different closed forms, depending on the values of n_1 and n_2. We consider two pairs of n_1 and n_2 values, one corresponding to `quicksort`'s best case, and the other to its worst case.

10.3.3 Quicksort's Best-case Performance

The best case for `quicksort` occurs when n_1 and n_2 have values that keep the $(n-1)+C(n_1)+C(n_2)$ part of Equation 10.17 as small as possible. This means making $C(n_1)$ and $C(n_2)$ as small as possible. Because of the $(n-1)$ term, $C(n)$ is an increasing function of n, and in fact a function that increases at least linearly with n. Therefore, keeping $C(n_1)$ and $C(n_2)$ small means keeping n_1 and n_2 themselves small. However, n_1 and n_2 can't both be small. This is because n_1 and n_2 are the sizes of the two subsections of an n-value array, and together those subsections contain $n-1$ values. Thus, $n_1 + n_2$ must equal $n-1$. This means that any decrease in n_1, and therefore in $C(n_1)$, is matched by an increase in n_2 and $C(n_2)$, as shown in Figure 10.5. Furthermore, in a function that grows at least linearly with n, the larger of n_1 and n_2 contributes most significantly to the overall value of $C(n)$, and so the smallest $C(n)$ arises when neither n_1 nor n_2 is larger than the other—when both equal $(n-1)/2$. (For a complete proof of this claim, do Exercise 10.10.)

Letting $n_1 = n_2 = (n-1)/2$, Equation 10.17 for quicksort's best case becomes:

$$C(n) = \begin{cases} 0 & \text{if } n \le 1 \\ (n-1)+C\left(\dfrac{n-1}{2}\right)+C\left(\dfrac{n-1}{2}\right) = (n-1)+2C\left(\dfrac{n-1}{2}\right) & \text{if } n > 1 \end{cases} \qquad (10.18)$$

Restricting n

Notice that $(n-1)/2$, the parameter to the recursive invocation of C in Equation 10.18, is not necessarily a natural number. This is a serious problem, because our

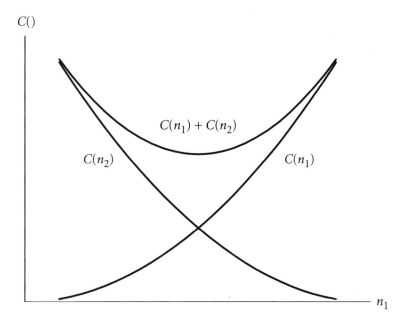

FIGURE 10.5 $C(n_1)+C(n_2)$ has its minimum value when $n_1 = n_2$.

technique for finding closed forms relies on induction, and so is only valid for recurrence relations defined on the natural numbers.

We can work around this problem by restricting Equation 10.18 to only certain values of n, namely those for which $(n-1)/2$ *is* a natural number, and so are the values used in subsequent recursive invocations of C—that is, the values:

$$\frac{(n-1)/2-1}{2}, \quad \frac{\frac{(n-1)/2-1}{2}-1}{2} \tag{10.19}$$

and so forth. Numbers of the form:

$$2^i - 1 \tag{10.20}$$

where i is any integer greater than or equal to 1, have this property (see Exercise 10.11). We will have to gamble that C's behavior restricted to these values represents its behavior as a whole. Since we are ultimately interested in C's asymptotic value, this is a reasonably safe gamble—for most functions occurring in practice, the restricted C will be asymptotically the same as the unrestricted C.

Guessing the Closed Form

We can now look for a pattern in the values of $C(n)$ for the restricted n values. Table 10.1 shows some values of $C(n)$. For each n, the table also shows the corresponding value of i (remember that every n equals $2^i - 1$ for some i), since the pattern might involve i as well as n:

TABLE 10.1 Some values of $C(n)$ for Quicksort's Best Case

$n = 2^i - 1$	$C(n)$
$1 = 2^1 - 1$	0
$3 = 2^2 - 1$	$(3-1) + 2C((3-1)/2) = 2 + 2C(1) = 2 + 2(0)$
$7 = 2^3 - 1$	$(7-1) + 2C(3) = 6 + 2(2 + 2(0)) = 6 + 2(2) + 2^2(0)$
$15 = 2^4 - 1$	$(15-1) + 2C(7) = 14 + 2(6 + 2(2) + 2^2(0))$
	$\quad = 14 + 2(6) + 2^2(2) + 2^3(0)$
$31 = 2^5 - 1$	$(31-1) + 2C(15) = 30 + 2(14 + 2(6) + 2^2(2) + 2^3(0))$
	$\quad = 30 + 2(14) + 2^2(6) + 2^3(2) + 2^4(0)$

The pattern emerges most clearly in the expressions for $C(15)$ and $C(31)$: $C(n)$ seems to be a sum of the recursively generated "$n-1$" terms (30, 14, 6, 2, and 0 for $C(31)$), each multiplied by a power of two. Decreasing $n-1$ values are multiplied by increasing powers of two. This pattern is easiest to write mathematically in terms of i, since i determines the relevant powers of two. Because n is always one less than some power of two, $n-1$ is that power of two minus two. In these terms, the apparent pattern is:

$$C\left(2^i-1\right)=\sum_{j=0}^{i-1}2^j\left(2^{i-j}-2\right) \tag{10.21}$$

Equation 10.21 simplifies as follows:

$$C\left(2^i-1\right)=\sum_{j=0}^{i-1}2^j\left(2^{i-j}-2\right) \qquad \text{Original equation.}$$

$$=\sum_{j=0}^{i-1}\left(2^i-2\cdot 2^j\right) \qquad \text{Distributing } 2^j \text{ through } \left(2^{i-j}-2\right) \text{ and simplifying.}$$

$$=\sum_{j=0}^{i-1}2^i-\sum_{j=0}^{i-1}2\cdot 2^j \qquad \text{Splitting the summation of } 2^i-2\cdot 2^j \text{ into separate summations of } 2^i \text{ and } 2\cdot 2^j.$$

$$=2^i\sum_{j=0}^{i-1}1-\sum_{j=0}^{i-1}2\cdot 2^j \qquad \text{Factoring the constant term } 2^i \text{ out of the first summation (this term is constant within that summation because the summation variable is } j, \text{ not } i).$$

$$=i\cdot 2^i-\sum_{j=0}^{i-1}2\cdot 2^j \qquad \text{The first summation is just } i \text{ 1s added together, or } i.$$

$$=i\cdot 2^i-2\sum_{j=0}^{i-1}2^j \qquad \text{Factoring the constant coefficient 2 out of the remaining summation.}$$

$$=i\cdot 2^i-2\left(2^i-1\right) \qquad \text{The sum of the first powers of two has a well-known closed form, } 2^i-1 \text{ (see Section 7.1.1).}$$

$$=i\cdot 2^i-2\cdot 2^i+2 \qquad \text{Distributing 2 through } 2^i-1 \text{ and removing parentheses.}$$

$$= (i-2)\cdot 2^i + 2 \qquad \text{Combining } i\cdot 2^i \text{ and } 2\cdot 2^i.$$

Proving the Closed Form

$(i-2)\cdot 2^i + 2$ is still only a guess about the closed form for $C(2^i - 1)$. We need to prove that this guess is correct.

THEOREM: $C(2^i - 1) = (i-2)\cdot 2^i + 2$, when C is defined by Equation 10.18, and $i \geq 1$. $\square$

PROOF: The proof is by induction on i.

Base Case: Suppose $i = 1$ (1 being the smallest value of i allowed by the theorem, although in fact the closed form also works for $i = 0$—see Exercise 10.12). $C(2^1 - 1) = C(1) = 0$, from the first line of Equation 10.18. $(i-2)\cdot 2^i + 2 = (1-2)\cdot 2^1 + 2 = (-1)\cdot 2 + 2 = 0$, also.

Induction Step: Assume that for some $k-1 \geq 1$, $C(2^{k-1} - 1) = ((k-1)-2)\cdot 2^{k-1} + 2$, which simplifies to $(k-3)\cdot 2^{k-1} + 2$. We show that $C(2^k - 1) = (k-2)\cdot 2^k + 2$. We begin with the recurrence relation's definition of $C(2^k - 1)$, which comes from the second line of Equation 10.18, since $2^k - 1 > 1$ when $k-1 \geq 1$:

$$C(2^k - 1) = ((2^k - 1) - 1) + 2C\left(\frac{(2^k - 1) - 1}{2}\right) \qquad \text{Equation 10.18.}$$

$$= 2^k - 2 + 2C\left(\frac{2^k - 2}{2}\right) \qquad \text{Simplifying } (2^k - 1) - 1 \text{ to } 2^k - 2, \text{ in two places.}$$

$$= 2^k - 2 + 2C(2^{k-1} - 1) \qquad \text{Simplifying } (2^k - 2)/2 \text{ to } 2^{k-1} - 1.$$

$$= 2^k - 2 + 2((k-3)\cdot 2^{k-1} + 2) \qquad \begin{array}{l} \text{Using the induction hypothesis to} \\ \text{replace } C(2^{k-1} - 1) \text{ with} \\ (k-3)\cdot 2^{k-1} + 2. \end{array}$$

$$= 2^k - 2 + (k-3)\cdot 2^k + 4 \qquad \text{Distributing 2 into } (k-3)\cdot 2^{k-1} + 2.$$

$$= (k-2)\cdot 2^k + 2 \qquad \begin{array}{l} \text{Combining } 2^k \text{ with } (k-3)\cdot 2^k, \text{ and} \\ -2 \text{ with 4. } \blacksquare \end{array}$$

The Closed Form in Terms of n

It would now be nice to phrase the closed form for Equation 10.18 in terms of n, because that is the parameter that directly measures the size of the array being sorted, and an expression in n should describe at least the general growth in the amount of work quicksort does even for n's for which the closed form is not exact. To write the closed form in terms of n, we will find an expression for i as a function of n, and then replace i with that expression in the closed form. We start by recalling Equation 10.20, which tells us that:

$$n = 2^i - 1 \qquad (10.22)$$

Adding 1 to both sides yields:

$$n + 1 = 2^i \qquad (10.23)$$

Finally, we can get i out of the exponent by taking base 2 logarithms of both sides (remember that logarithms and exponentiation cancel each other out):

$$\log_2 (n+1) = i \qquad (10.24)$$

Thus, we can replace i with $\log_2 (n+1)$ in the closed form to see the closed form in terms of n:

$$C(n) = \left(\log_2 (n+1) - 2\right) \cdot 2^{\log_2 (n+1)} + 2 \qquad (10.25)$$

Equation 10.25 simplifies to:

$$C(n) = n\log_2 (n+1) - 2n + \log_2 (n+1) \qquad (10.26)$$

The right-hand side of Equation 10.26 is asymptotically $\Theta(n\log n)$. Since this is the number of comparisons quicksort does in the best case, its best-case execution time should also be $\Theta(n\log n)$. Indeed it is (see the experiment in Exercise 10.18), and quicksort can run much faster than any of the $\Theta(n^2)$ algorithms you saw earlier in this text. Even better, quicksort usually performs close to this best case when sorting random data. Thus, quicksort is a far more practical way to sort than are the earlier algorithms.

10.3.4 Quicksort's Worst-case Performance

We noted in deriving quicksort's best-case execution time that the value of $C(n)$ is mainly determined by the largest term in $(n-1) + C(n_1) + C(n_2)$. By this reasoning, quicksort's worst case should happen when the larger of n_1 and n_2 is as large as possible. This happens when $n_1 = n-1$ and $n_2 = 0$, or vice versa. Both situations lead to the same result; we will analyze the one where $n_1 = n-1$ and $n_2 = 0$.

When $n_1 = n-1$ and $n_2 = 0$, Equation 10.17 becomes:

$$C(n) = \begin{cases} 0 & \text{if } n \leq 1 \\ (n-1) + C(n-1) + C(0) = (n-1) + C(n-1) & \text{if } n > 1 \end{cases} \qquad (10.27)$$

Identifying a pattern in the values produced by Equation 10.27 is straightforward, as Table 10.2 shows:

TABLE 10.2 Some Values of $C(n)$ for Quicksort's Worst Case

n	$C(n)$
1	0
2	$1 + C(0) = 1 + 0$
3	$2 + C(2) = 2 + 1 + 0$
4	$3 + C(3) = 3 + 2 + 1 + 0$

It appears that $C(n)$ is simply the sum of the integers between 0 and $n-1$, at least when $n \geq 1$ (and also when $n = 0$, because the sum of the integers between 0 and -1 is vacuously 0). We state and prove this guess formally as:

THEOREM: For $C(n)$ defined by Equation 10.27, and $n \geq 1$:

$$C(n) = \sum_{i=0}^{n-1} i \quad \square \qquad (10.28)$$

PROOF: The proof is by induction on n.

Base Case: $n = 1$. $C(1) = 0$, from Equation 10.27, and:

$$\sum_{i=0}^{1-1} i = \sum_{i=0}^{0} i = 0 \qquad (10.29)$$

Induction Step: Assume that for some $k - 1 \geq 1$:

$$C(k-1) = \sum_{i=0}^{k-2} i \tag{10.30}$$

Using this assumption, we show that:

$$C(k) = \sum_{i=0}^{k-1} i \tag{10.31}$$

$C(k) = (k-1) + C(k-1)$ $k > 1$, so $C(k)$ is defined by the second line of Equation 10.27.

$\displaystyle = (k-1) + \sum_{i=0}^{k-2} i$ Using the induction hypothesis to replace $C(k-1)$ with the sum of the integers between 0 and $k-2$.

$\displaystyle = \sum_{i=0}^{k-1} i$ $k-1$ is the next term in the summation. ∎

The sum of the integers between 0 and $n-1$ is (see Section 7.1.1):

$$\frac{n(n-1)}{2} \tag{10.32}$$

Equation 10.32 is asymptotically $\Theta(n^2)$. This is significantly worse than quicksort's best case, and indeed is no better than the simpler sorting algorithms you have already seen. This fact is quicksort's Achilles heel—it performs very well on most arrays, but its performance deteriorates badly in pathological cases (do Exercise 10.19 to characterize those pathological cases).

Exercises

10.9.   A sorting algorithm's performance can also be characterized by the number of times that algorithm swaps elements of an array.

1.   Derive the best- and worst-case number of swap messages that partition sends, as functions of the number of values in the section being partitioned.

2.   Derive the best- and worst-case number of swap message that quicksort causes to be sent, as functions of the number of values in the section being sorted.

10.10. Suppose $f(x)$ is a function that grows at least linearly with x. Prove that over the interval $0 \le x \le c$, where c is a constant, the expression $f(x) + f(c-x)$ has a minimum value at $c/2$. (Hint: Think about the derivatives of f. In particular, "growing at least linearly with x" means that f's second derivative is always greater than or equal to 0.)

10.11. Prove that for all numbers x of the form $2^i - 1$, where i is any integer greater than or equal to 1, $(x-1)/2$ is also of the form $2^j - 1$, for some natural number j. Explain why this property implies that you can take such an x and repeat the "subtract one and divide by two" operation as many times as you wish (until the result is 0), and always get a natural number as the result.

10.12. Show that $C(2^0 - 1) = (0-2) \cdot 2^0 + 2$, when $C()$ is defined by Equation 10.18.

10.13. Give a complete derivation of Equation 10.26 from Equation 10.25.

10.14. By restricting parameter values, estimate closed forms for the following recurrence relations:

1. $f(n) = \begin{cases} 1 & \text{if } n \le 1 \\ 2f\left(\dfrac{n}{2}\right) & \text{if } n > 1 \end{cases}$

2. $f(n) = \begin{cases} 1 & \text{if } n \le 1 \\ 1 + f\left(\dfrac{n}{2}\right) & \text{if } n > 1 \end{cases}$

3. $f(n) = \begin{cases} 1 & \text{if } n \le 1 \\ n + 2f\left(\dfrac{n}{2}\right) & \text{if } n > 1 \end{cases}$

4. $f(n) = \begin{cases} 0 & \text{if } n \le 1 \\ 1 + f\left(\dfrac{n}{3}\right) & \text{if } n > 1 \end{cases}$

5. $f(n) = \begin{cases} 0 & \text{if } n = 0 \\ 1 + f(n-2) & \text{if } n > 0 \end{cases}$

10.15. Find, and prove correct, closed forms for the following recurrence relations:

1. $f(n) = \begin{cases} 0 & \text{if } n = 0 \\ 2n + f(n-1) & \text{if } n > 0 \end{cases}$

2. $f(n) = \begin{cases} 0 & \text{if } n = 2 \\ n + f(n-1) & \text{if } n > 2 \end{cases}$

3. $f(n) = \begin{cases} 14 & \text{if } n = 2 \\ n + f(n-1) & \text{if } n > 2 \end{cases}$

4. $f(n) = \begin{cases} 0 & \text{if } n = 0 \\ n^2 + f(n-1) & \text{if } n > 0 \end{cases}$

10.16. One can write Binary Search (from Section 8.1) as a recursive algorithm that searches a section of an extended array. The (inclusive) lower and upper bounds for the section are parameters to the algorithm:

```
// In class ExtendedArray...
public boolean binarySearch(int x, int low, int high) {
    int mid = (low + high) / 2;
    if (x == contents[mid]) {
        return true;
    }
    else if (x < contents[mid]) {
        return this.binarySearch(x, low, mid-1);
    }
    else {
        return this.binarySearch(x, mid+1, high);
    }
}
```

Set up a recurrence relation for the number of comparisons between array elements and x that this version of binarySearch executes, as a function of the size of the array section. Find a closed form for your recurrence.

10.17. Design an algorithm that initializes an array in such a manner that quicksort will exhibit its best-case execution time when sorting that array. The array size should be a parameter to your algorithm.

10.18. Conduct an experiment to test the hypothesis that the best-case execution time of quicksort is $\Theta(n \log n)$. The algorithm from Exercise 10.17 will be a helpful tool in this experiment.

10.19. What initial order(s) of values in an array will lead to quicksort's worst-case execution time?

10.20. Phineas Phoole is designing an algorithm to reverse the order of the values in an array. He reasons thus: "I'll need to move the first value to the last position, but before I do that I have to move the value that was in the last position out of the way. I can do that by shifting all values except the first toward the beginning of the array. Then I put the old first value in the last position. This leaves the correct value in the last position, but all positions except the last still have to be reversed." This thinking leads to the following algorithm:

> To reverse positions 0 through n (inclusive) in array A...
>> if n > 0
>>> temp = A[0]
>>> for i = 0 to n − 1
>>>> A[i] = A[i + 1]
>>> A[n] = temp
>>> Reverse positions 0 through n − 1 in the array

Derive the asymptotic execution time of this algorithm, as a function of n. Do you think it is possible to reverse an array asymptotically more efficiently? If so, devise an algorithm that does so and derive its asymptotic execution time.

10.4 MERGESORT

Mergesort avoids Quicksort's $\Theta(n^2)$ worst case by always dividing arrays into equal-size parts. Mergesort is able to divide arrays evenly because it does not care what values go in each part. However, this indifference to where values go requires Mergesort to recombine sorted subarrays by *merging* them, that is, by interleaving their elements into the result array in a way that makes the result a sorted combination of the two subarrays.

10.4.1 Overall Design

Mergesort has a number of variants. The simplest divides an array at the middle, recursively sorts the two halves, and then merges the sorted halves. Mergesort uses recursion to sort sections of the array, so the algorithm receives parameters that tell it the first and last positions in the section to sort.

A Mergesort Method

Here is the Mergesort just outlined, as a method for the ExtendedArray class:

```
// In class ExtendedArray...
public void mergesort(int first, int last) {
    if (first < last) {
        int mid = (first + last) / 2;
        this.mergesort(first, mid);
```

```
        this.mergesort(mid+1, last);
        this.merge(first, mid, last);
    }
}
```

This `mergesort` assumes a `merge` message that merges two adjacent array sections. This message takes as parameters the first position in the first section, the last position in the first section, and the last position in the second section (`merge` doesn't need to receive the first position in the second section explicitly, because it is immediately after the last position in the first section). The `merge` message replaces the two sections with the merged result, as Figure 10.6 illustrates.

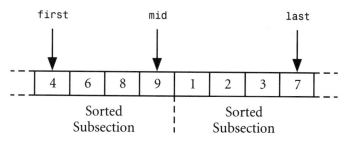

A. An array section with two subsections ready to merge

B. The section after merging

FIGURE 10.6 `merge` combines sorted subsections of an array into a sorted whole.

Correctness

With the foregoing description of `merge`, we can show that the main `mergesort` algorithm is correct. We outline the proof; Exercise 10.21 and Exercise 10.22 help you construct your own, more formal proof.

PRECONDITION: $0 \leq \text{first} \leq \text{last} < n$, where n is the size of an `ExtendedArray`'s contents array.

THEOREM: After the `ExtendedArray` handles the message `mergesort(first, last)`, $contents[i] \le contents[i+1]$ for all i such that $first \le i \le last-1$. □

PROOF: The proof is by induction on the size of the section being sorted.

Base Case: The base cases are sections of zero or one values, both of which are trivially sorted and so need (and get) no sorting.

Induction Step: The induction step shows that a section of size $k > 1$ becomes correctly sorted, assuming that sections of size approximately $k/2$ do. The `mergesort` algorithm divides the size k section into two subsections of size approximately $k/2$, sorts them (by the induction hypothesis), and then merges them. Because the subsections are sorted and adjacent, `merge` creates a single sorted section from them. ■

10.4.2 The Merge Algorithm

The `merge` algorithm interleaves two small sorted array sections into a larger sorted section.

Design

As with Quicksort's `partition` algorithm, generalizing `merge`'s postcondition into a loop invariant helps us discover a merging algorithm. The postcondition is, informally, that the large, merged section contains all the values in the subsections, in sorted order. We can generalize this postcondition to say that while merging is in progress, the first few values in the merged section are the first values from the subsections, in sorted order.

To create a loop based on this invariant, imagine merging "fronts" passing through each subsection, indicating the next value from that subsection to place into the merged section. Each iteration of the merging loop moves the smallest of the "front" values to the merged section. Figure 10.7 illustrates this idea. Lightly shaded values in a subsection have already been moved to the merged section, while dark values have not; dark values in the merged section have come from a subsection, while light positions still need to be filled.

The full `merge` algorithm has several additional subtleties. First, although the algorithm eventually places the merged data into array `contents` in place of the subsections, it is easiest to create the merged section in a separate temporary array, and then copy that array back to the section of `contents`. If the algorithm built the merged section in `contents` directly, it would overwrite not-yet-merged values from

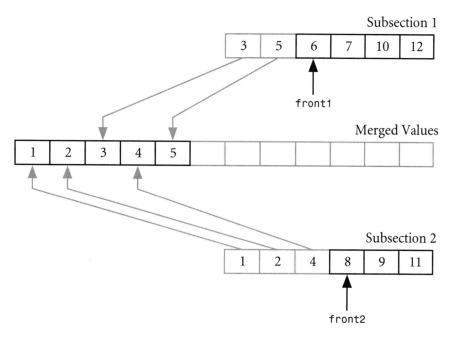

FIGURE 10.7 The merge algorithm interleaves two array subsections.

one of the subsections with values from the other.[3] The merge algorithm also has to handle the possibility that one "front" reaches the end of its subsection before the other does. The final algorithm looks like this:

```
// In class ExtendedArray...
private void merge(int first, int mid, int last) {
    int[] temp = new int[last - first + 1];
    int front1 = first;
    int front2 = mid + 1;
    // Merge values from subsections into temporary array:
    for (int t = 0; t < temp.length; t++) {
        if (front1 <= mid && front2 <= last) {
            if (contents[front1] < contents[front2]) {
                temp[t] = contents[front1++];
            }
            else {
```

---

[3] It is possible to merge directly in contents, but beyond the scope of an introduction to Mergesort. The "Further Reading" section at the end of this chapter provides a reference for those who are interested.

```
                    temp[t] = contents[front2++];
            }
        }
        else if (front1 <= mid) {
            // Section 2 is finished
            temp[t] = contents[front1++];
        }
        else {
            // Section 1 is finished
            temp[t] = contents[front2++];
        }
    }
    // Copy the temporary array back into the main one:
    for (int c = 0; c < temp.length; c++) {
        contents[first+c] = temp[c];
    }
}
```

Correctness

We outline a correctness argument for merge, and invite you to create a more detailed proof in Exercise 10.24 through Exercise 10.29. The first, merging loop terminates because t cannot equal or exceed n, where n is the number of values in the two subsections, and every iteration increases t by one. The main loop invariant, that temp contains a partial merger of the subsections, can be stated precisely as positions 0 through t−1 of temp contain the values from positions first through front1−1 and mid+1 through front2−1 of contents, in sorted order. When the loop exits, t is the size of the section being sorted, front1 = mid+1, and front2 = last+1, so all values from the subsections have been merged into sorted order in temp. The second loop copies these values back into contents, producing merge's result.

10.4.3 Performance

As usual, we can determine mergesort's theoretical execution time by counting the number of comparisons between array elements that it executes (but see Exercise 10.34 for an alternative operation to count).

The Number of Comparisons in merge

We start by deriving the number of comparisons that merge executes as a function of section size, n. The merge method combines two subsections of roughly $n/2$ elements. You can find the precise sizes of the subsections in Exercise 10.22, but $n/2$ is correct for even-length sections, and a close enough approximation for odd-length ones.

In merge's best case, all values in one subsection are less than all values in the other, so after $n/2$ comparisons one "front" reaches the end of its subsection and no further comparisons are needed. In the worst case, neither "front" reaches the end of its subsection until the last possible moment. Since one "front" must reach its limit slightly before the other does, there are $n-1$ comparisons in this case. We complete the best-case analysis next, and let you explore the worst case in Exercise 10.31.

Mergesort's Best-case Performance

Our mergesort causes no comparisons if the array section contains 0 or 1 values. If the section is larger, mergesort indirectly causes the $n/2$ comparisons that merge does in its best case, and also recursively mergesorts two $(n/2)$-value subsections. Letting $C(n)$ stand for the number of comparisons that mergesort causes, we summarize these observations with the following recurrence relation:

$$C(n) = \begin{cases} 0 & \text{if } n \le 1 \\ \dfrac{n}{2} + 2C\left(\dfrac{n}{2}\right) & \text{if } n > 1 \end{cases} \qquad (10.33)$$

To ensure that the parameters to the recursive invocations of C (i.e., $n/2$, $(n/2)/2$, and so on) are natural numbers, we restrict this recurrence to arguments of the form:

$$n = 2^i \qquad (10.34)$$

where i is any natural number. We can then look for a pattern in the values of the restricted $C(n)$, as shown in Table 10.3:

TABLE 10.3 Some Values of $C(n)$ for Mergesort's Best Case

$n = 2^i$	$C(n)$
$1 = 2^0$	0
$2 = 2^1$	$1 + 2C(1) = 1 + 2(0) = 1$
$4 = 2^2$	$2 + 2C(2) = 2 + 2(1) = 2 + 2$
$8 = 2^3$	$4 + 2C(4) = 4 + 2(2+2) = 4 + 4 + 4$
$16 = 2^4$	$8 + 2C(8) = 8 + 2(4+4+4) = 8 + 8 + 8 + 8$

The pattern seems to be that $C(2^i)$ equals i copies of $n/2$ added together. In more formal terms:

$$C(2^i) = i\frac{n}{2} = i\frac{2^i}{2} = i \cdot 2^{i-1} \qquad (10.35)$$

You can prove by induction that $i \cdot 2^{i-1}$ is indeed the closed form for the restricted Equation 10.33. See Exercise 10.32.

Finally, you can rewrite the closed form in terms of n by noting that $i = \log_2 n$:

$$i \cdot 2^{i-1} = (\log_2 n) \cdot 2^{\log_2 n - 1} \qquad \text{Substituting } \log_2 n \text{ for } i.$$

$$= (\log_2 n)\frac{2^{\log_2 n}}{2} \qquad \text{Applying the fact that } 2^{x-1} = 2^x/2 \text{ to } 2^{\log_2 n - 1}$$

$$= \frac{n}{2}\log_2 n \qquad \text{Noting that } 2^{\log_2 n} = n$$

Thus, at least when n is a power of two:

$$C(n) = \frac{n}{2}\log_2 n \qquad (10.36)$$

The right-hand side of Equation 10.36 is $\Theta(n\log n)$, so mergesort has the same asymptotic best-case performance as Quicksort. The worst-case performance of mergesort is also $\Theta(n\log n)$ (see Exercise 10.31), so mergesort has an advantage over Quicksort in guaranteeing good performance even in the worst case. In choosing a sorting algorithm for practical use, however, this guarantee must be balanced against the likelihood of Quicksort actually encountering worst-case data, and the cost of providing the extra memory that mergesort needs for merging.

Exercises

10.21. Formalize what the merge message does by stating its preconditions and postconditions.

10.22. Determine exactly what sizes the subsections that mergesort recursively sorts can have. Use this information to state a precise induction hypothesis for the proof that mergesort is correct, and use that induction hypothesis to rigorously phrase the induction step in mergesort's correctness proof. You will also need the pre- and postconditions for merge from Exercise 10.21.

10.23. Trace the merge algorithm by hand on the array subsections shown in Figure 10.7. Verify that the algorithm reaches the state shown in the figure, and continue tracing until the merge is complete.

10.24. Prove that the first loop in merge maintains the loop invariant that front1 $\leq$ mid+1.

10.25. State a loop invariant for merge's first loop that relates t, front1, and front2 by asserting formally that t is the total number of values copied from the two subsections of contents. Prove that the loop maintains this loop invariant.

10.26. Use the results of Exercise 10.24 and Exercise 10.25 to prove that front2 $\leq$ last+1 is also a loop invariant for merge's first loop. Further show that if t $<n$ (so the loop doesn't exit at the very beginning of the iteration) and front1 $>$ mid, then front2 $\leq$ last.

10.27. Prove rigorously that the first loop in merge maintains the loop invariant that positions 0 through t-1 of temp contain the data from positions first through front1-1 and mid+1 through front2-1 of contents, in sorted order. You will find the result from Exercise 10.26 technically useful, and you may restate the loop invariant more formally, if it helps.

10.28. Use the loop invariants proved in Exercise 10.24 through Exercise 10.26 to prove that upon exit from merge's first loop, front1 $=$ mid+1 and front2 $=$ last+1.

10.29. Prove that merge's second loop copies all values in temp into positions first through last of contents, preserving their order.

10.30. There are several iterative variants of Mergesort, among them:

1. "Straight merge sort" makes a series of merging passes over the array. The first pass merges pairs of values into sorted sections containing two values. The second pass then merges pairs of these two-value sections into four-value sorted sections. Subsequent passes merge larger and larger sections until finally the whole array consists of just one sorted section. Design and prove correct an implementation of straight merge sort.

2. "Natural merge sort" takes advantage of the fact that an unsorted array typically contains sequences of values that are in sorted order just by accident. These sorted sequences are known as *runs*. Natural merge sort makes a series of passes over the array, much like straight merge sort, except that each pass merges pairs of runs into larger runs. The algorithm stops when the array contains only one run. Design and prove correct an implementation of natural merge sort.

10.31. Derive the number of comparisons that mergesort executes in its worst case.

10.32. Prove that $C(2^i) = i \cdot 2^{i-1}$ is a closed form for Equation 10.33.

10.33. Conduct an experiment to test the hypothesis that mergesort's execution time is $\Theta(n\log n)$ for all n, not just those of the form $n = 2^i$.

10.34. More than most sorting algorithms, mergesort works by moving values from the array. It is therefore interesting to analyze mergesort's performance by counting the number of times it either assigns to an element of contents, or copies an element of contents to somewhere else. Analyze mergesort in these terms.

10.35. The recurrence relation encountered in analyzing mergesort's best case generalizes to a family of recurrences of the form:

$$f(n) = \begin{cases} 0 & \text{if } n = 1 \\ kn + cf\left(\dfrac{n}{c}\right) & \text{if } n > 1 \end{cases} \tag{10.37}$$

where k and c are constants. Prove that all such recurrences have closed forms:

$$f(n) = kn\log_c n \tag{10.38}$$

when restricted to ns of the form c^i for any natural number i.

10.5 CONCLUDING REMARKS

Finding efficient sorting algorithms is not trivial. Even the general idea behind the algorithms (dividing an array into halves and recursively sorting) is one whose value would only be recognized by someone who understands mathematically how the execution time of other sorting algorithms grows. Applying the general idea in specific algorithms requires discovering loops that can create or combine parts of arrays and that interact with recursive main algorithms. The correctness of the complete algorithms is not immediately obvious, and it is even less obvious that the algorithms perform as efficiently as intended. Algorithms such as Quicksort and Mergesort thus draw together the design and analysis techniques for recursion and iteration presented in earlier chapters to successfully attack a difficult design problem.

How would divide-and-conquer sorts perform in the 5-million-item sorting problem with which this chapter opened? Suppose that, like our Selection Sort, a hypothetical $\Theta(n\log n)$ sort takes 4800 microseconds to sort 512 records. $512\log_2 512 = 512 \times 9 = 4608$, while $5,000,000\log_2 5,000,000$ is about $110,000,000$. Thus, the $\Theta(n\log n)$ sort should take $110,000,000/4608$, or about 23,872 times longer to sort 5 million records than to sort 512. At 4800 microseconds for 512 records, this works out to about 115 seconds, under two minutes, to sort the 5-million-record data set. Quite an improvement over the five days we predicted for the $\Theta(n^2)$ algorithm! While this example is fictitious, it reflects reality well—sorting problems that are effectively impossible for the $\Theta(n^2)$ algorithms really do become trivial for the $\Theta(n \log n)$ ones.

By now, you know a great deal about the design and analysis of algorithms. Much of this knowledge relies on structure—on using conditionals, recursion, and loops to organize primitive steps into larger structures, and on using mathematics that parallels the algorithmic structures to organize your thinking about the algorithms. Computer scientists also impose structure on data in order to gain the benefits of organized, structured thinking when dealing with large data sets and the algorithms that process them. All that you have learned of computer science's methods of inquiry and algorithms also applies to studying data structures. The next section of this book takes up that study, designing and analyzing some classic data structures and their algorithms.

10.6 FURTHER READING

Sorting is a very old problem. Mechanical sorting machines were used before electronic computers existed. John von Neumann, one of the founders of modern computing, apparently used Mergesort as a benchmark in designing one of the first computers, as described in:

Donald Knuth, "Von Neumann's First Computer Program," *ACM Computing Surveys*, Dec. 1970.

Sorting remains an important application of computers, and Quicksort and Mergesort are among the most widely used sorting algorithms. Introductory and intermediate textbooks on algorithms cover them, along with many other ways of sorting. One of the most complete treatments is:

Donald Knuth, *Sorting and Searching* (*The Art of Computer Programming*, Vol. 3), Addison-Wesley, 1973.

For a good discussion of divide-and-conquer sorting algorithms, see Chapter 19 of:

Sartaj Sahni, *Data Structures, Algorithms, and Applications in Java*, McGraw-Hill, 2000.

Quicksort was invented by C. A. R. Hoare, and was first described in:

C. A. R. Hoare, "Quicksort", *Computer Journal*, 1962.

The idea that Quicksort's partitioning algorithm can be developed from a loop invariant that is a generalization of the postcondition is from:

David Gries, *The Science of Programming*, Springer-Verlag, 1981.

The earliest versions of Mergesort were iterative, such as those in Exercise 10.30. At the time, files were stored on magnetic tape, which had to be read sequentially (in other words, values had to be retrieved in the order they were stored on the tape), and main memories were too small to hold more than a fraction of a file. Iterative Mergesorts suit these technologies perfectly, because they only need a few values in memory at once (the "front" values for the merge), and they make a small number of sequential passes through a file. Recursive Mergesorts, such as the one studied in this text, became popular later, when sorting was less constrained by storage technology.

For a merging algorithm that does not need a temporary array, see:

Bing-Chao Huang and Michael Langston, "Practical In-place Merging," *Communications of the ACM*, March 1988.

For a formal justification of Section 10.3.3's "gamble" that $C(2^i - 1)$ is asymptotically the same as the general $C(n)$, and of the assertion that such an equivalence holds "for most functions occurring in practice," see the discussion of "eventually increasing" and "smooth" functions in Section 3.4 of:

Gilles Brassard and Paul Bratley, *Fundamentals of Algorithmics*, Prentice Hall, 1996.

III

Introduction to Data Structures

The emphasis of the first half of this text has been on actions (methods or algorithms): types of actions, defining new actions, predicting results, and evaluating actions. But the objects manipulated by algorithms can be quite interesting in their own right. In fact some algorithms all but require new perspectives on the nature of objects. This section expands the concept of object and investigates the implications of that expansion on the algorithms that manipulate them.

Thus far, objects have been viewed as fixed entities, fully specified by their class. The internal structure of an object does not change over time. A robot can't grow a new wheel, develop a new color palette, or rearrange its internal components. But some problems do require such references to or manipulation of the relationship of an object's subparts to each other or to the object as a whole. Part III describes techniques that enable an object to change in important ways. The resulting object classes with internally addressable structures are called *data structures*: subparts can be added, removed, reordered, or queried. The three methods of inquiry developed in Parts I and II continue to provide the cornerstone of the investigation, but the four chapters of Part III also add to that collection of tools to describe four classes of data structures and conclude by using those tools in new situations, developing new problem solutions.

11 Lists

We all have an intuitive notion of "list," as in a grocery list or a "to do" list. This chapter uses that simple notion as the starting point for creating a more formal or abstract concept of list, one of the basic building blocks for data structures in computer science. As formal objects, lists share several properties that make them both interesting and conceptually different from objects you have dealt with previously. Each list has subparts: the series of items that make up the list. That property, by itself, is not new; many objects can be described as a whole, and those same objects can be described in terms of their subparts. What is new is that relationships among the subparts of a list or between those subparts and the list as a whole also can be described or even manipulated.

11.1 EXAMPLES OF LISTS OR SEQUENCES

Examples of listlike structures can be found everywhere and include some entities that do not initially seem like lists. This section first looks to the world as a whole and then considers several examples of special importance for computer science and computer programming.

11.1.1 Real World Lists

Consider several real-world objects:

- Shopping list
- "To do" list
- Table of contents for a book
- List of items to take on a trip

and even:

- A railroad train

Train

To envision the universal properties of lists, consider the least listlike but most concrete of these examples: the railroad train. A train is an object made up of a series of other objects: the cars. There is no specific number of cars that make up a train. They do not have any inherent or fixed order (although at any given time they are necessarily in some order). Cars can be added or cars can be removed, but it is still a train. We can make statements about the train in its entirety:

> *It is on track 13.*
> *It is moving 60 miles per hour.*
> *It is headed to St. Louis…*

and about an individual car within the train:

> *This one is carrying wood.*
> *That one weighs 10 tons.*
> *Another one is 10 years old…*

These are not surprising. What is different is that we can also say something about the relationship of the train to its individual cars, or the cars to each other:

> *The first car is the engine.*
> *One carries wood, and the following one does, too.*
> *The third car weighs more than the fourth car.*
> *The train has (at the moment) a total of 17 cars…*

Most importantly, these are not fixed relationships, but ones that may change over time. Just as there are things that we can tell a train to do (move to a new location, speed up) and things we can say to a car (dump its cargo, close its coupler), we may want to reorganize a train. Specifically, cars can be added, removed, or reordered; one train can be combined with another, etc.

Grocery List

Now consider something that really does seem like a list: a shopping list, which turns out to be a surprisingly similar concept. At any moment, the shopping list contains the names of things needed from the store. Perhaps the following:

- Bread
- Eggs
- Milk
- Ice cream

New items can be added to the list. For example, adding "Pizza" results in:

- Bread
- Eggs
- Milk
- Ice cream
- Pizza

Existing items can be removed from the list. For example, if we removed "Ice cream" and "Pizza," we get:

- Bread
- Eggs
- Milk

The list can even be rewritten in a different order:

- Ice cream
- Bread
- Eggs
- Milk

Table of Contents

A table of contents provides yet another common example of a list. It contains the names for each chapter of a book. As the author rethinks the book, the table of contents will also change. Not only will chapters get new titles, but they may be reordered, added, or deleted. It's still the table of contents for the same book, but it reflects a changed order.

11.1.2 Of Special Importance to Computer Scientists

The generic concept of list is of special interest for computer science because lists appear naturally in many different computer applications. Some of these may be obvious: a list of incoming e-mail messages clearly seems to be a list. Some are not so obvious: a computer program can be thought of as a list of individual statements (statements can be added, deleted, reordered, or modified). Consider the workings of an e-mail system in a bit more detail:

- Each incoming message is an interesting object in its own right. It has a sender, a time stamp, a subject, a body, and perhaps other things such as who received "carbon copies," a priority, attachments, etc. Indeed, it may actually have a list of attachments.

■ At any given moment, the program can display the headers for all the messages in the inbox.

■ When a new message arrives, it must be added to the list.

■ When you delete a message, it is removed.

■ If you file a message, it is removed from the inbox list and added to a very similar list (perhaps "personal" or "my cs class").

■ Most e-mail systems can display the messages in any of several orders, such as by sender, by time, by subject, or by size. This requires a mechanism to reorder the list.

A moment's reflection will reveal many similar lists maintained within every computer system. Each of these shares many of the same requirements we just witnessed for e-mail messages. Consider a few:

■ Files within a folder

■ Files waiting to be printed

■ Users allowed to access the machine

■ Applications running right now (or applications installed on the machine)

■ Windows within an application

■ Words in a word processor

■ Characters on a screen or window

■ History list in a Web browser (or bookmarks or favorites)

■ Lines of code in a program

and of course: the preceding list itself. The bottom line here is that lists are ubiquitous in computing systems and therefore, understanding lists is essential. Using lists to represent collections of information forms the basis of an entire way of looking at data: *list processing*.

Exercises

11.1. Select five of the computer-oriented lists described in this section. For each, describe actions or relationships relevant to the list that are similar to those of a grocery list or a train.

11.2. Make a list of books you have read in the past two months. Describe how this list would change over time.

11.3. Think of five additional lists or sequences of items. Name or describe the lists as a whole and name or describe the individual items within the lists. Consider the implications of each of these on computer programming.

11.2 DEVELOPING THE CONCEPT OF A LIST

Looking ahead to formalizing the concept and ultimately creating a formal class definition, it should be clear that we will eventually need to define methods applicable to a list class. Although a list itself is an object like any other, it also has some more unique characteristics that pose special problems. In particular, we need tools for referring to and manipulating the subparts of the list. The subparts of a list are generically called *elements*, and so far, elements are no different from variables of any other class—except that the number of elements can change. Figure 11.1 illustrates the beginnings of this concept.

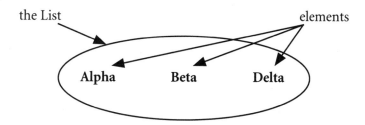

FIGURE 11.1 A list is made up of individual items.

Unfortunately, so far we have no way to change the number of member variables (or otherwise dynamically change any relationships between them) within an object. Most classes have methods that manipulate instances of the class, perhaps setting an internal (member) variable or printing out some information, and every member variable has a type—perhaps a class with its own appropriate methods. Although every class provides a mechanism for referring to the object itself (e.g., via an object variable, or the word "this" within a method) and to its individual subparts (the member variables or methods), none of these allow the object to reorganize or change its internal organization. Clearly, any list class will need some extra capabilities.

11.2.1 Manipulating Lists

Fortunately, the required access tools are remarkably similar for every list. Common operations for lists include: adding and deleting elements, combining two lists, measuring the size of a list, referring to one specific element of the list, and most importantly, visiting every element within a list.

Add a New Object to the List

Clearly, whether inserting a new item in a grocery list or coupling a car into a train, it must be possible to build a list incrementally, as represented generically in Figure 11.2.

Remove an Object from the List

An item can be crossed off a grocery list or an e-mail message deleted. Generically, we remove or *delete* an item from a list, as represented in Figure 11.3.

Combine Two Lists

Imagine stapling two grocery lists together, or coupling a train with a whole series of cars already linked together, generically shown in Figure 11.4. Combining two lists to make one large list goes by many names, including *join* (usually applied to unordered collections or sets), *concatenate* (usually applied to sequences of characters or words), and *append*. But the basic idea is the same no matter what the specific features of the list: start with two separate lists and end up with one long list containing all the elements of both lists.

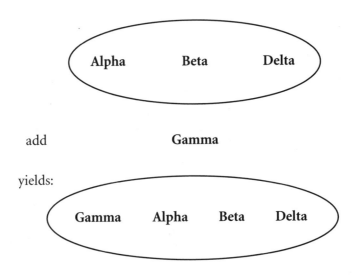

FIGURE 11.2 Adding an item to a list.

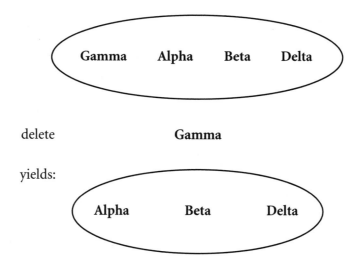

FIGURE 11.3   Removing an item from a list.

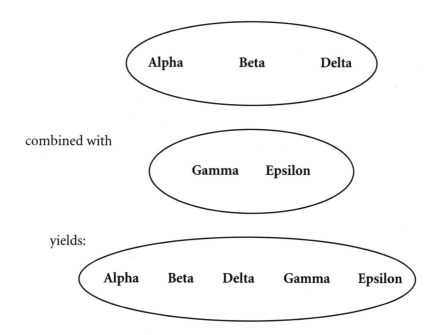

FIGURE 11.4   Combining two lists.

Visit the Elements

Any number of related actions, collectively called *visiting* or *traversing*, require accessing every element in the list individually, perhaps to print them out, perhaps to make a change to each item, or perhaps simply to find one particular value within the list. It is not the specific action, such as printing, that is important here. Rather, we need a general means of traversal through the list: a tool that enables us to access each element one at a time. In fact, this may be the most important of all the capabilities described here.

As we develop the concept of list further and ultimately create a List class, we will want to make sure that the resulting class facilitates these basic operations.

11.2.2 Visiting the Subparts

Traversal of a list is especially important because it is the means for accessing the elements even though their number or order may change. Perhaps the best way to assure that every element is reachable is to provide a way to visit each of them in a specific sequence. This suggests a path through the list: starting with some first element, each element is *linked* or connected to a next, as in Figure 11.5.

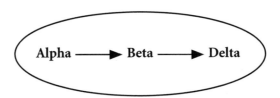

FIGURE 11.5 Links in a list.

Every element in the list should be on the path once—and no more than once. This requirement assures that we can visit every element by following the path from the first element to the last. Performing some operation on every element in the list can be accomplished by processing each element and then following the path to the next.

So far, this says nothing about the actual construction of a link, which might be accomplished in any of several ways. In a grocery list, items are linked simply by their position on the page; train cars are connected by a physical coupling device. Such links are probably not a new concept to most readers. If you have ever clicked on a link on a Web page you have followed a link. If you have ever followed directions that included something like "go to step 3," you have followed a link. In the figure and most other graphical representations, a link is represented as an arrow.

Humans can intuitively follow the arrows with no special instructions, but it may not be immediately clear how an arrow should best be represented in a computer. Any representation of a list class will require some computer equivalent to "arrow", some mechanism that says, "When looking at a given element, this is how to find the next in the sequence." Thus, every element in a list has an associated aspect or property: the link to the next element. These two items, element and link, taken together are often thought of as a single unit, called a *node*. But we will soon see an alternative representation that is more amenable to an object-oriented environment.

Find the Next Element

We need a specific tool that effectively says "follow the link." It must somehow explain how to get from "Alpha" in Figure 11.5 to "Beta". This single tool is the enabling tool for any algorithm that requires visiting every element of a list.

Using Lists

Given a tool for getting to the next element, most list-processing algorithms are very simple. Perhaps more importantly, they have remarkably similar structures, and with a little experience, can be built almost intuitively. A simple example might be something like:

> *Algorithm to find the total cost of groceries:*
> *Initialize the total cost to zero.*
> *Start at the first element.*
> *While there are more groceries on the list:*
> *Set total = total plus cost of current element.*
> *Find (visit) the next element.*

Recursive versions of most list algorithms are even simpler and look something like:

> *Algorithm totalCost (groceryList):*
> *If there are no more elements in the list*
> *Set total cost to 0.*
> *otherwise*
> *set total cost = cost of this element + cost of all following elements.*

This algorithm contains the question, "Are there any elements remaining to be visited?" Hidden within that question are at least two assumptions: that a list may not have any elements at all and that we can recognize when it doesn't. With those assumptions, the general structure of almost any traversing algorithm is almost identical:

> *Algorithm genericProcess:*
> *If the list has more elements to be visited*
> *then   Process this element,*
> *genericProcess the remaining elements.*

Only the details of the specific action performed during the visit will change. In fact, the simplicity of recursive algorithms for list processing is one of the features that make both lists and recursion popular tools. For example, one algorithm to print out all the items on a grocery list looks like:

> *Algorithm to print all element names:*
> *If there are elements remaining to print*
> *then   Print the current name,*
> *Print the names of the remaining elements.*

11.2.3 A Unifying Observation

Before we actually attempt a formal definition of a list, let's consider the question:

What follows an element in a list?

There are two possible answers:

- The next element
- A series of elements starting with the next element and running to the last element in the list

This second answer, while perhaps less intuitive, is more interesting, because it can be stated as: each element is followed by another list (possibly empty). Consider the train example yet again: each car within a train has a coupling device capable of hanging onto—or letting go of—the following car. By closing this coupler at the right moment, the car can attach itself to another car. But if that additional car happens to be the first car of a train, attaching it also adds that entire train. Each car in a train is followed not just by the next car but all the remaining cars in the train. Those remaining cars can collectively be thought of as a train.

The first answer to the question seems to correspond directly to the original concept of list. The second answer leads to an alternative description of list, that while consistent with the previous use, enables a much more powerful development of a list class. Just as each car in a train can be thought of as the first car of another smaller train, a list can be thought of as composed of a series of lists, each of which is an element followed by another list (rather than simply by an element), as illustrated in Figure 11.6. Notice that just as the list ovals in the figure are simply superimposed on the original list of elements (recall Figure 11.5), this vision of list can be superimposed on the original. The sublist provides the mechanism for visiting the remaining elements; each sublist of any given list contains all of the elements that follow the first element. Instead of representing a list as a series of individual elements, we will think of it as a nested series of lists.

By tradition, the two parts of a list are called the *head* and the *tail*.[1] The head is the first element of the list, while the tail—the rest of the list—is actually another list. In this view, every element is the head of some list, as in Figure 11.7. "Alpha" is the head of the list, "Beta" is the head of the tail of that first list. "Delta" is the head

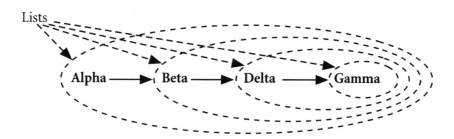

FIGURE 11.6 A recursive vision of list.

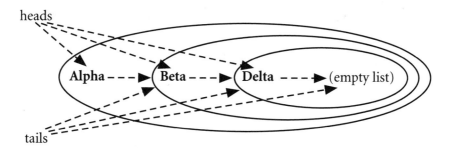

Beta is the head of the tail of the outer list.

FIGURE 11.7 The list as sequence of lists.

---

[1] The names are suggestive of the old question: Where does a snake's tail begin? Answer: right behind the head.

of the next list. In general, we can refer to any element of the original series as the head of some tail within the list. On occasion we may continue to visualize the physical list as a sequence of elements. In fact, we may even refer to "the next element of the list," but you should remember that by "the next element" we mean the head of the next sublist (or, "the head of the tail") following the current element.

11.2.4 The Empty List

The new definition is a recursive definition, and any recursive definition must terminate somehow. A list, like so many objects we have discussed in this text, may be empty—a list with no elements. A train with no cars is one that hasn't been put together yet (but perhaps is scheduled, in which case the switching yard needs to know about it); a character string with no characters is the null string (represented in most compilers as " "); a folder with no files in it yet is an empty list of files; and hopefully at the end of a shopping trip the shopping list is empty (all items have been crossed off). If we require that the last (innermost) list within a list be the empty or null list, we can avoid any infinite regression. In general a list may be:

> *an element—followed by a list*

or

> *the empty (null) list.*

Requiring that every list terminate with the empty list provides an easy way to recognize the end of a path through the list: if the current list is the empty list, we must be at the end.

A list made up of lists lends itself perfectly to recursive algorithms. The *printList* algorithm nears its final form as:

> *Algorithm printList:*
>   *If the list is not empty*
>   *then Print the current name (the head),*
>   *printList the next list (the tail).*

Exercises

11.4.   For each of the previous real-world examples of lists (train, shopping list, computer program, table of contents, words in a word processor, and letters on a screen), give an example of each of the basic list operations. Repeat for the computer-specific lists.

11.5. Draw schematic representations of three of the lists from Section 11.1. Be sure to include the list ovals superimposed on the sequence.

11.6. Describe, as a recursive algorithm, the process of buying all the items on a grocery list. Describe each element of that list in terms of heads and tails.

11.3 A FORMAL DEFINITION OF THE CLASS LIST

We can now use this recursive conceptualization of a list to start formalizing a Java List class. Before investigating the actual internal construction of the class, we will first consider the interface as seen by the client.

11.3.1 Basic Methods

The methods corresponding to the algorithms of Section 11.2 are all straightforward and are described here. The subsequent two sections illustrate those methods' use from the client's perspective by constructing some additional methods.

Constructor

Every class needs a constructor. A brand new list (corresponding perhaps to the point when a human creator reaches for the pad of paper on which to write the list) has nothing in it, so the basic constructor should create an empty list:

```
// constructor for the basic List class
public List() { ...
```

For example, a client can create a new grocery list with a statement like:

```
List todaysGroceries = new List();
```

The constructor is completely predictable, because every class needs one. Now consider the methods that reflect the more interesting properties of a list.

Recognize the Empty List

Some lists have no elements and some lists have actual content. The recursive traversal algorithms of the previous section terminated when there were no elements left to process, that is, when they encountered an empty list. By tradition, the method to test a list (or any other data structure) for content is called *isEmpty*. The definition within the List class looks like:

```
//this and all following methods are in the basic List class
public boolean isEmpty() { ...
```

`isEmpty` returns true if and only if the list contains no elements at all. If, immediately after creating `todaysGroceries`, a client asked if it were empty or not:

```
List todaysGroceries = new List();
System.out.print(todaysGroceries.isEmpty());
```

the result would be "true", since as yet nothing has been put into `todaysGroceries`.

Add a New Object to a List:

The actual construction of a list requires a mechanism for adding an element to an existing `List`:

```
public void addItem(Object newItem) { ...
```

Even though `newItem` is an `Object`, the method creates a new sublist each time a new element is added (remember that a list must have as many nested lists as there are elements). Even an empty list is a list, so new items can be added to a list as soon as it is created.

Access an item in a list

We also need the ability to access an item from a list. The public method `getFirst` provides this capability.

```
public Object getFirst() {...
```

This value-producing method does not alter the list but simply delivers the value of the head of the list. Clearly, we need to access more then the first element in the list. But since every element is the head of some list, `getFirst` is actually the primary tool for accessing any element of a list. Obviously, a precondition for accessing any element is that the list actually contains at least one element (i.e., that the list not empty). It is up to the client to ensure that this precondition holds (usually by using `isEmpty`).

Remove an Item

For removal of an element:

```
public void removeItem() { ...
```

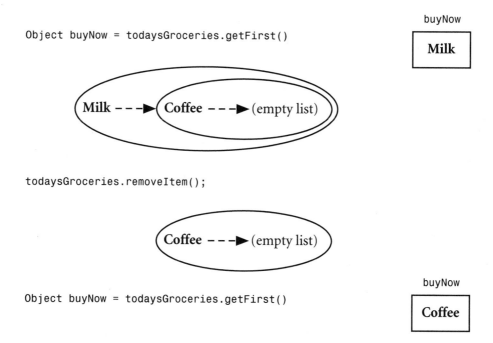

```
Object buyNow = todaysGroceries.getFirst()
```

buyNow

Milk

Milk - - -▶ Coffee - - -▶ (empty list)

```
todaysGroceries.removeItem();
```

Coffee - - -▶ (empty list)

buyNow

Coffee

```
Object buyNow = todaysGroceries.getFirst()
```

FIGURE 11.8 Removing items from a list.

removes one item (the head) from the List (and effectively throws it away). That is, removeItem is a side-effect-producing method: it changes the List but it does not actually deliver a value to the client, as seen in Figure 11.8.

In practice, removing an element from a list and then using the value of that element is such a common operation that the two methods are often combined into a single method:

```
public Object getAndRemove() { ...
```

Conceptually, getAndRemove combines the two methods getFirst and removeItem. This does violate the usual admonition against methods that are both side-effect- and value-producing. However, the operation is so basic in list processing that we will allow the violation. You may prefer to think of getAndRemove as splitting a list into its two constituent parts by returning the list's head, and replacing the original list with its own tail.

Access the Rest of a List

Finally, in order to access any element other than the head, we need a method to access the tail of the List. The method getRest accomplishes this important service:

```
public List getRest() { ...
```

getRest simply returns the tail without modifying the list itself in any way, as illustrated in Figure 11.9.

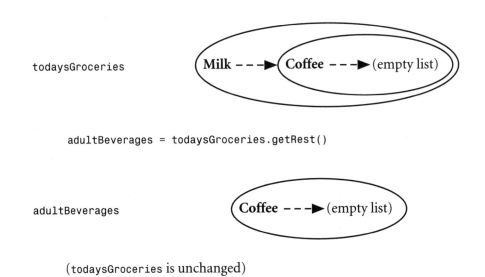

todaysGroceries

adultBeverages = todaysGroceries.getRest()

adultBeverages

(todaysGroceries is unchanged)

FIGURE 11.9 Using getRest to find a sublist.

Order of the List

Thus far, we have not specifically defined where in a list a new item is inserted by addItem, nor which item is removed by removeItem. And often, it doesn't matter. When a person builds a grocery list, it is just a list with no necessarily first nor last item. But the order of cars in a train does matter, and it also seems to matter for the definition we adopted in which a list is an element followed by a list. It is important that all operations be consistent and provide predictable results. If we execute printList twice, it should behave the same way both times. Traditionally, removeItem is thought of as the inverse of addItem. That is, adding an element and then removing an element:

```
groceries.addItem("ice cream");
groceries.removeItem();
```

should leave the list just as it was before these two statements were executed. Although this still seems to allow adding an element anywhere in the list, we will assume that `addItem` adds an element at the head of the list. Thus, `getFirst` should return the item just placed on a list, as it seems to do in Figure 11.8. Similarly, we will assume that `removeItem` removes the head of the list. Exercise 11.22 explores an alternative representation: adding and removing from the back of the list.

You Can't Change the First Item

The class deliberately does not have a method to change the first element of a list. The reason for this omission is not that the first item can't change, nor that there is never a need for change. Altering an element in the list should not be thought of as replacing it with another element. One doesn't change "ice cream" to "coffee" on a grocery list; one crosses "ice cream" off the list and adds "coffee." To completely replace the first item in the list, one can use `removeItem` followed by `addItem`.

SetRest

It is only occasionally necessary to alter the tail of a list. The method `setRest` does just that. Its argument is not an element value, as with `addItem` or `delete`, but another list. The interface looks like:

```
public void setRest(List secondList) { ...
```

`setRest` is not particularly intuitive and it is not needed very often, but there are at least a few circumstances that require it. One such situation is described in Section 11.3.2.

We will leave the actual implementations of the `List` methods until later. In fact, Java provides an interface called (not coincidentally) `List` that contains methods equivalent to each of those described here (plus others), so if we only wanted to know how to use a list (as opposed to understanding how to create the class), we could just use any of several library classes that implement that interface.

11.3.2 Examples

In spite of the leanness of this collection of methods, they are actually sufficient for creating most list algorithms. The complete `List` class that we will ultimately define does include a few additional methods, but those can be built from this basic set. Constructing the additional methods helps show the power of this basic set.

Building a Simple List

A list typically has several elements. Building a list is simply a matter of adding new elements as needed:

Algorithm buildList
    If another item for the list exists
        then   addItem (the new Item) to the list,
           buildList.

The details of this algorithm really depend more on the method of acquisition of new elements than on the list. For example, if the new items are coming from the keyboard, they would be acquired very differently than if they were coming from an existing list. But the new list itself is built in the same way in all cases.

List Traversal

Many uses of a list require traversal—visiting every element contained in the list. For example, we have seen the basic *printList* algorithm already, and it can easily be written in Java using the basic methods of the last section:

```
//in the basic List class
public void printList() {
    if (!this.isEmpty()) {
        System.out.println(this.getFirst());
        this.getRest().printList();
    }
}
```

Study this algorithm very carefully, because it embodies the essence of almost every list-processing algorithm, as suggested in Section 11.2.2. Traversal algorithms process a list by doing something with the head of the list, and then treating the tail as another, shorter, list—which, being a list, can be processed recursively. Consider a few more examples.

Count

How many items are in a list? That's easy—an empty list contains no elements, while a nonempty list contains one head plus whatever is in the tail. This recursive description is easily captured in the method:

```
//in the basic List class
public int count() {
    if (this.isEmpty())
        return 0;
    else
        return 1 + this.getRest().count();
}
```

Sum

Or perhaps you want to find the total of a list of numbers:

Algorithm sum:
    If the list isEmpty
        then Return 0.
        else Return getFirst + sum of getRest.

The Java version of *sum* is left to an exercise.

Even proofs of correctness are simple and straightforward for the List class. For example, showing that *sum* returns the correct value can be done easily.

THEOREM: *Sum returns the total of all values in a list.* □

PROOF: Proof is by induction on the length of the list.

Base Case: The empty list contains no elements, and the sum of zero things must be zero. When the list is empty, the algorithm returns zero, as needed.

Induction Step: Assume that the result is true for all lists of length $n-1$. Let L be a list of length n. In that case, the length of the tail of L must be $n-1$, so the proposition must hold for the tail. Thus, *getRest().sum()* returns the sum of all elements in the tail. *getFirst()* returns the only other element of the list. That element plus the sum of the tail elements is the sum of all values in the list. ∎

Performance analysis for list algorithms is just as straightforward.

THEOREM: *Sum runs in* $\Theta(n)$ *time.* □

PROOF: The proof is by induction on the length of the list. We will count the number of additions.

Base Case: If n is 0, then the list is empty. The algorithm performs no additions.

Induction Step: Assume the proposition is true for lists of length $n-1$. In particular, assume that a list of length $n-1$ requires $n-1$ additions. Let L be a list of length n. By definition, *L.tail* has length $n-1$, so the proposition is true for *sum.L.tail*, which must perform its calculation in $n-1$ additions. The calculation for L requires one more addition, for a total of n. ∎

Find

Boolean list methods often have three conditions to test for: success, "not yet," and "encountered the empty list." The algorithm to determine if an item is in a list illustrates the basic idea:

> *Algorithm find (value):*
>   *If the list is empty*
>   *then (the item must not be in the list, so)*
>   *return false.*
>   *otherwise If the first item is the desired value*
>   *then (we found it, so) return true.*
>   *otherwise look in the rest of the list.*

Notice how the first clause makes an implicit observation: nothing is in the empty list, so the target can't possibly be. Other than that, it is almost the same as the earlier algorithms. Java implementation of `find` is included in Section 11.5.2. We will see this "three part test" format over and over:

> *Generic value producing method:*
>   *If the list is empty*
>   *return false. [must have reached the end without*
>   *finding the goal]*
>   *otherwise if the first element satisfies the goal*
>   *then return whatever is found there*
>   *otherwise recursively look at the rest of the list.*

Some algorithms may use the same structure, but with almost exactly reversed interpretations. For example, an algorithm that asks if every item in a list satisfies some criterion would return with failure as soon as it found an inappropriate element. Exercise 11.16 explores such a possibility.

Delete By Value

Sometimes it is necessary to delete an element with a specific value, where that element is not necessarily the head, but any arbitrary element in the list (e.g., cross an item off a grocery list). To do that, use the familiar traversal structure: simply search the list and delete the desired item when it is found (it will be at the head of some sublist).

```
public void deleteItem(Object target) {
    if (!this.isEmpty())
        if (this.getFirst().equals(target))
            this.removeItem();
        else
            this.getRest().deleteItem(target);
}
```

Combining Two Lists

It may seem surprising that deleting an element from the middle of a list does not require altering a tail. But there is one situation that does require changing a tail: combining two lists. Surprisingly, combining two lists is no harder than any other list algorithm. As Figure 11.10 shows, there really is very little work to do.

The general concatenation algorithm is just:

Find the end of one list, and
Link to the (front of) the other.

The fist step can be achieved with the usual traversal algorithm, so the complete method can be written:

```
//first attempt
public void concat(List extraList) {
    if (this.getRest().isEmpty())
        this.setRest(extraList);
    else
        this.getRest().concat(extraList);
}
```

Actually this algorithm works except for one small case: if the original first list is empty. Extending the algorithm for that case is left to an exercise.

One aspect of this implementation that surprises some students is that it seems to make lists overlap. Specifically, notice in the figure that the right hand list is actually a sublist of the left hand list. This means that if either list changes, they both change. For example if "OJ" were removed from the second list and replaced with "Coffee," that change would be reflected in the first list, and vice versa.

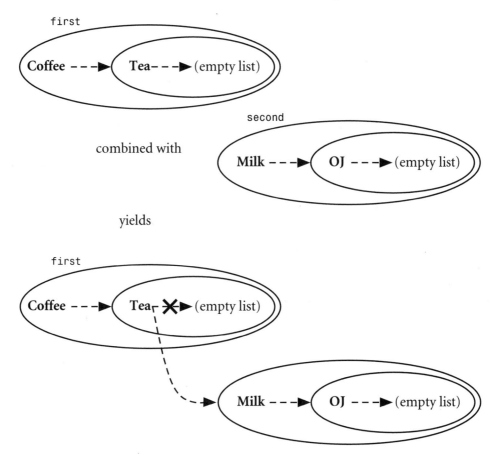

FIGURE 11.10 Concatenating two lists.

Exercises

11.7. printList, as defined, prints elements from the front of the list to the back. Since items are added at the front, that turns out to be upside down from how one would picture a list (such as a grocery list). Rewrite printList so that it prints back to front (hint: recall the general descriptions of recursive algorithms from Chapter 6).

11.8. Write an algorithm to find the third item in a list. If there are fewer than three items in the list, your algorithm should return null.

11.9. Write an algorithm that directs a list to create a duplicate of itself, but in the "duplicate," the order of the elements should be reversed from the original.

11.10. Write an algorithm to find the maximum value in a list.

11.11. Use the Java methods of this section to create a grocery list. Then print out all of the items in the list.

11.12. Create a method to find the position of a given element within the list. If the element doesn't appear at all, your method should return 0.

11.13. Write a Java method that finds the sum of all elements in the list.

11.14. Create a method that determines which of two elements occurs first in a list. Your method should return 1 or 2 according to whether its first or second argument occurs first in the list, and zero if they are both absent (if neither is present, neither can be first).

11.15. As stated, the concatenation algorithm will not work if the first list is empty. Explain the problem. Create two different solutions that will work in all cases.

11.16. Create a method allEven that returns true if every item in the list is even.

11.4 IMPLEMENTING THE CLASS

Now that we have defined the class List from the client perspective and have seen how it can be used, it is time to see how one could implement the class. It would of course be possible to use the class provided by Java. But, of course, someone had to implement that class (why not you?). But more importantly, there is much to be learned by "looking under the hood."

11.4.1 Constructing a Basic List Class

The class declaration includes two private member variables representing the two parts of a list:

```
public class List {
    private Object head;
    private List tail;
```

The explicit use of the List object as a member variable provides the necessary link. (You may want to see the Appendix for more on the relationship between Java objects and pointers.) The class also contains the basic methods.

Constructors

The basic constructor is straightforward. When a list is created, it is empty. So the constructor needs to build a list with no content (its head is null) and no next element (its tail is also null). Any element whose head is empty (i.e., null) should also have a null tail. More formally, we say that a class invariant for the List class is that: *no List satisfies: head = null and tail ≠ null*.

```
// basic new list
public List() {
    head = null;
    tail = null;
}
```

The empty list could have been represented differently (and other possibilities are discussed in Section 11.6.1), but any representation must be consistent with the test for emptiness.

isEmpty

The empty list is always exactly the same as that created by the constructor. So the isEmpty method simply needs to ask if a List looks like the one created by the constructor:

```
public boolean isEmpty() {
    return (head == null && tail == null);
}
```

getFirst

The first item of every list is the head. Since head is private, an access method, trivial as it is, is actually called for by good programming practice.

```
public Object getFirst() {
    return head;
}
```

getRest

Because it makes lists so easy to use, getRest may actually be the most important method. Yet all it does is return the value of the private variable.

```
public List getRest() {
    return tail;
}
```

setRest

The method setRest is seldom needed, but it is simple enough to include here without further explanation.

```
public void setRest(List newList) {
    tail = newList;
}
```

removeItem

Recall that removeItem deletes the first item in the list but does not return the value. The instinct of many programmers would be to try to write something like:

Bad Algorithm removeItem():
   Set this = this.tail.

That is, since the desired result is the tail of the current list, the algorithm asks the current list to replace itself with the list pointed to by its own tail. Alas, it is not possible for an object to replace itself; it can only replace its subparts. The method defined below works by changing both the head and the tail of the list. It copies the second element to the head (thus erasing the old head value), and then changes the tail to skip over the old second element (which now duplicates the new head), as illustrated in Figure 11.11.

```
public void removeItem() {
    head = tail.head;
    tail = tail.tail;
}
```

The deleted item does not cease to exist; it is just removed from the list. The element may or may not still be accessible by some other route. For example, if groceryList looked like the list at the top of Figure 11.11, then the statements:

```
smallList = groceryList.getRest();
groceryList.removeItem();
```

would leave groceryList as at the bottom of the figure but smallList would still be the inner list headed by "tea."

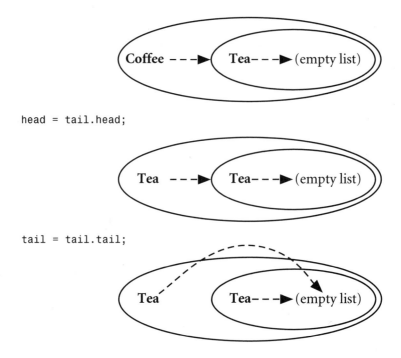

FIGURE 11.11 The steps of removeItem.

getAndRemove

The frequently needed getAndRemove is just a combination of getFirst and removeItem, and is left as an exercise.

addItem

addItem is tricky in a way similar to removeItem. Again, the intuition of the new programmer can get in the way. The first attempt may look like:

> *Bad Algorithm addItem:*
> *Create new list.*
> *Set head of new list to be the new value.*
> *Set tail of the new list to be the old list.*

That is, just place the item in front of the current list. Again, remember that an object cannot replace itself; it can only change the values of its individual parts (member variables). Although the proposed algorithm would create a new list of the correct form, the current list object does not refer to that new list. The corrected algorithm, coded in Java correctly, adds to a list by creating a copy of the first element and placing the copy second in the list. It then changes the head of the list to contain the new value, as illustrated in Figure 11.12.

```
public void addItem(Object newItem) {
    List temp = new List();
    temp.head = this.head;
    temp.tail = this.tail;
    this.head = newItem;
    this.tail = temp;
}
```

```
List todaysGroceries = new List();
```

(empty list)

```
todaysGroceries.addItem("Coffee");
```

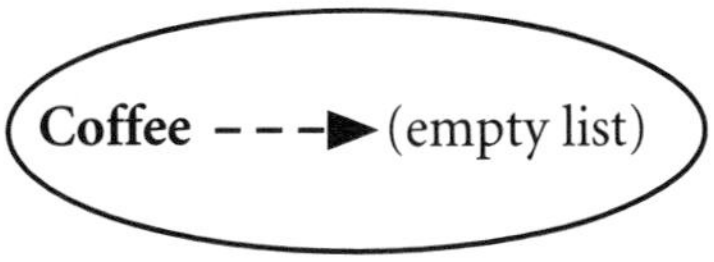

```
todaysGroceries.addItem("Milk");
```

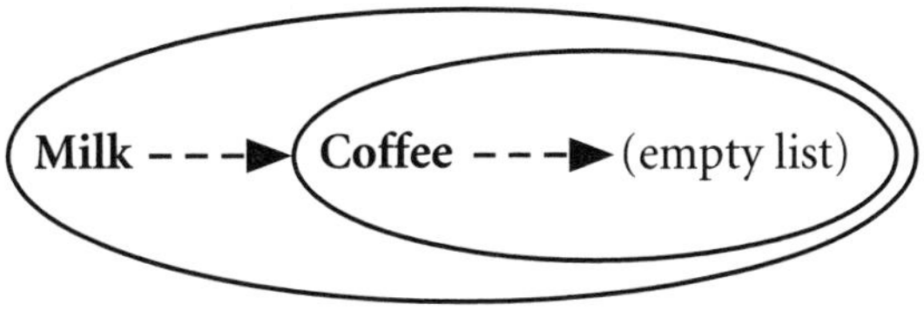

FIGURE 11.12 Building a list.

Exercises

11.17. Implement getAndRemove for the basic list class.

11.18. When creating a new List, a client is likely to want to add a new element immediately. Write a new constructor that accepts an object and initializes a List containing that one object.

11.19. In practice, many list classes would support a whole family of constructors allowing the client to create a new list with multiple elements already in it. Thus:

```
List foo = new List (A B);
```

would be equivalent to

```
List foo = new List ();
foo.addItem(A);
foo.addItem(B);
```

Create two more new constructors, List (one two) and List (one two three) that initialize List objects with two and three elements, respectively.

11.20. The text states that the concat method will not work as given if the original list is empty. Explain why not.

11.21. Improve the concat method so that it works even if the original list is empty.

11.22. Rewrite the List class so that additions and deletions are performed at the back of the list.

11.5 MAKING AN EXTENDABLE LIST CLASS

Almost certainly, in any real use of lists, the client is likely to want to build methods for performing specialized operations applicable to that client's specific use of lists. For example, printing the list in a specialized format, or using each element in a specific operation (creating the product of all elements, finding the largest element, sending an e-mail to each entry in the phone book, etc.). Constructing additional methods for lists requires extending the class. Unfortunately, extending the generic or basic List class to a specialized class tailored to your own specific needs is one of those places where the devil is in the details. Problems of extension fall into two categories:

- Adding methods for manipulating the list
- Extending the possible classes of entities that can be elements in the list

Accommodating these details actually impacts the proper definition of the List class in ways that didn't impact previous class definitions. This section explores the needed improvements.

11.5.1 Creating New Methods for Lists

Unfortunately, in Java (and some other languages), defining and then extending recursive classes such as List creates a small, but seemingly disastrous, conflict. Even though the members of the subclass may be structurally identical to those of the superclass, the methods themselves have a problem. Some methods of the class List return results of type List (e.g., getRest). When the client defines a new class, say UsableList, the objects of that class will obviously be of type UsableList—not List. The List returned by getRest is likely to conflict with the UsableList required by new methods. Consider a simple example. The method printList prints the elements from head to tail (typically, the inverse of the order in which they were added to the list). Suppose a client also wanted a generic method to print them tail to head (i.e., the same order in which they were created). One would expect this to be a simple modification of the printList method, something like:

```
//in class UsableList
//first attempt
public void printListForward() {
    if (!this.isEmpty()) {
        this.getRest().printListForward();      // *problem*
        System.out.println(this.getFirst());
    }
}
```

The diligent programmer will create a new class, UsableList, which extends List and includes this new method. Obviously, the new method is not part of the definition of the original class List; it is only defined for members of the class UsableList. This seems reasonable. After all, printListForward will only be used within the subclass. But there is a problem in the marked line. Although the programmer knows that the sublists of a UsableList should also be UsableLists, the original definition of getRest specifies only that it will return a List—and not necessarily a UsableList. On the other hand, the new method printListForward() is only defined for UsableLists. Thus, the recursive call:

```
this.getRest().printListForward()
```

causes a conflict: the message printListForward is defined for UsableLists but is sent to (what the compiler believes to be) a basic List. How can this problem be fixed? Enabling the List class to respond to the printListForward message requires changing the definition of the original class. But that violates the spirit of object-oriented programming (and may not even be possible for a client who does not have access to the full superclass definition). Similarly using static methods violates the object-oriented spirit. Alternatively, we could try to override getRest with a new version:

```
public UsableList getRest() {...
```

But this, too, has a problem: you cannot override a method with a given signature (getRest()) with one of the same signature but a different return type (UsableList instead of List).

Casting Within an Extension

Although the programmer knows that this particular use of getRest will always return a sublist of a UsableList (which therefore should be a UsableList), the compiler does not know this. It is possible to explicitly provide an assurance to the compiler by *casting* the List as a UsableList:

```
((UsableList) this.getRest()).printListForward();
```

This syntax is a *cast*, which tells the Java compiler that this particular use of getRest will always return, not just a List, but a UsableList. The seemingly extra set of parentheses show that the scope of the cast is this.getRest(). The statement effectively says: find the tail of the current List, treat that as a UsableList and send it the message printListForward. You will want to similarly cast every List returned within any new recursive algorithm. (See Section 5 in the Appendix for more details about casting.) The corrected method then is:

```
//in the class UsableList
public void printListForward() {
    if (!this.isEmpty()) {
        ((UsableList) this.getRest()).printListForward();
        System.out.println(this.getFirst());
    }
}
```

Constructing New Lists

Casting works—as far as it goes: printListForward does print out an existing UsableList. Unfortunately, there is an even larger problem when it comes to constructing a list within a subclass. Methods such as addItem create a new List. As written in the basic List class, addItem contains the line:

```
List temp = new List();
```

```
List demo = new UsableList();
demo.AddItem("Delta");
demo.AddItem("Beta");
demo.AddItem("Alpha");
```

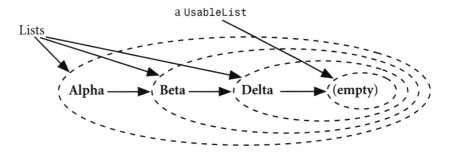

FIGURE 11.13 An incorrectly constructed `UsableList`.

which creates, not a `UsableList`, but a `List`. Thus, as a `UsableList` is built up, the created structure (except for the innermost empty list) is actually composed of `Lists`, not `UsableLists`, as illustrated in Figure 11.13.

This is a problem of object-oriented programming that seldom occurs—except when building data structures within a subclass. The problem can happen when extending any class in which methods (e.g., `addItem`) of the superclass may create new instances of that class. The solution is, in effect, to find a way to create new instances of the appropriate subclass. The approach is simple, but not very intuitive. Break the constructor into two parts: the basic constructor as before:

```
public List() {
    head = null;
    tail = null;
}
```

and a second generic helper:

```
//in class List
public List makeNewList() {
    return new List();
}
```

This method does nothing except call the constructor for `List`. The intent is that any method in the class `List` that needs to create a new list will use `makeNewList` instead of using the actual constructor (List()) directly. This may seem like a super-fluous complication. However, any extension of the List class should then override this single method, something like:

```
//in class UsableList
public List makeNewList() {
    return new UsableList();
}
```

Then any makeNewList message sent to a UsableList will be handled by this new definition of makeNewList, thus creating a new UsableList, rather than a new List. The method addItem also needs to be changed to use this new approach:

```
//in Class List
public void addItem(Object newItem) {
    List temp = this.makeNewList();
    temp.head = this.head;
    temp.tail = this.tail;
    this.head = newItem;
    this.tail = temp;
}
```

When a UsableList executes the corrected addItem method, the special variable this refers to a UsableList. Thus, this.makeNewList() will return a UsableList, correctly adding a new UsableList, not a new List, to the original UsableList. The final version of the List class in Section 11.5.2 (and on the Web site for this book) includes these improvements.

11.5.2 The Final List Class

The improvements needed to enable proper creation of subclasses do require that the designers of the original List class anticipate that the class will be extended. And well they should. After all, that is the whole point of object-oriented programming. The final List class—with the improvements— therefore looks like:

```
public class List {
    private Object head;
    protected List tail;
```

```
// constructors

// basic new list
public List() {
    head = null;
    tail = null;
}

// dummy for use with subclasses

public List makeNewList() {
    return new List();
}

// Basic public functions

// access functions
public Object getFirst() {
    return this.head;
}

public List getRest() {
    return this.tail;
}

public boolean isEmpty() {
    return (this.head == null && this.tail == null);
}

// remove an item
public void removeItem() {
    this.head = this.tail.head;
    this.tail = this.tail.tail;
}

public Object getAndRemove() {
    Object temp = head;
    this.head = this.tail.head;
    this.tail = this.tail.tail;
    return temp;
}
```

```java
public void addItem(Object newItem) {
    List temp = this.makeNewList();
    temp.head = this.head;
    temp.tail = this.tail;
    this.head = newItem;
    this.tail = temp;
}

protected void setRest(List newTail) {
    this.tail = newTail;
}

// traversal extensions building from base set

protected void concat(List extraList) {
    if (tail.isEmpty())
        tail = extraList;
    else
        tail.concat(extraList);
}

public void printList() {
    if (!this.isEmpty()) {
        System.out.println(this.getFirst());
        this.getRest().printList();
    }
}

// search the list for a given target
public boolean find(Object target) {
    if (this.isEmpty())
        return false;
    else if (this.getFirst().equals(target))
        return true;
    else
        return this.getRest().find(target);
}
```

```
// remove a node by value

public void delete(Object value) {
if (!this.isEmpty())
    if (this.getFirst().equals(value))
        this.removeItem();
    else
        this.getRest().delete(value);
}


}   // end of List class
```

11.5.3 Ordered List as an Extension of List

Sometimes in the real world, the exact order of items in a list makes a difference: If
a list were not a grocery list but a class-enrollment list, the owner of the list would
probably want to have the names in alphabetic order. Initially, it may seem unlikely
that additions and deletions at the front of the list would be sufficient to keep the
list in order. Maintaining order within a list seems to require access to elements
other than the first. For example, if a list currently contains

> Chris
> Terry

adding Mike, while maintaining the alphabetic order, requires that Mike must go
after, not before, Chris. For an ordered list, we want to add the class invariant: *not*
(*this.head > this.tail.head*). Notice that this wording allows equal values and also
applies to the last element. Surprisingly, maintaining an ordered list does not require changing any methods of the basic List class, but it does require that we build
a subclass of the basic class, containing one additional method—just as we needed
to do in order to add printListForward.

Insertion

Maintaining an ordered list requires the ability to insert an element at a specific
location in the list, for example, the alphabetically correct location. Since addItem
always inserts items at the head of the list, we need to construct a tool for insertion.
How can we insert an element into a list in alphabetic order if we can only add it at
the front? The trick is to remember that every element is actually the first element
of some list. That means insertion at an internal position can be achieved by adding
the element at the head of the appropriate sublist—but first we need to find that
sublist. To insert an element before Terry in the figure, simply add it to the list cur-

rently headed by Terry. The important thing is to remember that the tail at Chris refers—not to the element Terry but—to the list headed by Terry. When that list is altered by adding the new element at its the front, the tail at "Chris" still refers to the same list, but that list now has a new first element. The basic algorithm, illustrated in Figure 11.14, is structurally much like other list-processing algorithms:

> *Algorithm: insertAlphabetically:*
>   *If the new item alphabetically precedes the head of the list*
>   *then add the new element at the front of the list*
>   *otherwise insert it later in the list.*

There is one additional problem: the elements in a List may be any Object, but Objects are not necessarily comparable or ordered. If the objects in a list are not comparable to each other, it makes no sense to try to keep the list ordered. For example, a list may be composed of windows or e-mail messages, but neither of those classes has an inherent ordering. We need to restrict ordered lists to contain only comparable objects. With that restriction in mind, the method for inserting an object into an ordered list becomes:

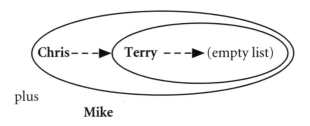

plus

Mike

yields

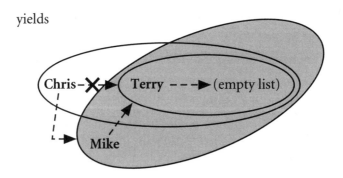

FIGURE 11.14 Inserting an element into a list.

```
//in class OrderedList
public void insert(Comparable newItem) {
    if (this.isEmpty())
        this.addItem(newItem);
    else {
        Comparable firstItem = (Comparable)this.getFirst();
        if (firstItem.compareTo(newItem) > 0)
            this.addItem(newItem);
        else
            ((OrderedList)this.getRest()).insert(newItem);
    }
}
```

There are two points to notice about this method. First, it takes advantage of the Java language interface Comparable (see the Appendix for more on interfaces) to ensure that insert only adds new items that are orderable. Any class that implements the Comparable interface must define a compareTo method as a standard means of comparing two objects. Second, there are two separate casts, one of the results of getRest as an OrderedList, and the other of getFirst as a Comparable.

Although insert is the only additional method that must be defined to create an OrderedList class, at least two other methods, find and delete, could be improved within such an extension. In an ordered list, searches for a specific value need not search the entire list. Once either algorithm encounters a value that should occur after the target value, it may quit, since the target cannot appear later in the list. On average, that should cut the number of recursions in half. Exercise 11.27 and Exercise 11.28 ask you to design such methods and empirically test this claim.

There is one final observation that you should consider. Creation of an OrderedList class does not assure that the elements of a list are indeed ordered. It is the client's responsibility to assure that nodes are never added to an ordered list except through the use of insert. Completion of the class OrderedList is left to the reader (Exercise 11.26).

11.5.4 Complex Elements

A list is a series of objects. In practice, these objects themselves are likely to be complex entities. Consider the problem of building a personal phone book, that is, a list containing the names, plus phone numbers and perhaps addresses or other special information about your friends. This task seems ideally suited for a list; items can be added or removed as you acquire new friends and lose contact with old ones.

Complex elements introduce an important new capability. The search key (e.g., in a class PhoneEntry, a person's name may serve as the key) is only one part of the full entry, which also contains additional information (e.g., phone number and address). *Find* returns true when an item is found. But the identical logic could be used to find and return the entire contents of a `PhoneEntry` object. In fact, that is exactly how one uses a phone book. The relevant question is unlikely to be, "Is Bill in my phone book?" A far more likely question is: "What is Bill's phone number?" That is: find Bill in the list and return the phone information (or more) from his entry.

Even in such a small extension, a few complications do creep in. Almost certainly, a task such as creating and using a phone will require a client-defined class. The new *find-and-return* method must be distinct from `find` because it can't have the same signature. The client will probably need to implement the *comparable* interface (see the Appendix), and will want to include the methods `compareTo` (to enable insertion), `equals` (to enable *find*) and probably `toString` (to enable human-readable output). Exercise 11.29 and 11.30 explore this task.

11.5.5 Case Study: Insertion Sort

Chapter 10 explored several sorting algorithms. One use for which ordered lists offer a different approach is not quite sorting, but "resorting." In particular, they offer an alternative to sorting in the usual sense. The concept behind an ordered list is that it is always sorted. The sorted list may be accessed, a new item added, and then the list used again—still sorted. Whenever a new element needs to be added, the list is already sorted—except for that one additional item. Using most sorting algorithms, the entire collection needs to be resorted at that point. But the single new item may simply be inserted directly into the correct position of an ordered list. Even with Quicksort, resorting a collection of n items after adding one new item requires $\Theta(n \log n)$ steps. But inserting a single new item into the correct position in an ordered list requires on average just $\Theta(n)$ steps: search about half way down the list ($n/2$ elements) and insert the new value. Thus, ordered lists are well suited for maintaining a collection where new items are added occasionally but intervening processing may require that the data always be in the appropriate order. If the list needs to be ordered between occasional additions or deletions, insertion may be more appropriate than appending and resorting.

In fact, this suggests an alternative sorting algorithm: the *insertion sort*. This algorithm uses the observations that a newly formed list contains no elements, and that at any point as the list is built, all existing elements are in order. As the list is built, it can be built in any order simply by inserting each new element at the correct location. This sort can be implemented trivially by simply creating the list in order: as each item is added to the list, it is added in order. Thus, as the list is created, the current list is always in order and the algorithm does not rely on continual reshuffling of values. The basic algorithm is usually written:

Algorithm insertionSort:
    For each new element to be added:
        If the new item alphabetically precedes the head of the list
           then add the new element at the front of the list.
           otherwise insert it later in the list.

but the bulk of this algorithm is just the algorithm for `insert`. So the algorithm can be rewritten as just:

Algorithm insertionSort:
    For each new element to be added:
        Insert the value into the list.

Creating the Java version is left to an exercise.

THEOREM: The elements in a list built using insertion sort will always be sorted. □

PROOF: Use induction on the length of the list.

Base Case: A list of no elements is clearly in order.

Induction Step: Assume that *insertionSort* works for all lists of length $n-1$, and that `insert` has been correctly coded. If insertion sort is applied to a list of n elements, then the n-th element is added to an existing list of length $n-1$, so the existing list in is order by assumption. *insert* then correctly adds the n-th element, clearly resulting in a list of length n that is in the correct order. ∎

As we just saw, a new element can be placed into the middle of the existing list of length n in approximately $\Theta(n)$ time. So the time required to insert n items is $\Theta(n^2)$. This is the same as several other sorts—all relatively inefficient. It would not be recommended for general situations. However, most sorting algorithms cannot take advantage of the knowledge that a list is currently sorted, except for one newly added item. If the list must be maintained in order between the arrival of new items, insertion sort may offer a unique advantage. For example, as new e-mail messages arrive, they must be displayed in order. It is not possible to wait until all messages have arrived before sorting the list. Exercise 11.24 asks you to demonstrate empirically both of these claims regarding insertion sort execution times.

Exercises

11.23. Extend the list class to work with a list of your music recordings. Each entry should have a title, an artist, running time, and where you obtained it. Printing the list should create a multiline, legible guide to your recordings in alphabetical order.

11.24. Construct and run an empirical test of the claimed times for insertion sort. Use methods of the class java.util.Random to generate a long sequence of random numbers. As you generate each number, insert it into a sorted list. Periodically, measure the time required to insert the next 10 elements. Skipping gaps between measurements creates a manageable data set but covers a wide variety of list lengths. Since the run-time estimates are for the average insertion, measuring for a set of consecutive elements helps smooth out the variations due to the random numbers. (Remember that insertion sort is a $\Theta(n^2)$ algorithm. Do not blindly test extremely large collections).

11.25. The definitive Java Web site is: *http://java.sun.com/j2se/1.3/docs/api/ index.html*. Find the definition of the List class there. Using only the methods described in this section, implement the methods described there but not defined in this chapter.

11.26. Complete the implementation of the OrderedList class.

11.27. Rewrite the methods find and delete to take advantage of an OrderedList.

11.28. Construct and run an empirical test of the claim that redefining find and delete for an OrderedList should cut the average number of recursions in half.

11.29. Build a class PhoneEntry containing at least names, phone numbers, and addresses. It should include compareTo, equals, and toString methods as described in Section 11.5.4.

11.30. Build and demonstrate a class PhoneList that extends OrderedList to include elements of a type PhoneEntry (see Section 11.5.4 and Exercise 11.29).

11.6 VARIANTS ON THE CONCEPT OF LIST

The class List is a basic and almost universal class. In fact, it is so universal that several variations are also common. The next three chapters explore some standard data structures based on lists. Some are extensions of lists and some are standard data structures motivated by lists. This section explores some of the more common variations on the idea of a simple list, and in doing so, lays the groundwork for the upcoming chapters.

11.6.1 Alternate Representations of the Base Class

The particular implementation of List presented in this chapter is not necessarily the most common. Some alternatives are older and better adapted to array implementations (see Section 14.2.1) or are more compact but less amenable to proofs. We mention a couple that you are likely to see.

Functional Programming Style

The methods addItem and removeItem may seem strangely complex in the List class. These complexities can be avoided (or exchanged for other problems) by using a functional programming style in which all methods are assumed to be value producing. For example, the method addItem could be written very simply as:

```
public List addItem(Object newItem) {
    List temp = new List();
    temp.head = newItem;
    temp.tail = this;
    return temp;
}
```

which alters the client interface so that a node would be added via an assignment statement:

```
todaysGroceries = todaysGroceries.addItem("Coffee");
```

Representation of the Empty List

Although it may seem wasteful for every list to have as a sublist another list that is empty, it turned out to make the programming easier, or more straightforward. It is possible to use a null pointer to represent the empty list, but it requires thinking of most list algorithms differently. In particular, there is no way to ask within an algorithm "if this node is empty, then…" The question must be asked by the client before sending the message. In general, such implementations define a list as a pointer to a node, and a node to be as we defined list in this chapter: a value and a pointer to another node. Exercise 11.31 explores this variation.

11.6.2 Two-way Lists

Lists as we defined them are traversable—but only in one direction. There is no nice way to visit the elements of a list in reverse order (for example, to ask, "What is the element before *B* in the list?" or to delete the last node satisfying some condition). One way to deal with such problems is to create two-way lists in which each head is associated with two other lists, one going forward and one going backwards, as illustrated in Figure 11.15. It probably isn't convenient to create a two-way list as an extension of List. Instead, we can talk in terms of the nodes in the figure. The structure of each node thus has a content part, plus two links, one forward and one backwards. Two traversal algorithms could follow the two sets of pointers. The *delete* algorithm deletes an element in a two-way list by making the links from both the node before and the node after the current node jump over it as in Figure 11.16. But fortunately, each of those nodes is accessible from the current node. Thus, the crucial section of the *delete* method would look something like:

```
this.previousPartOfList.tail = this.tail.tail;
this.tail.previousPartOfList = this.previousPartOfList;
```

The details of the implementation is left to the reader (Exercise 11.34).

The List

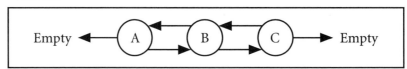

FIGURE 11.15 A two-way list.

The List

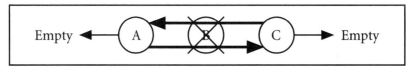

FIGURE 11.16 Deleting an item in a two-way list.

Exercises

11.31. The problems of empty lists described in Section 11.6.1 can be circumvented (albeit with some complications). Rewrite the basic list methods (List(), addItem(newItem), removeItem(), and isEmpty()) using null as the end of list mark.

11.32. The methods of the proposed List implementation do not guarantee that there will be no problems. Step through the concat method when invoked by the message `foo.concat(foo)`. Explain the problem (drawing a picture might help). Describe how traversing `foo` would fail after that call.

11.33. Rewrite the basic methods assuming that new items are added to the back (rather than the front) of a list and that items are removed from the same end.

11.34. Implement a two-way list class.

11.7 CONCLUDING REMARKS

Data structures are collections of data items. Dynamic data structures provide methods by which clients can alter the collection (e.g., add items to it, remove items, perhaps change the order of items), and find individual items within it. They allow for storing arbitrary collections of data where the size of the collection is not known at design time.

Lists are one of the fundamental data structures in computer science. The basic concept may not be obvious, but it is incredibly simple once worked out. The idea is to think of any collection of information as a first item (head), followed by all the rest of the data (tail). The definition is recursive and the structure almost begs for recursive methods to manipulate the structure.

As with any design process, a list data structure should be designed first and then implemented. The actual implementation of lists requires some new object-oriented techniques, but once you have built one list, building subsequent lists is very straightforward.

Lists are the basis for building a number of other data structures, and the inspiration for still more. The next three chapters examine some of these structures, beginning with simple variations on lists called "stacks" and "queues." Your understanding of the mechanisms employed with lists will be used repeatedly in these chapters.

11.8 FURTHER READING

John McCarthy first specified the basics of the Lisp (LISt Processing) programming language in 1956, making it one of the oldest programming languages in use today. The standard or classic reference manual for many years was:

McCarthy, John: *Lisp 1.5 Programmer's Manual*, MIT Press (Cambridge, MA), 1962.

Variants on Lisp, including Scheme, remain to this day standards in certain areas of computer science, notably artificial intelligence, where the list-processing model of human cognition hit its peak with:

Norman, D. & D. Rumelhart (eds). *Explorations in Cognition.* San Francisco: Freeman, 1975.

and

Schank, R. and K. Colby. *Computer Models of Thought and Language.* Freeman 1973.

List processing has continued to provide a primary view of computer science. In fact, one Scheme-based text has remained a classic for introducing the basic foundation of computer science to new students:

Abelson, Harold, Gerald Sussman and Julie Sussman. *Structure and Interpretation of Computer Programs.* McGraw Hill, 1985.

12 Queues and Stacks

The list data structure may be thought of as an ordered container. Its most important aspects are the *current* content and possibly the positional structure of that content. Some lists, however, seem to have an additional characteristic: content not only changes, but it does so as an orderly progression through the list. Consider the checkout line at a supermarket. It clearly can be described as a list: it contains a varying number of items (shoppers). At any moment, each person in the line has a relationship with the rest of the line in terms of his position compared to the other shoppers. But the checkout line also has a definite—and well-understood—front (or head) of the line and a distinct back (or end). By the accepted conventions, people join the line at the rear. As they wait, they slowly move to the front of the line. When they reach the front, they leave the line, are served, take their purchases and go home. The important and almost universal characteristic of such waiting lines is this progression from back to front—and then out—of the line. This structure is so ubiquitous that it warrants a special name, *queue*,[1] and is an important object of study in computer science.

In contrast, other lists, which also seem to have an orderly or predictable progression of their content, behave very differently. Consider a pile of plates on your kitchen shelf or in a cafeteria. Typically, there are almost always (at least a few) plates in this stack. When you want a clean plate, you simply take the top one off the stack. Fine, but where do you put the clean plates after you have washed them? They go back on top of the stack—the same place they are taken from. You don't put them under the stack. If the pile of plates were a queue, you would need to take the inconvenient step of lifting the pile and sliding the clean plate under it. You never (or very seldom) insert plates into the middle of the stack. Nor do you reorder the stack as you might a general list. People will almost certainly continue to both place clean dishes on, and take new ones from, the same place: the top of the stack. And *stack* is exactly what computer scientists call any data structure that behaves in that way.

This chapter explores these two extensions to the concept of list, first the conceptually more obvious—yet trickier to create—queue structure, and then the simpler—but more interesting—stack structure.

---

[1] The word "queue" is actually used in British English in almost exactly the same way Americans use the word "line" as in waiting lines (or waiting queues).

12.1 QUEUES

A queue is really the personification of the phrase "first come first served." Therefore, it is also called a *first-in-first-out* (FIFO) list. This section first motivates, and then develops, an implementation of a class for representing first-in-first-out collections of data.

12.1.1 Motivation from the Real World

The line at the supermarket is certainly not the only common example of queue that is a truly ubiquitous concept. In our culture, people line up or queue up for almost any service, from getting on a bus to waiting at the bank. Queues are useful for any list in which "fairness" seems to be important, that is, where the item, person, or process that has been waiting the longest somehow deserves to go next. Any first-come-first-served service or event uses a queue. When a service provider might not be able to service one client before the next arrives, a queue is needed—the lack of a queue generates pandemonium. Imagine the result at the supermarket if a clerk served a random person (or the one who shouted the loudest) next. Even the variation, in which a customer is served by the next available server—not just the single cashier at the head of the line, uses the same principle: the customer joins at the end, moves progressively to the front, and finally gets helped by the server. Another example from the grocery store: stock clerks normally restock the shelves from the rear, placing new merchandise in back of older merchandise so that the older stuff will sell first. Otherwise a bottle of milk could end up at the back for months as new bottles are placed in front of it—with a very unpleasant result. In fact, even when fairness is not essential, a queue can be used to assure that all items get processed eventually. For example, you might keep a "to do" list and discipline yourself by saying you will always do the item that has been on the list the longest. This would assure that you never put off any particular task indefinitely.

12.1.2 Computer Science Examples

But what does this have to do with computing? Everything—even where it is not obvious. Clearly, modeling a grocery store waiting line requires a queue. But queues have far more pertinent uses than that. When a person calls a company on the phone, the customer is told, "You will be helped by the next available representative." The customer is kept in a conceptual queue awaiting a turn with the representative. "Conceptual" here means that there is no physical queue, but the logical effect is the same: the people on the phone are waiting in a queue. The service probably uses a computer to keep track of those waiting customers and to make the connection to the awaiting operators. That computing system uses a queue data structure to keep track of the customers. We need queues anytime we model a queue-like, real-world situation such as the phone queue, but there are also many computing-specific uses of queues. You are probably at least casually aware of a number of these.

A List of Items Waiting to be Printed

Generally, a user can request that one item be printed and then request an additional document before the first is completed. The list of items waiting to be printed is a queue.

Mouse Clicks

If you rapidly click the mouse twice, once on each of two "buttons," and the first button requires some time to respond, the second click is kept in a queue until it can be processed. You can actually witness this in some systems. Try it: rapidly click on the close boxes for several windows. Or use the 'multiple close' command. It is usually apparent that the windows close one at a time. Clearly, the system must be keeping track of the windows remaining to be closed.

Any application using a list that has an unknown or highly varying length, but which must be completely traversed so that all items that enter the list must eventually be processed, is a candidate for a queue.

Key Stroke Buffer

Generally, any resource that may sometimes be requested more frequently than it can be processed is a candidate for a queue. Let's consider one example in a bit more detail. Some users type very fast. What happens if the human gets ahead of the computer's ability to process those characters? While few people (if any) could actually type that fast with a typical word processing program, the situation could occur with any program that processed each character in some complicated or time-consuming way. You may have witnessed this situation when network activity interrupts your typing, say, in an input box within a Web browser window. The text field remains blank (leaving you wondering for a moment if something is wrong). Then suddenly the system catches up, displaying the backlogged characters in the correct order. What actually happens is that all incoming characters are placed in a queue until the system has an opportunity to process them. Such an input queue is known as a *buffer*, since it protects (or buffers) the input against delays in the process or output. The main process loop conceptually looks something like:

> *Repeat the following forever:*
>   *If a new input character exists*
>   *Then put it in the queue (at back).*
>   *If the queue is not empty*

Then remove character from front of queue, and
Display (or process) that character.

While this demonstrates the general idea, there is still a problem if several extra inputs arrive during the time a single item is being processed. It is entirely possible that some input could still be lost. Dealing with that problem is beyond the scope of this text, but upper-level computer science courses such as Operating Systems or Computer Organization address this problem in detail.

A Score Separator

Suppose a professor has an electronic grade book, including a list of the scores students received on a test, and that he wishes to print two separate sheets as alphabetic lists: one containing all of the passing scores and the other containing the nonpassing scores. One way to do this would be to scan the string, printing the passing entries, and placing the nonpassing ones in a queue, to be printed after the passing group:

While any names remain:
    Get the next name.
    If the score is passing
        then print the info on that student.
        otherwise add the entry to the back of the nonpassing queue.
Start a new printed page.
While the nonpassing queue not empty:
    Remove one entry from the queue.
    Print the entry.

12.1.3 The Client Interface for a Queue Class

From the last two examples in Section 12.1.2, we can form a picture of the methods needed by any queue class.

addToBack:[2] *Add a new item to the back of a queue.*
removeFromFront: Remove an item from the front of a queue.

and

---

[2] In the literature, the terms *enqueue* and *dequeque* are frequently used rather than *addToBack* and *removeFromFront* respectively. While those two terms do make it clear that we are working with a queue, *removeFromFront* and *addToBack* make their relationship to each other clearer, and will be used throughout this section.

isEmpty: Determine if the queue is empty or not.

What the Queue and List Client Interfaces Tell Us

A queue is very similar to a list, and at first glance, building `Queue` as a subclass of `List` seems like a reasonable approach. Is it really? We can make a good start by considering the needed methods. Queues will need to handle at least three basic operations.

There are two restrictions on these methods. First, the `removeFromFront` method must retrieve the item from the *opposite* end of the list from the end used by the `addToBack` method. Second, in order to maintain the strict ordering or progression through the queue, the items in the queue may not be accessed by any other method (e.g., there is no cutting in line).

These restrictions on queue methods mean that queues are, in fact, not appropriately implemented as a subclass of `List` (at least as defined in Chapter 11). Our `List` class methods `removeItem` and `addItem` add or remove items from the same end of a list. Although the definition does not require it, virtually all implementations of the `List` class follow this convention. This means that either adding a node to or removing an element from a queue must work differently than does the analogous basic method in our `List` class. So a queue will need at least one completely new method. And at least one `List` method will need to be explicitly excluded.

12.1.4 Implementation and Efficiency

Even if `Queue` can't be appropriately constructed as an explicit subclass of `List`, we may still want to use many of the same concepts. It is, after all, a related dynamic data structure; elements can be added and removed, and the transition from back to front is reminiscent of the traversal algorithms. It would make sense to try to use the algorithms of the `List` class as primary building blocks for the methods of `Queue`. But when we analyze these *obvious* implementation ideas, we discover some underlying efficiency problems.

First Attempt: Using Listlike Methods

Both the `Queue` and `List` classes need methods to add and remove a node and to check if the structure is empty. Two of the three methods—*removeFromFront* and *isEmpty*—are logically identical to their `List` equivalents, and their algorithms can be borrowed with no modification at all. Even the preconditions and postconditions are the same. For example, a precondition for *removeFromFront* is that the queue must not be empty.

Unfortunately, *addToBack* is a bit more complex. Since our `List` implementations adds and removes nodes from the same end, but queues add new nodes to the opposite end, *addToBack* must be defined differently. The simplest conceptual approach is to find the back by starting at the front and traversing the queue until the end is found, something like:

> *Algorithm addToBack(new value)   [First attempt]:*
>   *If the queue is empty*
>   *then add the new value to the queue.*
>   *otherwise addToBack (new value) of the tail of the queue.*

Analysis of the Proposed *addToBack*

Unfortunately, this approach dictates that every insertion requires a recursion through the entire queue, meaning that insertion time for a new element is linear with the length of the queue. Since insertion at the back of the queue is a basic operation, this is likely to be very expensive as a basic operation for building a long queue: if a queue grew to n items before any items were removed, the i-th insertion would require i calls to *addToBack*. The n items would require a total of:

$$\sum_{i=1}^{n} i = \frac{n(n+1)}{2} \qquad (12.1)$$

recursive calls to add all the items. That is, building a queue by adding items to the end requires $\Theta(n^2)$ steps, clearly a very expensive approach.

Second Attempt: Adding an Extra Link

We might try to improve the required time for building a queue by keeping track of its end. Since items can only be added at the end, it should be easy to keep track of where the most recent item was added. One potential solution might be to include a link to the back of the queue, which would enable direct access to the end of the queue, as illustrated in Figure 12.1. Unfortunately, this approach has a small—but critical—problem. Recall that List was defined so that every list was composed of two parts: a head and a tail. That *tail* is not another node, but another list. Therefore, every tail also has two parts: its own head and tail. If we define *Queue* recursively as we did List, but with three parts, every subqueue will also have three parts: a head, a tail—plus an *endOfQueue* link of its own. Further, each *endOfQueue* actually refers to the same endpoint. While maintaining multiple links to the same location may be slightly wasteful, the approach actually has a much more significant problem: adding a new node to the back of a queue would require changing the *endOfQueue* link for every one of those subqueues. So adding a node would still require recursing the full length of the queue, changing the *endOfQueue* link for each of the n subqueues. It is just as slow as the first attempt.

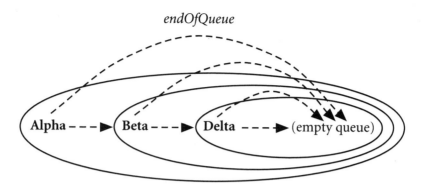

FIGURE 12.1 The redundant *endOfQueue* links.

12.1.5 A Workable Definition

We use these observations to build a better implementation, which gets around the problem of quadratic run-time costs. The class Queue is not defined as a subclass of List, or even recursively like List. Instead, we define Queue as a class that incorporates a List as a member variable and also maintains a single, separate link to the end of the queue (that is, to the last node in the List). Figure 12.2 represents this schematically. The member variable content is simply a List. The member variable endOfQueue will also be of type List because it refers to the last element of the list *content*, and that last element is, of course, a list. In fact, endOfQueue is always an empty list—but not always the same empty list, an observation that will become important as we attempt the implementation.

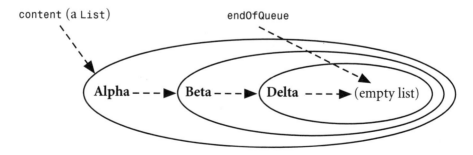

FIGURE 12.2 A queue containing a list.

In a very real sense, this approach combines the best features of the other approaches. *addtoback* and *isEmpty* will be able to use the corresponding List methods; the endOfQueue link provides a direct connection to the back of the queue, thereby avoiding the long recursions required for removal; and there are no redundant links.

12.1.6 Implementing the Queue Class

The Queue class definition begins simply with:

```
public class Queue {
    private List content;
    private List endOfQueue;
```

and development of most of the methods for the Queue class is straightforward.

isEmpty

A queue is empty if and only if its member list, content, is empty, so isEmpty can be just:

```
public boolean isEmpty() {
    return content.isEmpty();
}
```

addToBack

addToBack is only a little more complex. It must add a node to the current endOfQueue list and then reset endOfQueue to refer to the new end.

> *Algorithm addToBack:*
> *Add the new Item to the back of the queue.*
> *Reset endOfQueue to the end of queue.*

The first step takes advantage of the fact that *endOfQueue* already refers directly to the empty list at the end of the queue. The need for the second step may seem surprising. But recall that the List method addNewItem actually changes a list. So at the completion of the first step, *endOfQueue* refers to a list that now contains an element. This list is no longer the empty list at the end of the queue, its tail is. Figure 12.3 illustrates the process. Using this algorithm, adding a new node to the queue can be done in constant time, independent of the length of the queue.

At start of `addToBack()`:

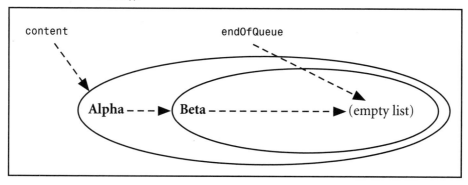

After `addItem(Delta)`:

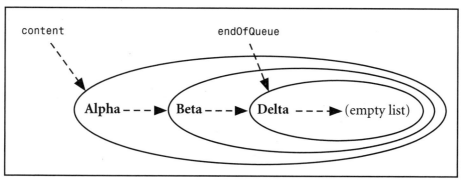

At completion of `addToBack()`:

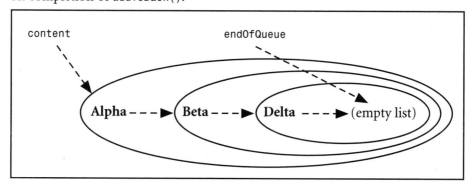

FIGURE 12.3 Adding a new node to the back.

In Java, the corresponding method is:

```java
public void addToBack(Object newItem) {
    endOfQueue.addItem(newItem);
    endOfQueue = endOfQueue.getRest();
}
```

At start:

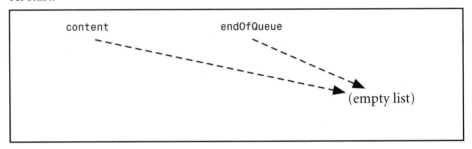

After `addItem(Alpha)`:

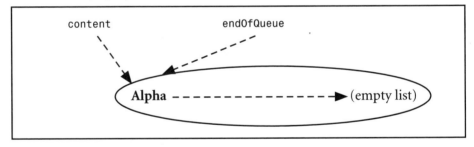

At the end:

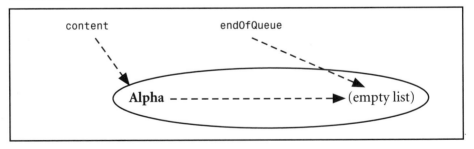

FIGURE 12.4 Adding a new node to the empty list.

The boundary cases deserve careful examination. For adding a node, the boundary case occurs when the entire list is empty. Normally, adding to the back should leave the front of the queue unaffected. But when the queue is empty, adding an item to the back will also change the front. Fortunately, when the queue is empty, both content and endOfQueue are the same; changing one will change the other.[3] Figure 12.4 helps illustrate this case. The important observation is that the first step conveniently changes the head of the list as well as the last item. This means that no special action is required for the boundary case.

removeFromFront

At first glance, the *removeFromFront* algorithm seems like it should be very simple, something like:

> *Algorithm removeFromFront   [first attempt]*
>   *getAndRemoveItem from the list.*

However, this time the boundary case does represent a problem. In general, removing an item impacts only the front of the queue and leaves the back of the queue unaffected. But if there is only one item left in the queue, then removing that one item also changes the end of the queue, as seen in Figure 12.5. This is subtle: after removing the last item from content, both content and endOfList are empty lists—but they are different empty lists. The two variables must be made to point to the same empty list.

> *Algorithm removeFromFront:*
>   *Get And RemoveItem the first item.*
>   *If the resulting list is empty*
>   *then reset the endOfList to refer to the List.*

Notice that the method can't return the retrieved value until after the conditional step, which in turn requires saving the result in a temporary variable:

```
public Object removeFromFront() {
    Object temp = content.getAndRemove();
    if (content.isEmpty())
        endOfQueue = content;
    return temp;
}
```

---

[3] If this is unclear, it may be a good time to look up the implementation of Java objects in Appendix A.

At start:

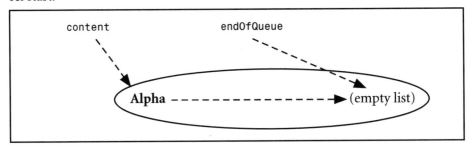

After `getAndRemoveItem`:

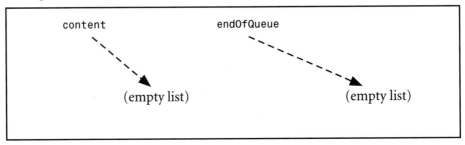

At the end:

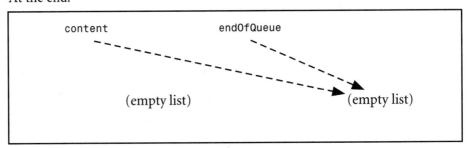

FIGURE 12.5 Removing the only item in a list.

Remaining Methods

Most other methods for the class `Queue` can be built by simply invoking their counterparts in the class `List`. For example, `printQueue` is just:

```
public void printQueue() {
    content.printList();
}
```

Exercises

12.1. Suppose you are modeling a grocery store checkout line. If the average line has ten people in it, how many steps will it take to add and remove 10 new customers with Queue defined as in Section 12.1.6? How many if defined as an extension of the List class?

12.2. Complete the definition of the Queue class.

12.3. Prove that queues actually maintain the first-in-first-out property. That is, show that if two items a_i and a_j arrive at times i and j, respectively, and $i < j$, then a_i must exit the queue before a_j.

12.4. Chapter 11 described a possible extension of the List class that included two-way links. Write algorithms for Queue as an extension of TwoWayList.

12.5. Some radio talk shows use a delay to record conversation but not distribute it publicly for a few minutes (either to first verify the accuracy of the information or to give the corporate brass a few minutes head start). Write a program that records discrete events (as opposed to conversation) to a queue and then prints them out after a user-settable amount of time.

12.6. Help out the professor in Section 12.1.2 by creating a program to separate all test scores into separate grade piles: one for each of the five standard letter grades. Assume that the "grade book" is an alphabetical list of student names and scores (you may want to define a class for this). The program should create five queues, one for each letter grade; read the grade list and place each element in the appropriate queue (keeping the entries in each queue in alphabetic order), and then print out the information from each queue.

12.2 STACKS

At first glance, a stack—a last-in-first-out structure—may seem like a strange tool, but it is actually considerably more interesting than a queue. In fact, the stack may be the most important data structure in computer science.

12.2.1 Real World Motivations for Stacks

Perhaps because stacks enable some interesting algorithms, they seem to be ubiquitous. As with any ubiquitous concept, stacks are known by several names, including some that are more descriptive of their behavior: *first-in-last-out (FILO)* lists or *last-in-first-out* (LIFO) lists. Consider a few real world examples:

Storage Shelves

Any collection of physical objects that are stored and reused will likely behave like the stack of plates—everything from underwear in your drawer to plates on the shelf. And any program modeling such things may need a stack.

Employment

When a company falls on hard times and needs to lay off workers, it will usually give preference to those employees who have been on the job the longest. Thus, the first workers fired are those who were most recently hired—last in, first out!

Maze

After walking into a maze, one can find the way out just as Hansel & Gretel tried to do: leave markers on the way in and follow the markers in reverse order to get back.

Work Order

The steps of many human tasks seem to have the same property. As you get ready to perform a task, you put on work clothes, go to garage, get out your tools, and finally do the actual task. But once done with the task, you put your tools away, return to the house from the garage, change back into your everyday clothes—exactly the reverse order.

Inbox

The classic *inbox*[4] on a desk is actually a stack. When new items arrive, they are simply dropped on top of the existing stack of documents in the inbox. When you are ready to deal with another task, you might take the top document off the stack. Oops, that means the last request gets processed first.

12.2.2 Stacks and Computer Science

And these real-world examples pale in comparison to the computer science uses. It is the power of stacks as a conceptual model for solving common computational problems that truly makes them important. Consider a simple example:

---

[4] Like so many computer desktop terms, the computer email term, inbox, is named after its real or physical world counterpart. For those who have not had the opportunity to witness a large office workplace, an inbox is a tray on a worker's desk. When an office boy or errand runner brings papers to that worker for processing he simply drops them in the inbox. There may also be an outbox for completed documents waiting for pick up by the same errand runner.

Reversing a String

Let's start with an example that illustrates the most important and central property of a stack, the first-in-last-out behavior, using a stack to reverse a string. Given the input "String" such a program would produce "gnirtS". A stack seems like a natural tool for this, since the first character must become the last. The algorithm reverses the string by placing each character on the stack and then grabbing them all off—in reverse order.

> *Algorithm reverseIt:*
> *While more characters exist*
> *Get the next character,*
> *Push it on the stack.*
> *While the stack is not empty*
> *Pop one character off the stack,*
> *Output the character.*

As the input is arriving, the stack would look like:

Stack Content	Action
(empty)	input S
S	input t
S t	input r
S t r	input i
S t r i	input n
S t r i n	input g
S t r i n g	

Then, as the characters are popped off the top (right side, in this case) of the stack, the algorithm generates the results:

Stack Content	Action
S t r i n g	output g
S t r i n	output n
S t r i	output i
S t r	output r
S t	output t
S	output S
(empty)	quit

Palindromes

A *palindrome* is a string that reads the same forward and backwards. One simple way to generate palindromes is to take any sequence of characters and output the original string followed by its reverse. The string "cat" would yield "cattac". Notice that solving this problem requires solving the last problem, reversing a string.

> *Algorithm palindrome:*
>   *(generate the first half)*
>   *While more characters remain:*
>   *Get one character.*
>   *Output that character, and*
>   *Push the character on a stack.*
>   *(now generate the second half)*
>   *While the stack is nonempty:*
>   *Pop one character from the stack.*
>   *Output that character.*

12.2.3   Designing the Stack Class

The class `Stack` is simple to construct. In fact, it looks remarkably like the class `List` or the class `Queue`—publicly, only the names have been changed. The class must contain 3 essential methods:

> *push (object):*[5] *Put a new item on top of the stack.*
> *pop: Remove and return the value of the top item on the stack.*
> *isEmpty: Check to see if the stack is empty.*

And for ease of programming, many implementations include the ability to simply look at the top of the stack without actually removing it:

> *peek: Return the value of the item on top of the stack.*

The only significant logical difference between the class definitions of stacks and queues is that items *must* be added and removed from the same—rather than the opposite—end of the stack. A much smaller difference is the way that the structures are visualized: whereas queues and lists are typically visualized as horizontal structures with a back and a front, stacks are almost always envisioned as vertical

---

[5] *Push* and *pop* are the traditional terms used in the computer science field for adding to or removing from a stack. We could have used names more parallel to the names we used for queues, e.g. *addToTop* and *removeFromTop*. But in this case the "fromTop" or "toTop" parts would add no additional meaning, since both are performed at the same end.

structures with a top and bottom. This, of course, follows from the analogy of a physical stack of objects in which it is physically difficult to remove any item without first removing everything above it in the stack. Since items are added and removed from the same end (the top) of a stack, there is no need for a separate link to keep track of the back end as there is with a queue. In fact, the class List as defined in the previous chapter assumed that new objects were added and removed from the same end of the list—exactly what is needed for a stack.[6]

12.2.4 Implementing the Class Stack

With the exception of the few name changes, the operations on stacks are almost exactly a subset of the allowable operations on lists. In fact, if we didn't want to use the traditional names for stack operations, we could just use the List class directly, treating it as a stack. We can very simply introduce the stack terminology as:

```
public class Stack extends List    {

    public void push(Object newItem) {
        this.addItem(newItem);
    }

    public Object pop() {
        return this.getAndRemove();
    }

    public Object peek() {
        return this.getFirst();
    }
}
```

There is no need to define isEmpty for the class Stack, because it has the same name as its List counterpart. As with queues, we will not allow access to the nodes of a stack by any other methods.[7]

---

[6] If some implementation for a List class used the opposite logic—adding and removing elements from opposite ends—the respective implications for Queue and Stack would be reversed: Queue could be a subclass of List, but Stack would require a different implementation.

[7] Presumably in this implementation, one might also override most of the other public List methods to make them unavailable. That way, clients won't inadvertently use the stack as if it were a list, thereby altering some of the unique characteristics of a stack. If avoiding such a perversion of the definition is important to you, you may wish to define Stack from scratch, using code almost identical to the corresponding parts of List. Or for a totally independent implementation see Section 14.2.3.

Using these basic methods, it is easy to build Java versions of our earlier algorithms. Thus, *reverseIt* can be coded as:

```java
public static String reverseIt(String original) {
    Stack reversingStack = new Stack();
    while (original.length() > 0) {
        reversingStack.push(original.substring(0,1));
        original = original.substring(1);
    }
    String result = "";
    while (!reversingStack.isEmpty()) {
        result = result + reversingStack.pop();
    }
    return result;
}
```

12.2.5 Stacks and Recursion

reverseIt and *palindrome* share a common characteristic: they reverse the order of things as those things are processed. The observant reader probably noticed that these examples of stack usage are very similar to some of the basic examples used to illustrate recursion in Chapter 6. *reverseIt* could have been written:

> *Algorithm reverseIt:*
> > *If any more characters exist*
> > > *Get the next character.*
> > > *reverseIt.*
> > > *Output the character.*

Or in Java:

```java
public static String reverseIt(String original) {
    if (original.length() == 0)
        return "";
    else return reverseIt(original.substring(1)) +
            original.substring(0,1);
}
```

This similarity is no coincidence. Java provides a hidden stack that is used to implement recursion. Each time a method is called, its local variables and parameters are pushed on the stack. When a method returns, its variables and parameters are popped off the stack. In a series of recursive calls, the stack acts like a record of the path taken to reach that point, with the most recent call on top and the oldest on the bottom. In fact, every computer maintains a stack for that specific purpose. Figure 12.6 illustrates the general concept, showing how the stack would evolve as *reverseIt* reverses the string "cat". Compare these examples with those of Chapter 6 and watch for this characteristic in other algorithms that incorporate stacks. In general, a recursive algorithm will have the advantage that the user does not have to explicitly refer to the stack, because the language compiler or computing system automatically maintains the stack for you. For purposes of illustration, most of the remaining examples in this chapter will use an explicit stack rather than recursion using the system stack. In real-world situations, the recursive versions will usually be more desirable. In some, the recursive equivalent may be obvious; in others, it may be obscure or even very difficult to create.

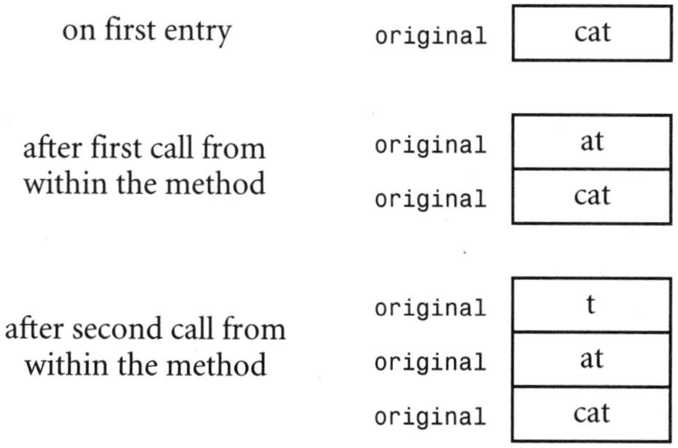

on first entry	original	cat

after first call from within the method	original	at
	original	cat

	original	t
after second call from within the method	original	at
	original	cat

FIGURE 12.6 The system stack holds local information for methods.

12.2.6 Implications of Stacks for Common Computing Problems

Stacks turn out to be very useful structures for computer science. In fact, they may be one of the most widely used—and studied—data structures in the field. In addition to providing a tool for creating algorithms, stacks provide guidance for both design and theoretical evaluation.

Formal Languages

In the theory of computation,[8] problems are categorized by how difficult they are to solve. One important theoretical measure of the difficulty of a problem is whether

---

[8] Most computer science programs offer an upper-division course devoted to this subject.

or not you can solve it without a stack. In particular, a large family of problems, called *context free*, turns out to be too hard to solve without using a stack, but solvable using one. This is especially interesting because this family is roughly equivalent to parsing a class of formal languages called *context free languages*. It turns out that most programming languages (and certainly any interesting one), contain context free segments. Thus, a compiler requires at least that much complexity: it must invoke a stack just to parse the input. To see this, we look at a typical context free language and then at some problems involved in parsing a programming language.

A prototypical example of a context free language is the set of all strings of the form $a^n bc^n$. That is, any string of "a"s followed by a single "b" followed by a string of "c"s exactly as long as the string of "a"s. So, abc, aabcc, aaabccc are all legal strings in this language (as is, by the way, "b-" which starts with zero "a"s and ends with zero "c"s). One algorithm for recognizing strings in this language pushes all the "a"s on a stack, in effect counting them. Then it pops them off, in effect counting off an equal number of "c"s:

Algorithm contextFree:
    While next character is an "a"
        Push the "a" onto the stack.
    If the next character is not a "b"
        fail. (a "b" was required by the definition)
    While there are more characters to examine
        If the stack is empty
            then fail. (too few "c"s)
        Pop one item.
        Get one more character
        If the next character is not a "c"
            then fail. (extraneous character)
    If the stack is empty
        then succeed
        otherwise fail. (too many "c"s)

Matching Delimiters

The interpreter or compiler for any computer language must perform several predictable tasks[9] that are very similar to the *contextFree* algorithm. One aspect of compiling, called *parsing*, is the identification of the various subparts of the expression. For example, a Web browser must interpret the HTML language used to describe individual Web pages. One aspect of parsing requires matching opening

---

[9] Most computer science departments offer an upper division course called "Compilers." Problems such as this are central to the issues covered in such a course.

"tags" with closing tags. For example, matching a <b> (the start of a bold segment) with the corresponding </b> (the end of a bold segment). It is not enough that the number of opening tags of a given type match the number of closing tags of the same type. Each closing tag must match a specific opening tag. And no two pairs may overlap. For example, the expression:

```
The <b>bold should contain <i>the italic</i> words</b>!
```

would be legal and corresponds to a rendered sentence:

The **bold should contain *the italic* words**!

but

```
The <b>bold <i>overlaps</b> the italics</i>!
```

which was probably intended to render as:

The **bold *overlaps* the italics**!

would not be legal because two segments overlap: the italics starts within the bold segment but ends outside of it.

One algorithm to solve this is very similar to *contextFree*: push all opening tags onto a stack; as closing tags are encountered, pop the corresponding opening markers off. Whenever a closing tag is encountered, the matching opening tag must be on top of the stack. When the end of the string is encountered, the stack should be empty (otherwise there is an unmatched opening tag). An algorithm that accomplishes this is:

Algorithm isBalanced:
    While more input exists
        If the next input item is an opening tag
            then Push the tag.
            otherwise if the next input item is a closing tag
                then if the stack is empty
                    Signal failure (there is no matching opening tag)
                otherwise Pop the top tag off the stack
                    if it doesn't match
                        then fail
            otherwise the input is not a tag, ignore it

> *If (after processing all input) the stack is empty*
> *then return success*
> *otherwise return fail (since there must be more*
> *opening tags than closing)*

Using the Balance Information

The *isBalanced* algorithm can easily be modified to do more than just verify that the input is balanced or count the number of occurrences. Suppose the stack holds not just the opening tag itself but also its position within the input string. When an

Input:

```
<p>This<b> is <font size="+1">a concocted</font>
example</b> designed <i>to <font color="gray">show
nested</font> HTML</i> tags.</p>
```

Stack states:

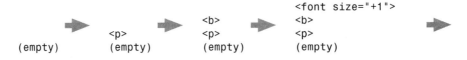

Rendered result:

This **is a concocted example** designed *to show nested* HTML tags.

FIGURE 12.7 A stack matching HTML tags.

opening tag is popped off the stack, the program has processed the input up through the matching closing tag. At that moment, the processing program has immediate access to the type of segment, its beginning position and ending position as well as the corresponding information for any enclosed segments. So in addition to verifying the legality of the input, the algorithm has the information it needs to render the segment on the screen. Figure 12.7 provides a sample of an HTML string and the series of stack states that accomplish its rendering.

Arithmetic Expressions

A second compilation issue relates to evaluating a parenthesized arithmetic expression, which must among other things match opening and closing parentheses. For this simple example, assume that there are no implied precedence issues. In most computing languages, the expression:

```
3+4*5
```

will evaluate to 23. That is, in interpreting the expression, the compiler will invoke the rule that multiplication takes precedence over addition, and is therefore performed first. For this example, assume that all operations are always performed left to right and that a writer who wants an expression to be evaluated in another order will make that explicit by using parentheses:

```
3+(4*5)
```

The following algorithm uses two stacks, one for operators and one for operands, to evaluate a parenthesized expression:

Algorithm evalExpression:
    Get next item.
    Case: Item is left paren:
                Push paren on operator stack.
                evalExpression.
                Get a right paren and pop left paren from operator stack
                (if there is no paren to pop here, there must be an error).
        Item is value:
                Push value on operand stack.
                If there is more input
                Get operator.
                Push on operator stack.
                evalExpression (yes, this is a recursive call).
                Pop two values from operand stack.

> *Pop operator.*
> *Perform operation on the two values.*
> *Push the result on operand stack.*
> *Item is anything else:*
> *Signal failure.*
> *Pop value and return.*

In the example, the stacks would fill as:

Numbers	Operators	
3		
3	+	(recursive call here)
3	+ (	(recursive call here)
3, 4	+ (	
3, 4	+ (*	
3, 4, 5	+ (*	
3, 20	+ (	(return from recursive call here)
3, 20	+	(return from recursive call here)
23		

Creation of Java code corresponding to this algorithm is left as an exercise.

Prefix and Postfix Notation

In the usual representation of arithmetic (called *infix notation*), each operator is placed between its operands: $a+b$. Computer scientists and mathematicians also use two variations on that form, *prefix* and *postfix* notation.[10] In prefix notation, the operator goes before rather than between the two operands: $+AB$.[11] In postfix notation, the operator follows the operands: $AB+$. One advantage of this form is that no parenthesis are needed. Each operator is followed immediately by its two operands—even when the operands are themselves expressions. Those operands may be simple numbers or variables, but they also may be another expression: an operator followed by two operands. Thus, in:

$$+{}^{*}AB{-}CD$$

---

[10] Also called *Polish* and *reverse Polish* notation, after the Polish logician J. Lukasiewicz.

[11] Some handheld calculators work in an analogous way: enter the two operands and then the operation.

the first operand of the operator + is *AB, and the second is –CD. The expression as a whole is the sum of the product of A * B plus the difference C – D, the same as:

$$(A*B)+(C-D)$$

in the infix representation. An interesting aspect of postfix notation is that the left-to-right ordering of the operators is exactly the order in which the operations must be performed during evaluation. That is, converting an infix expression to postfix is equivalent to finding the series of operations a computer must perform to evaluate the expression.

The final advantage of prefix representation is that it is ideally suited to stack processing—for both creating and evaluating the expression. The basic approach for evaluation is: get the next item, push the operands in one stack and the operators in another; whenever there are two operands, pop the most recent operator off the stack, perform the indicated operation and place the result back on the stack:

Algorithm evaluatePrefix
 Get the next input.
 If it is a value (operand)
  push on operand stack (and this procedure must be done).
 If it is an operator
  Push it on operator stack,
  evaluatePrefix,   *(get first operand)*
  evaluatePrefix,   *(get second operand)*
  Pop the operator,
  Pop two operands,   *(these are the two values*
            corresponding to the operator)
  Perform the operation, *(evaluate current expression)*
  push result on the stack.

Given the incoming sequence + * 3 4 – 6 5, the stacks should progressively contain:

Operators	Values
+	
+ *	
+ *	3 4
+	12
+ –	12, 6, 5
+	12 1
(empty)	13

The bottom line is that stacks are not just a useful data structure. They provide an important tool for determining the difficulty of a problem or showing problems equivalent. This classification actually tells us, for certain problems, that we must use some form of stack.

Exercises

12.7. Write a Java program equivalent to the algorithm *palindrome* from Section 12.2.2. You may use the class definition provided for stack.

12.8. Show that the algorithm *reverseIt* (Section 12.2.2) is its own inverse. That is, if one were using this algorithm to create a secret code, exactly the same algorithm could decode the result to obtain the original sequence. Show this (a) by writing a demonstration program and (b) proving it mathematically.

12.9. Prove by induction on the length of the input that *reverseIt* does indeed reverse the input.

12.10. Pick any recursive program that you wrote in conjunction with Chapter 6 and describe its behavior in terms of a stack.

12.11. Model the precedence free expression algorithm for the following input expressions:

1. (1+(2+(3+(4+5))))
2. ((((1+2)+3)+4)+5)
3. (2*3)+((4-2)*(5+6))

12.12. Model the prefix expression evaluator for the following input expressions:

1. + + + + 1 2 3 4 5
2. + 1 + 2 + 3 + 4 5
3. + + 1 * 2 3 * 4 5

12.13. Write the Java code for the prefix expression evaluator.

12.14. Rewrite the stack class, using the identical logic as the version in this section, but not as a subclass of the List class.

12.15. Rewrite *isBalanced* in a way that might be just a bit more intuitive: scan for tags. Then, once one is found, treat it appropriately depending on whether it is an opening or closing tag.

12.16. Prove that stacks actually reverse order properly. That is, show that if two items a_i and a_j arrive at times i and j, respectively, and $i < j$, that a_i must exit the stack after a_j (if it exits at all).

12.17. Prove, by induction on the number of operators, that the prefix interpreter algorithm is correct.

12.18. Prove, by induction on the number of operators, that the precedence free expression evaluator algorithm is correct.

12.19. Rewrite the prefix algorithm for postfix expressions.

12.20. Write Java code to implement the context free language recognizer.

12.21. Write an algorithm to recognize strings of the form $a^n bc^{2n}$.

12.22. Write an algorithm to recognize strings of the form $a^n (bc)^n$.

12.23. Draw a visual representation of a list, a queue, and a stack. Include representations for all needed links (both into the structure and within the structure). Now make similar drawings for structures that violate various list conventions: first a list containing a node whose "next" node actually comes earlier in the list, and then a "list" in which each node has two "next" nodes.

12.3 CONCLUDING REMARKS

Stacks and queues added a "life cycle" concept to the basic list concepts. The original list definitions allowed for maintaining a collection, and in the case of ordered lists, of sorting or rearranging the collection. But implicit in the definitions of both queues and stacks was the relationship between the orders of insertion and removal of data items. Additionally, they both explicitly disallow the fundamental internal reorganization methods available for lists.

12.3.1 Queues vs. Stacks

The obvious difference between stacks and queues comes from their basic definition: stacks are last-in-first-out and queues are first-in-first-out. That is, the distinction between them lies in which item can be accessed next. And the direct result of that is the apparent "reversing" behavior of stacks, but the "in-order" behavior of queues.

Another distinction is that any item placed in a queue is guaranteed to pop out the other end eventually. As long as the queue continues to be accessed, items will move through it. Every time an item is removed, every item in the queue moves forward one step. If, when an item joins a queue, there are already $n-1$ items in the queue, the new item becomes item n and it will be the n-th item to be removed. With a stack however, an item could theoretically stay in the stack forever. Consider a stack in which three items were added immediately, and after that, new items were added at exactly the same rate as old ones were popped off. In that case the size of the stack would oscillate between four and three items—but the ones removed would always be those new items. The original three items would just stay where they were.

Thus, a queue is preferable to a stack whenever it is important that all items get processed eventually, even if it is not important that items be processed in exactly the same order they were received. Consider, for example: a fastidious person may discipline himself by always working on the oldest task first. It may not actually be important that the task that was noticed first be done first, but keeping them in a queue does assure that every task will get done eventually and not be simply forgotten among the sea of things needing to be done (assuming it makes it into the queue at all).

Stacks, in contrast, are useful for any situation where recentness is the important identifier, the same situations that lend themselves to recursion.

Every computing system maintains both stacks and queues; the former for implementing recursion, and the latter for all those items that need to be buffered or held until the system is ready to process them.

12.3.2 Looking Ahead to Other Structures

Lists, queues, and stacks all assume an underlying structure in which the individual items are nodes or elements; each has a value variable and a link variable: a means of finding *the* specific other node that is next.

Are there any other basic data structures? Well, yes, and we will see some of them almost immediately. But before exploring specific other structures, consider the restrictions that were placed on the structures we have seen thus far: each node has a value and a specific relation to a *single* other node. What happens if we remove that restriction? What if a node can be explicitly related to more than one other node? Could a node have two "next" nodes? Could the "next" node be one that also occurs earlier in the sequence?

In addition, we will investigate the nature of links. What happens if we implement links by means other than Java object references?

12.4 FURTHER READING

Stacks have been a staple of computing systems for almost a half century. Bauer and Samelson first described a scheme using a pushdown stack for the translation and interpretation of arithmetic expressions, which first appeared in German, but was translated into English as:

F.L. Bauer and K. Samelson "Sequential Formula Translation," in *Communications of The Association for Computing Machinery*, vol.3 (1960), pp.76–83.

It is interesting to note that that is the same year as the publication of the "The Algol Report," which may have been the first language specification that explicitly called for a stack.

For more detailed information specific to the two data structures of this chapter, see any good data structures book such as:

Richard Gilberg and Behrouz Forouzan. *Data Structures: A Pseudocode Approach With C.* Brooks/Cole, 1998.

For the relationship of stacks to the complexity of problems, see any theory of computation text, such as:

J. Hopcroft, R. Motwani, J. Ullman & Rotwani. *Introduction to Automata Theory, Languages, and Computation.* Addison-Wesley, 2000.

For the application of stacks to compiler design, see any compiler text such as the classic:

Alfred V. Aho, Ravi Sethi, Jeffrey D. Ullman. *Compilers*, Addison-Wesley, 1986.

or the newer and Java-specific:

Andrew Appel and Jens Palsberg. *Modern Compiler Implementation in Java.* Cambridge University Press, 2003.

The mathematical analysis of queues and the systems that employ them is called queuing theory. A good introduction may be found in:

Frederick Hillier and Gerald Lieberman. *Introduction to Operations Research.* McGraw-Hill, 2002.

13 Binary Trees

The data structures queue and stack expand the concept of list in straightforward ways, and therefore necessarily share the essential characteristics of lists: linearity, access only via the end points, etc. Some data collections have characteristics or interrelationships that are not linear and cannot readily be represented in a list. Even when the data collection is linear, more efficient search strategies than those possible with lists may be needed. The *tree* structure or *hierarchical organization* often meets these needs. As a result, it is perhaps the most ubiquitous and useful of all data structures (also the most studied).

13.1 HIERARCHICAL ORGANIZATION

This section starts our investigation of trees by examining several examples from everyday life. It then develops some nomenclature before looking at examples that are specifically useful in computer science.

13.1.1 Real World Trees

Tree structures occur almost everywhere one looks. Consider just a few examples.

Sports Tournament

The 2003 Major League Baseball Playoffs, summarized in Figure 13.1, have fewer teams in each round: eight qualifying teams started, but only four were left in the second (league championships), then two entered the World Series, leaving a single national champion (in the most important position of the chart). The natural relationship among the entries in the tournament is not a linear list of teams, but rather the relation between teams from one round of the tournament to the next: it shows who won! Sports trees, such as the baseball playoffs, are very common. Any single-elimination sports tournament (e.g., Wimbledon tennis tournament, playoffs for the National Football League, and quite likely your local darts tournament) fits this format: each individual or team plays an opening game, but only the victors move onto the second round; only the winners of that round advance to the third round,

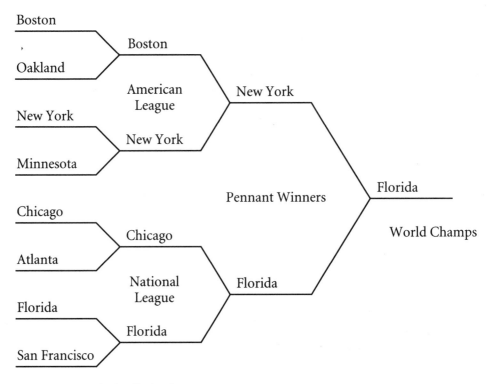

FIGURE 13.1 A single-elimination sports tournament.

and so on until there is only a single team left. Perhaps the most famous is the NCAA basketball tournaments, which start with 64 teams and after 6 rounds have reduced the field to a single winning team.

Family Trees

Perhaps the most familiar treelike data structure is the *family tree,* or *genealogy.* Figure 13.2 depicts a blank family tree (you can fill in your own ancestors if you so desire). Often a family tree is even drawn as if it were the arboreal variety of tree, with branches representing the hereditary relationships between individuals, and even leaves in the background. The person whose ancestry it represents holds the singular position (often depicted as the root of the tree) with the oldest ancestors up the high branches. An individual's parents are exactly those persons one *level* (generation) away, connected to the individual by a single branch (toward the leaves). Grandparents are found in the obvious way: the parents of the parents, or by looking back two levels. One obvious property of the genealogy tree is particularly interesting to computer scientists, it is *binary*: each person has exactly two parents, providing a very uniform and predictable structure. The figure emphasizes the fact that the number of entries at any level expands rapidly with the length of the paths.

Family relationships may also be drawn as *descendant* trees: rather than showing all of the ancestors for one individual, the descendant tree shows all of the descendants of a given individual. Such a tree starts with one person at the top, with multiple links to that person's children and then grandchildren, great grandchildren, and so on. So, for example, George Washington might be at the top and all of his currently living descendants at the wide bottom. Clearly, such a tree is not binary since one person may have any number of children.

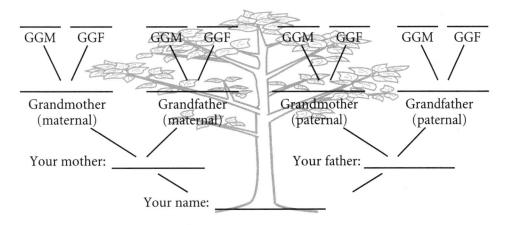

FIGURE 13.2   A family tree.

Corporate Organization

Corporations or business entities often represent their internal organization in terms of a corporate hierarchy, similar to that in Figure 13.3, with the president or CEO at the top and the rank-and-file employees at the bottom. Each connecting link represents a supervisory relationship. In general, each person has only one immediate boss, but each boss may have several underlings. Notice that the structure shows relative information about the individual employees: roughly, the closer a person is to the top of the tree, the higher the position in the chart—and on the *corporate ladder*. This particular mixed metaphor seems to make sense: a corporate hierarchy describes the corporation as a whole and is tree-structured, but "corporate ladder" views that same structure from the perspective of a single individual. In particular, it shows the linear path to the top. The chart even shows which persons are approximately equal in the organization; even though they have unrelated job titles and work in different divisions, they are placed at the same level of the tree.

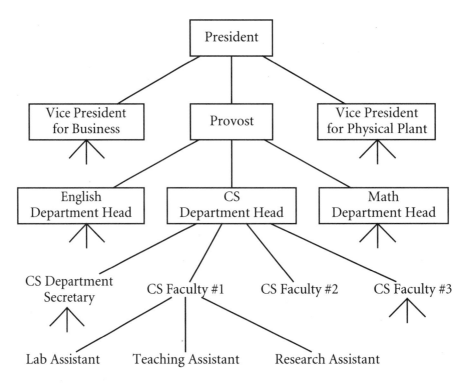

FIGURE 13.3 A corporate hierarchy.

Outlines

Some hierarchical relationships are really trees, even though the branches are not explicitly drawn in. An *outline* is a summary of a document, usually broken down into headings and subheadings. For example, a table of contents, such as the partial one shown in Figure 13.4, is a form of outline. Outlines don't necessarily show the page numbers, but they do show the structure and relationships among the sections. The highest level is the title of the book, the next level is the chapter headings, and each chapter has subsection types and possible sub-subsections (this book has three levels below the chapter level).

13.1.2 Trees as Analogies

Since trees are structurally more complex than lists, they have a more extensive nomenclature for referring to their various subparts. Generally speaking, the names are direct analogies drawn from two sources: the parts of arboreal trees and genealogical relationships. While this certainly creates a mixed metaphor, it does provide a powerful and flexible vocabulary for describing trees.

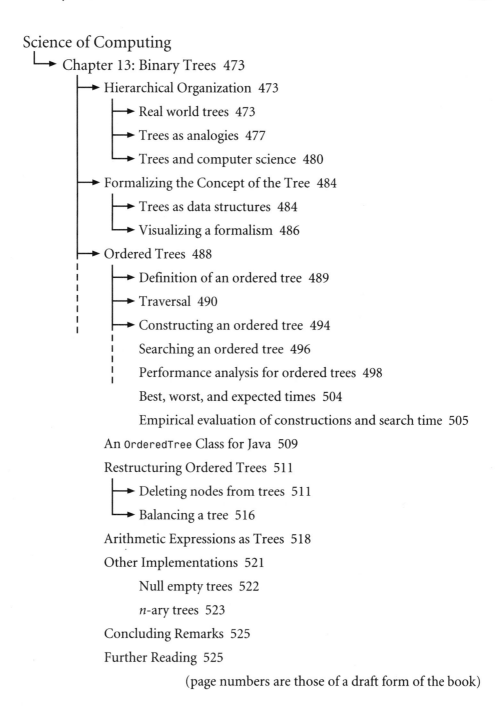

(page numbers are those of a draft form of the book)

FIGURE 13.4 The outline or table of contents as a tree.

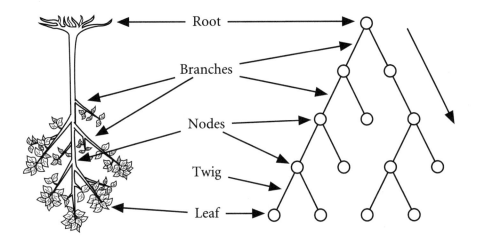

FIGURE 13.5 Component parts of a tree.

The analogy between tree data structures and arboreal trees extends well beyond their common name, as can be seen in Figure 13.5. Specifically most of the names of the parts of a tree come from this source.

Root

Just as arboreal trees are connected to the ground at a single point, the *root* of a tree data structure is the most important single point of the tree structure. By definition a (nonempty) tree has only one root (e.g., tournament winner, CEO, or founding father), and that root is the reference point for the entire tree, with all other points defined relative to the root. Computer scientists emphasize this aspect by drawing trees "upside down," thus accenting the all-important root at the top.

Nodes

The junction of two branches is a *node*. Although this biological term is less well known than the others, it is one of the most important for data structures. In a tree structure, data is associated, or stored, with the node. Conceptually, the root is a node, as are all of its subordinates.

Leaves

At the extreme ends of branches, furthest from the root (e.g., all eight teams in the playoff) are the *leaves*. In our models, we will treat the leaf as an identifiable subset of node.

Branches and Twigs

The *branches*, or *edges*, of a tree connect two nodes together. Schematically, they are drawn as lines; conceptually, they represent the logical relationship between two nodes (e.g., winner of the game, supervisor-subordinate, parent-child, etc.). Branch is a better word than edge because branches are directional: one end is the superior and one the subordinate. The further one gets from the root, the more numerous (and less significant) are the branches. The smallest (farthest from the root) branches are sometimes called *twigs*.

Genealogical Terms

While the parts of a tree structure take their names from their arboreal analogs, the names for relationships between any two nodes are usually drawn from the descendant tree as illustrated in Figure 13.6. If two nodes are directly connected by a branch, the *parent* is the node above and the *child* is the node below. *Grandparent* nodes are two levels above; *grandchildren* two below. All children of a single parent are *siblings*.[1] If any (series of branches) exists between two nodes, the upper one is

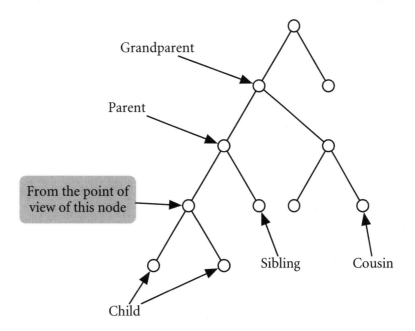

FIGURE 13.6 Genealogical tree nomenclature.

---

[1] Traditionally, gender-based terms were more common than the gender-neutral terms used here, and are still found occasionally in the literature, e.g., *Mother* and *daughter* instead of parent and child, or *sister* rather than sibling.

called the *ancestor* and the lower one the *descendant*. One can even extend the family relations to uncles, aunts, cousins, great-grandparents, and so on. The root is the only node with no parents, and it is an ancestor of all other nodes. All other nodes have exactly one parent. Leaves are the only nodes with no children.

Path, Pathlength and Height

A series of branches connecting a parent to its child to the grandchild and so on is called a *path*. The number of branches on a single path is called its *pathlength*. The longest path (including root and leaf) dictates the *height* of the tree: for nonempty trees, the height is one more than the longest path. A tree with just one node (and no path) has height 1, while the empty tree will have height zero. For example, the World Series has height 4, but only three rounds in the tournament—or branches in the path. The *level* of the node is the same as its height. Note that this means that the root is at level 0, and the furthest leaves at level *h*. Beware of one side effect of this convention in some mathematical derivations: a node at a higher numeric level is visually located below those with lower levels, and vice versa.

13.1.3 Trees and Computer Science

Tree structures are especially important in computer science, and several uses are probably already familiar to you (but it is very possible you have never thought about their "treeness"). As with an outline, the common uses often do not include an explicit visual representation of the branches.

File Structures

Figure 13.7 shows a subset of one user's files, represented as a hierarchy, with arrows added to indicate parental relationships. In general, a computer directory has a single root (the desktop). Below that are each of the individual disks (the nodes). Each disk may contain multiple folders (more nodes); each folder can itself contain more folders (still more nodes); but some folders must ultimately contain only documents (finally, leaves). In a command-line interface, the fully qualified file name identifies the path from root to leaf.

Decision Trees

An important problem-solving methodology uses a *decision tree*. The methodology systematically homes in on the desired answer by eliminating incorrect answers through a nested series of questions. The answer to each of these questions reduces the number of candidate solutions. For example, the *Pacific Coast Tree Finder* (by Tom Watts) helps its readers identify a tree (the arboreal kind) by asking a series of questions:

(My class work)

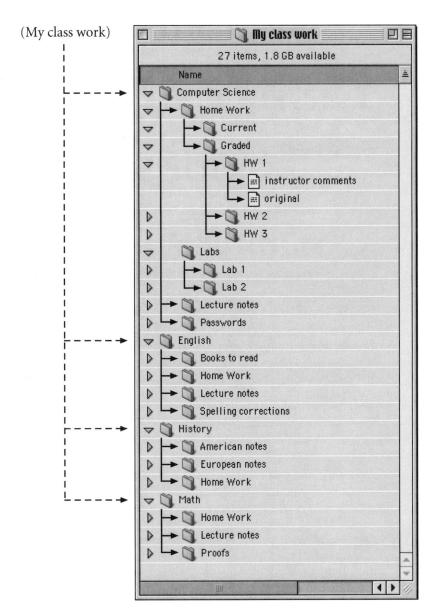

FIGURE 13.7 A hierarchy of files.

Does it have leaves or needles?
Are the leaves pinnate or palmate?
Are they smooth or serrated?
Is the bark furrowed or smooth?

The answer to each question sends the reader to another page or section of the book. For example, it might direct the reader to page 10 if the tree has needles, but to page 60 if it has leaves. At each stage the process reduces the candidate set of trees until only one tree fitting the description remains. In this case, the search tree is described by the recursive algorithm:

Algorithm decisionSearch:
    If you have identified the answer
        then return that answer (success).
        otherwise Answer the current yes/no (or other two-possibility) question.
            If the answer is yes (or first choice)
                then   Follow the "yes" branch to a child,
                    decisionSearch from that point.
                otherwise   Follow the "no" branch to a child,
                    decisionSearch from that point.

(The alert reader may recognize this algorithm as a generalization of the Binary Search algorithm described in Section 8.1.)

Computational Linguistics and Formal Languages

In the field of computational linguistics, a grammar is a collection of rules that describe trees, which in turn represent sentence structures. For example, a very small subset of English can be described by a set of rules:

sentence → noun phrase + verb phrase
noun phrase → article + noun + (prepositional phrase)
prepositional phrase → preposition + noun phrase
verb phrase → verb + adverb

meaning a sentence can be a noun phrase followed by a verb phrase; a noun phrase can be an article followed by a noun, and (optionally) a prepositional phrase, and so on. The rules can be used to either generate or recognize the sentence shown by the tree shown in Figure 13.8.

Computer languages can similarly be defined as tree structures. For example, one might include:

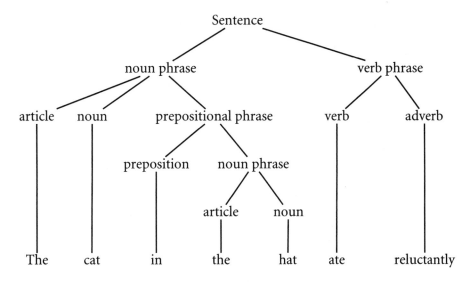

FIGURE 13.8 A tree structure for an English sentence.

statement → conditional | assignment | iteration | compound …
conditional → "if" + "(" + Boolean expression + ")" + statement

meaning that a statement can be a conditional statement, assignment, iteration structure, or a compound statement (e.g., enclosed in braces). Similarly a conditional starts with the word "if" and contains a Boolean expression and another statement. Such formal descriptions help make computer languages consistent, proofs involving their correctness easier, and compilation more straightforward.

Exercises

13.1. Sports teams from your college or university probably participate in tournaments. Find a tree representing one such tournament and identify all parts of the tree using computer science terminology.

13.2. Describe your college or university faculty in terms of a tree structure (most of the information can be found in the catalog).

13.3. Build a decision tree for recognizing geometric shapes. It should include at least: square, rectangle, rhombus, trapezoid, simple triangle, isosceles triangle, equilateral triangle, right triangle, pentagon, circle, and ellipse.

13.4. Draw the file structure of your own file directory that you use with this course as a tree.

13.5. Build a family tree for your own family.

13.2 FORMALIZING THE CONCEPT OF TREE

We can define the notion of "tree" in much the way we defined "list." While a tree is certainly a more complex structure than a list, the two formalisms share many of the same features.

13.2.1 Trees as Data Structures

We have seen several important properties of trees that we want to capture:

- Every tree has exactly one root.
- Every node other than the root has exactly one parent.
- No node can be its own descendant (or ancestor).
- No two nodes can have the same child.

Among other things, these properties mean that there are no *cycles*, that is, no series of branches or edges that lead from one node through other nodes and back to the original node. Figure 13.9 illustrates some way these properties may fail to be met. In general, any attempt to define tree formally will want to capture these properties.

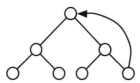
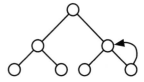

Root has a parent   One node has two parents

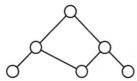
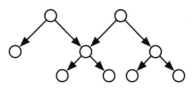

Two nodes have the same child   Two roots

FIGURE 13.9 Some structures that are not trees.

Binary Trees

In general, a node can have any number of children, and a tree with an upper bound of n on the number of possible children for any one node is called an *n-ary tree*. The *binary tree* (a tree with no more than two children for any node, such as the sports tournaments, genealogy, or decision tree) is especially important in computer science. While *n*-ary trees can be cumbersome, binary trees are easy to write and reason about. And as we will see in Section 13.7.2, any *n*-ary tree has an equivalent binary tree. For these reasons, the next several sections reason about binary trees exclusively.

13.2.2 Visualizing a Formalism

The tree structure can be envisioned much like the list structure—especially when restricted to binary trees. Just as a list is conceptually a series of lists, each with a nested, or next list, a tree should be envisioned as a collection of trees, each composed of a root value and two children, each of which is itself a tree.

Any class definition for a treelike data structure would start just as the list class does, with member variables corresponding to these three pieces:

>   *root:*   *any object*
>   *left:*   *a tree*
>   *right:*   *another tree*

Just as a list could be empty, so can a tree. Notice that just as each node in a list is actually another list, each node in a tree is another (sub)tree. Generally we will say *child*, *subtree*, or *node* depending on which aspect we wish to emphasize.

Figure 13.10 shows this recursive view of a tree, with empty trees represented by "(empty)". Even from this small tree, it may be obvious that the total number of these empty subtrees may be very large (Section 13.7.1 explores just how large). For that reason, we may often simplify the graphical representations as in Figure 13.11, omitting the explicit ovals representing subtrees, and empty trees along with the links to them. However, as we reason about trees, it will be important to take care to recognize whether we are talking about all nodes (subtrees) or just the nonempty ones. Similarly, when we say *leaf*, we need to be clear as to whether we mean the empty trees at the end of each path, or the last node with content. "Leaf" will usually mean the last nonempty node. However, many of the algorithms will actually visit the empty trees, and that fact will need to be considered when evaluating execution times.

The uniformity of the tree structure is key to most proofs involving trees. For example, the following lemma is used implicitly in most proofs in this chapter.

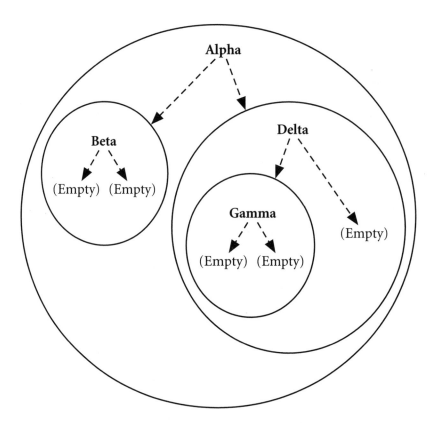

FIGURE 13.10 Schematic representation of a tree structure.

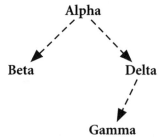

FIGURE 13.11 Simplified graphic representation of a tree.

LEMMA: The height of a tree is strictly greater than that of either of its children. □

PROOF: Let T be a tree and let T' be the taller of its subtrees (if they have the same height, select the left subtree) and let h be the height of T'. Let P be the longest path in T'. By definition, P has pathlength $h-1$. The path formed by joining P and the branch from the T to T' must be one longer than $h-1$. So the height of T must be greater than that of T', which by definition is at least as high as the other subtree. ■

Since every node is actually a tree, proofs involving nodes can usually be stated in terms of the subtree that has the node of interest at its root. For example, one particular place this change of reference is useful is where any two nodes in a tree have a common ancestor. That common ancestor is the root of the smallest tree that contains both nodes. In particular, for any two nodes in a tree, there is a unique smallest (shortest) subtree containing both nodes. To see this, start at the two nodes, A and B in Figure 13.12, and trace upwards until a common ancestor is located. Within that smallest tree, the two nodes cannot share any common path (otherwise they could share in an even smaller tree). Thus, they must either be in opposite sides of their common subtree, or one must be its root.

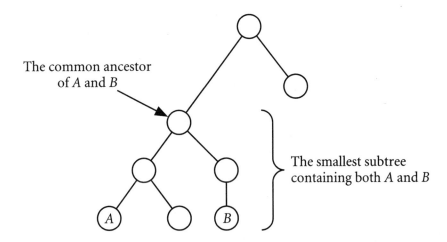

FIGURE 13.12 Reasoning about relationships between nodes.

13.3 ORDERED TREES

The most impressive use of binary trees comes as a surprise to many students: they can be used to maintain sorted data collections. In other words, trees can be used for purposes almost identical to those of OrderedLists. Even more surprising: they are dramatically more efficient. In particular, trees are very useful for building a sorted data collection that enables either searching for a given item or visiting every item in order.

13.3.1 Definition of an Ordered Tree

When we think of sorting, we normally mean organizing data into a linear sequence (as in a list or array), such that the values increase as one works through the sequence from first to last. Normally, we say that a sequence $a_1 \ldots a_n$, is sorted if $a_i < a_j$ whenever $1 \le i < j \le n$. A tree clearly is not a linear sequence, so that definition can't apply here. In order to use a tree for sorting, we need to restate the definition of "sorted" in terms of functionality rather than in terms of a static or positional description. In particular, we say that a collection $a_1 \ldots a_n$ is (functionally) sorted if the organization facilitates sequential traversal, that is:

■ Every element of the collection can be visited in order: a_1 is visited before a_n if and only if $a_1 < a_n$ (for example, print out a list in alphabetical order) in no more than $\Theta(n)$ time.

We will show that not only can we build trees that meet this functional definition, but that doing so provides a great advantage over other data structures. In general, we can use trees to sort any set of items for which an ordering definition exists: integers ($<$), strings (alphabetic order), etc. To establish this, we will create a pair of intermediate definitions. We say a tree is *inorder*, if:

■ Its left subtree contains exactly those values that are less than its root.
■ Its right subtree contains exactly those values that are greater than its root.

And we say a tree satisfies the *sort property* if every node in the tree is inorder. We will then show that any tree satisfying the sort property is in fact (functionally) sorted. For illustration purposes, we will use the tree depicted in Figure 13.13, which contains just the names of students in a class. To see that this tree satisfies the sort property, notice that the names in Mary's left subtree (Dave, Adam, and Francis) all come before Mary; those in Dave's left subtree (just Adam) come before Dave, and so on.

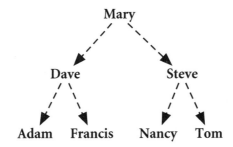

FIGURE 13.13 An ordered tree containing names.

Although the sort property was defined in terms of "every node of the tree," we can restate it in terms of the root and its children:

THEOREM: A tree satisfies the sort property if and only if it is empty or the root node is in order and both children satisfy the sort property. □

PROOF: The proof is by induction on the height of the tree.

Base Case: The empty tree satisfies both clauses. First, it has no nodes. Therefore, all of its nodes are inorder and it therefore satisfies the sort property. If the tree satisfies the sort property and is empty, then by declaration it is empty.

Induction Step: Assume the proposition is true for all trees of height h, $0 \leq h < H$. Let T be a tree of height H. If T satisfies the sort property, then all nodes within T are inorder. Specifically, the root and all nodes within each of T's children are inorder. By the induction hypothesis, each of T's children satisfy the sort property. Therefore, the root is inorder and both children satisfy the sort property.

Now assume that T's root is inorder and both children satisfy the sort property. Then by the induction hypothesis, every node within the left subtree is inorder. Likewise, every node in the right subtree is inorder. Since the root is also inorder, every node is inorder, and T satisfies the sort property. ∎

The importance of this observation is that although every node must indeed be structured correctly, we need not talk in terms of "every node," but can define *sorted* in terms of the overall tree structure: the root and its immediate children. Thus, we can say that a class invariant of ordered trees is: if a is the root of a tree, then $b < a$ is in the tree if and only if b is contained within the left subtree corresponding to a. Similarly for $b > a$ in the right subtree.

13.3.2 Traversal

We will first show that a tree satisfying the sort property is functionally sorted (traversable in linear time). We will then show that construction of such a tree is almost as easy as traversing it (and that may come as a surprise). Finally, we will show that finding a value in such a tree is not only easy, it is very fast.

So, assume for the moment that we have a tree satisfying the sort property. The basic principle of any tree traversal uses the fact that every value in any tree must be the root or in one of the subtrees. The traversal algorithm presented here recognizes that all values less than the root must be in the left subtree and therefore it visits them first. Then it visits the root, and finally the right subtree:

> *Algorithm traverse:*
>   *If the tree is not empty*
>   *then   traverse all nodes in the left child,*
>   *Visit the root,*
>   *traverse all nodes in the right child.*

As with lists, many traversal applications will be structurally identically. So, for example, all the nodes can be printed in order simply as:

> *Algorithm printTree:*
>   *If the tree is not empty*
>   *then   printTree the left child,*
>   *Print the root,*
>   *printTree the right child.*[2]

We now show that the *traverse* algorithm (and any algorithm with the same structure) not only visits every node, it visits them in the comparison order for the tree (alphabetical, in the example). Thus, the *printTree* algorithm will print the entire alphabetical listing of the students: Adam, Dave, Francis, Mary, Nancy, Steve, Tom. We address this one aspect at a time.

LEMMA: The *traverse* algorithm visits every node of any tree. □

PROOF: The proof is by induction on the height of the tree.

Base Case: If the tree is empty (height = 0), the algorithm clearly visits every node (since there are none), so the proposition is (vacuously) satisfied.

---

[2] This algorithm, and most others presented in this section are coded into Java in Section 13.4.

Induction Step: Assume that the proposition holds for all trees of height h, such that $0 \leq h < H$. Let T be a tree of height H. Since $H > 0$, T cannot be the empty tree, and therefore the algorithm attempts to traverse both children as well as visiting the root. The height of the left child, L, must be less than H, so by the induction hypothesis, the algorithm visits every node in L. Similarly, it visits the entire right subtree. Since the only parts of a tree are the root and the two children, the algorithm visits every node in the entire tree. ∎

Now that we have shown that the algorithm visits every node, we show that it doesn't duplicate its efforts by visiting any node twice. Combined, the two lemmas imply that *traverse* visits every node exactly once.

LEMMA: When applied to any tree, *traverse* visits no node twice. □

PROOF: The proof is by contradiction. Let T be a tree. Suppose there exists a node k and that *traverse* visits k twice. If k is the root, then k must also be visited during the traversal of one of T's children. Thus, k would have to be its own descendant which contradicts the definition of tree. If k is visited by two separate calls to *traverse*, then it is visited twice, once each as the child of two other nodes. That is, k has two parents, which again violates the definition. ∎

Combined, the two lemmas imply that *traverse* visits every node exactly once.

LEMMA: The *traverse* algorithm makes exactly n visits. □

PROOF: There are n nodes. Since the algorithm visits every node, it must make at least n visits. Since it visits no node more than once, it can make no more than n visits. Therefore, the number of visits must be exactly n. ∎

Since we now know that *traverse* will visit every node in linear time, all that remains to show is that it does so in the appropriate order, specifically, if two nodes in the tree have values $a_i < a_j$, then the *traverse* algorithm visits a_i before a_j.

THEOREM: Any tree satisfying the sort property is a functionally sorted collection: □

PROOF: Let T be a tree satisfying the sort property. We have already established that *traverse* visits every node exactly once, so all that is left is to show that it visits them in the correct order. Let $a_i < a_j$ be two values contained in T. And let T' be the smallest subtree containing both values. Either one of the two values is the root of T' or one is in each of T's children (otherwise there would be a smaller tree containing both values). If a_i is the root of T' then by construction, all nodes greater than a_i must be in the right subtree. The algorithm visits those nodes after the root so it prints a_i before a_j. Similarly if a_j is the root, then a_i must be printed first, since it must be in the left subtree. If neither is the root, then a_i must be in the left subtree and a_j must be in the right subtree. Again a_i is printed before a_j. ■

Notice that nothing in the proofs of the lemmas requires the sort property. Thus, in fact, *traverse* will successfully traverse any tree, visiting every node exactly once (although not necessarily in a particular order), an observation that will be useful in Section 13.6. For now, simply notice that the tree could clearly be printed in reverse order using a small variant on the traversal algorithm:

> *Algorithm printTreeReverse:*
> > *If the tree is not empty*
> > > *then   printTreeReverse the right subtree,*
> > > *Print the root,*
> > > *printTreeReverse the left subtree.*

The proof is left to an exercise.

13.3.3 Constructing an Ordered Tree

Traversing a tree requires the same amount of time as traversing a list of the same total size. But it is in the construction and search processes that trees truly excel. The algorithms for building and searching the tree are almost identical—and both are amazingly fast, a property that follows from the simple definition of ordered trees. The basic idea is that the tree is built one node at a time. Each new value gets placed recursively into the left or right subtree depending on its value relative to the root: values less than the root are placed in the left subtree and those greater than the root in the right subtree. The position within the subtree is determined by recursively applying the insert process. Thus, the algorithm for adding a new value to a tree is simply:

> *Algorithm addNode (newValue):*
> > *If the root is empty*
> > > *then   Place a new tree containing just the new value here.*
> > > *otherwise   If the new value is less than the root*
> > > > *then addNode(newValue) to the left subtree,*
> > > > *otherwise addNode(newValue) to the right subtree.*

Figure 13.14 illustrates the successive configurations of a tree resulting from adding with *addNode* the values Mary, Dave, Steve, Nancy, Tom, Francis, Adam, in that order, to an initially empty tree. For the moment, we will assume no value is added to a tree twice (e.g., no two students have the same name), but it is a simple matter to extend the algorithm to allow duplicate values.

> **THEOREM:** If T is a tree satisfying the sort property, then after adding a new node using the *addNode* algorithm, T still satisfies the sort property. □

> **PROOF:** The proof is by induction on the height of the tree.

> **Base Case:** If T is empty, then it satisfies the sort property. If a new node is added, then the new value becomes the root. T then contains one value, and T trivially satisfies the sort property.

> **Induction Step:** Suppose all trees of height $0 \le h < H$ satisfy the proposition. Let T be a tree of height H satisfying the sort property. Now suppose a new value, v, is added to T by means of the *addNode* algorithm. By definition, T is not empty. v is either less than or greater than the root. If v is less than the root, the algorithm attempts to add v to the left child, which is what the sort property requires. So the root is still inorder. Since the left subtree necessarily has height less than H, by assumption v will be correctly placed within that subtree so that the entire left subtree continues to satisfy the sort property. Neither the root nor any of the right subtree are changed. Thus, T itself must still satisfy the sort property. The analogous argument applies if v is greater than the root and the node is inserted in the right child. Either way, T still satisfies the sort property. ■

13.3.4 Searching an Ordered Tree

Given the construction of a sorted tree, finding a value is simply a matter of "looking where we put it!" The algorithm for finding a value is almost identical to that for adding a value:

Algorithm find (value)
    If the tree is empty
        then Return failure (no value can be in the empty tree)
        otherwise If the value is the same as the root
               then Return success.
               otherwise If the value is less than the root
                       then find (value) in the left subtree.
                       otherwise find (value) in the right subtree.

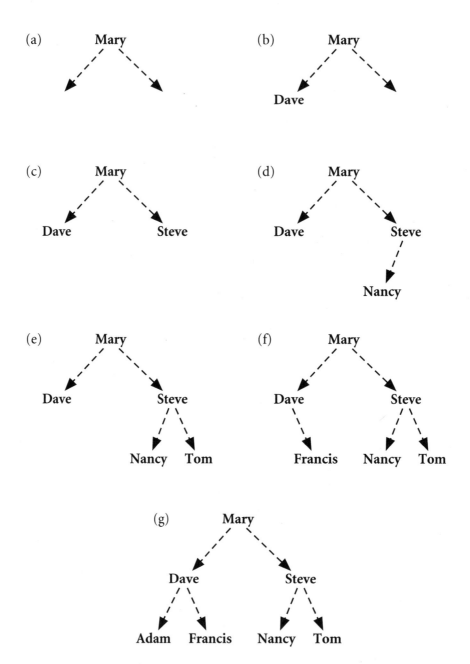

FIGURE 13.14 Building an ordered tree.

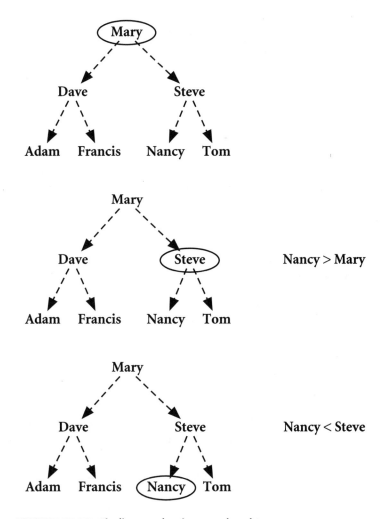

FIGURE 13.15 Finding a value in an ordered tree.

Figure 13.15 illustrates the use of this algorithm to find "Nancy." The proof of correctness for *find* is almost as easy as that for *addNode*.

THEOREM: When applied to any tree satisfying the sort property, *find*(*x*) returns true if and only if the tree contains *x*. □

PROOF: The proof again is by induction on the height of the tree.

Base Case: If the tree is empty, then it satisfies the sort property, but no target value can be in the tree. *find* returns failure when searching an empty tree, as needed.

Induction Step: Suppose all trees of height $0 \leq h < H$ satisfy the proposition. Let T be a tree of height H satisfying the sort property. Let v be a target value to be sought within T. If v is equal to the root value, then the algorithm returns success and the proposition is trivially satisfied. Otherwise v is either greater than or less than the root value. If v is less than the root, then the algorithm searches in the left subtree. By definition, if the value is in the tree at all, it must be in the left subtree. Since that subtree must have height $h < H$, by assumption, the algorithm will find the value if and only if it appears in that subtree. Similarly, values greater than the root will be in the tree if and only if they are in the right subtree of the root. ■

Information Retrieval

We saw in Section 11.5.4 that the list algorithm *find* could be modified to return the contents of an element, not just the presence of the target value in the tree. The same observations hold for finding elements in a tree. Thus, *find* could be used as an algorithm for retrieving data associated with the key. This sort of retrieval is explored in the exercises.

Duplicate Values

We have tacitly assumed that any two nodes in a tree have distinct values. In fact, we can allow duplicate values; we just need to assure that *addNode*, *find* and *traverse* are all defined consistently. For example, *addNode* actually treats equal values the same as it treats greater values (the test in construction was "if *newValue < root*"). *find* will locate the first (lowest level) among the duplicates. A search to find all nodes with a given value must search right children. Proof that traversal will print duplicate values consecutively is left to the reader (Exercise 13.21). These distinctions are not important for simple objects, but if a node contains complex objects, such as a phone entry, then the distinctions are critical.

13.3.5 Performance Analysis for Ordered Trees

Trees turn out to support incredibly efficient searches, and the reason lies in the relationship between a tree's height and its total number of nodes. *find* does not search every node, as did the corresponding algorithm for lists (or even half the nodes as with ordered lists); it visits only those nodes on the direct path from root to the target node, or if the target isn't present, to a leaf. An examination of the shape and proportions of a binary tree will lead directly to the expected construction and search times. A linear structure, such as a list, has only one relevant measure of size: the total number of nodes. A hierarchical organization is not so straight-forward: a tree has size, but it also has shape. Potentially, a tree may be tall and thin or short and squat. Search time will depend more on the height of the tree than its total size. Fortunately, under the right conditions, there are clear relationships between the size and the shape of the tree.

Height

Recall that the *height* of a tree is the maximum number of distinct levels contained in the tree. Clearly, the height of a tree will tell us how far we might have to search. Unfortunately, we cannot make a blanket statement about the exact relation between height and total number of nodes. But if we make some simple assumptions about the shape of the tree, we can say a lot about this relationship, and therefore about search time.

Fully Balanced Trees

Some trees are completely symmetrical and completely filled in (e.g., the World Series tree or the one in Figure 13.16). Intuitively, the bottom row of leaves in a balanced tree is completely filled in, with no paths extending further and none terminating earlier. We will, however, base the formal definition of fully balanced not on the leaves, but on the overall tree structure. We define a tree of height h to be *fully balanced* if every node at a level less than h has exactly two children. The tree in Figure 13.11 is not fully balanced because the node "Delta" has just one child (and matches the intuition because the bottom row has only one node), but the World Series tree fits the requirement (and the bottom (left) row is completely uniform). We can show that the formal definition matches the intuitive concept, but does so in a more computationally useful manner. We first show (as we did with the sort property) that we need not talk in terms of every node in the tree, but can use recursive definitions based on immediate subtrees.

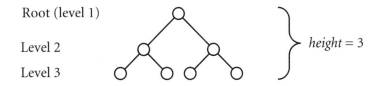

FIGURE 13.16 A small but fully balanced binary tree.

LEMMA: A binary tree is fully balanced if and only if either it is empty or both of its subtrees are fully balanced and have the same height. □

PROOF: The proof is by induction on the height of the tree.

Base Case: An empty tree explicitly satisfies the proposition.

Induction Step: Suppose that the proposition holds for all trees of height h, such that $0 \leq h < H$. Let T be a binary tree of height H, with two children L and R, both of which are fully balanced trees with height (L) = height (R). The height of L is necessarily less than H. Therefore, since L is fully balanced, all of L's nonleaf descendants have two children. The same argument applies to R. The root of T has two children by assumption. Thus, all nonleaf nodes in T have two children. So T is fully balanced.

Now suppose T is fully balanced. Then all nonleaf nodes within T have two children. In particular, all nonleaf nodes within T's left child, L, have two children. By the induction hypothesis, L must be fully balanced. The same argument applies to R.

It remains to show that L and R have the same height. If T is fully balanced, then by definition all nodes below level h must have two children (and therefore cannot be leaves). Since T has height h, no node (leaf or otherwise) can be at a level greater than h. Therefore, all leaves of T must be at the same level, h. Now suppose L and R have different heights, denoted as h_l and h_r respectively. By definition, the leaves of L are at level h_l (with respect to L) and those of R at h_r. With respect to T, these leaves are at $h_l + 1$ and $h_r + 1$, respectively. Since all leaves of T must be at the same level (h), it must be that $h_l + 1 = h_2 + 1$, and $h_l = h_r$, which contradicts the assumption. So both subtrees must be the same height. ■

We can now make a bound on pathlengths in a fully balanced tree.

LEMMA: In a fully balanced tree, every path from root to leaf has the same length. □

PROOF: Once again, the proof is by induction on the height of the tree.

Base Case: If a tree is empty, then there are no paths, so they are (vacuously) all the same length.

Induction Step: Assume that the proposition holds for all trees of height h, $0 \leq h < H$. Let T be a tree of height H. If T is fully balanced then it must have two children, L and R, which must have the same height. By the assumption, all pathlengths in L are equal, and all pathlengths in R are equal. Since the two trees have the same height, all paths in either tree have the same length. Any path in T must have one more edge than the paths of L or R. Thus, all paths within T have the same length. ∎

This is almost the property we want. It still remains to be shown that every possible node at the highest level has been filled in.

> **THEOREM:** In a fully balanced tree with height h, every possible path of length $h-1$ exists. □

> **PROOF:** Let T be a fully balanced tree of height h. Now suppose there is a potential path of length $h-1$ that does not actually exist. An unfilled path implies that there is a node somewhere at a level less than h that does not presently have two children. Filling in the potential path to level h would give that node more children. But by definition every node at a level less than h has two children. ∎

Size

For a fully balanced tree, there is a definite—and derivable—relationship between the total number of nodes in a tree and the height of that tree. We will first derive these relationships and then see how they apply to trees that are not fully balanced. The tree in Figure 13.16 has one node at level 1, 2 nodes at level 2, and 4 nodes at level 3. Since each node can have two children, it should be clear that the 4 nodes at level 3 could have 8 children at level 4. In general, the number of nodes doubles at each level and the number of nodes, n, at level h is described by the recurrence relation:

$$n(h) = \begin{cases} 1 & \text{if } h = 1 \\ 2n(h-1) & \text{if } h > 1 \end{cases} \qquad (13.1)$$

But this is just an instance of the result from Exercise 7.15 in Section 7.2. Using the result of that exercise to find a closed form yields:

$$n(h) = 2^{h-1} \qquad (13.2)$$

The total number of nodes, n, in an entire tree is simply the sum of the numbers of nodes at each level. So a tree of height 4 would have the sum of levels 1, 2, 3, and 4:

$$2^0 + 2^1 + 2^2 + 2^3$$
$$= 1 + 2 + 4 + 8 = 15 \qquad (13.3)$$

Equation 7.4 in Section 7.1, is the almost identical:

$$\sum_{i=0}^{n} 2^i = 2^{n+1} - 1 \qquad (13.4)$$

Substituting $j = i+1$ into this yields:

$$\sum_{j=1}^{n+1} 2^{j-1} = 2^{n+1} - 1 \qquad (13.5)$$

and then substituting $h = n+1$, yields the final form:

$$\sum_{i=1}^{h} 2^{i-1} = 2^h - 1 \qquad (13.6)$$

which evaluates to 1, 3, 7, 15, respectively, for trees of heights 1 through 4. From this, we can also see that the nonleaves comprise a tree of height $h-1$, so there are:

$$\sum_{i=1}^{h-1} 2^{i-1} = 2^{h-1} - 1 \qquad (13.7)$$

nonleaves, which is exactly one less than the number of leaves. Think about that: the number of leaves is not only twice the number of nodes in the level of their parents, it is actually more (by 1) than the total of all nonleaf nodes. As a rule of thumb, a fully balanced binary tree has almost exactly as many leaves as nonleaves.

We can also ask the opposite question: what is the height of a fully balanced tree containing n nodes? We can solve Equation 13.7 for h:

$$n = 2^h - 1 \qquad (13.8)$$

$$2^h = n+1 \qquad (13.9)$$

$$h = h\log_2(2) = \log_2(n+1) \qquad (13.10)$$

Thus, the height, h, of a fully balanced tree containing n nodes is $\log_2(n+1)$. Since a fully balanced tree always contains one less than a power of 2 nodes, and the logarithm of any power of two is an integer, the pathlength calculation yields an integer as expected. For example, a tree with 15 nodes has height $= \log_2 16 = 4$.

Search Time

The relationship between height and size of a tree gives us an immediate method for calculating the search time. In a fully balanced tree of n nodes, all the paths are the same length: $\log_2(n+1) = $ height. The *find* algorithm follows the path exactly with no backtracking. For a fully balanced tree containing n nodes, a search should require no more comparisons than the length of the path. It makes one comparison (target vs. current root) at each recursion. If *find* locates the target before it reaches a leaf, then it must make fewer than $\log_2(n+1)$ comparisons. If the target is a leaf, then *find* makes exactly $\log_2(n+1)$ comparisons. If *find* doesn't find the target, it again makes $\log_2(n+1)$ comparisons (the algorithm quits after reaching a leaf). The worst-case search time in a (fully balanced) tree, therefore, is just $\log_2(n+1)$ steps—the same as the height. How much better than a list search is that? Significantly! For example, if there are 1000 values (approximately 2^{10}) in the data structure, a search in an ordered list requires on average 500 comparisons. In a tree, the worst-case search requires $\log_2 1000$, or 10, steps. And of course the advantage gets even larger with larger collections: searching a million elements ($\sim 2^{20}$) requires no more than 20 comparisons rather than the expected 500,000.

The best-case search time isn't very interesting: it is just 1 (when the target value is found at the root). The average search time must be somewhere between 1 and $\log_2(n+1)$. The obvious first guess is $(\log_2 n)/2$. However, a moment's reflection points out that half the nodes are leaves requiring $\log_2 n$ comparisons and half of the remaining nodes each require $\log_2 n - 1$. Almost all the nodes are more than halfway down the list. The actual average time is more like $\log_2 n - 1$ (see Exercise 13.23). In reality, the average time will also depend on other factors, such as the likelihood that the target value is actually present.

Construction Time for an Ordered Tree

Not only is the search time for an ordered tree extraordinarily good, the time to construct the tree is also as good as can be accomplished for any structure satisfying the sort property. Recall that the best sorting algorithms of Chapter 10 required $\Theta(n\log_2 n)$ time. So how long does it take to build a tree satisfying the sort property? The worst-case nodes are the leaves, each of which requires $\log_2 n$ time to insert. For a tree of size n, there are:

$$\left\lceil \frac{n}{2} \right\rceil \tag{13.11}$$

leaves. Inserting just the leaves, therefore, requires $\log_2 n$ steps for each leaf. Thus, the time, t, for construction of the entire tree must require at least that much time:

$$t \geq \left\lceil \frac{n}{2} \times \log_2 n \right\rceil \tag{13.12}$$

On the other hand, since the leaves require the longest time, then the time for each of the other $n/2$ nodes must be less than $\log_2 n$ and the total time for adding all n nodes must be:

$$t \le \lceil n \times \log_2 n \rceil \tag{13.13}$$

Thus, the total is bounded by $n/2 \times \log_2 n$ and $n \log_2 n$. This satisfies the definition of $\Theta(n \log n)$, meaning that we can build an ordered tree from a collection of values as quickly as any of the previously discussed sort algorithms can create a sorted collection in the usual form.

13.3.6 Trees that Are not Fully Balanced

Unfortunately, most trees cannot be fully balanced—only those containing exactly $2^k - 1$ nodes for some h. What is the relevance of the fully balanced tree results for other trees?

Balanced Trees

We will define a close cousin of the fully balanced tree, the balanced tree, and show that the results apply almost as well to any tree in that class. We say tree of height h is *balanced* if every node with level $< h - 1$ has two children. The intuitive idea is that a balanced tree is fully balanced down to the last row, but that the bottom row is not itself full. In general, trees may be fully balanced, balanced, or neither, as illustrated by Figure 13.17.

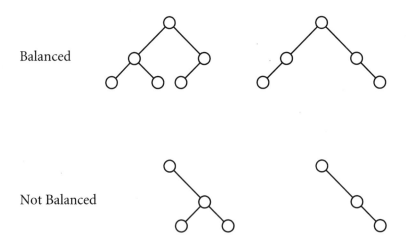

FIGURE 13.17 Balanced and unbalanced trees.

Search Time for Balanced Trees

A balanced tree of size n can be thought of as a fully balanced tree with a few nodes missing—all of which would be in the bottom row. Recall that the height of a tree was defined based on the longest path. Since *every* node with level less than $h-1$ has two children, if T is a balanced tree with height h, then all leaves are either at level h or $h-1$. The nodes down to (including) the $h-1$ level comprise a fully balanced tree. The worst-case times are either h or $h-1$—almost identical to that of the fully balanced tree.

Size of a Balanced Tree

From the way we defined it, any balanced (but not fully balanced tree) with n nodes must have a height, h, satisfying:

$$2^{h-1} \leq n < 2^h - 1 \tag{13.14}$$

$$h - 1 \leq \log_2 n < h \tag{13.15}$$

The upper bound is the size of a fully balanced tree of height h, and the lower bound the size of a fully balanced tree of height $h-1$. By definition, the balanced tree must have all of the nodes of the latter but not all of the nodes of the former.

Construction Time for Balanced Trees

A balanced tree of height h contains an entire fully balanced tree of height $h-1$. Informally, we already know that we can construct that tree in $\Theta(n\log n)$ steps. The bottom row contains no more than $n/2$ nodes, and each of those can be added in $\log_2 n$ steps, so the total time is less $2n\log_2 n$, which fits the definition of $\Theta(n\log n)$—the same as a fully balanced tree, height h. The bottom line is that the same construction time derived for fully balanced trees also holds for any balanced tree. Exercise 13.24 calls for a more formal proof of this claim.

13.3.7 Empirical Evaluation of Construction and Search Time

The actual time required to build or search a tree may differ widely from the theoretical values derived thus far for at least two reasons. The tree may not be balanced, and target values may not be generated uniformly.

The worst case for either constructing or searching occurs at a surprising time: when the items to be added to the tree are actually added in already sorted order. Assume that L is an ordered collection in increasing order. Further assume that the tree construction algorithm receives the values (in order) from L. In that case, each new item is greater than all values already in the tree. That means that in adding a new value, every comparison will result in following the path toward the right child.

Every new value will be added as the rightmost leaf of the tree. In other words, every node has only one child (the right one). The tree, in fact, degenerates to be logically identical to a list. The tree will have height n and the time to construct it will be the:

$$\sum_{i=1}^{n} i = \frac{n^2 + n}{2} \tag{13.16}$$

(see Section 11.5.5 and Section 7.1.1).

Few real trees are fully balanced, but on the other hand, hopefully one seldom uses *addNode* to create a tree from data that is already completely sorted. Real situations will fall somewhere in between these two extremes. Determination of expected times for building and searching a tree is possible, but complicated, and beyond the scope of this text. This is certainly one of those cases that calls for empirical methods. But note that any empirically determined time will depend not just on the size of the tree, but on how close it is to being balanced, which, in turn, depends on the randomness of the arrival of new items. Some of the exercises explore such empirical results.

Search Time

Once again, the best possible search time is not very interesting: it is always 1 and occurs when the target happens to be the root. So instead of asking what the search times are for successful searches, let's consider the time for unsuccessful searches. In those cases, the search must flow all the way to a leaf. For unsuccessful searches, balanced trees have the best worst-case time. That is, the worst-case search time for a balanced tree is less than the worst-case search time for an unbalanced tree. Why is that necessarily true? In a balanced tree of height h, every possible position through level $h-1$ is occupied. If another tree with the same number of nodes is not balanced, then some path must be longer and some other path shorter. That longer path creates a worse case. The absolute worst case occurs, as with construction, when the tree degenerates to a list. In that case, the unsuccessful search could require n steps.

Exercises

13.6. Earlier chapters defined sorted as: a collection $a_1 \ldots a_n$, is sorted if $a_i < a_i + 1$ for $1 \le i < n$ (or 0 to $n-1$, for collections defined on that range). This chapter claimed it is sorted if $a_i < a_j$ whenever $1 \le i < j \le n$. Show that the two definitions are exactly equivalent. Hint: one direction is trivial; for the other, use induction on the difference between i and j.

13.7. Design and run an experiment to find the time required to build an ordered tree. Build trees containing real numbers generated using Java's Random routines. Note that since expected time $(n\log_2 n)$ contains a logarithmic factor, you will need to build relatively large trees in order to obtain results that are truly graphable. Build trees of heights ranging from 1 to 25 and graph the results. Also use ratios between measured time and $\Theta(n\log n)$, as described in Section 9.2.3, to determine whether the construction time has the expected asymptotic behavior.

13.8. Design and run an experiment to search for values in the tree built in Exercise 13.7. Graph the results. Be sure to construct trees large enough so that the graph will smooth out. As in Exercise 13.7, use ratios to determine whether the search times have the expected asymptotic behavior.

13.9. Design and run an experiment to validate the claims about worst-case trees (both construction and search times). Conduct the experiment twice. In one case, use a sequence of consecutive integers. In the second, build the tree from entries from a standard dictionary.

13.10. Create a single graph containing both the results of Exercise 13.9 and the search times for balanced trees plotted against the same axes. What does the result tell you?

13.11. Prove that the reverse traversal algorithm can be used to print the values in an ordered tree in descending order.

13.12. Assume a tree of students' names allows duplicate names. Show that building a tree by adding all new values greater than or equal to the root in the right-hand subtree creates a correctly ordered tree. Demonstrate the claim by building and printing the tree in order.

13.13. Duplicate Exercise 13.12 assuming that duplicate nodes should be placed in the left-hand subtree.

13.14. Modify *find* to return the value found. Use it to find values of type PhoneEntry (see Exercise 11.29 and 11.30).

13.15. Extend Exercise 13.12 or 13.13 to find and print all occurrences of equal valued nodes.

13.16. How many levels in a fully balanced binary tree of 127 nodes? What is the pathlength in that tree?

13.17. How many nodes can be held in a tree of eight levels?

13.18. It is tempting to define fully balanced as "all leaves have identical pathlengths." What is wrong with this definition? Give an example of a tree that fits the definition but isn't fully balanced. Is there an equivalent situation for balanced trees? If so, give an example.

13.19. Trees built from items arriving in order are not the only trees with poor search and construction times. Consider the tree constructed by inserting the values 1, 100, 2, 99, 3, 98, …, 50, 51, in that order. Draw the first several layers of the tree. How many comparisons are required to construct the tree? What is the worst-case number of comparisons to search the tree?

13.20. The sort property required that ordered traversal be accomplished in $\Theta(n)$ time. In fact, even an unordered collection can be printed out in order. Describe a generic algorithm that will print (in order) the elements of an unordered collection, even though it requires more than $\Theta(n)$ time.

13.21. Prove that if a tree contains duplicate values, then the *printTree* algorithm will print any duplicates consecutively.

13.22. Prove that if a tree contains duplicate values, then the *find* algorithm will find the occurrence at the highest level.

13.23. In a fully balanced tree of n nodes, $n/2$ of the nodes are leaves (at a distance $\log_2 n$; $n/4$ nodes are one level closer ($\log_2 n-1$); $n/8$ are at $\log_2 n-2$, and so on. State the average search time as an equation involving the sum of the above terms. Then find the closed form.

13.24. Prove formally the claim that all balanced trees can be constructed in $\Theta(n\log_2 n)$ time.

13.4 AN ORDEREDTREE CLASS FOR JAVA

We have designed an entire class and shown not only the correctness of its basic algorithms, but calculated its performance characteristics. With this foundation, the implementation of the class in Java is straightforward. In fact, it is little more than the direct line-by-line translation of the algorithms from Section 13.3. The biggest complications are those needed to construct new Tree objects as parts of existing structures, as we did with List (Section 11.5).

Clearly, an ordered collection of objects requires Comparable objects such as a String, Integer, or PhoneEntry (see Chapter 11). Here are relevant methods of one Java implementation of a class OrderedTree:

```
public class OrderedTree {

    private Comparable root;
    private OrderedTree left;
    private OrderedTree right;

    // Constructor routines

    public OrderedTree() {
        root = null;
```

```java
        left = null;
        right = null;
    }

    // makeNewTree fills the same role as did makeNewList
    public OrderedTree makeNewTree() {
        return new OrderedTree();
    }

    // Access functions

    public Comparable getRoot() {
        return root;
    }

    public OrderedTree getLeft() {
        return left;
    }

    public OrderedTree getRight() {
        return right;
    }

    public boolean isEmpty() {
        return (root == null && left == null && right == null);
    }

    public void printTree() {
        if (!this.isEmpty()) {
            left.printTree();
            System.out.println(root);
            right.printTree();
        }
    }

    public void insertValue(String newNode) {
        root = newNode;
        left = this.makeNewTree();
        right = this.makeNewTree();
    }
```

```
public void addNode(Comparable newValue) {
    if (this.isEmpty()) {
        this.insertValue(newValue);
    }
    else if (root.compareTo(newValue) > 0) {
        left.addNode(newValue);
    }
    else {
        right.addNode(newValue);
    }
}

public boolean find(Comparable target) {
    if (this.isEmpty())
        return false;
    else if (root.equals(target))
        return true;
    else if (root.compareTo(target) > 0)
        return left.find(target);
    else return right.find(target);
}
}³
```

Exercises

13.25. Build a Java class Tree that can contain any form of object (not just comparables). Rewrite OrderedTree as a subclass of that class.

13.5 RESTRUCTURING ORDERED TREES

Although building, searching, and traversing trees are simple and straightforward, one basic operation is a bit more problematic: restructuring an existing tree (e.g., moving the contents of an existing node to a new position, possibly changing the shape of the tree). The most obvious need arises when deleting an internal node, but restructuring can also occur as a result of efficiency considerations.

---

³ We note that a conscientious designer would have defined a basic tree class first and then defined ordered trees as an extension of that class. However, OrderedTree is the central topic in this chapter. For clarity in explaining the ordered tree algorithms, the base class Tree was omitted entirely (except as an exercise).

13.5.1 Deleting Nodes from Trees

Deleting a node from a list was straightforward—the deleted value was effectively skipped over—we just changed the node before the deleted node so that it was followed immediately by the node that had followed the deleted node. But a moment's reflection shows that trees present a more problematic situation. A node has only one parent—but it might have two children. When an element, *N*, is deleted, it isn't possible for both of *N*'s children to become children of *N*'s parent. Although that parent is permitted two children, one of those children may already be defined. Nor can the node simply be left empty, because the basic algorithms depend on the value at each node for determining the appropriate child to visit.

We can, however, construct a deletion algorithm by considering the various cases it must handle, starting with the simplest. Recall that every node is actually the root of some (sub) tree. We can always describe a deletion situation in terms of that subtree. Assume we have located the node, *N*, to be deleted. *N* is the root of a subtree. If *N* is also a leaf, then it has no children, so we can just throw the node away (make it into the empty tree, identical to those created by the constructor) and no further work is needed. For example:

>   *N.root = null.*
>   *N.left = null.*
>   *N.right = null.*

If there is exactly one nonempty child (assume for discussion that it is a right child), there is no need to do anything fancy; just replace *N* by that child. But remember that even though *N* had only one child, it may have any number of descendants through that child and those must all be correctly referenced:

>   *N.root = N.right.root.*
>   *N.left = N.right.left.*
>   *N.right = N.right.right.*

Notice first that the old right child itself is no longer in the tree because nothing refers to it and the order of these steps is essential. Since the first two steps use N's *right child*, that child itself should not be removed until after the first two steps. Similar arguments apply when there is only a left child.

The interesting part comes when there are two children. The obvious approach would be to move one of the two children up. But then that child would have to be replaced by one of its own children. It could be necessary to recursively replace an entire sequence of values all the way down to a leaf.

Instead, we will find a node that can play the same role in searches as the deleted node. For example, suppose that you wanted to delete the value at the root

(64) in Figure 13.18. The root value must be replaced by one that preserves the structure and maintains the sort property. Specifically, it should assure that any future search for any value currently in the tree behaves in exactly the same way after deletion as it did before. That is, a search for any value larger than the old root must still search in the right child, and similarly with smaller values and the left child. We want to replace the root with a value that is larger than any value in its left subtree and smaller than any value in its right subtree. We can do this by replacing the root with the largest node that is less than the node to be deleted (or alternatively, the smallest node greater than the node to be deleted). Clearly, the desired node must be somewhere in the left subtree (since all smaller nodes are in that subtree). In fact, within that subtree, the largest node is the rightmost. When seeking the largest node within a tree (or in this case, a subtree), at every step, the right child must be larger than the current node. Combining the selection of the left subtree followed by the search for the largest value in that subtree gives:

> *Start at the root (64 in the figure),*
> *Find the left child.*
> *While the current node has a right child:*
> > *Move to that right child.*

The value of the root (not the entire node, since the general structure should be maintained) can be replaced by the found value (56):

> *N.root = found value.root*

That of course leaves the position that originally held 56 empty. Fortunately, although that node can have children, it can have only one immediate child (a left child, since the algorithm assures that there is no right child). The found node can be replaced by its left child.

> *Parent of the found node.right = found node.left*

Finally, since the algorithm searches left and then to the right, we also must address the special case in which *N* has two children but *N*'s left child has no right children. In that case, we just want to replace *N* by its left child:

> *root = left.root.*
> *left = left.right.*

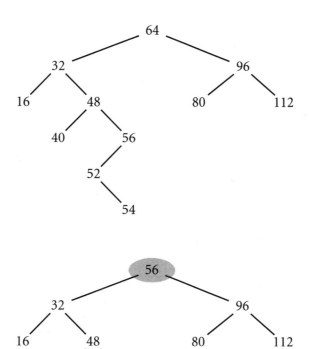

FIGURE 13.18 Deleting a value in an ordered tree.

Putting all these pieces together and coding it in Java gives:

```java
// in class OrderedTree
public void cutAndRaise() {
    if (this.isEmpty()) {
        root = null;
        right = null;
        left = null;
    }
    else if (left.isEmpty()) {
        root = right.root;
        left = right.left;
        right = right.right;
    }
```

```
    else if (right.isEmpty()) {
        root = left.root;
        right = left.right;
        left = left.left;
    }
    else if (left.right.isEmpty()) {
        root = left.root;
        left = left.right;
    }
    else {
        OrderedTree secondLargest = this;
        OrderedTree largest = left;
        while (!largest.right.isEmpty()) {
            secondLargest = largest;
            largest = largest.right;
        }
        root = largest.root;
        secondLargest.right = largest.left;
        largest.left = null;
    }
}
```

13.5.2 Balancing a Tree

Most of the performance analysis for trees—especially the parts that claimed excellent performance—made the assumption that trees were balanced. Unfortunately, nothing in the construction algorithms assures that trees will be balanced when built. Even if balanced when constructed, a tree can become unbalanced through deletions. Since in the most perverse case, a tree can degenerate into a list, thereby losing the significant advantage of the structure, it is important that trees be kept reasonably close to balanced.

The designer of a tree has two choices for dealing with badly balanced trees: periodically completely restructure the tree to create a better balance, or prevent it from becoming too unbalanced. The full techniques for these processes are beyond the scope of this text, but we will provide a brief overview of some of the essential aspects.

First, we want to convince you that it is always possible to balance a tree (remember, the goal here is balance, not fully balanced). We demonstrate this by what mathematicians call an *existence proof,* an example that accomplishes the task even if you would not want to use the example in practice.

THEOREM: Any ordered tree can be reconstructed as an equivalent balanced tree. □

PROOF: Let T be a sorted, but unbalanced, tree containing n values. We know that the traversal algorithms will visit each node of a sorted tree in order, but those algorithms don't require the tree to be balanced. So, traverse the tree. As each node is visited, copy its value into successive positions of an array A of size n. Thus, A is a sorted array. Half the values are above the midpoint of that array, and half below. Use the value at the midpoint as the root of a new tree T'. Build two (equal sized) subtrees of T' containing the values from the first and second halves of the array, respectively. Build these two subtrees recursively using the same algorithm: find the midpoint of the values to be inserted and place half the values in each of two subtrees. ■

Unfortunately, this algorithm is slow. Since the tree is completely reconstructed, every node is removed and placed back into the tree, the balancing must require at least $\Theta(n)$ steps. For a large tree, it clearly is not cost-effective to run such an algorithm very often. It wouldn't be too bad if checking for balance were a one-time task (e.g., if once a tree is built, it never changed). But that defeats much of the purpose of trees as dynamic data structures. If the data collection never changes, an array using binary search would work as well.

Maintaining "Near Balance"

Several special forms of tree have been designed that provide an alternative to either complete or frequent balancing. The general idea of each is that we can keep the tree "nearly balanced." This accomplishes two things: (a) it prevents a tree from becoming too unbalanced before interceding to restructure it, making the corrective action faster than resorting the entire tree, and (b) since these forms need not maintain complete balance, it may be possible to keep them "close enough" to balanced in less time than it would take to completely rebalance a tree. By "close enough" we mean that no path is much longer than $\log_2 n$. So for example, suppose we maintain the restriction that every path have a length, l, from root to leaf in the range $\log_2 n - 2 \le l \le \log_2 n + 2$. In that case, worst-case search time would be $\Theta(\log_2 n + 2)$, which is still technically $\Theta(\log n)$. A balanced tree of a million nodes has a worst-case search time of $\log_2 2^{20} = 20$. In our hypothetical, nearly balanced search tree, the worst case becomes 22—still extraordinarily good when compared to any linear search.

Tree Variants for Maintaining Balance

There are several specialized trees designed to keep the tree "nearly balanced" and when it gets too far out of balance, to restructure it. While any detailed discussion of these variants is beyond the scope of this book (advanced courses such as analysis of algorithms will spend ample time on them), it may be important to mention some of them—*AVL trees*, *Red black trees*, *2-3 trees*, and *B trees*—simply because their names will appear frequently in your computer science career. You can learn more about these in a later analysis of algorithms course or from the references in Section 13.9 (Further Reading).

13.6 ARITHMETIC EXPRESSIONS AS TREES

Although searching and sorting is where trees really shine as a data structure, there are many other uses for trees in computer science. One of the more interesting is the representation of arithmetic expressions. Section 12.2.6 claimed that expression evaluation is a central problem in computer science and showed how two stacks could be used to evaluate fully parenthesized arithmetic expressions. Trees can also be used to evaluate expressions, perhaps with an even clearer algorithm. You already know that every arithmetic expression has a standard unambiguous interpretation, indicating the order in which operations must be performed. A tree can represent that interpretation and guide the evaluation of the expression. A simple example:

3 + 4 * 5 (or alternatively, its equivalent parenthesized form: 3 + (4 * 5))

can be represented as in Figure 13.19. The operands of each operator appear as its children. The parent-child relationships in the tree reflect the precedence relationships in the expression. Thus, the children of the multiplication operator are 4 and 5. One child of the addition operator is a simple leaf containing a number, the other is the multiplication operator indicating the product. Note that in such a tree, every leaf should be a number and every nonleaf should be an operator.

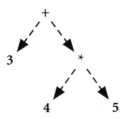

FIGURE 13.19 An arithmetic expression as a tree.

In order to evaluate any tree, one must first evaluate both of its subtrees. This suggests an extraordinarily simple algorithm:

Algorithm evaluate:
> *If the node is a leaf [i.e., a number]*
>> *then return that number.*
>> *otherwise*
>>> *evaluate the left child,*
>>> *evaluate the right child,*
>>> *Perform the indicated operation on the two values,*
>>> *Return that value.*

Of course, this assumes that the tree has been correctly built prior to executing the algorithm. Many algorithms exist for building such a tree from a standard expression, but we will not present them here. Instead, we will show how such a tree can be used for converting from one notational form to another.

Forms of Traversal

If the contents of an expression are printed using the traversal algorithm of Section 13.2.1, the results will be the expression printed in the usual order: 3 + 4 * 5 for the example. Now recall that Section 12.2.6 introduced prefix and postfix notation in which expressions are represented with the operators before or after the operands, respectively:

- infix: 3 + 4 * 5
- prefix: + 3 * 4 5
- postfix: 3 4 5 * +

Interestingly, all three representations can be produced from a single tree using minor variations on a single traversal algorithm. The standard *traversal* algorithm produced the traditional (infix) representation for the expression. For that reason, *traversal* is often called *inorder traversal*. The prefix representation is obtained by a *preorder traversal*, printing the root of each tree and then both of its subtrees:

Algorithm preorder:
> *If the tree is not empty*
>> *then   Process the root,*
>>>>> *Process the left child,*
>>>>> *Process the right child.*

The *postfix* representation is created using a *postorder traversal,* printing the root operator after both subtrees. The proof of these claims is straightforward and is left to an exercise.

These variants on the traversal algorithm have many uses. For example, a postorder traversal enables a very simple algorithm for counting the number of nodes in a tree:

> *Algorithm count:*
> > *If tree is empty*
> > > *then Return 0.*
> > > *otherwise count the left child.*
> > > > *count the right child.*
> > > > *Return the sum of the two children + 1*

Or to find the longest path in a tree:

> *Algorithm longestPath:*
> > *If tree is empty*
> > > *then Return 0.*
> > > *otherwise Find longestPath of the left child.*
> > > > *Find longestPath of the right child.*
> > > > *Return the longer of the two, plus 1.*

Perhaps most importantly, the postorder traversal can be used for evaluating the arithmetic expression. In general, any calculation that depends on both children is a candidate for a postorder traversal.

Exercises

13.26. Build inorder, preorder, and postorder traversal routines for the Tree class defined in Exercise 13.25 and demonstrate that infix, prefix, and postfix notations all can be printed from a single tree representing an arithmetic expression.

13.27. Prove that printing an arithmetic expression with the preorder traversal algorithm does in fact create a prefix representation. Similarly prove that postorder produces a postfix representation.

13.28. This chapter describes three distinct traversals (and certainly they are the most common three). How many possible traversals are there for a binary tree? Describe the missing traversals.

13.29. Write a Java program to evaluate arithmetic expressions represented as trees.

13.7 OTHER IMPLEMENTATIONS

As with the other data structures, there are many possible implementations for a tree. At least three variations on the basic implementation are worth investigating.

13.7.1 Null Empty Trees

The implementation for trees used in this chapter is a direct extension of the List implementation from Chapter 11. Unfortunately, following List as a model for trees leads to very inefficient use of memory, because of the explicit representation of empty trees. A list of n actual values needed only $n+1$ lists total, including the empty list at the end. But in a tree there are twice as many empty trees as there are leaves. Alternatively stated, there is one more empty tree than there are actual nodes. This may suggest attempting to represent empty trees with the special value null (indicating the absence of any object), instead of by explicit empty-tree objects. Such consolidation would reduce the actual storage required for a tree by about 50%. Accomplishing that change requires relatively few changes to our Java code. The most important is that a completely empty tree is represented as null, which in turn means that the tree being nonempty is a precondition for sending it any message, since null is not an object and so cannot handle messages. Thus, *printTree* would have to be rewritten as:

> *Algorithm printTree:*
> *If the left subtree is not empty*
> *then printTree the left subtree.*
> *Print the root.*
> *If the right subtree is not empty*
> *then printTree the right subtree.*

And of course before sending a *printTree* message, the calling routine would need to verify that the tree was not empty. Construction of this variant on the tree class is left to an exercise.

13.7.2 *n*-ary Trees

As indicated in Section 13.2.1, trees need not be restricted to binary trees; a tree having up to n children per node is called an n-ary tree. There are cases where n-ary trees would be desirable. For example, suppose each node represented a question for which there were three possible answers, or suppose that the targets were decimal numbers and at each level of a 10-ary tree the next digit determined which child to visit. In such a tree, all the numbers between, say, 2340 and 2349 would have a common parent.

It might seem at first glance that an n-ary tree would have dramatically shorter pathlengths. Surprisingly, the improvement over binary trees isn't nearly as impressive as might be expected and is almost insignificant when compared to that achieved by binary trees over lists. An n-ary tree could have a potential total n^i nodes at level i. This would be mean a total of:

$$\sum_{i=0}^{h-1} n^i = \frac{n^h - 1}{n - 1} \tag{13.17}$$

nodes in the full tree (proof is left to Exercise 13.33). Now consider two balanced trees, one binary and one n-ary, each with T total nodes. We already know that the binary tree would have height approximately $h = \log_2 T$. Analogously, the n-ary tree would have height approximately $k = \log_n T$, then:

$2^h = n^k$ From the relationship between trees' heights and number of nodes.

$h = \log_2 n^k$ Taking base 2 logarithms of both sides.

$h = k \log_2 n$ In any base, $\log x^y = y \log x$.

$k = \dfrac{h}{\log_2 n}$ Dividing both sides by $\log_2 n$.

That is, an n-ary tree reduces the number of levels by less than a factor of $1/\log_2 n$. Thus, a 16-ary tree would need one-fourth as many levels. The suggested 10-ary tree would need about a third as many. The height is still proportional to the log of n and search time would still be $\Theta(\log n)$, while representing a million node collection as a binary tree rather than a list improved expected search time from 500,000 comparisons to 20, allowing 16 children for each node decreases it by another quarter to 5. Implementing n-ary trees therefore does not provide much improvement in performance over binary trees, but it may better represent the logic of some problems. In general, for any n-ary tree, an equivalent binary tree can be built by breaking each n-ary choice into a series of binary choices. For example, a 4-ary tree could be replaced by a binary tree if two levels of selection can be found to replace a single question from the original tree.

Exercises

13.30. Build an OrderedTree class in Java that uses null to represent the empty tree. Describe any needed changes in the interface.

13.31. Build an N-OrderedTree class that holds *n*-ary trees. In particular, make it so that each node can have 10 children. Use it to sort a collection of random integers so that all values are stored in leaves, and the search and insert algorithms use the *n*-th digit of the integer to select the node at level *n*.

13.32. Prove the claim that there is one more empty node needed for a binary tree than there are nodes with content. Be sure that your proof applies to all trees, not just balanced trees.

13.33. Prove that Equation 13.17 describes the number of nodes in an *n*-ary tree. Hint: look at the derivations in Exercise 7.4.

13.8 CONCLUDING REMARKS

Trees may be the most common data structure in all of computer science—and they are certainly the most interesting. Trees provide a very simple and straightforward mechanism for both sorting in $\Theta(n \log n)$ time and searching in logarithmic time, making them among the fastest structures for organizing and retrieving data (see Table 13.1). Trees in general (ordered and unordered) are probably the most widely studied structure in computer science.

All data structures raise a collection of related issues, most notably the need for links between nodes, a representation for empty structures, algorithms that lend themselves to recursive definitions, and the need for some special techniques within object-oriented languages. The material learned in these three chapters can often be extended to other data structures. Lists and trees may be the most common and useful, as well as studied, data structures. But there are other structures that are also of interest. Fortunately, the concepts developed in these last three chapters can be extended or applied to those other data structures. The next chapter will explore three applications of these principles.

TABLE 13.1 Summary of Data Structure Performance Characteristics

Structure	add	remove	find by value	delete by value	build	sort	inorder traverse
Basic List	$\Theta(1)$	$\Theta(1)$	$\Theta(n)$	$\Theta(n)$	$\Theta(n)$	n/a	n/a
Ordered List	$\Theta(n)$	n/a	$\Theta(n)$	$\Theta(n)$	$\Theta(n^2)$	$\Theta(n^2)$	$\Theta(n)$
Queue	$\Theta(1)$	$\Theta(1)$	n/a	n/a	$\Theta(n)$	n/a	n/a
Stack	$\Theta(1)$	$\Theta(1)$	n/a	n/a	$\Theta(n)$	n/a	n/a
Tree	$\Theta(\log n)$	n/a	$\Theta(\log n)$	$\Theta(\log n)$	$\Theta(n \log n)$	$\Theta(\log n)$	$\Theta(n)$

13.9 FURTHER READING

As with so many algorithmic and data structure topics, the most frequently cited source is:

Donald Knuth, *Sorting and Searching* (*The Art of Computer Programming*, Vol. 3), Addison-Wesley, 1973.

Although the specialized trees designed for improved balancing will be covered in later courses, the original sources can be useful, too. An *AVL tree* (after their creators: Adelson-Velskii and Landis) is replaced by one of its immediate subtrees, and the tree "rotated" to accommodate the replacement (typically the left-right grandchild of the root becomes the right-left grandchild of the new root).

G.M. Adelson-Velskii & Y.M. Landis. "An Algorithm for the Organization of Information," English translation in *Soviet Math. Dokl* (3) 1259-1262.

Red black trees use a novel way of counting the height that approximates the actual height for any node. As long as the approximation holds, the tree is treated as if it is balanced. *2-3 trees* allow up to two values to be stored in a node and up to three children for each node. Just as the root value in a binary tree classified all search keys into two groups (greater than or less than the root), the two values break all keys into three possible groups (the additional group is between the two keys). The 2-3 tree is always kept balanced, with reorganization required only when a third value is added to a given node.

Bayer, R., McCreight, E. "Organization and Maintenance of Large Ordered Indexes," *Acta Informatica*, 1 (1972), 173–189.

B trees are a generalization of 2-3 trees with many children allowed for each node.

R. Bayer. "Symmetric Binary B-trees: Data Structures and Maintenance Algorithms," *Acta Informatica*, 1 (1972) 290-306).

Many textbooks aimed at sophomore (plus or minus a semester) computer science students focus on data structures. Among these are:

Michael T. Goodrich & Roberto Tamassia. *Data Structures and Algorithms in Java*. Wiley, 2004.

Sartaj Sahni, *Data Structures, Algorithms, and Applications in Java*, McGraw-Hill, 2000.

For an extended sample of a decision tree, see:

Watts, Tom. *Pacific Coast Tree Finder a Manual for Identifying Pacific Coast Trees*. Nature Study Guild June, 2003 (latest edition).

Or if the Pacific coast has little importance for you, see any of several other guides by the same author.

14 Case Studies in Design: Abstracting Indirection

S ometimes it may seem that computer science courses deal in idealized situations with only limited applications to the real world. A better way to view idealized solutions is as building blocks for more complex situations or as tools to be added to your toolbox. Although the past three chapters dealt with specific data structures, the tools for building those structures can be used in conjunction with the methods of inquiry used throughout this book to create alternate solutions to similar problems or even build solutions to very different problems. Sometimes the resulting new direction seems like a trivial extension, but other times it opens up seemingly completely new approaches to a problem. This chapter looks at three groups of problems, each based on concepts presented in the data structures part of this text. It outlines or motivates solutions to these problems, but generally leaves the actual details—the design, the proofs, or the experiments—to you.

14.1 INDIRECTION WITHOUT FORMAL POINTERS

Although Java tends to mask the concept, all of the data structures presented in earlier chapters used formal pointers to locate data. This powerful concept, called *indirection*, appears throughout computer science, but not always in Java's form. Java provides a specific tool for indirection, but some problems or situations may be better attacked using other approaches. We first generalize the concept of pointers and indirection, and then discuss both some alternative approaches and criteria for matching an approach to the problem.

14.1.1 Review of Indirection in Java

Before attempting to build alternative forms of indirection, we should first make sure we understand the form used implicitly by Java. Any computing situation requires a mechanism for locating items in storage. Simple variables have an address that for all practical purposes remains constant for the life of an application. Each reference to a simple nonobject variable (e.g., an int) is translated by the compiler into a reference to a specific storage location. But it is also possible to refer to a stored value indirectly by using a second location to hold the address of—or a pointer to—the primary location. Then, in effect, the client can say, "Find the item pointed to by the address held in the variable."

This approach is so pervasive in Java that it is usually invisible to the client. Every reference to an object variable in Java actually uses indirection. A declaration such as:

```
SomeClass obj = new SomeClass();
```

reserves two chunks of memory, as illustrated in Figure 14.1. One location holds all the members of a single SomeClass object, including all the values of the object's member variables, and information about how to find the code for the object's methods. The second memory location, the one actually named obj, holds information about where in memory to find that collection. When you refer to an object by name in Java you are really saying: follow this pointer and find the items you really want. A reference like thisList.head actually means, "Use the information stored at thisList to find a block of information describing a specific List object, and within that structure, find the item called head." This is the form of link or pointer used in the past three chapters.

Indirection is not just a more complicated way of referencing a data item; it makes true dynamic data structures possible. Assignments involving objects actually copy *pointers*, not objects. For instance:

```
myList.tail = new List();
```

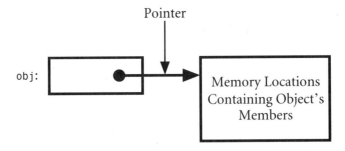

FIGURE 14.1 An object variable is a pointer to the object's members.

creates a new List, but it doesn't actually insert the new list into myList. Instead, it changes myList's tail pointer to point to that new List object, as shown in Figure 14.2. Actually inserting the new list into myList would cause some problems: specifically, there may not be enough storage at the original location allocated to myList, forcing the system to move the entire structure. Similarly, changing tail would necessitate copying the entire new list into myList. With indirection, only the pointer is changed, and it always fits. Similarly, when you pass an object as a parameter to a message, or return an object as a message's result, it is really a pointer to the object, not a copy of the object, that is passed or returned. Although we think of a list as containing its sublists, it is actually implemented with a pointer to another list.

This distinction between pointers and objects also explains why Java has two equality comparisons. The == operator applied to two objects tests whether two pointers themselves are the same (i.e., point to the same storage location), not whether the contents of two structures are the same. This can be useful if you need

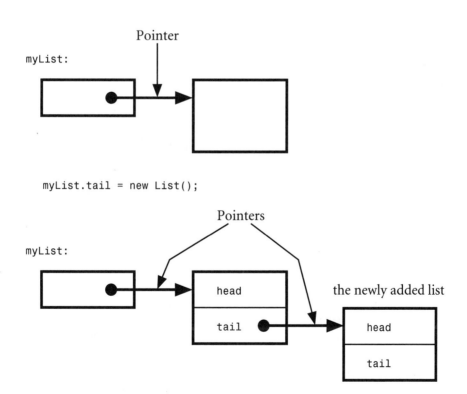

FIGURE 14.2 Inserting an object using a pointer.

to determine whether two references to objects really refer to the same single object. In contrast, the equals method determines if two objects have the same contents. The method returns a Boolean result: true if the two objects are equal "piece by piece," and false otherwise. (For further discussion of pointers, indirection, and equality in Java, see Appendix A.)

14.1.2 Abstracting the Concept of Indirection

Formal pointers are not the only way to achieve dynamic reference or indirection. Although you may not have thought of them in this way, you have already seen the most familiar example of indirect reference: array indices. The array index, in effect, points to a specific location within an array—just as a Java pointer points to a location in a more general memory. The index tells how to find a needed element. Thus, instead of describing the code segment:

```
for (int pos = 1; pos < 10; pos++) {
    System.out.println(block[pos]);
}
```

in the usual way, we could describe it as: let pos be a pointer into the storage area collectively known as block, and use that pointer to access the various locations within block by repeatedly changing pos.

Why We Didn't Use Arrays

Before going any further, note that a student might reasonably ask: can we use an array and an index to achieve the indirection needed for a dynamic data structure? If so, is it a better or worse approach? And since an array is already familiar, why didn't we start with it? The answer to the first question is: yes, with certain limitations. The answer to the others will take a bit more time to develop.

Building a dynamic data structure such as a List as an extension of an array may be the first instinct for some programmers. After all, both arrays and dynamic structures are collections of objects. In fact, this approach has certainly been done—and not just by beginners. But there are also many reasons for describing dynamic data structures without using arrays. The most important of these is that formal or abstract data structures are not just containers for information. Each data structure also represents a model—or the abstract embodiment— of an approach to thinking about a problem. In these respects, lists and arrays suggest very different approaches to solving any given problem. Arrays suggest a uniform, contiguous fixed-size structure; no element holds the special position of head of the structure. Arrays are random access: no path through the collection is inherently preferable to others. They do not lend themselves to recursive definitions for data structures (since you cannot build one array within another) or algorithms. Historically, every array has a maximum size.[1] But the spirit of a dynamic data structure requires that it vary in size. A very small maximum array size (e.g., no train can have more than 10 cars) would be ridiculously restrictive. A very large maximum (if every list needed to have 100,000 storage cells, say) might be wasteful of storage space. In contrast, a list uses only as much storage as is needed. While insertion, delete by value, and concatenation are not natural array operations, they are core ideas for lists. So even though arrays are a familiar concept, they actually might be a misleading approach for thinking about lists and other data structures. Now that you understand the basic data structure concepts, using an array to implement abstract data structures is not so likely to be misleading.

14.2 USING ARRAYS TO HOLD DYNAMIC DATA STRUCTURES

Under certain circumstances, arrays may actually provide a good foundation for a dynamic data structure, and indeed may even enable improvements. In fact, each of the data structures of the past three chapters can indeed be implemented using an array. By examining an array-based representation, we can compare the methods and determine when it may be as good or even a superior method compared to those of recent chapters. While reading, remember that even though the implementation details can be quite different, the abstract concepts for each structure remain the same.

14.2.1 Arrays as Lists

Suppose that the elements of a list are held in the first n positions of an array. Keeping the implementation as close as possible to the original described in Section 11.3, we will add and delete items at the head. Therefore, it is easier to keep the tail constant at position 0 of the array as in Figure 14.3.[2] An array index head can serve as a pointer to the logical head of the list. getFirst then is simple:

> *Algorithm getFirst:*
>   *Return content[head].*

---

[1] Vectors avoid part of this problem: although they can expand automatically as needed, they do not contract automatically when the space becomes free (the user can explicitly trim it); nor do they support the concepts of head and tail.

[2] This order of the list, with head on the right and tail at the left, seems unnatural to some. And in fact many implementations go the other way, as explored in Exercise 14.6.

content:

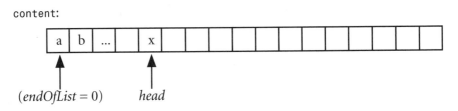

FIGURE 14.3   A list held within an array.

and *addItem* might be written as:

> *Algorithm addItem(value):*
> *Increment head.*
> *content [head] = value.*

removeItem would be defined analogously. Notice that as illustrated (Figure 14.3), in a list containing a single element, head would point to position 0 (same as the *endOfList*), so presumably in the empty list the head must point to the nonexistent position −1. Although easy to define, *isEmpty* will not have the prominent role it has with the recursively defined structure.

Traversal

Traversal takes on a different character. An array-based list is not composed of a head, and a tail as a pointer to another list. So, list methods that return a list or traverse through a list will need to have a very different character. We must think of the entire list as a single entity, with pointers to the first and last elements, with an extra pointer, *currentFocus*, to keep track of how far through the list the traversal has progressed, perhaps starting with:

> *Algorithm startAtFront:*
> *currentFocus = head.*

Moving to the next element (from head toward tail) is simply a matter of decrementing the index:

> *Algorithm moveToNext:*
> *Decrement currentFocus.*

and actually retrieving the element:

Algorithm getCurrentItem:
   Return content [currentFocus].

The last two methods have the precondition that *currentFocus* be a valid pointer into the list, i.e., *endOfList* ≤ *currentFocus* ≤ *head*.[3] While it is reasonable to require a nonempty list as a precondition for *removeItem*, it may not be so reasonable to require that the client check to make sure there is room to add a new node—a test which seems to defy the definition of list. An implementation might rely on an assumption that the array is of sufficient size, or the *addItem* method could have an additional test to provide a warning:

If the head > size of array
   then signal error.

But the Java implementation of error processing is beyond the scope of this text.
   A recursive version of a traversal algorithm might look something like:

Algorithm traverse:
   If currentFocus ≥ 0
       then   Process getCurrentItem
             moveToNext
             traverse.

Notice, however, that this algorithm has one more idiosyncrasy. In order to traverse the full list, *currentFocus* must initially point to the head of the list (e.g., *startAtFront* is called first).

Ordered Lists

Ordered lists are much trickier. For example, inserting an element by value requires opening up a space for the new value. In order to do this, every later item must be moved forward one position. Once the desired position has been found and *currentFocus* set to that position, the actual insertion can be accomplished as:

---

[3] Some implementations allow clients to maintain their own version of *currentFocus*, and pass that value as a parameter to a more general *getItem* method. That avoids some problems that could occur with the method presented here if, for example, a client wanted to have two traversals with overlapping scopes. The given implementation stays closer to the abstract definition of list. Exercise 14.8 explores the alternative version.

> *For counter = head to currentFocus:*
>   *content [counter + 1] = content [counter].*
>   *Decrement counter.*
> *content[currentFocus] = newValue.*
> *Increment head.*

Similarly, delete-by-value leaves a hole in the array, requiring filling in the resultant gap by moving all later elements back. There are any number of variations, for example, deletion could be simplified by using some special value to indicate an empty cell, etc. That simplification comes at the expense of any traversal/processing routines which must ask, "Is this a real value or a space holder?"

Costs

Most of the costs associated with an array-based list are straightforward—and identical asymptotically to the dynamic version. Adding or deleting an item at the head of a basic list can be accomplished in $\Theta(1)$ (constant) time. Building an entire (unordered) list of n elements is $\Theta(n)$ (linear), as is simple traversal. For insertion into an ordered list, locating the desired position requires $\Theta(n)$ time. Then moving the contents forward one position also requires $\Theta(n)$ time. Creation of the ordered list by insertion sort is quadratic ($\Theta(n^2)$) (see Exercise 14.12).

Evaluation

How should a programmer decide if using an array to hold a list is a good idea or not? Perhaps the most distinct requirement is predictability of size of the list. An array has a fixed size and that size must be declared before the array is filled. Second, if the list will require very little reordering, inserting, or deleting, an array might work well. At the other extreme, if the collection will be completely resorted (as opposed to insertions) frequently an array may actually be better since it can take advantage of better sort algorithms. (Exercise 14.1 through 14.12 ask you to build and work with array-based lists.)

14.2.2 Circle Queue

The situations in which array-based lists looked the least promising were those in which the order changed frequently or which had many insertions and deletions. By definition, queues do not allow changes in the internal order or internal insertions and deletions. The maximum size may or may not be bounded. For example, in the input buffer (Section 12.1.2) the total number of positions to hold characters needed may be relatively small. So a queue may be a good candidate for an array-based implementation. As with the list, the queue can be stored in an array, this time with separate indices, *frontOfQueue* and *backOfQueue*, pointing to the front and back of the queue as shown in Figure 14.4. Each index must be a legal index for the array containing the queue. For reasons that will become clearer as we proceed, we will treat the two links slightly differently. *frontOfQueue* will point to the actual first item in the queue, but *backOfQueue* will point to the first available *unused* location—the place where a new item will be added. Thus, *removeFromFront* uses the *frontOfQueue* pointer rather than a constant 0. Notice that the queue apparently does not need *currentFocus*. *isEmpty* works by checking if the first location actually in use and the first available location are the same.

> *Algorithm isEmpty:*
>   *If backOfQueue = frontOfQueue*
>   *then Return true.*
>   *otherwise Return false.*

Although this implementation seems to be much simpler, it does have a major problem: as items enter and leave the queue over time, both links to the queue are repeatedly incremented—but never decremented. Thus, the section of the array containing the current queue content will continuously move up (to the right). Eventually, *backOfQueue* will reach the end of the array. The problem is easily addressed—assuming an upper bound is known for the number of items that might ever be in the queue at any one time—in an improved form called a *circle queue*. Envision the array used to implement the queue as if it were bent into a circle so that the last item in the queue is followed by the first, as in Figure 14.5.

For example, if the array contains 100 items (numbered 0 to 99) after adding a new value at location 99, the next value will be added at location 0. The mod operator is a natural for this situation. This requires only a minor modification to *addToBack*:

> *Algorithm addToBack (new value):*
>   *Set array [backOfQueue] = new value.*
>   *Increment backOfQueue mod 100.*

And of course *removeFromFront* is modified in the analogous manner.

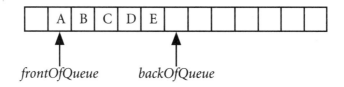

FIGURE 14.4 An array-based implementation of queue.

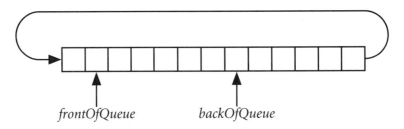

FIGURE 14.5 A circle queue.

As with lists, the use of fixed-size arrays dictates an added precondition for insertion: that the size of the queue before insertion is less than the maximum allowable size. This prevents wraparound—the inadvertent overwriting of existing items in the queue due to overfilling. In spite of the radically different approach, the resulting full class definition in Java can have the same interface to the client as the original implementation (all public methods are the same). Exercise 14.15 through Exercise 14.18 address the implementation of circle queues.

14.2.3 Stacks

Stacks, like queues, do not allow arbitrary insertion or deletion, so it is not surprising that they too are sometimes implemented as arrays. Again, this is only feasible if there is a practical or understood upper bound on the number of items that may be contained in the stack at any given moment.

Like the circle queue, an array-based implementation would use a link, usually called *topOfStack* or *tos*, to keep track of the current top of the stack. Since the bottom of the stack is fixed, no explicit *bottom of stack* link is needed. Adding items to the stack increments the link and removing them decrements the link. Generally the bottom of stack "link" is just the position below the lower bound of the array (e.g., in a stack built in an array with legal subscripts 0 to 99, the *bottomOfStack* position could be a constant −1). Figure 14.6 illustrates the general idea, but the details are left to the exercises (14.19 through 14.21).

Many systems provide hardware commands or addressing modes that, in effect, fetch an item and increment (or decrement) an index in a single operation. The existence of such instructions both reflects the universality of stacks and queues and makes the array-based implementation that much more attractive.

Costs

Array implementations of both queues and stacks require the same times as did the originals: $\Theta(1)$ (constant) time for insertion or deletion and $\Theta(n)$ linear time for building a collection. (See Exercise 14.16 and 14.20.)

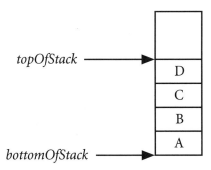

FIGURE 14.6 An array-based implementation of a stack.

14.2.4 Array-based Trees

Binary trees offer a more surprising opportunity for array-based data structures—even though arrays are inherently linear and trees clearly are not. In the previous array-based data structures, traversal was roughly equivalent to incrementing the index, which is really the classic method of visiting cells in any array. If we construct the tree appropriately, the location of both child and parent can be determined by a calculation based on the location of the current node. Recall that since each node can have two children, each level can have twice as many nodes as the level above it. Adding one extra row doubles the number of possible nodes. This means that in a linear structure, the positions of the nodes in one row are twice those of the previous row. Therefore, starting with the root at location 1, the nodes for level h can be stored in cells 2^{k-1} through $2^k - 1$ as shown in Table 14.1.

TABLE 14.1 Positions of Nodes in a Tree by Row

Level	Starts at location 2^{k-1}	Ends at location $2^k - 1$
1	1	1
2	2	3
3	4	7
4	8	15
5	16	31

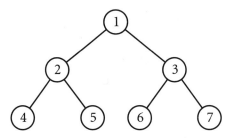

FIGURE 14.7 Node positions in an array.

The immediate children of the root go at locations 2 and 3. The grandchildren are stored at locations 4 through 7 (2's children at 4 and 5, 3's children at 6 and 7) and so on as illustrated in Figure 14.7. In general, for any node stored at location n, its left child is stored at location:

$$left = 2n \qquad (14.1)$$

and the right child at:

$$right = 2n+1 \qquad (14.2)$$

n's parent can similarly be found using the inverse:

$$parent = \left\lfloor \frac{n}{2} \right\rfloor \qquad (14.3)$$

Note that using integer arithmetic guarantees that both children map to the same parent. Such a representation eliminates the need for each node to store explicit references to its children. Instead, it calculates all needed locations based on the current location.

To be practical, this approach does require storage space for each possible node of the balanced tree, not just for those that actually exist. This dictates that the tree be reasonably balanced and have a predictable size range—otherwise it wastes too much storage. For example, a tree with 1000 nodes but a longest path of 13 (3 more than optimal) would need 8000 storage locations. Exercises 14.23 through 14.26 address array-based trees.

Costs

The cost of adding, deleting, or finding a node ($\Theta(\log n)$), as well as traversing an entire tree ($\Theta(n)$), are the same as for the original implementations (Section 13.3.5). Proof is left to reader.

Exercises

14.1. Define an interface for an array-based implementation of List. Try to stay as close to the definition from Chapter 11 as possible.

14.2. Define the private variables and methods needed for an array-based implementation of a list.

14.3. State the invariants needed for traversing an array-based list using Exercise 14.2. State the pre– and postconditions for a traversal.

14.4. Implement an array-based version of the basic List class.

14.5. Use of vectors simplifies some of the methods discussed in this section. For example, the Java vector methods insertElementAt and remove can be used in place of the algorithms for inserting and deleting code. Build a vector based implementation of List.

14.6. Implement a variation of Exercise 14.4 such that later items in the list are stored at higher values, i.e., with head at position 0.

14.7. Modify *addItem* (for a list) to check to make sure that the array size has not been exceeded. Either throw an exception or print an error message to the client.

14.8. Modify the array-based list implementation to allow clients to maintain their own position counter and request nodes based on that counter.

14.9. Demonstrate empirically that the timing results for lists (Chapter 11) still hold.

14.10. Implement ordered list using an array.

14.11. Modify the implementation of Exercise 14.10 so that deletion is accomplished via a "no value" indicator.

14.12. Prove formally that the timing results for ordered lists (Chapter 11) still hold.

14.13. Derive and prove the execution time needed for insertion sort when implemented in an array-based list (don't forget the time needed for pushing items down the list during insertion).

14.14. Construct an experiment to test the results of Exercise 14.13.

14.15. Build an array-based implementation of a circle queue.

14.16. Prove formally that the timing results for queues (from Section 12.1) hold when implemented in an array.

14.17. Some implementations of circle queues assume that the *backOfQueue* link points to the last item added and that the *frontOfQueue* link points to the now-empty location where the most recent item was before it was removed. Rewrite the code from Exercise 14.15 based on this change.

14.18. The implementation of circle queue as given had a problem if the capacity were ever exceeded. Modify the class definition to avoid this problem by using a vector, but continue to ensure that the size of the queue will not grow unnecessarily.

14.19. Implement the stack data structure using an array. Keep the same client interface.

14.20. Prove formally that the timing results for stacks (from Section 12.2) hold when implemented in an array.

14.21. Use the stack implementation in Exercise 14.19 as a basis for a program to solve Exercise 12.13 through 12.15.

14.22. Demonstrate empirically that the timing results from Chapter 13 still hold for trees implemented in an array.

14.23. Write methods `left` and `right` that given an element location in an array-based tree return pointers (integers) to the left and right children, respectively.

14.24. Incorporating the methods of Exercise 14.23, implement an array-based version of the tree structure. It should be possible to use exactly the same interface as presented in Chapter 13.

14.25. Prove that Equation 14.1, 14.2, and 14.3 for children and parents work correctly, specifically that for any node n, parent (child (n)) = n, and vice versa; and that no two children ever get placed in the same location.

14.26. In a worst-case situation, what is the storage cost of an array-based tree of n items?

14.3 HASH CODING

Recall that Chapter 13 described the essential criteria for a collection to be considered "ordered": traversability in linear time. For many purposes, in both everyday life and computing, traversability is a stronger requirement than is actually needed. Consider a customer service hotline: customers phone in with their problems concerning a product. When a customer calls a second time, the service person needs to access the history of their earlier conversations. Typically, this involves the customer's name or a confirmation number. Thus, the system must be able to use that name or number to find a specific transaction. But it is unlikely that the company has a need to print out the service records of all customers in alphabetic order. For situations such as this, searchability is important, but traversability is not.

Observations on Previous Structures

From Table 13.1, we see that not every data structure facilitated traversal. In fact, the structures with the fastest insertion and removal times (e.g., basic list, stack, and queue), did not even support in-order traversal. Being searchable may be a lesser requirement than being completely sorted. Clearly, any traversable structure is searchable (simply traverse the collection until the target is found), but not every searchable structure is necessarily traversable in order (in linear time). Of the traversable structures, trees had the best insertion and retrieval times ($\Theta(\log n)$) and the best construction time ($\Theta(n \log n)$)—all slower than the corresponding times needed for the non-in-order-traversable structures. Perhaps we can find better retrieval performance than is possible with trees if we do not need to traverse the entire collection. This suggests trying to combine the best characteristic of traversable and nontraversable structures.

A very reasonable question to ask is: if we do not require linear time traversal, might we be able to get better (faster) results for search operations?

This simpler requirement actually occurs more frequently than one might expect. Consider a few examples: when you put dishes away, you probably put the plates on one shelf, the glasses on another and the silverware in a drawer. When you want to use a utensil, you go directly to the appropriate shelf or drawer. But you never need to traverse your entire collection of utensils. It is not even clear what the order would be (plates before glasses or vice versa?). Similarly at tax time, a taxpayer may wish to sort his bills and receipts into several piles: automobile related, medical, charity, payroll, receipts, etc. The exact order within each set may not be important, nor may it be relevant where each stack is placed—just that each stack contains only one sort of bill, and that he can locate the desired stack. A professor may sort exams into piles of approximately equal scores ("A"s in one stack, "B"s in another, and so on). He may want to compare the "A"s to make sure that they are of similar quality, but he is not likely to traverse the pile from highest to lowest. An Internet search engine builds extensive indices of Web pages. For any keyword, it must be able to locate the relevant Web pages, but it does not need to traverse the entire collection. In each of these examples, insertions and retrieval are essential, but traversal is not. This section investigates the implications of just such a relaxation of the sorting requirement.

14.3.1 Content-based Pointers

Section 14.1 abstracted the concept of indirection from a stored pointer (as with Java Object reference) to include array indices. Section 14.2 calculated pointer values based on the location of the current node (e.g., a child goes at location $2n$). Even with these extensions, every example so far was designed primarily for traversability. In lists, stacks, and queues, pointers point directly to the next element in traversal order. In trees, pointers serve both to locate a desired target and to facilitate traversal. For array-based structures, the locations of data were carefully organized so that the location of the next item in traversal order was easy to calculate. For the examples in this section, searching, not traversal, is the criteria of primary importance.

Is it possible to construct a pointer to optimize or facilitate retrieval rather than traversal? Not only is it possible, but under the right conditions such a construction is an extraordinarily powerful tool. The technique, called *hashing*, is: decide where to store an element based strictly on its own content or key. Then use the same principle used for placement in and retrieval from a search tree: "Look for an item where we put it." For a very simple example, suppose that you had 26 storage locations, numbered 1 to 26. Then using the `String` method, `charAt`, and treating the result as an `int`, something as simple as:

```
static int hash(String key) {
    return ((int) key.charAt(0))-64;
}⁴
```

could select one of the 26 locations. In the standard internal coding "A" will return 1 and "Z" 26. The name Adam begins with "A" so it can be placed in location 1, "Betty" starts with "B", so her name goes into location 2, "Carl" into 3 and so on. To find an element, use an almost identical process: use the hash function to calculate where the element should be stored if it exists and look there.

As suggested by the method name, a hash function chops a key up into pieces and returns a result based on a mixture of the pieces. In this simple example, the only piece used was the first character, but we will soon see that much more complicated versions are possible—and desirable. In an improbable case with only 26 items in the collection and each starting with a different letter, this simple technique selects a unique location for each item. But it clearly won't work for more realistic situations. Nonetheless, the idea opens up a whole new approach to organizing data.

The example showed that the hash function must accomplish two subtasks:

1. Convert a string (or other type) into an index (or other pointer type).
2. Map the index into an appropriate range.

In the sample, the conversion was accomplished by the cast and the translation by subtracting 64. In practice, the two parts may or may not be so easily separable. The example function maps elements into the same order: B was stored in the position immediately after A, C after that and so on. But there is no need that that be so. In fact, we will soon see examples that do not necessarily store items in order. In fact,

---

⁴ This method finds the zeroth (leftmost) character of the string and treats it as an integer. Every variable is represented internally as a series of binary digits (*bits*) and can therefore be interpreted as a binary number (an integer). It turns out that in the classic representation, the (upper case) letters A–Z have the same internal representations as the integers 65–91. Thus *hash* returns an integer between 1 and 26 (inclusive).

hashing is sometimes called *randomizing*, although that term gives the impression that data locations are selected randomly, which they are not. But we will also see that there are other constraints on the values a hash function may return.

14.3.2 Collisions

What happens when we attempt to build a hash function for larger data sets? Suppose the original hash function was expected to handle not only Adam, Betty, and Carl, but also Bill. Unfortunately, hash will map Betty and Bill to the same location (2), a situation known as a *collision*. Collisions have two different, but interrelated, causes. First, as in this example, there may be more keys than distinct storage locations (there are just 26 distinct storage locations, but arbitrarily many names). Second, the hash function may not produce a uniformly distributed result. For example, the particular hashing algorithm used in the first example was particularly poor. It would have failed even with just the four keys used here. Consider how many (English) names start with A or B. Compare that to the number starting with Q or X or Z. It is clear that names are not uniformly distributed across the alphabet. The example hash function will not map the numbers uniformly into any integer range. Theoretically, sufficient available storage should side-step the first problem, but even with sufficient storage, a bad mapping could still generate excessive collisions. Clearly, every hash system will need to deal with collisions.

14.3.3 Uneven Distribution

Theoretically, if there are n elements and each has a unique key, we should be able to construct a hash function that maps the n keys onto n distinct storage locations. But as we saw, unequal distribution of keys makes that improbable, especially before the distribution of actual keys is known. In general, there is no known hash function that can guarantee perfectly equal distribution without excessive unused space. But it is possible to find functions that do much better than our first example.

Use More of the Key

If the hash code depends on more of the key, a better distribution is likely. For example, a hash function that depends on the first two letters might be better than one that depends on just one character. Thus:

```
static int hash(String key) {
    return (key.charAt(0)-64)*100 + key.charAt(1)-64;
}⁵
```

generates a value that depends on the first two characters. Notice that the function maps the first character into the range: 100–2600 and the second character maps to the range 1–26. No two pairs of characters can map to the same location. So any two keys starting with a unique pair of characters will map to distinct locations. But of course this version still produces a very poor distribution since many combinations of characters (e.g., "qx" or "zb") just don't occur very often. Using the first and third rather than the first and second might be an improvement since there are very few three letter patterns in English. In addition, no combination in this version maps to any of the values 0–99, 127–199, 227–299, ... That problem could be reduced by multiplying the first character by 27 rather than 100 (assuming all upper case characters). But even with these improvements, every word with the same first two (or first and third) characters still maps to the same storage location.

Select Mixed Sections of the Key

Just as we were able to interpret individual characters as integers and use only selected ones of those, we can also break a string up in other ways. The standard operators bitwise and (&), bitwise or (|) and shift (>>>) can be used to interpret the entire string as a collection of individual bits, and then combine any subset of those bits to be interpreted as an integer. For example, when treated as a series of bits, the upper case letters map to the binary sequences 01000001 through 01011010. Notice that the first two bits are always the same. They can be thrown away without any loss. Bitwise operations can avoid the 8- and 16-bit repetitions common with character patterns. Techniques of this form are common, but beyond the scope of this text. You will encounter these tools again in your first computer organization course.

Full Key Mapping

Java provides a better solution than any of these simple combinations. The String[6] method hashCode is a standard method, which as of version Java 1.3, returns the improbable looking:

$$s[0] \times 31^{n-1} + s[1] \times 31^{n-2} + \cdots + s[n-1] \qquad (14.4)$$

---

[5] Although Java often requires explicit casts, it will cast a character into an integer without an explicit instruction. The example in Section 14.3.1 used explicit casts for clarity to the human reader.

[6] Actually Java defines a method hashcode for the class Object. But the String method overrides the general method. In fact, while String.hashcode is very interesting, Object.hashcode is not.

where $s[i]$ is the i-th character of the string treated as an integer, n is the length of the string. In spite of being a major computation, this approach has the advantage of basing the hash on the entire key. For a single character key, this degenerates to almost the same thing as the earlier examples, but for longer strings, every character contributes to the answer. Thus, `"BA".hashCode()` yields 63, but `"Bill".hashcode()` returns 3490947 (note that upper- and lower-case letter have distinct values).

Java's method does indeed break up the patterns of character distribution of English words. Part of this result follows from throwing away portions of the data that are not related to the pattern. Any string with about six or more characters will yield a value too large to be stored in an integer storage location. When the results of an integer multiplication exceed the size that can be held in an integer storage location, the result is truncated and the extra digits are lost. Part of the success comes from the large space into which hashCode maps the collection of keys. hashCode generates a value in the range approximately negative 2 billion to positive 2 billion (actually -2^{31} to $+2^{31}-1$). This makes it highly unlikely (but not impossible) that any two keys in the collection will map to the same value, but it does generate a very large range of values. The client is unlikely to want to use 4 billion storage locations to store just a few million elements.

Costs

With no collisions, then both store and find would be possible in an incredible $\Theta(1)$ (constant) time. Unfortunately, as we will see, we can't guarantee a collision-free environment. In addition, the storage costs of ensuring a collision-free environment are prohibitively high.

Array Size

The usual next step is to reduce the number of storage locations. Clearly, billions or even millions of distinct addresses is too many for most implementations, both because it probably isn't feasible to use that many locations within an array, and because that may be way more locations than there are values to place in them. Mapping the New York City phone book into 4 billion locations would probably require about 1000 storage locations for every key. We need to map the result of Java's hashCode or any other hash function into an appropriate number of storage locations. If the calculated codes are truly random, then simply finding:

$$\text{number of possible values} \bmod \text{number of storage locations} \qquad (14.5)$$

will reduce the number of needed storage locations. Thus, $4 \cdot 10^9 \bmod 10^3$ reduces the range of possible values to 0–999. Unfortunately, no matter how hard we try, most hash codes are not truly random. Some of those 1000 locations will be empty, while others will have collisions. One common technique to improve the situation is to choose the number of locations to be a prime number, say 1009 rather than simply 1000. Then taking the hash value mod 1009 will destroy many patterns.

Unfortunately, mapping a large number of potential hash values into a smaller one will also increase the likelihood of collision. In fact, between elements with coincidentally identical hash values, and limitations on the number of locations possible, collisions are simply a fact of life with hashing. We simply have to allow for the possibility.

14.3.4 Dealing with Collisions

Any attempt to map an arbitrary key into a finite integer will result in at least some collisions. Any successful system will need recovery tools for dealing with collisions when they do occur. Typically, these involve arranging the storage space to accommodate the collisions.

Bins

One approach is to use an array larger than the range of possible hash values and space out the results. For example, starting with the first sample hash function, use an array of 260 possibilities and let hash return 10 times its original result (10–260 rather than 1–26) as illustrated in Figure 14.8. Names starting with "A" map to location 10, those starting with "B" map to location 20, "C" to 30, and so on. While Bill and Betty both map to location 20, there is room for both of them (plus 8 others) in locations 20–29. So the second key encountered is actually stored at location 21. Such a combined storage location is called a *bin*. The algorithm for storing an item then goes something like:

> *Algorithm hashWithBin:*
> > *Calculate the appropriate bin using hash.*
> > *Set a counter to first storage location within the bin.*
> > *While bin [counter] already contains an element:*
> > > *Move to next location (that is, increment the counter)*
> > *Insert new element at position counter.*

In theory, the items within a single bin could be sorted, providing performance improvements based on principles from earlier chapters (e.g., ordered list over list). It would still take one step to locate the bin, but instead of looping as many times as there are items in the bin, it would only be necessary to loop until the key has been passed (an expected 50% improvement (see Section 11.5.3). Similarly the time to sort many small bins is less than the time to sort one large one (see Section 10.1). Unfortunately, such sorting is seldom worth the effort. The asymptotic cost does not change.

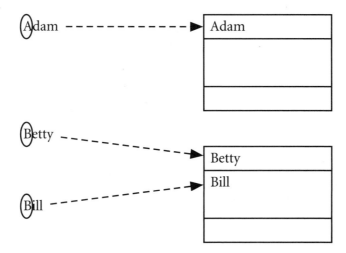

FIGURE 14.8 Mapping to a bin of elements.

Overflow

Unfortunately, even with bins, there can be no guarantee that a given bin is always large enough to hold every element that maps to it (e.g., more than 10 people whose names start with "B"). Since keys are not likely to be distributed completely uniformly, any successful hash table must allow for overflow of the bin. One solution would be to simply place the value in the next (or other algorithmically selected) bin. But retrieval can then be difficult. Another solution would be to have a special overflow bin and any item that overflows from any bin gets placed in the overflow bin.

A List for Each Bin

Instead of a fixed-sized multicell bin, each bin could be a list: that is a value and a pointer to another list. The entire collection is then stored in an array of relatively short lists, as in Figure 14.9. At the abstract level, the insertion algorithm is essentially the same as for the bin: hashing to the appropriate bin is the same, but the new item is simply inserted at the head of a list rather than searching through an array segment. This approach uses a more complex data structure (each item is now a list not just a key value) but it avoids a major problem with the array-segment approach: there is no upper bound on the number of items that can map to any given bin. If there are more items, the list just gets longer.

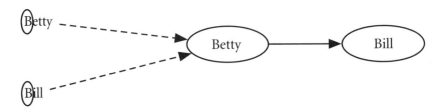

FIGURE 14.9 A list representation of bins.

Load Factor

One quantifiable factor in hash performance is *load factor*: the ratio of items stored in a hash table to the number of available slots. This is key to the performance of any hash scheme. A low enough ratio will ensure a low rate of collisions—even for relatively poor hash functions. A high ratio assures more collisions—even when the hash function is well chosen. The question becomes one of balancing the memory use against search time. Surprisingly, the load factor needn't be as low as one might expect: you can generally expect $\Theta(1)$ search times if the load factor is around 1 or less; etc. It isn't necessary to eliminate all collisions—you just need to keep the number relatively low. For example, if there were many bins containing two elements (but very few with more), then the bulk of searches need look at only one or two locations. If most bins hold only one element, it isn't so problematic if an occasional bin holds several.

14.3.5 Hashing and Empirical Results

The nature of hash coding makes much of the classic theoretical analysis more difficult. Perhaps it is better to say that both best-case and worst-case analysis are uninteresting or uninformative. As we saw earlier, the best case is a surprising constant $\Theta(1)$. But that assumes that collisions do not increase as n grows, which requires both a perfect hashing algorithm and sufficient storage space. This simply is not very likely. On the other hand, the worst-case situation occurs only if every value somehow maps to the same bin but creates prohibitive search times of $\Theta(n)$. This is a very large range and tells us almost nothing about the usefulness of the technique. The perceived performance actually depends less on the size of the input than on the expected collision rate. That rate in turn is dependent on both the size of the bins, the quality of the particular hash function used, and the actual set of keys. A well-chosen hash function with an appropriate load factor can yield a result much closer to the constant than the linear function, but it is very hard to evaluate theoretically. For that reason, empirical results are almost essential. When building a hash table, it is imperative to actually test the performance. Exercise 14.30 and 14.31 explore such experiments.

More advanced courses in the analysis of algorithms will discuss in considerable detail both the selection of specific hash functions and the selection of collision resolution algorithms.

Exercises

14.27. Define a client interface for a "hash table" class.

14.28. The Java hashCode method for strings described in Section 14.3.3 is theoretically that used within Java 1.3. Build a test to determine if it is indeed used in your version of Java. You may want to consult a table of Unicode values or you can find the appropriate values for single characters by sending the message to strings containing just the appropriate character.

14.29. Use a hash function to map English words into an array. Populate the table by using a built-in dictionary such as provided with many operating systems and selecting, say, every 100th word. Then test the table to see if it can find specific words.

14.30. Test the claim that, with a low enough load factor, hashing locates keys in constant time. To do this, create a very large table. Test it with progressively larger collections of values. As the load factor increases, the number of collisions will eventually rise. Determine for your collection at what point efficiency starts to break down.

14.31. Modify Exercise 14.30 and substitute each of the various hash functions presented in this section, plus at least one of your own invention. Can you find differences in performance? Differences are likely to show up as different rates of collisions.

14.4 PRIORITY QUEUES

If you have ever traveled on an airline, you may have noticed that at the check-in counter, the airline maintained a sort of "double queue": a short queue for the first-class passengers and a much longer one for the rest of us "coach" passengers. When a clerk is free, he looks first to see if there are any first-class passengers waiting. If so the first-class passenger gets taken care of ahead of all the coach passengers, even though the latter may have been waiting much longer. In general, a situation in which items are queued not just by time of receipt, but on the basis of a value or priority is called a *priority queue*. A priority queue isn't a queue as defined in Section 12.1, because queues do not permit access to items in any order other than the arrival order. But queues—and other data structures we have looked at—might suggest some ideas for its implementation. We will examine (and ultimately reject) a couple obvious ones, and then explore an interesting solution in an unexpected place.

14.4.1 The Public Interface

In order to find a new data structure with better performance, we can start by describing the needed interface—the public methods that will ultimately define the class—and develop the details later. There are only two and neither is very surprising.

addItem

Add one new item to the queue. The priority must be either a part of the item or calculable from the item.

> preconditions: *P is a properly formed priority queue.*
>   *I is a new item to be added.*
> postcondition: *P is still a properly formed priority queue, containing I.*

retrieveByPriority

Remove the highest priority item from the queue.

> precondition: *P is a nonempty properly formed priority queue.*
> post condition: *P is still a properly formed priority queue.*
>   *The highest priority item is removed and returned.*

isEmpty

Determine if there are any elements in the queue.

Amazingly that is all there is. Nothing in the description allows user access to any other elements, or to general information such as the total size of the priority queue.

14.4.2 What We Already Know Might Help Us

Before starting the task of investigating possible implementations, we might do well to survey some of the material we have seen in the Data Structures part of the book. Specifically, several seemingly unrelated observations will prove useful as we search for the best way to implement a priority queue.

Stacks and Queues

On the surface, this problem sounds like a queue. Both insertion and deletion from queues were accomplished in constant time. Unfortunately, a priority queue clearly requires more. In particular, neither stack nor queue supported a find-by-value operation (or since ultimately, priority is a value: find-by-priority). Only the absolute oldest (for queues) or newest (for stacks) element can be removed. It seems safe to conclude that we need something more than a queue.

Traversal vs. Retrieval

Section 14.3 showed that if we don't need traversal we can sometimes achieve faster retrieval. Priority queues do not seem to need traversal. The criteria for priority queues call for finding a specific node, but it is very unlikely that we will want to traverse the structure—much like the criteria for hash tables. This distinction led to significant improvements in the time requirements for storing and retrieving using hash tables.

Array Embedding

By embedding a dynamic structure within an array, we were able to calculate the storage location of one element from that of another (Section 14.1 and 14.2). In the case of trees at least, this meant we didn't need to actually store the pointers. In addition, the calculation enabled locating a parent when starting at a child, which was not possible with the original implementations of any data structure. And although we didn't do it, we could clearly have calculated sibling locations in a similar way.

14.4.3 Some Nice Ideas and What's Wrong with Them

A double queue system could be a straightforward modification of the queue algorithms with added checks such as:

> *If firstClassQueue is not empty*
> > *then get next from firstClassQueue.*
> > *else if coachClassQueue is not empty*
> > > *then get next from coachClassQueue.*

Now suppose there are not two, but several, priorities. The basic concept seems obvious, but it is just as obvious that extending this approach will rapidly become awkward, with multiple nested conditionals. If we further assume that the number of classes is arbitrarily large or contains an unpredictable set of values, the situation becomes worse than awkward. For an extreme example, suppose a bank prioritized customers by their check book balance. The suggested algorithm falls apart altogether, because there is no way to set up the full set of potential queues in advance, and therefore one can't write code that explicitly nests all of the potential conditionals.

A Single Ordered List

The simplest possibility is probably to implement a priority queue as a minor variation on an ordered list: ordered on the priority of the key. As each new item is received, the standard addItem method inserts the item after any other element with the same priority but before any items of lesser priority. Then retrieveByPriority can return the first element in the list: one with the highest priority, and among those with the highest priorities, the one that has been in the list longest. Unfortunately, as we have seen, the insertion cost is quite high.

A List of Queues

Suppose we had a structure resembling that of Figure 14.10. The left-hand column represents a list of queues. Each row is a queue containing all of the elements having the same priority. Although this may look like a completely new structure, it really isn't. In fact, it turns out to be essentially the same as one solution that we applied to the hash collision problem in Section 14.3.4, specifically the multiple bin solution shown in Figure 14.9. In this structure, each node of the list is the head of a queue. But this small change does generate an improvement.

Inserting an item is simple: add it to the back of the appropriate queue. Removal of an item simply takes the first item from the front of the first queue. Thus, the time required for either operation is proportional to the number of queues: search the list until the appropriate queue is found and retrieve the first element, or insert the element at the end. If there are m queues (one for each distinct priority), then the time for selecting a queue is proportional to m. If m is bounded, for example, 10 distinct values, then finding the right queue has a constant search time (i.e., $\Theta(10) = \Theta(1)$). On the other hand, if the number of possible priorities does not have a fixed bound (say, it is half of the number of elements), the time required to select the desired queue is proportional to n and the insertion and removal times degenerates to $\Theta(n)$. (Proof of these claims are left to Exercise 14.32). Unfortunately, the latter case is typical of many uses of priority queues in which the priority is calculated based on multiple factors.

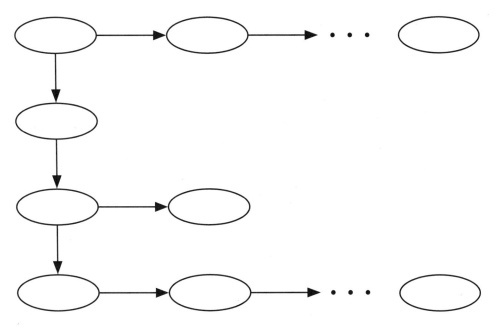

FIGURE 14.10 A priority queue as a list of queues.

What We Have Accomplished So Far

If your glass is half empty, you may feel like the above was a waste of time: it produced no significant improvements (e.g., no mathematically distinct retrieval time). Those of us with glasses half full realize that we combined the computer science design techniques with our knowledge of data structures to create candidate algorithms. Then we used our knowledge of the performance of algorithms combined with our ability to derive one result from another to conclude that these were not productive approaches. That means we neither spent time coding the unproductive approach nor built any empirical tests. We now know more about what we need from our eventual final approach—and we haven't used all of our hints yet.

14.4.4 The Heap Approach

A search tree organization is appealing because it yields such good insertion and retrieval results for an ordered collection, but unfortunately, it just doesn't seem appropriate for a queue. Can we take advantage of what we know about trees? The root is easy to locate; the leaves take the longest. Suppose we could create a tree in such a way that the highest-priority node was always at the root. Then accessing the highest-priority node would be easy (and would only require constant time). Unfortunately, removing the value would leave the root empty, but we already solved that problem (or one very much like it): deletion of an element from an ordered tree left a hole that had to be filled in logarithmic time (see Section 13.5.1). That's not as good as an ordered queue, but it is not bad. New items can be added to a tree in logarithmic time—and adding nodes is where our previous attempts broke down. Our previous attempts were unproductive because insertion was so expensive, but inserting in a binary tree was logarithmic, and that is encouraging.

A variant on the tree structure called a *heap*[7] is ideal for this problem. We will define heap as a balanced tree in which both children of the root are also heaps and the roots of each have key values less than or equal to their parent, as illustrated by Figure 14.11. If the value used for organizing the heap is the priority of an element, a heap's definition guarantees that a highest-priority node is always at the root (Exercise 14.34).[8]

It is actually easier to see how to remove an item, so let's look at that first. The only node to be deleted will be the one with the highest priority—the root. The basic algorithm for removal, illustrated in Figure 14.12, is:

> *Algorithm deleteNode:*
> > *Remove the root.*
> > *Raise an element from the bottom row to the root position.*
> > *Focus on that new root*
> > *While either child of current focus has a higher priority:*
> > > *Switch the current node and that child.*
> > > *Focus on the child.*

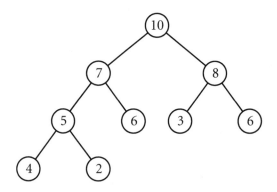

FIGURE 14.11 A simple heap.

---

[7] Not to be confused with the memory organization technique with the same name.
[8] Note that this says "*a* highest priority node," not "*the* highest." A heap approach by itself does not guarantee a fifo-like behavior. However this is an addressable problem (see Section 14.4.5).

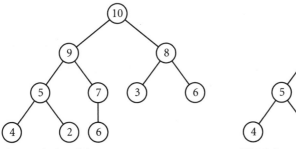

(a) Heap before deletion

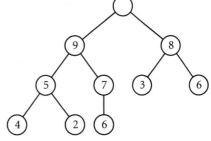

(b) Highest value is deleted, leaving empty root

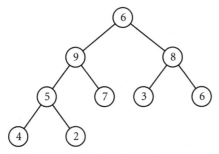

(c) Node moved up from lowest row

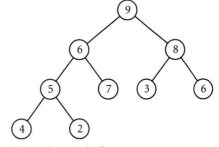

(d) 9 and 6 switched

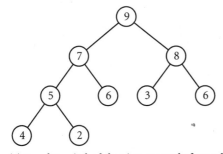

(e) 7 and 6 switched, leaving correctly formed heap

FIGURE 14.12 Removing a node from a heap.

Although the actual deletion takes just one step, filling in the missing value and letting it sink to its appropriate priority level takes more time. The bottom row of a balanced tree of n nodes must be at level:

$$h = \log\lceil n+1 \rceil \qquad (14.6)$$

After raising a node to the root, it will take at most $h-1$ iterations for the value to drift down. The total time for deletion is $\Theta(\log n)$ (see Exercise 14.38 and 14.40). Finally, notice two things about the shape of the tree. First, we have not yet specified exactly which node is raised, just that it is in the bottom row. Second, raising the selected node to the root is the only step that changes the shape of the tree. Since the drifting process is composed of swaps, it will not change the shape at all.

Insertion

The needed criterion for a heap is that the tree must always have the highest priority node at the top (even after multiple additions and removals). When adding a new value to a search tree, the new value was always added as a leaf, but the definition of a priority queue requires that the new value needs to be placed at the appropriate level. We need mechanisms for finding that point and handling any reorganization of the tree that might be needed if the new value replaces an internal node. We could try to start at the root and work down to the needed level, but when inserting into an already appropriately structured priority queue, we would expect that the elements close to the root are in approximately the right order. So it might be better to select a leaf position. More importantly, when starting at the root, there is no obvious method for deciding which branch to follow. Instead, we will start at a leaf position and work up until we reach the desired level:

> *Algorithm insertNode:*
>   *Insert the new element as a new leaf at the first available empty location.*
>   *Focus on that new node.*
>   *While the priority of the current focus is higher than its parent's:*
>   *Switch the child and parent.*
>   *Focus on the parent.*

Thus, we will insert the value at the bottom and let it drift up until it finds the appropriate level as illustrated in Figure 14.13. After an element drifts up, its priority will always be greater than any of its children and less than or equal to its parent. This looks very much like the deletion algorithm and it should not be surprising that it is also a logarithmic function (see Exercise 14.37). As with deletion, the drifting process will not change the shape of the tree.

Since both insertion and deletion traverse a single path from root partway to leaf or from leaf toward the root, both must work in logarithmic time, a result independent of the relative number of possible values compared to the total number of nodes (see Exercise 14.37 and 14.38). Construction of an entire tree should be no worse than $\Theta(n \log n)$.

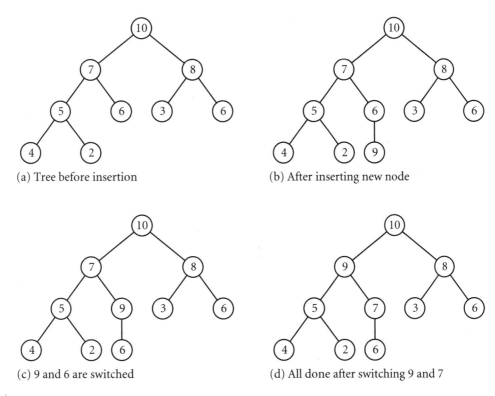

(a) Tree before insertion

(b) After inserting new node

(c) 9 and 6 are switched

(d) All done after switching 9 and 7

FIGURE 14.13 Inserting a new node into a heap.

Pointers for a Heap

We swept a couple of details under the rug. First, we did not specify exactly how to select the position for inserting a new node, nor for selecting the node to be raised during a deletion. Second, in the original tree class, all links pointed from parent to child, but in a heap both insertion and deletion require starting with an element in the bottom row. In addition, the insertion algorithm allowed elements to bubble up, which requires locating parents. The trick here is that although we could theoretically place the node anywhere in the bottom row, we will always select the "last" node in the tree. By the definition we used, a heap must be kept balanced. We will push that one step further. As new elements are added, insert them in the last row, and within that row, always add them from left to right. This will ensure that the leaves occupy consecutive left-hand positions of the bottom row (a balanced tree with all nodes of the bottom row occupying the leftmost positions is sometimes called a *complete tree*). Using an array implementation, the possible positions of the bottom row are in locations 2^k to $2^{k+1} - 1$ (see Section 14.2.4). The k leftmost positions are in locations 2^k to $2^k + k$ (see Exercise 14.42). When we insert a new node, we insert it at $2^k + k + 1$. When we raise an element to the root position after deletion, we select the last (rightmost) node in the last row, at location $2^k + k$. It is easy to keep track of that value: it is the node with the largest subscript and is therefore the same as the total number of nodes in the tree. This requires a private counter *size*, and private method `getSize`, which returns the value of *size*. Clearly, `addItem` and `removeItem` will need to alter `size`. This technique has the added advantage that from any node, the parent of the node at position n is easily located at location:

$$\left\lfloor \frac{n}{2} \right\rfloor \tag{14.7}$$

A Surprise Bonus

Given the construction time for an ordered tree (Section 13.3.5), one might expect the time to construct an entire priority queue to be $\Theta(n \log n)$. And so it would be, if the tree were constructed using repeated insertions as above. That approach would be needed if nodes were concurrently added to and removed from the priority queue. But if a priority queue was created from a large collection of values all at once, it can be built even faster:

> *Place half of all nodes into the lowest row*
> *While there are elements left to add:*
> > *Place half of all remaining nodes in next row above*
> > *For each of these newly added nodes*
> > > *"heapify" the tree rooted at the node*
> > > *That is: let the root element drift down to the appropriate position*

This approach yields a surprising linear time.

THEOREM: Construction time for a heap is $\Theta(n)$. □

PROOF: The proof uses induction and is only outlined here. Use as the base case a tree of size 1, which clearly requires 1 step. Then assume the proposition is true for trees of size:

$$\left\lfloor \frac{n}{2} \right\rfloor \tag{14.8}$$

and prove true for trees of size n. Constructing a tree of size n requires the time to insert a new root, the time to build each child tree, and the time for the value at the root to drift down:

$$1 + 2 \times \left\lfloor \frac{n}{2} \right\rfloor + \log n \qquad (14.9)$$

which is less than $2n$. The full proof is left to the reader (Exercise 14.39). ∎

14.4.5 One Final Detail: Finding the Oldest

The original problem was motivated by a need to retrieve the oldest node of highest priority (as at the check-in counter). But the heap approach only guaranteed that it would return *a* node of highest priority (not necessarily the oldest). Under many circumstances, this is sufficient, or is close enough, but it doesn't guarantee perfect results—even in the simple two-queue example of the airline check-in counter.

One solution is to incorporate two stages into the comparison. Instead of simply comparing two single values with a response based on that single comparison, the algorithm could use multiple steps, based on separate aspects:

> *if priority$_1$ ≠ priority$_2$*
> > *then return node with the higher priority*
> > *otherwise return the node that has been in the queue the longest.*

Exercises

14.32. Prove the execution times claimed for insertion, retrieval, and construction using the "list of queues" approach to priority queues.

14.33. Build a priority queue class in Java.

14.34. Prove using induction that the definition given for heap guarantees that the element with maximum priority is at the root.

14.35. Prove that the insertion operation for priority queues work correctly: i.e., that adding a node to a heap with insert results in a heap.

14.36. Prove that deletion works correctly for priority queues: that removal of a node from a heap (a) leaves the resulting structure as a heap, (b) returns the node with highest priority.

14.37. Prove formally that insertion into a priority queue can be accomplished in logarithmic time.

14.38. Prove formally that deletion in a priority queue requires logarithmic time.

14.39. Prove formally that creation of a priority queue can be accomplished in linear time.

14.40. Design and run an experiment to verify the claims of execution time for a priority queue. Note that an accurate measurement will require large n, so you will want to use simple keys and generate them with a random number generator.

14.41. Create a method `compareTo` that incorporates both the original priority and the arrival time.

14.42. Prove that both `insertNode` and `deleteNode` preserve the completeness of the heap.

14.5 CONCLUDING REMARKS

Hopefully, you had an opportunity to actually work through a number of the exercises in this chapter. In so doing, you were able to build upon the basic building blocks from many previous chapters in order to explore and even implement new solutions to both old and new problems. You have learned that you can attack problems even though you have not seen the explicit tools. In all cases, you—not the text—demonstrated the correctness and performance of the approaches.

Along the way, we discussed several additional topics of data structures: new ways of implementing pointers (as array addresses, as calculations, and based directly on a key), new storage organization for rapid retrieval (hashing), and a new form of queuelike structure for maintaining items in an order.

In this chapter, we used known data structures, algorithms, and execution times to motivate better solutions for new problems. Starting with the next chapter, the final part of the book explores the inverse problem: what happens when the proposed solution to a problem seems expensive? Can we always find an improvement? If not, is it reasonable to just accept the results we find?

14.6 FURTHER READING

As you may be realizing by now, the classic source for information on many algorithmic topics in computer science is:

Donald Knuth, *The Art of Computer Programming*, Addison-Wesley, 1973.

This pattern continues with both hashing and heaps (both of which occur in *Volume 3: sorting and searching*).

Sorting and retrieval are among the oldest areas of computer science research. Perhaps, then, it shouldn't come as too big a surprise that Williams published his first article on heapsort and the use of heaps to implement priority queues in 1964:

J.W.J Williams, "Algorithm 232: Heapsort," in *Communications of the ACM* (Vol 7, num 6),1964.

The earliest published reference to hash functions is even older:

A. I. Dumey, *Computers and Automation* (vol 5), December 1956.

A general survey of hash codes and collision resolution can be found in:

Michael T. Goodrich & Roberto Tamassia. *Data Structures and Algorithms in Java*. Wiley, 2004.

Part

IV

The Limits of Computer Science

One of the themes running through this book has been that you can start solving a problem by designing a simple but perhaps inefficient algorithm, uncover the algorithm's weaknesses through theoretical and empirical analysis, and then, with further design and analysis, improve on the algorithm until you have a truly excellent solution to the problem. For instance, you saw this theme in the progression from $\Theta(n^2)$ to $\Theta(n\log n)$ sorting, and from lists to trees to hash tables for searching. You might expect that with enough cleverness, the ideal algorithm can be discovered for any problem. Surprisingly, this is not true. There are problems that are impossible to solve efficiently, and there are even problems that are impossible to solve at all.

The fact that there are limits to what algorithms can do has important practical and philosophical implications. Practically, many unsolvable problems are ones that it would be very nice to have solutions to. This has lured many a programmer (and company) into wasting time and money trying to do things that they should have known were undoable. Philosophically, it is interesting that computer science has limits other than those of human cleverness, but that computer science's methods of inquiry (particularly theory) are powerful enough to discover and explore those limits.

The remaining chapters of this book study the limits of computation. Chapter 15 introduces algorithms that do an amazing amount of work with a very small amount of code but at a horrendous cost in execution time. Chapter 16 then explores why such horrendous execution times are sometimes inevitable, and Chapter 17 introduces an even more serious limit—the existence of problems that cannot be solved in any amount of time.

15 Exponential Growth

Figure 15.1 is a picture of a tree, created entirely by a computer program. The algorithm that generated this picture is about 20 lines of pseudocode. The picture, on the other hand, consists of over 72,000 line segments, and took over six seconds of computer time to create. It probably comes as no surprise to you by now that the trick to getting such a complex result from so little code is recursion. This chapter explores ways to use recursion to design very concise algorithms for some complicated problems, and the serious consequences for execution time that can ensue.

FIGURE 15.1 An algorithmically generated tree.

15.1 WARM-UP: THE TOWERS OF HANOI

We begin discussing recursive solutions to complicated problems with a puzzle called the Towers of Hanoi. The puzzle is easy to describe, but its solution is not at all obvious to most people. Thinking recursively, however, reveals a straightforward solution that can be phrased as an almost embarrassingly short algorithm.

15.1.1 The Problem

Legend tells of an ageless temple in the city of Hanoi. Within this temple are three poles of diamond piercing 64 golden disks of varying sizes. At the moment of creation, the disks were stacked smaller-on-top-of-larger on the leftmost pole, as in Figure 15.2.

Since then, the monks of the temple have been moving the disks from the left pole to the right pole, subject to the following rules:

- The monks only move one disk at a time.
- Every disk taken off a pole has to be put back on some pole before moving another disk.
- The monks never put a disk on top of a smaller one.

When all the disks have been moved to the right-hand pole, the purpose of creation will be fulfilled and the universe will end.

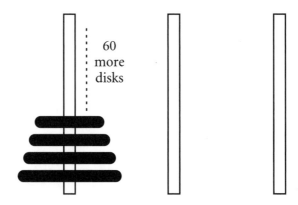

FIGURE 15.2 The Towers of Hanoi.

It's not immediately obvious how (or even if) the monks can move the disks to the right-hand pole while obeying all the rules. The Towers of Hanoi puzzle amounts to figuring out a way. It isn't essential to the puzzle that there are 64 disks, and in fact a 64-disk tower would be quite unwieldy. Thus, the problem is usually posed without reference to the specific number of disks, as follows:

Given n disks stacked smaller-on-larger on the left-most of three poles, move all the disks to the right-most pole, subject to the rules given above.

15.1.2 The Algorithm

Solving the Towers of Hanoi nicely illustrates the power of recursive thinking. Without recursion, it is very hard to solve the puzzle; with recursion, the solution is almost trivial.

Discovering the Algorithm

The Towers of Hanoi would be easy to solve if you could move more than one disk at a time. Then you could simply do the following (see Figure 15.3):

Move the top $n-1$ disks from the left pole to the middle one.
Move the biggest disk from the left pole to the right pole.
Move the $n-1$ disks from the middle pole to the right one.

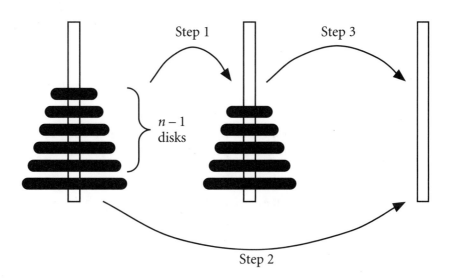

FIGURE 15.3 A summary of the Towers of Hanoi algorithm.

But, alas, the rules of the puzzle say you *can't* move more than one disk at a time, so this solution seems like wishful thinking—until you take a broader view of the problem. Don't think of it as moving a tower from left to right, possibly using the middle pole. Instead, think of it as moving a tower from a source pole to a destination, possibly using a spare pole. Now "move the top $n-1$ disks from the left pole to the middle one" is just another instance of the problem—moving a tower (albeit smaller than the original one) from a source to a destination. This instance of the problem moves the smaller tower from the same source (left), but to a different destination (middle), and with a different spare (right). Similarly, "move the $n-1$ disks from the middle pole to the right one" is also an instance of the broadened problem. The natural tool for solving any problem that contains other instances of itself is recursion. Suddenly, the solution above seems much more plausible, like this:

> *To move an n-disk tower from a source pole to a destination pole via a spare pole:*
>   *Recursively move an $(n-1)$-disk tower from the source*
>   *pole to the spare pole via the destination pole.*
>   *Move 1 disk from the source pole to the destination pole.*
>   *Recursively move an $(n-1)$-disk tower from the spare pole*
>   *to the destination pole via the source pole.*

All this needs in order to make a complete algorithm is a base case. As usual, you can identify a base case by asking yourself what instances of the problem are so small that they can be solved in a few simple steps. The smallest instance of the Towers of Hanoi is a tower of no disks—you literally need to do nothing to "move" such a tower:

> *To move an n-disk tower from a source pole to a destination pole via a spare pole:*
>   *if $n = 0$*
>   *Do nothing*
>   *else*
>   *Recursively move an $(n-1)$-disk tower from the source*
>   *pole to the spare pole via the destination pole.*
>   *Move 1 disk from the source pole to the destination pole.*
>   *Recursively move an $(n-1)$-disk tower from the spare*
>   *pole to the destination pole via the source pole.*

Correctness

You now have a complete, if rather abstract, algorithm for solving the Towers of Hanoi. At this point in the design process we should make sure that the algorithm is correct. When you invent a new algorithm, a quick and fairly casual check is often enough to convince yourself of its correctness. Such checks use the logic and proof techniques introduced earlier in this book, but not necessarily in great detail—detailed logic can be saved for cases in which the casual check raises questions, where an incorrect algorithm would have particularly serious consequences, or where a skeptical audience needs to be convinced. Because this casual approach is a very practical way to apply "proofs" in day-to-day computing, we use it here; Exercise 15.6 through 15.9 invite you to pursue some of the missing details.

You can show by induction on n that the algorithm correctly moves an n-disk tower from the source pole to the destination pole. In the base case, $n = 0$, the algorithm does nothing, and so is trivially correct—zero disks need to be moved, and zero disks do move. When $n > 0$, the algorithm executes its recursive arm. Assume that the algorithm correctly moves towers of $k-1$ disks, and show that the recursive arm correctly moves a tower of k disks. The first step in the recursive arm moves $k-1$ disks to the spare pole, and the induction hypothesis guarantees that this happens correctly. The algorithm then moves the largest disk to the destination pole, which is a legal move because all smaller disks are on the spare pole. Finally, the algorithm moves the $k-1$ smaller disks from the spare pole to the destination; this is legal because all of those disks are smaller than the one now on the destination, and other aspects of the move are correct by the induction hypothesis.

Notice that this proof used its induction hypothesis twice, once for each step in which the algorithm recursively moves a tower. There is nothing wrong with using an induction hypothesis multiple times, and it is in fact a natural thing to do when reasoning about any algorithm in which some arm involves multiple recursions.

A Concrete Algorithm

You can make the Towers of Hanoi algorithm more concrete by making it a method of some class. Think of the entire puzzle as an object, of class HanoiPuzzle. The main primitive action one performs on Towers of Hanoi puzzles is to move a disk from one pole to another, so let HanoiPuzzle objects handle a move message that does that. The parameters to this message are the pole to move from and the pole to move to. Such a HanoiPuzzle class is easy to implement (see Exercise 15.5). You can then phrase the solution algorithm as a solve method for the HanoiPuzzle class (note that we assume here that poles are identified by string names):

```
// In class HanoiPuzzle...
public void solve(int n,        // Number of disks to move
            String source,      // Pole to move from
            String dest,        // Pole to move to
            String spare) {     // Third pole
```

```
    if (n > 0) {
        this.solve(n-1, source, spare, dest);
        this.move(source, dest);
        this.solve(n-1, spare, dest, source);
    }
}
```

Discussion

The Towers of Hanoi algorithm demonstrates a valuable problem-solving trick: sometimes making a problem more general makes it easier. As originally stated (move the tower from left to right), the Towers of Hanoi didn't have an obvious legal solution—but it did have a solution that seemed illegal. However, the apparently illegal steps were instances of a more general problem (move a tower from any source pole to any destination pole). An algorithm for the more general problem could therefore carry out the questionable steps perfectly legally, using recursion. Try generalizing and using recursion whenever a solution to some problem runs into subproblems that are almost, but not quite, instances of the original problem.

15.1.3 Execution Time

If you were surprised by how short the Towers of Hanoi algorithm is, you will find a complementary surprise in its execution time—it's huge. To see just how huge, we will derive an asymptotic expression for the algorithm's execution time; you can then test this expression empirically in an experiment.

Analysis

Because the algorithm does its work by sending move messages, the number of such messages it sends should be a good estimate of its execution time. The algorithm is a recursion driven by n, so a recurrence relation that gives the number of move messages as a function of n is the natural way to count moves. Call the function $M(n)$. When $n = 0$, the algorithm sends no move messages, so $M(0) = 0$. When $n > 0$, the algorithm sends one move message directly, plus however many the two recursive solve messages engender. The number-of-disks parameter to each of the recursive solve messages is $n-1$, so each generates $M(n-1)$ move messages. 1 direct move, plus $M(n-1)$ for each of 2 recursive messages, yields $M(n) = 1 + 2M(n-1)$ when $n > 0$. The complete recurrence relation is therefore:

$$M(n) = \begin{cases} 0 & \text{if } n = 0 \\ 1 + 2M(n-1) & \text{if } n > 0 \end{cases} \tag{15.1}$$

You have seen this recurrence relation before, namely in Equation 7.16. There, we expanded the recurrence for some small values of n, and it appeared that:

$$M(n) = \sum_{i=0}^{n-1} 2^i \qquad (15.2)$$

This sum in turn simplified to:

$$M(n) = 2^n - 1 \qquad (15.3)$$

We proved by induction that Equation 15.3 is indeed equivalent to Equation 15.1. Chapter 7 provides further details of this derivation.

Asymptotically:

$$2^n - 1 = \Theta\left(2^n\right) \qquad (15.4)$$

We therefore conclude that the execution time of the Towers of Hanoi algorithm is $\Theta\left(2^n\right)$.

Mathematically, 2^n is an example of an *exponential* function. An exponential function is a function of the form:

$$f(n) = \Theta\left(c^{p(n)}\right) \qquad (15.5)$$

where c is a constant and $p(n)$ is a polynomial. For example:

$$2^n \qquad (15.6)$$

$$3^{n^2} \qquad (15.7)$$

and

$$2^{n-1} \qquad (15.8)$$

are all exponential functions of n. The important feature that makes these functions exponential is that the function's argument, n, appears in the exponent of some constant.

Discussion

2^n or $2^n - 1$ may not seem like particularly large numbers at first, but a few examples demonstrate that they are. Recall the legend that says that when an order of monks finish moving a 64-disk tower, the universe will end. Let's assume that the monks move one disk per second, and see how long the universe will last. If the tower had started with 1, 2, or 3 disks, the universe would have lasted 1, 3, or 7 seconds, respectively. However, were the tower 5 disks tall, the universe would survive for half a minute, and if the tower contained 10 disks the universe would have lasted for better than a quarter of a hour. None of these times is particularly impressive by itself, but notice how fast they grow. For the full 64 disks, $2^{64}-1$ seconds turns out to be approximately 585 billion years.

You can trace the Towers of Hanoi algorithm's exponential execution time to a particular feature of the algorithm. Intuitively, Equation 15.1 defines an exponential function because each value of $M(n)$ is roughly two times the previous value. This, in turn, reflects the fact that the algorithm's recursive arm sends two recursive messages. This is the root cause of the exponential execution time—moving a tower moves the next smaller tower twice, and so takes roughly two times as long. The general rule, applicable to many algorithms, is that whenever an algorithm solves a problem of size n by recursively solving multiple problems of size $n-1$, you can expect something exponential in that algorithm's execution time.

Exercises

15.1.   Carry out the Towers of Hanoi algorithm by hand on a physical Towers of Hanoi puzzle.

15.2.   Our Towers of Hanoi algorithm uses $n=0$ as its base case. Design a Towers of Hanoi algorithm that uses $n=1$ as its base case.

15.3.   Suppose the Towers of Hanoi started with the disks distributed over all three poles, with the only restriction being that no disk was on top of a smaller one. The goal is to put all the disks into a tower on the right-hand pole, with the same rules for moving disks as in the original puzzle. Design an algorithm that solves this version of the Towers of Hanoi. You may use pseudocode, or specify some additional helper methods for the HanoiPuzzle class.

15.4.   Design an algorithm for solving the Towers of Hanoi with two spare poles (in other words, four poles total). All the disks still start on the left-hand pole, and finish on the right-hand one.

15.5.   Design and code a HanoiPuzzle class. In the simplest class, move could just output text saying what poles a disk is moving between (for instance, "Moving from pole 'Left' to pole 'Middle'"); the pole parameters to move and solve in this class are just character strings that contain one of the names "Left," "Middle," or "Right." For more challenge, keep track of which disks are on which poles, or draw pictures of the poles and their disks after each move instead of printing textual descriptions.

15.6.   State precisely what it means for a Towers of Hanoi algorithm to "correctly" solve the puzzle.

15.7. State the preconditions that the Towers of Hanoi algorithm requires in order to solve the puzzle.

15.8. The recursion in our Towers of Hanoi algorithm does not usually move all the disks in the puzzle. For example, solving a puzzle containing 6 disks requires recursively moving towers of 5 disks, leaving the sixth disk untouched (one hopes). Similarly, moving the 5-disk towers involves recursions that move 4-disk towers, leaving the fifth and sixth disks untouched, and so on. The induction step in our correctness argument for the Towers of Hanoi algorithm glossed over this fact that there will generally be disks present that aren't part of the tower being moved. Put another way, n might not be the whole number of disks in the puzzle. Redo the proof in enough detail to show that this isn't a problem, that is, that the algorithm really is correct even if the puzzle contains disks not included in the tower being moved. (Hint: The algorithm's preconditions—see Exercise 15.7—may be helpful.)

15.9. Explain rigorously why the disk moved by the "Move 1 disk from the source pole to the destination pole" step in our Towers of Hanoi algorithm is necessarily the largest of the n disks.

15.10. Give casual correctness arguments for any algorithms you designed for Exercise 15.3 or 15.4.

15.11. Suppose you had a list (see Chapter 11) of numbers, and wanted to find the largest number in the list. Here is one algorithm you could use:

> *Algorithm findLargest:*
>   *(Precondition: The list contains at least one element)*
>   *if getRest() is empty*
>   *return getFirst()*
>   *else if getFirst() > the getRest().findLargest()*
>   *return getFirst()*
>   *else*
>   *return getRest().findLargest()*

Derive the worst-case number of ">" comparisons this algorithm executes, as a function of the length of the list.

15.12. Here is an algorithm that moves one of the robots introduced in Chapter 2 a long distance:

```
// In class ExtendedRobot...
public void moveFar(int n) {
    if (n == 1) {
        this.move();
    }
```

```
else {
    this.moveFar(n-1);
    this.moveFar(n-1);
}
}
```

How many meters does this move the robot, as a function of *n*? Recall that each move message moves a robot one meter.

15.13. Given a set, *S*, the following algorithm prints all the subsets of *S*. For example, if *S* were the set {*a*,*b*,*c*}, the algorithm would print {}, {*a*}, {*b*}, {*c*}, {*a*,*b*}, {*a*,*c*}, {*b*,*c*}, and {*a*,*b*,*c*}. The algorithm is based on the idea that if *x* is a member of set *S*, then there are two kinds of subset of *S*: subsets that contain *x*, and subsets that don't. The subsets that do not contain *x* are just the subsets of *S*−{*x*} (*S* with *x* removed). The subsets that do contain *x* can be constructed by adding *x* to each of the subsets of *S*−{*x*}. The algorithm recursively enumerates subsets by adding (or not) each element of *S* to a growing "candidate subset," which should initially be empty. When *S* itself is empty, the candidate contains one of *S*'s subsets. Derive the asymptotic execution time of this algorithm, as a function of the number of elements in *S*.

> *To print all the subsets of S, using candidate subset C...*
> > *if S is empty*
> > > *Output C*
> > *else*
> > > *Let X be any element of S*
> > > *Let S2 be all the elements of S except X*
> > > *Recursively print all the subsets of S2, using*
> > > > *candidate subset C union {X}*
> > > *Recursively print all the subsets of S2 using*
> > > > *candidate subset C*

15.14. Phineas Phoole is hiring a temporary programmer. The programmer suggests the following payment terms to Phineas: for the first day of the job, Phineas will pay the programmer one penny. For the second day Phineas will pay two pennies, for the third day four, and in general for the *n*-th day Phineas will pay twice as many pennies as for the (*n*−1)-th. How much will the programmer earn if Phineas accepts these terms, and the job lasts for 30 days?

15.15. Derive asymptotic execution times for any algorithms you designed in Exercise 15.2 through 15.4.

15.2 DRAWING TREES

One of the distinctive features of the Towers of Hanoi algorithm is that it solves a
large instance of its problem by recursively solving *multiple* smaller instances. Trees,
such as the one pictured at the beginning of this chapter, are similar—you can elegantly draw trees if you think of a tree as recursively containing multiple smaller
trees.

Before delving far into designing an algorithm for drawing trees, however, you
should have some idea of how an algorithm can draw. One possibility is for the algorithm to use a class that represents simple drawings, and that provides messages
that perform basic drawing operations. This is by no means the only option, but it
is simple, and code for such a class really exists (see the sidebar). The code doesn't
include a method for drawing entire trees, but you can easily write one in a subclass
that extends the abilities of the basic class.

15.2.1 The Algorithm

Intuitively, a tree consists of a trunk with some branches coming off of it. Each
branch in turn consists of a main branch with smaller branches coming off of it;
these smaller branches have even smaller branches, and so on, until leaves come off

---

A Line Drawing Class

A class that represents simple line drawings is available to accompany this text,
in file LineDrawing.java on the text's Web page. This class is based on the
metaphor of a pen that draws colored lines in a window.

The most important message to line drawings is movePen(*distance*), which
moves the pen the specified distance, drawing a line as it does so. The pen's
position can be described by *x* and *y* coordinates in the drawing window; you
can set this position without drawing a line via the setPosition(*x*, *y*) message.
Distances and coordinates are measured in *pixels*, the smallest points that the
computer can draw. The drawing window is typically a few hundred pixels
wide and high, with the coordinate origin at its center.

The direction the pen moves is described by an angle counterclockwise
from straight right. You can set this angle via the setAngle(*angle*) message.

You can set the color in which the pen will draw via the setColor(*color*)
message.

Finally, you can find out the current settings of pen parameters with
getAngle, getColor, getPositionX, and getPositionY messages.

Complete documentation for this class is at this text's Web site.

of the smallest branches. This idea of branches that fork into smaller branches is a recursive way of thinking of a tree, which we can formalize as follows:

A tree is either:

- A trunk/branch with several smaller trees forking off of one end, or
- A leaf.

Figure 15.4 illustrates the recursive part of this definition, showing three smaller trees forking off of a trunk.

Discovering the Algorithm

An initial outline of an algorithm for drawing trees follows the recursive description closely:

> *To draw a tree...*
> > *if the tree is very small*
> > > *Draw a leaf*
> > *else*
> > > *Draw a straight line (the trunk)*
> > > *Recursively draw two or more smaller trees at the*
> > > > *end of the trunk, making various angles to it.*

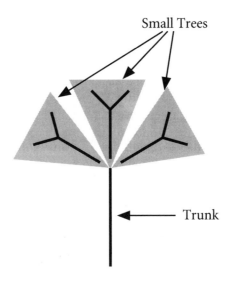

FIGURE 15.4 A recursive way of thinking of a tree.

The next step in designing this algorithm is to define precisely what constitutes a "very small" tree. If we specify the tree's size via a parameter to the algorithm, then a low value for the parameter (say one) can indicate a "very small" tree. Furthermore, we can make the recursive subtrees smaller than the main tree by simply subtracting one from the parameter when passing it to the recursive messages. These ideas lead to the following refined algorithm:

> *To draw a tree of size n...*
> > *if $n \leq 1$*
> > > *Draw a leaf*
> > *else*
> > > *Draw a straight line (the trunk)*
> > > *Recursively draw two or more trees of size $n-1$ at*
> > > > *the end of the trunk, making various angles to it.*

We use *n* in this algorithm to specify the size of a tree, without saying precisely what "size" is. One simple definition is to let *n* correspond to the length of the tree's trunk (with a "trunk" of length one really being a leaf). For now, let the length of the trunk be measured in some arbitrary "trunk units," which the tree-drawing algorithm will convert to the units needed for drawing (for example, pixels) when necessary.

Correctness

This is really the complete tree-drawing algorithm. You can use induction on the tree's size to convince yourself that it draws pictures that satisfy the recursive description of a tree. For the smallest trees ($n \leq 1$), the algorithm draws a leaf, consistent with the recursive description's base case. For larger trees, assume that the algorithm draws correct trees of size $k-1$, and consider what happens when it is asked to draw a tree of size k. The algorithm draws a trunk, with trees of size $k-1$ at one end. These smaller trees are positioned where the recursive description says they should be, and are drawn correctly by the induction hypothesis.

A Concrete Algorithm

Many details must still be provided in order to turn the algorithm into concrete code, but those details either adjust the aesthetics of the drawings (for example, the number of branches a trunk splits into or the angles the branches make with the trunk) or spell out the drawing steps in terms of a particular set of graphics operations (for example, the exact messages used to draw a trunk or leaf). These details do not alter the fundamental design of the algorithm.

For example, consider concrete code for this algorithm that draws via the line drawing class from the sidebar "A Line Drawing Class." In this context, the tree-drawing algorithm might appear as a `drawTree` method of some subclass of `LineDrawing`. All parts of a tree will be drawn as lines—trunks and branches as gray lines whose length in pixels is *n* times the number of pixels in a trunk unit, and leaves as green lines of some fixed length. The pseudocode below uses the following names for the numbers of pixels in a leaf and a trunk unit:

- `leafPixels` is the number of pixels in a leaf. This value was 4 in the program that drew the tree shown at the beginning of this chapter (Figure 15.1).
- `pixelsPerTrunkUnit` is the number of pixels in one "trunk unit." This value is 6 in Figure 15.1.

It is also helpful to define a constant for the number of branches that a trunk forks into:

- `branches` is the number of branches that a trunk forks into, typically somewhere between 2 and 5.

You can choose the angles at which branches fork from a trunk randomly, to make the trees look more natural. This is what the expression `random.nextGaussian()*15.0` does in the concrete code. The concrete method now looks like this:

```
// In class ExtendedDrawing, a subclass of LineDrawing...
private java.util.Random random = new Random();
public void drawTree(int n) {
    final double leafPixels = 4.0;
    final double pixelsPerTrunkUnit = 6.0;
    final int branches = 5;
    if (n <= 1) {
        // Draw a leaf:
        this.setColor(java.awt.Color.green);
        this.movePen(LeafPixels);
    }
    else {
        // Draw the trunk:
        this.setColor(java.awt.Color.gray);
        this.movePen(n * pixelsPerTrunkUnit);
        // Remember where the end of the trunk is,
        // and the direction in which it grows:
        double trunkHeading = this.getAngle();
        double x = this.getPositionX();
```

```
        double y = this.getPositionY();
        // Draw the branches:
        for (int i =0; i < branches; i++) {
            this.setPosition(x, y);
            double offset = random.nextGaussian() * 15.0;
            this.setAngle(trunkHeading + offset);
            this.drawTree(n - 1);
        }
    }
}
```

15.2.2 The Execution Time of the Tree-drawing Algorithm

Just as the two recursive messages in the Towers of Hanoi algorithm caused it to have an exponential execution time, so too one would expect the multiple recursive messages in the tree-drawing algorithm to give it an exponential execution time. The analysis of this algorithm is more general than the analysis of Towers of Hanoi, however, because different variations on the algorithm can involve different numbers of recursive messages—the number of recursive messages is just the number of branches at each fork in the tree. In the concrete algorithm drawTree method, it was set by constant branches. To analyze the running time of the tree-drawing algorithm, we therefore call the number of branches b, and study how the execution time of the algorithm depends on both b and n (the size of the tree).

The work each invocation of this algorithm does is embodied in drawing one thing, either a leaf or a trunk/branch, so we can estimate the algorithm's execution time by counting the number of items it draws. Since the algorithm's recursion is driven by n (the tree's size), we will describe the number of items it draws as a function of n, although we will use b (the amount of branching) in the function, too.[1] Call the number of items drawn $D(n)$. If $n=1$ the algorithm just draws a leaf, so $D(1)=1$. For larger trees, the algorithm draws one trunk/branch, and then recursively draws b additional trees of size $n-1$. Thus, for $n>1$, $D(n)=1+bD(n-1)$. Combining these observations produces the following recurrence relation for $D(n)$:

$$D(n)=\begin{cases}1 & \text{if } n=1 \\ 1+bD(n-1) & \text{if } n>1\end{cases} \tag{15.9}$$

As usual, expanding the recurrence for a few small values of n helps identify a candidate closed form, as shown in Table 15.1.

---

[1] Thus, a more formal analysis should make the number of items drawn a function of both n and b, $D(n,b)$.

TABLE 15.1 Some Values of $D(n)$, as defined by Equation 15.9

n	$D(n)$
1	1
2	$1 + bD(1) = 1 + b \times 1 = 1 + b$
3	$1 + bD(2) = 1 + b(1 + b) = 1 + b + b^2$
4	$1 + bD(3) = 1 + b(1 + b + b^2) = 1 + b + b^2 + b^3$

Noticing that $1 = b^0$ and $b = b^1$, it looks as if $D(n)$ is simply the sum of the powers of b from the 0-th through the $(n-1)$-th:

$$D(n) = \sum_{i=0}^{n-1} b^i \tag{15.10}$$

Such "geometric series" have well-known closed forms (see Exercise 7.4, item 3), yielding, in this case:

$$D(n) = \frac{b^n - 1}{b - 1} \tag{15.11}$$

We now need to prove that this candidate really is a correct closed form for Equation 15.9:

THEOREM: $D(n)$ as defined by Equation 15.9 is equal to:

$$\frac{b^n - 1}{b - 1} \quad \square \tag{15.12}$$

PROOF: The proof is by induction on n.

Base Case: $n = 1$. $D(1) = 1$, by Equation 15.9, and:

$$\frac{b^1 - 1}{b - 1} = \frac{b - 1}{b - 1} = 1 \tag{15.13}$$

Induction Step: Assume that for some $k - 1 \geq 1$:

$$D(k-1) = \frac{b^{k-1}-1}{b-1} \qquad (15.14)$$

Show that:

$$D(k) = \frac{b^k - 1}{b-1} \qquad (15.15)$$

$D(k) = 1 + bD(k-1)$	From Equation 15.9 and the fact that k must be greater than 1 if $k-1 \geq 1$.
$= 1 + b\left(\dfrac{b^{k-1}-1}{b-1}\right)$	Using the induction hypothesis to replace $D(k-1)$ with $\left(b^{k-1}-1\right)/(b-1)$.
$= 1 + \dfrac{b^k - b}{b-1}$	Multiplying b through $\left(b^{k-1}-1\right)$.
$= \dfrac{b-1}{b-1} + \dfrac{b^k - b}{b-1}$	Replacing 1 with $(b-1)/(b-1)$ to get a common denominator for the addition.
$= \dfrac{b-1+b^k - b}{b-1}$	Placing both operands to the addition over their now-common denominator.
$= \dfrac{b^k - 1}{b-1}$	Cancelling b and $-b$ in the numerator, and rearranging its remaining terms. ∎

A tree-drawing algorithm with branching factor b thus draws:

$$= \frac{b^n - 1}{b-1} \qquad (15.16)$$

items when drawing a tree of height n. Asymptotically, this is:

$$\Theta\left(b^n\right) \qquad (15.17)$$

Since we are using the number of items as an estimator of execution time, we conclude that the tree-drawing algorithm's execution time is also $\Theta\left(b^n\right)$.

The Towers of Hanoi algorithm suggested a general rule of thumb about multiple recursive messages leading to exponential execution time. The analysis of the tree-drawing algorithm suggests a more precise form of this rule: if an algorithm solves a problem of size n by recursively solving c problems of size $n-1$, then the execution time of the algorithm is likely to be $\Theta(c^n)$. This rule of thumb reflects the intuition that each unit increase in n in such an algorithm multiplies the amount of work the algorithm does by c.

15.2.3 A Variation on the Algorithm

The above tree-drawing algorithm decreases tree size by a fixed amount (one trunk unit) with each recursion. An alternative, which produces slightly more natural-looking pictures, is to decrease tree size to a fraction of its original value—in other words, instead of the parameter to the recursive messages being $n-1$, make it n/f, where f is a real number slightly larger than 1 (the authors like values around 1.4 to 1.6).

The New Algorithm

Decreasing tree size to a fraction of its original value yields an algorithm that looks like this:

To draw a tree of size n...
    if n ≤ 1
        Draw a leaf
    else
        Draw a straight line (the trunk)
        Recursively draw two or more trees of size n/f
            at the end of the trunk, making various angles to it.

Execution Time Analysis

This change has a surprising impact on the algorithm's execution time. To see that impact, one can try to proceed as with the original algorithm, namely set up and solve a recurrence relation for $D(n)$, the number of items the algorithm draws. The natural recurrence is the following (where b is the branching factor, as before):

$$D(n) = \begin{cases} 1 & \text{if } n \leq 1 \\ 1 + bD\left(\dfrac{n}{f}\right) & \text{if } n > 1 \end{cases} \tag{15.18}$$

Unfortunately, there is a problem with this recurrence: n/f is not necessarily a natural number. You saw a similar problem in Chapter 10, when analyzing Quicksort's best-case execution time. Fortunately, the solution used there helps here as well. In particular, you can restrict attention to just those values of n that are of the form:

$$n = f^i \qquad (15.19)$$

for some natural number i, and trust that the closed form derived for these restricted ns will be asymptotically equivalent to the unrestricted closed form. In terms of the restricted parameter, Equation 15.18 becomes:

$$D(f^i) = \begin{cases} 1 & \text{if } f^i \leq 1 \\ 1 + bD\left(\dfrac{f^i}{f}\right) = 1 + bD(f^{i-1}) & \text{if } f^i > 1 \end{cases} \qquad (15.20)$$

Rephrasing the recurrence in this way allows you to remove the division from the recursive "$D(n/f)$" term (see the second line of Equation 15.20). However, because f is a real number, f^i is still not generally a natural number. Fortunately, though, i is a natural number, and you can try to find a closed form for Equation 15.20 by looking for a pattern that relates the value of D to i. More specifically, you can list the values of $D(f^i)$ for some small values of i, and try to spot a pattern in the list, as seen in Table 15.2:[2]

TABLE 15.2 Some values of $D(f^i)$, for D as defined in Equation 15.20

i	$D(f^i)$
0	$D(f^0) = D(1) = 1$
1	$D(f^1) = 1 + bD(f^0) = 1 + b$
2	$D(f^2) = 1 + bD(f^1) = 1 + b(1+b) = 1 + b + b^2$
3	$D(f^3) = 1 + bD(f^2) = 1 + b(1+b+b^2) = 1 + b + b^2 + b^3$

As with the original tree-drawing algorithm, the pattern seems to involve a sum of powers of b, from b^0 up to b^i. In other words, it appears that:

$$D(f^i) = \sum_{j=0}^{i} b^j \qquad (15.21)$$

---

[2] To do the same thing more formally, define a new function, $B(i)$, as $B(i) = D(f^i)$. You can construct a recurrence relation for B from Equation 15.20. Then find a closed form for B, and use it and the definition $B(i) = D(f^i)$ to work back to a closed form for D.

Equation 15.21 has a closed form:

$$D(f^i) = \frac{b^{i+1} - 1}{b - 1} \tag{15.22}$$

This equation is indeed provably equivalent to Equation 15.18 whenever $n = f^i$ (see Exercise 15.21).

Execution Time is No Longer Exponential

Equation 15.22 differs from the closed form for the original tree-drawing algorithm because the exponent involves i rather than n. To make the two closed forms easier to compare, rewrite Equation 15.22 in terms of n by recalling that $n = f^i$, and so:

$$i = \log_f n \tag{15.23}$$

Thus, you can replace i with $\log_f n$ (and f^i with n) in Equation 15.22, and simplify the result:

$$D(n) = \frac{b^{\log_f n + 1} - 1}{b - 1} \qquad \text{Replacing } f^i \text{ with } n \text{ and } i \text{ with } \log_f n.$$

$$= \frac{b \cdot b^{\log_f n} - 1}{b - 1} \qquad \text{Adding exponents is equivalent to multiplying,} \\ \text{so } b^{\log_f n + 1} = b \cdot b^{\log_f n}.$$

$$= \frac{b\left(f^{\log_f b}\right)^{\log_f n} - 1}{b - 1} \qquad \text{Replacing } b \text{ with } f^{\log_f b} \text{ (From the definition of} \\ \text{``logarithm'', } \log_f b \text{ is the power } f \text{ must be} \\ \text{raised to in order to make } b.)$$

$$= \frac{b\left(f^{\log_f n}\right)^{\log_f b} - 1}{b - 1} \qquad \text{Interchanging the exponents of } f.$$

$$= \frac{bn^{\log_f b} - 1}{b - 1} \qquad \text{By the definition of ``logarithm,'' } f^{\log_f n} = n.$$

Asymptotically:

$$\frac{bn^{\log_f b} - 1}{b - 1} = \Theta\left(n^{\log_f b}\right) \tag{15.24}$$

Notice that this is no longer an exponential function. Rather, because f and b are both constants, $\log_f b$ is too, and so:

$$n^{\log_f b} \tag{15.25}$$

is a polynomial. For example, if f were 2 and b were 4, then:

$$\log_f b = \log_2 4 = 2 \tag{15.26}$$

and so the new algorithm would execute in $\Theta(n^2)$ time. Because we restricted n to only certain values in deriving the closed form for $D(n)$, we can use that closed form for the new algorithm's asymptotic behavior, but not its exact behavior. However, just knowing the asymptotic execution time is still valuable: every polynomial is smaller than any exponential function, so the new algorithm is far faster than the original.

This analysis illustrates another rule of thumb about the execution times of recursive algorithms. If an algorithm solves problems of size n by recursively solving subproblems of size n/c, for some constant c, then expect the algorithm's execution time to somehow depend on $\log_c n$. Logarithms and exponential functions are inverses of each other, so, as you saw in this example, this logarithmic behavior can cancel out the exponential growth normally caused by multiple recursive messages.

Exercises

15.16. A *Koch curve* is a jagged line whose exact shape is defined by the following recursion (also see Figure 15.5):

- (Base Case) An order 0 Koch curve is a straight line, as illustrated in Part B of Figure 15.5.
- (Recursive Case) An order n Koch curve is created by replacing every straight line in an order $n-1$ Koch curve with four lines as shown in Part A of Figure 15.5. Each new line is one-third as long as the line from the order $n-1$ curve, and the angles between the new lines are as shown in the figure. The first and last of the new lines head in the same direction as the line from the order $n-1$ curve.

For example, Part B of Figure 15.5 illustrates order 0, order 1 and order 2 Koch curves.

Design and code an algorithm for drawing Koch curves. Your algorithm should take the order of the curve as a parameter. You may use a line-drawing class such as the one introduced in this section in your design.

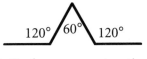

A. Koch curve construction.

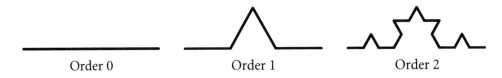

Order 0   Order 1   Order 2

B. Example Koch curves.

FIGURE 15.5 Koch curves.

15.17. A *Dragon curve* (so called because sufficiently large ones look a bit like drag-
ons) is a jagged line defined by the following recursion (also see Figure
15.6):

- ◾ (Base Case) An order 1 dragon curve is two straight lines meeting at a
  90° angle, as shown in Part B of Figure 15.6.
- ◾ (Recursive Case) An order n dragon curve is created by replacing each
  straight line in an order $n-1$ dragon curve with a pair of lines. Each line
  is $\sqrt{2}/2$ times as long as the lines in the order $n-1$ curve would be. Part
  A of Figure 15.6 shows how fragments of order n dragon curve (heavy
  lines) evolve from fragments of order $n-1$ curve (dashed lines). Note
  that the right part of an order n curve bends in the opposite direction
  from the left part.

For example, Part B of Figure 15.6 illustrates order 1, order 2, and order 3
dragon curves.

Design and code an algorithm for drawing dragon curves. Your algorithm should take the order of the curve as a parameter. You may use a line-
drawing class such as the one introduced in this section in your design.

15.18. You can think of a maze as a network of passages and intersections. Passages
are what you move along as you explore a maze. Intersections are where ex-
plorers must make choices of which direction to go next, that is, they are
places where passages meet.

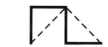

A. Dragon curve construction.

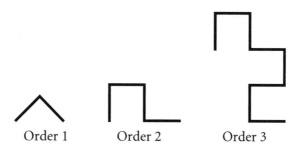

Order 1   Order 2   Order 3

B. Example dragon curves.

FIGURE 15.6 Dragon curves.

Design a recursive algorithm for exploring mazes. You may write your algorithm in an abstract enough pseudocode that you needn't explain how to represent a maze, you may simply assume that whatever executes the algorithm can follow passages, recognize intersections, etc. Your algorithm will need to handle two particular problems in mazes though:

■ Passages can have dead ends, and there can be some intersections from which all passages lead to dead ends. Thus, invocations of your algorithm may need to tell their invoker whether they eventually (possibly after several recursions) found a way out of the maze, or whether everything they could explore eventually came to a dead end. Designing the algorithm to return a value that provides this information might be a good idea. You may assume that whatever executes your algorithm can detect dead ends and exits from the maze.

■ Passages can loop back to places the explorer has already visited. If your algorithm needs to recognize such "cycles," you may assume that it can mark passages or intersections (for instance, by writing on the wall of the maze, dropping a crumb on the ground, etc.), and can tell whether a passage or intersection is marked.

15.19. Derive an expression for just the number of leaves (but not trunks and branches) in a tree of height n and branching factor b drawn by Section 15.2.1's tree-drawing algorithm.

15.20. Derive asymptotic execution times for any algorithms you designed in Exercise 15.16 or 15.17. Express execution time as a function of the order of the Koch or dragon curve.

15.21. Prove that Equation 15.22 gives the correct closed form for the recurrence relation defined in Equation 15.18 for ns that are exact powers of f. (Hint: What should you do induction on?)

15.22. Design and conduct an experiment to test the hypothesis that Equation 15.24 gives the asymptotic execution time of the variant tree-drawing algorithm for all tree sizes, not just those that are powers of f.

15.23. The text illustrates how the variant tree-drawing algorithm can have an execution time that is a quadratic function of tree size. Can the execution time be related to tree size by polynomials of other degrees? If so, give some examples and explain how they could arise.

15.24. The text asserts that "any exponential function is larger than every polynomial." What this means precisely is that any exponential function is *asymptotically* larger than every polynomial, i.e., if $f(n)$ is some exponential function of n, and $p(n)$ is a polynomial, then for every positive number c there is some value n_0 such that $f(n) \geq cp(n)$ for all $n \geq n_0$. Prove this.

15.25. Here is an algorithm that prints a non-negative integer, n, as a base b numeral:

```
public static void printAsBase(int n, int b) {
    if (n < b) {
        System.out.print(n);
    }
    else {
        printAsBase(n / b, b);
        System.out.print(n % b);
    }
}
```

Derive the asymptotic execution time of this algorithm, as a function of n and b.

15.3 THE EMPIRICAL SIGNIFICANCE OF EXPONENTIAL TIME

As a practical matter, exponential execution time means that an algorithm is too slow for serious use. The best way to appreciate why is to compare actual running times of exponential-time programs to running times of faster programs. To this end, we discuss some concrete execution time measurements taken from a family of algorithms whose theoretical execution times range from $\Theta(n)$ to $\Theta(2^n)$.

The algorithms we timed were implemented as static methods in Java (they are available on this book's Web site, in file Counters.java). All compute simple numeric functions of natural numbers. One simply returns its parameter, n; one computes n^2; the third computes 2^n. All the methods basically perform their computations by counting. For example, the method that returns n is:

```java
private static int countN(int n) {
    int result = 0;
    for (int i = 0; i < n; i++) {
        result = result + 1;
    }
    return result;
}
```

The method that computes n^2 builds on countN, thus:

```java
private static int countNSquared(int n) {
    int result = 0;
    for (int i = 0; i < n; i++) {
        result = result + countN(n);
    }
    return result;
}
```

The method that computes 2^n is essentially Chapter 7's powerOf2 method. Each of the methods theoretically runs in time proportional to the mathematical function it computes (Exercise 15.26 allows you to verify this). Specifically, the method that returns n runs in $\Theta(n)$ time, the n^2 method in $\Theta(n^2)$ time, and the 2^n function in $\Theta(2^n)$ time. The measured times thus reflect two polynomial growth rates and an exponential one.

We measured running times for each of these methods on values of n between 2 and 9. We collected all times using Section 9.3's iterative technique for measuring short times. We averaged 25 measurements of each function's execution time for each n. We made all the measurements on a 550 MHz Macintosh PowerBook G4 computer with 768 megabytes of main memory and 256 kilobytes of level-2 cache. Table 15.3 presents the results.

TABLE 15.3 Average Times to Compute n, n^2, and 2^n

n	Microseconds to Compute...		
	n	n^2	2^n
2	0.05	0.13	0.23
3	0.05	0.19	0.28
4	0.06	0.28	1.18
5	0.07	0.39	2.06
6	0.08	0.52	6.91
7	0.09	0.66	7.73
8	0.10	0.84	27.56
9	0.11	1.02	30.90

Exponential execution time is of an utterly different magnitude than polynomial time. Figure 15.7 plots execution time versus n for the algorithms in Table 15.3. While the polynomial times all fit on the same graph, the curve for the exponential time climbs almost literally straight off the graph. This is a concrete example of the previously mentioned fact that exponential functions always grow faster than polynomials. Also notice that in order to get manageably small times from the exponential time algorithm, we had to use small values of n in our experiment (2 to 9, in contrast to problem sizes of hundreds or thousands of items elsewhere in this text).

Exercises

15.26. Derive expressions for the number of addition operations that the countN and countNSquared methods perform, as functions of n. Check that these expressions have the asymptotic forms we claimed.

15.27. Extend the text's time measurements for the 2^n algorithm beyond $n = 9$. The times will probably soon become long enough that you won't need to measure them iteratively any more. You can get Java code for the algorithm from the text's Web site, or can use Chapter 7's powerOf2 method. How large does n get before you can no longer afford the time required to run your program?

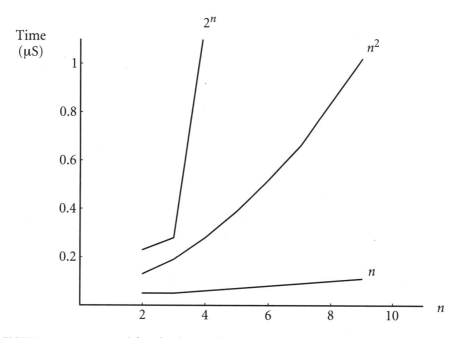

FIGURE 15.7 Exponential and polynomial times to compute certain numeric functions.

15.4 REDUCING EXPONENTIAL COSTS

As the times in Section 15.3 suggest, exponential execution time is a "kiss of death" for an algorithm—an algorithm with an exponential execution time cannot solve problems of the sizes people normally want. This means that as an algorithm designer, you need to recognize when your algorithms have exponential execution times, and abandon any that do in favor of more efficient ones. There is no universal way of reducing exponential time to subexponential, but a technique known as "dynamic programming" helps in some cases. Full treatment of dynamic programming is beyond the scope of this book, but this section introduces the technique by way of an example, in hopes of inspiring you to learn more about it later.

15.4.1 The Fibonacci Numbers

In 1202, Leonardo of Pisa, also known as Fibonacci, wrote a book of arithmetic examples. One example concerned a family of rabbits in which each pair breeds exactly one pair of babies every month, starting in their second month of life. Thus, the number of pairs of rabbits in month m is the number in month $m-1$ (all existing rabbits survive from month to month), plus the number in month $m-2$ (the number of pairs old enough to breed in month m, and so the number of new baby pairs). In formal terms:

$$F(m) = F(m-1) + F(m-2) \tag{15.27}$$

where $F(m)$ is the number of pairs of rabbits in month m (F is the traditional name for this function, in honor of Fibonacci). Fibonacci started his example with one pair of babies at the beginning of time ($F(0) = 1$), and thus still one pair in the first month ($F(1) = 1$, because the babies aren't old enough to breed until the second month). With this information we can describe the number of pairs of rabbits with a recurrence relation, usually given as:

$$F(m) = \begin{cases} 1 & \text{if } m = 0 \\ 1 & \text{if } m = 1 \\ F(m-1) + F(m-2) & \text{if } m > 1 \end{cases} \tag{15.28}$$

The values of $F(m)$ are known as the *Fibonacci numbers*.

15.4.2 An Obvious Fibonacci Number Algorithm

It requires hardly any thought to transcribe Equation 15.28 into an algorithm for computing the m-th Fibonacci number. To do so in Java, we define a MoreMath class that provides mathematical calculations not included in Java's standard Math class; the Fibonacci method will be a static method of this class. The method returns a long integer because Fibonacci numbers can be very large:

```
// In class MoreMath...
// Precondition: m is a natural number.
public static long fibonacci(int m) {
    if (m == 0) {
        return 1;
    }
    else if (m == 1) {
        return 1;
    }
    else {
        return fibonacci(m-1) + fibonacci(m-2);
    }
}
```

Execution Time

The two recursions in the last arm of the conditional should make you suspect that this algorithm has an exponential execution time. To see if this suspicion is correct, count the number of additions the algorithm does. The number of additions depends on m. When m is 0 or 1, the algorithm does no additions. When m is larger than 1, the algorithm does as many additions as needed to compute `fibonacci`$(m-1)$, plus the number needed to compute `fibonacci`$(m-2)$, plus one more to add those two Fibonacci numbers. Calling the number of additions $A(m)$, the following recurrence relation summarizes this thinking:

$$A(m) = \begin{cases} 0 & \text{if } m \le 1 \\ 1 + A(m-1) + A(m-2) & \text{if } m > 1 \end{cases} \tag{15.29}$$

In Equation 15.29 we have finally come to a recurrence relation that cannot be solved by expanding some examples and looking for a pattern. Techniques for solving this recurrence do exist (see the "Further Reading" section), but we can show the exponential execution time of the Fibonacci algorithm in an easier way: by showing that it is greater than one exponential function, but less than another.

To find both functions, notice that $A(m)$ is nondecreasing. In other words, $A(m) \ge A(m-1)$ whenever $A(m)$ and $A(m-1)$ are both defined. This means that the right-hand side of the recursive part of Equation 15.29, $1 + A(m-1) + A(m-2)$, is less than or equal to what it would be if its $A(m-2)$ were replaced by the larger $A(m-1)$ (making the expression $1 + A(m-1) + A(m-1)$, which equals $1 + 2A(m-1)$), and greater than or equal to what it would be if the $A(m-1)$ were replaced by $A(m-2)$ (making the expression $1 + 2A(m-2)$). Thus, we can define a function $G(m)$ that is greater than (or equal to) $A(m)$, and a function $L(m)$ that is less than (or equal to) $A(m)$, as follows:

$$G(m) = \begin{cases} 0 & \text{if } m \le 1 \\ 1 + 2G(m-1) & \text{if } m > 1 \end{cases} \tag{15.30}$$

$$L(m) = \begin{cases} 0 & \text{if } m \le 1 \\ 1 + 2L(m-2) & \text{if } m > 1 \end{cases} \tag{15.31}$$

The Closed Form for *G(m)*

The definition of $G(m)$ looks very familiar by now. It's essentially Equation 15.1, except that $G(m)$ starts growing when $m > 1$ rather than when $m > 0$. This suggests that $G(m)$'s closed form should be similar to Equation 15.1's, but lag one factor of two behind it. In other words, since Equation 15.1's closed form is $2^n - 1$, the closed form for $G(m)$ should be:

$$G(m) = 2^{m-1} - 1 \qquad (15.32)$$

(at least whenever $m \geq 1$; the reasoning that $G(m)$ grows like Equation 15.1 doesn't take $G(0)$ into account at all). You can prove by induction that this guess about $G(m)$'s closed form is correct (see Exercise 15.28).

The Closed Form for L(m)

You can find a closed form for $L(m)$ by the usual strategy of expanding L for some small values of m and looking for a pattern. Table 15.4 shows the results.

TABLE 15.4 Some values of $L(m)$, as defined by Equation 15.31

m	$L(m)$
0	0
1	0
2	$1 + 2L(0) = 1 + 2 \times 0 = 1$
3	$1 + 2L(1) = 1 + 2 \times 0 = 1$
4	$1 + 2L(2) = 1 + 2 \times 1 = 1 + 2$
5	$1 + 2L(3) = 1 + 2 \times 1 = 1 + 2$
6	$1 + 2L(4) = 1 + 2(1+2) = 1 + 2 + 2^2$
7	$1 + 2L(5) = 1 + 2(1+2) = 1 + 2 + 2^2$
8	$1 + 2L(6) = 1 + 2(1+2+2^2) = 1 + 2 + 2^2 + 2^3$
9	$1 + 2L(7) = 1 + 2(1+2+2^2) = 1 + 2 + 2^2 + 2^3$

Once again the pattern seems to involve sums of powers of two. However, the sums don't add a new power of two for every line in the table, but rather for every other line. The highest exponent in the sums is:

$$\left\lfloor \frac{m}{2} \right\rfloor - 1 \qquad (15.33)$$

(Recall that "$\lfloor \ldots \rfloor$" indicates truncating away any fractional part of a number—see Section 5.4.1.) Thus, the closed form for $L(m)$ appears to be:

$$L(m) = \sum_{i=0}^{\lfloor m/2 \rfloor - 1} 2^i \qquad (15.34)$$

Equation 15.34 in turn simplifies to:

$$L(m) = 2^{\lfloor m/2 \rfloor} - 1 \qquad (15.35)$$

To prove that Equation 15.35 really is the closed form for Equation 15.31, use induction on m. However, the induction must be slightly different from previous inductions we have done. It will have two base cases, corresponding to Equation 15.31's two base cases ($m = 0$ and $m = 1$), and the induction step will use an assumption about $k - 2$ to prove a conclusion about k, since the equation defines $L(m)$ from $L(m-2)$. Such a proof is a valid induction, but each part is essential: the $m = 0$ base case combines with the induction step to prove that the closed form is correct for all even numbers, but proves nothing about odd numbers; the $m = 1$ base case and induction step prove the closed form correct for odd numbers, but say nothing about even ones.

THEOREM: $L(m)$, as defined by the recurrence in Equation 15.31, is equal to $2^{\lfloor m/2 \rfloor} - 1$. $\square$

PROOF: The proof is by induction on m.

Base Case: $m = 0$.

$2^{\lfloor m/2 \rfloor} - 1 = 2^0 - 1$ Because $m = 0$ and $\lfloor 0/2 \rfloor = 0$.

        $= 1 - 1$ Replacing 2^0 with 1.

        $= 0$

        $= L(0)$ From the base case in Equation 15.31.

Base Case: $m = 1$.

$2^{\lfloor m/2 \rfloor} - 1 = 0$ Because $m = 1$ and $\lfloor 1/2 \rfloor = 0$.

        $= L(1)$ From the base case in Equation 15.31.

Induction Step: Assume that for some $k - 2 \geq 0$,

$$L(k-2) = 2^{\lfloor (k-2)/2 \rfloor} - 1 \qquad (15.36)$$

Show that:

$$L(k) = 2^{\lfloor k/2 \rfloor} - 1 \tag{15.37}$$

$k - 2 \geq 0$ implies that $k > 1$, so $L(k)$ is defined by the recursive arm of Equation 15.31:

$L(k) = 1 + 2L(k-2)$ Equation 15.31.

$\quad = 1 + 2\left(2^{\lfloor (k-2)/2 \rfloor} - 1\right)$ Using the induction hypothesis to replace $L(k-2)$.

$\quad = 1 + 2 \cdot 2^{\lfloor (k-2)/2 \rfloor} - 2$ Distributing 2 into $2^{\lfloor (k-2)/2 \rfloor} - 1$.

$\quad = 1 + 2^{\lfloor (k-2)/2 \rfloor + 1} - 2$ Because $2 \cdot 2^{\lfloor (k-2)/2 \rfloor} = 2^{\lfloor (k-2)/2 \rfloor + 1}$.

$\quad = 1 + 2^{\lfloor (k-2)/2 + 1 \rfloor} - 2$ Integers added to a "floor" can be moved inside the floor operator.

$\quad = 1 + 2^{\lfloor (k-2)/2 + 2/2 \rfloor} - 2$ Giving $(k-2)/2$ and 1 a common denominator.

$\quad = 1 + 2^{\lfloor k/2 \rfloor} - 2$ Adding $(k-2)/2$ to $2/2$ and simplifying.

$\quad = 2^{\lfloor k/2 \rfloor} - 1$ Combining 1 and -2. ■

Asymptotically:

$$2^{\lfloor m/2 \rfloor} - 1 = \Theta\left(2^{m/2}\right) \tag{15.38}$$

This provides our lower limit on the execution time of this Fibonacci algorithm. Since $2^{m/2}$ is the same as $\sqrt{2}^{\,m}$, you can also express this limit as:

$$\Theta\left(\sqrt{2}^{\,m}\right) \tag{15.39}$$

The upper limit on the algorithm's execution time was $\Theta(2^m)$, so the execution time is indeed exponential, with the base for the exponentiation lying somewhere between $\sqrt{2}$ and 2. You can elegantly complement this mathematical analysis with empirical measurements to determine the base more precisely, as outlined in Exercise 15.30.

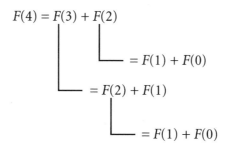

FIGURE 15.8 Redundant computations in computing $F(4)$.

15.4.3 The Dynamic Programming Algorithm

The previous section's Fibonacci algorithm does a lot of redundant work. For example, Figure 15.8 illustrates how the algorithm computes $F(4)$ (the fourth Fibonacci number): first, it computes $F(3)$, which requires computing $F(2)$ and $F(1)$. Computing $F(2)$ requires computing $F(1)$ again and $F(0)$. After computing $F(3)$, the algorithm computes $F(2)$ all over again, to add to $F(3)$. The essence of dynamic programming is to recognize when an algorithm makes redundant recursive calls such as these, and to save the results the first time they are computed, so they can be reused instead of recomputed when they are needed again.

For Fibonacci numbers, all you need to save in order to compute $F(m)$ are the values of $F(m-1)$ and $F(m-2)$. You use these to compute $F(m)$, then use $F(m)$ and $F(m-1)$ to compute $F(m+1)$, and so forth. This reasoning suggests that you don't really need recursion to compute Fibonacci numbers, you can do it in a loop based on an invariant that at the beginning of the k-th iteration the values of $F(k-1)$ and $F(k-2)$ are present in two variables, f1 and f2. If the loop exits just as it is about to begin its $(m+1)$-th iteration, then f1 will contain the desired $F(m)$. At the beginning of the first iteration, the loop invariant implies that f1 and f2 should be initialized to $F(0)$ and $F(-1)$, respectively. "$F(-1)$" isn't defined, but treating it as 0 allows you to compute $F(1)$ from the Fibonacci recurrence, in other words, as:

$$F(1) = F(0) + F(-1) \tag{15.40}$$

These ideas lead to a new Fibonacci method, namely:

```
// In class MoreMath...
// Precondition: m is a natural number.
public static long fibonacci(int m) {
    long f2 = 0;
    long f1 = 1;
```

```
for (int k = 1; k <= m; k++) {
    long next = f1 + f2;       // The next Fibonacci number
    f2 = f1;                   // Update f1 and f2 to
    f1 = next;                 // maintain loop invariant
}
return f1;
}
```

Dynamic programming often helps designers replace recursion with iteration, as it did in this case. Figuring out how to save values that need to be reused forces you to understand the order in which those values are used, which often leads to an iterative strategy for generating them.

You can derive the execution time of this algorithm by counting the number of times it executes the `long next = f1 + f2` statement. We count this statement because it seems to do the central job (computing a Fibonacci number), and because it is executed the same number of times as the whole body of the algorithm's loop. The statement gets executed once per iteration of the loop, and the loop iterates m times. The net execution time is thus $\Theta(m)$, an astonishing improvement over the exponential execution time of the obvious algorithm.[3]

Exercises

15.28. Prove rigorously that $G(m)$, as defined in Equation 15.30, is equal to $2^{m-1} - 1$ whenever $m \geq 1$.

15.29. With Equation 15.31, you saw recursion of the form $f(n-c)$ in a recurrence relation, where c is a constant, lead to division of the form n/c in the closed form. This illustrates a general relationship between expressions in a recurrence relation and in its closed form, and can help you guess closed forms for many recurrences. Prove the following examples:

1. Recurrence relations of the form:

$$f(n) = \begin{cases} 0 & \text{if } n < c \\ 1 + 2f(n-c) & \text{if } n \geq c \end{cases}$$

where c is a constant, have closed forms of the form:

---

[3] Some people incorrectly use this difference in execution times as evidence that iteration is more efficient than recursion. However, the difference doesn't arise from one algorithm being iterative and the other recursive, it arises from the two algorithms being fundamentally different ways of computing Fibonacci numbers. See Exercise 15.31.

$$f(n) = 2^{\lfloor n/c \rfloor} - 1$$

2. Recurrence relations of the form:

$$f(n) = \begin{cases} 0 & \text{if } n < c \\ 1 + f(n-c) & \text{if } n \geq c \end{cases}$$

where c is a constant, have closed forms of the form:

$$f(n) = \left\lfloor \frac{n}{c} \right\rfloor$$

15.30. If the execution time of Section 15.4.2's Fibonacci algorithm really is exponential, it means that the execution time is given by an expression of the form cb^m, where c is a constant of proportionality, and b is the base that lies somewhere between $\sqrt{2}$ and 2. Then, the ratio of the execution times for two consecutive values of m, say $m = k$ and $m = k+1$, should be:

$$\frac{cb^{k+1}}{cb^k} \tag{15.41}$$

which is just b. Use this idea, and some running times you measure for the Fibonacci algorithm, to estimate the base for the exponential execution time empirically.

15.31. Design a recursive version of the dynamic programming algorithm for Fibonacci numbers. Show that its execution time is still $\Theta(m)$.

15.32. The number of ways you can choose c items out of a population of n, written:

$$\binom{n}{c} \tag{15.42}$$

shows up in many places. For example, one of the authors lives in a state whose lottery involves guessing which 6 numbers between 1 and 59 the lottery authority will pick in the next drawing—that is, the chances of winning depend on how many ways there are to pick 6 numbers from a population of 59. There are many ways to evaluate Equation 15.42, one being to use the following recurrence relation:

$$
\binom{n}{c} = \begin{cases} 1 & \text{if } c = 0 \\ 1 & \text{if } c = n \\ \binom{n-1}{c-1} + \binom{n-1}{c} & \text{if } 0 < c < n \\ 0 & \text{in all other cases} \end{cases} \tag{15.43}
$$

Just as with Fibonacci numbers, this recurrence can be directly transcribed into a algorithm, and just as with Fibonacci numbers that algorithm has an exponential execution time. Use dynamic programming to design an algorithm that is based on Equation 15.43, but that runs in less than exponential time. Hint: consider using a two-dimensional array to save values of

$$
\binom{m}{k}
$$

for m ranging from 0 to n and k ranging from 0 to c.

15.5 CONCLUDING REMARKS

Exponential growth is a very powerful thing. Because exponential functions grow faster than almost all other common functions, an algorithm or calculation whose result is exponentially related to its input can produce a startlingly large amount of that result from a very small amount of input.

The work an algorithm does can grow exponentially when a single arm of the algorithm recursively invokes that same algorithm more than once. Such algorithms often have a skeleton similar to this:

```
SomeAlgorithm(n)
    if ...
        SomeAlgorithm(n−1)
        SomeAlgorithm(n−1)
    else
        ...
```

The multiple recursions may also be caused by a loop:

```
SomeAlgorithm(n)
    if ...
        for i = 1 to b
            SomeAlgorithm(n − 1)
    else
        ...
```

Wherever they come from, multiple recursions can allow a very short algorithm to produce a very large or complicated result; alternatively, they may allow a very small input to yield the large or complicated result.

Unfortunately, exponential growth in the work an algorithm does implies exponential execution time, too. Exponential-time algorithms are generally too slow to be practical. Thus, you should be suspicious of algorithms with structures characteristic of exponential growth, and if you verify that an algorithm has an exponential execution time you should find some way to reduce that time to less than exponential. Sometimes clever algorithm design reveals a nonexponential solution. In other cases, the problem itself is to blame for the exponential execution time, and no amount of algorithmic cleverness can produce a practical solution. This latter possibility, and how to recognize it, is the subject of the next chapter.

15.6 FURTHER READING

The Towers of Hanoi puzzle was invented by French mathematician Édouard Lucas. It was published posthumously in:

E. Lucas, *Récréations Mathématiques*, Vol. 3, Gauthier-Villars et Fils, 1893, pp. 55–59.

This essay describes the puzzle, gives the algorithm for solving it that we discuss in this chapter, and presents an informal analysis of its execution time. The "legend" about the temple in Hanoi is a combination of two completely fictitious stories from Lucas. Other algorithms also solve the puzzle. For example, a short iterative algorithm, and its correctness proof, appear in:

P. Buneman and L. Levy, "The Towers of Hanoi Puzzle," *Information Processing Letters*, July 1980, pp. 243–244.

For a sophisticated treatment of recursive trees, and recursive plants in general, see:

P. Prusinkiewicz and A. Lindenmayer, *The Algorithmic Beauty of Plants*, Springer-Verlag, 1990.

This book also presents an interesting and powerful way of treating Koch curves, dragon curves, and similar recursive lines as "sentences" in certain "languages." You can also find descriptions of Koch curves and similar shapes in:

F. S. Hill, *Computer Graphics Using OpenGL*, Prentice-Hall, 2001.

For an English translation of Fibonacci's problem, see:

D. Struik (ed.), *A Source Book in Mathematics, 1200–1800*, Harvard University Press, 1969.

Additional historical information on the Fibonacci numbers appears in:

Parmanand Singh, "The So-Called Fibonacci Numbers in Ancient and Medieval India," *Historia Mathematica*, Aug. 1985.

This article makes a convincing case that the Fibonacci numbers were known in India, in relation to metric schemes in traditional poetry, before they appeared in Europe.

There is a good treatment of "homogeneous" and "inhomogeneous" recurrence relations, with which you can find closed forms for Equation 15.29 and the Fibonacci recurrence itself, in:

G. Brassard and P. Bratley, *Fundamentals of Algorithmics*, Prentice Hall, 1996.

Brassard and Bratley's book also offers a good discussion of dynamic programming—Exercise 15.32 is taken from one of their examples. Most other advanced algorithm design and analysis texts also address dynamic programming, for example:

T. Cormen, C. Leiserson, R. Rivest, and C. Stein, *Introduction to Algorithms* (2nd ed.), MIT Press, 2001.

S. Skiena, *The Algorithm Design Manual*, TELOS/Springer-Verlag, 1997.

16   Limits to Performance

C ould you design an algorithm to solve the Towers of Hanoi in less than exponential time? Could anyone? These questions ask what might be possible with algorithms not yet discovered. Answers to such questions have important implications, no matter what those answers are. Affirmative answers, showing that it is possible to do something, advance the state of the art in computer science. Negative answers, showing that it is not possible to do something, describe the limits of computer science. While it may seem that any answer to a question about not-yet-discovered algorithms must be a matter of opinion, it turns out, surprisingly, that objective, provable answers are sometimes possible. This chapter discusses how computer scientists find such answers and introduces some important unanswered questions.

16.1   PRELIMINARY REMARKS

This chapter and the next require you to shift your attention in a subtle but important way. Previous chapters concentrated on individual algorithms; now we change the focus and concentrate on *problems*. Remember that a problem is a general situation requiring a solution or answer. For example, the problem of searching in arrays might be posed as, "Given an array and a piece of data, determine whether that data is present in the array." An algorithm, on the other hand, is a process for solving a problem. Typically, there are many algorithms that solve any given problem. For example, the problem of searching in arrays can be solved by Sequential Search, Binary Search, and other algorithms.

The central question in this chapter is no longer how fast a particular algorithm is, but instead how fast a problem can be solved. For instance, instead of wanting to know that Binary Search in an n item array takes $\Theta(\log n)$ time, we now want to know the shortest time in which *any* algorithm can search an array. Remember that answers to such questions must apply to *all possible* algorithms for solving the problem, including algorithms that have not yet been discovered.

Two terms are useful when talking about how quickly one can solve a problem:

- A *lower bound* on the time for solving a problem is an asymptotic expression, $\Theta(f(n))$, in which n is the problem size, such that every algorithm that solves the problem has a worst-case execution time of at least $\Theta(f(n))$.
- An algorithm is *optimal* for a problem if its worst-case execution time is a lower bound for that problem.

For example, it turns out that no matter how cleverly you search arrays, as long as you obey certain rules on how you examine data, there will always be some searches that take at least $\Theta(\log n)$ time. Thus, $\Theta(\log n)$ is a lower bound for searching under those rules. This in turn means that Binary Search is an optimal searching algorithm.

Exercises

16.1. Which of the following are problems, and which are algorithms?

1. Quicksort.
2. Sorting an array into ascending order.
3. Listing all the prime numbers less than or equal to some natural number.
4. Deciding whether one number evenly divides another.
5. "To factor a natural number, n, into prime factors, make a list of the prime numbers less than or equal to n. Then step through this list until you find a prime, p, that evenly divides n. Add p to a list of prime factors, and then repeat on n/p."
6. Playing a winning game of chess.
7. The following Java code fragment:

   ```
   int total = 0;
   for (int i = 1; i <= n; i++) total = total + i;
   ```

8. Finding and correcting the bugs in a computer program.

16.2. Every array searching algorithm that the authors know of completes some searches in constant ($\Theta(1)$) time. Does this fact contradict the claim that the lower bound for searching arrays is $\Theta(\log n)$?

16.3. Is it correct to say that $\Theta(1)$ is also a lower bound for searching arrays? If so, is $\Theta(1)$ as interesting a lower bound as $\Theta(\log n)$? Why or why not?

16.4. Suppose you learned of a problem for which $\Theta(1)$ was not a lower bound. What does this tell you about how the execution time of some algorithm for solving that problem behaves? Do you think it likely that such problems exist?

16.2   FINDING LOWER BOUNDS AND PROVING OPTIMALITY

Finding nontrivial lower bounds on problem solution time is tricky. The general idea is to identify features of the problem that force any solution to perform some minimum number of steps. Identifying such features requires very precise specifications of the problem and of the operations that algorithms may use. If one can derive a lower bound, however, it is easy to show that an algorithm is optimal by showing that its worst-case execution time is the lower bound. This section introduces lower-bound analysis by deriving in detail the lower bound for solving the Towers of Hanoi and by summarizing lower-bound arguments for several other problems.

16.2.1   The Towers of Hanoi

The Towers of Hanoi (Section 15.1) provides a good introduction to lower bounds, because the problem is precisely described by a few simple rules. Most importantly, these rules imply that no matter how you solve the problem, you ultimately have to do it in terms of one operation: moving one disk at a time from one pole to another. Thus, the lower-bound analysis amounts to deducing the minimum number of such moves required to solve an instance of the puzzle. This minimum will probably depend on n, the number of disks in the puzzle, so let's call it $M(n)$.

Analyzing the Problem

We now need to identify features of the Towers of Hanoi puzzle that constrain the possible value of $M(n)$. More specifically, we want to find features that limit how small $M(n)$ can get. For example, all the disks start on the source pole and end on a different destination pole. This means that we would have to move each disk at least once in order to solve the puzzle, requiring a total of at least n moves—in other words, $M(n) \geq n$.

We can deduce more about $M(n)$ by taking other rules of the puzzle into account (see Figure 16.1). For instance, think about moving the largest disk off of the source pole. The other $n-1$ disks must be off of the source at this time, since you can't move the largest disk while anything is still on top of it. You can't put the largest disk on top of any of the others (it can't be on top of anything smaller than itself), so the $n-1$ other disks must all be on whichever pole the largest is not moving to; they necessarily form a tower on this pole (because large disks can't be on top of small ones). In short, you have to move an $n-1$ disk tower from the source pole to some other pole before you can move the largest disk. Even without knowing exactly how you should move this tower, you know that it will take at least $M(n-1)$ moves (because M gives the *minimum* number of moves for moving any

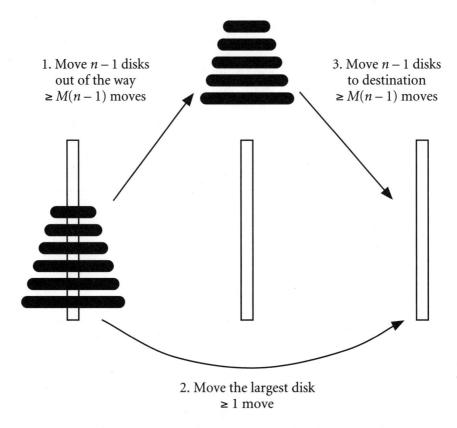

1. Move $n-1$ disks
out of the way
$\geq M(n-1)$ moves

3. Move $n-1$ disks
to destination
$\geq M(n-1)$ moves

2. Move the largest disk
≥ 1 move

FIGURE 16.1   The minimum number of moves to solve the Towers of Hanoi.

size tower). Since moving the largest disk takes one move itself, we have just discovered that $M(n)$ must be at least $M(n-1)+1$.

Continuing in this vein, think about moving the largest disk on to the destination pole. Immediately after this move, the other $n-1$ disks form a tower on some other pole. The reasons are similar to those for why they formed a tower immediately before moving the largest disk off of the source pole—they can't be on the pole you're moving the largest disk to, nor can they be on the pole you're moving it from, so they must all be in a tower on the third pole. To finish solving the puzzle, you have to move this $n-1$ disk tower to the destination pole. As before, moving it requires at least $M(n-1)$ moves. Adding these moves to the $1+M(n-1)$ moves previously deduced, we find that $M(n)$ must be at least:

$$1+M(n-1)+M(n-1)=1+2M(n-1) \tag{16.1}$$

$M(n) \geq 1 + 2M(n-1)$ is part of a recursive definition of $M(n)$. This definition still needs a base case, but one is easy to discover: the simplest possible puzzle, one with no disks, can be "solved" with no moves. The minimum number of moves needed to solve the Towers of Hanoi can therefore be described as:

$$M(n) = 0 \qquad \text{if } n = 0$$
$$M(n) \geq 1 + 2M(n-1) \qquad \text{if } n > 0$$

(16.2)

Equation 16.2 is a recurrence relation. The only difference between it and recurrences you have seen before is the use of "$M(n) \geq \ldots$" instead of "$M(n) = \ldots$" in the recursive part. This difference's only effect is that the closed form will also look like "$M(n) \geq \ldots$". Thus, this is really the same recurrence relation as the one for the number of moves performed by Chapter 15's Towers of Hanoi algorithm. This similarity immediately tells us that the closed form for Equation 16.2 is:

$$M(n) \geq 2^n - 1$$

(16.3)

More interestingly, our analysis tells us that Chapter 15's algorithm is optimal. Despite the intolerable time it required, no one can ever solve the Towers of Hanoi faster than we did in Chapter 15!

Discussion

Although the derivation of the minimum number of moves for solving the Towers of Hanoi ended with the same expression as Chapter 15's analysis of a particular Towers of Hanoi algorithm, there are important differences between the two analyses. The most important is that Chapter 15 started its analysis with specific steps in a specific algorithm, while here we started with the puzzle's rules. Those rules led to conclusions about numbers of moves, but said little about what disks should be moved, what poles should be involved, or similar algorithmic issues. As the separate lines of reasoning progressed, however, their consequences became more and more similar. This happened because Chapter 15's algorithm is optimal—it does exactly what is minimally necessary to solve the puzzle. Only by deriving the lower bound, however, could we find out what the minimally necessary actions are. As this example demonstrates, pinpointing necessary actions via lower bound analyses can guide one to optimal algorithms.

16.2.2 Other Problems

That the Towers of Hanoi has an exponential lower bound is bad news for people who need to solve the puzzle, but there aren't many such people—the problem just isn't of great practical importance. However, lower bound analyses do exist for more important problems. Two particularly significant examples are searching and sorting. Both often serve as parts of larger algorithms, so lower bounds on how quickly one can search or sort limit how fast those algorithms can be as well.

Searching

To derive a lower bound for searching, think of the problem as a game between a searcher and an evil adversary. The searcher wants to find some item, which we will call the target, in a set of data; the adversary wants to delay the searcher for as long as possible. Both players know the target value. The adversary controls the data set, divulging its contents to the searcher one item at a time. The searcher identifies items he or she wants to see by their position in the data set (for example, "Show me the seventh item"). These rules reflect the way computer hardware and programming languages access most data structures. Figure 16.2 illustrates the game. Because the searcher knows the contents of the data set only at those positions about which he or she has asked, the adversary doesn't have to decide what value is in a position unless and until asked about it. The only constraints on how the adversary can manage the data set are that it must be sorted (reflecting the fact that most real searching happens in sorted data sets—Exercise 16.11 considers unsorted searches), and the adversary can't change values after they have been revealed. Under these rules, the adversary should assign values to positions in the data set in a way that keeps the section in which the target could lie as large as possible. For example, if the searcher asks for a value from a position near the beginning of the data

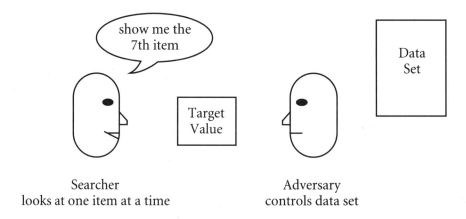

Searcher   Adversary
looks at one item at a time   controls data set

FIGURE 16.2 Searching as a game between a searcher and an adversary.

set, the adversary should reply with a value less than the target, and if the searcher asks about a position near the end, the adversary should answer with a value greater than the target. The best the searcher can now do is to always ask for the middle item in the section that might contain the target, thus splitting that section in half (otherwise the adversary will force the searcher into a subsection bigger than half the original). This requires the searcher to ask for enough items to successively halve an n item data set down to a one-item section, in other words, to ask $\Theta(\log n)$ questions.

Adversary arguments such as the one above are an illuminating way to pose many lower-bound analyses. While this argument and the analysis for Towers of Hanoi appear quite different, they have important underlying similarities. For example, precisely identifying the rules of a problem is critical to both. Also, notice how the analysis for searching ends by describing what is basically Binary Search, much as the analysis for Towers of Hanoi leads to Chapter 15's algorithm—both analyses produce optimal algorithms as a side effect. However, the lower bound for searching lets us conclude not only that Binary Search is optimal, but that searching in a balanced binary search tree is, too, since it also has the optimal $\Theta(\log n)$ execution time.[1] A properly constructed lower-bound analysis can produce results applicable to many algorithms, despite not directly analyzing any of them.

Sorting

Sorting's lower-bound derivation is quite abstract, so we summarize it very briefly. A reference in the "Further Reading" section provides details if you want them. To begin, think about how many different arrangements, or *permutations*, n distinct data items could have. Any of the n items could be first. For each of these choices of a first item, there are $n-1$ choices for the second item, for a total of $n(n-1)$ ways of arranging the first two items. Continuing this reasoning, there are $n \times (n-1) \times (n-2) \times \cdots \times 2 \times 1$, or $n!$, different ways of arranging all n items. Sorting turns out to be equivalent to determining which of these $n!$ permutations the items are initially in. Assuming that sorting must use Boolean tests (such as the comparison operations in typical programming languages) to determine the permutation, it takes at least $\log_2(n!)$ tests to isolate that permutation (see Exercise 16.12). $\log_2(n!)$ turns out to be $\Theta(n \log n)$. Unlike the Towers of Hanoi and searching, this analysis doesn't lead to an optimal algorithm. However, the analysis does show that independently discovered $\Theta(n \log n)$ sorting algorithms are optimal.

---

[1] It may not seem so at first, but binary tree search follows all the rules for searching used in the lower-bound analysis. A binary search tree is a sorted data set, searches examine one item at a time, and the links between nodes provide position-based access to the data (albeit only those positions that an optimal search needs to examine, in exactly the order such a search needs them).

Exercises

16.5. In deriving $M(n)$ for $n > 0$, we identified three stages in solving the Towers of Hanoi (moving $n-1$ disks off the source pole, moving the biggest disk, and moving $n-1$ disks to the destination) and added the minimum number of moves in each stage. But such addition is incorrect if the stages can overlap—in other words, if operations done in one stage can also contribute to completing another stage. Explain why the stages used in the above derivation cannot overlap.

16.6. Suppose the Towers of Hanoi had the following additional rule: every move must move a disk either from the source pole to the spare, from the spare to the destination, or from the destination to the source; no other moves are permitted. Derive a lower bound for the time needed to solve this version of the puzzle.

16.7. Suppose the Towers of Hanoi allowed large disks to be on top of smaller ones (even in the final stack on the destination pole). Derive a lower bound on the time needed to solve this version of the puzzle.

16.8. Find closed forms for the following recurrence relations. Use induction to prove that each of your closed forms satisfies the equalities and inequalities in its recurrence.

1. $$\begin{array}{ll} f(n)=0 & \text{if } n=0 \\ f(n)\geq 1+f(n-1) & \text{if } n>0 \end{array}$$

2. $$\begin{array}{ll} f(n)=1 & \text{if } n=0 \\ f(n)\geq 2f(n-1) & \text{if } n>0 \end{array}$$

3. $$\begin{array}{ll} f(n)\geq 1 & \text{if } n=0 \\ f(n)\geq 2+f(n-1) & \text{if } n>0 \end{array}$$

16.9. Play the searcher-and-adversary game with a friend (the adversary can record the data set on a piece of paper). Play until neither player can improve their performance against the other. Does it take roughly $\log_2 n$ questions to play a game at this point?

16.10. Write a computer program that plays the adversary role in the searcher-and-adversary game. The program should start by reading the data set size and target value from the user. Then the program should repeatedly read a position from the user and respond with the value at that position in the data set, until the user claims to know whether the target is in the data set or not. The program should then print a complete data set that is in ascending order and that contains the values that the program showed to the user in the positions the program claimed for them. If at all possible, the user's claim about whether the target is in this data set or not should be wrong. The data set can store whatever type of data you wish, although real numbers seem a particularly good choice.

16.11. Derive a lower bound for how long it takes to search an unsorted n item data set. Except for the unsorted data, assume that this form of searching obeys the main text's rules for searching.

16.12. Prove that it takes at least $\log_2 m$ Boolean tests to narrow a set of m items down to a single item.

16.13. Derive lower bounds on the time required to do the following. In each case, define your own rules for solving the problem, but keep those rules representative of how real programs and computers work.

1. Finding the largest value in an unordered set of n items.
2. Determining whether a sequence of n items is in ascending order.
3. Determining whether an n character string is a palindrome.
4. Computing the intersection of two sets, of sizes n and m.

16.14. Name an optimal sorting algorithm.

16.15. Derive a lower bound on the number of assignments to elements of the data set for sorting. Do you know of any sorting algorithms that achieve your bound (at least asymptotically)?

16.16. Show that the lower bound for the time to build a binary search tree from an unordered set of n input values must be $\Theta(n \log n)$. Hint: Can you think of a way to sort the input values by building a binary search tree?

16.17. Suppose you have won seven sports trophies. In how many orders can you display them on a shelf?

16.3 OPEN QUESTIONS

Some of the most interesting questions about lower bounds are *open*, or not yet answered. That these questions remain open is testimony to how hard lower bounds can be to find. This section introduces two such questions, both with surprisingly important consequences. The first is whether factoring integers is tractable (that is, doable in practical amounts of time)—if it is, then private information you send through the Internet might be read by eavesdroppers. The second question is whether a certain optimization problem is tractable—if it is, so are thousands of other problems of importance to business, computer science, and other fields, and the theoretical limits of computing are very different from what most people expect. While these are among the most important open questions about lower bounds, they are by no means the only ones—lower bounds on the time to solve many, if not most, problems are still unknown.

16.3.1 Tractable and Intractable Problems

As you saw in Chapter 15, an algorithm with an exponential execution time is too slow to be useful. On the other hand, while execution times that are polynomial functions of problem size can also be slow, the ones that occur in practice are fast enough that you can wait them out if the problem is important enough. Thus, computer scientists use the following rule of thumb to distinguish problems that algorithms can realistically solve from problems algorithms can't realistically solve:

A problem is *tractable*, or rapidly enough solvable to consider solving, if the lower bound on its solution time is a polynomial function of the problem size; a problem is *intractable*, or not solvable in practice, if the lower bound on its solution time is larger than any polynomial function of problem size (for example, exponential).

These notions of tractability and intractability mean that the most important distinction between problems is the distinction between problems with polynomial lower bounds and ones without. Frustratingly, the problems below resist even this coarse characterization, leaving open not only questions of their exact lower bounds, but significantly, the question of whether they can be solved in practice at all.

16.3.2 Factoring and Cryptography

Cryptography is the use of secret codes to protect information. Figure 16.3 illustrates cryptography as practiced around 1970. Alice has a secret message for Bob. To protect her message from spies, Alice *encrypts* it, in other words, turns it into a form that appears to be gibberish to anyone who doesn't know how it was encrypted. When Bob, who knows how the message was encrypted, receives it, he uses his knowledge of the encryption strategy to *decrypt* it back into meaningful text. The knowledge that Alice and Bob share in order to encrypt and decrypt messages is called the *key* to their code.

Unfortunately, Alice's message isn't very safe in this system. Anyone who knows the key can decrypt the message, and there are many opportunities for a spy to learn the key. The spy could steal it from either Alice or Bob, or could trick one of them into revealing it. Furthermore, Alice and Bob have to agree on a key before they can communicate securely; a spy could learn the proposed key during this stage just by eavesdropping.

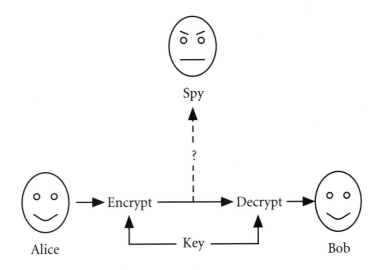

FIGURE 16.3 Cryptography, ca. 1970.

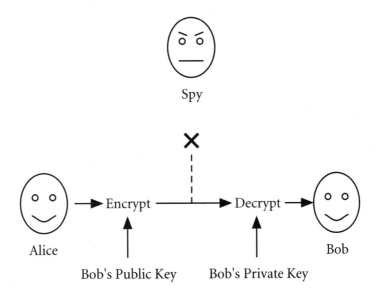

FIGURE 16.4 Public-key cryptography.

A more secure form of cryptography, called *public-key cryptography*, was invented in the late 1970s. Figure 16.4 illustrates public-key cryptography. To use public-key cryptography, Bob needs two keys—a "public" key and a "private" key. Messages encrypted with Bob's public key can only be decrypted with his private key. Furthermore, and quite surprisingly, knowing Bob's public key doesn't help a spy deduce his private key. Bob can therefore share his public key with everyone, but tells no one his private key. When Alice wants to send Bob a message, she looks up his public key and encrypts the message with it. Bob is the only person who can decrypt this message, because only he knows the necessary private key. Public-key cryptography eliminates the need to agree on keys (so there are no preliminary discussions for a spy to eavesdrop on), or to ever share knowledge of how to decrypt a message (making it all but impossible to trick Bob into revealing his private key).

Although publishing encryption keys without giving away the secret of decryption sounds like magic, public-key cryptosystems really do exist. The most popular is the *RSA cryptosystem* (named after its inventors, Ronald Rivest, Adi Shamir, and Leonard Adelman). RSA is widely used to set up secure communications on the Internet. For example, if you buy something on the Internet, your Web browser probably uses RSA to verify that the server it is talking to is who you think it is (so you don't get swindled by a con artist masquerading as your favorite on-line store), and to securely choose a key for encrypting private information (such as credit card numbers) that you send to the seller.[2]

To generate a public/private key pair in an RSA cryptosystem, one finds a large (around 300 digits) integer that has only two factors and calculates the keys from the factors. The only apparent way to discover someone's private key is to factor that person's large integer and rederive the keys from the factors.

The designers of RSA believed that factoring was intractable and that their cryptosystem was therefore secure. Research since then has steadily decreased the time that it takes to factor, but today's fastest factoring algorithms are still slower than polynomial in the number of digits in the number being factored. Therefore, factoring still appears intractable, and RSA cryptography is widely accepted as secure. However, no one knows for sure what the lower bound for factoring is, and so someone might someday find a polynomial-time factoring algorithm. If this ever happens, every user of RSA cryptography will immediately be exposed to spies. Millions of computer users bet their money and privacy every day on factoring being intractable!

16.3.3 The Travelling Sales Representative and NP-Hard Problems

The "Travelling Sales Representative Problem" is a famous *optimization* problem, in other words, a problem that involves finding the best way to do something. Related optimization problems are important in business, computing, and other fields. Unfortunately, the best algorithms presently known for solving any of these

---

[2] Browsers encrypt most data using conventional cryptography rather than RSA, because the conventional schemes are much faster. But the browser and server use RSA to securely agree on a key for the conventional encryption.

problems have exponential execution times. Nobody knows whether this is because the problems are inherently intractable, or just because fast algorithms haven't been found yet. However, most computer scientists believe that fast solutions do not exist, even though slow ones are easy to find.

Problem Definition

Imagine a company that sends a sales representative to visit clients in several cities. Because the company pays for their representative's travel, they want to find the cheapest trip that includes all the cities. The trip needs to start and end in the representative's home city, and must visit every other city exactly once. The cost of travel between cities varies according to the cities involved. For example, the travel options and costs for visiting New York, Paris, Cairo, Beijing, and Rio de Janeiro might be as shown in Figure 16.5, where lines indicate airplane flights that the representative can take and their costs. One possible trip is New York – Paris – Beijing – Cairo – Rio – New York, with a total cost of $2,300, but a cheaper possibility is New York – Cairo – Beijing – Paris – Rio – New York, with a cost of only $2,000.

A Travelling Sales Representative Algorithm

Here is an outline of one algorithm that solves the Travelling Sales Representative problem:

For each possible trip
    If this trip is the cheapest seen so far
        Remember this trip for possible return
Return the cheapest trip found

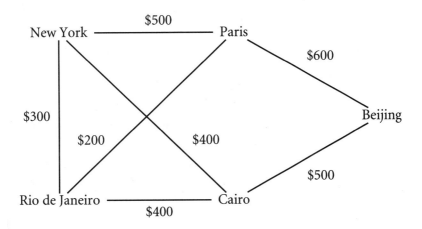

FIGURE 16.5 A travelling sales representative problem.

While it takes a little thought to devise concrete code to enumerate all possible trips (see Exercise 16.22), this algorithm is not hard to implement. The problem is its execution time: because there can be up to $n!$ different trips through n cities, the worst-case execution time is $\Theta(n!)$.

Nondeterminism

We could reduce the outrageous cost of the Travelling Sales Representative algorithm to something practical if we had a computer with one special feature. Specifically, if our computer could process all the trips at the same time, automatically returning the cheapest, we could solve the problem in $\Theta(n)$ time. The ability to process all the options in a problem at once and automatically select the one that turns out to be "right" is the essence of something called *nondeterminism*.[3] The interesting thing about nondeterminism and the Travelling Sales Representative is how a problem that seemed hopelessly intractable without nondeterminism became supremely tractable with it.

Many other problems (notably including other intractable optimization problems) also become tractable if solved nondeterministically. In fact, nondeterminism makes such a large set of problems tractable that computer scientists have given that set a name—NP, the *N*ondeterministically *P*olynomial-time-solvable problems. NP is a very large set. Nondeterministic computers aren't obligated to use nondeterminism when solving a problem, so NP contains all the problems that are tractable for ordinary computers (a set named P) plus, presumably, many other problems that are only tractable with nondeterminism.

NP-Hardness

The Travelling Sales Representative has one other very intriguing feature: if it has a polynomial time solution, then so does every problem in NP. This is because every problem in NP "reduces" to the Travelling Sales Representative. Informally, problem *A* *reduces* to problem *B* if one way to solve *A* involves calling a subroutine that solves *B*, with any computation outside of that subroutine taking only polynomial time. For example, there is a variant of the Travelling Sales Representative[4] that doesn't find the cheapest trip, but rather asks whether any trip exists whose cost is less than a specified limit. This variant is reducible to our Travelling Sales Representative problem because we can solve the variant by first using a subroutine that solves our version of the problem to find the cheapest trip, and then checking

---

[3] This isn't the exact definition of nondeterminism, but it is close enough that the properties we develop with it are also properties of true nondeterminism. References in the "Further Reading" section contain complete treatments of nondeterminism, if you want to learn more about it.

[4] In reality, this "variant" is the official version of the problem in theoretical computer science, and our version is a variation on it.

whether that trip's cost is less than the limit. Problems to which everything in NP reduces are called *NP-Hard*; the Travelling Sales Representative is a classic example of an NP-Hard problem.

Being NP-Hard has two implications. First, an NP-Hard problem is at least as hard (in the sense of being time-consuming) to solve as any problem in NP. This is because any problem in NP reduces to the NP-Hard problem, and so, at the worst, can be solved by doing the reduction and solving the NP-Hard problem. Saying that a problem is NP-Hard is thus tantamount to saying that it is among the most stubbornly intractable problems known. But on the other hand, the reward for finding a polynomial-time solution to an NP-Hard problem would be huge: it would instantly make every problem in NP tractable, and by doing so would prove that nondeterminism provides no real advantage over ordinary computing.

Because it intuitively seems that nondeterminism should be more powerful than ordinary computing, and because no one has yet found a polynomial-time solution to any NP-Hard problem, most computer scientists believe that the NP-Hard problems are inherently intractable. However, no one has been able to prove it, despite intense effort over many years. Nonetheless, the belief has important consequences for both applied computing and theoretical computer science. In applied computing, businesses and other computer users often need solutions to NP-Hard optimization problems. But because these problems are NP-Hard, people have largely abandoned efforts to compute exact solutions, concentrating instead on approximations (which can often be found quickly). Theoretically, computer scientists accept that NP is a bigger set than P, establishing a "complexity hierarchy" of problems. Whether the NP-Hard problems are really intractable or not is probably the most important open question in computer science.

Exercises

16.18. Design an algorithm that factors natural numbers. Derive its worst-case asymptotic execution time as a function of the number of digits in the number.

16.19. Look up the details of the RSA cryptosystem (see the "Further Reading" section at the end of this chapter for some references), and write programs to encrypt and decrypt text using RSA. Your programs can work with numbers that fit in `long` variables, even though this means that your cryptosystem won't be very secure.

16.20. One can use private keys, not just public ones, to encrypt messages; messages thus encrypted can be decrypted only with the corresponding public key. Use this property to devise a way for people to "sign" messages electronically, without actually hand writing signatures.

16.21. Does the Travelling Sales Representative problem illustrated in Figure 16.5 allow any trips other than the two described in the text and their reversals (assuming that the sales representative's home is in New York)?

16.22. Code in Java the Travelling Sales Representative algorithm outlined in this section. There is an elegant recursive way of generating the possible trips.

16.23. A school bus needs to pick up a set of children and bring them to school. The school knows how much time it takes the bus to drive from the school to or from each child's home, and how much time it takes to drive from any home to any other. The school wants to find a route for the bus to follow that takes the least total time. The bus starts at the school. Call this problem the "School Bus Routing problem."

1. Show that the School Bus Routing problem reduces to the Travelling Sales Representative.
2. Show that the Travelling Sales Representative also reduces to School Bus Routing.
3. Explain why the reduction in Step 2 proves that School Bus Routing is NP-Hard.

16.4 CONCLUDING REMARKS

The fact that there are limits to how quickly algorithms can solve problems has important practical, theoretical, and philosophical implications. Practically, lower bounds on how quickly one can do such things as searching or sorting limit some of the most widespread applications of computing. Theoretically, lower bounds on solution time provide a way to rank problems by their difficulty—problems with high lower bounds are harder than problems with low ones. In the coarsest classification, computer scientists consider problems tractable (practical to solve) or not according to whether they are solvable in polynomial time. Philosophically, it is interesting that computer science has limits other than those of human cleverness, but that computer science's methods of inquiry are powerful enough to discover and explore those limits.

Some of the most important open questions in computer science concern whether certain problems are tractable or not. These questions bear directly on socially and economically important applications of computing. RSA cryptography's reliance on factoring illustrates how a problem's presumed intractability can be used to advantage; the NP-Hard optimization problems illustrate how presumed intractability can be a disadvantage. In both cases, people act on plausible assumptions, but not proofs, about intractability. While these assumptions are probably good ones, some nasty (in the case of cryptography) or welcome (in the case of NP-Hardness) surprises could still await those who make them.

In this chapter, you have seen one definitely intractable problem (the Towers of Hanoi), and several others that are probably intractable. There are also problems that are even worse than intractable—problems that algorithms cannot solve at all. The next chapter introduces this phenomenon, and with it concludes our introduction to the science of computing.

16.5 FURTHER READING

For a thorough treatment of lower-bound analysis, including techniques for doing the analysis and analyses for searching, sorting, and a number of other problems, see:

S. Baase, *Computer Algorithms: Introduction to Design and Analysis* (2nd ed.), Addison-Wesley, 1989.

Adversary techniques seem to date from the 1960s—see the early presentation of one and related citations in Section 5.3.2 of:

D. Knuth, *Sorting and Searching* (*The Art of Computer Programming*, Vol. 3), Addison-Wesley, 1973.

The original description of the RSA cryptosystem is:

R. Rivest, A. Shamir, and L. Adelman, "A Method for Obtaining Digital Signatures and Public-key Cryptosystems," *Communications of the ACM*, Feb. 1978.

For an introduction to cryptography in general (including RSA) and its underlying math, see:

P. Garret, *Making, Breaking Codes: An Introduction to Cryptology*, Prentice Hall, 2001.

For a less mathematical introduction to cryptography, but more material on its applications to Internet and computer security, see:

W. Stallings, *Cryptography and Network Security: Principles and Practice* (2nd ed.), Prentice Hall, 1999.

Nondeterminism is an important idea in the subfield of computer science known as *theory of computation*. You can find a comprehensive survey of this subfield, including nondeterminism, in:

M. Sipser, *Introduction to the Theory of Computation*, PWS Publishing Company, 1997.

Sipser's book also introduces *computational complexity*, the subfield of computer science that studies such sets of problems as P and NP.

The Travelling Sales Representative problem has apparently been known for a long time. It appears as a recreational puzzle in:

S. Lloyd, *Entertaining Evenings at Home*, published by the Brooklyn Daily Eagle, 1919.

The formal study of NP-Hardness (or, more accurately, a closely related notion of "NP-Completeness") began with:

S. Cook, "The Complexity of Theorem-proving Procedures," *Proceedings of the 3rd ACM Symposium on the Theory of Computing*, 1971.

Understanding of NP-Completeness and the NP-Complete problems advanced rapidly in the following decade. The definitive text on the subject is now:

M. Garey and D. Johnson, *Computers and Intractability: A Guide to the Theory of NP-Completeness*, W. H. Freeman and Company, 1979.

17 The Halting Problem

Consider for a moment the developmental path we have taken from the beginning of this course through this point. We started with basic program-writing skills, and advanced to proving that algorithms were correct and demonstrating empirically how much time they required. We discovered that we could show not only that an algorithm is correct, but also that it can solve the problem in a definable time frame, without even running the program. We discovered the dramatic differences in that time for various algorithms. Then we showed that for many problems we could even find a lower bound on the time required to solve the problem—independent of the algorithm. Finally, we were able to classify problems on the basis of that time. We even showed that some problems are demonstrably equivalent in terms of their difficulty.

This chapter extends that progression—with a result that comes as a surprise to many students. In particular, we show that there are problems that, on the one hand, seem meaningful and well-described, but on the other hand, cannot be computed by any computer, no matter how fast the computer nor how much time is available.

17.1 APPLYING COMPUTER SCIENCE TO COMPUTER SCIENCE

At this point, a student might ask, "Where next?" You very reasonably may want to know if we can extend these tools. You might also ask if we can apply them directly to the development of programs central to computer science in general—perhaps to problems such as compiling a program. That is, instead of asking about the time required to search a list or solve the Towers of Hanoi, it might be useful to calculate the time required to compile a program. Or perhaps we should attempt to prove that a compiler correctly compiles any valid program? A compiler is a very large program and any such proof will be quite complex, but if we attack the problem systematically (e.g., building up the correctness of each method employed by the compiler) we might be able to achieve such a goal.

While we are trying to apply our methodologies to developing programs useful to computer scientists, how hard would it be to ask a compiler to apply techniques analogous to the proof techniques (similar to ones we ourselves have used for evaluating algorithms) to evaluate the correctness of the input code during the compilation process? That is, perhaps we should try to make compilers that not only check the legality of the code, but also prove the validity of the algorithm represented by the program. While this is clearly a huge task, steps in the right direction might include:

> A *"method analyzer": a method that looks at another method and calculates its run time.*

Or if we are really feeling optimistic:

> A *"correctness prover": a method that looks at another method or algorithm, together with a statement of its required pre- and postconditions, and proves the correctness of the code?*

Notice that these questions do not ask:

> *Can you personally solve this problem?*

or

> *How long will it take to develop these improvements?*

The questions we are asking are not about the skill of any particular or current programmer. Nor are they questions about what has been done in the past, or even the present state of affairs. They are questions about the future, about any future programmer solving these tasks by any method. And that makes the results we will eventually discover all the more surprising.

17.1.1 Programs as Strings

Before addressing the actual task of asking a compiler to evaluate proposed algorithms, let's consider the nature of the task:

> *What does it mean for one algorithm to analyze a method or another algorithm?*

Word processors and compilers are both programs that manipulate text as strings of characters. The text may describe very complex ideas, but the text itself is represented by a string and it is that string that a compiler manipulates. Any concept that can be put into words (or other strings of characters) can, in some sense, be manipulated by a word processor, or more importantly for this discussion, a compiler.

An algorithm contains information—information about how to solve a problem. Just as any other well-defined information can be represented in a computer, every algorithm has a computer representation. In particular, a computer program is a representation of an algorithm written in a formal computing language, a representation that can be manipulated as text. Any program is just a series of characters, and as such, can be treated as data. For example, consider the following Java method:

```java
public static void metaHello() {
    System.out.println("public static void hello() {");
    System.out.print("    System.out.println");
    System.out.println("(\"Hello World!\");");
    System.out.println();
    System.out.println("}");
}
```

which prints out the familiar and simpler "Hello world" method:

```java
public static void hello() {
    System.out.println("Hello World!");
}
```

As far as `metaHello` is concerned, the `hello` method is just a series of characters—even though that series of characters represents a method that could be executed by a computer.

A compiler or interpreter accepts as input a program written in a high-level language, such as Java, and produces as output a machine language version of the program, a version capable of running on the given computer. Correctness of a single compilation could be demonstrated by showing that the input and output indeed represented equivalent series of instructions. Calculations of the execution time required by a compiler could be measured in terms of the size of the input, say, the number of characters or lines. Proof of complete correctness of the compiler would require demonstrating that it must always generate the correct result. Finally, if we make improvements in the compiler (say, an extension in its capabilities), we will need to evaluate the improvement, too.

Compiler Warning Messages

One of the tasks performed by every compiler is a syntax check: the compiler checks to make sure that the input program is grammatically legal code (as defined by the particular language) and produces error messages describing inconsistencies. The syntax analyzer clearly treats the program as data, as a character string.

Many compilers check for more than just the grammatical legality of a program. Many analyze the code and produce warnings that alert programmers to the possibility that a program, while legal, may contain problematic sections. For example, in C++, the conditional test:

```
if (a = 1) ...
```

is legal but very likely doesn't do what the programmer intended. It means:

Assign 1 to a.
If a then contains a nonzero value, then ...

The programmer very likely meant to write:

```
if (a == 1)
```

meaning:

If a is equal to 1:[1]

This is a common error, and some C++ compilers will warn the programmer of this potential problem. Almost every new compiler includes new or improved capabilities for checking programs for potential problems. In effect, such compilers do not just investigate the syntactic legality of the code, but they also attempt to predict the performance of that code (or sections of it).

Such checks for dangerous conditions seem to be relatively straightforward, and they probably do not add much to the cost of compiling a program. We might want to inquire about the cost of some further–reaching error checking.

17.1.2 A Proposed Tool: Checking for Infinite Loops

One possible step in the improvement process that would be especially interesting would be a check for nonterminating programs. This certainly seems like a reasonable prerequisite for calculating the execution time or correctness. In fact, for the remainder of this chapter, we will focus on questions related to that specific improvement, questions such as:

---

[1] Java has a related problem, which you may have experienced already. Java interprets the a = 1 as an assignment, which would return the value 1. But Java does not permit casting an integer as a Boolean, so the compiler generates an error message something like "invalid cast from int to boolean" which of course makes little sense to the new programmer, who wasn't attempting to cast anything.

How do we write (and evaluate) an algorithm to determine if another algorithm will ever terminate?

The definition of *algorithm* requires that it execute in finite time; any program should do likewise. In fact, the question of how long an algorithm will run doesn't even make sense unless we know that it will terminate. And it certainly can't be a correct algorithm unless it terminates. Let's consider the nature of algorithms that we might add to a compiler to determine if a method fed to the compiler will run to completion or if it will get stuck in an infinite loop. The question we want the compiler to answer is simply:

Will the input program terminate?

Alternatively stated, the question might be:

Does a given program contain an infinite loop?

We will postpone the question of the cost of adding such an improvement to a compiler until after we better understand the nature of the algorithms needed to accomplish the task.

Infinite loops are among the most common errors in programs. If we can figure out how to add to a compiler the capability to find and report infinite loops, we will greatly ease program testing and debugging. But the problem is not quite as simple as checking: "Is the test for a while loop of the form: 1=2?" Consider the following method intended to print out a declining series of integers:

```
public static void decline(int current) {
    while (current != 0) {
        System.out.println(current);
        current = current - 2;
    }
}
```

On the surface, decline might not look too bad. But if called with:

```
decline(9);
```

current will never equal 0 because it will always be odd: 9, 7, 5, 3, 1, −1, −3, ... In that case, decline will loop forever.

A compiler that can recognize situations such as those created by decline would save programmers much grief, just as the simpler warning messages do. But at what cost? Clearly, it will not be a simple task to check for every possible infinite loop. What would it cost (amount of extra time to compile) to add such a capability? We might even wonder if it is tractable (recall that *tractable* means roughly "performable in polynomial time"). Finally, once we develop the algorithm, how do we prove it is correct?

The `decline` method demonstrates that, at a minimum, the compiler would need some information about possible input to the method. Perhaps the general question needs to be restricted a little:

> *How hard is it to determine if an algorithm will stop—assuming we know the input?*

terminate

Let's consider first how such a program would work by looking at its abstract description. Define *terminate* to be a method that accepts two inputs and returns a true/false result. One input, which we will call *candidate*, is a proposed method. Since any algorithm or method is representable as a string of characters, we will assume `candidate` is a string. The second input, which we will call *inputString*, is also a string representing the proposed input to `candidate`. For visualization purposes, as a Java program, `terminate` might look something like:

```
public boolean terminate(String candidate, String input) {
    if (/* whatever code is needed to determine
            if candidate(proposedInput) would terminate) */)
        return true
    else return false;
}
```

Consider the behavior of `terminate` if it is asked to evaluate a method, `silly`:

```
public static void silly(int someValue) {
    if (someValue != 1) {
        while (true) { }
    }
}
```

If `terminate` were passed the method `silly` and the input 1, perhaps as:

```
terminate(silly, 1)
```

terminate would return the answer true because `silly` would return without entering the infinite loop in its then clause. But if it were passed 0:

```
terminate(silly, 0)
```

terminate would return false because `silly` would loop forever. If terminate were passed a program to calculate the decimal equivalent of 1/3, it would return false (because any such method prints an infinite series of digits, "0.33333...," which would require an infinite time to print out.

Before we add a tool such as terminate to a compiler, we probably should find out how much it will cost. Is the algorithm represented by terminate tractable? Intractable? And how will we prove it correct?

17.2 THE HALTING PROBLEM (AT LAST)

The questions just described collide head-on with one of the most famous problems in computer science, *the halting problem*, providing the startling conclusion:

We can't put a cost on terminate—because no such program is possible!

This result has ramifications for the entire discipline. Just as startling, it is possible to prove this result mathematically.

17.2.1 A Preview: Dealing with Paradoxical Questions

The proof of this claim uses a variant on proof by contradiction (see Section 3.5.1). The usual technique shows that a result must be true because any alternative is impossible. In this case, we show that the attempt to answer a question (such as whether there is an infinite loop) leads to a problem, a problem so big that it suggests the original question was malformed. The classic form of this problem is called "The Barber of Seville":[2]

---

[2] The problem was first put forward by the British logician Bertrand Russell (1872–1970) as an instance of an important problem of set theory that has come to be known as *Russell's paradox*.

It is said that Juan Valdez,[3] "The Barber of Seville," shaves every man in Seville who does not shave himself—and only those men. The original problem asked:

Who shaves the barber?

If he does shave himself, then he is a man in Seville who does not shave himself. On the other hand, if he does not shave himself, then the barber shaves him. But since he is the barber, he must shave himself.

Either way, the Barber of Seville seems to present a paradox or a conundrum or perhaps just a bizarre question with no answer. But if instead of asking who shaves the barber, we ask if there can possibly be such a barber, we get a much more specific answer.

THEOREM: There is no person matching the description of the Barber of Seville. □

PROOF: The proof parallels the description of the conundrum.

Assumption #1: There is such a barber. Either the barber shaves himself or he does not shave himself.

We now show that either case leads to a contradiction.

Assumption #2: The barber shaves himself. By definition, the barber shaves only those men who do not shave themselves. Therefore, the barber does not shave himself. This contradicts Assumption #2.

Assumption #3: Alternatively, suppose the barber does not shave himself. Again the description of the barber says he shaves all those who do not shave themselves. Therefore, the barber must shave himself, contradicting Assumption #3.

But assumptions 2 and 3 exhaust all possible cases for the barber (i.e., either he shaves himself or he does not shave himself). Both assumption #2, and its negation (assumption #3) lead to contradictions. Since both alternatives lead to a contradiction, the original assumption must always lead to a contradiction. Assumption #1 must be false: there is no such barber. ■

---

[3] At the time of the original formulation of this problem, people did not seem to realize that the barber could be a woman. The use here of the male name, Juan, is intended to make it clear that we are still only looking at male barbers. We are not looking for any semantic tricks such as "the barber is a woman so she cannot shave himself."

The bottom line is that the original question, "Who shaves the barber?" was malformed. We should not have asked about what happens to the barber, we should have asked if he even exists. Similarly we will see that questions about the cost of looking for infinite loops were also malformed. Before conjecturing about the cost of such tests, we should have asked if we could create such tests at all.

17.2.2 Resolving the Halting Problem

The informal wording of the halting problem asks:

> *Is it possible to write a method (or algorithm) that can examine another method and state whether or not that second method will halt.*

As we saw in the case of decline, whether or not an algorithm will halt may depend on the input to that algorithm. Clearly, if we can solve the problem in general we should be able to solve it for a subset of those cases—specifically those for which we know the input. So let's ask a more specific question (which is actually the more common formulation of the halting problem):

> *Is it possible to write a method (or algorithm) that can examine another method— together with a possible input—and state whether or not that second method will halt with the specific input.*

The answer to this question is:

> *No! No such method can possibly exist!*

Any proposed general solution must fail for (at least) some combination of method and input. We will now prove this result by showing, for any possible version of *terminate*, how to construct a method that terminate can't evaluate correctly.

> **THEOREM:** No algorithm can examine an arbitrary method—together with a possible input—and determine whether or not that method will halt with the specific input. □

> **PROOF:** The proof is by contradiction. Assume *terminate* (any algorithmic version of the program terminate) exists and works correctly. The definition is repeated here in algorithmic form for reference:

> *Algorithm terminate (algorithm candidate, String input):*
> *   if candidate (proposedInput) will terminate*
> *   then   return true.*
> *   otherwise   return false.*

Now define a second algorithm, *enigma*, as follows:

> *Algorithm enigma (someInput):*
> > *If terminate (someInput, someInput) returns true*
> > > *then   loop forever.*
> > > *otherwise   return immediately.*

Assuming only that *terminate* is a valid program or method written in an appropriate language, *enigma* can be a very simple program, writable in any language. For example, in Java, it might look something like:

```
public static void enigma(String enigmasInput) {
    if (terminate(enigmasInput, enigmasInput))
        while (true) { }
    else { }
}
```

Consider `enigma`'s behavior carefully. *enigma* receives a single string, *enigmasInput*, and immediately passes it to `terminate`—twice, once as each of *terminate*'s two parameters. In effect, `enigma` asks *terminate*, "Will the program described by *enigmasInput* halt if given a copy of itself as input?" *enigma*'s behavior will clearly depend on the results of the call to *terminate*. If *terminate* determines that the program *enigmasInput* would halt when given the string *enigmasInput* as input, then `enigma` runs forever. If `terminate` determines that the method described by *enigmasInput* will not halt when invoked with input string `enigmasInput`, `enigma` itself finishes and returns immediately. In a rough sense, *enigma* behaves in the opposite manner from the program *enigmasInput*: `enigma` halts on the given input if and only if *enigmasInput* does not halt on its input.

Now consider a call to the method *enigma* with a copy of itself as input:

> *enigma (enigma).*

That is, `enigma`'s parameter is a string representing `enigma`. `enigma` will immediately invoke `terminate` with the message:

> *terminate (enigma, enigma).*

By definition, *terminate* always returns either true or false, so consider the two cases separately:

Case 1: Suppose *terminate*(*enigma*, *enigma*) returns true (that is, *terminate* concludes that *enigma* with the given input will terminate in finite time). Then *enigma* enters its "then clause" and loops forever, never terminating. Thus, *terminate* must be wrong, contradicting the original assumption.

Case 2: Suppose *terminate*(*enigma*, *enigma*) returns false (that is, *terminate* concludes that *enigma* will not terminate in finite time). In that case, *enigma* enters its else clause and immediately terminates. Specifically, it terminates in finite time—again contradicting the assumption that *terminate* would work correctly.

In either case, *enigma* terminates in finite time if and only if it does not terminate in finite time. Something must be wrong. In particular, the only assumption—that terminate exists—must be false. Therefore, the method *terminate* cannot possibly exist.[4] ∎

The interpretation of this result is that no algorithm can correctly decide, for every possible method and input combination, if the method will terminate. We can't even tell if an algorithm will terminate if we know in advance what the input will be. This does not mean that we can't create an algorithm, *semiTerminate,* that can often answer the question; it just means that we can't always answer the question.

The result does show that our original collection of questions were misdirected: we wanted to know how expensive it would be to add the termination checker to a compiler. But if we can't build *terminate*, then we can't discuss its correctness or its running time. And if the compiler can't decide if an input program will terminate, then it clearly can't determine the running time or correctness of the input. Since *terminate* can't exist, its tractability is not even a valid question. We can never completely automate such questions.

17.3 IMPLICATIONS OF THE HALTING PROBLEM FOR COMPUTER SCIENCE

We say that the halting problem is *undecidable.* That is, no program can decide if another (arbitrary) program will halt. Although this may be the first time you have ever seen a demonstration that it is impossible to solve a problem, it will not be the

---

[4] Proof of the impossibility of any program like *terminate* was first proven by the British mathematician Alan Turing (1912–54) in 1936. Although the field didn't even exist then, today computer scientists claim him as one of their own. Some might go so far as to call him the founder of the field.

last time you see such a result in computer science. It is very interesting that not only can we prove many solutions correct, for other problems we can show that no solution is possible. That's really a pretty amazing result.

The undecidability of the abstract halting problem provides the answer to the practical question that opened this chapter: "Is it feasible to build a termination-checker into a compiler?" Since terminate cannot exist, it is impossible to add the feature to a compiler. Such methods are useful before attempting to develop a complicated algorithm. For example, it is rumored that a major computer software company did in fact spend many thousands of dollars attempting to build such a checker into their compilers before someone pointed out to them the impossibility of the task.

Hopefully, the undecidability of the halting problem will whet your appetite for future explorations in computer science. It is by no means the last of the strange and surprising results that you will encounter. Investigation of such problems is an important theme in computer science because the answers have direct implications for the question: What can be computed? The halting problem has far reaching implications for the entire field of computer science. In particular, it shows that there are problems that, although apparently well formed, have no solution. That is, even though it may be possible to provide a formal and detailed description of a problem, it still may not be possible to find a solution—no matter how good the programmer.

While now is not the time to investigate those other surprising results in detail, we mention a small sampling of things to come. Some, but not all are direct corollaries of the halting problem.

17.3.1 Some Problems Just Cannot Be Computed

Even though some problems sound reasonable, they may have no algorithmic solution. The halting problem is just one example. In fact, one favorite technique for proving that a proposed algorithm is impossible is to prove that it is equivalent to the halting problem:

> *Assume the proposed algorithm can be written.*
> *Demonstrate that terminate must also exist.*
> *Conclude by contradiction that the first algorithm can't exist either.*

Tractable, Intractable, and Undecidable

Previous chapters divided problems into tractable (computable in reasonable time, e.g., searching, or even sorting) and intractable (requiring infeasible amounts of time, for example, the Towers of Hanoi). Undecidable problems such as the halting problem form yet another class. Even though intractable problems are considered to be impossible in practice, undecidable problems are impossible in an even stronger sense. If you were willing to wait a very long time, intractable problems could be computed. Yes, the wait could be truly outrageous, but in theory you could do it. But undecidable problems cannot be computed period—even if you were willing to wait forever or some astonishingly fast machine were invented.

17.3.2 There are More Functions than There are Programs.

This claim is not quite the syntactic paradox that it may appear to be at first. It does not mean that there are more sequences of the form:

>   *Define function Foo to be …*

than there are of the form:

>   *Define method Foo to be …*

It means there are more mathematical functions (e.g., sin, cos, log, …) than there are possible written programs. Put another way: there are well-defined mathematical functions that no computer program can describe. Given the discussion of the halting problem, this result may not be too surprising. After all, the function `terminate` must be a function with no corresponding program. On the other hand, for every computable function, there are many programs that compute exactly the same function (e.g., the two algorithms for computing Fibonacci numbers in Section 15.4). But the total number of logically possible functions is still larger than the total number of possible programs—even allowing such alternate versions.

17.3.3 Computable Problems

Several different definitions have been presented for the words *computing* or *computable*. The proof of the halting problem depended on the definition of algorithm, but it never explicitly defined the term *computable*. What does it mean to be computable? What does it mean to say there is an algorithm for a function? Many candidate definitions predate the first computer or the field of computer science. Several researchers have asked the reasonable question: Which of these definitions is correct? Or, can we even define what can be computed? It turns out that every proposed definition of computability is equivalent. No one has proposed a formal definition of the term "computable" that both satisfies the everyday intuition about what the word must mean and is different from any other definition in terms of what it does or does not allow to be computed. Every proposed definition is provably equivalent to all others. Although it is still unknown if some other definition is possible, the Church-Turing[5] hypothesis is the widely accepted belief that none can be.

17.3.4 All Computers are Equivalent

Every computer that has ever been designed is exactly equivalent in terms of the set of problems that it can solve (assuming only sufficient external storage). In fact, they are all equivalent to a simple machine (called a *Turing machine*) that can do no more than read and write to a tape and change states. This does not say they are all equally as fast—just that if a problem can be solved on one machine, it can be solved on any other (given enough time). No additional feature increases the theoretical computational power of a machine (although it may improve its speed or ease of use). It does not matter what the exact instruction set is. It does not matter how wide the bus is. And surprisingly, Alan Turing defined the Turing machine, proved the limits of its power, and the equivalence to other machines all before any actual computer was ever manufactured. A variant of this result states that every computing language that has ever been designed is exactly equivalent in terms of the set of problems that it can solve.

17.3.5 Mathematics is Incomplete

We are taught that mathematics is a universal language, that all of science can be described mathematically in a consistent manner. In fact, such a universal description was one of the goals of major nineteenth-century mathematicians such as David Hilbert and Gottlob Frege. However, the Austrian-American mathematician Kurt Gödel (1906–78) proved that every reasonably rich mathematical domain is necessarily inconsistent. For example, a representation rich enough to describe, say, algebra, must have internal inconsistencies. Alternatively stated, given any consistent language and universe, there are concepts that are true in that universe, but which cannot be proven in the language. In fact, Gödel's result, which preceded Turing's by just five years, actually contributed to Turing's thought on the question. His proof (although much more complicated then the following would suggest) actually amounted to creating the mathematical equivalent to, "This sentence is false!"—perhaps not all that different from, "This program will terminate only if it doesn't terminate."

---

[5] After Turing and the American logician Alonzo Church (1903–1995). Both men generated essentially the same result in the same year.

17.4 CONCLUDING REMARKS

The results of this chapter conclude our explorations into the three methods of inquiry of computer science. But for most students, it will not be your last encounter with any of them.

Unfortunately, in many (or most) curricula, the individual topics often appear to be segregated. Few students will be surprised by the presence of design in their future courses. They may be more surprised by the relative lack of courses aimed at the design of computer programs. They will, however, recognize the basic principles of design in courses in the area of Software Engineering. On the other hand, the vast majority of their courses will simply assume design capabilities as one of the prerequisite tools.

Theory, in most curricula, has at least two courses dedicated explicitly to it. Typically, these are called "analysis of algorithms" and "theory of computation." These course titles seem to suggest that they are about theory, divorced from design and empirical approaches. Certainly at least the first of these will inevitably contain significant aspects of design. The theory of computation will investigate abstract models of computation (such as the Turing machine mentioned earlier).

Unfortunately, empirical study has often received short shrift—at least in terms of being the topic of a course. Often it is relegated to a senior capstone course. It most commonly appears, not as verification of expected run time as in Θ calculations, but in areas where the run time is heavily impacted by factors external to the program and its input, such as operating systems, parallel processing, networks, and human factors.

But no matter what the apparent focus of the course, you will find that experiences in each of the other methods of inquiry will be useful. Each will help with problems that appear on the surface to relate primarily to the others.

We wish you a pleasant journey of exploration through the world of computing.

17.5 FURTHER READING

This chapter represents a very small peek into the world of great results in computer science. Many of the results described are standard reading for every computer scientist, if not in the original, then in an explanatory version. For example, Turing's original 1936 paper is available:

Alan Turing. "On Computable Numbers, With an Application to the Entscheidungsproblem," in *Proceedings of the London Mathematical Society*. (2) 42 pp 230–265 (1936–7).

Gödel's original paper on undecidability was published in German as:

"Über formal unentscheidbare Sätze der Principia Mathematica und verwandter Systeme," in *Monatshefte für Mathematik und Physik*, vol. 38 (1931).

Fortunately it is available in English translation at:

http://home.ddc.net/ygg/etext/godel/

Each result has been reworked many times and is available in many other versions. For example Gödel's work is described in:

Ernest Nagel and James Newman. *Gödel's Proof*. New York University Press, 1967.

Turing's result (or its equivalent) appear in most theory of computation texts, such as:

J. Hopcroft, R. Motwani, J. Ullman & Rotwani. *Introduction to Automata Theory, Languages, and Computation*. Addison-Wesley, 2000.

Alan Turing was one of the most remarkable men of the twentieth century. His accomplishments include not just the proof of the undecidability of the halting problem (at the age of 23!), but also the formulation of the "Turing test" (a distinction that has become the traditional criterion for defining "machine intelligence"), the formulation of what it means to be computable, and heading the Enigma project—(the most significant Allied attempt to decode intercepted German correspondence during World War II). In spite of his many accomplishments, he committed suicide at the age of 42—a direct result of persecution due to his sexual orientation. Today the Association for Computing Machinery annually gives its most significant honor, The Turing Award, to an outstanding computer scientist. You can read more about his fascinating life in:

Andrew Hodges. *Alan Turing: the Enigma*. New York: Walker and Company, 2000.

There is even a play about him, *The Code Breakers*.

Appendix A

Object-oriented Programming in Java

Readers come to this book with a wide variety of programming backgrounds. All readers have almost certainly had some programming experience. However, for some that experience was in Java, for others it was in another object-oriented language such as C++, and for still others it was in a procedural (i.e., not object-oriented) language such as C. This appendix helps those readers who are new to Java read and write it well enough to understand the examples and do the exercises elsewhere in this book. The appendix is not a complete course on Java, however. It does not cover advanced or little-used features of the language. The "Further Reading" section cites some comprehensive Java references from which you can learn more about the language if you wish.

We assume in this appendix that you already know how to program in some language. We also assume that you understand the object-oriented programming concepts covered in Chapter 2 and Section 3.4—you may wish to read those parts of the book in conjunction with this appendix.

The best way to learn any programming language is to use it. While this appendix does not explain how to use particular Java development tools, you should have access to some (and to instructions on their use), and you should use them to try the example programs here. You can find copies of all the examples at this book's Web site.

A.1 PROGRAM STRUCTURE

The ideal object-oriented program consists of a collection of objects that exchange messages with each other in order to accomplish some task. However, something has to create these objects in the first place, or at least send messages that cause pre-existing objects to do things. In Java, this "something" is a "main method" that runs when a program starts.

A.1.1 A First Program

Listing A.1 presents a Java program that consists of only a main method. The program prints "Hello world" when run.

LISTING A.1 A Java Program Consisting of Only One Method

```
// A simple Java program that prints "Hello world."
class Hello {
    public static void main(String[] args) {
        System.out.println("Hello world.");
    }
}
```

The main method in this program begins at the phrase:

```
public static void main(String[] args)
```

Its body is the *block* of code (i.e., code enclosed between "{" and "}"—in this case, a single statement) after that phrase. The main method in a Java program is always named main, and always has a single parameter consisting of an array of strings (the "[]" indicates an array). If you run a Java program from a command line, these strings contain any arguments provided to the program on the command line. Non-command-line environments may offer some other way to specify these strings or may simply pass main an empty array.

Unlike most methods, main methods aren't executed by objects. If they were, there would be an awkward paradox: a program's main method could only run after an object existed to run it, but such an object could only be created by running the main method. This problem is resolved by the word static in main's declaration, which indicates that the method executes independently of any object.

Everything in Java must be part of some class. Even though main isn't executed by an object, it still must be defined inside a class. Listing A.1 declares main in a class named Hello.

The statement:

```
System.out.println("Hello world");
```

causes the program to produce its output. System.out.println writes a string to the screen, and then tells the output window to put subsequent text on a new line.

Finally, the line:

```
// A simple Java program that prints "Hello world."
```

is a comment. Comments in Java begin with the characters "//", and continue until the end of the line.

A.1.2 Naming Source Files

A Java program consists of one or more text files containing Java statements (such files are also known as *source files*). Java programmers usually write each class in its own source file. The file's name is the class's name followed by ".java". For example, the introductory program presented in Listing A.1 consists of a class named `Hello`, and so it would be in a source file named Hello.java.

At this book's Web site, all the classes from this appendix (and the rest of the book) follow this convention. For instance, the introductory program is in file Hello.java at the Web site.

A.2 NONOBJECT FEATURES

Many of Java's data types, expressions, and control structures aren't unique to object-oriented programming—they are similar to features found in nearly every programming language. This section surveys these familiar features in just enough detail to give you a rudimentary ability to read and write procedural Java.

A.2.1 Data Types and Expressions

Every computation works on some kind of data. Tools for representing, describing, and manipulating data such as variables, expressions, and data types are therefore the heart of every programming language.

Declarations

You must declare variables before you use them in Java. Here is a template[1] for writing variable declarations:

<type> <name> ;

Any words between "<" and ">" in such templates are placeholders that you replace with your own text in concrete programs. Note that the "<" and ">" are part of the placeholder, they should *not* appear in concrete Java. Text not between "<"

---

[1] We use such templates to describe Java syntax throughout this appendix. These templates are skeletal pieces of Java code, containing placeholders that you replace with text of your own in order to create real Java code.

and ">" appears in concrete code exactly the way it appears in the template. In the template above, *<type>* stands for the name of any data type, and *<name>* stands for a variable name. Thus some concrete Java variable declarations that conform to this template are:

```
int i;          // Variable "i" will hold an integer
char initial;   // "initial" will hold a character
```

Pay particular attention to the semicolon in the above template and examples. Every Java statement must end with a semicolon, so it is an important part of the syntax that the template describes.

The scope of a variable declaration (i.e., the part of the program in which you can use the variable) extends from the declaration statement to the end of the block containing the declaration.

Java has two kinds of data types: simple types (like those found in procedural languages) and classes. Table A.1 describes some of the most frequently used simple types.

TABLE A.1   Some of Java's Simple Data Types

Type Name	Meaning	Notation for Values
int	Integer	Standard decimal integers, e.g., 3, 12, −1
char	Character	Any character in single quotation marks, e.g., 'A'
boolean	Boolean Value	The words true and false
double	Real Number	Standard decimal notation, e.g., 1.414, 3.0

Assignment and Initialization

A template for assigning a value to a variable in Java is:

$$<name> = <value> ;$$

<name> is a variable name, and *<value>* is the value or expression you want to assign to that variable. *<value>* can be any expression (of any complexity), as long as it produces a result of the same type as the variable. For example:

```
i = 3;
x = y + 4 * z;
```

You can combine declaration and assignment in one statement to initialize a variable at the moment you declare it. Doing so ensures that the variable won't be used before it has a value. The syntax for such statements is a combination of that for declaring a variable and that for assignment:

<type> *<name>* = *<value>* ;

For example:

```
int counter = 0;
boolean flag = false;
```

If a "variable" is really a constant, i.e., its value will not change once it is initialized, you can declare it as such by adding the word `final` to the declaration. Such declarations must include an initialization, because you cannot assign values to constants after their declarations (if you could, they wouldn't be constant). For example:

```
final int TABLE_SIZE = 1024;
```

Arrays

To indicate an array of a certain type, write the type name followed by an empty pair of square brackets ("[]"). You can use these array types in declarations just like other types. For example, here is a declaration that a is an array of integers:

```
int[] a;
```

Unlike in other languages, an array declaration does not specify the number of elements in the array. In fact, declaring an array doesn't create (i.e., reserve and initialize memory for) the array at all. This is a peculiar feature of arrays and objects[2] in Java; Java does create variables with simple types when you declare them. You create an array and specify its size with an assignment of the form:

<name> = new *<type>* [*<size>*] ;

where *<name>* is the name of the array, *<type>* is the type of element it contains, and *<size>* is the number of elements you want it to hold. The word `new` indicates creating an array or object. For example, to make an array big enough to hold five integers, you could write:

---

[2] In fact, arrays are really just a special kind of object in Java.

```
a = new int[5];
```

You typically declare an array and create it in a single statement:

```
char[] decimalDigits = new char[10];
```

You cannot access the elements of an array until you have created it.

An access to an array element has the form:

<name> [*<index>*]

where *<name>* is the name of the array and *<index>* is an expression that computes the index of the element you want. For example:

```
a[3] = 17;
x = a[i];
middleElement = a[(first+last)/2];
```

Array indices start at 0, so the legal indices for an array of n elements are the integers between 0 and $n-1$.

You can find out how big an array is with an expression of the form:

<name> . length

where *<name>* is the name of the array. For example:

```
int numberOfElements = a.length;
```

Expressions

Table A.2 presents some of Java's most important operations on simple types.

TABLE A.2 Some Common Java Operations

Operator(s)	Remarks
*, /, %	Multiplication, Division, Remainder
+, −	Addition, Subtraction ("+" also concatenates strings)
<, <=, ==, >=, >, !=	Comparisons ("==" compares for equality, "!=" for inequality)
&&, ||, !	Boolean "and", "or", "not"

A.2.2 Control Structures

Java's basic control structures include conditionals and loops, both of which behave similarly to their counterparts in other languages.

Conditionals

The most general conditional in Java is an "if" that has the following forms:

```
if ( <test> ) { <statements> } else { <statements> }
```

or

```
if ( <test> ) { <statements> }
```

In both of these templates, *<test>* is any expression that produces a Boolean result, and *<statements>* stands for any number of statements. The second template illustrates that the "else" part of a Java conditional is optional. Also notice that there is no semicolon after either form of conditional. You need semicolons after each statement within a conditional, but you never put a semicolon after "}" in Java. Here are some example conditionals:

```
if (x > 0) {
    total = total + x;
    count = count + 1;
}

if (0 <= i && i < 10) {
    System.out.println(a[i]);
}
else {
    System.out.println("i is not a legal index into a");
}
```

Loops

Java has several kinds of loop. To iterate while some condition holds, use a loop of the form:

```
while ( <test> ) { <statements> }
```

where *<test>* is any Boolean expression, and *<statements>* is any sequence of Java statements. For example:

```
while (i < 10) {
    i = i + 1;
}
```

Java "`while`" loops evaluate <*test*> before each repetition of <*statements*>; if <test> is false before the first repetition, then <*statements*> won't execute at all.[3]

Java includes a generalization of the classic "`for`" loop, which iterates while some condition holds, but also initializes the loop's state before the first iteration and changes the state after every iteration. This loop has the form:

for (<*initialization*> ; <*test*> ; <*change*>) { <*statements*> }

<*statements*> is the loop's body and can be any sequence of statements. <*test*> is a Boolean expression evaluated before each iteration; the loop will repeat as long as this expression is true. <*initialization*> is typically an assignment that initializes something (e.g., a loop control variable) before the loop's first iteration. <*initialization*> can declare as well as initialize a loop variable. The scope of such a variable is the loop's body. Finally, <*change*> is an expression whose side effects change the loop's state after each iteration. For example, the next loop steps i from 0 up to $n-1$, setting elements of array a to 0 as it goes. ("++" in the <*change*> part of this loop is a unary operator that increments its operand):

```
for (int i = 0; i < n; i++) {
    a[i] = 0;
}
```

A.3 USING OBJECTS

At a bare minimum, object-oriented programming means writing programs that use objects—in other words, programs that declare variables that represent objects, initialize those variables, and send messages to the objects (see Section 2.1 for the general concepts of objects and messages). The program in Listing A.2 demonstrates object declarations, initializations, and messages in Java. This program creates a copy of a string with all the spaces removed, by copying all the nonspace characters in a string named text to a StringBuffer named compressed. (String and StringBuffer are classes from the Java library that represent strings of characters.

---

[3] Java also has a "do" loop that is similar to "while," except it evaluates the test *after* each repetition of the body, thus guaranteeing that the body will be executed at least once. See the "Further Reading" references for details.

String represents unchangeable strings, while StringBuffer represents changeable ones.) The program initializes text to a constant string, and compressed to an empty StringBuffer. Then the program examines the characters in text, appending those that are not spaces to the end of compressed. After processing every character in this fashion, the program prints compressed.

LISTING A.2 Declaring, Creating, and Sending Messages to Objects

```
class RemoveSpace {
    public static void main(String[] args) {
        String text = "To be or not to be";
        StringBuffer compressed = new StringBuffer();
        for (int source = 0; source < text.length(); source++) {
            if (text.charAt(source) != ' ') {
                compressed.append(text.charAt(source));
            }
        }
        System.out.println("Compressed text: " + compressed);
    }
}
```

The following sections explain key features of this example in more detail.

A.3.1 Declaring Objects

All variable declarations have the syntax you learned in Section A.2.1. You declare object variables in a manner exactly analogous to simple variables: the type just identifies a class rather than a simple type. For example, the parts of Listing A.2 that read:

```
String text
```

and

```
StringBuffer compressed
```

are what declare text to be a String and compressed to be a StringBuffer, respectively. Note that we combined both declarations with initializations.

A.3.2 Creating Objects

Declaring object variables and creating objects are separate things in Java. Unlike many other languages, Java does not automatically create an object when you declare an object variable—you must write an explicit command to create the object and assign the result to the variable. You can, however, do this as an initialization in the statement that declares the variable.

The "new" Operator

The command to create an object in Java is the new operator. When used to create objects, new has the syntax:

new *<class>* (*<arguments>*)

Here, *<class>* is the name of the class from which you are creating the object, and *<arguments>* is a comma-separated list of arguments to the class's constructor (see Section 3.4 for information on constructors). The constructor will be called for you by new. For example, Listing A.2 uses the statement

```
StringBuffer compressed = new StringBuffer();
```

to create a StringBuffer, passing no arguments to the constructor. (When a constructor has no arguments, you still write parentheses after the class name, but there is nothing between them.)

Some other examples of new include:

```
StringBuffer nonEmpty = new StringBuffer("Some text");
Point corner = new Point(100, 50);
```

The first of these statements creates a StringBuffer initialized to contain the text "Some text." The second creates an object that represents the two-dimensional point (100,50) (Point is a Java library class that represents geometric points).

Other Object Values

Object variables can also be assigned values other than those produced by new. For example, Listing A.2 initializes text to a literal string with the statement:

```
String text = "To be or not to be";
```

You can also assign one object variable to another, as in the last line of this example:

```
Point p = new Point(100, 50);
Point q;
q = p;
```

Beware, however, that such assignments don't mean quite what you may expect. See Section A.7.2 for a complete explanation.

Java has a special value, null, that stands for the absence of any object. You can thus make a variable *not* refer to any object by assigning null to it. For example:

```
String nameToReadLater = null;
someObject = null;
```

A.3.3 Sending Messages to Objects

Java's syntax for sending a message to an object is:

<object> . *<message>* (*<arguments>*)

where *<object>* is the object to which you wish to send the message, *<message>* is the name of the message, and *<arguments>* is a comma-separated list of arguments to the message. For example, the expression:

```
text.charAt(source)
```

in Listing A.2 sends a charAt message to string text; the argument to this message is source, the position of a character in text (charAt retrieves the character at a specified position in a String or StringBuffer).

Messages such as charAt that return values can appear wherever their values are needed. For example, the statement:

```
compressed.append(text.charAt(source));
```

sends two messages: an append message that adds a character to the end of compressed, and a charAt that produces the character.

When you send a message with no parameters, you still write a pair of parentheses, but with nothing between them. For example, the expression:

```
text.length()
```

sends a parameterless length message to string text, to find out how many characters text contains.

Finally, note that Listing A.2's statement:

```
System.out.println("Compressed text: " + compressed);
```

also sends a message. Namely, it sends a `println` message to an object named `System.out`. (Output in Java is just a matter of sending appropriate messages—such as `println`—to objects that represent the devices or files to which you want to send data. `System.out` is a predefined object that represents the computer's display screen).

A.4 DEFINING CLASSES

Writing object-oriented programs of any real complexity requires defining your own classes. Chapter 2 discusses classes, their members, and why a programmer would want to define their own classes. To illustrate what such definitions look like in Java, Listing A.3 shows a class that represents simple counters—objects that store an integer value that they increment in response to `increment` messages.

LISTING A.3 A Counter Defined as a Java Class

```
class Counter {

    private int value;

    // A constructor
    public Counter() {
        value = 0;
    }

    // Increment a counter by n
    public void increment(int n) {
        if (n > 0) {
            value = value + n;
        }
    }

    // Increment a counter by 1
    public void increment() {
        this.increment(1);
    }
```

```
        // Report a counter's count
        public int getValue() {
            return value;
        }

        // Change a counter's count to a new value
        protected void setValue(int newValue) {
            value = newValue;
        }
    }
```

A.4.1 Overall Form

A class declaration in Java has the overall form:

```
class <name> { <members> }
```

In this template, *<name>* is the name of the class, for example `Counter` for the counter class. *<members>* is a series of declarations of member variables or methods. For example, the statement:

```
private int value;
```

in Listing A.3 is a member variable declaration, while the code segments beginning:

```
public Counter() ...

public void increment(int n) ...

public void increment() ...

public int getValue() ...
```

and

```
protected void setValue(int newValue) ...
```

are constructor or method declarations.

A.4.2 Member Variables

You must declare member variables before using them, just as you must declare other variables. The syntax for declaring and using member variables is similar to declaration and use of regular variables, albeit with a few features necessitated by the fact that member variables are contained in objects.

Because objects usually encapsulate (i.e., hide) information, programmers have to decide what code is allowed to access each member variable. Can it only be accessed by methods in the object's class (a "private" member variable, fully encapsulated)? Can it be accessed directly by clients of the object as well as by code in the object's class (a "public" member variable, no encapsulation)? Section 2.5 and Section 3.4 discuss why member variables should generally be private, but Java doesn't force them to be. Java even provides a third level of encapsulation, intermediate between public and private: "protected," meaning that the variable can be accessed by methods in the class, in subclasses of the class, or in the same "package" as the class (see Section A.6 for information on packages). In effect, a protected member variable can be accessed by code that is closely related to the class that declares the variable, but not by arbitrary clients.

Declarations

Member variable declarations begin with an *access specifier* that indicates which other parts of a program can directly access the variable. The syntax for a member variable declaration is:

> *<access> <type> <name>* ;

where *<access>* is the access specifier, and *<type>* and *<name>* are the type and name of the variable. Some access specifiers include:

- `private`, meaning that the variable is private
- `public`, meaning that the variable is public
- `protected`, meaning that the variable is protected

For example, the statement:

```
private int value;
```

in Listing A.3 declares an integer member variable named `value` that can only be used by code inside the `Counter` class.

Access

Refer to member variables just as you would any variable.[4] For example, the statement:

```
value = value + n;
```

from Listing A.3's first `increment` method accesses the `value` member variable once to fetch its value, and a second time to store the incremented value back into the member variable.

A.4.3 Method Declarations

Method declarations look much like function declarations in other languages.

Syntax

The template for a method declaration is:

<access> *<type>* *<name>* (*<parameters>*) { *<body>* }

where

- *<access>* is an access specifier. Java allows programmers to control what code can send messages to objects (i.e., invoke methods), using exactly the same access specifiers, with the same meanings, as for member variables.
- *<type>* indicates what type of value this method returns, if any. If a method doesn't return anything, use the dummy type `void`.
- *<name>* is the method's name. The method will be invoked by a message of the same name.
- *<parameters>* is a comma-separated list of parameter declarations. Individual parameter declarations have a form parallel to that of variable declarations, namely:

  <type> *<name>*

- *<body>* is the sequence of statements to execute when this method is invoked.

For example, the part of Listing A.3 that reads:

---

[4] At least when the access is from a method within the same class or a subclass. The syntax for accessing a public member variable from client code is slightly more elaborate—see the "Further Reading" references for details.

```
public void increment(int n) {
    if (n > 0) {
        value = value + n;
    }
}
```

declares a method named increment. This method has one integer parameter, and no return value. It can be invoked by clients of Counter, or by other methods within Counter. When invoked, the method checks that its parameter is positive, and if so, adds the parameter to the value member variable.

The method:

```
protected void setValue(int newValue) {
    value = newValue;
}
```

gives code closely related to Counter a way to arbitrarily change a counter's value, while general clients can only increment counters. Providing special powers to closely related code is a typical reason for using protected methods.

Returning Values

Listing A.3's declaration:

```
public int getValue() {
    return value;
}
```

declares the getValue method, which has no parameters but does return an integer. Within this method, the statement:

```
return value;
```

is what actually returns the integer (in this case, the contents of the value member variable). Statements of the form:

```
return <result> ;
```

where <result> is an expression, cause a method to exit and return the value computed by <result>.

Multiple Methods with the Same Name

A class may define several methods with the same name as long as they differ in the number or types of their parameters. When an object receives a message with this name, the object executes whichever method has the same number and types of parameters as the message. For example, Listing A.3 contains methods:

```java
public void increment(int n) {
    if (n > 0) {
        value = value + n;
    }
}
```

and

```java
public void increment() {
    this.increment(1);
}
```

These methods are both named `increment`, but one has one parameter, and the other has none. Therefore, if a `Counter` object receives an `increment` message with one integer parameter, that object will execute the first method, whereas if the object receives an increment message with no parameters, it will execute the second method.

The Special Object "this"

Within a method, the name `this` refers to the object executing the method (recall from Section 2.4 that an object executes a method when that object receives a message—the *recipient* of the message, not the sender, is the object that executes the method). For example, the statement:

```java
this.increment(1);
```

in Listing A.3's second `increment` method causes objects executing that method to send themselves an `increment` message with parameter 1 (i.e., the version of `increment` that always increments by 1 simply invokes the more general `increment` with a parameter that makes it increment by 1. It is important that the parameterless `increment` sends the message `this.increment(1)`, not just `this.increment()`—the latter would invoke the parameterless `increment` method again, in an endless recursion.)

A.4.4 Constructors

Constructors (see Section 3.4) aren't quite methods, but their declarations look like method declarations, except for two things:

- Constructors must have the same name as the class they initialize.
- Constructors do not have a result type.

For example, the constructor for the Counter class is declared:

```
public Counter() {
    value = 0;
}
```

Just as classes can have multiple methods with the same name, classes can have multiple constructors. As with methods, the constructors must differ in the number or types of their parameters.

A.4.5 Subclasses

Section 2.3 explains how subclasses are specialized subsets of a class. Imagine a subclass of Counter in which the count increases from 0 to 9, but then wraps back to 0 instead of passing 10. Listing A.4 demonstrates how one could write this subclass in Java:

LISTING A.4 A Special Kind of Counter that Counts from 0 to 9

```
class OneDigitCounter extends Counter {

    // A constructor for one-digit counters
    public OneDigitCounter() {
        super();
    }

    // Increment a one-digit counter by n
    public void increment(int n) {
        super.increment(n);
        this.setValue(this.getValue() % 10);
    }
```

```
    // Report the maximum value a one-digit counter can reach
    public int getMaxValue() {
        return 9;
    }
}
```

Declaring a Subclass

The keyword extends in a class declaration makes the declared class a subclass of some other class. The syntax is

class *<name>* extends *<superclass>* { *<members>* }

where *<name>* and *<members>* are the same as in any class, and *<superclass>* is the superclass's name. Classes in Java can only have one superclass.

OneDigitCounter's declaration demonstrates this syntax, with OneDigitCounter being the subclass, and Counter the superclass. Class OneDigitCounter defines its own constructor and increment and getMaxValue methods, and inherits other features from Counter.

Methods and Member Variables

Subclasses in Java ordinarily inherit all of the features of their superclass. In other words, instances of the subclass will have all of the member variables and methods of the superclass (although code in the subclass does not have direct access to the superclass's private member variables or private methods—it can only access them indirectly, by invoking a public or protected method that uses them). For example, OneDigitCounter objects handle getValue, setValue, and parameterless increment messages with the same methods that other Counter objects do.

You can override an inherited method by writing a new definition of it in the subclass. For example, Listing A.4 overrides Counter's one-parameter increment method with one that wraps the count around to 0 when it reaches 10. (This method will be invoked by the this.increment(1) statement in the inherited parameterless increment method, which means that both increment methods wrap the count around, even though Listing A.4 only overrides one of them.)

A subclass can also define additional member variables or methods beyond those inherited from its superclass. For example, Listing A.4 defines a getMaxValue method that is not present in other counters.

Accessing Superclass Features

Notice the statement:

```
super.increment(n);
```

in Listing A.4's one-parameter `increment` method. This statement causes the object executing that method (a `OneDigitCounter`) to send itself an `increment` message, but with the additional proviso that the message is to be handled by `Counter`'s one-parameter `increment` method (i.e., by the superclass's method). The word `super` is analogous to the word `this`, in that both allow the object executing a method to send itself messages, but `super` always handles the message with the method defined in the object's superclass, even if that method has been overridden. The word `super` is therefore only meaningful in a subclass.

Using `super` allows the `increment` method in `OneDigitCounter` to use the code already written for incrementing `Counter` objects. Afterwards, the statement:

```
this.setValue(this.getValue() % 10);
```

limits the result of this standard increment to the range 0 through 9 (because of the %, or remainder, operator).

A constructor in a subclass can use `super` to invoke one of the superclass's constructors. The syntax is:

```
super( <arguments> ) ;
```

where *<arguments>* is a comma-separated list of parameters to the superclass's constructor. Thus the statement:

```
super();
```

in Listing A.4's constructor means that a `OneDigitCounter` initializes itself by simply doing whatever is necessary to initialize a `Counter`. When one constructor invokes another via `super`, the invocation of `super` must be the first statement in the invoking constructor.

A.4.6 Static Members

Java allows programmers to create a variable or method associated with an entire class rather than a single object of that class. Such member variables or methods are distinguished by the word `static` in their declarations. For example, Listing A.5

defines both a static method (`printIndented`) and a static member variable (`SAMPLE_MESSAGE`).

LISTING A.5 A Java Class that Provides Indented Printing

```
class PrintTools {

    public static final String SAMPLE_MESSAGE = "Hello";

    // Print "msg" indented by "indent" spaces:
    public static void printIndented(String msg, int indent) {
        for (int i = 0; i < indent; i++) {
            System.out.print(" ");
        }
        System.out.println(msg);
    }
}
```

While every object in a class has its own copy of each of the class's ordinary member variables, all objects share a single copy of each static member variable. This is particularly useful when the member variable is a constant and so different objects won't have different values for it—e.g., SAMPLE_MESSAGE in Listing A.5. Similarly, static methods aren't executed by objects. Thus, a method that doesn't operate on an object's state anyhow—e.g., `printIndented` in Listing A.5—is easier for clients to invoke if it is static, because clients needn't create an object in which to invoke the method.

You invoke a static method with the syntax

<class> . *<method>* (*<arguments>*)

where *<class>* is the name of the *class* that defines the static method, *<method>* is the name of the method, and *<arguments>* is a comma-separated list of arguments to the method. For example, to call Listing A.5's `printIndented` method, you would write a statement such as

```
PrintTools.printIndented("Indented printing", 4);
```

Use a similar syntax for accessing static member variables, namely:

<class> . *<variable>*

For example, to refer to Listing A.5's `SAMPLE_MESSAGE` member variable, you would say:

```
PrintTools.SAMPLE_MESSAGE
```

The phrase `System.out` that you use when printing text is another example—it is really a reference to a static member variable named `out` in a class named `System`.

In general, static members have limitations and dangers that regular members don't (for example, you cannot use `this` or `super` in a static method; nonconstant static member variables can cause hard-to-debug interactions between objects). It is therefore best to avoid `static` unless you have to use it.

A.5 IMPRECISE CLASSES

Sometimes a program needs a way of specifying an object's class imprecisely. For example, suppose you want to define a data structure in which you can store arbitrary kinds of data—`String` objects, `Counter` objects, `Point` objects, anything that someone might someday represent as an object. The message that stores a piece of data into this structure cannot declare that data to be an instance of any one of these classes, because doing so would preclude storing instances of other classes in the structure. Nor can you declare different messages to store different kinds of data, because you can't know what classes future clients will define and want to store in your data structure. Similar problems arise in declaring messages that retrieve data from the structure, declaring the structure's member variables, etc. What you need is a way to declare parameters, results, and member variables that can be objects of *any* class, not just one class. Java provides several features that help programmers write such declarations.

A.5.1 Class "Object"

Java programmers use the class hierarchy (i.e., superclass/subclass relationships between classes) to specify classes imprecisely. In particular, something declared to be an instance of a superclass can actually be an instance of any of that superclass's subclasses (or subclasses of the subclasses, etc.).Therefore, if you don't know exactly what class some object will have, but you do know that it will be one of the subclasses of some general superclass, you can simply declare the object to be an instance of the superclass.

The most general superclass in Java is `Object`, which is the superclass of all other classes. Any class that doesn't extend something else is automatically a subclass of `Object`, so every class descends, either directly or indirectly, from `Object`.

For example, consider a simple data structure of the sort suggested in the introduction to this section. This structure holds data in an array, provides a `store` message to add an item to the array, and provides a `retrieve` message to fetch an item, given its position in the array. You could use `Object` to declare these features, as outlined in Listing A.6 (for the complete class definition and sample client code, see file SimpleStructure.java at this book's Web site).

LISTING A.6 An Outline of a Simple Generic Data Structure in Java

```
private Object[] data;                    // The array of items
public void store(Object newData) {       // The store method

   ...

}
public Object retrieve(int index) {       // The retrieve method

   ...

}
```

The actual values represented by something declared as `Object` will always really be instances of some subclass of `Object`. For example, here is a statement that adds a `String` to a simple data structure named container:

```
container.store("This is a string");
```

Note that this statement passes an ordinary `String` to `store`. This is a legal use of `store`, because `store` can receive any instance of `Object` as its parameter, and `String` is a subclass of `Object`—so all `String` objects are, indirectly, also instances of `Object`. Class `Object` is never used to create the value stored in the structure.

A.5.2 Casts

Imprecise classes sometimes leave a programmer knowing an object's class *more* precisely than is evident from a program. For example, suppose you are a client using Listing A.6's simple data structure to store strings. Your application will thus retrieve only strings from the data structure. Unfortunately, however, a Java compiler only knows that the `retrieve` message is declared as returning `Object`, it doesn't know how your application uses `retrieve`. Therefore, if you try to send string messages to the objects you retrieve, or assign those objects to string variables, the compiler will report an error and refuse to compile your program.

Java's solution to this problem is a *cast*. Casts let programmers assert that a value has a particular type. The syntax for writing a cast is:

(*<type>*) *<value>*

where *<value>* is an expression whose result is apparently of one type, and *<type>* is another type that *<value>* really has. For example, a client of the simple data structure who knew that every object stored in the structure was a string, and so wanted to assign objects retrieved from the structure to a string variable, could write:

```
String item = (String) container.retrieve(i);
```

Although you can sometimes use casts to convert one simple type to another (e.g., you can cast a char to an int, an int to a double), you should generally treat a cast as a promise by the programmer that an expression produces a result of a different type than the one the expression's operators or operands imply. You should *not* use casts to convert values of one type into values of a different type. Trying to do so can cause a program to abort with an error called a "class cast exception."

A.5.3 Interfaces

As you use either the standard Java libraries, or the classes provided with this text, you will encounter Java data types known as "interfaces." Like a class, an interface specifies messages that certain sets of objects handle. Unlike a class, however, an interface cannot define methods with which to handle these messages. Instead, other classes have to *implement* the interface, meaning that they provide methods for handling its messages.

You can use the names of interfaces as you would use the names of classes to declare objects whose exact class is unknown. Objects so declared can actually be instances of any class that implements the interface.

You probably won't need to define your own interfaces while using this book, but you may need to declare classes that implement other programmers' interfaces (recall that "implement" in this context is a technical term that means "provides methods for handling the interface's messages"). A class that implements an interface has a declaration that looks like:

```
class <name> implements <interfaces> { <members> }
```

or

```
class <name> extends <superclass> implements <interfaces>
    { <members> }
```

In these templates, *<name>*, *<superclass>*, and *<members>* are the class's name, the name of its superclass, and definitions of its member variables and methods, exactly as in other class declarations. *<interfaces>* is a comma-separated list of names of interfaces. A class can implement many interfaces, whereas it can only be a subclass of one class. For example:

```
class InterfaceExample implements Comparable, Serializable {
    ...
}
```

(Comparable and Serializable are interfaces from the Java library. Comparable represents objects with a "less than" relation. Serializable represents objects that can be written to and read from files.)

A.6 PACKAGES

Programmers are free to write their own libraries of Java classes, and to share those libraries with other programmers. For example, we have written a library that contains classes List, OrderedTree, LineDrawing, etc. for this book. As programmers all around the world write their own Java libraries, there will inevitably be *name conflicts*—situations in which two people use the same name to identify different entities.

Java's packages are a mechanism for reducing name conflicts. A *package* is a collection of related classes. Programmers place a class in a package by putting a special package statement at the beginning of the file that defines the class. All members of a package have names that, technically, include the package name. For example, the classes that accompany this book are all in a package named geneseo.cs.sc. The full name of the List class that accompanies this book is therefore geneseo.cs.sc.List.[5]

A.6.1 Using Classes from a Package

In order to use classes from a package, those classes must be installed on your computer. Unfortunately, exactly what "installed" means depends on your Java programming environment: in some environments, "installed" means that files containing the compiled classes have to be present in specific directories, in other environments it means that either the compiled or source files must be listed in "project files" that describe your program, etc. Consult your instructor, or the

---

[5] Packages only solve the problem of name conflicts if package names themselves don't give rise to conflicts. Fortunately there are published conventions for naming packages that make such conflicts unlikely.

documentation for your programming environment, if you want to install packages for yourself.

Once classes defined in a package are installed on your computer, you may use them by writing out their full names in your own programs. For example, you could declare an instance of this book's List class by writing code such as:

```
geneseo.cs.sc.List aList = new geneseo.cs.sc.List();
```

Such code quickly becomes painful to write and hard to read. Java therefore provides a way to *import* some or all of a package's definitions into a source file. After importing a definition, code in that file can refer to the imported entity by its short name. For example, after importing geneseo.cs.sc.List via the statement:

```
import geneseo.cs.sc.List;
```

you could write the above declaration as just:

```
List aList = new List();
```

To import a single class into a file, you write a statement of the form:

```
import <package> . <class> ;
```

at the beginning of the file. In this template, *<package>* is a package name, and *<class>* is the name of the class you want to import. For example:

```
import geneseo.cs.sc.List;
```

To import every class in a package, use an import statement of the form:

```
import <package> . * ;
```

where *<package>* is the name of the package. For example:

```
import geneseo.cs.sc.*;
```

A file can contain multiple import statements, if you need to import multiple classes, or need to import from multiple packages.

A.7   JAVA'S IMPLEMENTATION OF OBJECTS

Java's internal representation of objects has some consequences that can unpleasantly surprise programmers. Fortunately, knowing something about Java's implementation of objects reduces these surprises, and leads to more effective use of the language in general.

A.7.1   Object Variables are Pointers

Object variables in Java are more complicated, with more subtle behaviors, than simple variables. A simple variable is basically a place in the computer's memory to store the variable's value. For example, the statement

```
int i = 1;
```

sets aside enough memory to hold one integer, notes that henceforth the name i means that location in memory, and places the value 1 into that location. Figure A.1 diagrams these effects.

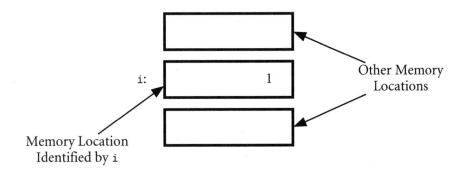

FIGURE A.1   A simple variable is a name for a memory location.

In contrast, Figure A.2 illustrates an object variable. A declaration such as

```
SomeClass obj = new SomeClass();
```

reserves *two* regions of memory. First, the new operation sets aside enough memory to hold all the members of one SomeClass object. This memory includes locations that store the values of the object's member variables, and locations that indicate where to find the code for the object's methods. Second, the declaration sets aside one memory location, named obj, that holds information about where in memory to find the members. Such information is called a *pointer*. Properly speaking, the object is the memory that holds the members; the variable is only a pointer to the object.

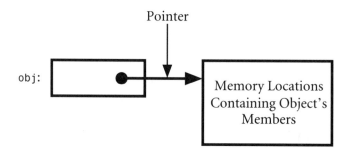

FIGURE A.2 An object variable is a pointer to the object's members.

A.7.2 Assignments to Object Variables

The distinction between pointers and objects shapes the way assignments to object variables work. Such assignments copy *pointers*, not objects. For instance, consider the statements:

```
SomeClass a = new SomeClass();
SomeClass b = a;
```

The assignment in the second statement copies the pointer a into variable b, but does not make a copy of the object a points to. In the end, there is only one object, but two different variables point to it, as illustrated in Figure A.3.

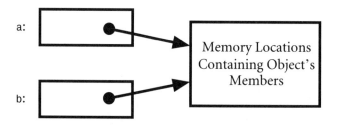

FIGURE A.3 Assignment makes two variables point to a single object.

Similarly, when you pass an object as a parameter to a message, or return an object as a message's result, it is really a pointer to the object, not a copy of the object, that is passed or returned.

Assigning pointers without copying objects means that several variables or parameters may all point to the same object. One important consequence is that you might use one variable (or parameter) to change an object, but also see the change via a different variable. For example, the following Java statements leave text1 and text2 both beginning with lowercase letters "a", even though the program appears to change only text2 (the program sends text2 a setCharAt message in order to change its first character; setCharAt replaces a character in a StringBuffer with a new character, given the position of the character to change):

```
StringBuffer text1 = new StringBuffer("ABCD");
StringBuffer text2 = text1;
text2.setCharAt(0, 'a');
```

A.7.3 Comparing Objects

The distinction between pointers and objects also affects comparisons between objects.

The == operator applied to two objects tests whether two pointers are the same, not whether the contents of two objects are the same. This can be useful if you need to determine whether two references to objects really refer to the same single object, but in other cases it can produce unexpected results. For example, consider this code:

```
String text1 = new String("XYZ");
String text2 = new String("XYZ");
if (text1 == text2) {
    System.out.println("The objects are the same");
}
else {
    System.out.println("The objects are different");
}
```

This code will print "The objects are different," even though text1 and text2 patently contain the same characters. This happens because even though they contain the same characters, text1 and text2 are distinct objects, and so any pointers to them are not equal (each new operation creates an object distinct from all others).

To see if two objects have the same contents, use the equals message. All Java objects handle this message. Send it to an object, with another object as the message's parameter. The message returns a Boolean result: generally true if the two objects have the same contents, and false otherwise.[6] For example, if you replace the conditional in the above example with:

```
if (text1.equals(text2)) ...
```

the resulting code will print "The objects are the same."

A.7.4 Null Pointers

Java's built-in constant `null` is a pointer that never points to anything. You can thus use `null` as a value for variables or parameters that shouldn't refer to any object. You can also compare pointers to `null`.

For example, Listing A.7 presents a class that represents employees in a company. Most employees have a boss, represented by the `boss` member variable. However, some employees (e.g., the company's CEO) don't have a boss. These employees will be represented by `Employee` objects with `null` in the `boss` member.

The constructor for class `Employee` receives an `Employee` object as its second parameter. Programmers can create `Employee` objects with no boss by using `null` as the value for this parameter. For example:

```
Employee ceo = new Employee("J. Mega Bucks", null);
```

The `findCEOName` method searches through bosses, bosses' bosses, etc., until it finds someone with no boss. The method uses the comparison:

```
currentEmployee.boss != null
```

to continue the search. Notice that comparisons to `null` are necessarily comparisons between pointers, not between objects' contents, since `null` doesn't point to an object. Therefore, you must always use `!=` or `==`, not an `equals` message, in such comparisons.

Because `null` denotes the absence of an object, you cannot send messages to `null`. Trying to do so causes programs to abort with an error known as a "null pointer exception."

---

[6] Things do not, however, always work this way. Classes inherit `equals` from `Object`, and should override the inherited method to test for equality of contents in a way appropriate to the class. However, if a class doesn't override the inherited `equals` method, what it inherits compares pointers exactly as "==" does. Furthermore, even if a class's implementor does override `equals`, there is no guarantee that their method behaves as it is supposed to.

LISTING A.7 A Java Class that Represents Employees

```java
class Employee {

    private String name;        // This employee's name
    private Employee boss;       // This employee's boss

    // A constructor.
    public Employee(String employeesName, Employee employeesBoss) {
        name = employeesName;
        boss = employeesBoss;
    }

    // Find CEO's name (i.e., name of the employee with no boss)
    public String findCEOName() {
        Employee currentEmployee = this;
        while (currentEmployee.boss != null) {
            currentEmployee = currentEmployee.boss;
        }
        return currentEmployee.name;
    }
}
```

A.8 FURTHER READING

The definitive reference for Java is:

Ken Arnold, James Gosling, and David Holmes, *The Java Programming Language* (3rd ed.), Addison-Wesley Longman, 2000.

This book is part of *The Java Series*, a collection of Java books authorized by Sun Microsystems, the company that developed Java. You can learn more about this series at the Java Web site mentioned later in this section or from Addison-Wesley Longman.

Experienced programmers who want a compact but complete introduction to Java should see:

David Flanagan, *Java in a Nutshell* (4th ed.), O'Reilly and Associates, 2002.

Sun Microsystems maintains up-to-the-minute documentation and tutorials for Java on the World Wide Web at:

http://java.sun.com/

This Web site is a particularly good source for documentation on the Java libraries.

Appendix

B About the Web Site

A complete course is more than just a textbook. In order for students to really learn, they need motivations to become actively engaged with the subject, they need exercises with which to practice new ideas, etc. As a source of some motivations and exercises, a companion Web site for this book has been set up at:

http://www.charlesriver.com/algorithms

B.1 WEB SITE CONTENTS

The material at the Web site includes laboratory exercises, complete Java code for many of the classes discussed in the book, and instructor notes for the laboratory exercises and classes. Most of this material is repeatedly used by one of the authors to teach a course based on this book. Additional material will appear at this Web site over time.

The documents available at the Web site can be classified as follows:

- The book's table of contents
- Laboratory exercises that give students direct, computer-based, experience with the concepts introduced in the book. The laboratory exercises include:
- Object Oriented Programming in Java. Exercises some basic object oriented programming concepts with the book's simulated robot.
- Introduction to Experimentation. Hands-on practice with basic experimental techniques for computer science.
- Elementary Recursion. Introductory practice designing and coding recursive algorithms.
- Intermediate Recursion. Practice designing and coding recursive algorithms.
- Intermediate Recursion with Line Drawings. Practice designing and coding recursive algorithms, using a simple graphics package.
- Recursive Treasure Hunts. Advanced practice designing, coding, and proving correctness of recursive algorithms, solving a "treasure hunt" problem for the simulated robot.

- Induction and Recursive Algorithms. Practice designing and coding recursive algorithms, and proving them correct.
- Recurrence Relations and Execution Time. An experiment that illustrates the practical significance of execution time analysis via recurrence relations, and also gives students practice setting up and solving recurrence relations.
- Debugging. An exercise in finding and correcting bugs in programs, with emphasis on how techniques for specifying and analyzing correctness theoretically can influence practical debugging.
- Introduction to Lists. An introduction to writing programs that use Chapter 11's recursive List class.
- Lists and the Sieve of Eratosthenes. An exercise in designing and coding subclasses of the List class, and applying one in an experiment concerning the behavior of prime numbers.
- Comparing Search Times for Lists and Trees. Experimental and theoretical analysis of worst-case search times for lists and balanced ordered trees.
- Advanced Recursion with Line Drawings. Advanced practice designing, coding, and analyzing execution time of recursive algorithms, in the context of drawing fractal shapes.
- Java source code that is used in many laboratory exercises, and that students can study or incorporate into their own programs. This code includes many of the classes discussed in the book, plus a few more. Complete documentation for all classes is also available on the Web site. The available classes are:
- LineDrawing. A class that supports simple line graphics, introduced in Chapter 15.
- List. The recursive list class described in Chapter 11.
- OrderedList. The ordered subclass of List also described in Chapter 11.
- OrderedTree. The ordered binary tree class described in Chapter 13.
- PhoneEntry. A simple record type that can be used to populate lists, trees, and other data structures.
- Robot. The simulated robot introduced in Chapter 2.
- RobotRoom. Environments in which the simulated robots move and act.
- WebPage. A class that provides simple access to World Wide Web pages.
- Instructor notes, explaining the authors' goals for laboratory exercises and Java classes, tips for using the exercises and classes, etc. The instructor notes include ones for:

  - Labs in general
  - The lab on object oriented programming in Java
  - The lab on introduction to experimentation
  - The labs on elementary and intermediate recursion
  - The lab on intermediate recursion with line drawings

- The lab on recursive treasure hunts
- The lab on induction and recursive algorithms
- The lab on recurrence relations and execution time
- The lab on debugging
- The lab on introduction to lists
- The lab on lists and the Sieve of Eratosthenes
- The lab on comparing search times for lists and trees
- The lab on advanced recursion with line drawings
- The Robot and RobotRoom library classes
- The LineDrawing library class
- The List library class
- The OrderedTree library class

B.2   WEB SITE ORGANIZATION

The "home page" (i.e., main entry point) for the entire Web site is

http://www.charlesriver.com/algorithms/index.html

All other documents and files are reachable from this page.

The site's organization is generally flat, meaning that most documents have URLs of the form

http://www.charlesriver.com/algorithms/document.html

where "document.html" is an individual document's name. A few files are in subdirectories, with the following subdirectories being the most important:

- doc. Contains all the documentation for Java classes.
- classes. Contains source code for the Java classes.
- testdata. Contains miscellaneous files of test data for laboratory exercises.

B.3   SYSTEM REQUIREMENTS

Most of the HTML files are XHTML 1.0 documents compatible with HTML 4.01, produced by Macromedia® Dreamweaver® MX 6.1. The notable exceptions are the class documentation files, which are HTML 4.01 documents produced by javadoc. All files are readable on any current browser—for example, we test them thoroughly with Safari™1.2 and Microsoft® Internet Explorer 5.2 for Mac® under Mac OS X, and have viewed them using Mozilla 1.5 under SunOS™, and Microsoft Internet Explorer® 6.0 under Windows XP®.

We used Java 1.4.2 as our reference for developing the Java classes, but in fact they use little if anything that is unique to Java 1.4.2, and run under most current Java development environments. We use Metrowerks™ CodeWarrior™ 8 under Mac OS X for development and testing, and also test thoroughly using the Java HotSpot™ virtual machine (Java 1.4.2) under SunOS. Students have successfully used the classes with CodeWarrior 8 under Windows XP and Eclipse 2.1.2 under Mac OS X.

Index